I0825143

"J. Gary Millar has given us a thoroughly accessible, readable, clear, and useful commentary that will be of practical use for preachers and pastors. He tackles the key interpretive issues with care and clarity and offers his judgments with humility. I warmly recommend this commentary."

—**Christopher Ash,** *writer in residence, Tyndale House, Cambridge, United Kingdom*

"This is a superb addition to commentary on an essential book: erudite, yet readable; expansive, yet detailed; firmly rooted in the world of the Old Testament, yet sensitive to matters of Christian theology and practice. Buy it, read it, have your heart stirred by the preaching of Moses, and be equipped to go and do likewise."

—**G. Geoffrey Harper,** *director of research and lecturer in Old Testament, Sydney Missionary and Bible College, Australia*

"J. Gary Millar's commentary is a needed resource for anyone who wants to understand, apply, and teach the book of Deuteronomy. Informed by his rigorous scholarship, yet written in a warm, pastoral manner, Millar takes readers by the hand and leads them into the biblical-theological riches of Moses's preaching, opening a spectacular vista onto the rest of the canon. This EBTC volume deftly navigates through Deuteronomy's trickier issues and gracefully maintains theological poise in teaching both a love of Torah–with the call to obey its 'beautiful life' and Israel's (and our) need for Messiah's redemption and new covenant—how Moses leads to Jesus. Millar's commentary is a sure and trustworthy guide for grasping what is perhaps the weightiest book of the Hebrew Scriptures!"

—**L. Michael Morales,** *professor of biblical studies, Greenville Presbyterian Theological Seminary*

"Gary Millar's commentary reflects a profound understanding of Deuteronomy's composition, rhetorical flow, theological message, and canonical significance. Careful exegesis and informed interpretation of the biblical text consistently model the very best of evangelical scholarship. The standout feature, however, is the way that the introduction and numerous bridging sections concisely highlight the gospel-shaped message of this seminal Old Testament book and facilitate a hermeneutically-informed appreciation of how this anticipates God's ultimate revelation of the gospel in Christ. If only it had been available in 2001, when I began teaching Deuteronomy at Moore College!"

—**Paul Williamson,** *lecturer in Hebrew, Aramaic, and Old Testament, Moore College, Australia*

DEUTERONOMY

DEUTERONOMY

Evangelical Biblical Theology Commentary

General Editors

T. Desmond Alexander, Thomas R. Schreiner, Andreas J. Köstenberger

Assistant Editors

James M. Hamilton, Kenneth A. Mathews, Terry L. Wilder

J. Gary Millar

Deuteronomy
Evangelical Biblical Theology Commentary

Lexham Academic, an imprint of Lexham Press 1313 Commercial St.,
Bellingham, WA 98225
LexhamPress.com

Print ISBN 9781683598220
Digital ISBN 9781683598237
Library of Congress Control Number 2024952173

General Editors: T. Desmond Alexander, Thomas R. Schreiner, Andreas J. Köstenberger
Assistant Editors: James M. Hamilton, Kenneth A. Mathews, Terry L. Wilder
Lexham Editorial: Derek Brown, John Barach, Mandi Newell
Cover Design: Jonathan Myers
Typesetting: Justin Marr

25 26 27 28 29 30 31 / IN / 12 11 10 9 8 7 6 5 4 3 2 1

For the students, graduates and staff of Queensland Theological College

CONTENTS

GENERAL EDITORS' PREFACE

In recent years biblical theology has seen a remarkable resurgence. Whereas, in 1970, Brevard Childs wrote *Biblical Theology in Crisis*, the quest for the Bible's own theology has witnessed increasing vitality since Childs prematurely decried the demise of the movement. Nowhere has this been truer than in evangelical circles. It could be argued that evangelicals, with their commitment to biblical inerrancy and inspiration, are perfectly positioned to explore the Bible's unified message. At the same time, as D. A. Carson has aptly noted, perhaps the greatest challenge faced by biblical theologians is how to handle the Bible's manifest diversity and how to navigate the tension between its unity and diversity in a way that does justice to both.[1]

What is biblical theology? And how is biblical theology different from related disciplines such as systematic theology? These two exceedingly important questions must be answered by anyone who would make a significant contribution to the discipline. Regarding the first question, the most basic answer might assert that biblical theology, in essence, is *the theology of the Bible*, that is, the theology expressed by the respective writers of the various biblical books *on their own terms* and *in their own historical contexts*. Biblical theology is the attempt to understand and embrace *the interpretive perspective of the biblical authors*. What is more, biblical theology is the theology of the *entire* Bible, an exercise in *whole-Bible theology*. For this reason biblical theology is not just a modern academic discipline; its roots are found already in the use of earlier Old Testament portions

[1] D. A. Carson, "New Testament Theology," in *DLNT* 810.

in later Old Testament writings and in the use of the Old Testament in the New.

Biblical theology thus involves a close study of *the use of the Old Testament in the Old Testament* (that is, the use of, say, Deuteronomy by Jeremiah, or of the Pentateuch by Isaiah). Biblical theology also entails the investigation of *the use of the Old Testament in the New*, both in terms of individual passages and in terms of larger christological or soteriological themes. Biblical theology may proceed *book by book*, trace *central themes* in Scripture, or seek to place the contributions of individual biblical writers within the framework of the Bible's larger overarching *metanarrative*, that is, the Bible's developing story from Genesis through Revelation at whose core is *salvation* or *redemptive history*, the account of God's dealings with humanity and his people Israel and the church from creation to new creation.

In this quest for the Bible's own theology, we will be helped by the inquiries of those who have gone before us in the *history of the church*. While we can profitably study the efforts of interpreters over the entire sweep of the history of biblical interpretation since patristic times, we can also benefit from the labors of scholars since J. P. Gabler, whose programmatic inaugural address at the University of Altdorf, Germany, in 1787 marks the inception of the discipline in modern times. Gabler's address bore the title "On the Correct Distinction between Dogmatic and Biblical Theology and the Right Definition of Their Goals."[2] While few (if any) within evangelicalism would fully identify with Gabler's program, the proper distinction between dogmatic and biblical theology (that is, between biblical and systematic theology) continues to be an important issue to be adjudicated by practitioners of both disciplines, and especially biblical theology. We have already defined biblical theology as whole-Bible theology, describing the theology of the various biblical books *on their own terms* and *in their own historical contexts*. Systematic theology, by contrast, is more topically oriented and focused on contemporary contextualization. While there are different ways in which the relationship between biblical and systematic theology can be construed, maintaining a proper distinction between the two disciplines arguably continues to be vital if both are to achieve their objectives.

---

[2] The original Latin title was *Oratio de iusto discrimine theologiae biblicae et dogmaticae regundisque recte utriusque finibus.*

The present set of volumes constitutes an ambitious project, seeking to explore the theology of the Bible in considerable depth, spanning both Testaments. Authors come from a variety of backgrounds and perspectives, though all affirm the inerrancy and inspiration of Scripture. United in their high view of Scripture and in their belief in the underlying unity of Scripture, which is ultimately grounded in the unity of God himself, each author explores the contribution of a given book or group of books to the theology of Scripture as a whole. While conceived as stand-alone volumes, each volume thus also makes a contribution to the larger whole. All volumes provide a discussion of introductory matters, including the historical setting and the literary structure of a given book of Scripture. Also included is an exegetical treatment of all the relevant passages in succinct commentary-style format. The biblical theology approach of the series will also inform and play a role in the commentary proper. The commentator permits a discussion between the commentary proper and the biblical theology it reflects by a series of cross-references.

The major contribution of each volume, however, is a thorough discussion of the most important themes of the biblical book in relation to the canon as a whole. This format allows each contributor to ground biblical theology, as is proper, in an appropriate appraisal of the relevant historical and literary features of a particular book in Scripture while at the same time focusing on its major theological contribution to the entire Christian canon in the context of the larger salvation-historical metanarrative of Scripture. Within this overall format, there will be room for each individual contributor to explore the major themes of his or her particular corpus in the way he or she sees most appropriate for the material under consideration. For some books of the Bible, it may be best to have these theological themes set out in advance of the exegetical commentary. For other books it may be better to explain the theological themes after the commentary. Consequently, each contributor has the freedom to order these sections as best suits the biblical material under consideration so that the discussion of biblical-theological themes may precede or follow the exegetical commentary.

This format, in itself, would already be a valuable contribution to biblical theology. But other series try to accomplish a survey of the Bible's theology as well. What distinguishes the present series is its orientation toward Christian proclamation. This is the Evangelical Biblical Theology Commentary series! As a result, the ultimate purpose of this set of volumes is not exclusively, or even primarily, academic. Rather, we seek to relate biblical theology to our own lives and to the life of the church. Our desire is to equip those in Christian ministry who are called by God to preach and teach the precious truths of Scripture to their congregations, both in North America and in a global context.

The base translation for the Evangelical Biblical Theology Commentary series is the Christian Standard Bible (CSB). The CSB places equal value on faithfulness to the original languages and readability for a modern audience. The contributors, however, have the liberty to differ with the CSB as they comment on the biblical text. Note that, in the CSB, Old Testament passages that are quoted in the New Testament are set in boldface type.

We hope and pray that the forty volumes of this series, once completed, will bear witness to the unity in diversity of the canon of Scripture as they probe the individual contributions of each of its sixty-six books. The authors and editors are united in their desire that in so doing the series will magnify the name of Christ and bring glory to the triune God who revealed himself in Scripture so that everyone who calls on the name of the Lord will be saved—to the glory of God the Father and his Son, the Lord Jesus Christ, under the illumination of the Holy Spirit, and for the good of his church. To God alone be the glory: *soli Deo gloria.*

ACKNOWLEDGEMENTS

The voice of Moses through Deuteronomy has been my constant companion for most of my adult life. Since the first classes I took in Old Testament at Aberdeen University over thirty five years ago (with Professor Bill Johnstone and Dr Ken Aitken), the grace which God shows in this book to a people who are no more (and often less) impressive than any other has captivated me. God was so good as to lead me to Oxford to work with Professors John Barton (who whilst sharing almost none of my convictions about Deuteronomy was a wonderful doctoral supervisor) and Gordon McConville, whose generosity and encouragement was very precious. In more recent years, I have benefitted enormously from the work (and friendship) of Professor Dan Block, not least during his regular visits to Queensland, as he has opened up "the Gospel according to Moses" for me and countless others.

During all of these years, in God's kindness, I have been cheered on every step of the way by Fiona, my wife, who is unmatched in her desire to live the kind of beautiful life sketched out by Moses and now put within our grasp by the Lord Jesus as he pours out the Spirit on those who commit to him in faith. Our three (now adult) daughters, Lucy, Sophie and Rebekah have shared in this long-term journey of covenantal delight. I thank God for them, and for their constant love and encouragement.

Both during my 17 years as a Presbyterian Minister in Ireland and then, since 2012, in my role as Principal of QTC (Queensland Theological College), I have had the huge privilege of teaching this book multiple times both to theological students and to local churches, seeking to point them to Christ and all that God has done for us in him. I am deeply grateful for the ways in which God's people and, in particular, successive cohorts of QTC students, have adapted to the fact that the answer to every question is probably either "Deuteronomy" or "Jesus" and have helped me to grasp this book a little better and live out its teaching a little more faithfully as the years have gone by. It is with thankfulness that this attempt to proclaim the gospel from this epic sermon is dedicated to them.

I am also deeply grateful to the staff of QTC for years of friendship, support and partnership in the gospel. Particular thanks are due to Annette McGrath, our Librarian, Mel Waldeck who prepared the indices, and Doug Green, my OT colleague, for countless early morning conversations about preaching Christ from all the Scriptures! The QTC community (students, graduates and staff) is a special group of people.

LIST OF ABBREVIATIONS

AB	Anchor (Yale) Bible Commentary
AnBib	*Analecta Biblica*
ANE	Ancient Near East
ANET	*Ancient Near Eastern Texts Relating to the Old Testament.* Edited by James B. Pritchard. 3rd ed. Princeton: Princeton University Press, 1969
Ant.	*Jewish Antiquities* (Josephus)
AOTC	Apollos Old Testament Commentary
BDB	Brown, Francis, S. R. Driver, and Charles A. Briggs. *A Hebrew and English Lexicon of the Old Testament*. Oxford: Clarendon, 1906
BETL	Bibliotheca Ephemeridum Theologicarum Lovaniensium
CBR	*Currents in Biblical Research*
CTA	*Corpus des tablettes en cuneiformes alphabetiques decouvertes a Ras Shamra-Ugarit de 1929 a 1939.* Edited by Andree Herdner. Paris: Geuthner, 1963
DCH	*Dictionary of Classical Hebrew.* Edited by David J. A. Clines. 9 vols. Sheffield: Sheffield Phoenix Press, 1993–2016
DLNT	*Dictionary of the Later New Testament and Its Developments.* Edited by Ralph P. Martin and Peter H. Davids. Downers Grove, IL: InterVarsity Press, 1997
GKC	*Gesenius' Hebrew Grammar*. Edited by Emil Kautzsch. Translated by Arthur E. Cowley. 2nd ed. Oxford: Clarendon, 1910
HALOT	*The Hebrew and Aramaic Lexicon of the Old Testament*. Ludwig Koehler, Walter Baumgartner,

	and Johann J. Stamm. Translated and edited under the supervision of Mervyn E. J. Richardson. 5 vols. Leiden: Brill, 1994–2000
HL	Hittite Laws
Int	*Interpretation*
JBC	*Jerome Biblical Commentary*. Edited by Raymond E. Brown et al. Englewood Cliffs, NJ: Prentice-Hall, 1968
JETS	*Journal of the Evangelical Theological Society*
JPS	Jewish Publication Society. 1917
JQR	*Jewish Quarterly Review*
JSOT	*Journal for the Study of the Old Testament*
JSOTSup	*Journal for the Study of the Old Testament Supplement Series*
KBL	Koehler, Ludwig, and Walter Baumgartner. *Lexicon in Veteris Testamenti libros*. 2nd ed. Leiden, 1958
LXX	Septuagint
MT	Masoretic Text
NIDOTTE	*New International Dictionary of Old Testament Theology and Exegesis*. Edited by Willem A. VanGemeren. 5 vols. Grand Rapids: Zondervan, 1997
NDBT	*New Dictionary of Biblical Theology*. Edited by T. Desmond Alexander and Brian S. Rosner. Leicester, England: Inter-Varsity, 2000
NSBT	New Studies in Biblical Theology
OTL	Old Testament Library
SBAB	Stuttgarter biblische Aufsatzbände
TDOT	*Theological Dictionary of the Old Testament*. Edited by G. Johannes Botterweck and Helmer Ringgren. Translated by John T. Willis et al. 15 vols. Grand Rapids: Eerdmans, 1974–2006
TynBul	*Tyndale Bulletin*
TWOT	*Theological Wordbook of the Old Testament*. Edited by R. Laird Harris, Gleason L. Archer Jr., and Bruce K. Waltke. 2 vols. Chicago: Moody Press, 1980
VT	*Vetus Testamentum*
VTSup	*Supplements to Vetus Testamentum*
ZAW	*Zeitschrift für die alttestamentliche Wissenschaft*

INTRODUCTION

I have a confession to make: I am very impatient and so seldom read the introductions to commentaries! That's why I've tried to write an "introduction" for people who don't read introductions. I suspect that readers of this book will fall into one of three categories: (1) those who are reading because they want some help in teaching Deuteronomy in the context of the local church (I suspect this is also the group most like me, and therefore the least likely to spend time wading through the introduction; in fact, they may have already turned straight to the commentary on chapter 1, verse 1); (2) those who have picked up this volume either because they have to for a course at seminary or Bible college; or (3) those who are reading simply because they want to know more of this marvelous part of God's word. My aim in this introduction is to surprise and then keep the first group reading to the end, to give the second group what they need as succinctly and helpfully as possible, and to make sure that the third group (well, actually all three groups) are encouraged, strengthened, and nourished in Christ right from the beginning.

My approach in this volume is fairly simple: I have tried to write the kind of commentary that I would enjoy reading and would find helpful when I come to teach Deuteronomy. What does that look like? This book aims to hit three goals:

First, above all, I have aimed to unpack the text—all of it. Now being truly comprehensive is almost impossible to achieve (and where I've missed that goal, I am truly sorry), but I do know how frustrating it is when we turn to a commentary to find out what on earth verse 37 means, only to find that the writer has conveniently omitted any mention of verse 37! So I have done my level best to try to anticipate and answer any question you may have on the text.

Second, I have tried to do as much work as I possibly can for you. Before I started work at Queensland Theological College in Brisbane, I was a pastor for seventeen years. I realize that most people most of the time (especially pastors) demand a high return for the time they invest in studying—and especially in reading commentaries. And to be honest, while I do want those who preach to me to read carefully and widely, I also want them to spend plenty of time praying and thinking about how to communicate and apply the message. That's why I have tried to approach this commentary as a "one stop shop" for those who are going to lead a Bible study or give a talk on Deuteronomy. Not that this is "the definitive work" on Deuteronomy—far from it. But I have tried to make sure that if you work through this book, you will also have an awareness of where the tricky issues are and how others might come at them.[1] In particular, I have engaged thoroughly with what I regard to be the four major commentaries on Deuteronomy in English, written by Jack Lundbom (a "critical" scholar) and Jeffrey Tigay (a Jewish writer), as well as by two evangelicals—Gordon McConville, my fellow Ulsterman and former adviser during my doctoral studies, and Daniel Block, long-time professor at Wheaton Graduate School, whose creative output on Deuteronomy has been as stimulating as it has been voluminous! I would love you to engage with them on their own terms, but should you be short of time, please know (as will be obvious from the footnotes) that I stand on their shoulders.

Third, following on from that, I have sought to provide you with a "Goldilocks" commentary—one that is "just right"! Pitching a commentary at the right level is notoriously tricky. It really does depend on whom one is writing for and what they want to get out of their reading. Some commentaries I read are extremely technical and tell me plenty about the Hebrew and nothing about the application. Others are highly engaging and applicatory but tell me little or nothing about the text. For anyone who wants to grapple seriously with the text and/or to teach it to God's people, I think the EBTC aims at precisely the right spot: just the right

---

[1] As is the goal of this series, I have tried not to weigh the discussion down with endless footnotes, referring to all kinds of journal articles and academic treatises. Where I have included articles, it is simply to give credit where credit is due for key ideas.

amount of technical information about the text, and the meaning in context, how it fits with the flow of biblical theology, and how we might apply it to our challenging world. That is what I have aimed for; I will allow you to be the judge of how successful I have been.

I. Moses and the "Words" of Deuteronomy

The book of Deuteronomy is made up of the words of Moses. It is entirely appropriate that the Hebrew name for the book, taken from its opening sentence, is simply הַדְּבָרִים ("the words"). Apart from a few explanatory comments (e.g., 1:1–5; 2:10–12), linking sections (e.g., 4:44–49; 29:1), and the account of his death (34:1–12), the entire book consists of statements from the lips of Israel's greatest ever leader, as he speaks on behalf of the God of the covenant. This has some basic implications for the reader and interpreter:

A. It Is Oral

Deuteronomy is presented to us as an edited record of Moses's speeches on the edge of the Transjordan looking over the Jordan Valley near Jericho. Everything about the book feels spoken. The language is not complex but repetitive and relatively straightforward.[2] Reading the text aloud should be enough to pick up the rhythms and cadences of the speaker and to feel the urgency of much of his preaching (for that is what it is). There is irony, persuasion, exhortation, and command.

It is uncertain if the breaks in the book (at 4:40; 27:1; 27:9; 29:1; 31:1, 24; etc.) mark separate speeches or are simply a product of the literary processes by which Moses's words became the book. What is clear is that the whole book is now presented as the total of what Moses said prior to his death on the plains of Moab.[3]

---

[2] On pages lxxvi–xcv of his classic volume (*Deuteronomy*, International Critical Commentary [Edinburgh: T&T Clark, 1902]), S. R. Driver provides us with a helpful analysis of the vocabulary, language, and rhetoric of Deuteronomy that has never been surpassed (and is a good reminder that newer isn't necessarily better!). It is worth working carefully through Driver's discussion.

[3] Personally, I am not convinced that these literary markers carry particular significance. There are key transitions in the book (including, most obviously) between chapters 11 and 12, which are not marked like this.

One puzzling feature of Deuteronomy, which is surely a product of the oral origins of the text, is something often called by its German name: the *Numeruswechsel* ("number change").[4] At seemingly random points throughout the text, the Hebrew switches from singular to plural (and vice versa) without warning, and often without any obvious reason. Once thought to be a sign of (clumsy) editorial activity, it is now widely accepted that this is a slightly unusual stylistic device. When these words were first spoken, it presumably had the effect of underlining that these words were addressed both to the individual and to the entire community.

B. It Is Ancient Near Eastern

At the risk of stating the obvious, Deuteronomy is an *ancient Near Eastern* book. The shape of the book has been profoundly influenced by the thinking and conventions of the world in which it is set.

Since the 1950s, debate has raged over where precisely Deuteronomy (or parts thereof) fits both geographically and chronologically.[5] In particular, there has been significant discussion over whether the completed book is more like a Hittite treaty from the second millennium or an Assyrian from the first. This has obviously had significant ramifications for the dating of the book. These arguments have been rehearsed many times, and while, on balance, I find the resemblance to the Hittite vassal treaties much more persuasive (Assyrian treaties did not have historical prologues), there are also so many ways in which Deuteronomy is quite different from these ancient documents (in its rhetoric of persuasion, for example), that it seems unwise to tie too much to identifying specific parallels.

In any case, the fact that Deuteronomy itself places virtually no emphasis on the fact that Yahweh is Israel's king should give us some pause before making ancient vassal treaties the key to unlocking the meaning of Deuteronomy. The legislation concerning any future king in Israel (17:14–20) seems to be basically neutral (although the phrase "like all the other nations" may be a fairly muted criticism), and the only explicit mention of Yahweh as their king comes in the blessing of Moses

---

[4] The issue was raised by De Wette in 1805, and first applied by W. Staerk and C. Steuernagel (both writing in 1894), but the classic discussion is that of Minette de Tillesse ("Sections 'tu' et Sections 'vous' dans le Deutéronome," *VT* 12 (1962): 29–87).

[5] Gordon McConville's article on "The Theology of Deuteronomy" (*NIDOTTE*, 5:537–44) is a succinct and helpful starting place for this discussion.

(33:5) and is hardly in an emphatic position within the rhetorical flow of the book. This makes is unlikely that the form of the book has been deliberately shaped in order to present Yahweh as Israel's peerless king.

It would seem more helpful to understand Deuteronomy as a product of its wider environment, in which Yahweh's covenant with Israel (summed up by the simple formula "I will be your God, you will be my people" as addressed in the biblical-theological discussion of "Covenant" below) is understood and expounded in ways (and in categories) that are drawn from its immediate world and with which its readers would be deeply familiar. This includes not just covenantal materials, which have attracted most attention, but also (perhaps even more importantly) the world of ancient Near Eastern law, which is discussed more fully below.

C. It Is Essentially Mosaic

From beginning to end of Deuteronomy, Moses is front and center. However, the book we know as Deuteronomy came into existence (which we will discuss next), its uniform insistence is that it is made up almost entirely of words spoken by Moses, committed to writing and then handed down to subsequent generations. There is no real reason to dispute this.[6]

At multiple levels, the book itself supports its basic authenticity. The place names are clearly early (and not always easy to identify). The land itself is described from a vantage point in the Transjordan (apart from the editorial notes in Deut 2:22; 3:14; 10:8; 11:4; 29:4; 34:6, which are self-avowedly written from a post-conquest standpoint. The language (as we have seen) is repetitive and persuasive, as befits a speech.

It has also been pointed out that it would take someone like Moses to make such a speech, especially given the fact that even general parallels to the kind of treaty documents alluded to above would require access to court/diplomatic circles. Add to that the theological creativity and dynamism of the theology, and it narrows the pool still further. Kenneth Kitchen, in typically mischievous fashion, sums up the situation like this:

---

[6] The question of the origins of Deuteronomy then is much more straightforward than that of the Pentateuch as a whole. The book is presented as the lightly edited, published version of the words of Moses.

> In short, to explain what exists in our Hebrew documents, we need a Hebrew leader who had experience of life at the Egyptian court, mainly in the East Delta (hence at Pi-Ramesse), including a knowledge of treaty-type documents and their format, as well as of traditional Semitic legal/social usage more familiar to his own folk. In other words, somebody distressingly like that old "hero" of biblical tradition, Moses, is badly needed at this point to make sense of the situation as we have it. Or somebody in his position of the same or another name.[7]

In the pages that follow, Moses will loom large, for these are his words, as well as the words of Yahweh.

II. The Birth of a Biblical Book: How Did We Get Deuteronomy?

Deuteronomy is essentially "Mosaic," as we have seen. But that does raise a further question: how did the words spoken by the leader of Israel on the edge of Moab find their way into the form in which we now have them ("Deuteronomy") in the Bible? The short answer is "We don't know!"

At one level, we shouldn't be surprised by this. It is the undeniable (if often forgotten) reality that we simply do not know how the constitutive materials of the Old Testament found their way into what we refer to as the books of the Bible. So we simply do not know who actually *composed* the words of, say, Genesis 1, or who wrote the books of Kings, or whether Jonah himself was involved in writing the book that bears his name. There are, however, a couple of places where we get a glimpse of the processes going on behind the scenes.

Jeremiah 36 provides a fascinating window into the way in which God ordered things to bring his word to his people. The chapter opens with Yahweh instructing Jeremiah to record his ministry to date:

> [1] In the fourth year of Jehoiakim son of Josiah, king of Judah, this word came to Jeremiah from the LORD: [2] "Take a scroll, and write on it all the words I have spoken to you concerning Israel, Judah, and all the nations from the time I first spoke to you during Josiah's reign until today." (Jer 36:1–2)

---

[7] Kenneth A. Kitchen, *On the Reliability of the Old Testament* (Grand Rapids: Eerdmans, 2003), 295.

After Baruch (his scribe) copies down the words dictated by the prophet, he reads them aloud to the people at the temple (Jer 36:4, 8). Word quickly reaches King Jehoiakim, who procures the scroll, and has it read to him by one of his officials.

> [21] The king sent Jehudi to get the scroll, and he took it from the chamber of Elishama the scribe. Jehudi then read it in the hearing of the king and all the officials who were standing by the king. [22] Since it was the ninth month, the king was sitting in his winter quarters with a fire burning in front of him. [23] As soon as Jehudi would read three or four columns, Jehoiakim would cut the scroll with a scribe's knife and throw the columns into the fire in the hearth until the entire scroll was consumed by the fire in the hearth. (Jer 36:21–23)

In the wake of this blatant rejection of Yahweh's words, the response is fascinating, particularly with regard to the way in which the words of the prophet become Scripture:

> [27] After the king had burned the scroll and the words Baruch had written at Jeremiah's dictation, the word of the LORD came to Jeremiah: [28] "Take another scroll, and once again write on it the original words that were on the original scroll that King Jehoiakim of Judah burned." (Jer 36:27–28)

At this point, a supplement dealing with Jehoiakim directly is added, along with "many other words like them" (36:32).

At least three stages are visible here. The first is the initial pronouncement of the prophetic oracles. Then there is the first edition, dictated by Jeremiah to Baruch. After that, there is a subsequent edition (or editions?), which presumably brings us closer to what we now know as the book of Jeremiah.[8] This chain of events may well give us some pointers as to how the *book* of Deuteronomy was born.

Daniel I. Block has suggested one possible pathway from the speeches to the canonical text.[9] Working from the assumption that there are four

---

[8] Incidentally, this also gives a credible explanation for the existence of different textual traditions for the book of Jeremiah, with the LXX, of Alexandrian provenance, being significantly shorter (around 2700 words) than the MT, which reflects the Babylonian tradition.

[9] Daniel I. Block, "Recovering the Voice of Moses: The Genesis of Deuteronomy," in *The Gospel According to Moses* (Eugene: Cascade, 2012), 21–68.

speeches in the book, Block then traces how the central speech may have been expanded, as it was combined with additional addresses of Moses (e.g., the Song of ch. 32) to give us the finished product that we know as Deuteronomy.[10] There is also little reason to doubt that this took place in the years following Moses's death (as implied by, e.g., Deut 31:9, 22; Josh 8:32).

III. The Structure of Deuteronomy: A Simple Approach

There is a sense in which my approach to the structure should be entitled "Confessions of a Minimalist"! The normal requirements of the introduction to a commentary involve a detailed breakdown of the text to a micro-level, which often stretches to several pages. The problem with this approach is that it often relies on a degree of arbitrariness, as rhetorical, grammatical, and textual factors (including the masoretic apparatus) are weighed, along with clear shifts in content, in coming up with an externally imposed structure.[11] The results are often not easy to evaluate, nor do they have particular utility.[12]

Rather than offer a complex structural breakdown of the book then, I will simply map out the main sections of the book, putting a premium on the *content* instead of other factors.

Moses Preaches History (1:1–3:29)
- A Carefully Crafted Beginning (1:1-8)
- A Surprising Interlude (1:9-18)
- A Disastrous Choice (1:19-46)
- A Painful Lesson (2:1-23)
- Two Model Conquests (2:24-3:22)
- A Shocking Prohibition (3:23–29)

---

[10] Block readily admits that this schema cannot be proven. Personally, I remain unconvinced that the "speeches" in the book can be treated as independent units, but I am persuaded that some such process accounts well for the establishment of the torah of Moses (essentially Deuteronomy) taking its place as the foundational document of the people of God shortly after their settlement in Canaan.

[11] I am also not persuaded that giving a highly detailed micro-breakdown is particularly useful to the reader at this stage.

[12] An extreme example of this is Duane L. Christensen's attempts to show that the book is an elaborate system of chiasms. *Deuteronomy 1:1–21:9*, 2nd ed., Word Biblical Commentary 6a (Nashville: Thomas Nelson, 2001) and *Deuteronomy 21:10–34:12*, 2nd ed., Word Biblical Commentary 6b (Nashville: Thomas Nelson, 2002).

Moses Preaches Revelation (4:1–43)
- The Priority of Listening to God (4:1–4)
- Introducing the Beautiful Life with God (4:5–8)
- Listening as God's Template for Life (4:9–20)
- Painful Alternatives (and a Way Back to God) (4:21–31)
- Life with the God Who Speaks (4:32–40)
- Postscript: What Listening Looks Like (4:41–43)

Moses Preaches Covenant (4:44–11:32)
- The Headline Statement (4:44–49)
- The Basic Requirements of the Covenant (5:1–33)
- Horeb Applied: Covenantal Listening(6:1–25)
- Horeb Applied: Covenantal Faithfulness (7:1–26)
- Learning from the Wilderness: Covenantal Dependence (8:1–20)
- Learning from the Golden Calf: Covenantal Humility (9:1–10:11)
- What God Requires (10:12–11:7)
- Blessing or Curse? (11:8–32)

Moses Preaches Torah (12:1–26:19)
- Worshiping God's Way (12:1–32)
- Worshiping God Alone (13:1–18)
- Living as God's Treasured Possession (14:1–21)
- The Rhythm of Covenant Life (14:22–16:17)
- Living under God's Appointed Leaders (16:18–18:22)
- Death as the Ultimate Sanction (19:1–22:12)
- Righteousness in All of Life (22:13–25:19)
- Conclusion: Living All of Life for God (Firstfruits and Tithes) (26:1–19)

Moses Preaches Blessing and Curse (27:1–28:68)
Moses Preaches the New Covenant (29:1–30:20)
Postscript 1: The Inevitability of Failure (31:1–32:47)
Postscript 2: The Death of Moses (32:48–34:12)

This hopefully will orient the intrepid reader (who has made it this far!) with a useful overview of the book, as well as preparing the way for both the exposition ahead and also the comments at the end of the introduction on how one might go about preaching this vitally important book in the context of the local church.

IV. What Kind of Book is Deuteronomy? Narrative and Law in Deuteronomy

One of the unique features of the book of Deuteronomy is the way the narrative material (in the form of Moses's rehearsal of the recent history of Israel) in the so-called framework of the book, chapters 1–11 and 27–34, enfolds the legal material of chapters 12–26. As we shall see in the next section of this introduction, that is highly unusual in the ancient Near East, where collections of law generally have only the briefest preamble.[13]

In the history of the study of Deuteronomy, one unhelpful tendency has been to view the narrative and legal sections as having a different origin, purpose, and "feel."[14] Often this has led to setting the framework and the laws against each other—usually, with the central section of the book being caricatured as legalistic and at odds with the grace on display in the narrative sections. This unresolved tension has generally been ascribed to the literary history of the book.[15]

While these are important discussions, there are two basic problems with this approach: (1) it misunderstands the nature of biblical "law" and in particular the ways in which the laws in the Bible are both similar and markedly different at the level of purpose and expression from other extant ancient Near Eastern collections, and (2) it drives a wedge between the laws and the framework in a way that underestimates the similarity of theology and rhetorical approach across the whole book. We'll look at each of these in turn.

---

[13] So classically, the Law Code of Hammurabi, which dates to Babylon around 1750 BC, which is discussed in more detail below.

[14] So my doctoral supervisor, John Barton, argues that the laws are appended to earlier narratives to interpret them. The laws "have the function of explaining the divine reaction to the kinds of human action that the narrative illustrates and exemplifies. Whoever it was in Ancient Israel ... who put together the Pentateuch in the form we now have it, was evidently concerned to make sense of the story of Israel by setting beside it a set of norms in the light of which that story could be judged and found deficient." See John Barton, "Law and Narrative in the Pentateuch," *Communio Viatorum* 51 (2009): 137–38. For a counter-argument, see Gordon J. Wenham, *Story as Torah* (Grand Rapids: Baker, 2004), especially 151–155. Wenham essentially argues that the narratives embody, illustrate and back up the values enshrined in the law.

[15] This approach was typical of German scholarship in the twentieth century (so, e.g., Gerhard von Rad, *Deuteronomy*, OTL [London: SCM, 1966]), but can also be seen in the work of John Sailhamer, who argues that the book is the product of the supplanting of a legalistic Mosaic covenant by a more gracious "Moabite" version. See John H. Sailhamer, *The Meaning of the Pentateuch: Revelation, Composition and Interpretation* (Downers Grove: IVP Academic, 2009), 315; 537–62.

A. The Laws of Deuteronomy in Its World

Over the years, a significant body of ancient legal material has been discovered, particularly from Babylon and the surrounding area. Known as *Cuneiform Law* (after the style of script in which it is written; Akkadian, Sumerian, and Hittite all use a similar cuneiform script), it was generally inscribed on clay tablets or stone obelisks known as *stelae*. The most spectacular example of such a stele is found in the Law Code of Hammurabi. It is a black stone stele 2.25m tall, on which 282 rules of various kinds, followed by an epilogue singing the praises of King Hammurabi and threatening woe on any who defy him, are inscribed.[16]

The laws of Hammurabi are relatively straightforward. All 282 stipulations are essentially case law in the form "If you do x, then y will happen to you." There is no attempt at persuasion; the king is backed by his gods to enforce order for the "common good" (which essentially means the good of the king). The focus is clearly on restraining evil and promoting "peace," in the sense of unquestioning, submissive obedience.[17]

It is also striking that throughout the inscription, the tone of these laws (as is typical of cuneiform law) is neither self-deprecating nor modest. The king is at great pains to emphasize his own superiority, worthiness, and power to compel miscreants to conform—none of which is a feature of the biblical material.

Shalom Paul offers very helpful comparative summaries of the laws in the biblical law codes and cuneiform law,[18] which highlight the marked differences between them. One could summarize his conclusions about

---

[16] The stele itself is on display in the Louvre in Paris. The full translation is available here: http://avalon.law.yale.edu/subject_menus/hammenu.asp. See also Stanley A. Cook, *The Laws Of Moses and the Code Of Hammurabi* (London: A&C Black, 1903) for the classic comparison of the two sets of laws.

[17] The preface to the code reads: "When Anu the Sublime, King of the Anunaki, and Bel, the lord of Heaven and earth, who decreed the fate of the land, assigned to Marduk, the over-ruling son of Ea, God of righteousness, dominion over earthly man, and made him great among the Igigi, they called Babylon by his illustrious name, made it great on earth, and founded an everlasting kingdom in it, whose foundations are laid so solidly as those of heaven and earth; then Anu and Bel called by name me, Hammurabi, the exalted prince, who feared God, to bring about the rule of righteousness in the land, to destroy the wicked and the evil-doers; so that the strong should not harm the weak; so that I should rule over the black-headed people like Shamash, and enlighten the land, to further the well-being of mankind."

[18] Shalom M. Paul, *Studies in the Book of the Covenant in the Light of Cuneiform and Biblical Law, VTSup* 18 (Leiden: Brill, 1970), 37–39.

the following broad distinctive principles that undergird and mark biblical law as follows:

1. All crime is sin.
2. Biblical law covers all of life.
3. God runs the justice system.
4. Biblical law is given to the whole nation (not just the king).
5. Transparency in the justice system is vital.
6. Biblical law is designed to be taught and so to educate people.
7. All of life is sacred.
8. Individuals are responsible for their actions.
9. All people are equal.
10. Slaves are to be treated well.

Deuteronomy 12–26, then, while having some commonality with the world in which it was born, is actually quite dramatically different at a deep level from the comparative material. This is why it is slightly unfortunate that this book is known in English as "Deuteronomos" ("Second Law"). Based on the unfortunate translation of 17:18 (where the king is to make for himself a *copy* of the torah) in the Septuagint, it is misleading on every count. Not only is the scroll to be produced not a *second* law, it isn't really a *law* at all. As will become obvious throughout the commentary, the word תּוֹרָה is not the same thing as the Greek νομος.

The word "law" (whether in English or Greek) is essentially a negative or restrictive term. But through Deuteronomy, the "torah of Moses" is described in relentlessly positive terms. Deuteronomy 4:5–8 sets the tone for the whole book:

> 5 Look, I have taught you statutes and ordinances as the Lord my God has commanded me, so that you may follow them in the land you are entering to possess. 6 Carefully follow them, for this will show your wisdom and understanding in the eyes of the peoples. When they hear about all these statutes, they will say, "This great nation is indeed a wise and understanding people." 7 For what great nation is there that has a god near to it as the Lord our God is to us whenever we call to him? 8 And what great nation has righteous statutes and ordinances like this entire law I set before you today?"

"Torah" does not mean (in any simple sense) "law." Literally meaning "instruction," it carries the connotation of living richly within the right boundaries that God has laid down. It is an expansive and expanding idea, which clearly sets it apart from not only the laws of Hammurabi, but from the entire world of ancient law, which simply did not have this positive, freeing element.

In the Old Testament, the legal collections build from the Decalogue, to the book of the covenant, to the Holiness Code, to the collection of laws in Deuteronomy, in part at least to capture the fact that God's prescriptions for life adapt and expand to address the challenges and opportunities faced by every generation in every "today" that his people face. If we allow the Old Testament material to breathe and to speak on its own terms, it is clear that Torah is an ever-expanding description/depiction of the beautiful life that Yahweh has created us for and calls us to.

This material, then, rather than mimicking the power-plays and posturing of ancient kings, anticipates the beautiful life to which God calls his people, a beautiful life fulfilled by and embodied in the Lord Jesus Christ himself.

At a biblical-theological level, such an understanding of the shape and purpose of the laws in Deuteronomy prepares us to expect the New Testament to ask more of and offer more to those who have been brought to new life in Christ and made part of his new society, the church. The beautiful life we discover in Christ should be *more*. The all-encompassing, gospel-shaped life delivered to us by Christ should be more vivid, more joyful, more wholehearted, more far-reaching than that in the Old Testament. This expansionist reading of the Old Testament opens up all kinds of possibilities in applying the Old Testament responsibly to the life of God's new covenant people

This explains why the food laws are relaxed by Jesus in Mark 6:14–23. We can dispense with the markers of distinctiveness and eat anything we choose, because our distinctiveness is not now based on diet but rests on the transformation that flows from our union with Christ and possession of (and by) the Holy Spirit, which issues in love and the rest of the fruit of the Spirit.

The same principle is visible in James 2:8–13:

> [8] Indeed, if you fulfill the royal law prescribed in the Scripture, **Love your neighbor as yourself**, you are doing well. [9] If, however, you show favoritism, you commit sin and are convicted by the law as transgressors. [10] For whoever keeps the

> entire law, and yet stumbles at one point, is guilty of breaking it all. [11] For he who said, **Do not commit adultery**, also said, **Do not murder**. So if you do not commit adultery, but you murder, you are a lawbreaker. [12] Speak and act as those who are to be judged by the law of freedom. [13] For judgment is without mercy to the one who has not shown mercy. Mercy triumphs over judgment.

There are obviously some complexities in James's argument here, but for our purposes it is clear that his coining of the phrase "royal law" refers to something huge, and demanding, and yet ultimately both attractive and inherently good ("the law of freedom"). It is also a "law" (torah?) that is steeped in and operates on the principle of mercy. This is the mercy that we have been shown in Jesus Christ—mercy that puts this beautiful life within our grasp.

This approach provides a way of reading and teaching the legal material in the Old Testament and in Deuteronomy in particular that is both biblically-theologically appropriate but also morally powerful.

Incidentally, this understanding of the laws in Deuteronomy also highlights some of the weaknesses in the classic approach of the "threefold division of the law." This idea is almost certainly ancient, but it was around 1270 that Thomas Aquinas wrote:

> We must therefore distinguish three kinds of precept in the Old Law; viz. "moral" precepts, which are dictated by the natural law; "ceremonial" precepts, which are determinations of the Divine worship; and "judicial" precepts, which are determinations of the justice to be maintained among men.[19]

Of course, it is with some hesitancy that I criticize an idea that has been the consensus among many of God's people for generations. However, despite the clear usefulness of the scheme (e.g., it makes very clear that Christ has fulfilled the need for sacrifice to be offered, having paid the price for sin once for all; it also highlights the fact that the church is not a nation-state), it does have some unfortunate implications.

The primary drawback is that it creates the sense that Christ has released us from a large percentage of what God asked his covenant

---

[19] Thomas Aquinas, *Summa Theologica*, trans. Fathers of the English Dominican Province, (New York: Benziger Brothers, 1947), 1034 (I-II, 99, Art. 4).

people to do before Christ. This seems to suggest that, in some sense, life in Christ is *less* rather than *more.* Fulfillment of the law is reduced to releasing us *from* obligation, rather than equipping and empowering to live out all that God holds out to us. It also suggests that much of the revelation of the beautiful life before Christ is simply irrelevant to those of us who are gentiles—we can dispense with all that—rather than celebrating the fact that we get to share in the unimaginably rich *fulfillment* of all that was anticipated in the torah of Moses.

There is also the simple (but obstinate) fact that if one attempts to sort the laws into these three categories, there are some laws that stubbornly resist such classification (e.g., is 16:18–20 civil or moral? Or both? How does one deal with 25:5–13?). Even at a *prima facie* level, these difficulties suggest that these categories, no matter how broadly useful, are foreign to the world of the laws themselves and so of limited help in understanding the text as God has given it to us.

B. The Laws of Deuteronomy and the Rhetoric of Moses

The remaining stand-out feature of the instruction of Moses in these chapters is a simple one, but one that is massively important: these laws are quite clearly *preached.* This is reflected in the sheer variety that the material displays, all in the interests of wooing, cajoling, and commanding the people of Yahweh to listen to him and walk in his ways. Unlike the uniform approach of Hammurabi (all case or "casuistic" law), the legal material in Deuteronomy is a mixture of the following:

(i) Apodictic laws (simple direct commands)

> e.g., "*Do not move your neighbor's boundary marker*, established at the start in the inheritance you will receive in the land the Lord your God is giving you to possess" (19:14).

(ii) Laws with motive clauses attached

> e.g., "Do not regard it as a hardship when you set [your slave] free, because he worked for you six years—worth twice the wages of a hired worker. *Then the* Lord *your God will bless you in everything you do*" (15:18).

(iii) Similar laws repeated for effect

> e.g., "Do not charge your brother interest on silver, food, or anything that can earn interest. You may charge a foreigner interest, but you must not charge your brother Israelite interest, so that the LORD your God may bless you in everything you do in the land you are entering to possess" (23:19–20)
>
> "When you make a loan of any kind to your neighbor, do not enter his house to collect what he offers as security. Stand outside while the man you are making the loan to brings the security out to you. If he is a poor man, do not sleep with the garment he has given as security. Be sure to return it to him at sunset. Then he will sleep in it and bless you, and this will be counted as righteousness to you before the LORD your God" (24:10–13)

(iv) Successive applications of the same law

> e.g., chapter 13, where idolatry springs from the influence of (a) a false prophet, (b) a family member, (c) wicked city dwellers

(v) Hypothetical case law

> e.g., the bizarre provision of 25:11–12, which cannot have been a regular occurrence in Israel, but rather (as in 14:21) represents a wider principle

(vi) Laws derived from national experiences

> e.g., "Remember what the Amalekites did to you on the journey after you left Egypt. They met you along the way and attacked all your stragglers from behind when you were tired and weary. They did not fear God. When the LORD your God gives you rest from all the enemies around you in the land the LORD your God is giving you to possess as an inheritance, blot out the memory of Amalek under heaven. Do not forget" (25:17–19)

These laws, then, are clearly theologically shaped and are presented in such a way as to mount the most compelling case for Israel to live as Moses has called them to in the first eleven chapters of the book. As the commentary section will point out in due course, Moses appears to have very little interest in supplying the kind of detail necessary to enact all these laws. His overwhelming interest is in moving people's hearts to love and obey Yahweh, as has clearly been the case from the beginning of his preaching in Deuteronomy. He is not trying to be comprehensive. He is not setting out a national constitution, but painting a picture of life in the land (or perhaps providing a model for working out what to do in the land).

The more carefully one reads the laws, the more it becomes obvious that Moses's preaching in chapters 1–11 flows from the same source and has the same goal as his preaching in chapters 12–26. His preaching of torah is very clearly rooted in grace—something that is made explicit by the constant reminders of grace in the text (e.g., 14:1–2: "You are sons of the Lord your God; do not cut yourselves or make a bald spot on your head on behalf of the dead, for you are a holy people belonging to the Lord your God. The Lord has chosen you to be his own possession out of all the peoples on the face of the earth"). And like his preaching in chapters 1–11, his preaching of torah revolves around right worship, right relationships, and right behavior. The core issue is "righteousness" (e.g., 16:20), as it has been since 6:25.[20]

The theology of the laws dovetails perfectly with the theology of the rest of the book. In the laws, Yahweh is absolutely and utterly sovereign ("the place that the Lord your God chooses," 12:5–6), as he is when he chooses Israel (7:7–8). Idolatry is a terrible idea (7:1–6; 12:1–4; 29:16–18). Worshiping God his way is the only way to joy (see 16:9–12 and 28:47). Being God's much-loved people means loving those who are excluded and disadvantaged (10:17–20; 15:7–11). God is the best thing that the land has to offer, so even the king should concentrate on listening to and delighting in him (6:4–5; 17:14–20; 18:1–8). Rejecting Yahweh will lead to disaster, and ultimately even expulsion from the land (4:25–31; 11:18–25; 13:1–5).

Given all this, it seems reasonable to assert that the primary function of these chapters is to build on the preaching of the framework that calls God's people to wholehearted obedience, by painting a picture of the beautiful life with Yahweh in the land, lived in response to his grace, in step with his commands. James Watts, in his excellent short book *Reading Law* helpfully points out that:

---

[20] See See J. Gary Millar, "Deuteronomy" in *NDBT*, ed. Brian S. Rosner, T. Desmond Alexander, Graeme Goldsworthy, and D. A. Carson (Downers Grove: IVP Academic, 2000), 159-65.

> The combination of story and list [and divine sanction] ... should be regarded as a strategy of persuasion employed by many cultures in a variety of literary genres for the purpose of convincing readers and hearers of the document's, and its author's, authority. In other words, both law and narrative work together, employing complementary strategies of persuasion.[21]

He goes on to point out that when compared to other collections of law in the ANE generally, the Bible, with its variety of preached legal material, is "truly *sui generis*, without parallel in size, scale, contents in Israel's or any other culture's earlier or contemporary literature."[22]

So what kind of book is Deuteronomy? It is a book where Moses preaches history, theology, and law in an effort to shape the future life of Israel. It is all of a piece, even though there is variation and richness in the literature itself. Given all that we have seen, it seems reasonable to assert that the function of chapters 12–26 is to paint a picture of the beautiful life with Yahweh in the land, lived in response to his grace, in step with his commands—the same life that Moses calls people to in chapters 1–11 and from chapter 27 to the end.

The Mosaic vision here fits perfectly with the statement of James K. A. Smith that

> A vision of the good life captures our hearts and imaginations not by providing a set of rules or ideas, but by painting a picture of what it looks like for us to flourish and live well ... because we are affective before we are cognitive (and even while we are cognitive).[23]

V. The Audiences of Deuteronomy

Deuteronomy is a timeless book. The sense of contemporaneity is carefully constructed through the use of the word "today" (occurring over

---

[21] James W. Watts, *Reading Law: The Rhetorical Shaping of the Pentateuch* (Edinburgh: T&T Clark, 1999), 60.

[22] Watts, *Reading Law*, 60.

[23] James K. A. Smith, *Desiring the Kingdom: Worship, Worldview, and Cultural Formation* (Grand Rapids: Baker Academic, 2009), 53.

170 times in the book) and the artfully layered call to present, future, and distant future generations to listen to the voice of Yahweh.[24]

In the first place, the words of Moses were addressed to the Moab generation, as they camped on the verge of the land, prior to taking hold (finally) of the promises that Yahweh had made to their forefathers and was now delivering to them. The first "today" is the day when the people actually heard Moses deliver this sermon on the ridge above the Jordan. However, that is not the primary audience of the book.

It is important to remember that even though the words were first spoken to the Moab generation, when the book came into being, the people had actually moved into the land and "settled down," as we saw above from the editorial notes that helped fashion Moses's speeches into the book we have today. This changes the dominant tone of the book from "Let's go and take the land" to "Let's not take the land for granted, sliding into complacency, but rather press on to live the beautiful life with Yahweh." For most of Israel's history, they failed to take this clarion call seriously and, given the reality of 2 Kings 22:7–13, presumably resented it to the point that the book was actually suppressed and forgotten. This is the reason why Deuteronomy's easiest and most natural application is to followers of God for whom life is relatively comfortable and easy. However, we have not yet exhausted those to whom this book is addressed.

Such is the unique genius of this book that it is also addressed to those at some point in the future who have *already paid the price for rejecting Yahweh* and have experienced the curse of the covenant already. Not only does it speak to those in the land who are in danger of complacency, it also speaks to those who have already been scattered, offering them *a way back* from the places to which they have been scattered. So, for example:

> [27] The Lord will scatter you among the peoples, and you will be reduced to a few survivors among the nations where the Lord your God will drive you. [28] There you will worship man-made gods of wood and stone, which cannot see, hear, eat, or smell. [29] But from there, you will search for the Lord your God, and you will find him when you seek him with all your heart and all your soul. 30 When you are in distress and all these things have

[24] For the use of "today" in the book, see James Gordon McConville and J. G. Millar, *Time and Place in Deuteronomy*, *JSOTSup* 179 (Sheffield: JSOT Press, 1994).

> happened to you, in the future you will return to the Lord your God and obey him. (Deut 4:27–30)

> [1] When all these things happen to you—the blessings and curses I have set before you—and you come to your senses while you are in all the nations where the Lord your God has driven you, [2] and you and your children return to the Lord your God and obey him with all your heart and all your soul by doing everything I am commanding you today, [3] then he will restore your fortunes, have compassion on you, and gather you again from all the peoples where the Lord your God has scattered you. (Deut 30:1–3)

Notice that these passages are both quite general rather than reflecting any details of this future experience of scattering and regathering. They show every sign of being exactly what they purport to be: an early anticipation of the (theo)logical consequences of disobedience in Israel's new land, coupled with a strong encouragement to "return to Yahweh." This means that Deuteronomy also speaks clearly to those who are seeking to repent. But we still aren't quite finished.

As I will argue below, Deuteronomy also has a word for those who live *on the other side* of the dramatic intervention of God anticipated in 30:6 (the "circumcision of the heart"). In that sense, Deuteronomy even speaks directly to those of us upon whom "the end of the ages has come":

> [11] This command that I give you today is certainly not too difficult or beyond your reach. [12] It is not in heaven so that you have to ask, "Who will go up to heaven, get it for us, and proclaim it to us so that we may follow it?" [13] And it is not across the sea so that you have to ask, "Who will cross the sea, get it for us, and proclaim it to us so that we may follow it?" [14] But the message is very near you, in your mouth and in your heart, so that you may follow it. (Deut 30:11–14)

Deuteronomy is a call for those of us who are in Christ to choose life in him, the one who has already given us everything we need for life and godliness.

I should admit that this is not the way that most writers on Deuteronomy view these verses (seeing them rather as addressing the Moab generation, as 30:15–20 almost certainly seem to). But the lack of support from Old Testament scholars is outweighed by the rather more significant support of the apostle Paul (!), who writes this in Romans 10:

> [5] Moses writes about the righteousness that is from the law: **The one who does these things will live by them**. [6] But the righteousness that comes from faith speaks like this: **Do not say in your heart, "Who will go up to heaven?"** that is, to bring Christ down [7] or, **"Who will go down into the abyss?"** that is, to bring Christ up from the dead. [8] On the contrary, what does it say? **The message is near you, in your mouth and in your heart.** This is the message of faith that we proclaim: [9] If you confess with your mouth, "Jesus is Lord," and believe in your heart that God raised him from the dead, you will be saved.

This unique book, with its deliberate, dynamic way of addressing multiple audiences across history at the same time, is therefore a deeply precious resource for the people of God across time and space. This also goes some way to explaining the seminal importance this book has for much of the rest of the Old Testament.

VI. Deuteronomy and the Rest of the Old Testament

Deuteronomy is neither the longest, nor the most poetic, nor the most conceptually complex book in the Old Testament. But standing where it does as both the climax of the Pentateuch and the gateway to the historical books, as well as the inspiration behind the preaching of the prophets and the reflections of the wise, this perpetually fresh book is right at the heart of the theology of the Old Testament. There is a very real sense in which to grasp Deuteronomy is to grasp the flow and contours of the Old Testament. One could even say that Deuteronomy is the fountainhead of biblical theology. It is worth taking some time to reflect briefly on Deuteronomy in relation to the earlier books in the Pentateuch, then to the Former and Latter Prophets, and finally to the wisdom of Proverbs.[25]

A. Deuteronomy as the Rhetorical Climax of the Pentateuch

The collection of books we refer to as the Pentateuch (or "The Five Books of Moses") is not often recognized as the standout literary achievement

[25] Throughout this section, I am deeply indebted to Gary Schnittjer's marvelous resource, *Old Testament Use of the Old Testament: A Book by Book Guide* (Grand Rapids: Zondervan, 2021).

of the ancient world. The artistry and complexity of this multi-volume work is remarkable, and Deuteronomy stands at its head, gathering up and applying key themes that have guided its narrative.

Of course, as we have seen with Deuteronomy itself, we remain in the dark about the nature and timing of the processes by which this epic work took on its final shape.[26] How the blend of ancient history, genealogy, and patriarchal narratives flowing into the story of the nascent nation of Israel and the revelation of Yahweh at Sinai came together is not explicitly reported in the text. But what is unmistakable is that the dominant figure in this unfolding drama (at least from the beginning of Exodus) is Moses, and, as we have seen already, in Deuteronomy *Moses speaks.*

This ancient address sits as the capstone of this expansive literary work, picking up and developing the key themes of what has gone before. Interestingly, there is little direct interaction with the narratives of Genesis, although Moses repeatedly makes reference to the God of their "fathers" (CSB: "ancestors") and to the land that Yahweh had sworn to give to their "fathers," a term that generally, and occasionally specifically, refers to Abraham, Isaac, and Jacob.[27] In the Song of Moses, he also alludes to the creation narrative (32:10–11) and events in the wake of Babel (32:8), but apart from that, his interest is more focused on the fulfillment of the promises made to Abraham, Isaac, and Jacob than on the events of their lives. That is confirmed by the way in which Deuteronomy uses the material in Exodus.

The exodus itself is viewed as the foundational moment in the life of the people of Israel and is referred to regularly throughout the book in all kinds of contexts.[28] However, it is the events and the revelation at Sinai (which Moses refers to as Horeb in Deuteronomy) that occupy center stage.

---

[26] Mercifully, in the past twenty years, the preoccupation with identifying putative sources behind the text (generally the fabled J, E, D, and P sources) has waned, giving rise to a much greater appreciation of the literary and theological genius of the text itself.

[27] See Deut 1:8, 11, 21, 35; 4:1, 31, 37; 5:3, 9; 6:3, 10, 18, 23; 7:8, 12–13; 8:1, 3, 16, 18; 9:5; 10:11, 15, 22; 11:9, 21; 12:1; 13:6, 17; 19:8; 22:21, 30; 24:16; 26:3, 7, 15; 27:3, 20; 28:11, 36, 64; 29:13, 25; 30:5, 9, 20; 31:7, 16, 20; 32:17.

[28] Exodus language is everywhere in the book. Phrases like God "brought you out of the land of Egypt" (Deut 4:20, 37; 5:6, 15; 6:12; 7:8, 19; 8:14; 13:5, 10; 16:1), "a mighty hand and outstretched arm" (Deut 4:34; 5:15; 7:19; 11:2; 26:8) and references to the "signs and wonders" referring to the plagues and the defeat of the Egyptians (Deut 4:34; 6:22; 7:19; 26:8; 29:3; 34:11) litter the text.

The declaration of Exodus 19:5–6 ("Now if you will carefully listen to me and keep my covenant, you will be my own possession out of all the peoples, although the whole earth is mine, and you will be my kingdom of priests and my holy nation") provides the undergirding for Deuteronomy's depiction of the people of Yahweh (Deut 7:6; 14:2; 26:18). The "words" that are then spoken (first the Decalogue of Exod 20, and then the "book of the covenant" in chs. 21–24) form the "text" that is expounded by Moses at the core of the book.[29] In addition, the covenant ceremony in chapter 24 appears to be the template for the subsequent ritual to be carried out on Mount Ebal in Deuteronomy 27:1–8. On top of that, the events of Exodus 32–34 are revisited in some detail in Deuteronomy 9 and 10. There is a very real sense in which Deuteronomy then is an expansion and exposition of Exodus for the nation's impending new life in the land.

Explaining the relationship between Deuteronomy and Leviticus is one of the most challenging puzzles in the Old Testament, and one that is far beyond the remit of this introduction.[30] However, it does seem fair to say that in a similar vein to the way in which Deuteronomy has picked up several key theological threads and themes from Genesis and highlighted them in the context of life in the land, there is clear evidence that in his final sermon, Moses has also drawn on the traditions of Leviticus.

So, for example, the laws in Deuteronomy 14 clearly are from the same thought-world as Leviticus 11:1–28, and the covenant blessings and "consequences" of Leviticus 26 appear to lay the groundwork for the blessing and curse motif developed in Deuteronomy 11, 27, and 28. Even though the two books have dramatically different settings and preoccupations, there are clear theological links, which at a literary level at the very least, gives good grounds to say that Deuteronomy functions as the natural conclusion to the massive work of which Leviticus forms a central part.

Deuteronomy's relationship to Numbers is much more straightforward. The crucial events of the refusal to enter the land at Kadesh (Num 13–14),

---

[29] See the list of possible references to Exod 21–24 in the laws of Deuteronomy in Schnittjers, *Old Testament Use of the Old Testament*, 74–75.

[30] One unfortunate legacy of the focus on source criticism in Old Testament studies of the past 200 years has been the lack of any interest in exploring this relationship. Leviticus and Deuteronomy have been placed in hermetically sealed silos, with little thought about their interaction. A glorious exception has been J. Gordon McConville's work in *Law and Theology in Deuteronomy*, *JSOTSup* 33 (Sheffield: JSOT Press, 1984), but there has been little follow up to his work.

Moses's hubris when bringing water from the rock (Num 20), the passage around Edom and Moab (Num 20–21), and the Balaam incident and idolatry at Peor (Num 22–25) all feature in Moses's retrospect as he seeks to highlight the sinfulness of Israel and the enduring grace of Yahweh.

Deuteronomy then appears to function exactly as it presents itself, as an address (or series of addresses) given by the dominant figure of Israel's early history, which draws on key elements of their tradition and applies them in a fresh way to the life they are about to begin in the land of Canaan.

B. Deuteronomy as the Key to History

It has long been recognized that there is a strong link between Deuteronomy and the books that follow. Not only is there is an overlap of content and perspective with Joshua, but far beyond that, Deuteronomic language and concerns can be seen throughout the books of Judges, Samuel, and Kings.[31]

Once more, even though it is difficult to describe the literary history of these books with any certainty, at a canonical level, it seems clear that we are intended to read the subsequent events between occupation and exile through the lens of Moses's words to the people on the edge of the land.

Joshua picks up the events and language of Deuteronomy (so, e.g., chs. 1, 8, 24) but also exemplifies the very concerns that Moses has been airing so forcefully in Deuteronomy. There are moments when Israel obeys, and the conquest is straightforward (e.g., Josh 6), but there are others when the actions of the Israelites are foolish or dubious (e.g., the behavior of the spies in Josh 2, and Joshua himself with the Gibeonites in chapter 9) and their prospects a little more bleak. The fact that the account of the division and occupation of the land is punctuated by failure or a lack of completion amplifies the nagging doubts introduced by Moses at the end of his life.[32]

---

[31] There has been significant discussion over the years concerning the relationship between Deuteronomy and Joshua (should we really speak of a Hexateuch, with Joshua being the conclusion of the epic story of God bringing his people into the land?), and the nature of the continuous narrative running from Joshua to the end of 2 Kings (is it helpful to speak of a "Deuteronomic/Deuteronomistic History?" How did such a work come about? Etc.) These questions are beyond the scope of this volume, but see, for example, André Lemaire, Baruch Halpern, and Matthew J. Adams. *The Books of Kings: Sources, Composition, Historiography and Reception*, *VTSup* 129 (Leiden: Brill, 2010), for an exhaustive discussion.

[32] Other specific allusions to Deuteronomy include Josh 6:17; 9:6, 14;11:20; 24:13.

Similarly, from Judges on, there continue to be allusions to specific texts in Deuteronomy (e.g., Judg 2:6–9 picks up on Deut 11:7; 2 Sam 23:16–17 works from the principle of Deut 12:16, 23–25; 15:23); however, the *theological* influence of Deuteronomy runs much deeper.[33]

In the books of Samuel, the search for and appointment of a godly king is filtered through the criteria that were laid out in Deuteronomy 17:14–20, and in particular, the need for someone whose heart is neither turned aside nor lifted up (1 Sam 12:20, 24; 13:14; 16:7). In Kings, Solomon's reign is evaluated against the same standard (see 1 Kgs 10:26–11:10).

When the temple is constructed and dedicated, Solomon's prayer (probably his finest hour) in 1 Kings 8 is thoroughly Deuteronomic in theology right down to the emphasis on the presence of Yahweh at the heart of the nation, the inevitable consequence of disobedience (8:17–40) and even the possibility of return after losing the land (8:46–53).

It is also striking that when Elijah steps abruptly into the life of the nation (1 Kgs 17:1–2), his primary contribution is simply to bring the word of Yahweh. Elijah (and Elisha who follows him) are simply servants of the word: it is God who through the word does his work, again, a profoundly Deuteronomic idea. This influence is much deeper than mere allusion. Deuteronomy functions as the interpretive key for all that unfolds in the life of the people of Yahweh.

C. Deuteronomy as the Foundation of Prophecy

It is not surprising given the role of Deuteronomy in the history of the nation, that there are also strong connections between the book and many of the prophets, who were essentially *preachers of covenant*.[34]

Perhaps the clearest example of the effect Deuteronomy had in shaping the ministry of the prophets can be seen in the book of Jeremiah. Having seen the rediscovery of the book of torah as a young man (see 2 Kgs 22: this book was clearly at the very least Deuteronomy), and sharing in the excitement of Josiah's new reformation of the nation, Jeremiah lives and breathes Deuteronomy. According to Schnittjers, Jeremiah quotes Deuteronomy in 1:6–9; 2:5; 3:1; 7:5–6; 12:4; 13:11; 17:19–27; 20:7–8; 31:30–34; 34:14, and this really is only the start. There are numerous other

---

[33] For more examples, see Schnittjer, *Old Testament Use of the Old Testament*, 78–79.

[34] This is true, to a degree of Elijah and Elisha, from whom the prophetic "movement" grows. It is certainly true of the later (writing) prophets.

echoes and allusions to the book. The same could be said of the rest of the prophets. Even when it comes to quotations, it is not simply Jeremiah who quotes Deuteronomy: Isaiah, Ezekiel, Hosea, Amos, Habakkuk, Nahum, and Malachi all follow suit. The word of the Lord that comes through his prophets turns out to be essentially the same message that he delivered through Moses, and now the people must obey.

D. Deuteronomy as the Beginning of Wisdom

One final element of Deuteronomy's contribution to the Old Testament (and the unfolding of biblical theology) is often overlooked, downplayed, or even rejected. It is the connection between the final book of the Pentateuch and biblical wisdom, especially as developed in the book of Proverbs.[35] In particular, the similarities between Deuteronomy 6:6–9 and Proverbs 3:1–3, 21–24; 6:20–23 and 7:1–3 are striking, as is the emphasis on the importance of the fear of Yahweh (Deut 4:10; 5:29; 6:2, 13, 24; 7:19; 10:12, 20; 11:25; 13:4; 14:23; 17:19; 25:18; 31:12–13; and the classic statement of Prov 1:7). There is also some overlap between individual requirements of torah and "wisdom" (e.g., Deut 19:14 and Prov 22:28 are virtually the same).

Determining the direction of influence between schools of thought is notoriously difficult. Did the torah influence Proverbs? Or vice versa? Or were the published forms of both influenced by an older tradition? Sometimes the simplest solution is the best, and this is surely the case here. Moses came first, and it was his ancient preaching that mapped out important categories, which were then developed and extended by Solomon and others from his torah (a richly theological, "from first principles" picture of national life with Yahweh) to the daily "wisdom" of Proverbs, which deals primarily with the concrete, conflicting realities of ordinary life.

Deuteronomy then stands right at the center of the theological landscape of the Old Testament. To grasp the flow of biblical theology, means coming to terms with the spiritual contours of Deuteronomy and its influence.

---

[35] The classic discussion of this can be found in Moshe Weinfeld, *Deuteronomy and the Deuteronomic School* (Oxford: Clarendon, 1972), especially 244–319. Weinfeld's observations on the points of contact between Deuteronomy and Proverbs are extremely helpful, even if his reconstruction of how these connections arose is not persuasive.

VII. Deuteronomy and the New Testament

Not only is Deuteronomy regularly quoted in the New Testament, but the theology of Deuteronomy is reiterated, extended, and reapplied in the New Testament in the light of the coming of the Lord Jesus Christ. There are several lists of proposed quotations of and allusions to Deuteronomy in the New Testament, which are broadly similar.[36] A good proportion of these references use individual statements in Deuteronomy to illustrate a theological point or to commend a practice. Deuteronomy 25:4 (the prohibition of muzzling an ox while it is threshing grain) is quoted in both 1 Corinthians 9:9 and 1 Timothy 5:18 to encourage people to support those in teaching ministries. However, there are multiple places where the words of Deuteronomy are quoted and/or the theology of Deuteronomy is articulated in a way that is hugely significant for the emerging Christian church.

I would suggest that Deuteronomy is fundamental to New Testament biblical theology in the following areas:

A. The Temptations of Jesus, the New/True Israel

In both Matthew 4 and Luke 4, before Jesus begins his ministry, he encounters the devil in the wilderness for forty days. Both the place and the timeline suggest that Jesus is recapitulating Israel's experience. Three times, the devil seeks to entice him to use his power and authority for selfish gain; three times Jesus answers using the words of Deuteronomy (8:3; 6:13; 6:16):

> He answered, "It is written: **Man must not live on bread alone but on every word that comes from the mouth of God.**" (Matt 4:4)
>
> Jesus told him, "It is also written: **Do not test the Lord your God.**" (Matt 4:7)
>
> Then Jesus told him, "Go away, Satan! For it is written: **Worship the Lord your God**, and serve only him." 11 Then the

---

[36] See Schnittjers, *Old Testament Use of the Old Testament*, 77–78, and the fuller list in Jack R. Lundbom, *Deuteronomy: A Commentary* (Grand Rapids: Eerdmans, 2013), 950–55. The following verses are probably quoted or alluded to in the New Testament: 1:7, 31; 2:5; 4:2, 11, 24, 35; 5:16, 17, 18, 19, 20, 21, 22; 6:4, 5, 13, 16; 7:1; 8:3; 9:19; 10:17, 22; 11:14; 13:1–2, 5; 14:2; 15:11; 17:6; 18:13, 15, 19; 19:15, 21; 22:22, 23; 24:1, 15; 25:4, 5; 27:26; 28:35; 29:4, 18, 21; 30:4, 12, 14; 31:6, 8; 32:4, 5, 17, 21, 35, 36, 43.

> devil left him, and angels came and began to serve him. (Matt 4:10–11)

In each case, Jesus commits to doing precisely what Israel was told to do but had not managed to sustain successfully. The background of Deuteronomy helps establish that he is the one who will succeed where Israel fails.[37]

B. Jesus's Fulfillment of the Torah

It is true that Jesus does not quote Deuteronomy in Matthew 5:17–20, but when he claims to have fulfilled the law (presumably the torah), and also calls his people not to shred it but embrace it, so that "their righteousness exceeds that of the scribes and the Pharisees" and so they "get into the kingdom of heaven," the conceptual background to what he is saying is surely the fullest expression of the life to which God calls his people, which is Deuteronomy. As I will argue in the next section, unless we have a sufficiently full and positive view of "law" here (like that enunciated by Moses in Deuteronomy), these words are virtually meaningless.

C. "The New Covenant in My Blood"

When Jesus announces on the night before his death and resurrection, that he is about to establish a "new covenant in his blood," he makes no effort to explain precisely what he means. He assumes that those in the room with him understand how covenants work, why a new one might be needed, and why that might require the shedding of blood. And where were they to acquire this understanding? It is Deuteronomy, which provides the theological underpinnings for what Jesus says.

There are two crucial aspects to the covenantal thought of Deuteronomy that feed into our understanding of Jesus's death: (1) God's covenantal commitment to his people Israel is developing and dynamic: Horeb is refreshed at Moab, which in turn is renewed in the land at Shechem (Deut 27:1–8). The problem with this covenant (or series of covenants) is that they simply don't work. Moses makes it plain that people will not be able to obey wholeheartedly, and it will take God's own action (30:6) to enable the people to choose life with him. It will take a new covenant. (2) This covenant will need to be enacted by an accompanying sacrifice.

---

[37] Jesus may also be depicted here as the ideal King of Deut 17, who constantly meditates on the torah.

This was clearly the case from Exodus 24 onwards for the nation (as it had been prior to that for individuals, e.g., Gen 12:1–9; 15:9–12). Jesus is identifying himself as the sacrifice who establishes the new covenant. Of course, Deuteronomy is not the only influence here. Exodus 12–13 and the explanation of the nature of sacrifice from Leviticus are also important, but the covenant thinking of Deuteronomy is foundational.

D. "The Word Became Flesh"

When the prologue to John's Gospel announces that "the Word became flesh and dwelt among us. We observed his glory, the glory as the one and only Son from the Father, full of grace and truth" (John 1:14), it is not often noticed how conceptually close to Deuteronomy 4:32–40 John's thought is.

In Deuteronomy, God remains in heaven but makes his presence known on earth by speaking:

> 36 He let you hear his voice from heaven to instruct you. He showed you his great fire on earth, and you heard his words from the fire. 37 Because he loved your ancestors, he chose their descendants after them and brought you out of Egypt by his presence and great power, 38 to drive out before you nations greater and stronger than you and to bring you in and give you their land as an inheritance, as is now taking place. 39 Today, recognize and keep in mind that the Lord is God in heaven above and on earth below; there is no other. 40 Keep his statutes and commands, which I am giving you today, so that you and your children after you may prosper and so that you may live long in the land the Lord your God is giving you for all time. (Deut 4:36–40)

Again, while John does not quote from Deuteronomy 4, conceptually he is clearly drawing on the fact that by speaking, God can be present in two places at once: a glorious truth that was embodied in the incarnation of the Son.[38]

E. Paul's Doctrine of Salvation

If the links between Jesus's words at the Last Supper and John's prologue and Deuteronomy are theological and conceptual, rather than explicit

[38] The thinking is broadly similar in Heb 1:1–3.

quotations of the text, Paul's reliance on the logic of Deuteronomy at a key point in his letter to the Romans could not be clearer:

> [4] Christ is the end of the law for righteousness to everyone who believes, [5] since Moses writes about the righteousness that is from the law: **The one who does these things will live by them.** [6] But the righteousness that comes from faith speaks like this: **Do not say in your heart, "Who will go up to heaven?"** that is, to bring Christ down [7] or, **"Who will go down into the abyss?"** that is, to bring Christ up from the dead. [8] On the contrary, what does it say? **The message is near you, in your mouth and in your heart.** This is the message of faith that we proclaim: [9] If you confess with your mouth, "Jesus is Lord," and believe in your heart that God raised him from the dead, you will be saved. [10] One believes with the heart, resulting in righteousness, and one confesses with the mouth, resulting in salvation. ... [13] For everyone who calls on the name of the Lord will be saved. (Rom 10:4–10, 13)

In verse 5, Paul speaks of Moses's statement in Leviticus, which calls for wholehearted obedience; in essence, it simply urges people to live the beautiful life. However in verses 6–8, he quotes from Deuteronomy 30, explaining that "gospel righteousness" (unlike "torah righteousness") is built on the fact that Christ has already died, risen, and ascended, and has brought the message "near to us," putting it "in our mouths" and writing it "on our hearts." In the same way that in Deuteronomy 30 (especially verse 6), the action of Yahweh in circumcising the hearts of his people makes obedience possible, so the death and resurrection of Jesus puts transformation within our grasp and makes new life possible, as we are united to him by faith. Confessing that "Jesus is Lord" and entrusting oneself to him in faith is the key to this change, and to salvation itself.

The key thing for our purposes is to see that the *structure* of Paul's thought and that of Moses in Deuteronomy 30 are exactly the same: salvation depends entirely on God (see also Deut 29:4 quoted in Rom 11:8), and our part is simply to listen to his words and respond in faith.

F. The Circumcision of the Heart

In Colossians, Paul picks up the language of Deuteronomy 30 directly, and says explicitly what is implied elsewhere (including in Rom 10): it is Christ who performs the circumcision of the heart.

> [11] You were also circumcised in him with a circumcision not done
> with hands, by putting off the body of flesh, in the circumcision
> of Christ, [12] when you were buried with him in baptism, in which
> you were also raised with him through faith in the working of
> God, who raised him from the dead. [13] And when you were dead
> in trespasses and in the uncircumcision of your flesh, he made
> you alive with him and forgave us all our trespasses. [14] He erased
> the certificate of debt, with its obligations, that was against us
> and opposed to us, and has taken it away by nailing it to the cross.
> [15] He disarmed the rulers and authorities and disgraced them
> publicly; he triumphed over them in him. (Col 2:11–14)

In Christ, God has brought us to life, removed the charge sheet against us, and disarmed those who would attack us. We have been united to him in both his death and his resurrection through faith.

G. The Election of the People of God

It is in Deuteronomy (notably 7:6–11; 9:4–6; 14:2) that the doctrine of unconditional election is declared with crystal clarity. It is then clearly the theology of Deuteronomy that lays the foundation for the election of all those who are part of God's people in the New Testament. Ephesians 1 and 2, for example, borrow heavily from the thought and language of Deuteronomy 6 and 9:

> [1:3] Blessed is the God and Father of our Lord Jesus Christ, who has
> blessed us with every spiritual blessing in the heavens in Christ.
> [4] For he chose us in him, before the foundation of the world, to
> be holy and blameless in love before him. [5] He predestined us to
> be adopted as sons through Jesus Christ for himself, according to
> the good pleasure of his will, [6] to the praise of his glorious grace
> that he lavished on us in the Beloved One. ... [2:8] For you are saved
> by grace through faith, and this is not from yourselves; it is God's
> gift—[9] not from works, so that no one can boast. [10] For we are his
> workmanship, created in Christ Jesus for good works, which God
> prepared ahead of time for us to do. (Eph 1:3–6; 2:8–10)

In his letter to Titus, Paul quotes directly from Deuteronomy 14:2:

> He gave himself for us to redeem us from all lawlessness and to cleanse for himself a people for his own possession, eager to do good works. (Titus 2:14)[39]

---

[39] A similar sentiment is expressed in 1 Pet 2:9.

The way the apostle describes the people of God in the New Testament has been shaped by the way Yahweh speaks of his people in Deuteronomy.

H. The Removal of the Curse of the Covenant (A Substitutionary Atonement)

The elaborate system of blessing and curse that provides a real time index of Israel's obedience (or lack thereof) in Deuteronomy is not picked up directly in the New Testament. However, Moses's scheme is picked up, adapted, and applied to those who *rely* on the works of Yahweh in Galatians 3:10–14:

> For all who rely on the works of the law are under a curse, because it is written, **Everyone who does not do everything written in the book of the law is cursed.** (Gal 3:10)

The statement from the climax of the list of curses to be pronounced from Mount Ebal (Deut 27:26) makes it clear that trusting one's own righteousness is always going to be a bad idea because the standard one must attain to avoid being cursed is 100%. Paul then makes the distinction between the two basic ways to live (by grace or by works) from Galatians 3:11–12:

> 11 Now it is clear that no one is justified before God by the law, because **the righteous will live by faith.** 12 But the law is not based on faith; instead, **the one who does these things will live by them.**

The principle is simple: if you are going to try to justify yourself, you had better get it completely right, because if you come up short, you will be cursed! And of course, that means all of us will end up there. Which is why what comes next is so encouraging:

> 13 Christ redeemed us from the curse of the law by becoming a curse for us, because it is written, **Cursed is everyone who is hung on a tree.** 14 The purpose was that the blessing of Abraham would come to the Gentiles by Christ Jesus, so that we could receive the promised Spirit through faith.

In 21:22–23, Moses records the slightly odd law about anyone being hung on a tree is cursed. Now in Galatians 3, Paul uses it as an illustration. What was Jesus doing hanging on that vaguely tree-like instrument of execution? He was dealing with the curse, that is, the consequences that we all should face for trying to go it alone and coming up short, as enemies of

God. Once again, it seems that Deuteronomy has had a profound influence on the thinking of the apostles.

There is, of course, much more to be said about this, and the "Deuteronomic shape" of the New Testament. Ideas like God's faithfulness (32:5–8) are picked up repeatedly in Revelation (see, e.g., Rev 15:3; 16:5; 19:2), and the Song of Moses's insistence that vengeance belongs to God is a key idea in both Romans 12:19 and Hebrews 10:30. I hope you can see that whether Deuteronomy is quoted directly, alluded to, or simply mirrored, the message of this book has had a profound influence on the shape and message of the New Testament.

VIII. Preaching Christ and the Gospel from Deuteronomy

The goal of this book is to enable people to teach Deuteronomy in particular (and God's word in general) to God's people effectively and faithfully. But if we are to do that, it makes sense for us to give thought to the particular challenges in preaching Deuteronomy.

A. Breaking Up the Book

Breaking up any book (especially a longer one) is best done top down—that is, by breaking the book into large sections along the major seams of the text, and then continuing to subdivide those large sections into a roughly equal number of talks, depending on the particular needs of the group you are teaching at that time.

So for Deuteronomy, the text (I believe) falls into three large sections: 1–11; 12–26; 26–34 (see the Commentary for my reasons for dividing the sections on the basis of content, rather than along the lines of the assumed "speeches"). That means that if I were preaching a nine week series, my default would be to have three talks on each section, if a twelve week series, approximately four per section, and so on. However in this case (and given the fact that preaching chapters 12–26 is so hard), I would veer toward having only one or two sermons on the legal sections. So what then would, say, a ten week sermon series look like for me?

Week 1	Chapters 1–3
Week 2	Chapter 4
Week 3	Chapters 5–6
Week 4	Chapters 7–11
Week 5	Chapters 12–26 (part 1)

Week 6	Chapters 12–26 (part 2)
Week 7	Chapters 27 & 28
Week 8	Chapters 29 & 30
Week 9	Chapters 31 & 32
Week 10	Chapters 33 & 34

If the series needed to be extended, the logical place to expand would be in chapters 7–11. There are however, still some challenges with this model.

B. The Challenges of Preaching Deuteronomy

There are several quite obvious challenges in preaching Deuteronomy, that, although easy to spot, can be quite difficult to overcome:

1. Dealing with the collection of laws

The longest collection of laws in the Bible is hard to preach. Some parts are easier than others to preach on (e.g., 17:14–20; 26:1–11), but it is still a daunting task to attempt to understand the sprawling vision of these provisions.

2. Covering longer sections of text

In all but the most biblically literate congregations, a slow meander through Deuteronomy is going to be hard to pull off, especially when one thinks of the morass of laws.

3. Preaching "preaching"

Perhaps the most significant challenge is that the text of Deuteronomy is already in sermonic form. That introduces a layer of complexity that we aren't used to. The primary requirement of a "sermon on a sermon" is to let the voice of the original sermon be heard, without explaining it to death.[40]

4. Dealing with defeater beliefs

Some things in Deuteronomy are so-called *defeater beliefs*. A defeater belief is something that, unless it is resolved, will lead to people refusing to come to Christ or even to think through the

---

[40] A key purpose of any expository sermon is to recover the rhetorical effect experienced by the first hearers, and so to enable people now to respond to the text in the light of all that God has done for us in Christ.

wider implications of the message. The classic defeater belief in this part of the Bible is the judgment on the Canaanites.

5. Avoiding legalism

When dealing with a text that is largely exhortatory on the one hand and legal on the other, it would be remarkably easy to end up handling neither particularly well. It is incredibly hard not to send people away with the sense that we just need to try hard and do our best, rather than allowing the riches that God himself has given us to inform our thinking and empower our response.

6. Preaching Christ and the gospel from Deuteronomy

This of course is the ultimate challenge: to do this creatively and in a way that flows out of each text slightly differently, capturing readers in an inexorable flow to Christ, while remaining both true to the text and God-honoring.

C. Conclusion

This introduction has set out the approach taken to Deuteronomy in this commentary. These words come from the mouth of the greatest leader Israel has ever seen. They have been gathered together in a form that, while unique, is expressed in language and forms drawn from the world in which it is set. We do not know precisely how the book itself came together, other than that Moses's words dominated, and the entire book seems to have been finished during Israel's time in the land. The result is a theological work of real depth and power, which has been shown to have shaped not just the development of the Old Testament at multiple levels, but also the very fabric of the New Testament.

IX. Biblical-Theological Themes in Deuteronomy

A. Introduction

> The theological significance of Deuteronomy can scarcely be overestimated. Inasmuch as this book offers the most systematic presentation of theological truth in the entire Old Testament, we may compare it to Romans in the New Testament. On the other hand, ... like the Gospel of John, the book of Deuteronomy functions as a theological manifesto, calling on Israel to respond to God's grace with unreserved loyalty and love.

So says Daniel Block, in his essay "Deuteronomy: A Theological Introduction."[41] And that is not an overstatement.

Deuteronomy stands alongside Genesis, Isaiah, and the Psalms as one of the books that provides not just the backbone, but the whole musculo-skeletal system of the Old Testament. It could be argued, of course, with some justification, that Genesis is more foundational, that Isaiah's vision of God is more sweeping, and that the Psalter brings both the nature of the Davidic messiah and the human heart into sharper relief, but there is no book of the Bible that is quite so replete with rich biblical-theological themes as Deuteronomy.

I am quite convinced that Deuteronomy is *the* seminal book for understanding not just the Old Testament but the flow of biblical theology as a whole. Not everything in the book is original. Many of the ideas are hinted at in the preceding books of the Pentateuch. Not everything is thoroughly developed. There are lots of hints and nuances that Moses doesn't pause to spell out. But as the Old Testament unfolds, the rhythms, cadences, and concepts of Deuteronomy provide the soundtrack. Joshua–Kings is history viewed through the lens of Deuteronomy. The prophets (notably Jeremiah and Amos, but also almost all the others) preach the covenant in ways that have been profoundly shaped by Deuteronomy. Proverbs picks up a way of viewing the world that has its roots in Deuteronomy. When Christ comes, from the wilderness onwards, Deuteronomy is a key part of his playbook. When the apostles (and above all, Paul), seek to proclaim and explain the gospel, time after time, it is to this book of Deuteronomy, "the Gospel According to Moses" (to quote Block again) to which they turn.[42]

In order to illustrate this redemptive-historical richness, I want to highlight thirteen themes which are more or less prominent in Deuteronomy and have profound impact on the unfolding message of the Bible.

---

[41] See Daniel I. Block, *The Gospel According to Moses: Theological and Ethical Reflections on the Book of Deuteronomy* (Eugene: Cascade, 2012), 1.

[42] For example, Paul in Rom 10, bases his argument on Deut 30.

B. Grace

I start with "grace" because this is where it started for me when it came to Deuteronomy. It was in a theology lecture at the University of Aberdeen in 1990 that I was first blown away by the words of Deuteronomy 7:6–8:

> [6] For you are a holy people belonging to the LORD your God. The LORD your God has chosen you to be his own possession out of all the peoples on the face of the earth. [7] The LORD had his heart set on you and chose you, not because you were more numerous than all peoples, for you were the fewest of all peoples.
> [8] But because the LORD loved you and kept the oath he swore to your ancestors, he brought you out with a strong hand and redeemed you from the place of slavery, from the power of Pharaoh king of Egypt.

Nothing had quite prepared me for these words. Up to this point, I had operated with a misguided and reductionist view of the Old Testament as a rather long, pharisaical injunction to be good, before the gospel of grace exploded in the New Testament. At a stroke, Moses shattered my perceptions and sparked an interest in this book that has persisted for most of my life. Since then, when people have asked the question (as they often have) "Why Deuteronomy?" my answer has always begun with the glorious truth that it is a book that is saturated with the grace of God.

Of course, it is not alone in this. One could argue that all four of the preceding books in the Pentateuch display God's grace on almost every page. But it is in Deuteronomy that this grace is not only relentlessly articulated but also integrated into a deeply gospel-shaped theology.

Moses's retrospect on the post-exodus experiences of Israel is, on the one hand, searingly critical. But it is easy to overlook the fact that despite Israel's behavior (even when compared to Edom, Moab and Ammon), Yahweh is still committed to giving them the land and leading them into it. The preaching of the book rests on grace.

This grace only becomes clearer in chapter 4. In one of the key statements in the book in 4:6–8, Moses explains that because God has spoken, they should listen and obey,

> [6] This will show your wisdom and understanding in the eyes of the peoples. When they hear about all these statutes, they will say, "This great nation is indeed a wise and understanding

> people." [7] For what great nation is there that has a god near to it as the LORD our God is to us whenever we call to him? [8] And what great nation has righteous statutes and ordinances like this entire law I set before you today?

This provision is clearly undeserved. It flows from the fact that the God of grace has drawn near to them, has spoken to them at Horeb, and will continue to do so, making his presence with them obvious.

This divine grace continues to play a dominant note at every stage of the book. In 4:25–32, the idea of *exile* is introduced (which in Deuteronomy is a slightly vague future prospect of losing the land and being scattered among the nations). No sooner, however, is this terrible prospect introduced than God announces his intention to bring them back home. So 4:30–31 reads: "When you are in distress and all these things have happened to you, in the future you will return to the LORD your God and obey him. He will not leave you, destroy you, or forget the covenant with your ancestors that he swore to them by oath, because the LORD your God is a compassionate God." This is God's grace in action.

There are regular reminders of the undergirding, undeserved kindness of God throughout Moses's preaching. The oddly placed reminder of the provision of cities of refuge (4:41–43), for example, is a gentle pointer to grace in action. In 6:10–12, Moses urges the people not to take God's grace for granted, but to remember that all that they have is ultimately a gift from Yahweh:

> [10] And when the LORD your God brings you into the land he swore to your fathers, to Abraham, Isaac, and Jacob, that he would give you—a land with large and beautiful cities that you did not build, [11] houses full of every good thing that you did not fill them with, cisterns that you did not dig, and vineyards and olive groves that you did not plant—and when you eat and are satisfied, [12] be careful not to forget the LORD who brought you out of the land of Egypt, out of the place of slavery. (Deut 6:10–12)

In chapter 8, Moses goes to great lengths to emphasize the way God has cared for the people through the wilderness period (including, according to 8:3, preserving their clothing and providing preventative podiatric care!) None of this was deserved. The expansive generosity detailed from 8:7–10 is part of the overwhelming evidence that Israel's God is a God of grace:

> 7 For the Lord your God is bringing you into a good land, a land
> with streams, springs, and deep water sources, flowing in both
> valleys and hills; 8 a land of wheat, barley, vines, figs, and pome-
> granates; a land of olive oil and honey; 9 a land where you will
> eat food without shortage, where you will lack nothing; a land
> whose rocks are iron and from whose hills you will mine cop-
> per. 10 When you eat and are full, you will bless the Lord your
> God for the good land he has given you.

That significant space is given in chapters 9 and 10 to the sin and restoration of the nation, complete with a replacement set of stone tablets, ultimately speaks of God's long-suffering and grace. Israel has rebelled and reneged on commitments again and again, and yet Yahweh forgives and renews his commitment to them.

Even the avalanche of instructions in chapters 12–26 is peppered with motive clauses that remind God's people that they have been rescued from Egypt by Yahweh and brought into a good land, with the effect that even their obedience is born in and shaped as a response to the relentless grace of Yahweh. This is woven into the fabric of this book.

It is no surprise that the past and present grace is augmented by the future grace of chapter 30, which looks ahead to the day when God will finally resolve the most basic problem faced by God's people: that they are incapable of consistent obedience, and that they desperately need God himself to circumcise their hearts (30:6).

All of this leads eventually to Moses's final words at the end of the blessing in chapter 33, which provides a fitting climax to a book that, unlike any other, has set the trajectory of the Old Testament firmly on an arc of grace:

> 26 There is none like the God of Jeshurun,
> who rides the heavens to your aid,
> the clouds in his majesty.
> 27 The God of old is your dwelling place,
> and underneath are the everlasting arms.
> He drives out the enemy before you
> and commands, "Destroy!"
> 28 So Israel dwells securely;
> Jacob lives untroubled
> in a land of grain and new wine;
> even his skies drip with dew.

> [29] How happy you are, Israel!
> Who is like you,
> a people saved by the LORD?
> He is the shield that protects you,
> the sword you boast in.
> Your enemies will cringe before you,
> and you will tread on their backs.

There is a sense in which after Deuteronomy, it should be crystal clear that any careful and faithful reading of the Old Testament will be a grace-shaped reading. The sinfulness of the people has been well established, and we should not be surprised to see it repeatedly raising its ugly head in the books that follow, whether in the history books from Joshua to 2 Kings that are so shaped by Deuteronomy or the preaching of the prophets who provide God's real-time commentary on that history.

Already in Deuteronomy, the basic "gospel-shape," to use an anachronistic term, of the Old Testament has crystalized: God rescues sinful people, speaking to them, tracing out the shape of the life they must live, finding a way to forgive them when they find they cannot live in this way, and promising the resources they will need to do so. All this and more flows from the Deuteronomic doctrine of grace.

C. The Word of God

It is at Mount Sinai, at the very moment that the family of Jacob becomes God's covenant nation (e.g., Exod 19:6), that the words of Yahweh become the driving force of the life of Israel. It is, however, forty years later at Moab, that Moses's reflection on those events begins to articulate the theological importance of the word of God.

Before the events at Horeb, obviously God did speak. He spoke directly, intimately, and unmistakably to Adam, Noah, Abraham, Isaac, Jacob, and others. He also spoke directly to Moses, notably out of the burning bush in Exodus 3 and then repeatedly through the unfolding conflict with Pharaoh. But at Horeb, something different happens. At this point in redemptive history, Yahweh starts to speak to his people about the "nuts and bolts" of covenant life: what it means to live as his people, with him as their God, day after day in all the mundane details of life. This occupies much of the books of Exodus and Leviticus. But it is in Deuteronomy that Moses turns to the enduring theological significance of the fact that our God is a talking God.

Deuteronomy 4 is effectively an overture to the rest of the book. Most of the key theological themes that Moses expounds in the addresses that follow are anticipated here, but at the heart of the chapter is the Deuteronomic understanding of the word of Yahweh.

From 4:1, it is clear that listening to (which includes obeying) the word of Yahweh is the key to *life* for God's people: "Now, Israel, listen to the statutes and ordinances I am teaching you to follow, so that you may live, enter, and take possession of the land the Lord, the God of your ancestors, is giving you." It is listening and obeying that will "show your wisdom and understanding in the eyes of the peoples" (4:6). But more than that, it is the fact that God *speaks* to his people that really sets Israel apart: "For what great nation is there that has a god near to it as the Lord our God is to us whenever we call to him? And what great nation has righteous statutes and ordinances like this entire law I set before you today?" (4:7–8). There is a tight connection between God's *presence* and his *words.*

This leads to the next vital aspect of Moses's theology of the word: when God's words are present (whether freshly delivered or handed down through the generations), *God himself is present*. To have his torah (whether written down, announced at Horeb or expounded at Moab) is to have Yahweh.

Moses backs this key insight up by taking them back to Horeb, where the definitive experience of the people consisted of standing "before the Lord your God" and hearing his words (4:10). To underlines this, 4:12 states that "the Lord spoke to you from the fire. You kept hearing the sound of the words, but didn't see a form; there was only a voice." Listening to this voice is the single most important challenge facing them in the years to come. How they listen will determine whom (or what) they worship, and where they do it (e.g., 4:25–30). Their response to the word of Yahweh is their response to Yahweh himself. His word is *the* constitutive element of their relationship with him. When Yahweh speaks, he demonstrates that he is their God and he is with them. When they obey, they show that they are his people and so open up the riches of life to the full with him.

Moses confirms all this in one of the most important passages not just in the book of Deuteronomy, but in the entire Old Testament in 4:32–40. The exodus and the events at Horeb are woven together to make clear that their God is a rescuing, speaking God and that the key to enjoying life in the presence of this God is to embrace his word. It's worth reproducing in full:

> 32 Indeed, ask about the earlier days that preceded you, from
> the day God created mankind on the earth and from one end
> of the heavens to the other: Has anything like this great event
> ever happened, or has anything like it been heard of? 33 *Has*
> *a people heard God's voice speaking from the fire as you have, and*
> *lived?* 34 Or has a god attempted to go and take a nation as his
> own out of another nation, by trials, signs, wonders, and war,
> by a strong hand and an outstretched arm, by great terrors, as
> the LORD your God did for you in Egypt before your eyes? 35 You
> were shown these things *so that you would know that the LORD is*
> *God; there is no other besides him.* 36 *He let you hear his voice from*
> *heaven* to instruct you. He showed you his great fire on earth,
> and you heard his words from the fire. 37 Because he loved your
> ancestors, he chose their descendants after them and brought
> you out of Egypt by his presence and great power, 38 to drive
> out before you nations greater and stronger than you and to
> bring you in and give you their land as an inheritance, as is now
> taking place. 39 *Today, recognize and keep in mind that the LORD is*
> *God in heaven above and on earth below; there is no other.* 40 *Keep his*
> *statutes and commands, which I am giving you today, so that you and*
> *your children after you may prosper and so that you may live long in*
> *the land the LORD your God is giving you for all time.*

Verse 39 is crucial. Moses, with a previously unmatched clarity, explains that God is simultaneously present in heaven and on earth. But how does that work? During the exodus from Egypt and the wilderness period, that presence was expressed through cloud and fire at the head of their column and (at times) at the tabernacle. But now, God has demonstrated that he is with his people through his words. The God who reigns above makes his presence with his people below obvious when he speaks to them. When he speaks, he makes his presence felt. It is through his word that he offers life and judges and directs the nation. It is through his word that he brings joy through the assurance of his presence. There will more to say about the importance of God's presence in Deuteronomy below, but for now let's focus on the significance of the theology of the word.

Now that God has spoken from heaven and explained that the core of his covenant relationship is listening to and obeying his word today and every day, he has provided a lens through which to view the progress (or otherwise) of his people. This simple metric is then applied consistently through the books that follow to the unfolding events of Israel's history.[43] From God's perspective, the history of Israel is simply a history of her response (or lack thereof) to his word. There is, however, more to be said.

Although it mostly remains implicit in Deuteronomy, there is also a sense in which these words spoken from heaven direct the course of human history. God has spoken. The path of the future is set, with the only real variable being the response of the people.

This idea is picked up and developed at some length in the books of Kings. After the end of Solomon's reign, the text is punctuated by the phrase "according to the word of the Lord" (1 Kgs 12:24; 13:26; 14:18; 15:29; 16:12, 34; 17:16; 22:38; 2 Kgs 1:17; 7:16; 9:26; 10:17; 23:16; 24:2). The word is essentially personified, as the "one" who is doing God's work in the world. Kings may rise and fall, but Yahweh's powerful word continues to govern the course of events—an idea beautifully expressed in Isaiah 55:10–12.

It is surely this essentially Deuteronomic view of the "word" as carrying God's presence on earth and directing human history which (alongside Gen 1:1–3) lies behind John's use of the idea in the prologue to his Gospel (1:1–14):

> [1] In the beginning was the Word, and the Word was with God, and the Word was God. [2] He was with God in the beginning. [3] All things were created through him, and apart from him not one thing was created that has been created. [4] In him was life, and that life was the light of men. ... [9] The true light that gives light to everyone was coming into the world. ... [14] The Word became flesh and dwelt among us. We observed his glory, the glory as the one and only Son from the Father, full of grace and truth.

It is now in Christ, the living word, and through the Spirit, that God makes his presence with us known. He is the one who speaks to the church. He is the one who is the sum total of what God says to us and

---

[43] Scholars have long debated the relationship between Deuteronomy and the books that follow. Links and influence are so strong that in academic circles, Joshua–Kings are generally referred to as the "Deuteronomistic History." There are multiple theories on how these books (and the relationship with Deuteronomy) arose, but the simplest explanation remains far and away the best: Deuteronomy provided the theological categories and template for all who followed to evaluate the history of Israel. For a short and rich discussion of the issues involved, see J. Gordon McConville's *Grace in the End: A Study in Deuteronomic Theology* (Grand Rapids: Zondervan, 1993).

provides for us (so Heb 1:1–3). Through union with him, God's word is written on our hearts. This rich biblical theology of the word of God has its initial expression right here in Deuteronomy.

D. The Torah of Moses (and the Beautiful Life)

The primary reason, I suspect, for the relative lack of love among God's people today for the book of Deuteronomy is the massive collection of rules that runs from chapter 12 to the end of chapter 26. The expanding reach of the legal material in the Pentateuch (from the Decalogue, to Exod 21–24, via the holiness laws in Leviticus to Deut 12–26) is basically seen as restrictive and obsolete to those who have been set free in Christ. To rush to dismiss this so-called "legal" material in the opening sections of the Bible, however, is a biblical-theological misstep that will, unless we are very careful, leave us with a severely diminished view of the beautiful life to which God calls us in Christ.

One of the cross-cultural issues that we face in reading the Old Testament as evangelical Christians concerns the idea of "law." Most of us (rightly) have it drummed into us from our earliest days (whether as children or new converts) that we live by grace, *not* law. This, of course, is a thoroughly biblical position. "Legalism" (trying to gain our acceptance with God by what we do) is spiritually toxic, whether we're dealing with some first century Pharisees, Jewish believers in the first church plants, or contemporary Christians. When Paul highlights the contrast between legalism and the gospel of Christ, he makes it plain that trying to "be good" to get to God is disastrous. Used like that, the law can only bite you. But he is also at pains to say that "the law is ... holy, just and good" (Rom 7:12)! And that's where Deuteronomy (and actually, virtually all of the Old Testament) begins: with a rock solid confidence, and even an enthusiasm, for the goodness and beauty of God's torah or "instruction."

To be honest, even using the word "law" to describe this material isn't all that helpful.

The problem is that the English word "law," because it is essentially derived from how the Romans saw rules, is far distant from the way the Bible speaks of what God asks of us. In fact, the word usually translated "law" (*tôrâ*) doesn't even mean law at all. Deuteronomy 4:5–8 is very helpful here:

> [5] Look, I have taught you statutes and ordinances as the Lord my God has commanded me, so that you may follow them in

> the land you are entering to possess. 6 Carefully follow them,
> for this will show your wisdom and understanding in the eyes
> of the peoples. When they hear about all these statutes, they
> will say, "This great nation is indeed a wise and understanding
> people." 7 For what great nation is there that has a god near to
> it as the Lord our God is to us whenever we call to him? 8 And
> what great nation has righteous statutes and ordinances like
> this entire law I set before you today?

This "entire law" (torah) is presented as something wholesome and beneficial, describing life as it should be with Yahweh in the land. It is a good gift from Yahweh—so much so that a copy of it is to be placed beside (or in) the ark and read to the nation at least every seven years (31:9–13), so that they might enjoy life in covenant with Yahweh in the land. This instruction has got to be a wonderful thing! While it is true that ultimately this rich and beautiful life will prove beyond Israel's reach (condemning them in the process), if we are to understand Deuteronomy (and read the Old Testament well), we need to allow torah to be a good thing first!

Only if we do that, can we make any sense of passages like Psalm 19:7–11:

> 7 The instruction of the Lord is perfect,
> renewing one's life;
> the testimony of the Lord is trustworthy,
> making the inexperienced wise.
> 8 The precepts of the Lord are right,
> making the heart glad;
> the command of the Lord is radiant,
> making the eyes light up.
> 9 The fear of the Lord is pure,
> enduring forever;
> the ordinances of the Lord are reliable
> and altogether righteous.
> 10 They are more desirable than gold—
> than an abundance of pure gold;
> and sweeter than honey
> dripping from a honeycomb.
> 11 In addition, your servant is warned by them,
> and in keeping them there is an abundant reward.

From the headline statement of 4:8 all the way through the laws themselves in chapters 12–26 there is an enduring note of celebration and joy.

These laws describe *life*. The torah of Moses defines a response to God that can be summed up as "choosing life" (see 30:15–20). And yet doesn't this road lead only to death? The answer is clearly yes, but the problem, according to Deuteronomy (and, I would suggest, the rest of the Bible) isn't with the road, but with those traveling on it, who are unable to fear Yahweh, walk in his ways, love him, and worship him with all their heart and soul (10:12) The problem is that they can't circumcise their hearts (10:16). The good news, of course, is that God through Moses commits to do that for us (30:6), which takes us to the work of the Lord Jesus himself.

One of the most contested areas of biblical theology across the centuries has been the extent to which the Old Testament law(s) remain binding and/or helpful for new covenant believers. I would suggest that the way Jesus himself speaks of his relationship with torah/law sets this discussion on a firm foundation.

There is a clear progression from the earliest commands of God to Adam and Eve in the garden of Eden, to the Ten Words spoken (and written) by God on Sinai, expanded in the book of the covenant in Exodus 22–24, to the far-reaching provisions in the Levitical Code, culminating in the sweeping and expansive preached legislation of Deuteronomy 12—26. This in turn creates a strong sense that this torah, rather than being an exhaustive canon of legal prescriptions, presents Israel with a living, breathing template of covenant life. This torah is expansive and far-reaching, touching every part of life, providing the way to life, and tracing out the shape of the beautiful life that Yahweh offers. One implication of all of this is that while keeping the torah may be a wonderful and desirable thing, it is a massive task, which seems beyond the people of Yahweh even at their very best.

According to the Old Testament as a whole and Deuteronomy in particular, the basic problem is that human beings in general (including even God's people) cannot consistently keep this torah. It is simply too big and exacting, and for us as human beings, the task proves too demanding, given our flawed nature. The key question then is how Jesus understands his mission vis-à-vis the torah. Perhaps surprisingly, Jesus doesn't see his role as simply "doing away with" all of this. In fact, he says the very opposite!

According to Matthew's Gospel, Jesus understands his mission as "fulfilling" this law. Speaking at the beginning of the Sermon on the Mount in Matthew 5:17–20, Jesus says:

> [17] "Don't think that I came to abolish the Law or the Prophets. I did not come to abolish but to fulfill. [18] For truly I tell you, until heaven and earth pass away, not the smallest letter or one stroke of a letter will pass away from the law until all things are accomplished. [19] Therefore, whoever breaks one of the least of these commands and teaches others to do the same will be called least in the kingdom of heaven. But whoever does and teaches these commands will be called great in the kingdom of heaven. [20] For I tell you, unless your righteousness surpasses that of the scribes and Pharisees, you will never get into the kingdom of heaven.

What does "fulfilling the law" mean in this context? It surely must involve obeying it perfectly and thus removing the requirement that we keep it perfectly, while at the same time making it possible for us to live the beautiful life that God introduced us to in the Old Testament.[44] Jesus's own life, death, and resurrection brings the necessary radical change (Moses's "circumcision of the heart" or, as Paul calls it in Colossians 2:11–12, the "circumcision of Christ") to enable people like us to live the life that is anticipated by the torah.[45] This understanding is supported by what Jesus goes on to say next in the Sermon on the Mount.

Jesus's focus in these chapters is firmly on the moral life of his followers in comparison to that of the Pharisees. His intention seems to go beyond saying that we have reached a new point on the redemptive-historical timeline with the coming of the kingdom to a discussion of the very nature of kingdom life. This is confirmed by the subsequent verses in Matthew 5:

1. The soaring language of verse 18 ("until heaven and earth pass away") is most naturally taken to refer to the end of time. Given

[44] For a more detailed treatment, see J. Gary Millar, *Changed into His Likeness: A Biblical Theology of Personal Transformation*, NSBT 55 (London: Apollos, 2021), 123–28. Attempts to say that "fulfilling the law" means less than this are often theologically rather than exegetically driven.

[45] So John Nolland can write, "'Fulfil' must be taken in a manner that allows it to be an appropriate counterpart to annul. ... The fulfilment language constitutes a claim that Jesus's programmatic commitment, far from undercutting the role of the Law and the Prophets, is to enable God's people to live out the Law more effectively." *The Gospel of Matthew: A Commentary on the Greek Text*, New International Greek Testament Commentary (Grand Rapids: Eerdmans, 2005), 218–19.

that the law in this context endures until the establishment of the new heavens and the new earth, it is hard to see how Jesus can be emphasizing anything other than the enduring importance of the law for those who welcome his kingdom.

2. In verse 19, the choices on offer are either breaking these commands and teaching others to break them or doing them and teaching others to do the same. This makes absolutely no sense if the torah is being abolished.
3. The puzzling statement in verse 20 ("unless your righteousness surpasses that of the scribes and Pharisees, you will never get into the kingdom of heaven") suddenly becomes a real possibility: a statement ahead of time of the life that God will make possible through the power of the Spirit, rather than an impossibility that Jesus is calling people to, in some subtle tactical reverse psychology.

In the next phase of the Sermon (sometimes called the "antitheses"), Jesus takes the fascinating approach of accusing the Pharisees *not* of expecting too much from people, but rather of *being satisfied with far too little when it comes to obeying God's word.* His point is not that they are being too scrupulous and that we all need to relax. Rather, Jesus points out their narrow-minded reductionism, and highlights that it is in stark contrast to Jesus's expansive vision of a beautiful life with God that realizes, builds on, and exceeds what was described in the Old Testament torah, above all in Moses's vision of life with God in the land in Deuteronomy.

According to Jesus, in line with the expectation of the Old Testament (as expressed in, e.g., Jer 31:31–34), his mission is to bring about real change in the lives of those who welcome him, which will enable them to live the beautiful life anticipated in the torah. Or to quote John 10:10, "A thief comes only to steal and kill and destroy. I have come so that they may have life and have it in abundance."

E. Joy

What we have seen so far (that Yahweh is the God of grace who speaks to his people so that they might live the beautiful life with him in the land) is only highlighted by the fact that it is in Deuteronomy that Moses first articulates a biblical theology of *joy*. The ultimate goal of Moses's preaching is that his people might delight in Yahweh himself, as he reveals himself to them.

While there is a (solitary) reference to rejoicing before Yahweh in Leviticus (23:40, in the context of the Festival of Shelters), Deuteronomy takes this to a whole new level.

At the beginning of the collection of laws in chapter 12, the emphasis is on the fact that in the land, the people must worship Yahweh's way, and to do that by going to the "place which the Lord your God chooses from all your tribes to put his name for his dwelling." What is not often mentioned is the repeated insistence that God's people must rejoice in the presence of Yahweh:

> You will eat there in the presence of the Lord your God *and rejoice with your household in everything you do*, because the Lord your God has blessed you. (Deut 12:7, emphasis mine)

> *You will rejoice before the Lord your God*—you, your sons and daughters, your male and female slaves, and the Levite who is within your city gates, since he has no portion or inheritance among you. (Deut 12:12, emphasis mine)

> You are to eat them in the presence of the Lord your God at the place the Lord your God chooses—you, your son and daughter, your male and female slave, and the Levite who is within your city gates. *Rejoice before the Lord your God in everything you do.* (Deut 12:18, emphasis mine)

This joy is hardly peripheral: it is to mark every trip to the sanctuary, every aspect of the festival, and to include everyone in the community. Deuteronomy puts joy at the heart of the life of the covenant people of Yahweh. The same note is sounded repeatedly in subsequent chapters. Joy is to be the dominant note when the tithes are consumed (14:26), and at both the Festival of Weeks (16:11), and Shelters (16:14–15).

It is also striking that at the climax of the laws in 26:1–11 the ritual of the firstfruits, which embodies a wholehearted response to Yahweh's gracious word, culminates in an outpouring of joy:

> You, the Levites, and the resident aliens among you will rejoice in all the good things the Lord your God has given you and your household. (Deut 26:11)

When Moses turns to the ritual to be carried out on Mount Ebal, once the nation has actually entered the land, the emphasis remains exactly the same:

> There you are to sacrifice fellowship offerings, eat, and rejoice in the presence of the Lord your God. (Deut 27:7)

It is important to realize that this is a genuinely new thing. Up to this point, the focus when discussing Israel's life and worship has been firmly on Israel's obligation to respond to Yahweh's grace, primarily shown to them in the exodus, and the necessity of recognizing the holiness of God, with its requirement that they be holy as he is (e.g., Lev 19:2). Now the focus has well and truly shifted to the fact that Yahweh is a kind and generous God, who has given them a good land, and more than that, invites them to share its benefits *in his company*. That lays a different obligation on Israel.

Perhaps the most striking reference to joy in the book comes in the heart of the long list of covenant curses in 28:47–48:

> [47] Because you didn't serve the Lord your God with joy and a cheerful heart, even though you had an abundance of everything,
> [48] you will serve your enemies that the Lord will send against you,
> in famine, thirst, nakedness, and a lack of everything.

Such is the fundamental importance of joy in the Deuteronomic vision that to fail to display joy is actually culpable and must be punished. Joy in relationship with Yahweh is a basic part of being the covenant people of God, a fact that is confirmed in both the Song of Moses (32:43, which speaks of joy after deliverance) and the blessing (33:18, which prays for joy in all of life, specifically for Zebulun and Issachar).

This note of joy then sets the expectation for the rest of the Old Testament, and ultimately for what can be expected when Messiah comes. The Psalms and the Prophets relentlessly pursue this joy and announce that God will act in the future to bring (or restore) deep joy to his people. This message reaches a crescendo in the New Testament in the Lord Jesus Christ, whose own astonishing statement in John 15 puts joy at the very heart of his mission:

> I have told you these things so that my joy may be in you and your joy may be complete. (John 15:11)

The writer to the Hebrews takes this a step further, when explaining that Jesus Christ's own joy lay at the core of his motivation for his rescue mission:

> [1] Let us run with endurance the race that lies before us, [2] keeping our eyes on Jesus, the pioneer and perfecter of our faith.

> For the joy that lay before him, he endured the cross, despising the shame, and sat down at the right hand of the throne of God. (Heb 12:1–2)

It is no surprise then that throughout the New Testament, for every writer, this joy is fundamental to what it means to be the new covenant people of God:

> [4] Rejoice in the Lord always. I will say it again: Rejoice! [5] Let your graciousness be known to everyone. The Lord is near. [6] Don't worry about anything, but in everything, through prayer and petition with thanksgiving, present your requests to God. [7] And the peace of God, which surpasses all understanding, will guard your hearts and minds in Christ Jesus. (Phil 4:4–7)

> [2] Consider it a great joy, my brothers and sisters, whenever you experience various trials, [3] because you know that the testing of your faith produces endurance. (Jas 1:2–3)

> Though you have not seen him, you love him; though not seeing him now, you believe in him, and you rejoice with inexpressible and glorious joy ... (1 Pet 1:8)

> We are writing these things so that our joy may be complete. (1 John 1:4)

This key strand of biblical theology finds its source in Moses's preaching on the plains of Moab.

F. Land

Given the setting of the book, it is hardly surprising that the *land* dominates Moses's preaching from beginning to end. The land is both the evidence of God's grace and the context in which his enduring grace is to be enjoyed. The land is where God's words are to be listened to and lived out, and the place where life with God is to be enjoyed as part of the covenant people. Put simply, the land is not simply a place to live, *but a place to live with God.*

So, for example, Deuteronomy 11:8–12 says:

> [8] Keep every command I am giving you today, so that you may have the strength to cross into and possess the land you are to inherit, [9] and so that you may live long in the land the Lord

> swore to your ancestors to give them and their descendants, a land flowing with milk and honey. [10] For the land you are entering to possess is not like the land of Egypt, from which you have come, where you sowed your seed and irrigated by hand as in a vegetable garden. [11] But the land you are entering to possess is a land of mountains and valleys, watered by rain from the sky. [12] It is a land the Lord your God cares for. He is always watching over it from the beginning to the end of the year.

Similarly, we find the land described like this is Deuteronomy 8:7–10:

> [7] For the Lord your God is bringing you into a good land, a land with streams, springs, and deep water sources, flowing in both valleys and hills; [8] a land of wheat, barley, vines, figs, and pomegranates; a land of olive oil and honey; [9] a land where you will eat food without shortage, where you will lack nothing; a land whose rocks are iron and from whose hills you will mine copper. [10] When you eat and are full, you will bless the Lord your God for the good land he has given you.

The fact that the land is regularly referred to simply as "good" is probably an allusion to Genesis 1 (see, e.g., Deut 1:25, 35; 3:25; 4:21, 22; 6:18; 8:7, 10; 9:6; 11:17). In Deuteronomy, the land is essentially a new Eden: a "stopping-off point" between creation and new creation, which gives a glimpse of God's soaring intentions for his people.

In Deuteronomy, then, *land* and *relationship* are inseparable. This is confirmed by the strong emphasis on going to *the place* at the heart of the land to celebrate in the presence of the Lord, as we have seen. The journey to the land is recapitulated by a three times a year journey in the land, and the purpose (startlingly) is meeting with, feasting with, and worshiping Yahweh, the rescuing God of the covenant (so, e.g., 16:9–12). But this isn't the whole story in the book.

Alongside the pattern of the nation gathering three times a year in the presence of Yahweh at the place he chooses, there is another innovation. Given that they will soon be scattered in the land, provision is made in 12:20–21 for killing and eating animals away from Yahweh's chosen place.

> [20] When the Lord your God enlarges your territory as he has promised you, and you say, "I want to eat meat" because you have a strong desire to eat meat, you may eat it whenever you

> want. [21] If the place where the LORD your God chooses to put his name is too far from you, you may slaughter any of your herd or flock he has given you, as I have commanded you, and you may eat it within your city gates whenever you want.

The fact that the blood must be carefully handled underlines the fact that this is far from an "anything goes" approach. In fact, the term "desacralization of slaughter," which is often used, is highly misleading. It is more a case of the whole land becoming a holy place, even if not all holy places are equally holy! The place which Yahweh shall choose retains priority, even though the whole land is in some sense sanctified. This distinction ensures that enjoyment of the land points (in what is virtually a sacramental way) to the enjoyment of Yahweh himself at the heart of the land.

This idea is developed at some length by the role played by the Levites (in Deuteronomy in particular). The key text comes in Deuteronomy 18:

> [1] The Levitical priests, the whole tribe of Levi, will have no portion or inheritance with Israel. They will eat the LORD's food offerings; that is their inheritance. [2] Although Levi has no inheritance among his brothers, the LORD is his inheritance, as he promised him. [3] This is the priests' share from the people who offer a sacrifice, whether it is an ox, a sheep, or a goat; the priests are to be given the shoulder, jaws, and stomach. [4] You are to give him the firstfruits of your grain, new wine, and fresh oil, and the first sheared wool of your flock. [5] For the LORD your God has chosen him and his sons from all your tribes to stand and minister in his name from now on.

The Levites, who function as both the priests and teachers (guardians of the theological tradition) are a living visual aid of the fact that God has made this people his own and is committed to enabling them to enjoy life with him.

It is no accident that the climax to the collection of laws in chapter 26 is the ritual of the first fruits:

> [11] You, the Levites, and the resident aliens among you will rejoice in all the good things the LORD your God has given you and your household. [12] When you have finished paying all the tenth of your produce in the third year, the year of the tenth, you are to give it to the Levites, resident aliens, fatherless children, and widows, so that they may eat in your towns and be satisfied. [13] Then you will say in the presence of the Lord your

> God: "I have taken the consecrated portion out of my house; I have also given it to the Levites, resident aliens, fatherless children, and widows, according to all the commands you gave me. I have not violated or forgotten your commands. ... [15] Look down from your holy dwelling, from heaven, and bless your people Israel and the land you have given us as you swore to our ancestors, a land flowing with milk and honey."

The land, then, is primarily an expression of God's commitment to enable his covenant people to enjoy life with him. Or to put it slightly differently, at the most basic level, the land in Deuteronomy is a gift from Yahweh himself.

Promised to Abram (see Gen 12:1–3; 13:14–16; 15:18–21; 17:8; 26:3, 4, 24; 28:3–4, 13–15; 35:9–12), it is now freely given to Israel (so Deut 1:20–21, 25, 35; 3:18, 20; 4:1, 40; 6:1, 10, 18; 7:1, 8, 12; 8:1, 18; 9:5; 10:11; 11:9, 21; 12:1; 19:8; 26:3, 15; 27:3; 30:20; 31:17, 21, 23; 34:4). This is, of course, made possible by the fact that the land is his to give (see Exod 19:5; Lev 25:23; Deut 32:43).

As we have already seen, it is a "good land," which is described as "flowing with milk and honey" (Exod 3:8, 17; 13:5; 33:3; Lev 20:24; Num 13:27; 14:8; 16:13–14; Deut 6:3; 11:9–12; 26:9, 15; 27:3; 31:20). This good land is given to Israel "as an inheritance" (e.g., Deut 26:1). Inheritance language is very common when speaking about the land (see Num 26:53; 36:2; Deut 4:21, 38; 15:4; 19:10; 24:4; 25:19; 26:1), which further underlines that this gift is given to Israel as God's chosen son. Sonship, of course, is a privilege that also brings responsibility. The next question we must consider is the relationship of land (and in particular, its occupation) to obedience.

The land is a good gift from God, given without condition to his son Israel as his inheritance. However, it is also clear that enjoyment of life in the land with God is dependent on an appropriate response to this gift, expressed as "obedience," as Israel lives the beautiful life to which they are called—or does not. Christopher Wright helpfully comments: "What kind of relationship can it have been to produce this duality in which the indicative of God's grace is explicitly unconditional yet requires Israel's obedience and response? The answer, it seems, is to be found in the relationship of Israel's 'sonship of Yahweh,' which is expressed in many parts of the Old Testament. As a living, personal relationship, Israel's 'sonship of Yahweh' involves this organic tension or duality by its inherent nature."[46]

---

[46] Christopher J. H. Wright, *God's People in God's Land: Family, Land, and Property in the Old Testament* (Exeter: Paternoster, 1990), 15.

This relationship between the land and obedience can be characterized under three broad headings:

1. The land is the context for obedience (e.g., Deut 6:1; 12:1; 26:1; 27:1–3)
2. Obedience is the condition for entry into and occupation of the land (e.g., Deut 6:1–3; 8:1–3; 11:8–9; 12:1). The importance of this idea is reflected in the phrase "the land the LORD your God is giving you to possess" (see Deut 3:18; 5:31; 12:1; 15:4; 19:2, 14; 25:19, and also 1:39; 4:1; 17:14; 26:1).
3. Occupation of the land is a measure of obedience: the principle laid down in Lev 26:32–29 is developed in Deuteronomy (see especially chapters 4 and 30, and also 27–28).

This understanding of the land is fundamental for reading the rest of the Old Testament: from Joshua to 2 Kings, Israel's story in the land is played out from (partial) occupation to loss in the very categories established in Deuteronomy. The prophetic commentary on this history, both preexilic and exilic, is built on Moses's understanding of the significance of the land in Deuteronomy.[47]

Before we discuss briefly how this plays out in the coming of Christ in the New Testament, we need to complete our discussion of land by examining what Moses says about the potential loss—and recovery—of the land which Yahweh gifts to his people.

G. Exile and Homecoming

The theological trajectory for the loss of land and return to the land Yahweh set in Deuteronomy is probably one of the most important contributions this book makes to biblical theology. The theme is introduced in Deuteronomy 4:

> [25] When you have children and grandchildren and have been in the land a long time, and if you act corruptly, make an idol in the form of anything, and do what is evil in the sight of the LORD your God, angering him, [26] I call heaven and earth as witnesses against you today that you will quickly perish from the land

---

[47] Perhaps the prime illustration of this is Jeremiah, whose entire prophecy seems shaped by Deuteronomic categories.

> you are about to cross the Jordan to possess. You will not live long there, but you will certainly be destroyed. [27] The LORD will scatter you among the peoples, and you will be reduced to a few survivors among the nations where the LORD your God will drive you. [28] There you will worship man-made gods of wood and stone, which cannot see, hear, eat, or smell. [29] But from there, you will search for the LORD your God, and you will find him when you seek him with all your heart and all your soul. [30] When you are in distress and all these things have happened to you, in the future you will return to the LORD your God and obey him. [31] He will not leave you, destroy you, or forget the covenant with your ancestors that he swore to them by oath, because the LORD your God is a compassionate God.

As is often noted, the usual word for "exile" (from the verb גָּלָה) does not occur in Deuteronomy.[48] This is not simply a quirk of vocabulary, but reveals an important element of the theological world of this book. The truth is that exile in and of itself is of very little interest to Moses. His focus is well and truly on the danger of *losing the land*. Being scattered among the peoples (4:26) is hardly a pleasant prospect, but in Deuteronomy, it is more a case *of being expelled from the place where a relationship with Yahweh is to be enjoyed*, rather than being transported to another location. Losing the land (or "exile") then is more of a theological idea in Deuteronomy than a concrete reality.

This can be seen quite clearly in the list of curses of the covenant laid out in chapter 28. In 28:21, the dark prospect is that they are "exterminated ... from the land you are entering to possess." In 28:25, they are defeated and scattered, becoming an "object of horror" to all nations. A metaphorical "return to Egypt" is signaled in 28:27. It is only in verses 36–37 that anything like an exile proper is mentioned:

> [36] The LORD will bring you and your king that you have appointed to a nation neither you nor your ancestors have known, and there you will worship other gods, of wood and stone. [37] You will become an object of horror, scorn, and ridicule among all the peoples where the LORD will drive you.

[48] Unlike, e.g., Judg 18:30, which has no hesitation in displaying knowledge of the events following Nebuchadnezzar's incursion.

The focus, however, remains on the horror of defeat and the shame of losing their inheritance. So from verse 49, the vivid description of an attack from a foreign nation sent by God does not deal primarily with deportation, but deprivation in their own place. Similarly, when Moses returns to the idea of the "return to Egypt" in 28:60, and the reversal of the promises made to the patriarchs (28:62), the fate of Israel is described as being "ripped out of the land you are entering to possess" (28:63) and being scattered "among all peoples from one end of the earth to the other" (28:64). If further confirmation is needed that losing the land in Deuteronomy is a not a simple anticipation of the Babylonian deportation, it is provided in 28:68:

> The LORD will take you back in ships to Egypt by a route that I said you would never see again. There you will sell yourselves to your enemies as male and female slaves, but no one will buy you.

In the theological vision of Moses, disobedience will lead to an exit from the land—but this is depicted as utter destruction, a reversal of the exodus, deportation by sea to Egypt, as well as dislocation to a land they do not know, an idea that recurs at the end of chapter 29, as a future speech of the watching nations is envisaged:

> 28 The LORD uprooted them from their land in his anger, rage, and intense wrath, and threw them into another land where they are today.

It seems that here too, Deuteronomy proves a rich seedbed for ideas that are developed, expanded, and applied later in the Hebrew Scriptures, including the conviction that even though the judgment of Israel is inevitable and they will eventually lose the land, that will not be the end for them.[49] God's people can look forward to a "new exodus," which will consist of an even more dramatic rescue, a better covenant, and a fuller intimacy with Yahweh.[50] Deuteronomy 4:29–31 makes clear that beyond judgment lies *return*, an idea that finds its full expression in chapter 30:

---

[49] Chapter 32 contains multiple allusions to Israel being defeated, but not "exiled."

[50] As L. Michael Morales points out in his excellent (and seminal) book *Exodus Old and New: A Biblical Theology of Redemption* (Downers Grove: IVP Academic, 2020), it is ultimately the new exodus that is the macro-category that clarifies the kind of return for which Israel is waiting. This explains why limping back from Babylon doesn't even come close to meeting the expectations of God's people!

> 1 When all these things happen to you—the blessings and curs-
> es I have set before you—and you come to your senses while
> you are in all the nations where the Lord your God has driven
> you, 2 and you and your children return to the Lord your God
> and obey him with all your heart and all your soul by doing ev-
> erything I am commanding you today, 3 then he will restore
> your fortunes, have compassion on you, and gather you again
> from all the peoples where the Lord your God has scattered
> you. 4 Even if your exiles are at the farthest horizon, he will
> gather you and bring you back from there. 5 The Lord your God
> will bring you into the land your ancestors possessed, and you
> will take possession of it. He will cause you to prosper and mul-
> tiply you more than he did your ancestors.

This "return" involves changed attitudes and a changed commitment to listen and obey, as well as a physical return from wherever they have been scattered, as Yahweh brings them back home. What has brought this about? As I will argue below, 30:6 is the key event:

> The Lord your God will circumcise your heart and the hearts of your descendants, and you will love him with all your heart and all your soul so that you will live.

This return is triggered by the action of God himself bringing new life, and it is marked not so much by territory as by a renewed spirituality in Israel. It is also noticeable that God himself is the focus of the return. This is exactly what we find when Zechariah 1:1–6 redefines the return from exile in Babylon to a return to Yahweh himself in repentance and faith. The exile would provide a significant challenge to the self-understanding of Israel: Could they possibly still be God's son when they have blown their inheritance? Somehow their sonship remains intact, even if the land is effectively gone, and the Father is committed to enabling his son to come home.

That takes us to the massively important theme of covenant, which in Deuteronomy is where we see the delicate balance between Yahweh's unconditional, loving commitment and the conditional blessing that is attached to a proper response to that love. Before we move on, we do need to pause for a moment to reflect on how these key biblical-theological themes of land, exile, and homecoming (or return), developed so powerfully by Moses in Deuteronomy, play out in the rest of the Bible, and particularly in the coming of the Lord Jesus.

There is a sense in which the rest of the Old Testament simply plays out the pattern which has been anticipated by Deuteronomy. The only mystery is that it takes so long (in God's mercy) for the nation to lose first the northern kingdom to the Assyrians (where they are scattered) and then the southern kingdom of Judah, at which point some are deported, some scattered, and some literally flee to Egypt. The ministry of the prophets through this entire period is as "preachers of the covenant," urging God's people to face reality and return to him before it's too late (which, of course, they don't).

In the wake of the Babylonian captivity, after an initial surge of joy (e.g., Neh 8–10), life back in Judah (under constant foreign influence and even control) somehow never quite lives up to its potential. Astonishingly, as we noted above, Zechariah can still call the people to "return," even though they have been back in the land for years. Similarly, the prophet Malachi (in parallel with Chronicles) describes life after the return in a way which does not sound as if all the promises of God to restore them have been fulfilled. The sense of anticlimax is palpable. One can almost hear the people of Yahweh ask "Is this it?" Ultimately, they are looking not simply for a new location, but a new exodus.

The opening chapters of the New Testament answer the question in a stunning and entirely fresh way. As he narrates the earliest years of Jesus, Matthew quotes two Old Testament passages, one from Hosea and one from Jeremiah:

> [14] So he got up, took the child and his mother during the night, and escaped to Egypt. [15] He stayed there until Herod's death, so that what was spoken by the Lord through the prophet might be fulfilled: **Out of Egypt I called my Son.** [16] Then Herod, when he realized that he had been outwitted by the wise men, flew into a rage. He gave orders to massacre all the boys in and around Bethlehem who were two years old and under, in keeping with the time he had learned from the wise men. [17] Then what was spoken through Jeremiah the prophet was fulfilled: [18] **A voice was heard in Ramah, weeping, and great mourning, Rachel weeping for her children; and she refused to be consoled, because they are no more.** (Matt 2:14–18)

The Hosea quotation highlights that with Jesus's coming, the homecoming of God's people is at hand. Another exodus is taking place: this time, however, it is a "return from Egypt" after the curses of the covenant have been poured out. The words from Jeremiah recall the darkest days of the Babylonian invasion, but the clear implication is that as the events of the exile are a re-run, what must happen next is a new return—the return from exile that the people have been waiting for, which is no less than a new exodus.

What becomes more and more obvious as the New Testament continues is that it is in Jesus Christ that this new exodus and new return from exile are experienced. Those who come to him will discover and enjoy the rich relationship with God that was anticipated as Israel settled down in the land.

This is the understanding that undergirds Jesus's own words in Matthew 5:5: "Blessed are the humble, for they will inherit the earth." He is quoting Psalm 37, which spoke of inheriting the *land*. Now, by coming humbly to the one who is himself "humble in heart" (Matt 11:29), the humble will inherit the whole *earth*.

Gary Burge has also argued persuasively that in John 15, Jesus's encouragement to "remain in him" as the true vine is ultimately based on the reality that he himself is now the new promised land, and it is "in him" that all the land promises of flourishing and security are fulfilled.[51] This is supported by a series of other texts in which being *in Christ*, and belonging to *his kingdom* are described in language drawn from the Old Testament promises regarding the land:

> [1] Children, obey your parents *in the Lord*, because this is right. [2] **Honor your father and mother**, which is the first commandment with a promise, [3] **so that it may go well with you and that** you may have a long life in the land. (Eph 6:1–3)

> [13] He has rescued us from *the domain of darkness* and transferred us *into the kingdom of the Son he loves*. [14] In him we have redemption, the forgiveness of sins. (Col 1:13–14)

> [3] Blessed be the God and Father of our Lord Jesus Christ. Because of his great mercy he has given us new birth into a living hope through the resurrection of Jesus Christ from the dead [4] and into an inheritance that is imperishable, undefiled, and unfading, kept in heaven for you. (1 Pet 1:3–4)

> [8] For if Joshua had given them rest, God would not have spoken later about another day. [9] Therefore, a Sabbath rest remains for

[51] Gary M. Burge, *Jesus and the Land: The New Testament Challenge to "Holy Land" Theology* (Grand Rapids: Baker, 2010), 43–57.

> God's people. [10] For the person who has entered his rest has rested from his own works, just as God did from his. [11] Let us, then, make every effort to enter that rest, so that no one will fall into the same pattern of disobedience. ... [14] Therefore, since we have a great high priest who has passed through the heavens—Jesus the Son of God—let us hold fast to our confession. [15] For we do not have a high priest who is unable to sympathize with our weaknesses, but one who has been tempted in every way as we are, yet without sin. [16] Therefore, let us approach the throne of grace with boldness, so that we may receive mercy and find grace to help us in time of need. (Heb 4:8–11, 14–16)

It is in the Lord Jesus Christ that the promises of rest, flourishing and security in the land, which find their most developed expression in Deuteronomy, are ultimately fulfilled, as in Christ the new covenant, anticipated by Moses in Deuteronomy 30, is established.

H. Covenant (and New Covenant)

Undergirding almost everything we have said so far about the biblical-theological significance of Deuteronomy is the fundamental importance of God's covenant with his people. While it's often said that the overall trajectory of the Bible is dominated by God's kingdom (as shown by glancing at Gen 1–3, Mark 1, and Rev 21–22), it is equally clear that God advances his work in the world, building his kingdom, by making covenants (gracious commitments guaranteed by a promise, carrying significant obligations). In fact, I think it's fair to say that for the first half of the Bible at least, it is the idea of covenant that fills the theological frame. That is certainly true for Deuteronomy.

In the ancient Near East, for several thousand years before Christ, covenants were "in the air." All kinds of formal and informal covenant and treaty arrangements dominated life at home, nationally, and internationally.[52] It should come as no surprise to us then that the Scriptures come to us clothed in covenantal garb. Daniel Block captures this divinely inspired theological undergirding and atmosphere by coining the term "covenance," and he is surely "on the money"![53]

---

[52] This is reflected in the language of, e.g., Gen. 21:27, 32; 26:28; 31:44. See the helpful work of Paul Kalluveettil, *Declaration and Covenant: A Comprehensive Review of Covenant Formulae from the Old Testament and the Ancient Near East*, AnBib 88 (Rome: Pontifical Biblical Institute, 1982).

[53] See his magisterial discussion of covenant across the whole Bible, and in particular, the first ten pages in which he explains the idea of "covenance": Daniel I. Block, *Covenant: The Framework of God's Grand Plan of Redemption* (Grand Rapids: Baker, 2021).

This recognition has given rise to all kinds of work trying to map Deuteronomy onto various kinds of treaties and land grants (most notably Hittite vassal treaties from 1400–1300 BC and their later Assyrian counterparts from about 600 years later). The results, however, remain inconclusive. Often, those seeking to liken Deuteronomy to these other ancient documents tend to overplay the similarities and downplay the differences. The truth is that Deuteronomy is written on a much grander scale, with a much bigger agenda than any comparable document. Theologically, it breathes a different atmosphere. Rhetorically, it speaks a different language, seeking to move the heart of the people. Formally, it resists neat classification.[54]

It seems much more satisfactory to assume that Deuteronomy emerges from a common pool of covenant/treaty ideas, rather than attempting to establish a close literary dependence on any particular document at any moment in time. Deuteronomy really is one of a kind.

So how then does Deuteronomy seek to present the covenantal relationship that Yahweh enjoys with this chosen people? The biblical-theological importance of Deuteronomy in this context can hardly be overestimated, drawing together as it does the fairly disparate material from earlier in the Pentateuch and fashioning from it a theology of covenant that shapes not simply the rest of the Old Testament, but the entire Bible.[55]

From the beginning of Genesis, God's relationship with the people he creates in his image can broadly be described as "covenantal": he takes the initiative, makes promises, and attaches conditions for the enjoyment of the relationship that he has established by grace.[56] There has been much discussion over whether it is appropriate to speak of a "covenant with Adam" (often called the "covenant of works" in Reformed theology), but whether or not that terminology is justified, the shape of the

---

[54] See Block, *Covenant*, 234, for a nuanced and measured discussion of Deuteronomy as a treaty document, albeit one that has many distinctive features.

[55] Block, *Covenant*, 304 (and throughout) presents a compelling discussion of how the various covenants in the Old Testament (both those made with representative individuals and those made with God's people) fit together as expressions and aspects of "covenance," God's covenantal way of working in our world. While the way in which we express some of the details are quite different, our work is based on the same essential convictions about the nature of covenant.

[56] For a thoroughly biblical-theological (rather than systematic-theological) defense of these ideas, see Block, *Covenant*, 13–66.

relationship is clearly covenantal.[57] The same could be said of God's statements to Adam and Eve in the wake of their rejection of his authority in Genesis 3:14–19: the relationship is broadly covenantal, but the word "covenant" (בְּרִית) does not appear. It is actually in the Noah narrative that the word "covenant" first occurs (Gen 6:18; 9:9, 11–13, 15–17). What's interesting here is that from the beginning there is a looseness (or flexibility) in the way this commitment is described: in 6:18 (and 9:11–13), the covenant is very definitely with Noah and his family; by 9:17, the rainbow is said to be a sign of the covenant Yahweh has made with "every creature on earth." It seems that covenantal language can be used to denote *both* God's gracious dealings with humanity as a whole *and* specific, limited arrangements that express or enact one part of that all-encompassing relationship between God and his people.

This conception of "covenant" (Block's idea of "covenance") as the umbrella term to describe the way God unfolds his grand redemptive plan *and* the specific commitments he makes to individuals as part of that plan then plays out in Genesis and Exodus.

It is, of course, a matter of some controversy how the various promises and covenants made to the patriarchs intersect and interact.[58] The key commitments made to Abram/Abraham" in Genesis 12:1–3 do not actually use the term "covenant," although they seem closely related (even foundational to) many of the later allusions to covenant(s) made with the patriarchs. However, the designation "covenant" is used to describe specific commitments in both Genesis 15 and Genesis 17 (where in verses 10–14, circumcision is declared to be a "sign of the covenant"). Opinion is divided on whether these are two different covenants or aspects of the same divine commitment.[59] I am convinced that these are partial, complementary expressions of the same basic divine covenantal commitment.

This multifaceted Abrahamic covenant is then "refreshed" with Abraham's son, Isaac, and his grandson, Jacob (Gen 26:1–5; 28:10–21;

---

[57] The primary text that supports the existence of a covenant with Adam is Hos 6:7, but the Hebrew of this verse is notoriously ambiguous.

[58] For a careful and helpful discussion which comes to slightly different conclusions than this commentary see Paul R. Williamson, *Sealed with an Oath: Covenant in God's Unfolding Purpose*, NSBT 23 (Downers Grove: InterVarsity Press, 2007).

[59] My compatriots Desi Alexander (one of the series editors of EBTC) and Paul Williamson (*Sealed with an Oath*, 89–91) argue strongly that these are unrelated, whereas Block (*Covenant*, 94–104) sees them as complementary elements of the same interaction.

35:9–15; see also Exod 2:23–25). This covenant (or these covenants) are not static, but dynamic, expanding as God's work in his world advances.

Such an understanding of covenant in Genesis lays the foundation, I believe, for the fresh expression of covenant in Exodus 19:5–6 to anything which has gone before. The assumption is that the family of Jacob are the heirs of the covenant reiterated with Abraham, Isaac, and Jacob and now refreshed at this key moment in redemptive history, as the family becomes a nation (see also Exod 24:8, and the further development after the golden calf incident in Exod 34:10–28). It is slightly misleading (if ultimately necessary) to call this "the Mosaic covenant": covenant arrangements keep being "refreshed," but there is a strong sense of continuity and integration. These covenants are part of the same, seamless work of Yahweh.

This continuity is expressed in Deuteronomy both implicitly and explicitly. It is clear on the one hand that Israel is the heir to the promises made to Abraham, Isaac and Jacob (so, e.g., Deut 6:3; 9:5; 19:8; 27:3; 29:13). But on the other, it is explicitly stated to the Israelites Moses is addressing that the covenant at Horeb was made *with them*:

> [1] Moses summoned all Israel and said to them, "Israel, listen to the statutes and ordinances I am proclaiming as you hear them today. Learn and follow them carefully. [2] The Lord our God made a covenant with us at Horeb. [3] *He did not make this covenant with our ancestors, but with all of us who are alive here today.* [4] The Lord *spoke to you face to face* from the fire on the mountain. (Deut 5:1–4)

There can be no mistaking the fact that the covenant made at Horeb continues to be a present (and enduring) reality. But that does not make it a static thing. On the contrary, chapter 29 makes it very clear that in the same way that Horeb remains in force, so the covenant made at Moab will endure:

> [1] These are the words of the covenant that the Lord commanded Moses to make with the Israelites in the land of Moab, in addition to the covenant he had made with them at Horeb.

After rehearsing the events from Egypt to Moab, Moses adds this:

> [9] Therefore, observe the words of this covenant and follow them, so that you will succeed in everything you do. [10] "All of

> you are standing today before the Lord your God—your leaders, tribes, elders, officials, all the men of Israel, [11] your dependents, your wives, and the resident aliens in your camps who cut your wood and draw your water—[12] so that you may enter into the covenant of the Lord your God, which he is making with you today, so that you may enter into *his oath* [13] *and so that he may establish you today as his people and he may be your God as he promised you and as he swore to your ancestors Abraham, Isaac, and Jacob.* [14] *I am making this covenant and this oath not only with you,* [15] *but also with those who are standing here with us today in the presence of the Lord our God and with those who are not here today.* (Deut 29:9–15)

These words are probably the most neglected in discussions of the nature of the covenant Old Testament. The covenant at Horeb has not been superseded, but it has been expanded, extended, and enriched. The covenant *at Moab* is to guide the people through the procession of "todays" that lie ahead. Here the promises made to Abraham, Isaac, and Jacob are seamlessly blended with those made to the infant nation at Horeb and then applied to life in the land. This is among the richest expressions of covenant theology in the Hebrew Scriptures.

There is a tendency to set the Abrahamic and Mosaic covenants against one another.[60] However, given that (a) the Abrahamic covenant can go through multiple "refreshes," (b) Deuteronomy itself happily embraces both Abrahamic and Mosaic covenants, and (c) the Moab covenant in Deuteronomy 29:13–15 explicitly binds these together, it seems that the covenant is a multifaceted reality, rather than a series of sequential treaties at odds with one another.[61]

The "covenant at Moab" in Deuteronomy 29, then, is most naturally understood as the latest iteration in a series of grace-based promissory commitments that come with obligations that are progressively spelled out. Incidentally, basic elasticity allows for other covenantal

---

[60] See, e.g., Sailhamer, *Meaning of the Pentateuch*. Most Old Testament scholarship in the twentieth century operated with a similar underlying dichotomy between "law" and "grace."

[61] This might seem to be at odds with passages like Gal 3:17, where Paul opposes the "covenant" (Abrahamic) and the "law" (Mosaic). But the context makes clear that he is countering his first century opponents' approach of prioritizing law-keeping (however understood), arguing that the events of Sinai did not "invalidate a covenant previously established by God and thus cancel the promise." Paul is not attempting to expound Old Testament covenant theology as a whole or even to capture the entirety of the relationship between Abraham and Moses, but to deal with the live issues in Galatia.

arrangements (such as those with Noah and even the one with David in 2 Sam 7) to be accommodated in the overall covenantal structure of the Old Testament.

There is only one problem with this covenant at Moab: it doesn't work! No sooner has Moses uttered these words than he also exposes the inevitability of the failure of God's people to meet their obligations (29:16–29; also 31:14–22, as well as the Song of Moses in chapter 32). This, however, also gives rise to the first intimation of what will become known as the "new covenant" in 30:1–10.[62]

The classic statement of covenantal thinking in the Old Testament is "I will be your God, you will be my people" (so variously Exod 6:7; Jer 7:23; 11:4; 30:22; Ezek 36:28). There is no question that God keeps his side of this commitment. The problem is that Israel (and Judah) doesn't—or to be more accurate—*cannot* respond to Gods' grace in an appropriate way. What God asks of his people is a wholehearted, thoroughgoing response to his grace and mercy (e.g., Deut 6:1–5). The problem is that we can't pull this off (see also Luke 10:25–37). But the great news is that this is already anticipated in the text of the Old Testament itself. After calling on God's people to "circumcise their hearts" (Deut 10:16), God through Moses points to the ultimate solution:

> The Lord your God will circumcise your heart and the hearts of your descendants, and you will love him with all your heart and all your soul so that you will live. (Deut 30:6)

This is the earliest explicit expression of what becomes known as the "new covenant" in the Old Testament. Astonishingly, this new covenant thinking appears to lie dormant until it's picked up by the prophet Hosea in 2:16–23:

> 16 In that day—
> this is the Lord's declaration—
> you will call me "my husband,"
> and no longer call me "my Baal."
> 17 For I will remove the names of the Baals
> from her mouth;
> they will no longer be remembered by their names.
> 18 On that day I will make a covenant for them

---

62 It is important to remember that the concept of covenant can loom large even when the word itself does not appear (see also 26:17–19, which is clearly covenantal).

with the wild animals, the birds of the sky,
and the creatures that crawl on the ground.
I will shatter bow, sword,
and weapons of war in the land
and will enable the people to rest securely.
19 I will take you to be my wife forever.
I will take you to be my wife in righteousness,
justice, love, and compassion.
20 I will take you to be my wife in faithfulness,
and you will know the Lord.
21 On that day I will respond—
this is the Lord's declaration.
I will respond to the sky,
and it will respond to the earth.
22 The earth will respond to the grain,
the new wine, and the fresh oil,
and they will respond to Jezreel.
23 I will sow her in the land for myself,
and I will have compassion
on Lo-ruhamah;
I will say to Lo-ammi:
You are my people,
and he will say, "You are my God."

Jeremiah, who regularly picks up on ideas and images used by Hosea, develops this idea more fully, this time drawing more directly on Deuteronomy 30:

> 31 "Look, the days are coming"—this is the Lord's declara-
> tion—"when I will make a new covenant with the house of Is-
> rael and with the house of Judah. 32 This one will not be like the
> covenant I made with their ancestors on the day I took them by
> the hand to lead them out of the land of Egypt—my covenant
> that they broke even though I am their master"—the Lord's
> declaration. 33 "Instead, this is the covenant I will make with
> the house of Israel after those days"—the Lord's declaration. "I
> will put my teaching within them and write it on their hearts.
> I will be their God, and they will be my people. 34 No longer
> will one teach his neighbor or his brother, saying, "Know the
> Lord," for they will all know me, from the least to the greatest
> of them"—this is the Lord's declaration. "For I will forgive their
> iniquity and never again remember their sin." (Jer 31:31–34)

It is not only Jeremiah who announces this ultimate reboot of the covenant. Ezekiel picks up the same thread in two key passages:

> [25] I will make a covenant of peace with them and eliminate dangerous creatures from the land, so that they may live securely in the wilderness and sleep in the forest. [26] I will make them and the area around my hill a blessing: I will send down showers in their season; they will be showers of blessing. [27] The trees of the field will yield their fruit, and the land will yield its produce; my flock will be secure in their land. They will know that I am the Lord when I break the bars of their yoke and rescue them from the power of those who enslave them. [28] They will no longer be prey for the nations, and the wild creatures of the earth will not consume them. They will live securely, and no one will frighten them. [29] I will establish for them a place renowned for its agriculture, and they will no longer be victims of famine in the land. They will no longer endure the insults of the nations. [30] Then they will know that I, the Lord their God, am with them, and that they, the house of Israel, are my people. This is the declaration of the Lord God. [31] You are my flock, the human flock of my pasture, and I am your God. This is the declaration of the Lord God. (Ezek 34:25–31)

> [24] I will take you from the nations and gather you from all the countries, and will bring you into your own land. [25] I will also sprinkle clean water on you, and you will be clean. I will cleanse you from all your impurities and all your idols. [26] I will give you a new heart and put a new spirit within you; I will remove your heart of stone and give you a heart of flesh. [27] I will place my Spirit within you and cause you to follow my statutes and carefully observe my ordinances. [28] You will live in the land that I gave your ancestors; you will be my people, and I will be your God. (Ezek 36:24–27)

All of this flows from the preaching of Moses in Deuteronomy 30.[63] The question is, how do the earlier covenant(s) and this new covenant fit together? We have already hinted at the answer that Deuteronomy begins to articulate. The "new covenant" is essentially the ultimate articulation of the enduring commitment that "I will be your God, you will be my

[63] See also Joel 2:24–32, which is clearly dealing with similar ideas, but does so in different, if overlapping, categories.

people."[64] It is a refreshed, fully functional expression of God's determination to bring people like us to know and enjoy him forever. O. Palmer Robertson describes this relationship:

> Does some unity bind together the various covenantal administrations spread across human history? Are the covenants to be viewed as successive and distinctive commitments that replace one another in temporal sequence? Or do the covenants build the one on the other so that each successive covenant supplements its predecessors without at the same time supplanting the continuing role of the more ancient bond between God and his people? The cumulative evidence of the Scriptures points definitively toward the unified character of the biblical covenants. God's multiple bonds with his people ultimately unite into a single relationship.[65]

For us to have a relationship with God, God himself has to take the initiative. The Westminster Confession calls that sweeping initiative "the covenant of grace." The "covenant of grace" is a huge umbrella term for the way God makes it possible for people like us to know and enjoy him forever. When we read the Old Testament (and Deuteronomy in particular), we discover that this grand covenantal commitment is actually made up of multiple little ones, building in turn toward the moment when Jesus announces that his kingdom has broken in, through the "new covenant in my blood." This is the "new covenant" that Moses, Jeremiah, and the rest

---

[64] Expressing the continuity and discontinuity of the covenant(s) is obviously hotly debated, and my Reformed Baptist friends will quickly point to texts like Jer 31:32 and suggest that this is a radically different covenant. I think that is overstating the case and, as discussions of the breakdown of Israel's marriage speak freely of it being "over" and yet somehow "not over," the new covenant is both new and yet enduring.

[65] O. Palmer Robertson, *The Christ of the Covenants* (Phillipsburg: Presbyterian and Reformed, 1980), 28. The biblical-theological understanding set out here coheres with the more systematic language in chapter 7 of the Westminster Confession of Faith: "I. The distance between God and the creature is so great, that although reasonable creatures do owe obedience unto him as their Creator, yet they could never have any fruition of him, as their blessedness and reward, but by some voluntary condescension on God's part, which he hath been pleased to express by way of covenant. ... V. This covenant was differently administered in the time of the law, and in the time of the gospel; ... VI ... .There are not therefore two covenants of grace differing in substance, but one and the same under various dispensations." This is not so much a case of importing systematic theological categories as of having to find some way of expressing the continuity of covenantal thinking on display across the canon of Scripture.

spoke about, which is set up through Jesus's death and resurrection and is brought to life through the outpouring of the Spirit, as promised in Joel.

In much the same way that the Old Testament seems comfortable expressing both the privileges and responsibilities (or unconditionality and conditionality) of the covenant, the New Testament at points focuses on the continuity of this covenant (as in Luke 22, Acts 2, and elsewhere) and at other points on the discontinuity, as in Hebrews 8 and 9, where the defining feature of this new covenantal operating system is that it actually works.

The fact that we live under a new covenant arrangement is one of the single most important facets of biblical theology: We are not Israelites; we are Christians! And that changes everything. Of course, it is important to remember that the difference between life under the old covenant and that under the new covenant is *not* that we now enjoy God's grace: all the way through the OT, when God said "I will be your God and you will be my people," he was showing grace to the children he loved. The difference is much more nuanced than that.

The difference is not that God is now keeping his part of the promise (he always has done that); the difference is that in Christ's death and resurrection, God has made it possible for people like you and me to keep our part! Life under the new covenant is marked by the fact that we have been born again, united to Christ by faith, given life in the Spirit, and as a result are now able to live the life to which we have been called in Christ.

Under the old (gracious) arrangements, God rescued his people, gave them a land, and called them to live for him (warning that if they chose not to they would experience curse rather than blessing). Under the new (super-gracious) arrangements, God has brought us through a new exodus, rescuing us from death and bringing us to new life in Christ, establishing a new covenant that, through the Spirit, enables us to know him in a new way and to live in a way that fits with who we are in Christ, who is the mediator of this new covenant.[66] As the writer to the Hebrews says:

> [6] But Jesus has now obtained a superior ministry, and to that degree he is the mediator of a better covenant, which has

---

[66] See T. Desmond Alexander, *Face to Face with God: A Biblical Theology of Christ as Priest and Mediator* (Downers Grove: IVP Academic, 2022), 109–21. Deuteronomy's basic disinterest in the details of the role of the priesthood will come seen repeatedly throughout this commentary.

> been established on better promises. [7] For if that first covenant had been faultless, there would have been no occasion for a second one. (Heb 8:6–7)

I. Blessing and Curse

One oft-neglected feature of the theological contribution of Deuteronomy to the canon is the carefully constructed schema of "blessing" and "curse." Although the concept is first suggested in Leviticus 26, it is Deuteronomy that both develops these categories and fully exploits them as a motivation for God's people to live God's way in God's land. The end result is a clear exposition of the fact that as Yahweh's people, there are only two ways to live: either they obey (and experience blessing) or disobey (and taste the "curses of the covenant").

This is first properly articulated at the end of Deuteronomy 11, at the highpoint of Moses's preaching, which precedes the beginning of the laws:

> [26] Look, today I set before you a blessing and a curse: [27] there will be a blessing, if you obey the commands of the Lord your God I am giving you today, [28] and a curse, if you do not obey the commands of the Lord your God and you turn aside from the path I command you today by following other gods you have not known. [29] When the Lord your God brings you into the land you are entering to possess, you are to proclaim the blessing at Mount Gerizim and the curse at Mount Ebal. [30] Aren't these mountains across the Jordan, beyond the western road in the land of the Canaanites, who live in the Arabah, opposite Gilgal, near the oaks of Moreh? [31] For you are about to cross the Jordan to enter and take possession of the land the Lord your God is giving you. When you possess it and settle in it, [32] be careful to follow all the statutes and ordinances I set before you today.

This ritual, to be performed at the twin peaks above Shechem, enshrines these twin realities at the heart of the life of the people. That the details of this event are then spelled out again in chapter 27 and 28 (see the commentary on these passages for a discussion of what exactly is going on here) underlines how important they are if Israel is to live well with and for Yahweh in the land. This is highlighted once more at the very climax of the book in chapter 30:

> [19] I call heaven and earth as witnesses against you today that I have set before you life and death, blessing and curse. Choose life so that you and your descendants may live, [20] love the Lord your God, obey him, and remain faithful to him. For he is your life, and he will prolong your days as you live in the land the Lord swore to give to your ancestors Abraham, Isaac, and Jacob.

It is important to remember that "blessing" and "curse" are not the same things as "salvation" and "damnation." Rather, they are an index of the obedience (or disobedience) displayed by the people of Yahweh at any given time. So to live the "blessed life" in Matthew 5 at the beginning of the Sermon on the Mount is essentially to live in obedience to God in the way that he has revealed. Jesus's point is that if we live like this, it really will show. Once more, the problem is that we really aren't able to maintain that level of integrity.

To try to be good in our own strength, even in a Christian framework, is ultimately to choose failure and misery over life. This is precisely what Paul says in Galatians 3:

> [10] For all who rely on the works of the law are under a curse, because it is written, **Everyone who does not do everything written in the book of the law is cursed.** [11] Now it is clear that no one is justified before God by the law, because **the righteous will live by faith.** [12] But the law is not based on faith; instead, **the one who does these things will live by them.** [13] Christ redeemed us from the curse of the law by becoming a curse for us, because it is written, **Cursed is everyone who is hung on a tree.** [14] The purpose was that the blessing of Abraham would come to the Gentiles by Christ Jesus, so that we could receive the promised Spirit through faith.

The vision of the life of God's people that Moses sets out is one in which they are enabled by God to enjoy blessing, rather than curse, because Christ, the one who has flawlessly lived the beautiful life of torah, has also voluntarily substituted himself for us, dying in our place, placarding the fact that he dealt with the curse by the manner of his death. The incredible mercy of all this is that by living and dying like this, Jesus enables all those of us who are not Jewish to gain access to the blessed life, a foretaste of which was adumbrated in Deuteronomy, but can now be enjoyed by all who come to Christ in repentance and faith.

J. The Sovereignty of God

The sovereignty of God is on display in every book of the Bible, but it is on display in unique ways in Deuteronomy. There are two key ways in which Deuteronomy makes a unique contribution to this emerging doctrine:

(1) The election of Israel

While it is clearly present in the narratives of Exodus, the fact that Yahweh has chosen Israel freely (by grace, as we have seen) from all nations to be his people, is made explicit by Moses in his addresses on the verge of the land in Moab:

> [7] "The Lord had his heart set on you and chose you, not because you were more numerous than all peoples, for you were the fewest of all peoples. [8] But because the Lord loved you and kept the oath he swore to your ancestors, he brought you out with a strong hand and redeemed you from the place of slavery, from the power of Pharaoh king of Egypt. (Deut 7:7–8)

His election of Israel will also be demonstrated by him repeating his rescue act against the Canaanites (7:17–21). He has chosen to presence himself with and act for Israel against anyone who would oppose them.

This explains why arrogance or hubris is one of Moses's key concerns: a people chosen by God's free grace has no reason to become smug or self-assured, even in the wake of great victories (like those presumably about to happen in the land):

> [4] When the Lord your God drives them out before you, do not say to yourself, "The Lord brought me in to take possession of this land because of my righteousness." Instead, the Lord will drive out these nations before you because of their wickedness. [5] You are not going to take possession of their land because of your righteousness or your integrity. Instead, the Lord your God will drive out these nations before you because of their wickedness, in order to fulfill the promise he swore to your ancestors Abraham, Isaac, and Jacob. [6] Understand that the Lord your God is not giving you

> this good land to possess because of your righteousness, for you are a stiff-necked people. (Deut 9:4–6)

The sovereignty of Yahweh shines brightly against the dark background of the depravity of his people throughout Deuteronomy.[67] Nowhere is that clearer than in chapter 10:

> [14] The heavens, indeed the highest heavens, belong to the LORD your God, as does the earth and everything in it. [15] Yet the LORD had his heart set on your ancestors and loved them. He chose their descendants after them—he chose you out of all the peoples, as it is today. [16] Therefore, circumcise your hearts and don't be stiff-necked any longer. [17] For the LORD your God is the God of gods and Lord of lords, the great, mighty, and awe-inspiring God, showing no partiality and taking no bribe. ... [21] He is your praise and he is your God, who has done for you these great and awe-inspiring works your eyes have seen. [22] Your ancestors went down to Egypt, seventy people in all, and now the LORD your God has made you numerous, like the stars of the sky.

It is not just when Moses is preaching that we find this idea. In three places in the collection of laws, we also read of Yahweh "choosing":

> You are a holy people belonging to the LORD your God. The LORD has chosen you to be his own possession out of all the peoples on the face of the earth. (14:2)

This first example is another straightforward example of God choosing the nation of Israel. But the other two develop the theology of election a little further:

> The LORD your God has chosen him and his sons from all your tribes to stand and minister in his name from now on. (18:5)

> Then the priests, the sons of Levi, will come forward, for the LORD your God has chosen them to serve him and pronounce blessings in his name, and they are to give a ruling in every dispute and case of assault. (21:5)

---

[67] One could argue with some justification that the sinfulness of humanity is a key theme in Deuteronomy, but given the fact that it is also a major idea in each of the first five books of the Bible, I have chosen not to include it as a separate section in this discussion of key biblical-theological themes.

Moses insists that the Levites are chosen from among the other tribes to serve in particular ways, even as they are also chosen to enjoy a particular closeness to Yahweh:

> [1] "The Levitical priests, the whole tribe of Levi, will have no portion or inheritance with Israel. They will eat the LORD's food offerings; that is their inheritance. [2] Although Levi has no inheritance among his brothers, the LORD is his inheritance, as he promised him. (Deut 18:1–2)

In the same way that Israel is chosen to show the world what a relationship with Yahweh is like, the tribe of Levi is chosen to show the Israelites the goal of God's work in the world—to draw people like you and me into an intimate relationship with our God.

(2) THE PLACE WHERE YAHWEH WILL CHOOSE TO PUT HIS NAME

The other context in which Yahweh's sovereignty is placarded is in Moses's insistence that when they enter the land, Yahweh himself will decide how *and where* he is to be worshiped:

> [4] Don't worship the LORD your God this way. [5] Instead, turn to the place the LORD your God chooses from all your tribes to put his name for his dwelling and go there. [6] You are to bring there your burnt offerings and sacrifices, your tenths and personal contributions, your vow offerings and freewill offerings, and the firstborn of your herds and flocks. [7] You will eat there in the presence of the LORD your God and rejoice with your household in everything you do, because the LORD your God has blessed you. ... [10] When you cross the Jordan and live in the land the LORD your God is giving you to inherit, and he gives you rest from all the enemies around you and you live in security, [11] then the LORD your God will choose the place to have his name dwell. Bring there everything I command you: your burnt offerings, sacrifices, offerings of the tenth, personal contributions, and all your choice offerings you vow to the LORD. [12] You will rejoice before the LORD your God—you, your sons and daughters, your male and female slaves, and the Levite who is within your city gates, since he has no portion or inheritance among you. [13] Be careful not to offer your burnt offerings in all the sacred places you see. [14] You must offer your burnt offerings only in the place the Lord chooses in one of your tribes, and there you must do everything I command you. (Deut 12:4–7, 10–14)

This takes us to the heart of the Deuteronomic conception of the life of God's people in God's land *worshiping God's way*. This idea of the place chosen by Yahweh recurs in Deuteronomy 12:18, 21, 26; 14:23–25; 15:20; 16:2, 6–7, 11, 15–16; 17:8, 10; 18:6; 26:2, 4, 9–10. This is not a lame attempt to avoid naming Jerusalem: it is a deeply theological assertion of the right of God to determine how he should be worshiped.[68] It is a clear pointer to the nature of the God whom Moses describes like this in chapter 32:

> 39 See now that I alone am he;
> there is no God but me.
> I bring death and I give life;
> I wound and I heal.
> No one can rescue anyone from my power.
> 40 I raise my hand to heaven and declare:
> As surely as I live forever,
> 41 when I sharpen my flashing sword,
> and my hand takes hold of judgment,
> I will take vengeance on my adversaries
> and repay those who hate me.

There can really be no question: "there is none like the God of Jeshurun" (33:26). This is the same God who chose us before the foundation of the world in Christ, the same God who invites us to worship him in spirit and truth (John 4:23–34) of whom Paul writes in Ephesians 1:

> 3 Blessed is the God and Father of our Lord Jesus Christ, who has blessed us with every spiritual blessing in the heavens in Christ. 4 For he chose us in him, before the foundation of the world, to be holy and blameless in love before him. 5 He predestined us to be adopted as sons through Jesus Christ for himself, according to the good pleasure of his will, 6 to the praise of his glorious grace that he lavished on us in the Beloved One.

K. The Righteousness of God

One of the great areas of controversy in New Testament theology in recent years has been over precisely what Jesus and the apostles meant by "the righteousness of God" in the various contexts in which the phrase occurs. Part of the challenge has been doing justice to both those passages where it refers to a quality of God (his integrity) and those where it clearly

---

[68] It also accounts for the situation in Joshua, Judges and 1 Samuel, where the sanctuary of God is located at Shiloh (e.g., Josh 18:1).

has a declarative sense—where righteousness is not a personal quality, but a verdict announced (and often imputed) by God. Perhaps surprisingly, this complexity of meaning is already in evidence in Deuteronomy where various forms of the root צדק appear.

In Deuteronomy, righteousness in the first place belongs to God. It describes his character and the way in which he acts. This righteousness must then characterize the way in which Israel orders its life (and notably, the way in which its legal system is operated—in this context, it is often translated as "justice"). But there is a further *aspirational* dimension. Israel is urged to aim for, to choose or even possess this righteousness. The agenda which God has for his people is that they share in his quality of life. The problem is that Israel cannot actually pull this off. It becomes clear by the end of the book that if Israel is to enjoy this righteousness, it will have to be given to them by God.

This range of meanings for "righteousness" is quite obvious in the text. The first occurrence of the concept comes in 1:16 and is quite straightforward. Those given authority by Moses must act with *justice,* making decisions in a way which fits with God's righteousness.

The second passage where righteousness occurs is more complex. In 4:8 Moses asks the rhetorical question:

> And what great nation has righteous statutes and ordinances like this entire law I set before you today?

This cannot simply mean fair or just. These laws are remarkable because they reflect God's nature. The statutes and ordinances are *righteous* because the God who is their source is *righteous*. This link becomes explicit in verse 7, where it is tied to the proximity of the Lord our God in a completely unprecedented way. This pushes beyond the idea of judicial fairness to an affirmation that these laws allow the people to flourish, because they allow them to share in the kind of life which God himself enjoys.

It is one of the distinctive features of Deuteronomy that the righteous God invites his people to enjoy the life of righteousness with him. This idea recurs throughout Moses's preaching, as he invites God's people to choose life. This is the idea expressed in 6:25:

> Righteousness will be ours if we are careful to follow every one of these commands before the Lord our God, as he has commanded us.

As I'll argue in the Commentary below, this righteousness (e.g., unlike Gen 15:6) is not primarily forensic. It is an encouragement and an invitation to enjoy the righteous life with God by listening to and obeying his (righteous) words. The problem is, of course, that this will always prove beyond the reach of Israel, something Moses makes clear a few chapters later (see 9:4–6).

In his preaching, Moses both invites people to embrace God's righteous commands, to choose the righteous life, and warns them that they are not righteous and will not be able to live in a way that fits with, let alone displays, God's righteousness.

That tension takes us right to the heart of the sweeping vision of the laws of chapters 12–26, which are, in essence, part of this vibrant exposition of the righteousness of God, embodied and lived out in the life of the nation. That is implicit throughout, but explicit in a passage that stands near the center of the collection:

> [18] Appoint judges and officials for your tribes in all your towns the Lord your God is giving you. They are to judge the people with *righteous* judgment. [19] Do not deny justice or show partiality to anyone. Do not accept a bribe, for it blinds the eyes of the wise and twists the words of the *righteous.* [20] Pursue justice [*righteousness*] and justice [*righteousness*] alone, so that you will live and possess the land the Lord your God is giving you. (Deut 16:18–20)

Righteousness in the courts and the community are a key part of the life to which God is inviting (or better, calling) his people. In his land, things must be done his way. This is what righteousness looks like in action:

> Be sure to return [his garment] to him at sunset. Then he will sleep in it and bless you, and this will be counted as righteousness to you before the Lord your God. (Deut 24:13)

> You must have a full and honest weight, a full and honest dry measure, so that you may live long in the land the Lord your God is giving you. (Deut 25:15)

Confirmation that this is the full-orbed view of righteousness in Moses's mind comes in the opening lines of the song he teaches the nation in chapter 32:

> [4] The Rock—his work is perfect; all his ways are just.
> A faithful God, without bias, he is righteous and true.

This double emphasis—on the innate righteousness of God and his invitation and requirement for us to share in this righteousness—runs right through the Old Testament. Just two examples will suffice:

> Listen to me, you who pursue righteousness,
> you who seek the LORD:
> Look to the rock from which you were cut,
> and to the quarry from which you were dug. (Isa 51:1)

> [5] "Look, the days are coming"—this is the LORD's declaration—
> "when I will raise up a Righteous Branch for David.
> He will reign wisely as king
> and administer justice and righteousness in the land.
> [6] In his days Judah will be saved,
> and Israel will dwell securely.
> This is the name he will be called:
> The LORD Is Our Righteousness. (Jer 23:5–6)

In both these passages, God is both the one who possesses and gives righteousness. God models righteousness in all his actions and makes it possible for us to be declared righteous (or justified) and to live a truly righteous life. All this is gloriously brought together by the Lord Jesus Christ, as the apostle Paul explains in Romans 3:

> [21] But now, apart from the law, the righteousness of God has
> been revealed, attested by the Law and the Prophets. [22] The
> righteousness of God is through faith in Jesus Christ to all
> who believe, since there is no distinction. [23] For all have
> sinned and fall short of the glory of God; [24] they are justified
> freely by his grace through the redemption that is in Christ
> Jesus. [25] God presented him as the mercy seat by his blood,
> through faith, to demonstrate his righteousness, because in
> his restraint God passed over the sins previously committed.
> [26] God presented him to demonstrate his righteousness at the
> present time, so that he would be just and justify the one who
> has faith in Jesus.

Once more, Deuteronomy contains the raw materials that are eventually built into the superstructure of the gospel itself.

L. Leadership (Including Kingship)

It is one of the striking features of the plotline of the Old Testament that in a world where the achievements and character of leaders (especially kings) were routinely exaggerated and praised out of all proportion (especially by the kings themselves), those leaders who feature largest are also those who are portrayed so honestly as flawed human beings. Probably the two greatest leaders of the Hebrew Scriptures, David and Moses, are both described as brilliant but ultimately flawed individuals, whose greatest contribution was to point their people to the one and only God, who can be trusted.

In Moses's case, both he himself in his preaching and the finished version of the book go out of their way to relativize his significance. This is actually part of a surprisingly rich biblical theology of leadership, which has a profound influence on the rest of the Old Testament.

Almost at the beginning of the book, as Moses starts to reflect (mostly negatively) on the nation's experience from Horeb to Kadesh and back to Moab, he prefaces his travelogue with an explanation of how the responsibility of leading the nation became too much:

> 9 I said to you at that time: I can't bear the responsibility for
> you on my own. 10 The Lord your God has so multiplied you
> that today you are as numerous as the stars of the sky. 11 May
> the Lord, the God of your ancestors, increase you a thousand
> times more, and bless you as he promised you. 12 But how can
> I bear your troubles, burdens, and disputes by myself? 13 Ap-
> point for yourselves wise, understanding, and respected men
> from each of your tribes, and I will make them your leaders.
> (Deut 1:9–13)

Part of the purpose of this, as explained below, is surely to head off any attempt to blame Moses for the series of debacles that follow. But it also highlights the fact that the leadership of the nation has to involve more than one man, *even when that man is someone as remarkable as Moses.*

Add to that, however, the fact that Moses has already been excluded from the land by Yahweh (3:21–29; 32:48–52; 34:4), and it becomes clear that the book as a whole is not encouraging a particularly sanguine view of even the best of human leadership. The primary requirement of a leader is obviously to be godly. This is made crystal clear by the remarkable passage concerning any future kings of Israel.

In Deuteronomy 17:14–20, Moses lays down the requirements for any future ruler:

> 14 "When you enter the land the Lord your God is giving you, take possession of it, live in it, and say, "I will set a king over me like all the nations around me," 15 you are to appoint over you the king the Lord your God chooses. Appoint a king from your brothers. You are not to set a foreigner over you, or one who is not of your people. 16 However, he must not acquire many horses for himself or send the people back to Egypt to acquire many horses, for the Lord has told you, "You are never to go back that way again." 17 He must not acquire many wives for himself so that his heart won't go astray. He must not acquire very large amounts of silver and gold for himself. 18 When he is seated on his royal throne, he is to write a copy of this instruction for himself on a scroll in the presence of the Levitical priests. 19 It is to remain with him, and he is to read from it all the days of his life, so that he may learn to fear the Lord his God, to observe all the words of this instruction, and to do these statutes. 20 Then his heart will not be exalted above his countrymen, he will not turn from this command to the right or the left, and he and his sons will continue reigning many years in Israel.

The first thing to notice is that this king is to be appointed by Yahweh (further evidence of the sovereignty of God in this book), and the second is that he is to be chosen "from your brothers." This obviously entails being an ethnic Israelite, and therefore a worshiper of Yahweh, but beyond that, it seems to imply also that he continues to act like any other part of the family of God—a view that is confirmed by verse 20 ("his heart will not be exalted above his countrymen").

Yahweh instructs any future occupant of the throne to avoid seeking military power and international influence (and definitely not from Egypt) or being enticed by sex and pursuing wealth. Instead, he is to copy out Deuteronomy, have it certified, and read it constantly! The key here is the "heart" (essentially meaning the personality or character): it must not be turned aside by the pursuit of pleasure or the allure of power. Instead, he is to listen to Yahweh. This is how it must be for all leaders, which is implicitly indicated by three notes that all portray Moses as acting in concert with other leaders in the nation:

> Moses and the elders of Israel commanded the people, "Keep every command I am giving you today." (Deut 27:1)

> Moses and the Levitical priests spoke to all Israel, "Be silent, Israel, and listen! This day you have become the people of the LORD your God." (Deut 27:9)

> Moses wrote down this law and gave it to the priests, the sons of Levi, who carried the ark of the LORD's covenant, and to all the elders of Israel. (Deut 31:9)

Leadership in Israel (from the king down) is to be godly, humble, selfless leadership that is marked above all by listening to Yahweh, reading his word, and doing what it says—an ideal which was seldom, if ever, the case. But even though few leaders ever came close to this Deuteronomic ideal, from this point in salvation history this is the template against which all leaders are measured.

Part of the strangeness of Judges, for example, is the fact that none of the procession of leaders (culminating in the brutish Samson) ever give any hint that they have even heard of God's torah, living out the beautiful life, let alone have their own handwritten, Levite-certified copy! When we arrive in 1 Samuel, the choice of Saul as king is riddled with ambiguity. Although is clearly takes place with Yahweh's permission, the selection criteria used by the people appear to be "must be tall and good looking" (see 1 Sam 9:2), and so well suited to leading them into battle, rather than the guidelines laid down in Deuteronomy 17. It is only when we come to David that the heart of a future king comes into play (1 Sam 13:14; 16:7), and a man (though far from sinless) is appointed who is neither hubristic nor idolatrous.[69]

The Deuteronomic ideal is the template against which Solomon is measured, from the moment he marries Pharaoh's daughter in 1 Kings 3:1 to the damning words of 1 Kings 11:1–4:

> [1] King Solomon loved many foreign women in addition to Pharaoh's daughter: Moabite, Ammonite, Edomite, Sidonian, and Hittite women [2] from the nations about which the LORD had told the Israelites, "You must not intermarry with them, and they must not intermarry with you, because they will turn your heart away to follow their gods." To these women Solomon was deeply attached in love. [3] He had seven hundred

[69] In my view, the presentation of Saul's reign is almost uniformly negative in 1 Samuel.

> wives who were princesses and three hundred who were concubines, and they turned his heart away. [4] When Solomon was old, his wives turned his heart away to follow other gods. He was not wholeheartedly devoted to the Lord his God, as his father David had been.

Through the rest of Kings, David becomes the gold standard against which all kings are measured, because, in line with Deuteronomy 17, he followed Yahweh wholeheartedly (that is, his heart was neither turned away or lifted up). Sadly, no king manages to meet the requirements, until a king came not "to be served, but to serve, and to give his life as a ransom for many" (Mark 10:45), the one of whom God said "This is my Son: listen to him!" And he is the one who appoints under-shepherds to care for his sheep as he does:

> [1] I exhort the elders among you as a fellow elder and witness to the sufferings of Christ, as well as one who shares in the glory about to be revealed: [2] Shepherd God's flock among you, not overseeing out of compulsion but willingly, as God would have you; not out of greed for money but eagerly; [3] not lording it over those entrusted to you, but being examples to the flock. [4] And when the chief Shepherd appears, you will receive the unfading crown of glory. [5] In the same way, you who are younger, be subject to the elders. All of you clothe yourselves with humility toward one another. (1 Pet 5:1–5)[70]

As in Deuteronomy, it is the job of leaders in Christ's church to know and speak the words of God to his people:

> [7] Remember your leaders who have spoken God's word to you. As you carefully observe the outcome of their lives, imitate their faith. ... [17] Obey your leaders and submit to them, since they keep watch over your souls as those who will give an account, so that they can do this with joy and not with grief, for that would be unprofitable for you. (Heb 13:7, 17)

As the sweep of biblical theology unfolds, it becomes obvious that the foundations of the leadership of God's people began to be laid extremely early, primarily in the book of Deuteronomy.

---

[70] See also 1 Tim 3:1–13; 2 Tim 2:2; Titus 1:5–9.

M. Journey

The theology of Deuteronomy is permeated with a dynamic element. There is a sense in Deuteronomy in which the people of God are constantly seen to be on the move toward the land of promise, and the challenge for the people is to live out their lives in obedience to Yahweh even in the face of changing circumstances. The book itself is, of course, set in a moment of tremendous importance and change. The people are addressed at Moab, on the verge of the promised land. They are leaving behind the wilderness, the nomadic life, and the experience of slavery in Egypt. Their relationship with Yahweh will change upon their entry into the promised land. Whereas formerly the people had a tangible sense of Yahweh's presence in the form of the pillar of fire and cloud and the tent of meeting at the heart of their camp, they will soon find themselves settling into cities and villages (some distance from the "place which Yahweh will choose to make his name dwell there", and their sense of Yahweh's presence will necessarily change. Deuteronomy, then, addresses the people at a crucial turning point in the way they live out their lives as the people of Yahweh.

Moses's preaching begins by reminding them of the day when God had said "you have stayed at this mountain long enough" (1:6), at which point their journey, which had taken them to Horeb, resumed, as they were sent into the land. The fact that the first three chapters are a rehearsal of their tortuous journey (from Horeb to Kadesh to Moab) invests the whole book with a sense of movement.

Moses is also very careful to preserve that sense of movement in the land. From 12:1–7 onward, the people are to go the "place the Lord your God chooses." Their journey to the land is to be perpetuated by a constant journey to the place chosen by Yahweh within the land, where they will rejoice in his presence. There is a sense in which the journey of Israel never ends. Three times a year, they go to the place for the festivals (ch. 16); every year they go to present their tithes and firstfruits (ch. 26). When they are eventually scattered, they are to "return." To be God's people is to be a pilgrim people, always on the move.

As the covenant at Moab replaces (or refreshes) that at Horeb (29:1), their life is to be made up of a series of "todays" that encapsulate the past, present, and future of Israel's life.[71] All the important decisions are said

---

[71] I have developed these ideas much more fully in J. Gary Millar, *Now Choose Life: Theology and Ethics in Deuteronomy*, NSBT 6 (Leicester: Apollos, 1998), 73–98, and *Time and Place in Deuteronomy*.

to be urgent "today." Deuteronomy evokes the sense that its "today" at Moab is a decisive moment, but one that, paradoxically, the people face again and again in their journey with Yahweh. Moab is presented as the place where the past and future of Israel coalesce in a single moment, the place where the decision to follow Yahweh must be reaffirmed in every generation. Deuteronomy is God's instruction to his people at this stage—and at every future stage—in their ongoing journey both "into" and "in" the land.

It is the writer to the Hebrews who picks up this idea of the "journey" of God's people and develops it in fresh and creative ways. Speaking of the possibility of missing out on all that God offers us in Christ, he writes this:

> [8] For if Joshua had given them rest, God would not have spoken later about another day. [9] Therefore, a Sabbath rest remains for God's people. [10] For the person who has entered his rest has rested from his own works, just as God did from his. [11] Let us, then, make every effort to enter that rest, so that no one will fall into the same pattern of disobedience. ... [14] Therefore, since we have a great high priest who has passed through the heavens—Jesus the Son of God—let us hold fast to our confession. [15] For we do not have a high priest who is unable to sympathize with our weaknesses, but one who has been tempted in every way as we are, yet without sin. [16] Therefore, let us approach the throne of grace with boldness, so that we may receive mercy and find grace to help us in time of need. (Heb 4:8–11, 14–16)

The nuances of his argument are rich and complex, but for our purposes the point is clear. In the same way that God held out rest in the land to the people in the days of Moses and Joshua, he offers ultimate rest to us in the Lord Jesus. All we need to do is to come to Christ and keep coming to him, for he is the one who then brings us right into the presence of his father, enabling us to find all the resources we need to face the challenges of our world, including mercy and grace. The perpetual journey we need to make, then, is to take hold of Christ in repentance and faith, knowing that he has already blazed a trail for us to bring us to God.

N. The Nations

While it is true that there is significant awareness of "the nations" in Deuteronomy, Moses's words fall some way short of what one might describe as a missional concern. He speaks of those who are not part of the covenant people in four different ways:[72]

(1) *The Nations as an Audience*

The nations are spoken of as looking on and reacting as Yahweh deals with his people in both tenderness and discipline. So, for example, God says of the nations watching their progress through the wilderness:

> Today I will begin to put the fear and dread of you on the peoples everywhere under heaven. They will hear the report about you, tremble, and be in anguish because of you. (Deut 2:25)

Similarly, in chapter 29, the nations will be audience for Israel's future apostasy:

> 24 All the nations will ask, "Why has the Lord done this to this land? Why this intense outburst of anger?" 25 Then people will answer, "It is because they abandoned the covenant of the Lord, the God of their ancestors, which he had made with them when he brought them out of the land of Egypt. 26 They began to serve other gods, bowing in worship to gods they had not known—gods that the Lord had not permitted them to worship. 27 Therefore the Lord's anger burned against this land, and he brought every curse written in this book on it. 28 The Lord uprooted them from their land in his anger, rage, and intense wrath, and threw them into another land where they are today."

More positively, in 4:5–8, Moses envisages the nations being deeply impressed by the nature of Israel's torah, and (theoretically) the quality of life it produces:

> 6 Carefully follow [these laws], for this will show your wisdom and understanding in the eyes of the peoples. When they hear about all these statutes, they will say, "This great nation is indeed a wise and understanding people."

[72] There is also the consistent inclusion of those who are resident aliens in the festivals of Israel (e.g., 16:11). This does speak of the possibility of inclusion in God's people (that they get to rejoice in the presence of Yahweh points in this direction), but that is slightly different from the treatment of the nations per se.

(2) *The Nations as the Recipients of Blessing*

There are also a couple of moments in the book where the nations do actually receive some blessing.[73] The first comes in 2:5: "Don't provoke them, for I will not give you any of their land, not even a foot of it, because I have given Esau the hill country of Seir as his possession" (see also the Moabites in v. 9 and the Ammonites in v. 19), which is unique in the Old Testament.

This is the only place in the Old Testament where Yahweh is said to gift land to these peoples in the same way that he gave the land to Israel. A similar idea is probably alluded to in 32:8–9. There is some limited positivity to Egyptians and Moabites in 23:7–8, but it could hardly be described as "blessing."

(3) *The Nations as a Threat*

There is, however, much more material devoted to the nations as a threat—one example from chapter 7 and another from chapter 12 will suffice:

> [1] When the Lord your God brings you into the land you are entering to possess, and he drives out many nations before you—the Hethites, Girgashites, Amorites, Canaanites, Perizzites, Hivites and Jebusites, seven nations more numerous and powerful than you—[2] and when the Lord your God delivers them over to you and you defeat them, you must completely destroy them. Make no treaty with them and show them no mercy. [3] You must not intermarry with them, and you must not give your daughters to their sons or take their daughters for your sons, [4] because they will turn your sons away from me to worship other gods. Then the Lord's anger will burn against you, and he will swiftly destroy you. (Deut 7:1–4)

> [29] When the Lord your God annihilates the nations before you, which you are entering to take possession of, and you drive them out and live in their land, [30] be careful not to be ensnared by their ways after they have been destroyed before you. Do not inquire about their gods, asking, "How did these nations worship their gods? I'll also do the same." [31] You must not do the same to the Lord your God, because they practice every de-

[73] Whether or not Gen 12:3 anticipates the future blessing of the nations through Abram's descendants is heatedly contested. If this is in fact what that promise holds out, then this may be a partial fulfillment of it.

> testable act, which the LORD hates, for their gods. They even burn their sons and daughters in the fire to their gods. [32] Be careful to do everything I command you; do not add anything to it or take anything away from it. (Deut 12:29–32)

A large part of the reason every trace of the Canaanites and their cultic apparatus must be removed is the weakness of Israel.

(4) The Nations under Judgment

The final way in which the nations are discussed in Deuteronomy is as objects of Yahweh's wrath, who are about to be judged by him:

> [4] When the LORD your God drives them out before you, do not say to yourself, "The LORD brought me in to take possession of this land because of my righteousness." Instead, the LORD will drive out these nations before you because of their wickedness. [5] You are not going to take possession of their land because of your righteousness or your integrity. Instead, the LORD your God will drive out these nations before you because of their wickedness, in order to fulfill the promise he swore to your ancestors Abraham, Isaac, and Jacob. (Deut 9:4–5)

This takes us neatly to the "problem of the Canaanites" (e.g., 9:4–6). One of the most morally problematic elements of the Bible as a whole is Yahweh's repeated instructions to dispossess and kill those who occupied the land before Israel. Given that, it is vitally important that we examine very carefully what the Bible actually says.

Excursus: The Problem of the Canaanites

The issue with the Canaanites is flagged as early as Genesis 15:16: "In the fourth generation [your descendants] will return here, for the iniquity of the Amorites has not yet reached its full measure." Variously called the Amorites, Canaanites, Amalekites, the inhabitants of Canaan are designated from the beginning as particularly evil.[74]

This is picked up by Moses in Deuteronomy 7:1–7 and then again later in the chapter:

---

[74] See the helpful discussion of William Ford, "The Challenge of the Canaanites," *TynBul* 68, no. 2 (2017): 161–84.

> 16 You must destroy all the peoples the Lord your God gives over to you. Do not look on them with pity and do not serve their gods, for that will be a snare to you. … 22 The Lord your God will drive out those nations before you, little by little. You will not be allowed to eliminate them all at once, or the wild animals will multiply around you. 23 But the Lord your God will deliver them over to you, throwing them into great confusion until they are destroyed. 24 He will give their kings into your hand, and you will wipe out their names from under heaven. No one will be able to stand up against you; you will destroy them. 25 The images of their gods you are to burn in the fire. Do not covet the silver and gold on them, and do not take it for yourselves, or you will be ensnared by it, for it is detestable to the Lord your God. 26 Do not bring a detestable thing into your house or you, like it, will be set apart for destruction. Utterly abhor and detest it, for it is set apart for destruction. (Deut 7:16, 22–26)

The same note is sounded in 9:4–6; 12:1–4 and then in chapter 20:

> 10 When you approach a city to fight against it, make an offer of peace. 11 If it accepts your offer of peace and opens its gates to you, all the people found in it will become forced laborers for you and serve you. 12 However, if it does not make peace with you but wages war against you, lay siege to it. 13 When the Lord your God hands it over to you, strike down all its males with the sword. 14 But you may take the women, dependents, animals, and whatever else is in the city—all its spoil—as plunder. You may enjoy the spoil of your enemies that the Lord your God has given you. 15 This is how you are to treat all the cities that are far away from you and are not among the cities of these nations. 16 However, you must not let any living thing survive among the cities of these people the Lord your God is giving you as an inheritance. 17 You must completely destroy them—the Hethite, Amorite, Canaanite, Perizzite, Hivite, and Jebusite—as the Lord your God has commanded you, 18 so that they won't teach you to do all the detestable acts they do for their gods, and you sin against the Lord your God. 19 "When you lay siege to a city for a long time, fighting against it in order to capture it, do not destroy its trees by putting an ax to them, because you can get food from them. Do not cut them down. Are trees of the field human, to come under siege by you? 20 But you may destroy the

> trees that you know do not produce food. You may cut them down to build siege works against the city that is waging war against you, until it falls. (Deut 20:10–20)

Despite the ethical problems that these texts throw up for many today, the view of Deuteronomy is relatively simple: (1) God commands Israel to dispossess the tribes or nations that are currently occupying Canaan. (2) This is divine judgment. God the judge is punishing them for their wickedness (and in particular their brutality and idolatry). (3) God also says that this step is necessary because his people, Israel, are so prone to be led astray. (4) This is a single-generation event: Israel is specifically prohibited from following these orders in any campaign after the initial conquest of the land.[75] (5) The primary goal of this campaign is to eradicate the Canaanite religious system: God intends that Canaanite civilization and the independent existence of these tribes come to an end.

The most problematic element of the text is how the Israelites are to achieve this. And the answer? Actually it's not all that simple.

The Hebrew word used to describe what the Israelites are to do to the Canaanites is *herem*. The trouble is that translating it isn't so straightforward. Some translations use a phrase like "subjecting them to the ban," which is less than clear. Others use phrases like "totally destroy," but unfortunately that loses all nuance. *Herem* language is always used in connection with God's judgment. So to subject to the ban is simply to carry out what God has decreed concerning the object or person or nation concerned. *Herem* can mean "put beyond use" (as in an altar) or kill (of a person), but doesn't specify how this should be done. Leviticus 27:28–29 suggests that it operates as both a principle and a practice. However, when it comes to the Canaanites, God's command is explicit: they are be driven out, and in several cases, to be killed.

There are several factors that do bring some nuance to the discussion: (1) K. Lawson Younger has shown that these warfare accounts are written in stereotypical language (some of which is reflected in Joshua).[76] It seems that ancient wars were generally described in absolute terms that should not be read as a "blow by blow account" of what happened.[77]

---

[75] The term "holy war" is not found in the text and, in my view, is not particularly helpful.

[76] See K. Lawson Younger, *Ancient Conquest Accounts: A Study in Ancient Near Eastern and Biblical History Writing* (Sheffield: Sheffield Academic Press, 1990).

[77] This is a convention carried over to the way we speak about victory, even in sporting contexts (e.g., we "slaughtered them," a "crushing" victory, we were "annihilated").

(2) Reality was clearly much messier than the theory, All through Deuteronomy, for example, it's assumed that Israelites will have to live with the temptation that comes with the Canaanites *who survive*. The accounts in Joshua detail the complexities of taking the land over many years. Similarly, in 1 Samuel 15, even after Saul has applied the ban to the Amalekites it's implied that the king's mother is still alive. Which basically all means that the picture must be a little bit more complex than it might first seem. However, the plain teaching of the text still remains: God gave a specific command to his people to carry out a death sentence on an entire nation that was particularly evil.

This, of course, is not a unique event in the Bible. Over the 1500 years or so covered by Genesis 12 to the end of 2 Kings, there are two other examples of similar acts or decrees of judgment: Sodom and Gomorrah (Gen 18–19) and the Amalekites (1 Sam 15).[78] In each case, those on the receiving end are declared to be unusually evil (either in absolute terms in the case of Sodom and Gomorrah, or specifically in relation to their treatment of Israel, in the cases of the Egyptians and the Amalekites), despite the patience of God in pausing to allow time for them to repent, and the judgment carried out is dramatic and drastic.[79]

The issue for biblical theology, of course, is that the judgment threatened by Yahweh is much more widespread and more directly focused than even this. As Hebrews 9:27–28 says:

> And just as it is appointed for people to die once—and after this, judgment—so also Christ, having been offered once to bear the sins of many, will appear a second time, not to bear sin, but to bring salvation to those who are waiting for him.

It remains a terrible thing to fall into the hands of the living God.

X. Conclusion: The Deuteronomic Vision

Returning to the comment I made at the beginning, I am convinced there is no other book that has richer biblical-theological connections

---

[78] The death of the Egyptian firstborn in Exod 12–14 is similar in some ways, although the situation there is more complex, given that the threat is also made against the firstborn of Israel.

[79] For more details on recent work in this area, see Charles Trimm, "Recent Research on Warfare in the Old Testament," *CBR* 10 (2012): 1–46.

and pickings than Deuteronomy. Its grace-fueled, gospel-shaped theological framework, which beautifully integrates grace and torah under the umbrella of covenant, is a precious thing.

There are, of course, other threads that we have not had time to follow in this short discussion, but they are worth mentioning:

1. The presence of Yahweh (his actual presence) as he speaks through Moses is a very real and comforting thing.
2. The people of Yahweh are to be a tight-knit and yet deeply inclusive family (ask the resident aliens if that is true!), a "brotherhood" of believers.
3. There are strong affinities between Deuteronomy and Proverbs: the idea of wisdom itself is explicitly mentioned at a key point in the text (4:5–8); the language of father and son is a key wisdom idea; many of the categories of Proverbs (and some of the images in Deut 32 and 33, in particular) are very close to the wisdom book. It does read as if the writer of Proverbs drew inspiration from Deuteronomy.

No doubt there is much more we could mention, but for now, it might be better to spend some time gasping at the stunning revelation of the goodness and grace of God in the Lord Jesus Christ.

EXPOSITION

I. Moses Preaches History (1:1–3:29)

A. Outline

1:1–8	A Carefully Crafted Beginning
1:9–18	A Surprising Interlude
1:19–46	A Disastrous Choice
2:1–23	A Painful Lesson
2:24–3:22	Two Model Conquests
3:23–29	A Shocking Prohibition

B. Relation to Surrounding Context

The opening of Deuteronomy picks up where the end of Numbers leaves off, with the people having reached the Moab/Canaan border opposite Jericho. The final verse of Numbers 36:13 ("These are the commands and ordinances the Lord commanded the Israelites through Moses in the plains of Moab by the Jordan across from Jericho") both sets the scene for Deuteronomy, and anticipates its content, providing Israel with the necessary instructions to live well with and for God in the land.

These chapters are essentially a historical retrospect, in which Moses reflects on the lessons of the prolonged journey from Horeb to Moab and highlights some of the key themes that will be expounded in the rest of the book. There is a particular focus on the choice Israel faces "today" (in the light of the choices they have made in the past) and on the gift of the land God has given his people in fulfillment of the promises made to Abraham, Isaac, and Jacob. The sobering reality of Moses's own exclusion from the land (3:23–29) adds force to his preaching and brackets the book with an ominous theme (see 34:1–12).

It has been suggested that these chapters function as an introduction to the entire history to follow (Joshua–2 Kings) rather than the book of Deuteronomy itself.[1] While it is helpful to recognize the foundational importance of the theology of Deuteronomy for the historical narratives (and indeed, the rest of the Bible, as we shall see), the shape and content of Deuteronomy 1–3 are primarily concerned to introduce the message of Moses's preaching in this book.

C. Structure and Style

These chapters, along with the conclusion in chapters 33 and 34, are where the hand of the "publisher" of Deuteronomy is most visible. The opening details in 1:1–5 and the repeated explanatory notes in 2:10–12, 20–23, and 3:11 are designed to enable later readers to make sense of the implications of Moses's words. These helpful interruptions and the nature of the subject material—reported events packed with historical details—mean that the characteristic rhetorical language and vocabulary that dominate the rest of the book are less visible here, but not entirely absent.

The structure of this historical introduction is not complex. After some carefully chosen details to ground Moses's words in a geographical and theological context, he starts to speak (1:5–8). Surprisingly, he shifts immediately to a reminder of the leadership structure of the nation in 1:9–18, before a long rehearsal of how the journey to the land stalled the first time around, and kicked off the anti-exodus of the wilderness years. 2:1–23 contains a long reflection on their recent passage around the territories of Seir (Edom), Moab, and Ammon. Moses's narrative continues seamlessly to the conquest of the Transjordan in 2:24–3:22, before he concludes by referring to his own painful exclusion from the land in 3:23–29.

1. A Carefully Crafted Beginning (1:1–8)

> 1 These are the words Moses spoke to all Israel across the Jordan in the
> wilderness, in the Arabah opposite Suph, between Paran and Tophel,
> Laban, Hazeroth, and Di-zahab. 2 It is an eleven-day journey from
> Horeb to Kadesh-barnea by way of Mount Seir. 3 In the fortieth year, in

[1] See, famously, Martin Noth, *The Deuteronomistic History*, *JSOTSup* 15 (Sheffield: JSOT Press, 1981).

the eleventh month, on the first of the month, Moses told the Israelites everything the Lord had commanded him to say to them. 4 This was after he had defeated King Sihon of the Amorites, who lived in Heshbon, and King Og of Bashan, who lived in Ashtaroth, at Edrei. 5 Across the Jordan in the land of Moab, Moses began to explain this law, saying:

6 "The Lord our God spoke to us at Horeb: 'You have stayed at this mountain long enough. 7 Resume your journey and go to the hill country of the Amorites and their neighbors in the Arabah, the hill country, the Judean foothills, the Negev and the sea coast—to the land of the Canaanites and to Lebanon as far as the great river, the Euphrates River. 8 See, I have set the land before you. Enter and take possession of the land the Lord swore to give to your ancestors Abraham, Isaac, and Jacob and their future descendants.' "

1:1. The Hebrew name for Deuteronomy is simply "Words," which is completely appropriate, for the book consists almost entirely of the reported words of Moses.[2] This address (or series of addresses; see on 4:44; 5:1) is given live by Moses to "all Israel." This is not just an affirmation that the entire nation is gathered before their leader but also the first glimpse of the Deuteronomic doctrine of the people of God. This nation has been created, rescued, and established by God himself as his one holy nation—his "son" (see 8:5; 14:1; 32:19). God deals with them both as individuals and as a unit. As they enter the land, the fate of the nation will hinge on their behavior as individuals.

The setting for Moses's preaching is "across the Jordan," that is, on the east side of the river valley outside the land (showing that the book was assembled and published after the conquest). More specifically, Moses is said to have spoken "in the wilderness" (the opening words and the Hebrew name of Numbers), underlining the continuity with what has gone before, "in the Arabah opposite Suph." The Arabah is the rift valley that extends from the Sea of Galilee in the north all the way to the Gulf of Aqaba in the deep south. It encompasses both the Jordan Valley and the Dead Sea. But beyond that, it's fair to say that the place names don't help us to pin down the location. Suph may be in Moab, or connected with the Hebrew name for the Red Sea. Of the list of place names that follow, only Paran (Num 13:3, 26) and Hazeroth (Num 11:35; 12:16; 33:17–18) occur

[2] This is reflected in the fact that only 38 of the 645 references to the name "Moses" in the Pentateuch occur in Deuteronomy, and most (25) of those come in chs. 31–34. See Bill T. Arnold, "Deuteronomy as the 'Ipsissima Vox' of Moses," *Journal of Theological Interpretation* 4 (2010): 53–74.

elsewhere, although Laban may be related to Libnah (Num 33:20–21). There are two options: (a) these places are otherwise unknown areas in and around Mount Nebo in Moab[3] or (b) this is an allusion to "places on the way," with the sense of "having come via ..." Given the uniform insistence that Israel is at Moab (reiterated as soon as 1:5), the first option seems more likely.

1:2. It is then noted that it takes eleven days to walk from Horeb to Kadesh-barnea, the scene of Israel's refusal to enter the land in Numbers 13–14, via the Mount Seir route. Sinai is routinely referred to as Horeb in Deuteronomy (although see 33:2). It is not clear how the two are related, but the other Old Testament references to the name (see Exod 3:1; 17:6; 33:6; 1 Kgs 8:9; 19:8; 2 Chr 5:10; Ps 106:19; and Mal 4:4) suggest there is no particular theological significance in this choice. It is important to notice, however, that this is not simply a geographical detail added for completeness! As Moses's words are gathered for publication, the editor brilliantly prepares us for the tone of what will come next. The traditional site of Horeb (Jebel Musa) is around 160–170 miles (250–270 km) from the usual identification of Kadesh-barnea, which would, in theory, have allowed God's people to start the conquest within a couple of weeks of setting out. In reality, it has taken them forty years. This simple statement then casts a dark shadow over the historical material to follow.

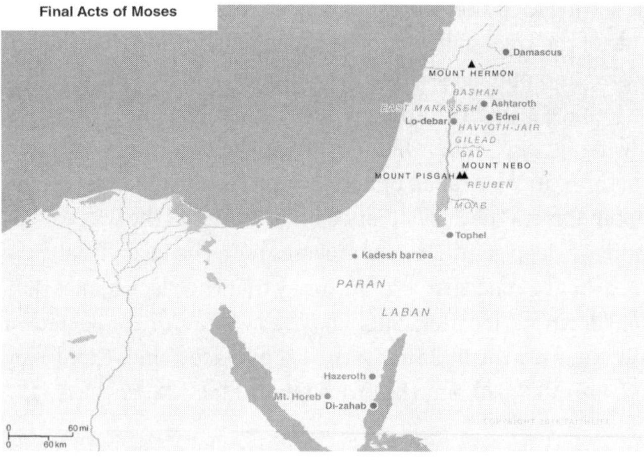

[3] This may be supported by some similarity to modern Arabic place names. See, e.g., Duane L. Christensen, *Deuteronomy 1:1–21:9*, 7.

1:3–4. Alongside the geographical details, the date on which Moses spoke is recorded. The "fortieth year" underlines that Israel's time in the wilderness is coming to an end. The day (the first day of the eleventh month) begins with Moses preaching and, according to 32:48, ends with his death.[4] The precise dating underlines the fact that this is a real speech given by a real person in real time. The fact that Moses "told the Israelites [lit. "sons of Israel"] everything the Lord had commanded him to say to them" matches the emphasis on location with an insistence on divine inspiration. Moses's words are equated with the command of God himself.

The first reference in the book to the Amorite kings Sihon and Og is slightly unexpected but typical of Deuteronomy. For Moses, Israel's experience with these two kings is a powerful reason to ensure that they press on into the land in confident obedience. The encounters with these kings have already been recorded in a fairly matter-of-fact way in Numbers 21:21–35. Moses's emphasis on these kings (see the discussion of 2:24–3:22) is anticipated here by the publisher, implying that the delay highlighted in 1:2 really was completely unnecessary.

1:5. It has been suggested by many that 1:1–8 has a chiastic structure. If this is the case, then verse 5 stands at the center of this section.[5] Once more, it is underlined that the nation is gathered on the high ground of Moab to the east of the Jordan Valley. From this area, Jericho is easily visible, as is Jerusalem to the south (on a clear day). In this setting, Moses began to "explain this law." The word "explain" here has the sense of "making clear." God's people are to be left in no doubt about what their master is asking of them. The next phrase is the first indication that in Deuteronomy "law" is much more than rules or commands. This torah actually contains narrative, persuasion, motivation, and expositions of grace, alongside specific instructions (making our English translation

[4] Jan van Goudoever, "The Liturgical Significance of the Date in Dt 1, 3," in *Das Deuteronomium: Einstehung, Gestalt und Botschaft*, ed. Norbert Lohfink, BETL 68 (Leuven: Leuven University Press, 1985), 145–46, points out that this is exactly ten weeks before the start of Passover, and suggests that this is then to be seen as a preparation for the first Passover in the land in Josh 5.

[5] The existence and significance of chiastic structures in Hebrew has long been debated. It is hard to tell the extent to which this is the result of artistry and where it is simply an unintended feature of good writing. In general, I prefer to prioritize content over structure in determining emphasis and meaning.

of the word slightly restrictive and wooden). It is more helpful to think of torah in terms of the "gospel according to Moses."[6]

1:6–8. Moses begins to speak in 1:6 and does so without interruption until 4:40. This section of text is often referred to as the "First Speech of Moses." However, given that the entire speech (or sermon) is delivered on the same day and that the rhetorical movements of the text tend to flow across breaks between speeches (as we will see in moving from ch. 4), it may be more helpful to think of the words of Moses as a single address.[7]

The first words from Moses's mouth are a quotation of God's own statement (which is alluded to, but not spelled out in Num 10:11–13). Horeb was the foundational moment in the life of the nation, but they could not stay there forever—they are to live as a "pilgrim people," constantly "moving forward" with God. The latest phase of this national journey began with God's defeat of the Egyptians but has its roots back in Genesis 11–12, with God's call of (and covenantal commitments to) Abram.[8]

The command to "resume" their journey (the verb is "turn," which is used repeatedly in this section: 1:24, 40; 2:1, 3, 8; 3:1) was initially designed to move the people on from Horeb, the mountain of God into the land. The fact that it can be reiterated and reapplied forty years later is a further indictment of their failure. They are to go to the "hill country of the Amorites." This is probably a general designation of the land (as in Gen 15:16, although the term can also refer to a smaller tribe and its possession, Gen 15:21). More specifically, this land is described as comprising the Arabah (the rift valley described in 1:1), the highlands as well as the foothills of Judah (the "mountain" and the "Shephelah"), the arid area of the Negeb and the coastal plains—in other words, all of the land of Canaan, which is then described as stretching from Lebanon to the Euphrates. As in Genesis 15:18 (also Exod 23:31; Deut 11:24; Josh 1:4; 1 Kgs 4:21), this is the classical shorthand for the extent of God's land-gift to his people.[9]

---

[6] A phrase coined by Daniel Block in the title of his collection of essays.

[7] I suspect that the disjunctions in the speech may be the result of the very understandable necessity for a 120-year-old man to have occasional "refreshment" breaks. It is, of course, difficult to prove this!

[8] And before that even, in the command to "multiply, fill the earth, and subdue it" in Gen 1:28.

[9] This raises an interesting question concerning the Transjordan. Moses will make clear that it is less than ideal to settle outside the land, and yet it is permissible. This may be on the basis of God's extravagant kindness in giving Israel jurisdiction over territory beyond the actual borders of Canaan.

The call to "see" (or "look") in 1:8 reflects their position overlooking the land, and emphasizes the importance of this moment in history (also 1:21; 2:24, 31; 30:15). God has "set" the land (the verb is נָתַן, "to give") before Israel as the most spectacular gift. Now it falls to them to receive it by going in and taking it (as their rightful possession or inheritance) on the basis of God's enduring covenant promises made to their ancestors Abraham, Isaac, and Jacob.[10] These three are also mentioned in Genesis 50:24, then repeatedly in the early chapters of Exodus (2:24; 3:6, 15, 16; 4:5; 6:3, 8; also 33:1), once in both Leviticus (26:42) and Numbers (32:11), but play a key role in Deuteronomy, as the phrase becomes a shorthand for all that God has promised to do in and through his people in the land (6:10; 9:5; 9:27; 29:13; 30:20; 34:4). The promises to the patriarchs form the theological context and foundation for all that follows.

Bridge

Deuteronomy opens with a clear assertion of the grace of God that has been displayed in creating one people and giving them a land, just as God had promised their ancestors. These people are clearly sinful, and yet God continues to extend his lovingkindness to them, leading them on and enabling them to take hold of what he has already given them. From the very first details in the opening verses, Deuteronomy is profoundly gospel-shaped. Since we are people who have been chosen and forgiven and who are being transformed by grace in Christ, God's dealings with Israel should fuel our amazement, honesty about our sin, and determination to put our confidence in him alone.

2. A Surprising Interlude (1:9–18)

> 9 "I said to you at that time: I can't bear the responsibility for you on
> my own. 10 The Lord your God has so multiplied you that today you are
> as numerous as the stars of the sky. 11 May the Lord, the God of your
> ancestors, increase you a thousand times more, and bless you as he
> promised you. 12 But how can I bear your troubles, burdens, and disputes
> by myself? 13 Appoint for yourselves wise, understanding, and respected
> men from each of your tribes, and I will make them your leaders.

---

[10] Daniel I. Block argues that the language here is adapted from an ancient land grant formula. This may be so, although it is difficult to tie down dependence/relationships between such ancient covenantal documents given the amount of surviving evidence. Block, *Deuteronomy*, NIV Application Commentary (Grand Rapids: Zondervan, 2012), 63.

> [14] "You replied to me, 'What you propose to do is good.'
>
> [15] "So I took the leaders of your tribes, wise and respected men, and set them over you as leaders: commanders for thousands, hundreds, fifties, and tens, and officers for your tribes. [16] I commanded your judges at that time: Hear the cases between your brothers, and judge rightly between a man and his brother or his resident alien. [17] Do not show partiality when deciding a case; listen to small and great alike. Do not be intimidated by anyone, for judgment belongs to God. Bring me any case too difficult for you, and I will hear it. [18] At that time I commanded you about all the things you were to do."

1:9–14. One of the enduring puzzles in Deuteronomy is the immediate interruption of the flow of Moses's address by details of a reorganization of the administrative/judicial life of the nation. The background to these events seems to be Exodus 18:13–26 (but see also the appointment of Elders in Num 11:10–25). As we might expect given the context, the focus is not on the mechanics of how the system was organized, but on the theological principles undergirding this move. It is quite clearly presented as the result of God fulfilling his promise to make Abraham and Isaac's descendants as "numerous as the stars in the sky" (see Gen 22:17; 26:4), and anticipating blessing to continue (Deut 1:11). But this can hardly be the only reason for its inclusion here, as Moses has just made that very point in the previous verses.

The phrase "at that time" (1:9, then repeated in verses 16 and 18) is used in Deuteronomy 1–11 to highlight particularly important moments in the history of the nation (2:34; 3:4, 8, 12, 18, 21, 23 of the conquest of the Transjordan as a precursor to the occupation of the land itself; 4:14 and 5:5 of God's self-revelation at Horeb; 9:20; 10:1, 8 of key events in the golden calf incident and its aftermath). This suggests that the placement and inclusion of 1:9–18 is more than simply a matter of there being nowhere else for it to go![11]

Moses's language in describing the challenges he is facing is telling: his issue was in bearing "your troubles, burdens, and disputes." The language here is drawn from earlier accounts of Israel's complaining (see Exod 17:2, 7; Num 11:11, 17; 20:3, 13), which leads Tigay to helpfully translate this threefold challenge as dealing with their "trouble, burden and

---

[11] The suggestion of Richard D. Nelson, *Deuteronomy*, OTL (Louisville: Westminster John Knox, 2002), 19. Most writers simply note the break in the flow. Christensen, *Deuteronomy 1:1–21:9*, 21, notes that 1:9-18 appears here because of Moses's complaint, which does, I think, point in the direction of this as a necessary but ultimately problematic development.

bickering."[12] The presenting issue is then the sinfulness of the people. The problem is that the solution also depends on the people. We have seen little so far in the narrative of the Pentateuch to suggest that there will be a ready supply of "wise, understanding, and respected men" (Deut 1:13) to be appointed as leaders ("heads") of God's people. The fact that the people readily welcome this scheme should not be given too much weight (see Josh 1:16–18; 24:16–18 on the reliability of the words of the people). As they begin their trek to the promised land, authority has been devolved from Moses himself to a people who are marked out by their discontent and disgruntlement. This would then explain why this unit is included at this point: it is part of the developing picture of the sinfulness and rebellion of the people (as hinted at in 1:2).

1:15–18. Moses recounts how he enacted this system, appointing those qualified as "leaders" of tribes to be "leaders" of the various "administrative" divisions of the people (from thousands down to tens), as well as appointing "officers" for their tribes. No detail is given about the extent of these roles, but they seem to be the basic authority structure of the nation, encompassing both judicial and military matters (see, e.g., 1 Sam 17:18; 18:13). The "officers" are probably junior appointees, who assist with organization and administration (see 16:8; 20:5, 8, 9; 29:9; 31:28).

That the purpose of this unit in Deuteronomy is rhetorical rather than simply to describe the detailed administrative structures comes to the fore again in 1:16. Moses's underlines that these officials have been duly appointed (by him), but are finally accountable for their decisions to God himself, "for judgment belongs to God" (1:17). All their judgments are to be marked by "righteousness" (צֶדֶק), the first mention of a term that is perhaps the most important in the book. This is not an insignificant task, as not only must God's people be treated as equals (without *any* prejudice), but the same privilege must also be extended to resident aliens. This is ultimately because the reputation of the righteous God depends on it. This explains why in 1:17 the option of fast-tracking any case straight to Moses is built into the system. The final phrase in 1:18 echoes that of 1:16, which confirms this way of reading the text. Moses's instructions were clear: the wise and discerning men of the nation were to share responsibility with him for the grassroots leadership of God's people. Given what happens next, the people must take their share of the responsibility.

[12] Jeffrey H. Tigay, *Deuteronomy*, JPS Torah (Philadelphia: JPS, 1996), 10.

Bridge

It is clear from the outset that God can be trusted to come through on his promises, but even the best of God's people cannot. We are wired for self-interest, prejudice, and favoritism. This, ultimately, is why Christ had to die and why in him alone we can find the strength and motivation to live a "righteous" life.

3. A Disastrous Choice (1:19–46)

> 19 "We then set out from Horeb and went across all the great and terrible wilderness you saw on the way to the hill country of the Amorites, just as the LORD our God had commanded us. When we reached Kadesh-barnea, 20 I said to you: You have reached the hill country of the Amorites, which the LORD our God is giving us. 21 See, the LORD your God has set the land before you. Go up and take possession of it as the LORD, the God of your ancestors, has told you. Do not be afraid or discouraged.
>
> 22 "Then all of you approached me and said, 'Let's send men ahead of us, so that they may explore the land for us and bring us back a report about the route we should go up and the cities we will come to.' 23 The plan seemed good to me, so I selected twelve men from among you, one man for each tribe. 24 They left and went up into the hill country and came to Eshcol Valley, scouting the land. 25 They took some of the fruit from the land in their hands, carried it down to us, and brought us back a report: 'The land the LORD our God is giving us is good.'
>
> 26 "But you were not willing to go up. You rebelled against the command of the LORD your God. 27 You grumbled in your tents and said, 'The LORD brought us out of the land of Egypt to hand us over to the Amorites in order to destroy us, because he hates us. 28 Where can we go? Our brothers have made us lose heart, saying: The people are larger and taller than we are; the cities are large, fortified to the heavens. We also saw the descendants of the Anakim there.'
>
> 29 "So I said to you: Don't be terrified or afraid of them! 30 The LORD your God who goes before you will fight for you, just as you saw him do for you in Egypt. 31 And you saw in the wilderness how the LORD your God carried you as a man carries his son all along the way you traveled until you reached this place. 32 But in spite of this you did not trust the LORD your God, 33 who went before you on the journey to seek out a place for you to camp. He went in the fire by night and in the cloud by day to guide you on the road you were to travel.
>
> 34 "When the LORD heard your words, he grew angry and swore an oath: 35 'None of these men in this evil generation will see the good land I swore to give your ancestors, 36 except Caleb the son of Jephunneh.

> He will see it, and I will give him and his descendants the land on which he has set foot, because he remained loyal to the LORD.'
>
> 37 "The LORD was angry with me also because of you and said, 'You will not enter there either. 38 Joshua son of Nun, who attends you, will enter it. Encourage him, for he will enable Israel to inherit it. 39 Your children, who you said would be plunder, your sons who don't yet know good from evil, will enter there. I will give them the land, and they will take possession of it. 40 But you are to turn back and head for the wilderness by way of the Red Sea.'
>
> 41 "You answered me, 'We have sinned against the LORD. We will go up and fight just as the LORD our God commanded us.' Then each of you put on his weapons of war and thought it would be easy to go up into the hill country.
>
> 42 "But the LORD said to me, 'Tell them: Don't go up and fight, for I am not with you to keep you from being defeated by your enemies.' 43 So I spoke to you, but you didn't listen. You rebelled against the LORD's command and defiantly went up into the hill country. 44 Then the Amorites who lived there came out against you and chased you like a swarm of bees. They routed you from Seir as far as Hormah. 45 When you returned, you wept before the LORD, but he didn't listen to your requests or pay attention to you. 46 For this reason you stayed in Kadesh as long as you did."

1:19–21. Without further ado, Moses reminds the people of how they set out together "across all the great and terrible wilderness," a phrase used to describe the Wilderness of Paran (Num 12:16) only here and in 8:15.[13] The striking language highlights the utter foolishness of the decision that would soon follow: they had seen the wilderness, would see the land and its produce, and yet would still choose the desert way. 1:19 sets the scene for the climactic announcement of 1:20–21. When they reached Kadesh-barnea (presumably in something close to the eleven days of 1:2), Moses called on the people to press on into the land. The call to "see" is emphatic here (as in 4:5; 11:26; 30:15; and possibly 32:39). Unlike at Moab, the view from Kadesh-barnea was probably not panoramic, so the "seeing" here is probably spiritual/metaphorical, focused on God's covenantal faithfulness to their ancestors as well as to their own experience of the exodus, which removed any reason to be afraid of what lay ahead.

[13] Although God himself is described in these terms in 7:21 and 10:17. Later, the day of the Lord is characterized as "great and terrible" (Joel 3:4; Mal 4:5 [Heb. 3:23]).

1:22–25. Moses states explicitly that the impetus to spy out the land came from the people. His concern throughout these chapters is to push the nation to take responsibility for their sinful rebellion, which started as soon as they left the land—and here that includes their attitude to this reconnaissance mission from beginning to end.

In Numbers 13:1–2, the initial idea seems to come from God himself, but there is no necessary contradiction here. Moses emphasizes the fact that the people seized on this idea and extended it. The sensible exercise of "scouting out" the land before marching in to obey God's command morphs into a slightly different exercise: this mission is to "explore the land *for us*" and "bring *us* back a report" about both the roads and the settlements. A subtle shift seems to be taking place, as the people shift their focus from simple obedience to seizing control.[14] Even the language of "sending men ahead of us" in the context of a journey in which God himself has promised to "go ahead" of them hints at a significant misstep.

According to 1:23, Moses's complicity in what happens next is confirmed as he affirms that "this seemed good to me" (echoing the people's verdict on his judicial system in 1:14) and that he then assembled a twelve-man team, with one representative from each tribe. The blame for what is about to happen is to be shared among the whole people.

The reconnaissance mission is summarized in 1:24–25, but even in this abbreviated version, the extremely limited nature of their discoveries is obvious (this is even clearer in Num 13:17–33). They explored only a tiny portion of the land, although the rich produce of one area (the Eshcol Valley) was more than enough to convince them that God's claims were true and that "the land the Lord our God is giving us is good." The Eden-like abundance of Canaan, even on a cursory inspection, once more makes their choice of the wilderness look even worse.

1:26–28. The conclusion of 1:26 is painfully blunt, containing just seven words in Hebrew: "But you were not willing to go up. You rebelled against the command [lit. "mouth"] of the Lord your God." Any doubt that Moses's primary goal in this section is to confront the people with their

---

[14] Support for reading 1:22 like this can be found in Nelson, *Deuteronomy*, 27; Block, *Deuteronomy*, 70; also J. Gordon McConville, *Deuteronomy*, AOTC (Leicester: IVP, 2002), 67–68; Telford Work, *Deuteronomy*, Brazos Theological Commentary on the Bible (Grand Rapids: Brazos, 2009), 33. Tigay, *Deuteronomy*, 15, helpfully comments that their action "contains the seeds of disaster."

sinful past is dispelled at this point! However, their sin does not end there, as they pile disgruntled blasphemy on top of raw disobedience in 1:27.[15]

The core of the national attempt to blame Yahweh for their stubbornness was the accusation that he "hates" them. The implication was that God was never serious about his stated intention to keep his covenant with them (to "love" them).[16] Instead, they alleged that God had lured them into a trap, in order to allow the Canaanites to kill them. Their self-justification had three dimensions (1:28): (1) God had led them into a dead-end: the implied answer to their question is "Nowhere!"; (2) The spies' (exaggerated) report had "made them lose heart" (lit., "made their hearts melt," which, ironically, is precisely the effect that news of their advance had on the natives of the land, according to Josh 2:11; 5:1). Given the fact that their mission may have taken them past Hebron, but not much further, the claim that the Canaanites' cities "reach into the heavens" sounds strained. (3) There were "giants" in the land. The "sons of the Anakim" were large and fearsome Canaanite fighters.[17] However, we must not thoughtlessly credit these spies with too much insight, given their clear penchant for hyperbole! For Moses, there was nothing invincible about these admittedly fearsome Canaanites. They could be overcome by simply obeying God and pressing on (as he will make clear in biting terms in ch. 2). This is what Joshua would do in Joshua 11:21–22 (and David would do in 1 Sam 17). Moses cuts right to the heart of the issue, reminding them of the military dynamic of the exodus (Exod 14:14) and the nature of God's fatherly care in the wilderness, carrying them "as a man carries his son." The Israelites' determination to justify their behavior, blaming God, each other and the opposition is sadly revealing.

1:29–33. It is hard to imagine a more powerful response to this willful rejection of God. Moses started by reminding them that there was absolutely no need to be scared (1:29; also 31:6, and the similar wording in Josh 1:9). Invoking the assurance of Exodus 14:14, 25 he underscored that

---

[15] The word for "grumbled" (or "murmured") here is a rare one, occurring elsewhere only in Ps 106:25; Prov 16:28; 18:8; 26:20, 22; and Isa 29:24. It may have the nuance of "slander."

[16] For the covenantal background of love/hate language, see the seminal article by William L. Moran, "The Ancient Near Eastern Background of the Love of God in Deuteronomy," *Catholic Bible Quarterly* 25 (1963): 77–87.

[17] This designation may imply a "supernatural" level of strength or prowess. According to the spies in Num 13:33, these Canaanites were descended from the Nephilim of Gen 6. I suspect the spies, in this as in other details, carelessly exaggerated in an attempt to strengthen their case. They presumably forgot that the Nephilim had perished in the flood.

Yahweh had committed to overcome all their potential enemies in the land (whether giants or not!), as he "goes before you" (again, rather than the spies). On top of that, his personal care for his people has been proven repeatedly, as he "carried you as a man carries his son." In Exodus 19:4 (and Deut 32:11), God carries his people like an eagle with its young; in Numbers 11:12, Moses implies that Yahweh's care is like a nursing mother and baby; here the picture is of a strong and protective father (for similar images see Isa 1:2; Jer 31:20; Hos 11:1–3). But his words fell on deaf ears. Israel was implacable, and their response remained the same: they did not trust their God. Moses's depiction of God seeking out a safe place for them to camp (the language is once more of "going before" them) and appearing in "fire by night" and "cloud by day," a theophanic guidance system without parallel (Exod 13:21; Num 10:32–33; 14:14), captures both the imminence and transcendence of God. Yet neither God's tenderness nor his awesome majesty were enough to move his people to obedience. Their unbelief was unshakeable.

1:34–36. The nature of God's covenant with his people means that their stubbornness must lead to temporal judgment and discipline. Yahweh's real-time response when he *heard* their words was to announce that none of them would *see* the good land (seeing and hearing are key ideas throughout Deuteronomy). God's anger is righteous by definition, and here led to the exclusion of an entire generation from the paradise that they should have enjoyed, in a way reminiscent of Adam and Eve's exclusion from Eden in Genesis 3. The present disobedience of the nation appeared to overcome the power of the promise to the patriarchs.

However, not all was lost. Caleb, son of Jephunneh, was given an exemption from this exclusion order. Up to this point, all we know of Caleb is that, along with Joshua (whose survival is explained in 1:38), he was the source of the minority report in Numbers 13, urging God's people to take the land as they had been commanded. The very mention of his name held out the possibility of obedience to the people, for he was one who (lit.) "filled up after Yahweh." This phrase also occurs in Numbers 14:24 and 32:11–12 as well as Joshua 14:14, and denotes wholehearted obedience.[18] Remarkably, according to Numbers 32, Caleb was

---

[18] Moshe Weinfeld ("The Covenant of Grant in the Old Testament and the Ancient Near East," *Journal of the American Oriental Society* 90 [1970]: 184–203) has shown that the language is typical of agreements associated with transferring land. In this case, it seems to

of Edomite descent (although a leader in the tribe of Judah, Num 13:6), and yet becomes the standard for Israelite obedience and receives the land "on which he has set foot" (see also 2:5; 11:24–25). In this case, the expression is literal, and refers to the city of Hebron (Josh 14:6–14).

1:37–40. By turning to his own exclusion from the land at this point, Moses adds even more rhetorical force to his sermon. His fate is bound up with his generation, as he faces not only God's wrath, but hears the crushing words "You will not enter there either." The implication is clear: the sinfulness of the people at Kadesh-barnea led not only to their death outside the land, but also ensured that Moses, their leader, perished east of the Jordan (a death, his hearers knew, that was imminent).

Is Moses attempting to evade responsibility for his own rash and hubristic actions in striking the rock in Numbers 20? That seems unlikely. His point is rather that the fateful events in the Wilderness of Zin could not have taken place had Israel chosen well at Kadesh, and he mentions his own impending death in order to hammer home the seriousness of these matters. That an entire adult generation, including their peerless leader, was to die outside the land was designed to have a sobering effect.

The fact that the other faithful spy, Joshua, is the one to lead the people into the land underlines the fundamental importance of listening to Yahweh and doing (exactly) what he says. This is the shape of covenantal faithfulness. Moses was to "encourage" (or strengthen) him for the task ahead, as he leads Israel into the land. The impact of Moses himself saying all this to the people he has led for so many years can't be underestimated.

1:39 is highly ironic. In Numbers 14:2–3 (see also 14:31), the "Kadesh generation" had cited concerns for the wellbeing of their children as a reason for not going into the land. They claimed that it would endanger those "who don't yet know good from evil," either those who are under twenty, and therefore not full-fledged members of the community eligible to fight in battle (Exod 30:14; Num 1:3) or simply those who are too immature to know right from wrong. It turns out that only the vulnerable group would make it into the land to take possession of it, while those who were "of age" would die in the wilderness. This is confirmed by the shocking command of 1:40. The opening words of 1:7 are repeated, but

---

be referring to Caleb's attitude to the land and God's promise in the wake of their mission, rather than making a general statement about his life and godliness.

rather than setting out for the land, Israel had gone into reverse. Having escaped slavery and near-certain death by crossing the Sea or Lake of Reeds (traditionally the Red Sea), they were to retrace their steps in an "anti-exodus."[19]

1:41–46. The emotional roller-coaster ride that has characterized this chapter continues as Moses describes their attempted repentance. Their response had three parts: an apparently straightforward confession: "We have sinned against Yahweh"; an expressed desire to obey God by following (belatedly) his command; and finally their strapping on their weapons in order to march on Canaan. However, what looked like repentance on the surface turned out to be a further expression of stubborn independence (also 1:43). Moses states baldly that they "thought it would be easy" to march right into the hill country of Canaan. But they were wrong. It was too late.

God's people clearly had not understood the nature of a covenantal relationship, in which obedience and disobedience both have real-time consequences (to be fleshed out later in this book, as at the end of Leviticus, in terms of blessing and curse). The fact that they thought a simple acknowledgement of such a catastrophic misstep would sort everything out bespeaks a deep-seated independence and presumption.

Yahweh now instructed Moses to inform them that the assurance of 1:30 (that he would fight for them against all-comers) no longer applied, and therefore they must *not* go up and fight. How have they forfeited their divine protection? They have denied the very heart of the covenant. When God spoke, they did not listen (and obey—the ideas are synonymous in Deuteronomy). This is tantamount to rebellion, a rebellion that was only exacerbated as they foolishly tried to take matters into their own hands, defiantly starting to fight on their own. But God had withdrawn his presence.[20] In 1:43, their disobedience was compounded, as they once more ignored the voice of God, rejected his command, and acted in blatant disregard of his will.

"The Amorites" is an ancient designation for the inhabitants of the land (see Gen 15:16). They came against the Israelites with the ferocity of an angry swarm of honey bees (as in Isa 7:18; Ps 118:12). Traditionally, Seir (also mentioned in 1:2; 2:1, 4) was part of the territory of Edom (Gen

---

[19] The precise location of the Sea of Reeds (יַם־סוּף) is uncertain, but the point here is clear.

[20] This is an important idea. See for example Exod 17:7; 33:3, 5; 34:9–10; Num 14:14, 42, 44.

36:8–9; Judg 5:4). Although Edom proper was to the east of Kadesh, it seems that Seir at this point extended much further west.[21] The Israelites are driven north as far as Hormah in the eastern Negeb (Num 21:1–3). Although the precise location of Hormah is uncertain, the irony of Israel being driven there by Canaanites would not have been missed by Hebrew speakers—the word Hormah shares a root with the word routinely used for the destruction of the Canaanites (חרם).

The actions of God's people clearly damaged the state of their covenantal relationship with God. Even though they "wept before Yahweh," he did not acknowledge or relieve their distress. The exodus had begun with the God of Abraham, Isaac and Jacob hearing their groaning in Egypt (Exod 2:24). As it now ground to a crashing halt, the same God was ignoring the cries of his people.

Israel was now left in limbo at Kadesh-barnea. Having refused to go into the land once, they were now banned from trying again. A (relatively) long hiatus began at this oasis, before they began their wilderness period proper.

Bridge

This section (1:19–46), along with the chapters which follow in the rest of Moses's introduction, is one of the most searing indictments of sin in the entire Bible. If one wants to know why Christ had to die, then reading Moses's rehearsal of the catastrophic decision to refuse to enter the good land that God was giving to his people, in line with the promises he had made repeatedly to their forefathers, powerfully unpacks the answer.

The sin of God's people is characterized in several ways: (1) refusal to hear/listen, (2) refusal to trust, and (3) refusal to obey. These fit perfectly with the three ways in which the Bible most often describes our propensity to turn away from God: idolatry (in which we elevate someone or something to the place of God, listening to them rather than God; unbelief, in which we refuse to accept that God is what he says he is; and rebellion, in which we deliberately go our way, not his. This exposition of the human problem prepares the way for one to come who not only listens to and perfectly obeys his Father, but speaks to us on his behalf, as we are called to listen to him; one who expresses perfect trust in his

[21] See Lundbom, *Deuteronomy*, 183. Also Num 20:16 is helpful, locating Kadesh on the Edomite border.

Father to the very point of death and one who does not rebel but gladly submits to his Father, even facing his wrath on our behalf. Jesus Christ is the only one who can resolve the problems displayed in this chapter.

The journey motif for life with God that was established in the exodus is now developed and filled out in powerful ways that lay the foundation for the rest of Deuteronomy, the Old Testament, and ultimately the pilgrim life. Peter's assessment that we are simply sojourners (1 Pet 1:1) and the encouragement of the writer to the Hebrews to press on that we might enjoy the rest of God himself are based on this model.

Caleb is held up in this chapter, along with Joshua, as one who made the right decision at a key moment in the life of the nation, and for that he is commended. However, his influence made no actual difference. The failure of the ten spies, the overwhelming choice of the nation, and even the exclusion of Moses himself from the land make clear that it will take someone far greater than Caleb to resolve the obvious issues which have already emerged in the life of the nation of Israel.

4. A Painful Lesson (2:1–23)

> [1] "Then we turned back and headed for the wilderness by way of the Red
> Sea, as the Lord had told me, and we traveled around the hill country of
> Seir for many days. [2] The Lord then said to me, [3] 'You've been traveling
> around this hill country long enough; turn north. [4] Command the peo-
> ple: You are about to travel through the territory of your brothers, the
> descendants of Esau, who live in Seir. They will be afraid of you, so be
> very careful. [5] Don't provoke them, for I will not give you any of their
> land, not even a foot of it, because I have given Esau the hill country of
> Seir as his possession. [6] You may purchase food from them, so that you
> may eat, and buy water from them to drink. [7] For the Lord your God has
> blessed you in all the work of your hands. He has watched over your
> journey through this immense wilderness. The Lord your God has been
> with you these past forty years, and you have lacked nothing.'
>
> [8] "So we bypassed our brothers, the descendants of Esau, who live in Seir.
> We turned away from the Arabah road and from Elath and Ezion-geb-
> er. We traveled along the road to the Wilderness of Moab. [9] The Lord
> said to me, "show no hostility toward Moab, and do not provoke them
> to battle, for I will not give you any of their land as a possession, since
> I have given Ar as a possession to the descendants of Lot.'
>
> [10] "The Emim, a great and numerous people as tall as the Anakim, had
> previously lived there. [11] They were also regarded as Rephaim, like the
> Anakim, though the Moabites called them Emim. [12] The Horites had

previously lived in Seir, but the descendants of Esau drove them out,
destroying them completely and settling in their place, just as Israel
did in the land of its possession the LORD gave them.

13 “The LORD said, ‘Now get up and cross the Zered Valley.’ So we crossed
the Zered Valley. 14 The time we spent traveling from Kadesh-barnea
until we crossed the Zered Valley was thirty-eight years until the entire
generation of fighting men had perished from the camp, as the LORD had
sworn to them. 15 Indeed, the LORD’s hand was against them, to eliminate them from the camp until they had all perished.

16 “When all the fighting men had died among the people, 17 the LORD
spoke to me, 18 ‘Today you are going to cross the border of Moab at
Ar. 19 When you get close to the Ammonites, don’t show any hostility
to them or provoke them, for I will not give you any of the Ammonites’
land as a possession; I have given it as a possession to the descendants
of Lot.’

20 “This too used to be regarded as the land of the Rephaim. The Rephaim lived there previously, though the Ammonites called them Zamzummim, 21 a great and numerous people, tall as the Anakim. The LORD
destroyed the Rephaim at the advance of the Ammonites, so that they
drove them out and settled in their place. 22 This was just as he had done
for the descendants of Esau who lived in Seir, when he destroyed the
Horites before them; they drove them out and have lived in their place
until now. 23 The Caphtorim, who came from Caphtor, destroyed the
Avvites, who lived in villages as far as Gaza, and settled in their place.”

2:1–8a. Very surprisingly, Moses deals with almost forty years spent in the wilderness to the south and west of Canaan in a single verse (unlike 1:46, “many days” here refers to an extended period of around thirty-eight years). Now Yahweh’s words, rather than bringing them freedom, took them back toward Egypt. The motion here was exactly the reverse of 1:7. The word “turn” is characteristic of this revisiting of the nation’s past (1:24; 2:1, 8; 3:1), and marks off the key moments in this journey. They traveled, initially at least, “by the Red Sea road,” which is probably part of what is often called the “Via Maris” (Way of the Sea), an ancient trade route that linked Egypt with Damascus, which in turn served as a gateway to Mesopotamia. The Israelites, however, neither traveled to Egypt nor all the way south to the Gulf of Aqaba, but eked out an existence in the fairly barren territory on the fringes of Edom (the “hill country of Seir” loosely marked the outskirts of the Edomite kingdom). “Traveled around” can have the sense of “skirted,” implying that they avoided any direct contact with the main Edomite centers of population at this point. This is supported by Numbers 20:14–21 where their request for safe passage through the Edomite heartland on the King's Highway, the main inland north-south trade route, is denied. The events at Meribah (which became proverbial for disobedience); the death of Aaron at Mount Hor; the victory over Arad/Hormah, and the Bronze Snake (Num 20–21) are all omitted. But it is clear in both Numbers and Deuteronomy that the period of wandering was a bleak interlude in the history of Israel. Daniel Block comments: "Yahweh had one primary goal for their desert wanderings—to get rid of that rebellious generation (vv. 14–16). For almost four decades Israel was a death camp, a walking mortuary, in which the dominant sound was the death wail. The irony is inescapable. So long as they were slaves in Egypt, the population mushroomed; as soon as they were free, it shrank."[22]

When God spoke again in 2:2–3, his message was simple: their time in the wilderness had served its purpose, and now was the moment for their journey north into the land to resume (the language of being here "long enough" echoes 1:6, as the journey to the land restarts). This new start is not recorded in Numbers, which is more interested in the defining moment of the census in 26:64–65, when the passing of the entire exodus generation is noted. Here in Deuteronomy, however, Moses's focus is on the journey of Israel itself, and the theological lessons that can be gleaned from it.

The Lord's command in 2:4 highlights both the brotherly connection between the Edomites and the Israelites as descendants of Isaac and the fact that even this nation would be "afraid of them," which was anticipated back in Exodus 15:14–16. This strengthens the sense that the Israelites' fear of the Canaanites was completely unconscionable. The idea that Edom and Israel are "brothers," and that Edom should benefit in some small way from this connection can presumably be traced back to the logic of Genesis 12:1–3, where blessing "flows" through Abraham and his descendants (initially Isaac, Jacob, and Joseph) to other nations. However, the call for Israel to "take great care" or "be on their guard" (see also 4:6, 9, 23) was a reminder that fear can produce all kinds of reactions.[23] "Seir" is the hilly region to the west of the Jordan Valley. Edom

---

[22] Block, *Deuteronomy*, 75.

[23] See the relatively positive provisions of Deut 23:7–8. As the Old Testament progresses, relations between Israel and Edom become progressively more hostile (see Jer 49:7–22; Obad 10; Ps 137:7–9; Mal 1:2–4).

"proper" is on the other side of the Jordan to the east (including the region in and around Petra, known for its reddish terrain). Numbers 20 details an encounter in the Petra region, but here, Moses is talking about the fringe area on the other side of the Jordan.

None of this prepares us for the stunning (and unprecedented) statement God made in 2:5. Israel was warned, in keeping with the non-aggression policy (against non–Canaanite nations) presented throughout the book, not to pick a fight with the Edomites. But it is the reason for this stance that is so remarkable. God said, "I will not give you any of their land ... because I have given Esau the hill country of Seir as his possession." Nowhere outside this chapter is it stated explicitly that any nation is given land like this "as a possession."[24] Despite the strong emphasis on God's choice of and care for Israel as his covenant people, from time to time, the insistence that he is also the God of all nations shines through. This is one of these places. This was why Israel was not allowed even to try to take a footprint-sized piece of land (for similar expressions see 11:24; 28:65; Josh 1:3). However, it is important to recognize that the primary reasons for stating this so starkly were to expose Israel's own ingratitude and to spur them on to make obedience the dominant note of their long-delayed entry to the land that God had given them.

This is apparent in 2:6–7, where God gave permission to barter (lit., "with silver") for provisions from the Edomites (because of their status of "brothers," and since they are not under the same judgment as the Canaanites). This is cited as evidence of God's ongoing care for his people, even while they are under his covenantal discipline. "All the work of your hands" encompasses every dimension of their national life and experience during this period (a typical expression in Deuteronomy: 14:29; 15:10; 16:15; 24:19; 28:12; 30:9; and also 12:7, 18; 15:10; 23:20; 28:8, 20). As the book goes on, this is generally shorthand for covenant faithfulness in the land. Here, it refers to their attempts to survive! Not only has God "watched over" (lit., "known"; also Ps 1:6) the full course of their wanderings through this "great" wilderness, but he has been with them every step of the way (see also 32:10–12). His care has ensured that "they lacked nothing" (lit., "you did not lack a thing/matter/word [Heb. דָּבָר]"), a phrase

---

[24] The word occurs fourteen times in the Old Testament: Num 24:18 (2x); Deut 2:5, 9, 12, 19; 3:20; Josh 1:15; 12:6–7; Judg 21:17 (heirs); Jer 32:8, always with the sense of continuing inheritance. Amos 9:7 comes close to making a similar statement, but stops short of saying that God gave other nations their lands.

that is repeated in 8:9 about his extravagant provision for them in the land itself. This highly positive take on what can only have been an extremely difficult period of eking out an existence in the desert is designed to highlight that God cannot be blamed in any way for their experience.

This fleeting encounter with their Edomite "brothers" (according to 2:8a they avoided main roads as they avoided the Seir area) should have impressed on them the generosity and kindness of Yahweh in sticking with them and giving them a land, reassured them of his relentless love over these past forty years, and motivated them to make every effort to take advantage of his grace this time around.

2:8b–9. Although the precise location of the "Arabah road" is uncertain, it does seem clear that the Israelites "turned off" the main route to avoid further dealings with the Edomites, headed north (away from Elath and Ezion-Geber, towns on the Gulf of Aqaba to the south), and made their way east of the Jordan and the Dead Sea to the desert/wilderness of Moab. As Driver notes, this land is on the edge of the Syrian/Arabian desert, but isn't, strictly speaking, desert itself. It was uncultivated land, which, in theory at least, would have allowed the Israelites to sustain their goats and sheep and probably given them access to wells.[25]

In 2:9, God prohibited Israel from instigating any provocative aggression or military action against Moab, in much the same way as he had done with Edom in the preceding verses. Any expansionist schemes are doomed to fail. God expressly said, "I will not give you any of their land as a possession." This establishes beyond any doubt that (1) Yahweh alone is sovereign; (2) The allocation of territory to nations is his business; and (3) There is no evidence of any divine sanction for a generalized campaign of land-grabbing by God's people. More specifically, the Moabites have been given "Ar" as their possession, The fact that they are now described as the "descendants of Lot," Abraham's nephew (Gen 11:27, 31; 12:4; also Gen 19:37, which details the sorry origins of Moab, Lot's son) in all likelihood ties them in to the promised patriarchal blessing of Genesis 12:1–3 through their association with Abraham himself. "Ar" (Num 21:15, 28 and perhaps also 22:36; Isa 15:1) was a city in the northern part of Moab, which is used to represent all of Moab here. At one time it seems that the Moabites controlled all of the land east of the Jordan, although Sihon had seized much of their territory in the north. This explains why the "plains

[25] Driver, *Deuteronomy*, 35.

of Moab," where Deuteronomy is set (Num 36:13; Deut 34:1), refers to an area opposite Jericho to the north of the Dead Sea, despite it being some distance from the borders of Moab at this time.[26]

There is scant reference to any direct interaction with the Moabites as a nation in Numbers, although the events involving Balaam (Num 22–24) and the idolatry at Peor (involving the "daughters of Moab"), coupled with the tradition of Judges 11:17–18 of a refused request for passage, lay the foundations for a fairly problematic relationship with their distant relatives and near neighbors in years to come (see, e.g., 2 Kgs 3).

2:10–12. This is the first in a series of parentheses in this chapter, presumably added when Moses's sermon was "published." These historical notes both supply some additional background detail that may not be known by the reader and also make explicit the implied criticisms of Israel's failure to take possession of the land.

First, we are told that the "Emim, a great and numerous people as tall as the Anakim," had occupied the territory now belonging to Moab. The phrase "great and numerous people" also occurs in 2:21 and echoes the results of God's blessing on the nation of Israel (e.g., 1:10).

According to verse 11, these "giants" were, like the Anakim, regarded as "Rephaim" (although the Moabites had their own name for them). The term "Rephaim" is first found in Genesis 14:5, where it appears alongside Emim in the list of those defeated by Chedorlaomer. The term also occurs in Genesis 15:20, in the demarcation of the land that God promises to give to Abraham. In neither place does the term "Rephaim" have any supernatural connotation. It seems simply to refer to a particularly large and fearsome warlike tribe. This is confirmed by Deuteronomy 3:11 and the reference to King Og and his large bed (see also Josh 13:12; 17:15; 1 Chr 20:4, and the references to the Rephaim Valley in Josh 15:8; 18:16; 2 Sam 23:13; 1 Chr 11:15; 14:9; Isa 17:5). With the Rephaim, we are dealing with real (albeit large!) people who lived in real places and were defeated in actual battles.[27]

But what about the Anakim? They are first mentioned in the context of the spies' mission and report (Num 13:22, 28). Like the Rephaim, they have names and live in real places. Like the Rephaim, while fearsome (Deut

---

[26] Tigay's discussion of this is most helpful (*Deuteronomy*, 26).

[27] It is true that the same word is used later in the Old Testament to refer to the spirits of the dead (e.g., Ps 88:10 [Heb. 88:11]; Job 26:5; Isa 26:14), but there appears to be no connection between these meanings.

9:2), they are certainly beatable, as Caleb and Joshua both demonstrate (Josh 15:13; 21:11; Judg 1:20; Josh 11:21–22; 14:12, 15). The only suggestion that the Anakim are any more than fearsome but normal human beings comes in Numbers 13:33: "We even saw the Nephilim there—the descendants of Anak come from the Nephilim! To ourselves we seemed like grasshoppers, and we must have seemed the same to them." Several things need to be said about this claim: (1) It comes at the climax of the fear-fueled attempt to dissuade the Israelites from entering the land. (2) It sounds like hyperbole. (3) It is the only reference to the Nephilim in the Old Testament outside Genesis 6. On balance, it seems best to ignore the report of the spies (as Israel should have done!), and read 2:10–12 and the similar statements later in the chapter as simply pointing out that the presence of large, aggressive fighters did not prevent the Moabites from taking their land (nor did they resort to superstition, legend, or misinterpretation of older traditions to justify their passivity).[28]

This interpretation is supported by the additional note in 2:12 that the Edomites had actually succeeded in dispossessing the Horites (Gen 14:6; 36:20–21; 29–30).[29] There is no connection between the Horites and any legendary group, and the parallelism suggests the simple point that, like the Moabites, the Edomites conquered and dispossessed the occupants of their land. The language of "destroying them completely" is not that of the commanded total annihilation of the Canaanites but is used elsewhere of the Israelite campaign in Canaan (Josh 24:8; Amos 2:9), as is that of replacing the locals in the land (Deut 2:21–23).

2:13–19. After this aside, Moses's reporting of Israel's journey continues, as God again commands his people to get up and get going, this time to cross the Zered Valley. The word is actually "river," but here almost certainly refers to a wadi, a river valley in which water flow is seasonal. The Zered marked the boundary between Edom in the south and Moab in the north. However before any interaction with Moab is

---

[28] The identity of the Nephilim in Gen 6 is itself a source of much dispute. Although there is clear evidence that some viewed them as mythical (and even supernatural) figures (so perhaps Num 13:33, and much later, 2 Pet and Jude), it is not clear that Gen 6 is describing angelic figures. It seems most plausible to me that Genesis is describing the same kind of legendary, powerful, and very human warriors who are also described here.

[29] There is some discussion of the link between the biblical Horites and the Hurrians, a dominant non-semitic race who occupied much of the Near East in the third and second millennia BC. For details see Lundbom, *Deuteronomy*, 196.

discussed, Moses raises some painful truths about Israel's past progress. The bald statement that it took thirty-eight years to make the short trip from Kadesh-barnea to the wadi at Zered (referring to their first visit to Kadesh in Num 13–14) is the flip-side of the assertion in 1:2 that it should have taken eleven days to travel from Horeb to Kadesh-barnea.[30] The sobering impact of this statement is compounded by the blunt reminder that the entire cohort of "fighting men" over twenty (Num 14:29) has now died, as Yahweh had decreed (Deut 1:34–35). As Tigay points out, the reference to "fighting men" is slightly ironic, as they had refused to do any fighting![31] Moses underlines the significance of this by intensifying his statement in 2:15. Yahweh's "hand was against them" (see also Judg 2:14–15, and more generally, Exod 9:3; 1 Sam 5:9) in order to completely confound them (המם, see also Exod 14:24 and Deut 7:23 for the by-form הום). The repeated reference to the "camp" picks up the idea prominent in Numbers (see especially chs. 1–11) that Israel's enjoyment of life with Yahweh (and progress into the land) is dependent on purity, symbolizing a right relationship with their God. The events of Numbers 13 and 14 had clearly rendered that impossible for the exodus generation.

The note of 2:16 is the third consecutive reference to the death of the exodus generation, which adds to the dominant downbeat tone of this part of Moses's address: the consequences of sin in the life of the nation can only be covenantally catastrophic. However, God's gracious commitment to his people was demonstrated yet again in the command to the new generation to press on into the land, as he once more "spoke" (the use of דִּבֵּר here is probably emphatic). Passing over any interaction with the Moabites for now, this new "day" for God's people began with leaving Moabite territory. The phrase "at Ar" is either, in contrast to 2:9, referring to the city rather than the region or repeating what has been already said "leaving Ar." Either way, they were now entering Ammon. Like the Moabites, the Ammonites were the product of a drunken Lot sleeping with his scheming daughters (Gen 19:30–38). The fact that God continues to treat these races with extra kindness because of their connection with Abraham is a powerful testimony to his grace.

---

[30] The uncertainty concerning the precise location of Kadesh-barnea makes it impossible to tie down the distance to the Zered Valley, but it is of the order of tens rather than hundreds of miles.

[31] Tigay, *Deuteronomy*, 28.

As with the Moabites, the Israelites were prohibited from launching any form of attack or showing any aggression to the Ammonites (2:18), because God had already given them the land in perpetuity. The Edomites, Moabites, and now the Ammonites have all (gratefully?) received gifts from Yahweh and gladly taken possession of them—unlike Israel, despite their unique relationship with him through Abraham, Isaac, and Jacob.

2:20–23. The second parenthesis starts by asserting that, like the Moabites, the Ammonites also dispossessed fearsome opponents when taking their land. These "Rephaim" were called "Zamzummim." This may be the tribal group referred to as the "Zuzim" in Genesis 14:5, but in any case, the point Moses is making is clear. As with the Emim in 1:10, this "great and numerous people," who were similarly large, were swept away. This time, however, this is attributed not to the military efficiency of the people group concerned, but to the direct action of God himself. "Yahweh destroyed the Rephaim" before the Ammonites. The editor of this part of Moses's sermon also makes explicit what was only implicit in the note of 2:10–12. This was not simply the case with the Zamzummim lining up against Ammon, but also with the Horites who opposed the Edomites (2:22). These nations who enjoyed few of the privileges of Israel, and certainly did not have the unique covenantal relationship with Yahweh, nonetheless recognized his generosity and allowed him to act for them.

A final note in 2:23 adds that even the Caphtorim (mentioned in the table of nations in Gen 10:14 as descended from one of the sons of Ham, and closely linked to the Philistines in Amos 9:7; Jer 47:4) managed to displace the Avvites (Josh 13:3). Caphtor was an ancient name for Crete, and this seems to refer to seafaring peoples (some of whom were the Philistines) who appeared on the eastern coastal territories of the Mediterranean around 1200 BC. It seems that even complete outsiders to the covenant of God (even *the Philistines*!) have done what Israel steadfastly refused to do.

Bridge

Deuteronomy 2:1–23 is an immensely powerful piece of rhetoric. Both Moses's own words, and the deceptively innocuous asides of 2:10–12 and 20–23, finally have the effect of confronting the Israelites with their disastrous past, in an attempt to move them to gratitude and determined obedience in the future. The problem was, of course, that all this could really do was expose their failure and guilt. This is what makes the chapter so challenging. God in this chapter is extravagantly, disturbingly (even annoyingly) gracious. He has shown kindness upon kindness to Israel (and remarkable kindness to all kinds of other nations). The question is: Will they respond?

These words ask the same basic question of us. God has been inexpressibly generous to us—not in giving us a place to enjoy him, but in drawing us to a person, the Lord Jesus Christ himself, in whom (as the true land) we get to enjoy life with God both now and forever. The challenge is, will we live in a way that fits with who we are, or will we act like we are outsiders (and ungrateful outsiders at that)? Paul, writing to the Corinthian church says this in 1 Corinthians 6:9–11:

> [9] Don't you know that the unrighteous will not inherit God's kingdom? Do not be deceived: No sexually immoral people, idolaters, adulterers, or males who have sex with males, [10] no thieves, greedy people, drunkards, verbally abusive people, or swindlers will inherit God's kingdom. [11] And some of you used to be like this. But you were washed, you were sanctified, you were justified in the name of the Lord Jesus Christ and by the Spirit of our God.

5. Two Model Conquests (2:24–3:22)

> [24] "The Lord also said, 'Get up, move out, and cross the Arnon Valley. See, I have handed the Amorites' King Sihon of Heshbon and his land over to you. Begin to take possession of it; engage him in battle. [25] Today I will begin to put the fear and dread of you on the peoples everywhere under heaven. They will hear the report about you, tremble, and be in anguish because of you.'
>
> [26] "So I sent messengers with an offer of peace to King Sihon of Heshbon from the Wilderness of Kedemoth, saying, [27] 'Let us travel through your land; we will keep strictly to the highway. We will not turn to the right or the left. [28] You can sell us food in exchange for silver so we may eat, and give us water for silver so we may drink. Only let us travel through on foot, [29] just as the descendants of Esau who live in Seir did for us, and the Moabites who live in Ar, until we cross the Jordan into the land the Lord our God is giving us.' [30] But King Sihon of Heshbon would not let us travel through his land, for the Lord your God had made his spirit stubborn and his heart obstinate in order to hand him over to you, as has now taken place.
>
> [31] "Then the Lord said to me, "See, I have begun to give Sihon and his land to you. Begin to take possession of it.' [32] So Sihon and his whole army came out against us for battle at Jahaz. [33] The Lord our God handed him over to us, and we defeated him, his sons, and his whole army. [34] At

that time we captured all his cities and completely destroyed the
people of every city, including the women and children. We left no
survivors. 35 We took only the livestock and the spoil from the cities
we captured as plunder for ourselves. 36 There was no city that was
inaccessible to us, from Aroer on the rim of the Arnon Valley, along
with the city in the valley, even as far as Gilead. The Lord our God gave
everything to us. 37 But you did not go near the Ammonites' land, all
along the bank of the Jabbok River, the cities of the hill country, or any
place that the Lord our God had forbidden.

3:1 "Then we turned and went up the road to Bashan, and King Og of
Bashan came out against us with his whole army to do battle at Edrei.
2 But the Lord said to me, 'Do not fear him, for I have handed him over
to you along with his whole army and his land. Do to him as you did
to King Sihon of the Amorites, who lived in Heshbon.' 3 So the Lord our
God also handed over King Og of Bashan and his whole army to us. We
struck him until there was no survivor left. 4 We captured all his cities at
that time. There wasn't a city that we didn't take from them: sixty cities,
the entire region of Argob, the kingdom of Og in Bashan. 5 All these
were fortified with high walls, gates, and bars, besides a large number
of rural villages. 6 We completely destroyed them, as we had done to
King Sihon of Heshbon, destroying the men, women, and children of
every city. 7 But we took all the livestock and the spoil from the cities
as plunder for ourselves.

8 "At that time we took the land from the two Amorite kings across the
Jordan, from the Arnon Valley as far as Mount Hermon, 9 which the
Sidonians call Sirion, but the Amorites call Senir, 10 all the cities of the
plateau, Gilead, and Bashan as far as Salecah and Edrei, cities of Og's
kingdom in Bashan. 11 (Only King Og of Bashan was left of the remnant
of the Rephaim. His bed was made of iron. Isn't it in Rabbah of the
Ammonites? It is 13 ½ feet long and 6 feet wide by a standard measure.)

12 "At that time we took possession of this land. I gave to the Reubenites
and Gadites the area extending from Aroer by the Arnon Valley, and
half the hill country of Gilead along with its cities. 13 I gave to half the
tribe of Manasseh the rest of Gilead and all Bashan, the kingdom of Og.
The entire region of Argob, the whole territory of Bashan, used to be
called the land of the Rephaim. 14 Jair, a descendant of Manasseh, took
over the entire region of Argob as far as the border of the Geshurites
and Maacathites. He called Bashan by his own name, Jair's Villages, as
it is today. 15 I gave Gilead to Machir, 16 and I gave to the Reubenites
and Gadites the area extending from Gilead to the Arnon Valley (the
middle of the valley was the border) and up to the Jabbok River, the
border of the Ammonites. 17 The Arabah and Jordan are also borders
from Chinnereth as far as the Sea of the Arabah, the Dead Sea, under
the slopes of Pisgah on the east.

[18] "I commanded you at that time: The LORD your God has given you this land to possess. All your valiant men will cross over in battle formation ahead of your brothers the Israelites. [19] But your wives, dependents, and livestock—I know that you have a lot of livestock—will remain in the cities I have given you [20] until the LORD gives rest to your brothers as he has to you, and they also take possession of the land the LORD your God is giving them across the Jordan. Then each of you may return to his possession that I have given you.

[21] "I commanded Joshua at that time: Your own eyes have seen everything the LORD your God has done to these two kings. The LORD will do the same to all the kingdoms you are about to enter. [22] Don't be afraid of them, for the LORD your God fights for you."

2:24–25. After the aside dealing with the Ammonites (and the Caphtorites), the review of Israel's journey resumes. Having passed on Yahweh's warning about the Ammonites (should they encounter them: there is no hint in the text that they actually did), verse 24 returns to a command to cross the Arnon River, the northern border of Moab, to the territory of Sihon of Heshbon. According to Numbers 21:26, this had formerly been part of Moab but had been stripped from them by Sihon in a previous campaign (according to Isa 16:8–9, which speaks of this area in an oracle which is addressed to Moab, it would eventually revert to them). There is a stark simplicity to Yahweh's statements. In marked contrast to the lands of Edom, Ammon, and Moab, God says he has given these lands to his people, and because of this divine gift, they should take it, beginning by engaging him in battle. As in 1:8; 4:5; 11:26; and 30:15, the imperative is used emphatically to underline the importance of this moment, as the conquest begins in earnest (albeit outside the land proper).

Similarly, the use of "today" at the start of 2:25 highlights the importance of the decision that Israel faced at that moment. This is a dry run for the land itself. As they cross a river to begin a conquest, thirty-eight years on from their refusal to enter, will they obey the command of God? There is no doubt that Yahweh was making it as easy as possible for his people by inspiring "fear and dread" of the Israelites in the minds of the Amorites, and then because of their experience, on the "peoples everywhere under heaven," who will literally "writhe," a word often used of the pains of childbirth (e.g., Isa 26:17; Jer 4:31). This has echoes of Exodus 14:14–16. The significance of this event for the future of Israel is massive. According to Joshua 2:10–11 (also Num 22:3), it was precisely these events that caused panic in Jericho and led to Rahab's response to the Israelite spies.

2:26–30. Moses's abbreviated account reflects the material in Numbers 21:21–32, although the reference to the "Wilderness of Kedemoth" is unique (but see Josh 13:18, which may suggest they had already crossed the Arnon when the envoy was dispatched). The approach made to Sihon, perhaps surprisingly, fits with the template of Deuteronomy 20:10–12 for dealing with nations outside Canaan who are not facing the judgment of God.[32] Moses requested safe passage on the main road (according to Num 21, the King's Highway, which has been a major north-south artery through the region since ancient times) and promises no deviation. The Hebrew expression is "by the road and only by the road."[33] The request to buy food and water is a standard one (as sanctioned by God in 2:6). No mention was made earlier in this chapter nor in Numbers 21 to any interaction with Moab. In Judges 11:13–23, Jephthah speaks in a similar diplomatic situation of an incident where the Moabites refuse to offer such a facility (and the events of Num 22–24 also show evidence of Moabite hostility to Israel). According to Numbers 21:14–21, Edom had also denied them this kind of easy passage. It may be that Moses was simply dealing shrewdly with Sihon, in line with ancient diplomatic practice when there is a possibility of war (as he had with Pharaoh in, e.g., Exod 9:24–29). However, given the other otherwise unknown details in this chapter (like the Wilderness of Kedemoth reference), it could also refer to non-official interactions with Edomites and Moabites over the extended period that Israel was in their general vicinity. In any case, Sihon rebuffed their request. Moses views this through the same lens as the nation's treatment at the hands of Pharaoh (Exod 4:21; 7:3; 9:12; 10:1, 20, 27; 11:10; 14:4, 8, 17; see also Josh 11:19–20). This ensures that God himself is given credit for the campaign, which they already know to have been a spectacular success. Contrary to their allegation in 1:27, when they trust God to do what he promises, progress is both guaranteed and miraculously smooth. The phrase "as it is to this day" occurs in 2:30; 4:20, 38; 6:24; 8:18; 10:15; and 29:28. It underlines the significance of past events for the present (and future) decisions of Israel.

2:31–37. In 2:31, God reiterated that he has given them this land in emphatic terms (as in 2:24, Israel is commanded to see what's before

---

[32] The use of "Amorites" as both a general designation for the occupants of the land and specific tribal groups may explain why the strictures of Gen 15:16, 21 do not seem to be taken as applying to Sihon and Og.

[33] See GKC §123e.

them) by giving them Sihon's land. As he had begun to give it to them, they had to begin to take hold of their new inheritance. Initially it did not look as though this would be straightforward, as the Amorites massed for the battle at Jahaz. Jahaz is mentioned in the Moabite Stone inscription (dated to around 900 BC), but its location is uncertain.[34] The account of the battle could not be more cursory: "The Lord our God handed him over to us, and we defeated him, his sons, and his whole army." It isn't that the battle was God's in some abstract sense: he is the one who determined the outcome.

The note in verse 34 explicitly states that *all* the cities were captured and *all* the inhabitants were "completely destroyed" (the verb is חָרַם).[35] This phrase is not used in the parallel account of Numbers 21, but is coined here by Moses to highlight the connection between this conflict and the one to come in Canaan, where the entire population was to be treated as coming under the condemnation of God.

The fact that Moses says explicitly that *all* the women and children were included and that they "left no survivors" is one of the most disturbing statements in the whole of the Bible.[36] While it is true that ancient warfare (like modern) was often described in sweeping, even hyperbolic terms (e.g., the fact that the enemy was "crushed," "obliterated," or "annihilated" need not imply that that life was actually squeezed out of them, nor even that every last enemy soldier was killed), the careful specificity of the text leaves no room for interpretation.[37] Moses's emphasis is on the fact that straightforward obedience to the sovereign God leads to a straightforward (and overwhelming) victory in line with his promise, but the jarring truth remains that terrible judgment was exacted on the kingdom of Sihon. The sin of the Amorites had clearly reached the threshold where facing God's wrath was inevitable (Gen 15:16). A deep-rooted

---

[34] See lines 19–21 in *ANET*[3] 320. The spelling here occurs in Jer 48:21 (Jahzah), but elsewhere is simply Jahaz, hence the rendering in most English versions.

[35] The word "all" is used seven times in this section. Interestingly, the verb חָרַם an equivalent Moabite verb also appears on the Moabite Stone, describing the wars of the Moabite King Mesha.

[36] This phrase is used where those concerned are under God's judgment: see also Josh 8:22; 10:28–40; 11:8 and also 2 Kgs 10:11 (referring to the house of Ahab).

[37] The classic work on this subject is Younger, *Ancient Conquest Accounts*. Younger points out that the language is like that of "Germany conquered France" during World War II. One could say that all resistance was crushed, but that does not deny the existence of the French Resistance!

confidence in the righteousness/justice of God is the only thing that allows us to read shocking texts like this without recoiling.

According to 2:35, the Israelites themselves were well aware of the uniqueness of these events, and, for once, acted in line with God's instructions (see, e.g., Deut 20:15). As a non–Canaanite nation who has instigated war on Israel outside the land, their possessions (both living and material) were fair game for God's people (in contrast to the way in which they are to apply the rules of חֵרֶם in the land proper).

The twin principles that these events teach God's people are reiterated in verses 36 and 37. First, because God himself fights for them, no city (or nation) can possibly stand against them when they are following his instructions. The point is not so much that the cities were hard to access (the verb is שָׂגַב, meaning "exalted") but rather that the claims of the spies (e.g., 1:28) that the cities in Canaan were impregnable were patently false. This was proven repeatedly, as they made their way from the city of Aroer close to the Moabite border in the south to the territory of Gilead, the southern half of which was under Sihon's rule (Num 21:24). In due course, Aroer would become the southern border of the Transjordan (Deut 3:12; Josh 13:15–16) in the territory of Reuben. The fact that "God gave everything to" them was a real-time demonstration of his covenant faithfulness, and in particular, a guarantee of both his willingness and ability to deliver the land that, according to Moses, he is giving to them today.

The second principle is that victory is predicated on obedience. When Israel does things God's way, Israel wins. It is that simple. In this case, adherence to God's strategy was expressed in a willingness to take on Sihon on the one hand, and to refrain from engaging the Ammonites to the north-west (or any other neighboring tribe) on the other.

3:1–11. Once again, Israel "turned" (1:40; 2:1, 3, 8, 27), this time heading for Bashan. Bashan was a hugely fertile highland area that extended from Hermon in the north to the Yarmuk river in the south (see 32:14; also Isa 2:13 and Amos's memorable if hardly politically correct language in 4:1). Og's territory also included northern Gilead, on the other side of the Jabbok to Sihon's territory, but didn't extend as far west (according to Deut 3:14, Maaca and Geshur lay between Og's kingdom and the Sea of Galilee, in what is now called the Golan Heights). Like Sihon, King Og attacked God's people with the full force at his disposal (see the repetition of "his whole army"). The confrontation took place at Edrei, one of Og's capital cities. God's instructions were clear: Israel was to do exactly what they did in their encounter with Sihon. God's intention in this incident was clearly to show that the conquest of Sihon was no fluke, and that taken together, these twin battles would provide a template that would guarantee a successful conquest of the land itself.

The account of the war against Og is perfectly in step with that against Sihon. In 3:3, the victory is ascribed entirely to God "handing" over the king, and led to Og's entire fighting force being wiped out. Not only was the army destroyed, but "every city" was taken, all sixty of the settlements in the region of the Argob, which was probably eastern Bashan (see also 1 Kgs 4:13). Moses then clarifies in 3:5 that these were not soft targets, but impressively defended with gates and even iron bars (as in 2:36–37). None of this could stop their advance, as they took possession of both the "cities" and the smaller, scattered settlements. The triumph of the Israelites was total. As in the previous verses, there were no survivors, and they freely seized the spoils of war (3:6–7).

In 3:8–10, Moses rehearses the extent of the territory taken from Sihon and Og, underlining the ease and success of the campaign. If the Transjordan could be occupied so easily, then why not the land? From the border of Moab at the Arnon Gorge to the slopes of Hermon (which separates Gilead from the land proper), the land was taken. The fact that the Sidonians and Amorites have different names for the mountain is a reminder that Israel's God is ultimately the God of all nations (these names can also be found in Deut 4:48; Ps 29:6; Song 4:8; Ezek 27:5; 1 Chr 5:23). In the sweeping language of 3:10, "the cities of the plateau" refers to the settlements in Sihon's kingdom, which, along with all of Gilead and Bashan, fell easily to the Israelites.

This unit concludes with another parenthetical note. Verse 11 adds that not only was Og a king, but he was also a "giant"! He is described as the last of the descendants of the Rephaim, presumably having survived the onslaughts of 2:10–11, 21. The fact that he slept in a very large iron bed (about 14 feet by 6 feet) simply highlights that he was a very large man—and yet Israel defeated him. Iron was just coming into use at this time, and the bed may have been made entirely of iron or supported by iron strips.[38] The writer adds that should any reader

[38] Alan R. Millard, "King Og's Bed and Other Ancient Ironmongery," in *Ascribe to the Lord: Biblical and Other Essays in Memory of Peter C. Craigie*, ed. Lyle Eslinger and Glen Taylor,

doubt this, at the time Deuteronomy was "published," it was still on display in the Ammonite capital.[39]

3:12–17. Moses then turns to the key moment (marked by "at that time") of the allocation of the Transjordan territories to Reuben, Gad, and half of the tribe of Manasseh. The lengthy discussions (and preconditions) of Numbers 32 concerning the validity of settling on the east of the Jordan are passed over here. In this address, the Transjordan is simply held up as a model of an ideal conquest and the annexation of these territories as part of the inheritance of Israel taken for granted. In 3:12, Reuben and Gad together were given an area roughly equivalent to the kingdom of Sihon, and in 3:13 Manasseh was granted the kingdom of Og.

At this point, another series of parenthetical historical details are included. Argob/Bashan, it seems, was formerly known as the land of the "Rephaim." Not only had Israel's cousins successfully dispossessed "giants" before, it turns out that God's people themselves had already proven that such a thing could be done through the obedience of faith! This is backed up by the actions of significant Manassites.[40]

The outstanding efforts of Manasseh's great-great grandson Jair (1 Chr 2:21–22) were crucial to this phase of the occupation (see also Num 32:41; Josh 13:30).[41] His actions anticipate the later actions of Caleb (Josh 14:13–15; 15:13–15) and provide another model for what would be required in the days to come.

Moses's words resume in 3:15, as he continues to describe the allocation of this territory. The leader's simple decision here is in contrast with the more convoluted process of drawing lots to determine Yahweh's will in Joshua. Gilead is again mentioned, this time in connection with the clan of Machir: like Jair, these people were model "occupiers" (Num 32:39–40). In 3:16–17, Moses details an extra provision of land given to the Reuben-Gad alliance: a narrow strip of the Arabah and the Jordan Valley traced from north to south (from the Sea of Galilee to the Dead Sea) in

---

JSOTSup 67 (Sheffield: JSOT Press, 1988): 481–92.

[39] This would suggest that Deuteronomy was "published" relatively soon after the Mosaic period. Block suggests the bed may have found its way to the Ammonite capital (modern Amman) during the time of Jephthah in Judg 10–12 (see *Deuteronomy*, 95).

[40] It seems likely that "Machir" refers to a clan rather than an individual (see Gen 50:23; Num 26:29). This is reflected in Num 32:40. Machir presumably had died long before.

[41] The reference to Jair, Manasseh's great-great grandson may be the same Jair mentioned in Judg 10:3–4, or another eponymous member of the clan.

the shadow of the range of mountains which included Mount Nebo (see 34:1). The inheritance of Reuben and Gad is described in much finer-grain detail in Joshua 13:15–28.

3:18–22. The conditions on which the two and a half tribes were allowed to settle in the Transjordan now come to the fore in 3:18. "At that time," Moses asserted that from this point on, this "land outside the land" should be regarded as God's promised gift to them. The condition for this settlement was that the Transjordan tribes *had to* play a full part in the conquest of the territory west of the Jordan. So their armed (rather than valiant) men had to take their place at the head of the Israelite nation. As a gracious concession, their families would be allowed to remain in their new-found home. The allusion to livestock reflects the discussions in Numbers 32:1–4, where the possibility of staying put first comes up in the context of the successful animal husbandry of Reuben and Gad, even during the wilderness years.

The criterion for assessing when Israel's mission is complete, allowing the Transjordan tribes to return home, would be their brothers being given the same rest by God that they now enjoy (see, e.g., Josh 11:23; 21:43–45). This goal is officially reached in Joshua 22, and the tribes cross back over the Jordan, despite the persistent challenge posed by the failure of God's people to take the whole land and follow God's commands to the letter.

Those issues, however, remain far in the future. Moses recounts how he called Joshua to model a right response to these events: having seen God deliver his people in real time and space when faced with Sihon and Og, he was to trust that God "will do the same to all the kingdoms you are about to enter." Echoing 1:29–30, Moses insisted that there were now two more reasons not to be afraid but to trust Yahweh. He had proven his willingness to fight for his people (as promised) beyond all reasonable doubt.

Bridge

Rather than rehearsing every detail of the victories over Sihon of Heshbon and Og of Bashan, Moses uses these events, like those of the exodus itself, to demonstrate that God is relentlessly for his people, that he is willing to fight for them, and that to experience his rescue (and ultimately his rest) all that his people need to do is trust in his provision and express that trust by obediently doing what they are told. Moses's approach is profoundly gospel-shaped. The call to all people is to trust wholeheartedly in God's rescuing provision for us in the Lord Jesus Christ and to express that justifying faith in wholehearted obedience. Sadly, as we shall see, exercising this faith often proved beyond Israel. But thanks be to God! In Jesus Christ he has not only given us the precious gift of faith, but all the resources we need for life and godliness.

6. A Shocking Prohibition (3:23–29)

> [23] "At that time I begged the Lord: [24] Lord God, you have begun to show
> your greatness and your strong hand to your servant, for what god is
> there in heaven or on earth who can perform deeds and mighty acts
> like yours? [25] Please let me cross over and see the beautiful land on the
> other side of the Jordan, that good hill country and Lebanon.
>
> [26] "But the Lord was angry with me because of you and would not listen
> to me. The Lord said to me, 'That's enough! Do not speak to me again
> about this matter. [27] Go to the top of Pisgah and look to the west, north,
> south, and east, and see it with your own eyes, for you will not cross the
> Jordan. [28] But commission Joshua and encourage and strengthen him,
> for he will cross over ahead of the people and enable them to inherit this
> land that you will see.' [29] So we stayed in the valley facing Beth-peor."

3:23–29. Although he has already alluded to his own exclusion from the land (1:37–39), it still comes as a shock when Moses returns to the subject at the end of chapter 3. After the rallying call of the Transjordan campaign, Moses's unsuccessful appeal to Yahweh to rescind his ban from Canaan is a real "downer." The rhetorical impact of hearing the nation's first and long-time leader not simply relate his punishment, but also the refusal of his plaintive appeal is extremely powerful.

Moses shares a private interaction with God in which his language was intense but his reasoning was not particularly persuasive (3:24). It is true that the sovereign God had "begun to show his greatness and strong hand" (the idea of beginning was expressed by God in 2:25, 31, and the phrase "strong hand" also occurs in 4:34; 5:15; 6:21; 7:8, 19; 9:26; 11:2; 26:8; 34:12), but actually, God had been doing exactly this since the time of the exodus (Moses uses the same language to describe the exodus event in 9:26 and 11:2) and even before. He had more than demonstrated both his uniqueness and supremacy over all the competition (specifically in his "deeds and mighty acts"). The plea of 3:25 is honest, if not compelling: Moses longed to "cross over" (one of the key phrases in chapters 1–3) to see the "beautiful" (lit., "good") land on the other side of the Jordan Valley, the "good" hill country as well as Lebanon to the north (parts of the land not visible from the plains of Moab). The phrase the "good land" is particularly powerful, as God had used the very words in speaking to Moses in Exodus 3:8, but also in Deuteronomy 1:35.[42] Yahweh's answer, however, is blunt.[43]

There is only one earlier instance of God being explicitly angry with Moses. In Exodus 4:14, after his repeated and stubborn refusal to speak to Pharaoh (on extremely dubious grounds), Moses incurred God's displeasure. This was a similar example of contesting a direct command of God, and God's response was intense. However, in this case, as in Deuteronomy 1:37, Moses attributed at least part of the responsibility for God's anger to the people ("because of you"). As we saw earlier, his point was not to shift all culpability away from himself, but simply to underline the consequences of the consistent sinfulness of the people. In this case, it led to the one to whom God had spoken "face to face" being ignored and, in the second half of 3:36, actually silenced by God. The implications of this are worrying: if God's spokesman cannot speak to God, and if the great leader cannot lead his people into the land because of their failure and his own, what hope is there for a successful overturning of their previous disobedience by a straightforward advance into the land?

God softened the impact a little by inviting Moses to climb up to the heights of the Pisgah (perhaps the ridge containing Mount Nebo, 34:1) to gaze over the full extent of the land "with his own eyes" (perhaps as in Gen 13:14–15). Looking to all four points of the compass again implies that the lands to the east (the Transjordan lands) are now considered part of God's land gift to his people.

The reminder that he was to hand over responsibility for leading the people to Joshua, and to encourage him for that extremely daunting task, has the effect of introducing a somber note to Moses's preaching. He is very close to death, and death outside the land at that. This tone is confirmed by the final line of this introductory section in 3:29: "So we stayed in the valley facing Beth-peor."

Moses's recapitulation of the journey of the past forty years is now complete, but his people have still not entered the land. Instead, they

---

[42] Although the territory today is fairly arid, the evidence is clear that in ancient times, the Jordan was a much, much larger river, and the view would have been stunningly green compared to Moab and the wilderness,

[43] The phrase "enough" may echo 1:6, 21, 26 and 2:3, where Israel had stayed "long enough" in one spot.

are camped near Beth-peor, a place synonymous with idolatry, which cannot bode well (see Num 25:1–9). This place was variously known as Baal-Peor (Deut 4:3; Hos 9:10), Beth-Peor (Deut 3:29; 4:46; 34:6; Josh 13:20) or simply Peor (Num 23:28; 25:3, 5, 18; 31:16; Josh 22:17; Ps 106:28). The overwhelming association of the location was unfaithfulness to Yahweh.

Bridge

From this point on, the death of Moses looms large over the entire book of Deuteronomy. It is easy for us to underestimate the impact of the fact that the great leader, the human architect of Israel as a nation, the mediator who brought them God's own words, is excluded from the land on the grounds that even he could not manage to obey those words. Moses himself presses home the fact that his failure is inextricably linked to that of the nation as a whole. The issue that he faces—like the nation—is ultimately one of original sin. This is why this section (and in fact chs. 1–3 as a whole) expose the fact at the outset that no leader is going to be able to solve the intractable problem of the unbelief that comes so naturally to God's people. There is a sense in which these chapters are a powerful answer to the question "Why did Jesus have to come?" The human problem is laid out before us in the attitudes, behavior, and experience of Israel. "For all have sinned and fall short of the glory of God" (Rom 3:23).

D. Conclusion to Chapters 1–3

The opening section of Deuteronomy sets the tone for what is to come. Israel's past failures have been abject, despite God's faithfulness. While there is no reason for them to fail again as they reach the borders of the land, their record (and even that of Moses) introduces an ominous note from the beginning and suggests that this may be the case. But as powerfully as sin is depicted in the opening section of Moses's address, it is also clear that God's relentless grace is at work: he has not abandoned his people; he remains true to his promises; he has fought for his people and is committed to doing so again; he is orchestrating not just the affairs of Israel but of all nations for his glory. Israel may be sinful; a whole generation including Moses may have experienced the "curse of the covenant," the painful discipline of God as they are excluded from the land; but God's covenantal commitment remains rock solid, and in that alone there is hope.

II. Moses Preaches Revelation (4:1–43)

A. Outline

4:1–4	The Priority of Listening to God
4:5–8	Introducing the Beautiful Life with God
4:9–20	Listening as God's Template for Life
4:21–31	Painful Alternatives (and a Way Back to God)
4:32–40	Life with the God Who Speaks
4:41–43	Postscript: What Listening Looks Like

B. Relation to Surrounding Context

Deuteronomy 4 is a stunning chapter, which builds on Moses's review of the nation's history in chapters 1–3 and then moves in a fresh direction to lay the foundation for the rest of the book. After sweeping through the past forty years in an attempt to provoke Israel to faithful obedience, Moses now returns to focus on the foundational moment at Horeb, when the family of Jacob became God's nation.

This chapter functions as an overture for the rest of Deuteronomy, as almost all of the key themes of the rest of the book are previewed and the basic theological shape of Moses's preaching becomes clear. The fundamental insights of Horeb are to form and control the future life of the nation. The God who appeared at Horeb is the God who speaks to Israel. This revelation is to determine the way they live, both for the sake of God's people and the reputation of God in the world. It is God's speaking that displays and guarantees his presence with them. It is their response, given shape in the "laws and the statutes," that defines the nature of the response that God requires.

As at the end of chapter 3, Moses's own failure is a dark warning about the possibility of future disobedience, which begins to seem inevitable. However, even in the gathering gloom, it is clearly foreshadowed that God will provide a way back for his people (4:29).

In the meantime, what God has revealed in the past, and is about to reveal for the future through Moses, is held out as the key to enjoying life with God in the land he has given.

C. Structure and Style

There is a clear break in the flow of Moses's address in 4:1 (which is marked by וְעַתָּה), as having traced Israel's journey back to the edge of the land, he returns to examine the events of Horeb in detail. As a result, there is an obvious change of pace, tone, and vocabulary at the beginning of the chapter.

Key words and phrases (which will dominate much of chs. 5–11) come to the fore: legal terms like "laws and statutes," calls to "listen" and "obey," injunctions to "watch carefully" and "guard yourselves," and instructions to pass on truth to succeeding generations are all prominent. The subtle (and not so subtle) irony of the first three chapters now gives way to forceful persuasion and direct command.

In addition, the expectation that God's people will endure a period outside the land before being brought home in resurgent obedience and faith is introduced and starts to exert its influence on the message of the book.

There is a sense in which Deuteronomy 1–3 operates as a Prologue, which flows smoothly into chapter 4, which acts as the Introduction proper, framing the main body of Moses's address in chapters 5–28 along with the Conclusion of chapters 29–30.

The structure of the argument of chapter 4 itself is coherent and moves from introducing the revelation to and through Moses (at both Horeb and Moab) in 4:1–4, before commending this revelation as the key to life with God in the land in 4:5–8.[44] After commending listening to/obeying this revelation as the key to life in the land (4:9–20), Moses provides a double warning of the consequences of failing to do that: his own experience and the (inevitable) future possibility of being expelled from the land (4:21–31). 4:32–40 is one of the most profound passages not only in Deuteronomy, but in the entire Bible, as Moses expounds the privilege and significance of encountering God through his words. The report of Moses's words pauses at 4:40, but the inclusion of the establishment of Cities of Refuge in 4:41–43 functions as an important postscript to his message.

1. The Priority of Listening to God (4:1–4)

> [1] "Now, Israel, listen to the statutes and ordinances I am teaching you
> to follow, so that you may live, enter, and take possession of the land
> the Lord, the God of your ancestors, is giving you. [2] You must not add
> anything to what I command you or take anything away from it, so
> that you may keep the commands of the Lord your God I am giving

---

[44] For a discussion of the phenomenon of "number-mixing" (the way in which the text switches randomly from singular to plural and vice versa and also has regular "rogue" forms even in the middle of sections that are otherwise consistent), see the introduction. I take this to be a purely stylistic variation and will not note it unless there is a strong reason to do so.

> you. 3 Your eyes have seen what the Lord did at Baal-peor, for the Lord your God destroyed every one of you who followed Baal of Peor. 4 But you who have remained faithful to the Lord your God are all alive today."

4:1. The lessons of "then" are now replaced by an urgent call in the "now" that will dominate the rest of this book. In particular, Israel is to "listen/hear/obey" (there is no distinction between these concepts in Hebrew: to hear is to listen is to obey). This word (שְׁמַע) occurs ten times in this chapter, in 5:1, and repeatedly in 5:24–28 before thundering out in the words of the Shema (6:3–4), which stands at the heart of the Old Testament and enduringly in Jewish piety. In particular, Israel is to listen to "the statutes and the ordinances" (אֶת־הַחֻקִּים וְאֶת־הַמִּשְׁפָּטִים). The word "statutes" is related to inscribing something permanently, and "ordinances" has the nuance of a legal decision forming a precedent. "Statutes and ordinances" is one of several fluid expressions used to describe the entire body of material that Moses passes on and applies to the people from here onward. We will come across other expressions, including "the commandment/s," "the torah," and "the laws". These terms are used virtually interchangeably at points. However, in some places, the particular phrase or combination chosen very deliberately reflects Moses's purpose.[45] At this point, the use of "the statutes and ordinances" is quite deliberate, serving as a headline for virtually everything that Moses has to say from chapters 4 to 30.

There are several important things to notice: (1) "The statutes and ordinances," according to 4:5, covers both what Moses has said up to this point and what is to follow in his sermon. Its use in 4:1, 5, 8, 14; 5:1, 31; 6:1; 7:11; 11:32; 12:1 and 26:16 (plus similar expressions in 4:45; 6:20; 8:11; 11:1; 26:17; 30:16) very deliberately ties together the revelation at Horeb (including the Ten Commandments in particular) with the revelation at Moab. God is still speaking, and his word carries ultimate authority. (2) Given that there are no actual rules or laws in chapter 4, but rather a large raft of persuasive or discursive material, "the statues and ordinances" seems to be an umbrella term for all that Moses is laying before them in order that they might live well in the land. The designation (like "torah," "command," etc.) embraces both detailed requirements and the broader appeals to live wholeheartedly for Yahweh. (3) As we shall see,

---

45 See the discussions in McConville and Millar, *Time and Place*, 69–89, and Millar, *Now Choose Life*, 80–88.

this careful use of language clearly identifies Moses's sermon (at least in chs. 12–26, if not 4–26) as a reapplication, development, and exposition of the Decalogue for life in the land that God was giving them.

The experience of the nation in the land from day one will be determined by their willingness to listen to and obey God's words. Moses's role is to "teach them to do" what God asks of them, which emphasizes the role he is to play at Horeb.

God's covenantal commitment, which started with their "ancestors" (lit., "fathers', i.e., Abraham, Isaac and Jacob, also 1:11) and now extended to them in rescuing them, shepherding them through the wilderness, and underwriting all attempts to take the land is clear. The required response, if they are to take possession of the land and live well with God in it, is nothing short of the wholehearted obedience that Moses fleshes out in the rest of his sermon.[46] The theme of "life," which is so much more than survival, is crucial to understanding this chapter, this book, and ultimately what the New Testament has to say about life in Christ. It is not new (see Lev 18:5), but in Deuteronomy it becomes the key category for being God's people in the land (see 30:15–20).

4:2. The dynamic nature of God's revelation, continuing at Horeb as Moses his servant passes on these "statutes and ordinances," must not be confused with mere human beings adding to what God has made known to them. The shape of obedience required is both total and comprehensive: they have no liberty to ignore, amend, or append anything to God's words (here called his "commands" [מִצְוֹת]). "Anything" here is literally "a word/matter" (דָּבָר). Only such an approach makes obedience possible. The fact that Moses and Yahweh can equally be described as giving these commands is indicative of the divine origin and human agency involved in this revelation. A similar word is found on Jesus's lips in Matthew 5:19.[47]

4:3–4 Throughout the chapter, Moses plays on the theme of seeing and hearing. Here, he appeals to the recent memory of twenty-four thousand deaths at Baal-peor (see Num 25:1–15). The name change makes this place's deadly history explicit. Men of Israel became sexually involved with women from Moab (a decision presumably driven by what they

---

[46] McConville comments that in Deuteronomy, "the gift of the land and the duty of obedience are interdependent" (*Deuteronomy*, 103).

[47] Dire warnings against altering the terms of a covenantal arrangement are found in several ANE contexts, including the Code of Hammurabi (see *ANET*^{3},178).

"saw"), which led in turn to them worshiping the gods of Moab, including the Baal of Peor. The faithful Israelites (those who "cleaved/stuck" to Yahweh"; see Deut 10:20; 11:22; 13:4; 30:20; see also Gen 2:24) who survived the wrath of Yahweh, expressed in a plague (Num 25:8–9) now need to learn from what they "saw," allowing God's words to set their agenda, as they enter a context where the temptations to flirt dangerously with foreign women and their gods will be everywhere. The way to life, as they have seen, is the way of faithfulness to the word of Yahweh "today" (and, by implication, every day).

Bridge

As Moses warms to the main theme of this sweeping sermon, the essentially gospel-shaped nature of his preaching comes into full view. The key to real life with God ("eternal life") is found in listening to his word, a theme that is powerfully developed in the gospels, as the Father says from heaven "This is my beloved Son; listen to him!" (Mark 9:7) and Jesus is declared to be the "Word made flesh" (John 1:14). The inseparability of saving faith and an overflowing response of love to God and others is also deeply enmeshed in the Deuteronomic doctrine of the land. God's grace both demands—and ultimately produces—a real-time response.

2. Introducing the Beautiful Life with God (4:5–8)

> [5] "Look, I have taught you statutes and ordinances as the Lord my God
> has commanded me, so that you may follow them in the land you are
> entering to possess. [6] Carefully follow them, for this will show your
> wisdom and understanding in the eyes of the peoples. When they hear
> about all these statutes, they will say, 'This great nation is indeed a
> wise and understanding people.' [7] For what great nation is there that
> has a god near to it as the Lord our God is to us whenever we call to
> him? [8] And what great nation has righteous statutes and ordinances
> like this entire law I set before you today?"

4:5–6 As in 1:8, 21; 2:24; 31, the call to "look" is emphatic (as is the expression "the Lord *my* God) and highlights the importance of *this moment* in the life of the nation. Moses now uses the perfect tense to underline the fact that although he will sharpen and extend God's prescriptions for a good life in his good land, they already know the basic shape of the beautiful life to which God is calling them.[48] In that sense, the "statutes and the ordinances" are not particularly new but are a fresh expression of the same vision that lay behind God's revelation from Horeb onwards.

What is new, however, is the emphasis on the impact of Israel's obedience on a watching world. The nation is to devote themselves to careful obedience, for this will lead to their wisdom (חָכְמָה) and understanding (בִּינָה) being recognized by the surrounding peoples. In fact, it will not only be acknowledged, but actually commended. The terms for Israel's acuity here (along with some other "wisdom"-like features, including the Father-Son language) have led some to suggest that Deuteronomy arose as a product of the wisdom tradition.[49] However, it seems much more likely that the foundational nature of Moses's theological preaching gave rise to a variety of later emphases, including that of "wisdom teachers."[50]

The emphatic declaration that Israel is a "great nation," coupled with the awareness of other nations, suggests that Moses is alluding to the fulfillment of the promises made to Abraham in Genesis 12:1–3.[51] The repetition of the phrase a "great nation" (Gen 12:2) and the positive impact ("blessing"?) on the nations makes this likely. This "greatness" however, should be read in the light of 7:7. It is not simply numerical but is derived from the fact that they are the covenant people of Yahweh. This statement may also recall the statements of Exodus 19:4–6, and the priestly role of Israel with respect to the nations.[52]

4:7. In the next verse, it is Moses himself who reflects on the privileges given to Israel, the beneficiaries of God's covenant commitments. Slightly surprisingly, he focuses first on God's *presence* with them rather than God's revelation to them. The rhetorical question highlights what sets

---

[48] For a contrary view, that the perfect simply refers to the act that is in progress, see Moshe Weinfeld, *Deuteronomy 1-11*, AB (New York: Doubleday, 1991), 201.

[49] Notably Moshe Weinfeld's *Deuteronomy and the Deuteronomic School.*

[50] The language is used earlier of Joseph in Gen 41:33, 39

[51] The discussion of Georg Braulik, *The Theology of Deuteronomy: Collected Essays of Georg Braulik* (Richland Hills: Bibal, 1994), 14–15 is helpful here.

[52] Christopher J. H. Wright, *Deuteronomy*, New International Biblical Commentary (Peabody: Hendrickson, 1996), 47, who sees this as part of the "missiological" agenda of the book. This is clearly hinted at, but to speak of a missiological agenda is probably a slight overstatement (see my *Now Choose Life*, 151–55). In addition, T. D. Alexander has clearly highlighted the difference between the mediatorial role of the high priest and the quite different role of the priesthood in general (upon which Israel's priestly ministry is patterned). See Alexander, *Face to Face with God*, 122–131.

Israel apart from other "great nations," for no other nation can boast in God himself being so close to them, poised to answer "whenever we call to him." The real presence of God with his people is a key Deuteronomic theme and dominates the final part of the chapter (4:32–40). It also lies at the heart of Moses's teaching on journeying regularly to worship "at the place that Yahweh shall choose" when they are in the land. But for now, he simply states this in general terms.

God's proximity is linked to hearing his people (with the implication that he will answer them) when they cry to him. This has been their lived experience from Exodus 2:23–25 onward, as God heard their cries in Egypt, rescued them from Pharaoh, and sustained them in the wilderness.

4:8. Not only is God close to his people, but he has revealed himself to them, speaking through his "*righteous* statutes and ordinances." This is the only place in the Old Testament that this form of the word (צַדִּיק) is used of anything other than a person. Righteousness is perhaps the single most important category in the book of Deuteronomy. It is because God is righteous that he can be trusted absolutely. It is because he reveals his righteousness to his people that they know how to live a righteous life in the land. Anything that does not fit with this righteousness must be dealt with instantly and decisively (as we shall see in due course).[53]

Having introduced the "statutes and ordinances" in 4:1, Moses now makes explicit that they are not simply a collection of helpful stipulations, but that they speak with one voice of the life to which God calls his people. He describes them as "this entire law" (תּוֹרָה). This word *tôrâ* is better translated as something like "instruction," and we must be careful not to import later (and particularly Western) legal ideas into the term.[54] In both Deuteronomy and the Old Testament as a whole, as we have already seen, the term embraces much more than rules and regulations: it is a shorthand for the revelation of Yahweh, which will persuade, enable, and instruct his people on living the kind of beautiful life that will make onlookers sit up and take notice. It is no accident that the term "the torah of Yahweh" (whether referring to some/all of Deuteronomy or a wider selection of pentateuchal material) is used glowingly in the Psalms (e.g., Ps 1:1–2; 19; 119). This has lead Block to helpfully characterize this torah

---

[53] Gordon McConville, *Deuteronomy*, 104, suggests that the claim that the righteous God has given righteous laws echoes (and subverts) the claims of Hammurabi (who called himself the "King of Righteousness").

[54] See, e.g., the discussion in *HALOT*.

as "the gospel according to Moses."[55] The choice that Moses "is setting before them today" is whether or not to embrace this "gospel."

Bridge

This short unit lays out God's agenda for his people in his land. They are to live in his strength, for his glory, displaying his righteousness, which in turn will embody both wisdom and understanding. In his grace, God is holding out his beautiful life to his people. The remarkable thing is that God does not simply give people his words. It is his empowering presence that offers the possibility of life. However, in the light of what Moses has already said in chapters 1–3, despite this awesome provision, God's people will never manage to live like this in the land. It will take Jesus, the true Israel, to live this beautiful life, fulfilling this law for us, and enabling his people to live out a previously unimagined righteousness (Matt 5:17, 20).[56]

3. Listening as God's Template for Life (4:9–20)

> 9 "Only be on your guard and diligently watch yourselves, so that you don't forget the things your eyes have seen and so that they don't slip from your mind as long as you live. Teach them to your children and your grandchildren.
> 10 The day you stood before the Lord your God at Horeb, the Lord said to me, 'Assemble the people before me, and I will let them hear my words, so that they may learn to fear me all the days they live on the earth and may instruct their children.'
> 11 You came near and stood at the base of the mountain, a mountain blazing with fire into the heavens and enveloped in a totally black cloud.
> 12 Then the Lord spoke to you from the fire. You kept hearing the sound of the words, but didn't see a form; there was only a voice.
> 13 He declared his covenant to you. He commanded you to follow the Ten Commandments, which he wrote on two stone tablets.
> 14 At that time the Lord commanded me to teach you statutes and ordinances for you to follow in the land you are about to cross into and possess.
>
> 15 "Diligently watch yourselves—because you did not see any form on the day the Lord spoke to you out of the fire at Horeb—
> 16 so you don't act corruptly and make an idol for yourselves in the shape of any figure: a male or female form,
> 17 or the form of any animal on the earth, any winged creature that flies in the sky,
> 18 any creature that crawls on the ground, or any fish in the waters under the earth.
> 19 When you look to

[55] Daniel I. Block, *How I Love Your Torah, O LORD! Studies in the Book of Deuteronomy* (Eugene: Wipf and Stock, 2011), xiii.; also *The Gospel According to Moses*, xiv.

[56] See the discussion in Millar, *Changed into His Likeness*, 124–148.

> the heavens and see the sun, moon, and stars—all the stars in the sky—do not be led astray to bow in worship to them and serve them. The Lord your God has provided them for all people everywhere under heaven. [20] But the Lord selected you and brought you out of Egypt's iron furnace to be a people for his inheritance, as you are today."

4:9. In 4:9, Moses turns to what is the primary spiritual danger in Deuteronomy: "forgetting."[57] They are to take every possible defensive measure to guard their "souls" (נֶפֶשׁ can function as a reflexive pronoun, but here probably has emphatic force) to ensure that the "things [their] eyes have seen" in the exodus and its aftermath on Horeb in particular, do not "slip from [their] mind" at any point during their lives. Even though all those aged twenty and over at the time of the exodus had died by this point, a significant number of Moses's listeners had seen these events as children. More important, however, is the conviction in Deuteronomy that "all Israel" has access to the words of God at Horeb through Moses's own testimony.[58] The "mind" here (lit., "heart") is the control center of the personality. To allow these memories to fade rather than shape us is to live a graceless life, marked only by ingratitude. The land, with its rich provision after the depredations of the wilderness, will pose all kinds of challenges to vibrant remembering (see, e.g., 6:10, 12; 8:1–11), so Israel must be proactive. They are to make a concerted effort to ensure that the dramatic demonstrations of God's remarkable, undeserved kindness in their own recent history are passed on to succeeding generations (a theme to which Moses returns in 6:6–9, 20–25).

4:10–14. Moses's concern, however, is to encourage God's people to remember not simply *events*, but *words* also, which is why he focuses on the specifics of their experience at Horeb. To "stand before" God in Deuteronomy is to have a significant encounter with him (see, e.g., 10:8; 18:7; 29:15), and in the case of Israel, this encounter is focused on God allowing his people to "hear his words." According to Exodus 20:18–21, this was a terrifying experience for the people, and one they were not craving! Moses does not focus on their attitude, but rather on the divine purpose in setting things up this way: the whole experience was designed to enable the people to "learn to fear me all the days they live on the

[57] 4:9–14 are one long sentence in Hebrew.

[58] In the same way, the covenantal commitments made at Horeb were "made with" those sitting before Moses at Horeb in 5:2–5.

earth" (see also Exod 20:20, and repeatedly in Deuteronomy, e.g., 5:29; 6:2, 13, 24; 8:6; 10:12, 20; 13:4; 14:23; 17:19; 28:58; 31:12–13). Tigay comments: "Reverence is man's response to God's power. It consists of both respect and awe at His grandeur and dread of His power, which serves as a deterrent to disobeying him."[59] According to God himself, the revelatory experience at Horeb is the key both to fearing God in the long-term and to the formation of their children mandated in 4:9.

The description of what the people saw in 4:11 is broadly similar to Exodus 19:16–19, but here Moses emphasizes the fire (reaching literally to "the heart of the heavens"), and the blackness of the cloud. The word "enveloped" doesn't appear in the Hebrew, which simply juxtaposes the bright fire and the deep black cloud. This prepares the way for what he is about to say about the relative importance of the words and the visual phenomena. As Lundbom insightfully points out, the language of "face to face" encounters in the Old Testament always refers to speaking and hearing rather than seeing.[60] To meet with Yahweh is to hear him speak.

The simple declaration that Yahweh "spoke to you from the fire" is foundational. The God of Deuteronomy is the speaking God, who is present with his people.[61] Moses ensures that his point cannot be missed by first spelling out that they heard words but "didn't see a form" (because of the darkness, not because God has no form), and then finally declaring "there was only a voice." It is by listening to the voice of Yahweh that this people can hope to live in the land now and in the future.

In 4:14, Moses moves on from the preeminence of the verbal revelation at Horeb to its content. Moses says that God "declared his covenant to you." This pregnant expression probably refers at least to Exodus 19:5–6 ("Now if you will carefully listen to me and keep my covenant, you will be my own possession out of all the peoples, although the whole earth is mine, and you will be my kingdom of priests and my holy nation"), probably embracing the Decalogue that follows. God's covenantal commitment to the people of Abraham obviously precedes this announcement, but at Horeb, this wonderfully elastic expression that sums up his relationship with them is expanded to accommodate their new status as a nation.

---

[59] Tigay, *Deuteronomy*, 47.

[60] Lundbom, *Deuteronomy*, 241.

[61] For a thorough discussion of this idea in Deuteronomy, see the excellent work of Ian Wilson, *Out of the Midst of the Fire: Divine Presence in Deuteronomy*, Society of Biblical Literature Dissertation Series 151 (Atlanta: Scholars Press, 1995).

The required response to God's covenantal initiative is mapped out for the first time in the Ten Commandments (lit., "Ten Words"), a phrase that surprisingly is found elsewhere only in Exodus 34:28 and Deuteronomy 10:4. The fact that these seminal instructions are both written by God himself and inscribed on stone speaks to their enduring importance in enabling the people to remember. This is part of the view of Deuteronomy that insists that "all Israel" has access to the events of Horeb—that God spoke to *them* (whether they were physically present or not)—and so they must continue to listen to him "today."

It is an enduring puzzle why the "Ten Words/Commandments" are not more prominent in the rest of the Old Testament.[62] This text points us in the direction of an answer. Rather than these ten "words" being a summary of God's desires for his people (and therefore the culmination of all Moses's words), they should rather be thought of as a road map or even a contents page that outlines the broad areas and principles to be fleshed out in the years ahead. The beautiful life God desires for his people is more sweeping and expansive than can be captured by the Ten Commandments (although the two tablets of stone do give an accurate sense of the shape of this life). Deuteronomy (and the rest of the Old Testament Scriptures) prefers expressions like "the torah of Moses" or even the "statutes and ordinances" to ensure that the scope of the beautiful life to which God calls (and for which he equips) his people is rich and broad. This is encapsulated in 4:14, as Moses links the Ten Commandments with the divine instruction given to him to teach them the "statutes and ordinances" to follow in the land—which most naturally refers to the contents of Deuteronomy.[63]

4:15–18. At the start of verse 15, Moses again calls on his audience to guard themselves (as in 4:9), but now turns to the negative implications of that command. In addition to listening to the words spoken by God, they are to make sure that they do not make any idols (which clearly cannot speak). The rationale for this is not primarily the prohibition of making images, as written on the stone tablets at Horeb, but the implications of Yahweh's chosen mode of revelation: he is a God who speaks, but whose form is not seen (and cannot be adequately represented by a crafted mute

[62] Block suggests the phrase should be translated the "ten declarations" or even "ten principles of covenant relationship." (*Deuteronomy*, 128).

[63] There is no need to exclude the book of the covenant (Exod 21–24) or the prescriptions of Leviticus from this, but it seems to have particular reference to Deuteronomy.

object). To do so would be to "act corruptly": the sense is to "ruin" or "spoil" their exclusive covenant relationship with God (see Gen 6:11–12, 17 and Deut 31:29, where Moses insists that eventually they will do this).

The list of forbidden objects to copy is broadly modelled on the order of creation in Genesis 1 in reverse: human beings (male or female) (4:17); animals, birds, insects, or fish (4:18); and then astral bodies (4:19). Literally "Lifting up your eyes to heaven" will raise the possibility, common in the ancient world, of worshiping not manmade idols but created objects (as in Job 31:26–27). The Israelites will also be tempted to gaze at them longingly, be seduced by them, bow before them, and even serve them. But neither sun, moon, nor stars ("all the stars of the sky," literally "none of the host of heaven," is added to underline this) can substitute for the God who made them.

The final phrase of 4:19 is difficult. The fact that God has "provided [or: allotted] them for [or: to] all people everywhere under heaven" (similar language is used in 32:8–9) has led some to suggest that this is approving the worship of other deities by other nations. However, this is completely at odds with the logic of the text. Moses's point is that it would be ridiculous for the people to whom the living God has spoken to worship anything else, whether made by people or created by God himself, including the stars that *he has* put in place for all to see.

The basic incongruity of Israel worshiping any other God is underlined by the dramatic statement of 4:20. Yahweh has chosen them, rescued them from the "iron furnace" (also 1 Kgs 8:51; Jer 11:4) of Egypt to make them "a people for his inheritance." The language is striking: Israel gets the land as their inheritance (4:21), but God gets his people in perpetuity (see a similar idea in Exod 34:9). This is another example of how this chapter establishes the theological framework for the whole book. The Israel-land relationship parallels that of God himself and his people. The addition of "as you are today" both alludes to God's faithfulness over the wilderness period and sharpens the decision now facing Israel on the plains of Moab.

Bridge

In order to enjoy the beautiful life with Yahweh in the land, his people have to listen to his words on the one hand and refuse to listen to false gods who cannot speak on the other. Trusting the God who rescued them and rejecting idolatry is to be the shape of a faithful life. This basic shape undergirds the whole Bible. In the New Testament, we are called to "remember Jesus Christ" (2 Tim 2:8) as the driving force of a gospel-shaped life, which also involves guarding ourselves from idols (1 John 5:21).

4. Painful Alternatives (and a Way Back to God) (4:21–31)

> [21] "The Lord was angry with me on your account. He swore that I would
> not cross the Jordan and enter the good land the Lord your God is giv-
> ing you as an inheritance. [22] I won't be crossing the Jordan because I
> am going to die in this land. But you are about to cross over and take
> possession of this good land. [23] Be careful not to forget the covenant of
> the Lord your God that he made with you, and make an idol for your-
> selves in the shape of anything he has forbidden you. [24] For the Lord
> your God is a consuming fire, a jealous God.
>
> [25] "When you have children and grandchildren and have been in the
> land a long time, and if you act corruptly, make an idol in the form
> of anything, and do what is evil in the sight of the Lord your God, an-
> gering him, [26] I call heaven and earth as witnesses against you today
> that you will quickly perish from the land you are about to cross the
> Jordan to possess. You will not live long there, but you will certainly be
> destroyed. [27] The Lord will scatter you among the peoples, and you will
> be reduced to a few survivors among the nations where the Lord your
> God will drive you. [28] There you will worship man-made gods of wood
> and stone, which cannot see, hear, eat, or smell. [29] But from there, you
> will search for the Lord your God, and you will find him when you seek
> him with all your heart and all your soul. [30] When you are in distress and
> all these things have happened to you, in the future you will return to
> the Lord your God and obey him. [31] He will not leave you, destroy you,
> or forget the covenant with your ancestors that he swore to them by
> oath, because the Lord your God is a compassionate God."

4:21–24. As in chapters 1 and 3, Moses raises the specter of his own exclusion from the land. It is hard to make any sense of this repetition outside the context of a real-time address to actual people at a specific moment in time. As in 3:23–28, the focus falls on what Moses is going to miss out on (the "good land" of both vv. 21 and 22), but there is now no mention of the transition of leadership to Joshua to enable entry to the land (see 1:37–39). The bluntness of Moses's words is clear: "I won't be crossing the Jordan because I am going to die in this land." Although the Transjordan has been subsumed in Yahweh's gift of land to Israel, for Moses, it is still Canaan that is the land "proper." The reason Moses returns to this theme becomes obvious at the end of 4:22.

Moses will not be crossing over the Jordan, but they will. They must. And as they go, Moses wants them to remember *him* (as well as the exodus and the wilderness experience) in order that they might not "forget the covenant" God has made with them. To "forget the covenant" in Deuteronomy means both undervaluing the grace God has shown in the past and ignoring the response that grace demands in the present and the future. The consequences of doing this are severe, as Moses's own story illustrates in the most graphic way possible.

The alternative to covenant faithfulness (whether the hubris is expressed in self-exaltation, like Moses in Num 20, or the fashioning of idols prompted by the practices of the Canaanites) is to experience the fact that "the Lord your God is a consuming fire, a jealous God." Similar fiery language is used in Exodus 24:17, Isaiah 33:14, and in the New Testament, in Hebrews 12:29. The jealousy of God is flagged in Exodus 20:5; 34:14; Deuteronomy 5:9; 6:15; 29:20; 32:16, 21; Joshua 24:19; Psalms 78:58; 79:5; Ezekiel 5:13; 8:3; 16:42; 39:25; and Nahum 1:2. Zephaniah 1:18 and 3:8 are probably closest to our text in speaking of the "fire of my jealousy."[64] The paucity of texts describing God in these terms adds to the shock of Moses's statement. The intense love of the covenant God can be experienced as grace or as burning wrath.

4:25–31. So far Moses has, for the most part, concentrated on the past failure and the present decisions facing Israel. In anticipation of one of the most important themes of the book—Israel's inevitable failure—his attention turns to the distant future.

4:25 looks ahead to an indeterminate point in the future (several generations on, when they have been in the land for "a long time," and presumably the novelty has worn off) and insists that the passage of time is no excuse for idolatry, nor will it mitigate Yahweh's reaction. The list of 4:16–19 is condensed to "an idol in the form of anything" (as in 4:23), and described as doing what is "evil in the sight of Yahweh." This becomes a normal way to describe idolatry (9:18; 17:2; 31:29; then Judg 3:12; 4:1; 6:1; 10:6; 1 Kgs 15:26, 34; 16:7, 19, 30, etc.), and as 4:24 made clear, it provokes God's pure anger (also 9:18 and 31:29). But how will this anger be expressed? Israel will lose the land (28:64; 30:3; also Lev 26:27–40).

---

[64] Although Block argues that this second part of the verbless clause should be translated as "he is Impassioned El" (*Deuteronomy*, 131). This is possible, but not certain.

Debate has long raged over the significance of 4:26–31. Is this a sign that Deuteronomy was written (or at least heavily edited) close to (or during, or even after) the time of the Babylonian exile?

The concept of "exile" existed long before the Babylonians perfected it in the sixth century BC, and it is hardly a huge conceptual leap from Israel's failure to take the land to the possibility that they might one day lose it! While this passage would have carried a special resonance for the Judean community after Nebuchadnezzar had conquered Jerusalem, the language of 4:26–31 does not seem to suggest (let alone require) a knowledge of the Babylonian exile: scattering among the nations and worshiping idols there (cf. Gen 15:7) are extremely general. Even the language of 4:31 does not seem tailored to the specifics of the later experience of the nation, but fits best with the perspective of a warning a long way ahead of time (as is also the case in 1 Kgs 8:46–53).[65]

Summoning "heaven and earth as witnesses" in 4:26 (also 30:19 and 31:28, and similarly 32:1), perhaps suggested by 4:19, is a typically Mosaic way of pressing home just how serious this possibility is for God's people, as they experience the curse of the covenant (although this language is not used until later in the book).[66] Similar intensive forms warn them that should they fall into idolatry, they will "quickly" (or perhaps "utterly") perish, and "certainly" (or perhaps "utterly") be destroyed. This "destruction" will entail effectively losing nationhood, as they are dispossessed, scattered all over the ancient world, and their population is massively diminished, in an undoing of the blessings of the covenant.[67] Rather than God acting against the present inhabitants of the land through them, they themselves will be "driven out" (also 28:37). Rather than choosing to worship idols, they will be consigned to serving powerless, silent gods who cannot deliver (4:28, 28:36, 64; see also Hos 4:12; Jer 2:27; 3:9; 16:13; Isa 37:19; 44:9–20).

Without explanation, at this point, Moses suddenly holds out solid hope of a reversal in Israel's fortunes even while they are "scattered" (although the grammar binds these verses tightly to 4:26–28). "From

[65] See J. G. McConville, "1 Kings VIII and the Deuteronomic Hope," *VT* 42 (1992): 67–69.

[66] This "heaven and earth" language is also found in many ancient treaty documents. See *ANET* 200–201; 205–6, 534–35; 538–41, 659–60.

[67] This bears little resemblance to the Babylonian exile. If anything, it is more like the experience of the northern kingdom at the hands of the Assyrians in 722 BC, but even then, there is little to suggest that it was written at or after that time.

there" (4:29) does not refer to a particular place, but their various locations outside the land. When they "seek" Yahweh, they will "find" him—on the condition that they "seek with all their heart and soul (נֶפֶשׁ)." This is the goal of Deuteronomic piety (see 10:12; 11:13; 13:3; 26:16; 30:2, 6, 10, and preeminently 6:5, which also adds "strength" [מְאֹד], and is also reflected in 1 Kgs 8:46–53 and Jer 29:11–14). The enduring question in the book is how Israel can manage to seek God like this.[68] This question is not answered yet, but Moses insists that they will "return" to Yahweh and "obey" him. The idea of "returning" (or "repenting")—the verb is שׁוּב—is vital not only to Deuteronomy (see the discussion of 30:1–10 below) but to the entire prophetic movement (e.g., Hos 6:1; Amos 4:6–12; Jer 3:22; 4:1), and ultimately the ministry of Jesus (e.g., Mark 1:14–15).[69]

This future moment ("when all these things/words have happened," lit. "at the end of days") will demonstrate the enduring quality of God's covenant commitment, as he refuses to "leave," "destroy," or "forget" the covenant with Abraham, Isaac, and Jacob. "He swore to them by oath" is a particularly forceful way of underlining God's faithfulness. He does all this because he is "compassionate" (also 30:3). This word depicts a deep (even maternal, derived from the same root as the Hebrew word for "womb") emotional attachment and is the root of all that happens in this section, as God is moved to remember his covenant, causing his people to seek him in repentance and faith and enabling them to obey his voice (see also Exod 34:6; Joel 2:13, also Hos 11:8–9). The point is not that the covenant with Abraham was unconditional and that made at Horeb conditional, but rather that the complexity of God's covenant relationship with his people can even handle and provide for their disobedience.

Bridge

Because of our deep-rooted sinfulness, rebellion against God (whether in the form of selfishness, idolatry, or unbelief) is inevitable. We have all provoked God's wrath and are separated from him, helpless to save ourselves. What we desperately need is for God in his kindness to bring us back to him, enabling us to "return" in repentance and faith. Praise

---

[68] This is illustrated beautifully in the parable of the Good Samaritan, where a teacher of the law identifies the requirements of the law perfectly (using Deut 6 and Lev 19), but appears oblivious to the fact that we are incapable of pulling this off on our own.

[69] See the excellent work of Mark J. Boda, *Return to Me: A Biblical Theology of Repentance*, NSBT 35, Downers Grove: IVP, 2015).

God that this is what he loves to do in and through the Lord Jesus Christ! (Luke 24:47; Acts 5:31; 11:18; Rom 2:4; 2 Tim 2:25).

5. Life with the God Who Speaks (4:32–40)

> 32 "Indeed, ask about the earlier days that preceded you, from the day
> God created mankind on the earth and from one end of the heavens to
> the other: Has anything like this great event ever happened, or has any-
> thing like it been heard of? 33 Has a people heard God's voice speaking
> from the fire as you have, and lived? 34 Or has a god attempted to go and
> take a nation as his own out of another nation, by trials, signs, wonders,
> and war, by a strong hand and an outstretched arm, by great terrors,
> as the LORD your God did for you in Egypt before your eyes? 35 You were
> shown these things so that you would know that the LORD is God; there
> is no other besides him. 36 He let you hear his voice from heaven to
> instruct you. He showed you his great fire on earth, and you heard his
> words from the fire. 37 Because he loved your ancestors, he chose their
> descendants after them and brought you out of Egypt by his presence
> and great power, 38 to drive out before you nations greater and stron-
> ger than you and to bring you in and give you their land as an inher-
> itance, as is now taking place. 39 Today, recognize and keep in mind
> that the LORD is God in heaven above and on earth below; there is no
> other. 40 Keep his statutes and commands, which I am giving you today,
> so that you and your children after you may prosper and so that you
> may live long in the land the LORD your God is giving you for all time."

4:32–34. As this part of his address reaches a climax, Moses returns to the theme of the uniqueness of Israel's experience of God (as in 4:5–8). He insists that the events of Horeb are completely unprecedented. Nothing like this has ever happened anytime (from the day of creation until now) or anywhere (probably from one end of the cosmos to the other [Ps 19:6], although the phrase "the end of heaven" can simply refer to the farthest imaginable point on earth [Deut 30:4; Isa 13:5; Neh 1:9]. In fact, this outstrips even the most outlandish rumor (nothing like this has even been "heard of"). At the core of this peerless event (4:33) is the fact that God has revealed himself to his people, speaking "from the fire," and that rather than overwhelming them or destroying them, this has introduced them to real life.[70] To make this revelation possible (and to undergird it), Yahweh

[70] Given the emphasis in Deuteronomy on "life," it is probable that this isn't simply a matter of not dying (see 5:24–27, and also Exod 3:6; 24:10–11; 33:20–23; Judg 6:22–23; 13:22; Isa 6:5) but is an allusion to the "life" Israel is called to (see, e.g., Deut 30:15–20).

had also gone to unparalleled lengths to "take a nation as his own out of another," using a string of means: trials that audaciously "tested" Egypt, signs and wonders, the usual description of the events surrounding the exodus itself, war, the "battle" at the Sea of Reeds in Exodus 14:21–25, terrors (cf. Deut 26:8; 34:12), and, in a phrase repeated in Deuteronomy 5:15 and 26:8 to sum up God's actions on their behalf, "a strong hand and an outstretched arm.". "Attempted" does not imply the possibility that God's mission could have failed, but rather that he is utterly superior to all other gods—for none of these non-gods would even have *attempted* such a thing, let alone been able to pull it off.

4:35–38. All of this, according to 4:35, was carefully arranged "so that you would know that the Lord is God," that he is the supreme lord of all, and there is "no other besides him," a phrase that is repeated in verse 39 and again in 32:39. He is peerless. Israel's attitude to God in the land must be based on this (also 4:10).

There has been much discussion of whether statements like this in Deuteronomy are a clear articulation of full-blown monotheism or are simply asserting the supremacy of Yahweh (over other gods, even though they are regarded as "non-gods"). In the last analysis, it is almost impossible to tell when monotheism actually crystallized in the minds and theology of Israel, but at the very least, Deuteronomy is an important step in that process, with its dramatic insistence on the radical differentness of Israel's God.

This is confirmed by Moses's explanation that God spoke to them from the place of all power and authority ("heaven") to "instruct [or better: discipline] them." The substance of this instruction was, in the first place, God's self-revelation: he introduced himself to them as the great covenant lord of all, who nonetheless spoke directly to them. This tension is captured slightly differently in Exodus (see 19:11, 18, 20; 20:19), where God both comes down to Horeb and speaks from heaven, but the theological concern to capture God's transcendence and immanence is consistent.

He is the God of Abraham, Isaac, and Jacob, and because of his loving commitment to them (4:37), he chose them (the first explicit mention of election in Deuteronomy), came personally to their aid, rescuing them "by his presence and great power," and now is in the process of driving out the Canaanites, handing their land over to Israel as a gift that doesn't stop giving (4:38). This collocation of love and choice will be expanded on in 7:6–13. Yahweh's personal and intimate involvement in all of this (rather than simply acting through emissaries, as in, e.g., Num 20:16) is striking. "As is now taking place" captures the sense that what has just happened in the Transjordan is the template for what they can expect in the land of Canaan itself.

This self-revelation demands a very specific response. Moses calls on the people to recognize and reflect on ("keep in mind," lit., "take to your heart") both Yahweh's transcendent sovereignty (that he is "God in heaven above") and that he is always with them on earth, speaking to them out of the midst of the fire (4:36). In other words, he is simultaneously ruling over them and with them. They owe him complete allegiance, which is to be expressed, according to 4:40, in keeping his "statutes and [this time] commands." The double reference to "today" underscores the urgency of responding faithfully to God right now and always. This is the key to both their quality of life in the land and the duration of that life (see also 5:29; 6:3, 18; 12:25, 28; 22:7; and also Jer 7:23). God's commitment to them is not in doubt—the land is a gift "for all time"—the question remains, can Israel do what she is told? At this point, Moses appears to pause.

Bridge

The God of the Bible is a God who is the sovereign ruler of the cosmos and yet stops at nothing to make himself present with us for our good. His transcendence and immanence lay the groundwork for the ultimate self-revelation of God in the incarnation of the Lord Jesus Christ, God made flesh. This chapter prepares us for what the writer to the Hebrews explains like this: "Long ago God spoke to our ancestors by the prophets at different times and in different ways. In these last days, he has spoken to us by his Son. God has appointed him heir of all things and made the universe through him. The Son is the radiance of God's glory and the exact expression of his nature, sustaining all things by his powerful word." (Heb 1:1–3) Listening to what God says and doing it remains the key to life.

6. Postscript: What Listening Looks Like (4:41–43)

> [41] Then Moses set apart three cities across the Jordan to the east. [42] Someone could flee there who committed manslaughter, killing his neighbor accidentally without previously hating him. He could flee to one of these cities and stay alive: [43] Bezer in the wilderness on the plateau land, belonging to the Reubenites; Ramoth in Gilead, belonging to the Gadites; or Golan in Bashan, belonging to the Manassites.

4:41–43. Given the careful arrangement and rhetorical flow of the chapter, it seems slightly jarring that the report of Moses's sermon (in direct speech) is interrupted by the details of some Transjordanian housekeeping. However, given the placement of 4:44–49 and the fact that Moses clearly *resumes* speaking in 5:1, the simplest explanation is that the aged leader *did* pause at this point to name these cities, which were not recorded *verbatim* in the record of the sermon proper. The details were included in the text at this point because theologically they fit well with the flow of thought and rhetorically they signal a break in the discourse.[71]

Before moving on to his magisterial exposition of the beautiful life in the land, which will occupy chapters 5–28, there is one loose end to be tied up in the Transjordan. If the lands granted to Reuben, Gad, and half of Manasseh are to be regarded as part of God's gift to Israel and to function in exactly the same way as the land, then Cities of Refuge need to be set aside.[72] This had been made clear in Numbers 35:9–34 and is now seamlessly absorbed into Moses's address (he will return to the subject in 19:1–13).

The legislation here in typical "Deuteronomy" style is highly abbreviated, explaining the basic principle behind the law. No mention is made of the key theological rationale of Numbers 35:34, which demands that the land be kept ritually clean, as Yahweh himself lives there. This is probably because in this address, the dominant categories are obedience/disobedience, remembering/forgetting, and promoting God's reputation/dragging it through the mud rather than cleanness/uncleanness (although, as we shall see in chs. 12–26, these categories are not completely absent).

The cities allocated to the Levites to operate for each tribe are Bezer (Reuben), Ramoth (Gad) and Golan (Manasseh), and they each recur in Joshua 20:8 (cf. 21:27, 38), in the complete list of such cities provided on both sides of the Jordan.[73] On the one hand, this list draws the historical retrospect and overture of chapters 1–4 to a fitting close,

---

[71] This is based on the argument, set out in the introduction, that the pattern of breaks in Moses's speeches is neither the result of a cumulative editorial processes nor the key to interpreting the book as a whole. The breaks should be taken rather as a consequence of the book's oral origins.

[72] It is important that we do not import our contemporary notion of cities as massive urban centers. The word עִיר basically describes a walled town.

[73] Bezer is mentioned on the Mesha Stele as having been retaken by the Moabites (see *ANET* 320–21). The precise locations of all these cities are uncertain.

with the optimism generated by the conquest of these lands providing strong motivation for the people to press on. But on the other, even the necessity of this provision may also be a subtle reminder that we live in a broken world, and even in this "beautiful land," all will not always be as it should be.

Bridge

These three cities are a clear statement both of the sinfulness of humanity and of God's gracious provision for sinful people to find safety, even in the middle of a broken world. This God truly is a refuge and provides us access to this refuge in the Lord Jesus.

D. Conclusion to 4:1–43

Chapter 4 is a stunning chapter that introduces the key theological themes that will dominate the rest of the book: the nature of the sovereign God who speaks; the importance and delight of living the beautiful life with God in the land; the loving election of God of a people who will eventually blow it; the toxicity of idolatry and the reality of the "wrath of the covenant"; the determination of God in his grace to provide a way back for his people; God's intention to display his glory to the nations through his people. I do not think there is a richer chapter anywhere in the Scriptures nor one that presents so clearly the gospel-shape of the Old Testament.

III. Moses Preaches Covenant (4:44–11:32)

A. Outline

4:44–49	The Headline Statement
5:1–33	Horeb: The Basic Requirements of the Covenant
6:1–25	Horeb Applied: Covenantal Listening
7:1–26	Horeb Applied: Covenantal Faithfulness
8:1–20	Learning from the Wilderness: Covenantal Dependence
9:1–10:11	Learning from the Golden Calf: Covenantal Humility
10:12–11:7	What God Requires
11:8–32	Blessing or Curse?

B. Relation to Surrounding Context

After the historical retrospect of chapters 1–3 flows into the "theological overture" of Deuteronomy 4, there is a clear break in Moses's address to the nation. The summary statement of 4:40 is followed by the rehearsal of the provision for cities of refuge in the Transjordan, which effectively concludes the introductory section of the book. The transitional section in 4:44–49 then functions as a recapitulation of the context and the salient points of the first phase of Moses's teaching before the leader starts to speak once again.

It would, however, be a mistake to overemphasize the disconnect between chapter 4 and what follows. While it is true that there is a break (both literary and "real-time"), the theological and rhetorical continuity is significant. Having established that the fact and manner of God's self-revelation at Horeb (through the word, rather than the image) is to shape the life of the nation, Moses now moves on to explain how the content of that revelation should also have a formative effect on God's people.

In chapter 4 (see vv. 13, 23, 31), the language of covenant was introduced to describe the relationship that God has instigated and maintained with his people.[74] In the long section running through to chapter 11, however, covenant becomes the controlling theological concept.

C. Structure and Style

This section of the book is dominated by the careful repetition of the Ten Commandments in full (with only slight "Deuteronomic" tweaks). Understanding why Moses does this, and why it occupies such a prominent position in the book, is crucial for appreciating the theological flow of both the book and this section in particular.

In the ancient world, it was common for significant agreements between two parties (whether formal diplomatic treaties or a whole range of other broadly covenantal arrangements) to be guaranteed by written terms. The most important of these documents were inscribed on stone and were usually deposited in the most sacred place available. In the context of the covenantal relationship between Yahweh and Israel, the

---

[74] Clearly the *concept* of covenant is present from the beginning of the book, but the language of covenant is only introduced in ch. 4.

terms of their relationship were mapped out in the "Ten Words" stipulated in Exodus 20.

Unusually (and probably uniquely), these Ten Words were not so much a *summary* of the requirements that this covenant relationship laid on Israel as an introduction (more like a table of contents, roadmap, or even a mission statement). No sooner had these been stones been engraved than Moses began to expound and expand on them (see Exod 21–23). This dynamic understanding of covenant obligations undergirds the logic and approach of the central core of the book of Deuteronomy.

The rehearsal of the Decalogue in chapter 5 is the launching pad for the exposition of Israel's covenantal responsibilities in the exhortations of chapters 6–11. But it is more than that. As we shall see, it is also the template for the development of the "statutes and ordinances" (including the motivational and exhortatory material) in chapters 12–26. One could argue that the movement begun in chapter 5 doesn't actually find its conclusion until chapter 30.[75]

The overall structure of chapters 5–11, as reflected in the outline, is relatively straightforward.[76] The rehearsal of the events of Horeb, and in particular the Ten Words, gives way to an extended discussion of the covenantal implications of those events that occupies all of chapters 6 and 7. At this point, the focus shifts to the covenantal implications of the wilderness period (ch. 8), and then, returning to Horeb, homes in on the golden calf rebellion. The broad similarity to the approach of chapters 1–3 is obvious, but here the goal has shifted decisively to future behavior, as is confirmed by the double conclusion of 10:12–22 and 11:1–25.

The blessing at Ebal and Gerizim in 11:26–32 both provides a ritual reinforcement of the message of the chapters and brackets the collection of laws to follow with a powerful symbolic act to be carried out on entering the land.

If chapters 1–3 are slightly sardonic and chapter 4 intensely theological, chapters 5–11 are highly rhetorical. Like any good preacher, Moses

---

[75] This is why I think it is ultimately unhelpful in Deuteronomy to attempt to be too dogmatic about the structure of the speeches or even the book as a whole. The oral character of the book does seem to reflect a fluid exposition of covenantal themes, and the overall coherence balances the structural markers of the various phases of the text.

[76] See Jason DeRouchie, *A Call to Covenant Love: Text Grammar and Literary Structure in Deuteronomy 5-11* (Piscataway: Gorgias, 2007).

knows and understands the power of repetition, slight variation, developing a theme and driving it home with powerful illustration and finally application. That's why these chapters are among the most compelling in the Old Testament, peppered with memorable one-liners, constantly reinforcing the shape of the covenant life and enabling us to hear the voice of God through the theologically rich cadences of arguably the greatest theological mind to lead the nation of Israel.

1. The Headline Statement (4:44–49)

> [44] This is the law Moses gave the Israelites. [45] These are the decrees, statutes, and ordinances Moses proclaimed to them after they came out of Egypt, [46] across the Jordan in the valley facing Beth-peor in the land of King Sihon of the Amorites. He lived in Heshbon, and Moses and the Israelites defeated him after they came out of Egypt. [47] They took possession of his land and the land of Og king of Bashan, the two Amorite kings who were across the Jordan to the east, [48] from Aroer on the rim of the Arnon Valley as far as Mount Sion (that is, Hermon) [49] and all the Arabah on the east side of the Jordan as far as the Dead Sea below the slopes of Pisgah.

4:44–49. Verse 44 functions as a "banner headline" for at least all of chapters 5–11, and perhaps for Moses's words all the way to the end of chapter 30.

As in 1:5 and 4:8, the entire content of Moses's sermon is designated as "the law [Heb. *tôrâ*] Moses gave the Israelites" (see also 17:11, 18, 19; 27:3, 8, 26; 28:58, 61; 29:21, 29; 30:10; 31:9, 11, 12, 24, 26; 32:46; 33:4, 10). Clearly, the word *tôrâ* here has a much broader reference than the English word "law." The "instruction" (probably the most literal translation of the word) here encompasses what God has done, what he asks of his people, and the reasons why doing what he says makes sense. It really is the Old Testament equivalent of the word "gospel" in the New. This is the foundation of the overwhelmingly positive attitude to the *torah of Yahweh* in, e.g., Psalm 1:2 ("his delight is in the Lord's instruction), as well as Psalms 19 and 119. Although a variety of terms for Moses's teaching are used interchangeably, each retains a particular nuance (we have already seen this with "statutes and ordinances"). In the case of torah, the emphasis is on the ultimate goal and benefits of "hearing" (as in embracing) all the words of God in order to enjoy the beautiful life he holds out to his people in the land.

This becomes clearer in verse 45, where it is added that this torah includes "decrees [lit., testimonies], statutes, and ordinances" (הָעֵדֹת וְהַחֻקִּים וְהַמִּשְׁפָּטִים). "Testimonies" (a plural form that occurs only here and in 6:17, 20 in the book) may be an allusion to Exodus 25:16, where the two stone tablets bearing the Ten Words are called "the tablets of the testimony" (singular; see also Exod 25:21; 31:18; 32:15; 34:29; and similarly the phrase "the ark of the testimony" in Exod 25:22; 26:33; 30:6, 26; 31:7; 39:35; 40:3, 5, 21; Num 4:5; 7:89). The fact that "testimonies" is followed immediately by the phrase "statutes and ordinances," which, as we have seen, is the shorthand for the specifically Deuteronomic application and expansion of the Ten Words to life in the land, is further evidence that Moses sees the Horeb revelation and his words at Moab as intrinsically linked. His new and fuller expression of the shape of covenant life is to be understood as a careful application of the seminal revelation at Horeb.[77]

The rest of 4:44–49 functions in a way similar to 1:1–8, but although some of the details are shared, the particular focus is on recapitulating the key insights of chapters 1–3. It is often argued that the "double introduction" of 1:1–8 and 4:44–49 is evidence of a complex literary history for Deuteronomy, with competing "voices" attempting to enlist Moses in their various political and theological causes. This is, ultimately, highly speculative and does not take proper account of the thematic unity of the address as a whole.[78] It is much more likely that these verses are included by the "publisher" of Deuteronomy as a "recap" ("Previously, in Moses's great address ... !") to enable the reader to recover the rhetorical flow of chapters 1–3, which was slightly arrested by both the foundational theological meditation of chapter 4 and the break in Moses's delivery.[79]

---

[77] This process of reapplication has already happened in the Book of Covenant of Exod 21–23.

[78] These issues are helpfully addressed by, e.g., Lundbom, who argues that 1:1–5 and 4:44–49 form an inclusion for the introduction to the book in chapters 1–4: "These verses—as most everyone recognises—essentially repeat the content of 1:1–5, making an inclusion for Deuteronomy's Prologue." (*Deuteronomy*, 260), and, in my view more compellingly, by Tigay, who sees these verses as a "recapitulation ... necessary because the Teaching was delayed by the long digression of 1:6–4:44" (*Deuteronomy*, 59).

[79] Block presents a fascinating and generally persuasive account of how the book of Deuteronomy itself gives us significant clues to its own genesis. See "Recovering the Voice of Moses," 43.

Verse 46 reminds the Israelites that they are still perilously close to Beth-peor (see 3:29), but that a repeat of their failure is not inevitable: they are standing on the land which was occupied through obedience. The geographical details summarize what has already been said (2:36; 3:8–9, 17). The name "Sion," referring to Hermon, occurs only here in the Bible. As in 1:5, the perspective of these editorial notes is west of the Jordan in the land itself.

Bridge

The positive intention of Moses's teaching in Deuteronomy really is "gospel-shaped." Rooted in God's initiative-taking grace, the double motives of gratitude and future joy that flow from living in his presence are the driving force for all Moses's preaching. As he has already anticipated, the fatal flaw is found not in his preaching, but in us as human beings. However, in the light of what Christ has done, is doing, and will do (not least in pouring out his Spirit into us, changing us and instigating a total change process), this life is not simply within our reach now, but in Christ, it has already begun.

2. The Basic Requirements of the Covenant (5:1–33)

> [1] Moses summoned all Israel and said to them, "Israel, listen to the statutes and ordinances I am proclaiming as you hear them today. Learn and follow them carefully. [2] The LORD our God made a covenant with us at Horeb. [3] He did not make this covenant with our ancestors, but with all of us who are alive here today. [4] The LORD spoke to you face to face from the fire on the mountain. [5] At that time I was standing between the LORD and you to report the word of the LORD to you, because you were afraid of the fire and did not go up the mountain. And he said:
>
> [6] 'I am the LORD your God, who brought you out of the land of Egypt, out of the place of slavery.
>
> [7] 'Do not have other gods besides me.
>
> [8] 'Do not make an idol for yourself in the shape of anything in the heavens above or on the earth below or in the waters under the earth. [9] Do not bow in worship to them, and do not serve them, because I, the LORD your God, am a jealous God, bringing the consequences of the fathers' iniquity on the children to the third and fourth generations of those who hate me, [10] but showing faithful love to a thousand generations of those who love me and keep my commands.

11 'Do not misuse the name of the LORD your God, because the LORD will
not leave anyone unpunished who misuses his name.

12 'Be careful to remember the Sabbath day, to keep it holy as the LORD
your God has commanded you. 13 You are to labor six days and do all
your work, 14 but the seventh day is a Sabbath to the LORD your God.
Do not do any work—you, your son or daughter, your male or female
slave, your ox or donkey, any of your livestock, or the resident alien
who lives within your city gates, so that your male and female slaves
may rest as you do.

15 'Remember that you were a slave in the land of Egypt, and the LORD
your God brought you out of there with a strong hand and an outstretched arm. That is why the LORD your God has commanded you to
keep the Sabbath day.

16 'Honor your father and your mother, as the LORD your God has commanded you, so that you may live long and so that you may prosper in
the land the LORD your God is giving you.

17 'Do not murder.

18 'Do not commit adultery.

19 'Do not steal.

20 'Do not give dishonest testimony against your neighbor.

21 'Do not covet your neighbor's wife or desire your neighbor's house,
his field, his male or female slave, his ox or donkey, or anything that
belongs to your neighbor.'

22 "The LORD spoke these commands in a loud voice to your entire assembly from the fire, cloud, and total darkness on the mountain; he added
nothing more. He wrote them on two stone tablets and gave them to
me. 23 All of you approached me with your tribal leaders and elders
when you heard the voice from the darkness and while the mountain
was blazing with fire. 24 You said, 'Look, the LORD our God has shown us
his glory and greatness, and we have heard his voice from the fire. Today we have seen that God speaks with a person, yet he still lives. 25 But
now, why should we die? This great fire will consume us and we will die
if we hear the voice of the LORD our God any longer. 26 For who out of all
humanity has heard the voice of the living God speaking from the fire,
as we have, and lived? 27 Go near and listen to everything the LORD our
God says. Then you can tell us everything the LORD our God tells you;
we will listen and obey.'

28 "The LORD heard your words when you spoke to me. He said to me, 'I
have heard the words that these people have spoken to you. Everything
they have said is right. 29 If only they had such a heart to fear me and
keep all my commands always, so that they and their children would

> prosper forever. [30] Go and tell them: Return to your tents. [31] But you stand here with me, and I will tell you every command—the statutes and ordinances—you are to teach them, so that they may follow them in the land I am giving them to possess.'
>
> [32] "Be careful to do as the LORD your God has commanded you; you are not to turn aside to the right or the left. [33] Follow the whole instruction the LORD your God has commanded you, so that you may live, prosper, and have a long life in the land you will possess."

5:1–5. As he will do again in 29:2 (after a similar break in the flow of his address), Moses reconvenes the people and repeats the command of 4:1: "Israel, listen to the statutes and ordinances." The identity of these rules will gradually become clear through the rest of the book. At this point in his address, the emphasis is firmly on the act of listening. The opening command (lit., "Hear, O Israel") recurs in 6:4 and 9:1 in this section and marks the major rhetorical shifts in the discourse. The language of the rest of verse 1 (lit., "that I am speaking in your ears today") presses home the importance of paying close attention in this very moment, in order that they might *learn* (a form of the same verb is used in 4:1 of Moses's teaching, but now the focus shifts to the people's responsibility to learn), and take great care in carrying them out.[80]

The statement of 5:2 is deceptively simple. The understanding of God's covenant that was developed and presented in chapter 4 is now made explicit. As in Exodus 19:5–6 and 34:10, 27, 28, Moses states that God made a covenant with the infant nation (either side of the golden calf incident) that both guaranteed their status (as God's special possession, a "kingdom of priests" and a "holy nation") and his future support in the conquest of the land he had promised to give them. The language of Exodus 34 establishes that this arrangement is genuinely new (34:10), but also is intricately linked with what has gone before (delivering on the land promise first made to Abraham, and then reiterated to Isaac and Jacob).

The phrase is literally to "cut" a covenant, which may well come from the practice of sealing an agreement like this by cutting an animal in two

---

[80] It is worth mentioning that the first command "Hear" is in the singular, but those that follow are in the plural. As discussed in the introduction, this is a particular feature of Deuteronomy, which is best understood as a stylistic device to emphasize both corporate and individual responsibility.

(see Gen 15:17–21, see also Jer 34:18–20), but was also used where other rituals were used to ratify the deal (e.g., Exod 24:1–8).

The striking element in Moses's exposition here is the assertion that this covenant was not made "with our ancestors, but with all of us [now including Moses himself] who are alive today." Given the covenantal context, and the fact that in Deuteronomy "ancestors" ("fathers") is usually a shorthand for Abraham, Isaac, and Jacob, this may be intended to tie the Horeb revelation to the covenantal commitments in Genesis. The main focus in the subsequent verses, however, is very firmly on the Horeb generation.

The problem with 5:3 is that, quite clearly, the covenant *was* made with the previous generation, all of whom had passed away outside the land (Num 14:28–29).[81] However, the thrust of Moses's claim is that it was not *only* made with them. God's commitment has an enduring, constantly fresh force, which is why the leader can insist that this covenant is made with *all* God's people *today*. In due course, this will be extended to the entire exodus experience (11:2–7).[82]

As discussed in the introduction, this dynamic view of covenant shows that the understanding of God's commitment to his people transcends any particular example of a treaty or grant arrangement in the ancient world. While clearly drawing on the patterns of international diplomacy, this theological conception pushes far beyond any ancient parallel. In particular, the perpetual now-ness of the covenant is grounded in the fact that God continues to speak to his people through his words, making his presence obvious, as he calls them *today* to continue to choose him (see 4:9–14).

This basic perspective is fleshed out in 5:4, where Moses insists that Yahweh "spoke to *you* [switching back to the second person] face to face" out of the fire on Mount Horeb. The actual phrase used here is unique (see Gen 32:30 [also 33:10]; Exod 33:11; Deut 34:10, 22; Judg 6:22; Ezek 20:35). The other examples of this kind of language are

---

[81] Given the fact that roughly forty years had passed, some of the teenagers who were not old enough for military service in Numbers (and therefore were not subject to the exclusion order) would now be approaching 60 years of age. Although they may have been "at Horeb" with their families, they were not formally part of the "assembly of Israel" then, and so in that sense, the covenant was not made with them.

[82] The thought is similar to Lam 3:22–24, where in the immediate aftermath of the exile, it is asserted that God's (covenant) mercies remain "new every morning."

slightly ambiguous: in the case of Jacob and Gideon, it is not entirely clear whether the encounter with the heavenly figure was a theophany; in the Ezekiel text, the promise emphasizes that Judah will have her "day before the Judge," which may or may not entail an intimate encounter with Yahweh. Even with Moses himself, who is said twice to have met with God "face to face" like an old friend, the narrative of Exodus 33:18–23, where he is denied the opportunity to see God's unalloyed glory (having to make do with a glimpse of his back!), suggests that the "face to face" language does not entail seeing God "as he is" (see also John 1:18; 1 John 4:12). Rather the language points to a real encounter with God in which he communicates a pressing message to his people (as in Num 12:8).

Deuteronomy 5:5 supports this interpretation, as the people's "face to face" encounter with God involves the words of Yahweh being reported by Moses. This is the key to the enduring nature of this encounter: this "face to face" conversation with God is ongoing, because God's words are being repeated to the people even as Moses speaks (and would continue to be repeated as they are written down and read to subsequent generations). As we have seen already, "at that time" is a marker of significant moments of decision in Deuteronomy (1:9, 16, 18; 2:34; 3:4, 8, 12, 21, 23; 4:14; and see also 9:20; 10:1, 8; 26:3).

Surprisingly, the reason for this revelation being mediated is that Israel was "afraid of the fire," refusing to draw any closer to God (see Exod 20:18–21). The people's understanding of what was going on, and their trust in God's covenantal commitment to them seems to have be somewhat shaky from the very beginning.

5:6–21. Moses then repeats (or almost repeats!) the words themselves that Yahweh spoke at Horeb. Before we come to the exegesis of the individual instructions themselves, it is important to address four important issues in the interpretation of the Ten Commandments (or more accurately, the Ten Words) as a whole, particularly in their Deuteronomic version.

The Ten Words in their covenantal context

These "words" are inscribed on two stone tablets and deposited in the ark of the "testimony." In some Hittite treaties from the second millennium before Christ, each party to a covenantal arrangement would be provided with a stone copy of their obligations, which would be deposited in their respective temples. This kind of practice is almost certainly in the background here.[83] This leads Block to view the Ten Words as the "Ten Principles of Covenant Relationship," which function akin to a "Bill of Rights" (rather than an ancient law code like that of Hammurabi).[84] Although this idea clearly has merit, the lack of reference to these commandments as a "collection" in the rest of the Old Testament suggests that the idea of a "Bill of Rights" is something of an overstatement. However, Block is surely right to insist on an essentially covenantal understanding of the Ten Words. This is reflected in the fact that they are addressed to the heads of family and couched as simple commands rather than as strictly legal stipulations. It may be more accurate to see them simply as the first rudimentary expression of the terms of Yahweh's covenant with Israel, which was then expanded on by subsequent expositions of what the Lord requires (in, e.g., the book of the covenant, the holiness teaching of Leviticus, and the torah of Deuteronomy itself, all of which are fundamentally covenantal, rather than legal).[85]

The numbering of the Ten Words

At least since the time of the translation of the Septuagint, there has been divergence on how the Ten Words should be broken down/counted, given that there are more than ten imperatives in the "collection." The majority of Jewish writers take the first word to be "I am Yahweh your God". Most Christian interpreters take this to be the introduction to the Ten Words, and start counting after that. As well as differences over the opening statement, there are also various views on whether the prohibitions of worshiping other gods and making images be taken together as part of the same "Word" (the Catholic/Lutheran view) or are they the first and second commandments (the Reformed view, which is

[83] See Meredith G. Kline, "The Two Tables of the Covenant," *Westminster Theological Journal* 22 (1960): 133–46. The parallel, however is not exact, given that *both tablets of stone* are deposited in the ark, rather than in separate locations.

[84] Daniel I. Block, "Reading the Decalogue from Left to Right: The Ten Principles of Covenant Relationship in the Hebrew Bible." In *How I Love Your Torah*, 21–60. Block (27–28) also suggests that the nuance of "testimony/ies" in the phrase "ark of the testimony" is actually "covenant obligation(s)."

[85] So Tigay, *Deuteronomy*, 63: "they introduce the Israelites to the areas governed by God's legislation and provide an apt introduction to the detailed laws (*huqqim* and *mishpatim*) that Moses will subsequently communicate to them."

also reflected in the Septuagint)? The other main point of contention concerns the command against coveting, which has crystallized into a Reformed/Orthodox view (which sees one prohibition of coveting) and a Catholic/Lutheran view (which sees two). To complicate matters further, Old Testament scholars from a wide variety of traditions can be found on all sides of the debate![86]

The issues here are complex, and it seems that from ancient times, interpreters have struggled to fit the text into a neat pattern of ten (as demanded by Deut 4:13; 10:4). The syntax of the passage is not straightforward and so does not decisively settle the question. That the version of the Decalogue in Deuteronomy is slightly different to that in Exodus is pertinent, as we shall see, but can be interpreted in various ways.[87] In my view, as will be set out in what follows, it is more likely that the opening statement is not to be counted as the "First Word," that the prohibition of worshiping other gods should be taken as a separate issue from making idols, and that despite some syntactical evidence pointing the other way, the commands not to covet or crave what is not yours should be taken together as the "Tenth Word." In other words, the Reformed/Orthodox numbering is probably to be preferred.

The two versions of the Ten Words

The very fact that the "Ten Words" are repeated is slightly puzzling. Given that Moses can refer to them (e.g., 4:13) in this way suggests they were well known and presumably did not *need* to be included in the transcript of his speech for the purposes of information. There must therefore be a rhetorical/theological purpose for their inclusion.

Then there is the fact that the version of Deuteronomy 5 is very similar *but not identical* to that of Exodus 20. Is this deliberate? What does this say about the status or nature of the Decalogue?

I would suggest that reading the Ten Commandments as a primary (perhaps even rudimentary?) expression of the implications and requirements of the newly clarified covenant relationship with Yahweh makes

---

[86] For a thorough discussion of the issues involved see, e.g., Block, "Reading the Decalogue," Appendix A, 56–60.

[87] For one interpretation of the difference, see Block in "'You Shall Not Covet Your Neighbor's Wife': A Study in Deuteronomic Domestic Ideology," in *The Gospel According to Moses*, 137–73.

most sense of the text both in Exodus and Deuteronomy and also explains the absence of the Ten Words in the rest of the Scriptures.

As I have suggested, Block's characterization of the "Ten Words" as a "Bill of Rights" is generally helpful but perhaps claims a little too much for the short collection. Even the text of Exodus seems to view the "Ten Words" as a template or starting point for the definition and description of the "beautiful life" to which God calls his covenant people in the land.[88] The fact that the Ten Words are immediately followed by a much longer series of prescriptions in the book of the covenant already suggests that the Decalogue is the *terminus a quo* for Israel's "legal tradition" (in a loose sense) rather than the quintessential expression of an ideal, to which they would make constant reference. In this, the Ten Words are more like the first edition of, say, Calvin's *Institutes*: extremely interesting in understanding the foundations and development of the larger work, but also dated, and not generally referred to once the definitive version is completed.

As Israel's "constitutional (covenantal) arrangements and requirements" are expanded from the Ten Words, through the book of the covenant, and the Holiness Code of Leviticus, to their fullest expression in the torah of Deuteronomy (which can be construed as either all of Moses's address(es) or simply the "statutes and ordinances" of chs. 12–26), at each stage, the latest version eclipses the previous one.

What then is the significance of the Decalogue? It remains foundational, as the first stage in the process of God's revelation to his covenantal people of how they should live. The stone tablets (in the ark) remind them of their covenantal responsibilities, although the particular expression of those responsibilities has expanded far beyond the original "sketch" of the Ten Words.

Why then would Moses repeat the Ten Words at this point? He is in the process of expounding the shape of covenantal faithfulness in the land which they are about to enter. For Moses, entry into the land will require a whole new expression of covenant faithfulness, which will be worked out in the face of a raft of previously unencountered challenges, such as living in houses they did not build (6:11) or coping with the apparatus of idolatry in their midst (7:5). How can the fundamental continuity between this fresh revelation of what God requires be integrated with what God

[88] Block, *Deuteronomy*, 159, calls the Decalogue "the fountainhead from which later revelation springs."

has already said? The simplest way of consolidating this connection is by tying the first edition of the Decalogue to the definitive, expansive revelation of his torah. The repetition of the Decalogue then, has a very specific function: it validates Moses's ongoing teaching by identifying it as the exposition and fullest expression of the same covenant loyalty sketched out in outline in the Ten Commandments.

So what are the differences in the two versions of the Decalogue? They are both relatively minor and disproportionately significant. After repeating the first three commandments verbatim (however they are construed), the Mosaic variations begin. At several points, Moses adds to the Exodus version of the Ten Words: in verses 12 and 16, the phrase "as the Lord your God has commanded you" strengthens the weight of the instructions; in verse 16, "prosper[ing] in the land" is added as a further incentive to honor parents and in verse 21 coveting a neighbor's field is included (obviously less of an issue before the occupation of the land). In other places, Moses appears to adapt the words of Exodus quite freely: (1) the Sabbath command is the most markedly different. As well as the addition already mentioned, the day is to be "kept" rather than "remembered" (שָׁמַר rather than זָכַר) and is grounded not on creation but on Yahweh's action in rescuing Israel in the exodus, and the enjoyment of rest is extended to any animal, including specifically the "ox and donkey," and to the entire household, specifically including servants, on the basis that Israel knows what it is like to be deprived of rest. (2) In verse 20, rather than false (שֶׁקֶר) testimony, "dishonest" (literally "empty" [שָׁוְא]) witness statements are banned. (3) In the discussion of coveting, "wife" now comes before "house," and in verse 21, rather than repeat the word "covet," a synonym (תַּאֲוָה, "desire") is used.

The significance of these variations has been much debated. However, it should be noted that, with the exception of the case of the Sabbath, the other changes or additions are the slightest of elaborations, already implied by the Exodus statement. There is little on which to rest a distinctively Deuteronomic recast of this earlier statement of covenant responsibility.

The differences in the Sabbath command are of a slightly different order. While the inclusion of servants in the rest day may simply be spelling out the implicit intention of the Exodus version, the switch in motivation from the pattern of creation to the freedom for which Israel was rescued from Egypt may be more significant. So is there an explanation for these differences?

I would suggest that two reasons stand behind these differences. The first is relatively obvious and quite straightforward. Presumably, Moses did not pause to go and read the Ten Words from the stone originals (which were in the ark in the holiest part of the Tent), which means he is speaking from memory. His concern is not to rehearse every word without error but to cite the Horeb revelation as a basis for the authority of God's ongoing words to his people.[89] The second reason is, I think, more significant. As Moses speaks (under God's authority), he does not view the "Ten Words" as the final word from God to his people but seems to hold something like the view set out above, where the Horeb revelation is a template for what follows rather than the perfect and complete expression of all that God has to say to his covenant people. Spelling out appropriate application, or adding motivation, or even listing the requirements in a different order, are all consistent with a dynamic view of God's torah—his sweeping prescriptions for future life, including unanticipated challenges, in the land itself.[90]

The enduring significance of the Ten Words

This view of the significance of the Ten Words finds substantial support in the remarkable absence of any clear citation of or even allusion to "the Ten" in the rest of the Hebrew Bible (or, in fact, the Scriptures as a whole).[91] There are, of course, allusions to or repetitions of individual commands, but there is no evidence that appeal was ever made to this putative "Bill of Rights" either to encourage or condemn specific behavior as God's covenant people (in contrast, for example, to the multiplicity of references to, e.g., the torah of Moses). This seems to point to a disjunction between the significance granted to the Ten Commandments in our modern Christian tradition and that within the text of the Bible itself.

In Exodus and Deuteronomy, the Decalogue is the launchpad for an expansive (and expanding) view of covenant responsibilities, which is

---

[89] See the comments of Block, *Deuteronomy*, 159.

[90] I also wonder if this slight looseness is responsible for some of the syntactical vagaries of the text. If so, this would tell against attempts to argue that there are two "coveting" commands on the basis of the syntax of Deut 5.

[91] Moshe Weinfeld, "The Decalogue: Its Significance, Uniqueness and Place in Israel's Tradition," in *Religion and Law: Biblical-Judaic and Islamic Perspectives*, ed. E. B. Firmage et al. (Winona Lake: Eisenbrauns, 1990), 3–47, assembles a range of Old Testament passages that he suggests cite the Decalogue, but none of them is convincing.

dynamic, rather than static. This explains why the Ten Words are never appealed to as the first and final word of covenant life.

Interestingly, in the New Testament, it becomes apparent that Jesus shares such an expansive view of what the good life of the covenant is all about. In Matthew 5:17–20, we read this:

> 17 "Don't think that I came to abolish the Law or the Prophets. I did not come to abolish but to fulfill. 18 For truly I tell you, until heaven and earth pass away, not the smallest letter or one stroke of a letter will pass away from the law until all things are accomplished. 19 Therefore, whoever breaks one of the least of these commands and teaches others to do the same will be called least in the kingdom of heaven. But whoever does and teaches these commands will be called great in the kingdom of heaven. 20 For I tell you, unless your righteousness surpasses that of the scribes and Pharisees, you will never get into the kingdom of heaven.

Jesus's expansive view of torah (and righteousness) is then reflected in the rest of the Sermon on the Mount, as he consistently asks *more* of even the Pharisees than they have so far managed. Even when the law is condensed to "love God and love your neighbor" (see, e.g., the parable of the Good Samaritan in Luke 10:25–37), the effect of this summary is actually to ask *more* of the listeners than they had previously thought possible. It is then the grace-filled mission of Jesus to inaugurate a new covenant that delivers on what previous iterations could not and puts this real, beautiful, covenantal, eternal life within reach of those who come to him.[92]

5:6 The bold statement of 5:6 begins with an affirmation that is characteristic of Leviticus (11:44; 18:2, 4, 30; 19:2, 3, 10, 25, 31, 34, 36; 20:7, 24; 23:22, 43; 25:17, 55; 26:1, 13) but is relatively rare elsewhere in the Old Testament (Exod 16:12; Num 10:10; 15:41; Judg 6:10; Ps 81:10; Isa 41:13; 43:3; 48:17; Ezek 20:5, 7, 19; 23:49; Joel 2:27; 3:17). There are a significant number of conceptual links between Leviticus and Deuteronomy that should not be underestimated.[93] Similar statements are also found in several ancient royal inscriptions, including the Mesha Stele and the Code of Hammurabi.[94]

---

[92] Block, *Deuteronomy*, 167, beautifully captures the expansive dynamic of the Old Testament material, but not the way in which Jesus continues that trajectory in his teaching.

[93] At points in the past, this has either been overlooked because of a deeply unhelpful rigidity produced by the Documentary Hypothesis or simply discussed in the context of the putative origin of Deuteronomy among Northern Levites. The theological worlds of the two books are much closer than is often allowed for.

[94] See the inscriptions of Yehawmilk of Byblos (*ANET*, 656); Kilamuwu (*ANET*, 654) as well as the Moabite Stone (*ANET*, 320) and the Code of Hammurabi (*ANET*, 177).

God has "brought [his people] out" (the classic exodus verb, יָצָא) from the "house of slaves" (lit.), the phrase used in Exodus 13:3, 14 and 20:2, but then picked up and used repeatedly by Moses in his sermon (see 6:12; 7:8; 8:14; 13:5, 10 [Heb. 13:6, 11]; also Josh 24:17; Judg 6:8; Jer 34:13; Mic 6:4). Unlike many ancient treaties, God's covenantal relationship with his people starts not with conquest, but with grace and rescue. As a result, the people belong not to Pharaoh, but to Yahweh.[95]

5:7 The phrase literally reads "There shall not be for you other gods before my face." Moses is extremely realistic about the propensity for his people to worship gods other than, or even as well as, Yahweh, mentioning this seventeen times. However, he routinely makes little comment about the foolishness of this, or the inferiority of other gods, which is just assumed. The question of their existence is not addressed explicitly. However, these non-gods are held in such abject contempt and are so utterly inferior to Yahweh, that there can be no question that Moses (or any other Israelite) gives any credence to the idea that they exist and are powerful. "Besides me" may simply mean "in addition to me" or may carry the added nuance of "before me," as in "in my presence." The latter seems more likely. The requirement of a covenant relationship with Yahweh is exclusive fidelity (compare the language of Gen 31:50), and to form a relationship with a rival, introducing them to Yahweh's "space," would be provocative in the extreme. Tigay rightly comments that "This prohibition, banning but all but one deity, is unique in the history of religion."[96]

5:8–10. The explicit prohibition of idolatry is expressed in terms of not making a פֶּסֶל, an idol that is usually carved out of wood or stone (as is completely fitting in a pre-Iron Age culture). The word "shape" (see 4:12, 15, 18, 23) clearly means "physical representation." In 4:15–18, Moses had expanded this basic formula, which covered flying, walking (including, presumably, human forms), and swimming creatures, presumably because he anticipated that this would be one particularly pertinent command as they walked into the land and were exposed to the settled idolatry of Canaan. However, it is not simply the making of such images that is in view.[97]

---

[95] See the discussion in Lundbom, *Deuteronomy*, 276.

[96] Tigay, *Deuteronomy*, 64.

[97] The language here ("image of any form") is slightly different from Exod 20:4 ("image or any form") but the point is not appreciably different.

Chapter 4 laid out a clear theological rationale for being a "word" people rather than a "physical/visual representation" people, but that, while it is a natural implication of this "Word," is not spelled out here. The concern is much more concrete: the problem with making an idol is that it will lead almost inexorably to worshiping or serving the non-god it represents. The verb "worship" here is the hishtafel form of חוה, which conveys the physical action of bowing down, and to "serve" is the default Old Testament word for wholehearted commitment and devotion.

The reason for this level of dedication to Yahweh has a slightly different nuance than in 5:7, although the ideas are similar. Rather than the sheer incongruity of introducing another god to the presence of the one and only Yahweh, the focus is now on Yahweh's own reaction to any possible relational unfaithfulness.

God here presents himself as a "jealous" or "impassioned" (קַנָּא) God (see Exod 20:5; 34:14; Deut 4:24; 6:15; see also the verbal forms in 29:20 [Heb. 29:19]; 32:16, 21).[98] The language interestingly does not necessarily conjure up a romantic or conjugal relationship. Rather the emphasis is on God's strong determination to ensure that his people do not betray him. As in Exodus 20 (and Exod 34), the nature of God's covenantal commitment entails both the possibility of both negative and positive consequences. Here, the negatives are God's response to those who "hate" him, which is demonstrated by their "iniquity" (עָוֹן). The language of "hate"/"love and keep my commands" is a typical way of expressing a choice of two options (so also, memorably, Mal 1:2), rather than a literal depiction of the emotional responses to God's revelation. "Bringing the consequences of" on successive generations is a most helpful translation of פָּקַד (traditionally rendered "visiting").

There is a tension between this principle and insistence of texts like Deuteronomy 24:16 and Ezekiel 18 that it would be unjust to punish people for things they did not do. This tension arises because of the overlap of individual responsibility (which is the focus of e.g. Deut 24:16) and the nature of Israel as the covenant people of God, operating under a national framework of blessing and curse. In this national framework, disobedience leads to the real time experience of covenantal curse, which will

[98] See also Josh 24:19; 1 Kgs 14:22; 2 Kgs 19:31; Isa 9:7; 27:11; 37:32; 42:13; 59:17; 63:15; Ps 69:9 [Heb. 69:10]; 78:58; 79:5; Ezek 5:13; 8:3, 5; 16:38, 42; 23:25; 36:5; 38:19; 39:25; Joel 2:18; Nah 1:2; Zeph 1:18; 3:8; Zech 1:14; 8:2. The adjectival form is only used of God in the Bible.

have an impact on the life of the community of God and their corporate witness for several generations. This is quite different to God holding individuals responsible for crimes they did not commit.

Notice too that there is clear asymmetry in God's responses here: he is clearly biased toward covenant love or faithfulness (חֶסֶד), in that his lavish treatment of those who obey him is essentially limitless,[99] while the consequences of "hating" him are felt for three or four generations (which may be intended to cover the lifespan of the offender, roughly the seventy or eighty years of Ps 90:10).[100] However, the asymmetry is not simply seen in the times involved: it seems that evil results in the punishment of those who are not yet born, whereas God's love is shown on an individual basis in real time. In a book that makes much of the righteousness of God, this problem is not insignificant.

So is this unfair? It is important to read these words in their covenantal context. This command warns Israel that covenant disloyalty will have ramifications that last for generations. This is another reason why they must not be unfaithful. But the consequences of covenant loyalty are much more straightforward: God's inexhaustible supply of steadfast love will continue to flow, as one obedient generation succeeds the next.

5:11. The third commandment is perhaps the one which is most elusive. The CSB ("Do not misuse the name of the Lord your God"). reflects the traditional interpretation, where "take" (נָשָׂא) is understood as speaking, and "in vain" (לַשָּׁוְא) refers to blasphemy, profanity, or perhaps simply invoking Yahweh in an oath or commitment inappropriately. The rest of the verse does not clarify the nature of what is being prohibited, as it simply confirms that the matter is a serious one, and that God will not allow offenders to get off scot-free, using exactly the same terminology as the first part of the command.

This understanding is not without merit.[101] Leviticus 19:12, for example, does connect the name of Yahweh and speaking truth ("Do not swear

---

[99] The text reads "to thousands," which may well imply to a thousand generations, a sense that is made explicit in 7:9.

[100] So for example Lundbom, *Deuteronomy*, 280. Block (*Deuteronomy*, 162) makes the interesting suggestion that the multiple generations here should be understood "horizontally" (within a multi-generational household) rather than "vertically" (successive generations over an extended period). Attractive though this is, it is hard to eliminate any sense of the progression of time.

[101] There is no doubt that oaths played an important role in the ancient world (Lundbom, *Deuteronomy*, 282–284).

falsely by my name, profaning the name of your God; I am the LORD." See also Zech 5:4). But the vocabulary here is quite different and, in addition, if that were the intention, one might expect the issue to figure more prominently in the rest of the Old Testament.

There is a long strand of Jewish interpretation that emerged in the Second Temple period that links this prohibition to speaking the name of Yahweh (the tetragrammaton, often represented as YHWH) aloud.[102] However two factors tell against this: first, there is no evidence that the verb "take" here ever means "pronounce"[103]; second, the proliferation of the divine name both in the text and in personal names in the Old Testament gives little support to the idea that it could not be said aloud. A more fruitful line of interpretation is suggested by Exodus 28:11–12, 29.[104]

> 28:11 Engrave the two stones with the names of Israel's sons as a gem cutter engraves a seal. Mount them, surrounded with gold filigree settings. 12 Fasten both stones on the shoulder pieces of the ephod as memorial stones for the Israelites. Aaron will *carry their names* on his two shoulders before the LORD as a reminder. ... 29 Whenever he enters the sanctuary, Aaron is *to carry the names* of Israel's sons over his heart on the breastpiece for decisions, as a continual reminder before the LORD.

In both cases, Aaron, as high priest, is to wear the breastplate as a *sign that he is representing Israel*. This suggests that the idiom in Exodus 20:7 and Deuteronomy 5:11 should be read as insisting that Israel, as God's representative in the world (Exod 19:5–6; Deut 4:5–8; 7:6; 26:19; 28:10), must not drag his reputation through the mud (lit., "lift it up to emptiness").[105] If this is the case, then the third commandment is elevated from a relatively minor ethical injunction to the biblical-theological heart of the Old Testament.

5:12–15. The Sabbath command not only shifts to the positive (like the command to honor parents) but displays the greatest degree of variation

---

[102] See the discussion in Tigay, *Deuteronomy*, Excursus 4, "The LORD," 431–32.

[103] There are places where the expression "take *on your lips*" is used (i.e., pronounce), e.g., Pss 16:4; 50:16.

[104] See Daniel I. Block, "Bearing the Name of the LORD with Honor," in *How I Love Your Torah, O LORD*, 61–72, for an extended discussion and defense of this reading. See also Carmen Joy Imes, *Bearing YHWH's Name at Sinai: A Reexamination of the Name Command of the Decalogue*, Bulletin for Biblical Research Supplement 19 (University Park: Eisenbrauns, 2018).

[105] This idea is clearly expressed in Lev 18:21; 24:11, 16 and developed at some length in Ezekiel (e.g., 36:17–23). See also Dan 9:16–19 and Ps 24:3–4, which speaks of lifting up the soul to "emptiness." See also the discussion in Imes, *Bearing YHWH's Name.*

from the wording of Exodus 20.[106] In the first place, although the CSB has "be careful to remember," the imperative "remember" in Exodus is replaced by the word "keep" (שָׁמַר). Although the nuance of the words is slightly different, emphasizing the practice of "keeping" the Sabbath, I have suggested above that this is certainly within the natural variation of a faithful oral reminder of the inscription on the tablets in the ark.[107]

The second difference comes in the details of the entitlement to rest (lit., "cease, desist"). The "ox and donkey" get a specific call-out, alongside the generic "livestock," but this, again, is not a substantial difference. The specific repetition of the right of male and female slaves to "rest as you do" does not alter the content of the instruction, but does underline both the new situation of life in the land (where having male and female servants was now a real possibility, presumably in contrast to both Egypt and the wilderness). This also reflects the particular Deuteronomic emphasis on protecting the weak.

The third departure from the Exodus version is by far the most significant. In Exodus 20:11, the explicit motivation for remembering the Sabbath is the pattern of creation in Genesis 1:1–2:3, and specifically, God's "rest" on the seventh day of the cycle. Not so in Deuteronomy. According to 5:15, keeping the Sabbath will flow from "remember[ing] that you were slaves in Egypt and the Lord your God brought you out of there with a strong hand and an outstretched arm." This is highlighted by the final clause, which insists that remembering God's rescue lies at the heart of the Sabbath command (and also supports the idea that Moses is developing the tradition of Exod 20).

There is no denying that the rationale for Sabbath-keeping in Exodus 20 and Deuteronomy 5 appears markedly different. However, this difference may be less substantial than first appears. In Exodus 20, it is the *prior action of God in setting the Israelites free from slavery* that allows God's people to establish a one in seven pattern of rest and work. The exodus *implicitly* allows the creation pattern to be observed. Moses in Deuteronomy 5, however, given the context forty years on and his preoccupation with the danger of forgetting, calls on the people *explicitly*

---

[106] According to Exod 16:22–30, the Israelites were already keeping a Sabbath before they arrived at Sinai. Other texts dealing with Sabbath are Exod 23:12; 31:12–17; Lev 19:3; 23:3; 26:2.

[107] The fact that the Decalogue was also rewritten by God after the golden calf incident may also provide an explanation for the variation in phrasing.

to remember the Sabbath as a sign that they are committed to living *as the rescued people of God. Implicitly*, this should lead to them living in line with the pattern of creation.[108]

In other words, the different motivation is the result of theological emphasis on one of two intrinsically related ideas—*rescue and rest*. In Exodus, *rest* is central and rescue assumed, whereas in Deuteronomy, the situation is reversed. In both cases, the day is to be set aside as "holy" in the sense of "dedicated to God." However one understands the different nuance of this command in each place, it is clear that God's rescue of his people in the exodus should lead them to participating in and enjoying his "Sabbath."

Again, the relative looseness of Moses's inspired citation of the stone tablets in the ark suggests that the Decalogue is best understood as "template" rather than the final (or purest) expression of torah. In addition, the connection between rescue and rest paves the way for the theological reinterpretation of these categories in the wake of Jesus's death and resurrection in Hebrews 4:1–11 in particular.[109]

5:16–21. As mentioned above, the wording of the fifth commandment is slightly expanded from the Exodus version. Like the previous instruction, appeal is made to Yahweh's earlier commands.[110] The phrase "so that you may prosper" is inserted, in addition to the promise of long life in the land. This phrase is literally "so that it may result in good for you." The idea that God is poised to make his people prosper is typically Deuteronomic (see e.g. 4:40; 5:29; 6:3, 18; 8:16; 12:25, 28; 22:7; 28:11, 63; 30:5, 9; 31:20). The authority of parents (and interestingly, contrary to many ancient societies, it is *parents*, and not just *fathers*, who are to be shown honor) is to be respected as the fundamental basis of life in the land as the people of Yahweh. Their authority, like that of the elders of Israel and even Moses himself, is delegated authority from God himself (see Matt 28:18–20; 1 Pet 5:1–5) and therefore must be acknowledged if

---

[108] The phrase "has commanded you" appears in Deuteronomy where an earlier text is being alluded to. In this, it may well suggest that Moses is aware that he is adding to the motivation for Sabbath keeping spelled out in Exod 20. This anticipates the treatment of the Sabbath in the rest of the Old Testament, where it is variously an opportunity to rest, a statement of living in step with Yahweh, a demonstration of covenant faithfulness, an expression of holiness, a celebration of rescue, and an opportunity to care for the marginalized.

[109] See the comments of McConville, *Deuteronomy*, 128.

[110] This may possibly be due to the influence of Lev 19:2–3, where the Sabbath command and the importance of honoring parents also occur side by side.

God's people are to enjoy the life to which he has called them. It is also striking that this command is expressed positively: this is not simply compliance based on fear of punishment, but an active submission that is to mirror our response to God himself. The importance of this command is underlined by 21:18–21, and the fact that it is cited six times in the New Testament (Matt 15:4; 19:19; Mark 7:10; 10:19; Luke 18:20; Eph 6:2–3).

Commandments six through eight (on the Reformed/Orthodox numbering system) are virtually identical to the wording in Exodus 20. The short, linked commands contrast with the developed persuasion of the previous statements, but also contribute to a "coherent consequentiality, and building up a total picture of the standards which need to be observed in the covenant community."[111]

The sixth commandment prohibits murder rather than all killing under any circumstance and is also stated in Exodus 21:12; Leviticus 24:17 and Numbers 35:30–34, which also call for a mandatory death sentence for the crime (underlining that the word cannot simply mean "kill," as translated in the King James Version and others). It is picked up by the New Testament in Matthew 5:21; 19:18; Mark 7:21; 10:19; Luke 18:20; Romans 13:9 and James 2:11.

The prohibition against adultery, developed in Deuteronomy 22 (see also Lev 18:20; 20:10 and also the evidence of John 8:3–11, which although probably not original to John's Gospel, is evidence that this view endured), is a reflection of the seriousness with which marital faithfulness is taken in Israel. The fact that, as with murder, no commuting of the death sentence is allowed is most likely a function of the fact that this is a breach of covenant faithfulness of the very kind that Yahweh shows to his people.

Commandments eight and nine extend the need for covenant faithfulness to the theft of property and speaking about others (particularly in a judicial setting). The variation in language in 5:20 ("empty," as in Exod 23:1, rather than "false" testimony in Exod 20:16) may simply be the result of Moses's dynamic rendering of the commands as he speaks.

The beautiful life to which God is calling his people in the land is one in which the life of human beings made in the image of God is precious (and murder is prohibited); relational fidelity (mirroring God's own covenant commitment) is vital, whether in public or private settings; respect for property, which is ultimately a gift from God, is basic; and speaking the

[111] McConville, *Deuteronomy*, 129.

truth, especially among God's people, is fundamental. What is clear is that all of this can be seen as an expression of God's own righteousness, lived out in the land by his people.[112]

The variations in the last of the Ten Words in 5:21, with two different verbs used ("covet" and "desire," rather than the repetition of "covet" in Exod 20), the prioritization of wives in the list, and the addition of the neighbor's "field" as a possible snare can again be ascribed to the oral nature of the speech. The word "neighbor" here cannot be limited to those living in immediate proximity, but rather is a general designation for "fellow Israelite." Moses appears to be deliberately updating, applying the commands to the new realities of life in the land, and in particular, to the prospect of the division of the land and permanent settlement. This command also uniquely deals with the inner motivations and temptations faced by God's people. The language of "desire" (see 7:25; Josh 7:21; also Gen 3:6; Prov 6:25) reveals a strong craving after an "idol of the heart," and takes us to the very root of the human problem.[113]

5:22–27 In Exodus 20:18–20, the reaction of the people (consisting largely of fear) takes center stage. As Moses reflects on the events here, his theological agenda comes to the fore. Once again, the word of God is central to his concerns.

Horeb is *the* definitive moment for the nation of Israel: it was at Horeb that God spoke audibly "to your entire assembly."[114] One God speaks to one nation at one key juncture in history. God spoke out of the "fire, cloud and total darkness."[115] But the spotlight is not on the phenomena which accompanied the revelation, but on the completeness of what Yahweh said ("he added nothing more"). Given the ongoing insistence that this torah needs to be applied and expanded for life in the land (and has already been augmented significantly in, e.g., Exod 21–24), this is best taken as further evidence of the foundational (rather than final) nature of the revelation at Horeb, and in particular the "Ten Words" of

---

[112] As expressed, for example, in the slogan of 16:20.

[113] See David Powlinson, "Revisiting Idols of the Heart and Vanity Fair," *JBC* 27:3 (2013): 37–42. See also Jesus's words in Matt 5:28; Luke 12:13–15, and the warnings of Paul in Rom 1:29; 7:7–8; 13:9; Eph 5:3, 5; Col 3:5; 1 Tim 6:6–10; as well as Jas 4:2.

[114] This is so important that in 9:10; 10:4 and 18:16 this day is simply referred to as "the Day of the Assembly."

[115] The combination of these elements is unique, although the language is drawn from Exod 20:21; Deut 4:11; etc.

the Decalogue.[116] The evidence that God has spoken, and the tangible reminder of the covenantal obligations under which Israel now lives are engraved on stone, entrusted to Moses (and now deposited in the ark).

As we have already seen in Moses's preaching (see 1:9–18), the emphasis falls not only on the people as a whole, but also the shared responsibility of *all* their leaders (including Moses himself). This is reflected in the added detail that the "tribal leaders and elders" played a crucial part in the post-Horeb dialogue.

As in chapter 4, rather than highlighting the fear of the people (which seems to be the dominant note in Exod 20), here Moses focuses on the fact that God reveals himself through speaking. It is his words, spoken out of the midst of the fire, that reveal his "glory and greatness," an unusual phrase (whose only real equivalent is Ezek 31:18). The question here is not "can a person see God and live?" but rather can a person *hear the living God speak* (see, e.g., 1 Sam 17:26, 36; Jer 10:10; Ps. 42:2). The answer in verse 24 could not be clearer: "Today we have seen that God speaks with a person, yet he still lives."

Moses's account of these events shows how strange the response of the people and leaders actually was to this realization. Even though their experience "today" consists of hearing God speak, they are terrified that they will die, consumed by fire and the sheer impact of continuing to hear the voice of Yahweh (see 5:4–5).

Rather like Eve in Genesis 3:3, the people seem to be jumping to their own (unwarranted) conclusion. There is nothing in the context, either here or in Exodus, to suggest that the likely result of continuing to listen to God speak out of the fire is their immediate death. The words of verse 26 are clearly true: "For who out of all humanity has heard the voice of the living God speaking from the fire, as we have, and lived?" The problem is that they appear to regard this as a peril rather than a privilege. There is a decided ambiguity in their plea to Moses to do their listening for them. One wonders why they think they are in any position to bargain with God. The insistence that they will "listen and obey" on the surface is admirable but hints of presumption and raises questions about their seriousness of engaging with the living God wholeheartedly.[117]

---

[116] Exod 24:3–7 spells out that Moses's conveyed the extra stipulations (of the book of the covenant initially) to the people at Horeb. He does not spell out how the laws of Deuteronomy came to him or how they are related to previous material.

[117] See also Exod 19:8; 24:3, 7.

5:28–33. According to 5:28, the "words" that Yahweh heard the people speak were "right" (better: "good"), a statement unparalleled in Exodus. This presumably refers to their commitment to listen to all God's words through Moses and obey them (rather than their assertion about their impending death). However 5:29 confirms the suggestion that all is not well. God's expressed desire that they had "such a heart to fear me and keep all my commands always" (lit., "all the days"), clearly implies that their heart (decision-making faculty) is fickle and unreliable.[118] The fact that Israel repeatedly speaks in these verses, rather than listens, may also support this. God's instruction to the people to go back to their tents to await the revelation mediated through Moses feels slightly sad. However, God is clearly committed to his people and is willing to accommodate their wrongheaded fear graciously, by speaking only through his servant.[119]

Moses then summarizes the lessons of Horeb for the Moab generation in 5:32–33. Echoing 5:1, the imagery is that of a journey: they are to follow "the whole instruction"—literally, "the whole way"—of Yahweh. Where the phrase "the way" is used previously (1:2, 19, 22, 31, 33, 40; 2:1, 8, 27; 3:1), it refers to the journey from Horeb to Canaan through the wilderness. Here, it is metaphorical for the ongoing journey of daily, lifelong obedience that Israel is called to continue after they have settled in the land. "Walking" in Yahweh's ways is one of Moses's favorite expressions for covenantal obedience (see, e.g., 8:6; 10:12; 11:22; 13:5; 19:9; 26:17; 28:9; 30:16).

Bridge

The African-American song "Were you there when they crucified my Lord?" neatly captures the theological underpinnings of Moses's preaching on the events—and the words—of Horeb. The God who speaks to his people at Horeb is speaking at Moab. The God who makes a covenant with his people at Horeb is refreshing the same covenant at Moab. The reassurance for every generation is that God's covenantal commitment to us is unshakeable. The question for every generation is: will we respond to the God who speaks to us (through his ancient words) today?

---

[118] In Deuteronomy, it is the "heart" (occasionally translated "mind" which is the seat of decision-making: see 6:6; 10:16; 28:67; 29:4). This "heart focus" also appears in e,g, Exod 16:3; Num 11:29; Job 6:8; 11:5; 13:5; 14:4; 19:23; 23:3. Yahweh eventually commits to change their hearts in Jer 32:39–40 (also Ezek 36).

[119] For the use of "command" in the singular, see 6:25; 8:1; 11:8, 22; 17:20; 19:9; 27:1; 30:11.

Those of us who have been united to Christ by faith are drawn into the same story (or to use Paul's language in Romans 11, "grafted in" to this same tree). The beautiful life sketched out in the Ten Words and then filled out in the rest of Deuteronomy has been brought to life in the flesh by the Lord Jesus, the one who calls us and empowers us to live his life after him. Unlike the Israelites, we can do more than make a commitment and hope for the best, because in Christ, and by the power of the Spirit, God has committed to bring about in us the "integrity of heart" we need to "fear [him] always" (Jer 32:39–40), so that God's covenantal commitments might be brought to fruition, and we might know and delight in him forever.

3. Horeb Applied: Covenantal Listening (6:1–25)

> [1] "This is the command—the statutes and ordinances—the Lord your God has commanded me to teach you, so that you may follow them in the land you are about to enter and possess. [2] Do this so that you may fear the Lord your God all the days of your life by keeping all his statutes and commands I am giving you, your son, and your grandson, and so that you may have a long life. [3] Listen, Israel, and be careful to follow them, so that you may prosper and multiply greatly, because the Lord, the God of your ancestors, has promised you a land flowing with milk and honey.
>
> [4] "Listen, Israel: The Lord our God, the Lord is one. [5] Love the Lord your God with all your heart, with all your soul, and with all your strength. [6] These words that I am giving you today are to be in your heart. [7] Repeat them to your children. Talk about them when you sit in your house and when you walk along the road, when you lie down and when you get up. [8] Bind them as a sign on your hand and let them be a symbol on your forehead. [9] Write them on the doorposts of your house and on your city gates.
>
> [10] "When the Lord your God brings you into the land he swore to your ancestors Abraham, Isaac, and Jacob that he would give you—a land with large and beautiful cities that you did not build, [11] houses full of every good thing that you did not fill them with, cisterns that you did not dig, and vineyards and olive groves that you did not plant—and when you eat and are satisfied, [12] be careful not to forget the Lord who brought you out of the land of Egypt, out of the place of slavery. [13] Fear the Lord your God, worship him, and take your oaths in his name. [14] Do not follow other gods, the gods of the peoples around you, [15] for the Lord your God, who is among you, is a jealous God. Otherwise, the Lord your God will become angry with you and obliterate you from the face of

the earth. 16 Do not test the LORD your God as you tested him at Massah. 17 Carefully observe the commands of the LORD your God, the decrees
and statutes he has commanded you. 18 Do what is right and good in
the LORD's sight, so that you may prosper and so that you may enter
and possess the good land the LORD your God swore to give your ancestors, 19 by driving out all your enemies before you, as the LORD has said.

20 "When your son asks you in the future, 'What is the meaning of the
decrees, statutes, and ordinances that the LORD our God has commanded you?' 21 tell him, 'We were slaves of Pharaoh in Egypt, but the LORD
brought us out of Egypt with a strong hand. 22 Before our eyes the LORD
inflicted great and devastating signs and wonders on Egypt, on Pharaoh,
and on all his household, 23 but he brought us from there in order to lead
us in and give us the land that he swore to our ancestors. 24 The LORD
commanded us to follow all these statutes and to fear the LORD our God
for our prosperity always and for our preservation, as it is today. 25 Righteousness will be ours if we are careful to follow every one of these
commands before the LORD our God, as he has commanded us.' "

6:1–3. Using similar language to 5:1 and 31, Moses now announces that "this is the command" (singular, although made up of the "statutes and ordinances" as we have seen) that God gave to him on Horeb.[120] This is an interesting statement, given that significant amounts of revelation have already been passed on by Moses (e.g., Exod 21:1; 34:3; Lev 1:1, etc.). But now explicitly, Moses is to *teach* this command (as in 4:1, 14; 5:2) as a single, overarching, integrated vision of the covenantal life both now and stretching into the future, so that the people can both enter and occupy the land successfully.[121]

The unfolding revelation of the shape of life in the land, then, is viewed as inseparable. God speaking at Horeb in the Decalogue, continuing to speak from Horeb in the book of the covenant and the prescriptions of Leviticus, and now at Moab as his servant preaches this torah are intrinsically linked. Rather than a static view of what covenant life looks like (set

---

120 Norbert Lohfink (*Das Hauptgebot: Eine Untersuchung literarischer Einleitungsfragen zu Deuteronomium 5–11*, AnBib 20 (Rome: Pontifical Biblical Institute, 1963), 67–68, argues that 5:27–6:3 is bound together by a chiastic arrangement of the verbs. See also Lundbom, *Deuteronomy*, 305; Christensen, *Deuteronomy 1:1–21:9*, 134. However, given that 6:3 is also bound to 5:1 and 11:2, and 6:1 seems to introduce a new phase of the argument, this may simply be the result of the interlocking and repetitive nature of Moses's rhetoric.

121 The land in Deuteronomy is, at the same time, a motivation to obey, an index of obedience, and a reward for obedience. See my article on "Land" in *New Dictionary of Biblical Theology: Exploring the Unity & Diversity of Scripture*, ed. Brian S. Rosner et al. (Downers Grove: IVP Academic, 2000), 623–26, and also *Now Choose Life*, 55–62.

in stone, perhaps!), the Pentateuch as a whole, and Deuteronomy in particular, presents a dynamic understanding of torah, in which God speaks into every new situation, making clear what their exclusive relationship with him demands (and looks like) in their context. This, incidentally, is why Deuteronomy is a vital component of any attempt to work out how to apply the ethics of the Old Testament as Christians.

The goal of Moses's teaching, as in 4:10 and 5:29, is to produce a healthy "fear" in God's people. This idea is vitally important in Deuteronomy (see 6:13, 24; 8:6; 10:12, 20; 13:4; 14:23; 17:19; 25:18; 28:58; 31:12, 13). It is to characterize Israel's relationship as individuals and as a community with God for the entire course of their lives; it is to be produced by and expressed in a wholehearted, all-encompassing obedience by every generation; and it holds the key to a "long life," which conveys both duration and quality of life. The "fear of Yahweh" is no small thing, but takes us to the very heart of the nature of this covenantal relationship.[122]

Any rich relationship is hard to sum up in a single word, and Moses does not try to reduce the complexity of Yahweh's commitment to Israel to a soundbite. But he does continue to hit some key notes: this relationship is built on Yahweh's love, covenant faithfulness, and righteousness, and the proper response to all of this encompasses returning this love, being faithful, pursuing righteousness, but also "fearing him"—displaying a healthy, affectionate awe toward the God who has rescued us and spoken to us. This fear, according to 6:2, is both produced by and expressed in obedience. It is by following God's commands that a healthy fear is lived out. A healthy fear of God drives people to obey. And what is it that oils the wheels of this kind of life? The answer is clear from 6:3. Israel is to listen to Yahweh.

This careful theological foundation laid in chapter 4 and underlined in chapter 5 is now focused in a sharp, practical application. God is the speaking God. Now Israel must be lifelong listeners, hanging on every word spoken by their covenant God, who has been working up to this moment for generations.

As they stand (or sit) on the plains of Moab, overlooking the lushness of the Jordan Valley, Moses reminds them again (see 1:10–11) that God's

---

[122] There is a deep link between covenant, sonship, and the fear of Yahweh that has its roots here but is spelled out in more detail both later in Deuteronomy and elsewhere in Scripture (e.g., Prov 1–3).

commitment to them has at its roots the promises he made to their forefathers (notably Abraham in Gen 12:1–3, Isaac, and Jacob), and prior to that, to Adam and Eve as our first parents (Gen 1:28). The land "flowing with milk and honey" (or perhaps "syrup") is a favorite designation of Canaan in Deuteronomy. Tigay proposes that it should be translated "oozing with milk and honey," which captures the sense beautifully.[123] It first occurs in Exodus (3:8, 17; 13:5; 33:3), but is picked up at key points in Moses's address (6:3; 11:9–15; 26:9, 15; 27:3; 31:20).[124]

6:4. The summary statement of 6:4 is both one of the most important and the most elusive statements in the whole of the Old Testament. In most Hebrew manuscripts, the last letter of both the first and last word are extra large (אֶחָד and שְׁמַע). This may be because the letters spell the Hebrew word for "witness" (עֵד) or simply for emphasis. Most of the interpretative issues stem from the fact that the six words contain a command "Hear/listen, Israel" followed by a verbless clause made up of four simple words in Hebrew: Yahweh (your) God Yahweh one.[125]

The seamless integration of the *shema* ("hear") with its context is achieved by the repetition of the injunction to listen to the talking God of Horeb. Listening is clearly to be Israel's way of life (see 4:1; 5:1; 9:1; 27:9). But the question remains: Does 6:4 identify the God to whom they are to listen, lay out some attributes or qualities of this God they need to understand, or perhaps a combination of both?

There is significant discussion over the translation of each part of the clause, as well as the relationship between the two "halves" of the clause.[126] So debate rages over whether the first clause should be translated "Yahweh is our God" or simply "Yahweh our God." Similarly, there is discussion over whether the second half should be related to the first by the verb "to be" (e.g., "Yahweh our God is one Yahweh"[127]) or simply taken appositionally

---

[123] Tigay, *Deuteronomy*, 75. See also S. Douglas Waterhouse, "A Land Flowing with Milk and Honey," *Andrews University Seminary Studies* 1 (1963): 152–66.

[124] The language is probably Egyptian in origin. See the second millennium description of the land by an Egyptian traveler of roughly the same period in William W. Hallo and K. Lawson Younger, eds., *The Context of Scripture* (Leiden: Brill, 1997), 1.38:79.

[125] "Your" is expressed in Hebrew using a suffix attached to the word "God," hence five words in English are needed to represent four in Hebrew.

[126] Or as some read it, between the two short (two-word) verbless clauses!

[127] The option preferred by Weinfeld, *Deuteronomy 1–11*, 330, 337–38 and Peter C. Craigie, *The Book of Deuteronomy*, New International Commentary on the Old Testament (Grand Rapids: Eerdmans, 1976), 168–69.

(e.g., "Yahweh our God, Yahweh is one," as in the CSB and the NIV[128]). Finally, there is significant divergence on whether the normal form of the cardinal number *one* should be taken as such (presumably referring then to the unity of God), or interpreted to mean "alone," as in unique, an idea already present in 4:35, 39, and is reflected by a few other Old Testament texts (e.g., Josh 22:20; 2 Sam 7:23; 1 Chr 29:1; Job 23:13; 31:15; Song 6:9; Zech 14:9). This level of uncertainty gives rise to a very large number of possibilities!

Linguistically, all of these variations are possible. Overall, the evidence seems strongest for the translation "Yahweh [is] our God; Yahweh alone." But the determining factors in settling on an interpretation will then necessarily be contextual and theological.[129] In my view, the most likely options are then reduced to the following:

1. The Shema identifies the one to whom Israel should listen (Yahweh the speaking God is the only one to whom Israel must listen).
2. The Shema explains why Israel should listen exclusively to Yahweh (Israel should listen because Yahweh alone is Israel's God).
3. The Shema makes specific theological claims about the nature of this God which then undergird the appeal to listen (Israel should listen because Yahweh is unique, or because of his "simplicity," i.e., there are no contradictions or tensions in him).[130] It could, however, also be an implicit expression of monotheism, although this is harder to demonstrate from *this* text (it is clearly present in 4:35, 39, as we have seen).

On balance, I prefer the first option on contextual grounds. The dominant idea in chapters 4 and 5, reiterated in 6:1–3, has been that of listening to the God who speaks: it surely makes sense to allow this to shape our reading of the Shema. On this understanding, 6:4 then becomes the climax of the theologically dense argument that has been building from the

---

[128] See also R. W. L. Moberly, "Yahweh is One: The Translation of the Shema," in *Studies in the Pentateuch*, ed. J. A Emerton, *VTSup* 41 (Leiden: Brill, 1990), 209–15; McConville, *Deuteronomy*, 137, 141.

[129] The superb article by Daniel I. Block ("How Many Is God?" in *How I Love Your Torah, O Lord!*, 73–97) makes this point convincingly.

[130] See McConville, *Deuteronomy*, 141–42, on this option.

beginning of chapter 4. Israel is to respond to Yahweh on the basis not primarily of his *nature* but of his *actions*—and above all, on the basis of the fact that their God has *spoken to them* (e.g., 4:5–8). It also provides the foundation for the rest of the chapter, which is essentially a practical plea to live a word-centered life. It makes perfect sense then, for the Shema to become the biblical slogan *par excellence* that undergirds the life of the covenant people. The second option would also dovetail neatly with the theological agenda of this part of the book: Yahweh is Israel's rescuer and covenant partner, and because of his unique commitment to them, Israel has every reason to listen. Perhaps in this case, the ambiguity is deliberate, and this slogan reminds Israel that the only God who speaks is their God, the God of the exodus, and they must listen to him alone.

Despite the obvious significance of 6:4, there are few clear references to it in the rest of the Old Testament (with Zech 14:9 the only undisputed quotation of the earlier text). However, the New Testament provides ample evidence of its enduring significance for Jews. In Mark 12:29–32, Jesus's quotation of the Shema follows the Septuagint ("Hear O Israel, the Lord our God is one Lord," but the context makes plain that, like Zechariah 14, this was understood in terms of exclusive allegiance. This is also the dominant idea in Paul's reflection on the text in 1 Corinthians 8:5–6, which astonishingly incorporates Jesus Christ into this most foundational expression of the faith of Israel.

6:5. This understanding of 6:4 as a call to listen to Yahweh, the one and only speaking God of Israel, is immediately supported by the call to covenant loyalty ("love") in verse 5. Strikingly, love can be commanded. It is true that love language was common in ancient treaties from early in the second millennium before Christ. But the idea of love here is simply borrowed from either a treaty context (essentially reducing it to obedience to a superior or self-interested respect for a peer) or a wisdom milieu (essentially reducing it to learning from a mentor).[131] However, the text does not allow a reductionistic understanding of the concept (whether the word used is אָהֵב, as here, or חֶסֶד). While the ancient conception of "love" was not driven by or born of the emotions, all emotional content

[131] For the background to this discussion see, e.g., R. Frankena, "The Vassal-Treaties of Esarhaddon and the Dating of Deuteronomy," *Old Testament Studies* 14 (1965): 122–54; Moran, "Ancient Near Eastern Background," 77–87; and J. W. McKay, "Man's Love for God in Deuteronomy and the Father/Teacher—Son/Pupil Relationship," *VT* (1972): 426–35. See also the succinct discussion in Lundbom, *Deuteronomy*, 310–11.

cannot be stripped from the term in the Old Testament (see, e.g., Hos 3:1; 11:1; Jer 2:2). This is an all-encompassing response to God. [132]

The "heart" was not seen as the seat of emotions as in current usage, but of the sum total of human capacities and personalities, including the will; the "soul" (נֶפֶשׁ) is a similarly broad term that often has the nuance of "life"; "strength" again implies "with all my resources."[133] The response God asks of us is all-embracing (as Josiah models in 2 Kgs 23:25). This is why in the rest of Deuteronomy, the idea of loving the God who has loved us becomes so very important (see 10:12; 11:1, 13, 22; 13:3; 19:9; and above all in the climax to the whole book, 30:6, 16, 20).

This expansive understanding of love lies behind Jesus's use of this statement in discussion both with individuals and the religious establishment in Judah (Matt 22:37; Mark 12:30–31; Luke 10:27). Jesus's insistence that they have not fulfilled the command to love God and neighbor is based not on a shortfall on obedience or diligence in studying the Scriptures, but on an abject failure to engage with and respond humbly—and lovingly—to the God of the Scriptures.

6:6–9. The importance of the words of Yahweh is hammered home in 6:6–9. The key to *loving* Yahweh with heart, soul, and strength is to ensure that "these words that I am giving you today are to be in your heart." This includes but is not limited to what we might call "internalization." Yes, they are to be taken to heart, an idea picked up in Proverbs (see 3:1; 4:4; 6:21; 7:3). But Moses is asking for more than this: God's words, conveyed through him, are to dominate very moment, every sphere, every aspect of national life (6:6).[134] This saturation of life with God's word is then expounded in the verses that follow.

"Repeat" in 6:7 is probably the root of the rare verb used here.[135] The sense is to drive them home to your children by constant reinforcement.

---

[132] For a similar use of "heart" in one of the Vassal Treaties of Esarhaddon, see *ANET*[3], 538 no. 34. See also Tigay, *Deuteronomy*, 77.

[133] See the discussion of Old Testament anthropology in Millar, *Changed Into His Likeness*, 39–48. Block ("How Many Is God?," 85–86) argues that "strength" here should be interpreted as "wealth," creating an outward progression from "mind" to "person" to "resources" (three spheres of human existence). However, this does not seem to be reflected in the way in which the New Testament uses the phrase.

[134] This is similar to the idea of 30:6, which is then picked up in the new covenant passages in Jer 31:33; Ezek 11:19; 18:31; 36:26.

[135] So Craigie, *Deuteronomy*, 170 n. 17. Contra BDB, Weinfeld, *Deuteronomy 1–11*, 332–33, who take the word to be derived from a root meaning "sharpen."

These words are to penetrate and have their effect (cf. Heb 4:12: "The word of God is living and effective and sharper than any double-edged sword, penetrating as far as the separation of soul and spirit, joints and marrow. It is able to judge the thoughts and intentions of the heart"), particularly in the next generation.

It seems inescapable to me that this statement really is intended to drive the new nation to invest heavily in passing on the words of Yahweh to every succeeding generation.[136] As becomes explicit in 6:20–25, the family is to be the primary context for ensuring that God's words retelling his mighty acts are remembered, embraced, and lived. Interestingly, incisively teaching children is the "headline statement," presumably because this is the foundation of the long-term future of faithfulness among the people of God. It is then backed up with a series of four pairs of instructions, each of which covers all of life.

In the first pair of commands, God's words are to dominate conversation both when sitting "at home" and when "out and about" ("when you walk along the road"). There is to be no public/private split when it comes to reminding one another of God's words and working out how to apply them. Similarly, this discussion must continue 24/7, not pausing "when you lie down" or only beginning "when you get up." This, incidentally, shows that these descriptions are a metaphorical description of a never-ending conversation: Moses does not intend to ban sleep![137]

In 6:8, God's people are instructed to tie God's words "as a sign on your hand" and "a symbol on your forehead." This is almost identical to the way refraining from eating leavened bread is described in Exodus 13:9, which is clearly symbolic. The word "symbol" is extremely rare, but clearly refers to something worn suspended between the eyes (often translated as "frontlets" in the past, but the term may mean "headband"). In the Jewish tradition, this verse has been applied literally in the use of phylacteries, small boxes containing copies of key texts of the Hebrew Scriptures (usually Deut 6:4–9; 11:13–21; Exod 13:1–16).[138] Contextually,

---

[136] The literary devices of Proverbs ("Hear, my son," e.g., 6:20–22) and Song of Songs ("Young women of Jerusalem, I charge you ...") may have been prompted by this language, but in Deuteronomy, it seems to be a clear example of Moses instructing fathers in particular to teach their children the words of God.

[137] In the same way that Paul's command to "Pray without ceasing" (1 Thess 5:17) does not call for 24-hour-a-day prayer for the rest of our lives.

[138] For support for a literal view, see Block, *Deuteronomy*, 185–86.

it seems much more likely to refer simply to Gods words governing all of life. Some care must be taken with the precise interpretation, however, for there is no evidence in Deuteronomy (or the rest of the Old Testament, for that matter) of a hands/head (practical/cerebral or actions/thoughts) contrast. "Hands" clearly can stand for general activity (the "works of our hands"), but rather than referring to mental processes, the "head" is either connected to (a) "authority" (Deut 28:44), making this an expression of submission to God; (b) God's verdict on our lives (Deut 33:16; Ps 27:6) making this an acknowledgement that God is sovereign; (c) the whole of our lives (Prov 10:6; 25:22), as in 6:5.

The final pair in 6:9 is more straightforward. Mirroring the "at home"/"on the road" pair with which the series began, the injunction to inscribe God's words on both domestic doorframes and the "city gates," a practice that has again been interpreted literally in Jewish tradition, with the word for "doorposts" (מְזוּזוֹת) eventually becoming the name for the box containing Scriptures from this passage and Deuteronomy 11 attached to the frame itself.[139] However, this is not simply another geographical designation, but rather a home/work distinction. The "city gates" in ancient walled towns describes the public space in which commercial and judicial activity takes place.[140] Moses's point is that God's word (and his righteousness) should govern both family life and civic affairs in the life of God's people.

6:10–12. Having painted a detailed picture of what a life of listening will look like, Moses starts to spell out why this matters so much in a long sentence that runs from verse 10 to verse 12. As they start to experience the fulfillment of God's land promise, first made to their ancestors Abraham, Isaac, and Jacob (1:8), Israel will also face an entirely new set of temptations. Life is about to get significantly easier. Rather than the realities of bonded labor in Egypt or the challenges of surviving in inhospitable environments *en route* to the land, Israel will now have to deal with comfort and prosperity (see also 8:7–18).

This is characterized in terms of four newfound advantages "inherited" from the previous inhabitants: (1) "large and beautiful cities"; (2) houses well stocked "with every good thing" (presumably produce from

---

[139] For a discussion of the possible Egyptian background to this practice and the evidence for it in Second Temple Judaism, see Lundbom, *Deuteronomy*, 315. It is sometimes suggested that it is hard to take this metaphorically, but this seems unpersuasive.

[140] See, e.g., 2 Sam 18:24; Prov 31:23, 31; Jer 15:7; Amos 5:12; Zech 8:16.

the previous harvests); (3) a secure water supply ("cisterns" to store the seasonal rain falling between October/November and April/May)[141]; and (4) mature vineyards and olive groves, which normally take years to establish. All of this will make it very easy for Israel to "eat and be satisfied" (6:11, also 8:10, 12; 11:15; 14:29; 26:12; 31:20), tasting the "good" life in the "good land" which Yahweh has given them. This should lead to gratitude, but also makes it terribly easy to forget Yahweh.

Living in a context that oozes grace opens up new possibilities for the archetypal sin in Deuteronomy, which is forgetting the God who rescued them from Egypt, which is again described as "the house of slaves" (see on 5:6).

6:13–19. The opposite (and antidote) to "forgetting" is, perhaps surprisingly, a threefold instruction to "fear" Yahweh, to "worship" (or serve) him, and to "swear in his name" (presumably rather than in the name of other non-gods). This triplet is repeated in 10:20 (for broadly similar expressions see also 10:12; 13:4; Josh 24:14; 1 Sam 12:14; 2 Kgs 17:25; Mal 3:5; also Rev 14:7). This uniquely Deuteronomic combination is aimed at ensuring that Israel stays faithful to the true God and is not sucked into the idolatry that is characteristic of the land they are entering. Fearing Yahweh has already been placarded as a key part of covenantal life in 4:10; 5:29; and 6:2: the basic stance of the people is to be one of reverent awe, which issues in both serving him and relying on him. "Serving Yahweh" is a key idea in Deuteronomy. It can have a general sense or, as here, refer specifically to worship (see also, e.g., 5:9; 7:4, 16; 8:19; 11:16; 17:3; 29:18). "Swearing in the name" of another god involves expressing both allegiance and dependence on this god (as prohibited in 5:11), and therefore looking to this god rather than Yahweh to provide (see Josh 23:7; Jer 5:7; 12:16; Amos 8:14; Zeph 1:5; also the positive equivalent in Isa 19:18; 45:23; Jer 12:16). The command is then to positively maintain a right attitude to the rescuing God (fearing and serving him) and actively reject any temptation to "sign up" with any other god. This will be a recurring theme in the rest of Moses's address.

The explicit challenge to reject the "gods of the peoples around you" shows that for the foreseeable future (see 7:22), Israel will have to cope

---

[141] Cisterns at Hazor and Taanach have been found that are Canaanite in origin. These "bottle shaped" excavations which served the whole community had a waterproof lining. See 2 Kgs 18:31; 2 Chr 26:10; Jer 2:13; 38:6 for later use in Israel.

with the enduring evidence of Canaanite worship in the land. "Following other gods" is highlighted in 11:28; 13:2; and 28:14, and picked up by Jeremiah in his preaching (e.g., 7:6, 9; 11:10; 13:10; 16:11; 25:6). The extent of their obedience will also determine both the degree and the duration of this temptation to idolatry in the land.[142] Moses is understandably keen to press them to deal decisively with these gods and their worship sites.

The reason he gives at this point is the same cited at 4:24 and 5:9: Yahweh, the God who is actually present with them (also 1:42; 7:21; 31:17) is a "jealous" God. In this context this can only mean that he demands relational exclusivity and loyalty. Anything other than covenant fidelity will provoke God's "anger" (the idiom is that the "nose" of Yahweh will be upon you, depicting God's wrath as a hot blast from his nostrils), which will, in turn, lead to their destruction.[143]

It is disturbing to read such blunt statements. But it is important for us to remember that an important (and ancient) part of the story of Israel's occupation of the land is the sinfulness of the Amorite occupants (Gen 15:16). It is a matter of justice that if Israel continues to act in exactly the same way, then they should suffer the same fate as those who have gone before and face the white-hot purity of the wrath of God. All the way through this sermon, Moses links God's extravagant grace with the terrible consequences of spurning that grace.

This truth needs to be embraced and allowed to shape Israel's attitudes, and in particular, to dissuade them from "testing" Yahweh.

The place name Massah (מַסָּה) is derived from the verb "to test" here (נָסָה). The command is not to test God as you did at "Testville." To "test" here is to provoke or even to "push" someone (in order to ascertain if someone will act in a specific way). God has the right to test individuals at key moments (e.g., Abraham in Gen 22:1; Israel in Exod 20:20; Deut 8:2), but humans do not have the right to treat God like this. In the past, Israel was "tested" by hardship; now they will be pushed to the limit by their experience of comfort.

---

142 The books of Kings narrate how this was an ongoing issue in and after the reign of Solomon; the northern kingdom was steeped in false worship from birth, and even the southern kingdom struggled to deal with the enduring issue of the high places.

143 Interestingly, the previous uses of the verb translated to "obliterate" in 2:1 and 2:21 described how the Edomites destroyed the Horites and how Yahweh himself destroyed the Rephaim before the Ammonites. Now his own people are threatened with the same fate if they behave like Canaanites. See also 7:4; 11:17; 13:12–17; 29:18–28.

The events which provided a paradigm of rebellion are described in Exodus 17:1–7 (see also Num 20:1–13; Deut 9:22; 32:51–52; 33:8; Ps 95:8; also 78:18). The incident started with complaining because of a lack of water and ended up with turmoil as people denied God's presence with and commitment to them and turned on Moses, God's appointed leader. Moses knows all too well that ingratitude quickly spills over into a sense of entitlement and then rage against both God's spokesman and even God himself.

But the best protection against future rebellion is careful obedience to the words of God in the present. This is spelled out in 6:17. The necessary response to God's action is summed up in a typically Deuteronomic expression, backed up with an unusual phrase in the next verse: only here, in 12:28, Proverbs 2:9 and 2 Chronicles 14:2 (concerning Asa) and 31:20 (concerning Hezekiah) do we get this combination of "good" and "right."[144] This behavior will make it possible for God's people to enter and possess the land promised to them by God and, more importantly, for them to enjoy the good life that God is holding out to them in the land (lit., that it might "go well with them"). The idea of "good" recurs in 6:10, 11 and now twice in this verse. This will, of course, involve driving out all their enemies, which will in turn help to ensure that they are not sucked into idolatry.[145]

6:20–25. Picking up his earlier encouragement to teach the next generation effectively, Moses then homes in on how to explain the nature and function of the "decrees, statutes, and ordinances," which, as we have seen, refers to his preaching of God's revelation to him in its entirety. As in the celebration of Passover (Exod 12:26–27; 13:14) and the later crossing of the Jordan (Josh 4:6–7, 20–24), it is envisaged that an inquisitive child will ask about the laws which shape the life of God's people. The Hebrew behind the question is slightly elusive, with the interrogative particle (מָה) having the sense of something like "what's with the decrees, etc.?" But it is reasonable to supply the word "meaning," as long as it is remembered that this is a bigger issue than just explaining the words (as in both Exodus and Joshua) .

Moses spells out the definitive answer in a form that is basically a simple creed (see also 26:5–11 for a similar approach). Verses 22–23

---

[144] Tigay suggests that this phrase refers to further application of torah to situations not explicitly covered, which may be correct (*Deuteronomy*, 82).

[145] This verse may pick up Exod 23:27–31.

step through the exodus experience, making it clear that God's dramatic rescue was linked intrinsically to the gracious promises made to the patriarchs. The "strong hand" of God recurs in 4:34; 7:8; 9:26 and 34:12. For Moses, God's rescue of his people from slavery in Egypt was the defining moment of their nation. But it is a moment that has ongoing ethical implications (see 5:15; 15:15; 16:12; 24:18, 22). Because they have been rescued by grace, this must shape the way in which they live, and in particular, the way in which they treat others. This is the "gospel-shape" of Deuteronomy.

God's stunning action on a global stage to subdue Pharaoh through "signs and wonders" was aimed ultimately to make it possible for the people he had chosen to occupy the land he had promised generations before to give to them as their own. In 6:24, Moses then sums up (and repeats) what Yahweh asks of his people as a response to his grace: obedience consistent with fearing Yahweh, which will guarantee both "prosperity" and "preservation." The real-time benefits of their covenant relationship with Yahweh will be both satisfaction and security, as they enjoy the good life (10:13) in the land with him.

In what proves to be a headline statement for the rest of the book, in 6:25 Moses states that "righteousness will be ours" if this formula is followed. This phrase (lit., "it will be righteousness for us") has sparked much discussion. What will obeying "all this commandment" lead to? Is this a similar idea to Genesis 15:6, where God "credits" righteousness to Abraham?

Righteousness in Deuteronomy is first and foremost God's own righteousness, which Israel is called to emulate. This is probably in view here. If God's people listen and obey, living with him and for him in the land that he gives before the watching world, they will be embodying (and even enjoying) the righteous life of God himself. This takes us to the heart of the theology of the book. Living the beautiful life described by God (listening to his word and doing what he says) results in a display of his righteousness, which is then publicly heralded by the righteous God himself (4:8; 24:13).

The idea here then (in contrast to Genesis) is not *primarily* forensic. However, given Moses's conviction, which becomes increasingly obvious through his speech, that God's people are not equipped to listen, obey and live (9:4–6), there is an unspoken implication that if Israel is ever to experience this righteousness, it will have to be given (by God), rather than achieved, an idea that becomes clear in chapter 7. The statement of

6:25 then is not at odds with Genesis 15:6, but rather begins to establish that if God's people are to taste this righteousness, then God himself will have to make this possible (as he did for Abraham).[146]

Bridge

Deuteronomy 6 is a stunning exposition of what covenant life with Yahweh, the righteous God, is all about—and it is profoundly gospel-shaped.

The living God who has kept his promises in enabling his people to flourish, bringing them to the edge of a new future in the land, is also the God who speaks to his people. Listening to his words (past, present, and future) is clearly the key to their existence—living in awe of his stunning grace, worshiping him alone, and obeying his every word. God's people are to live under the slogan "Yahweh is our God—Yahweh alone!" Yahweh commands their exclusive allegiance, attention, and obedience. Listening to him is the key to "remembering" rather than "forgetting," spiraling off into idolatry. This is to be the heartbeat of family life and national life, for this is the way of "righteousness."

However, Jesus's calls to righteousness in Matthew 5:18–20 are simultaneously deeply attractive and profoundly exposing. We simply do not have the resources in and of ourselves to maintain this kind of life. Ultimately, we know that righteousness needs to be given and received, rather than earned. So what are we to do?

At Jesus's transfiguration, Peter, James, and John, while standing on a mountain, hear a voice from heaven that says "This is my beloved Son, with whom I am well pleased. *Listen to him*!" Ultimately, it is only Jesus who speaks the word that can transform. It is only Jesus who can lead us into the kind of life sketched out so attractively in Deuteronomy. It is in coming to him, the one who has loved God with heart, soul, mind, and strength and who loved us as himself, that we find the beautiful life anticipated here. As Peter says in John 6:68, "Lord, to whom will we go? You have the words of eternal life."

This chapter then is a call to soak and saturate ourselves, and our families, and our churches, in the richness of the gospel, leaning hard on the only one who can give us what this chapter anticipates, which is both God's declaration that in Christ we are righteous and the moment

---

[146] God's righteousness here is "at once rectitude, acquittal and the condition brought about as a result." McConville, *Deuteronomy*, 145.

to moment experience of the righteous life with God, which starts now and endures forever.

4. Horeb Applied: Covenantal Faithfulness (7:1–26)

> 1 "When the Lord your God brings you into the land you are entering
> to possess, and he drives out many nations before you—the Hethites,
> Girgashites, Amorites, Canaanites, Perizzites, Hivites and Jebusites,
> seven nations more numerous and powerful than you— 2 and when
> the Lord your God delivers them over to you and you defeat them, you
> must completely destroy them. Make no treaty with them and show
> them no mercy. 3 You must not intermarry with them, and you must
> not give your daughters to their sons or take their daughters for your
> sons, 4 because they will turn your sons away from me to worship other
> gods. Then the Lord's anger will burn against you, and he will swiftly de-
> stroy you. 5 Instead, this is what you are to do to them: tear down their
> altars, smash their sacred pillars, cut down their Asherah poles, and
> burn their carved images. 6 For you are a holy people belonging to
> the Lord your God. The Lord your God has chosen you to be his own
> possession out of all the peoples on the face of the earth.
>
> 7 "The Lord had his heart set on you and chose you, not because you
> were more numerous than all peoples, for you were the fewest of all
> peoples. 8 But because the Lord loved you and kept the oath he swore
> to your ancestors, he brought you out with a strong hand and re-
> deemed you from the place of slavery, from the power of Pharaoh king
> of Egypt. 9 Know that the Lord your God is God, the faithful God who
> keeps his gracious covenant loyalty for a thousand generations with
> those who love him and keep his commands. 10 But he directly pays
> back and destroys those who hate him. He will not hesitate to pay back
> directly the one who hates him. 11 So keep the command—the statutes
> and ordinances—that I am giving you to follow today.
>
> 12 "If you listen to and are careful to keep these ordinances, the Lord
> your God will keep his covenant loyalty with you, as he swore to
> your ancestors. 13 He will love you, bless you, and multiply you. He
> will bless your offspring, and the produce of your land—your grain,
> new wine, and fresh oil—the young of your herds, and the newborn
> of your flocks, in the land he swore to your ancestors that he would
> give you. 14 You will be blessed above all peoples; there will be no
> infertile male or female among you or your livestock. 15 The Lord will
> remove all sickness from you; he will not put on you all the terrible
> diseases of Egypt that you know about, but he will inflict them on all
> who hate you. 16 You must destroy all the peoples the Lord your God is
> delivering over to you and not look on them with pity. Do not worship
> their gods, for that will be a snare to you.

> 17 "If you say to yourself, 'These nations are greater than I; how can I
> drive them out?' 18 do not be afraid of them. Be sure to remember what
> the Lord your God did to Pharaoh and all Egypt: 19 the great trials that
> you saw, the signs and wonders, the strong hand and outstretched arm,
> by which the Lord your God brought you out. The Lord your God will do
> the same to all the peoples you fear. 20 The Lord your God will also send
> hornets against them until all the survivors and those hiding from you
> perish. 21 Don't be terrified of them, for the Lord your God, a great and
> awesome God, is among you. 22 The Lord your God will drive out these
> nations before you little by little. You will not be able to destroy them
> all at once; otherwise, the wild animals will become too numerous for
> you. 23 The Lord your God will give them over to you and throw them
> into great confusion until they are destroyed. 24 He will hand their kings
> over to you, and you will wipe out their names under heaven. No one
> will be able to stand against you; you will annihilate them. 25 Burn up
> the carved images of their gods. Don't covet the silver and gold on the
> images and take it for yourself, or else you will be ensnared by it, for it
> is detestable to the Lord your God. 26 Do not bring any detestable thing
> into your house, or you will be set apart for destruction like it. You are
> to abhor and detest it utterly because it is set apart for destruction."

7:1–6. After pressing home the need for careful covenantal listening, Moses starts to deal with the specific challenges of occupying the land of Canaan. His overarching concern is to ensure that God's people grasp the fact that God's grace, demonstrated in both their election and the divine guarantee of success, demands an appropriate response. The required response is nothing less than complete commitment to Yahweh. This chapter as a whole shows key similarities with Exodus 23:20–33.[147]

In 7:1, the inhabitants of Canaan are represented as seven nations or tribal groups.[148] There is some fluidity in the terms (both "Canaanites" and "Amorites" are also used elsewhere to denote all the inhabitants of the land), but the list of seven nations may well be intended to designate a complete census of the present occupants of the land of promise.[149] Very similar lists occur in Joshua 3:10 and 24:11, (see also Exod 3:8, 17; 23:23; 34:11; Deut 20:17; Josh 9:1; 11:3; 12:8, where the Girgashites are

---

[147] Although this chapter has approximately 350 words, compared to 150 in the Exodus passage. As we have seen repeatedly, Moses is in effect preaching on the earlier text.

[148] See Gen 10:15–19. The "Hethites" is more commonly translated as the Hittites. This group is a remnant of the great Hittite Empire of the second millennium BC. For further discussion see, e.g., McConville, *Deuteronomy*, 152–53.

[149] For a judicious and exhaustive account of the identities and demography of these nations, see Lundbom, *Deuteronomy*, 328–32.

dropped from the list without explanation or replacement; also Exod 13:5 for a five member list). It seems fair to say that Moses has little interest in the fine distinctions or interrelations among these tribal groups. The main point for Moses is that these nations are "more numerous and powerful" than Israel. In that regard, they are clearly a potential obstacle to the fulfillment of God's promises both of population growth and occupation of this land. However, God is insistent that these nations who have long stood under his judgment (Gen 15:16) will not be able to hinder the progress of his plans for his people. In fact, it is God himself who will defeat them. In Exodus 23:20–23, God had promised to send an "angel" ahead of them. But now, in keeping with Moses's emphasis on the presence of God with his people, the spotlight falls not on the messenger, but on Yahweh himself.[150]

The insistence that God does the real fighting as he "delivers them over to you" is a basic part of the exodus tradition (see Exod 14:14) and has already been underlined in Moses's account of the campaigns in the Transjordan (Deut 2:24–25, 31). Now Moses maintains that the conquest of the land should be no different. Yahweh can be counted on absolutely to do his part. And the people? They must do theirs.

This brings us to the single most difficult and contested feature of the theology of Deuteronomy. Not only are the Israelites to subdue the Canaanites but "devote them to complete destruction."

This Hebrew phrase, which contains a double use of the verb חָרַם (a hiphil imperative absolute and a hiphil imperfect), is very difficult to translate. The central idea is that the object concerned is to be "devoted to God," which can either mean dedicated to his sole use or put beyond the use of others (i.e., destroyed, or at the very least, "decommissioned").[151]

This idea is set out in Leviticus 27:28–29, which is worth quoting in full:

> [28] Nothing that a man *permanently sets apart* to the Lord from all he owns, whether a person, an animal, or his inherited landholding, can be sold or redeemed; everything *set apart* is especially holy to the Lord. [29] No person

---

[150] T. Desmond Alexander, *Exodus*, AOTC (Downers Grove: InterVarsity, 2017), 532, highlights how some have argued that the presence of the "angel" in the exodus account can be understood as denoting that Yahweh himself is present.

[151] The concept was not limited to Israel. The word also appears on the Moabite stone, where Mesha applies the "ban" to 7000 Israelites, killing them in the name of Ashtar-Chemosh. See *ANET* 320. Also the discussion of similar issues arising from Deut 20 in Block, *Deuteronomy*, 474–79.

> who has been *set apart for destruction* [use of a nominal form חֵרֶם plus a hophal imperfect יָחֳרַם] is to be ransomed; he must be put to death.[152]

Some of the challenges in interpreting the application of this חָרַם principle in Deuteronomy can also be seen here in Leviticus. On the one hand, it seems to operate as a positive mechanism for designating something or someone as "belonging to Yahweh." Leviticus 27:28 makes clear that when this happens, it cannot be reversed for the benefit of the original owner. But the idea of destruction does not seem to be front and center. However, in the specific case outlined in 27:29, which seems to involve a stricter application of חָרַם (and accompanied by a double use of the root), there can be no mistaking the insistence that the person concerned should be executed. This slight ambiguity highlights that a translation like "completely destroy" may be a little wooden, and it might be better to stick with something like "subject them to the ban" or "apply the principle of *herem*."

In the rest of the Old Testament, it is important to note that for Israel, the application of the חָרַם principle is limited to the conquest of Canaan and the exceptional campaign against the Amalekites in 1 Samuel 15. But even during the Canaan campaign, at some points the requirements could be relaxed (Josh 6:25 and at others the reality was very different to what was envisaged, as the Canaanites resisted (and persisted; see Josh 16:10; 17:13; Judg 1:127–35; 1 Kgs 9:20–21). In addition, the fact that both Rahab (Josh 2) and the Gibeonites (Josh 9) are spared on the basis of a commitment given shows that the *details* of this kind of war are not moral absolutes and do not trump other ethical imperatives. This slightly messy ambiguity between the ideal and reality runs through this passage, and the rest of the book.

The fact that Deuteronomy 7:2–3 prohibits making a peace treaty with those already living in the land (and in particular prohibiting them from showing them mercy and/or intermarrying with them) is striking. The three commands (make no covenant/show no mercy/do not intermarry) could simply be parallel. However, each instruction has a markedly different nuance. First, "cutting a covenant" with the nations is ruled out. Although the word בְּרִית is clearly describing what we would call a treaty, in the context of Deuteronomy the use of the generic covenant word

---

[152] For a discussion of capital crimes in the torah, see Bruce Ballard, "The Death Penalty: God's Timeless Standard for the Nations?" *JETS* 43 (2000): 471–87.

brings basic issues of loyalty to Yahweh, the covenant God, firmly into view. Insisting that no mercy or grace (חָנַן) must be shown to these people (who stand under the judgment of Yahweh) is more than a simple requirement to carry out God's commands. It accentuates the exceptional nature of this situation. Normal service is suspended. The usual standing orders of Israel's warfare do not apply (see the discussion of ch. 20). However, the discussion of intermarriage seems to be addressing a slightly different challenge. This is not simply a hyperbolic or convoluted way of saying the same thing again.

The proscription of intermarriage is repetitive and slightly convoluted. A blanket ban is backed up by outlawing the joining of Israelite women to Canaanite men or Israelite men taking Canaanite wives. The family language (sons and daughters) is typical of Moses's conception of the people of Israel as the (extended) family of God. The emphasis placed on preventing this practice, and the smooth transition to the rationale behind the ban (that doing this would lead inexorably to Israel "turning away" from Yahweh to worshiping other gods; see also Deut 4:9; 5:32; 7:15; 9:12, 16; 11:16, 28; 17:11, 17, 20; 21:13; 28:14; 31:29), would seem to imply that this command cannot simply be a synonym for destroying them.[153]

Trying to tie down the precise nature of חֵרֶם in Deuteronomy (and the books that follow, particularly Joshua) is not easy. On the one hand, some of the language clearly demands divinely sanctioned, judicial killing of the entire Canaanite population (this is explicit both in 7:2, and in other texts such as 20:17; Josh 6:21). But on the other, there also seems to be the expectation that the reality on the ground will be messy and less than clear-cut. The conquest won't actually be the *blitzkrieg* that it could be (see 7:22). As the narratives of Joshua flesh out, there will be dubious deals made by fearful spies (Josh 2), disobedience leading to unanticipated defeats (Josh 7), and opportunistic Gibeonites (Josh 9) to deal with. Some pockets of Canaanite resistance will prove stubborn (like Jebus, Josh 15:63), and some tribes' attempts to take their land will be less than exemplary (e.g., Josh 19:40–48). How are we to resolve this tension?

It will not do on the one hand to try to argue that חֵרֶם is purely a metaphorical or even a spiritual idea. However, Leviticus 27:28–29 does suggest that there are grounds for understanding חֵרֶם as operating simultaneously

153 Exod 34:15–16 further supports the contention that this was a genuine (realistic) expectation, rather than simply another way of saying they must be destroyed.

at both an in principle level (judicially) and an extremely realistic (even mundane) level. The Canaanites are under the judgment of God. He has jurisdiction over them and has spoken. Canaanite civilization has been judged by God and is finished. It needs to be dismantled. That much is clear and beyond dispute. However, precisely how that is to be applied on the ground in a gradual conquest has yet to be worked out.

So for example, all the inhabitants of Jericho are put to death (Josh 6:21). Are the inhabitants of Jebus in the same situation? In theory, yes. But how is that to be worked out as they stubbornly resist the advances of Judah? How long does the command to put them to death remain in place? What should be done with people who flee to the hills or are encountered years into the occupation? Is it the Canaanite *civilization* that is to be destroyed totally or every individual (like the Israelite who is condemned to death in Lev 27:29)?[154] None of these questions is answered explicitly by the text of Deuteronomy. But this much is clear: Moses speaks from a standpoint where he is completely committed to God's ideal (as is reflected by the strength of language in 7:4, which picks up similar ideas to 6:15), but he is also divinely realistic in his expectation that God's verdict on the Canaanites will be worked out imperfectly by sinful people in a messed-up world.[155]

This basic concern with the sinful vulnerability to the influence of Canaanite idolatry is reflected in 7:5 (see also 20:17–18). Moses makes clear that as part of executing God's judgment against the Canaanites, Israel must permanently dismantle and destroy the apparatus of local idolatry (see also 12:2–3 and Exod 23:24; 34:13). This includes pulling down their sacrificial altars (basically tables on which to place offerings), smashing all symbols of the male deities ("pillars," which are probably phallic representations, although Gen 35:14 and Exod 24:4 may suggest the word has a more general reference) and those of the female gods.

The "Asherim" are probably poles matching the "pillars" and carved in the image of the goddess Asherah.[156] Asherah's particular significance

---

[154] Ford ("Challenge of the Canaanites," 161–84) highlights the fact that the focus of the action demanded by God through Moses in Deuteronomy is on intermarriage and idolatry, the twin dangers that most threaten Israel.

[155] The singular verbs of v. 3 give way to a plural in v. 4. This "number mixing" appears to have no particular significance and is best attributed to a fairly loose verbal style. It is also worth noticing that Moses's words and God's words at points are hard to distinguish (see also, e.g., 11:14–15).

[156] Some suggest that they may have been trees, but there is no clear evidence for this.

is that she was the wife of the high god El (and later, also, it seems, Baal) and mother of over seventy other Canaanite gods, whose images are also to be obliterated.[157] The unnerving implication of Moses's words (which fits with much of what we have already heard) is that if *any* vestige of this idolatry remains, it will only be a matter of time before Israel is ensnared, and this simply must not be.

The underlying rationale for this is given in 7:6, in terms that are strongly reminiscent of Exodus 19:5–6. Israel is a "holy people belonging to the Lord your God." [158] The contrast suggested in Leviticus 27:28–29 is underlined here: Israel, God's holy people, is set apart for Yahweh. The Canaanites are set apart for destruction. To be holy in this context means both to be utterly committed to Yahweh and also righteous (and by extension, morally pure) as he is. But Moses doesn't stop there, insisting that "The Lord your God has chosen you to be his own possession out of all the peoples on the face of the earth." In 4:37 the patriarchs were chosen. Now for the first time, the language is applied to the nation (see also 10:15; 14:2).[159]

The word "possession" (סְגֻלָּה) carries the connotation of "personal treasures" (which is what it means in a literal sense in Eccl 2:8; 1 Chr 29:3), but here is a striking representation of God's commitment to and love for his chosen people (see Exod 19:5; Deut 14:2; 26:18; also Ps 135:4 and Mal 3:17).[160] Opinion is divided as to whether or not the phrase "out of all the peoples on the face of the earth" effectively makes this statement concerning Israel "missional."[161] Given the context of commanding the Israelites to deal ruth-

---

[157] See Frank Moore Cross, *Canaanite Myth and Hebrew Epic* (Cambridge: Harvard University Press, 1973), 32.

[158] The people are also called "holy" in 14:2, 21; 26:18–19; 28:9; and designated Yahweh's own people in 9:29; 27:9; 29:13; 32:9; also 33:29. Block points out that the "warm" word for people (עַם) occurs here, whereas Exod 19 uses the "cold" political word for people or nation (גוֹי). Block, *Deuteronomy*, 208–10.

[159] In time, "election" language would also be applied to David (e.g., Ps 89:3) and Zion (e.g., Ps 132:13). In the Old Testament, however, the overarching category is God's choice of his *people*. See Amos 3:2 for another striking statement of this truth.

[160] The term is also found in a Hittite treaty from around 1300 BC (see Weinfeld, *Deuteronomy 1-11*, 368).

[161] See my discussion of this issue in *Now Choose Life*, 153–54. It is also interesting that the language of priesthood is not picked up here. This may be because the emphasis in Deuteronomy is on the presence of Yahweh, who displays his superiority through the nation as a whole, rather than it being mediated in a priestly fashion. The difference, however, is only one of emphasis. Ideas of priesthood and positional holiness can be found elsewhere in the book (e.g., chs. 14, 23).

lessly with the Canaanites, it is important not to overstate this, but there is a sense in which the international dimension of the promise made to Abraham in Genesis 12:1–3 is picked up in Exodus 19:6, and that note is sounded again here. This note is not dominant, but neither can it be dismissed.[162]

7:7–11. The explanation Moses gives of God's choice of Israel in 7:7–8 is probably the clearest, most remarkable, and most beautiful statement of the doctrine of election in the whole Bible. The language is strong and daring: literally, the Lord "desired" Israel (חָשַׁק), an expression that often refers to sexual desire (Gen 34:8; Deut 21:11) or personal ambition (when used of Solomon in 1 Kgs 9:1, 19; 2 Chr 8:6), but here and in Deuteronomy 10:15 of God's deep affection for his people, and in Psalm 91:14 of the affection of the faithful Israelite for God. There is nothing cold and clinical about God's electing love. It is born of profound interpersonal commitment to the people he created and chose. However, lest any of God's people (at this stage, or at any point in their history) start to slide into thinking that Yahweh recognized something admirable or attractive in them, Moses backs this up with an assertion that "you were the fewest of all peoples" (see also the phrase "other nations greater and stronger than you" in 4:38; 9:1; 11:23).

One might be tempted to dismiss this as hyperbole, but in the case of Israel, their origins as a single family (whether that of Abraham, or latterly, Jacob's family "going down into Egypt") mean that the words should probably be taken literally. The Egyptian population dwarfed that of Israel, even as they left. Presumably, the Canaanites when taken *en masse* did the same (hence the need to secure each part of the land carefully before pressing on). The promise to Abraham has been partially realized, but there is much farther to go.

The only reasons given for God's extravagant commitment to Israel are his love (or more accurately, that he "loved you") and his faithfulness to the promises made to their ancestors (particularly Abraham, Isaac, and Jacob), both of which were displayed in the exodus, which is described in Moses's favorite terms. Yahweh's "strong hand" once more frees his people from "the house of slavery" (see 4:34 and 7:19), although this time, Yahweh is also said to pry them out of the control of Pharaoh, "king of Egypt."[163] All of this is rooted in the nature of God himself and is an expression of pure, unmerited favor.

---

[162] For a vigorous (and at points compelling) case for understanding a missiological impetus in this text, see Wright, *Deuteronomy*, 111–15.

[163] The word here is פָּדָה, which can be translated "ransom" or "redeem" (see 9:26; 13:5 [Heb. 13:6]; 15:15; 21:8; 24:18).

This definitive experience of Yahweh in action should, according to Moses, lead to one basic theological realization and affirmation: that Yahweh, the God of Israel ("your God"), is "God." In this clause, perhaps surprisingly, the word for God in each case is אֱלֹהִים. Once more, at the very least, this is a claim to supremacy on the part of Yahweh (as in 4:49). This is further clarified in the rest of the verse, as he is called "the faithful God" (this time using the word אֵל, which usually designates the "Most High God" of the ancient Near Eastern pantheon, but here simply refers to the generic idea of "God"). The use of אֵל with the definite article is relatively unusual, but it heightens the implication that Yahweh is the one and only God.[164]

The expression "keeps his gracious covenant loyalty" builds on the classic expression of God's commitment to Israel in Exodus 34:6–7 but does so by speaking of Yahweh's unshakeable commitment to keep "the covenant" (הַבְּרִית) and "the steadfast love" (וְהַחֶסֶד). This striking phrase is then picked up by Solomon (1 Kgs 8:23; also 2 Chr 6:14), Daniel (Dan 9:4) and Nehemiah (Neh 9:32) in their epic covenantal prayers, but does not seem to appear elsewhere.[165]

The classic statement of Exodus 20:5–6 (also Exod 34:6–7; Deut 5:10) promising immense and limitless generosity to those who love him and keep his commands is accompanied by a much simpler statement of God's contrasting treatment of those who "hate him."[166] This time, there is no mention of the effect reverberating down through the generations (or across extended families, if that is what the text means). Instead, the focus is on God's direct and instant intervention against those who hate him. The repetition of the phrase "He will not hesitate to pay back directly the one who hates him" makes this an extremely emphatic idea. The use of שָׁלֵם here conveys the idea of an immediate, full, and personal reckoning for any "hate crime" against Yahweh, which is essentially any failure to listen to him, honoring him as the one and only God. The suffix on the verb makes clear that all God's enemies will pay a terrible price for hating him.

---

164 Similar uses with the article are found in Gen 31:13; 46:3; Deut 10:17; 2 Sam 22:31, 33, 48; Neh 1:5; 9:32; Pss 18:30, 32, 47; 68:19, 20; 77:14; 85:8; Isa 5:16; 42:5; Jer 32:18; Dan 9:4.

165 For a discussion of the nature of these prayers as asking God to come through on his covenant promises, see J. Gary Millar, *Calling on the Name of the Lord: A Biblical Theology of Prayer*, NSBT 38 (London: Apollos, 2016).

166 In Exodus (and Deut 5), the text simply says "thousands," which may imply a thousand generations or simply a large number. See, e.g., Alexander, *Exodus*, 389, 648.

In the context of impending judgment against the Canaanites after hundreds of years of such behavior, it seems clear that God's chosen people are to be held to higher standards. This means that the blunt conclusion of 7:11 is inevitable: Israel simply *must* keep "the command" (singular once more) fleshed out in the statutes and ordinances (also 5:31) that Moses is expounding and explaining at Moab.

It is clear that there can be no question of the unconditionality of Yahweh's commitment to Israel leading to a blasé disregard for his words. The relationship and the revelation have been given as a gift, but the enjoyment of these privileges is conditional on wholehearted obedience. Or to put it slightly differently, knowledge of God leads to obedience to God, which in turn leads to enjoying the blessing of God.

7:12–16. Having warned them of the consequences of "hating" rather than "loving" Yahweh, Moses turns again to the positive incentives for obedience.[167] Repeating the words of 7:9, Moses insists that "listening" to the words of God and the ensuing obedience *will* lead to his maintaining "covenant loyalty" or perhaps better, his "covenant of love" that originated with the patriarchs.[168] And what are the consequences of Yahweh keeping his covenant? Moses's language is both comprehensive and extravagant.

The promise that Yahweh will "love you" confirms the fact that אָהֵב is not merely a diplomatic term applied to treaty keeping or it would simply be duplicating the previous statement. The intention to "bless" initially recalls the promises made to Abraham in Genesis 12:1–3 (and subsequently echoed throughout Genesis), which is confirmed by the expansive exposition of these ancient promises in the phrases which follow. Although language of multiplication does not appear in Genesis 12 (being drawn rather from Gen 1:27 and elsewhere), the concept is front and center, as God promised to make a great nation from the "offspring" (seed) of the patriarch, as further stated in Genesis 15:5. However, the promises dealing with the fruitfulness of the land are a Mosaic expansion, based on ideas also found in Exodus 23:25–26 (see also Lev 26:1–13), which

---

[167] Although it is almost impossible to capture in English, 7:12 opens with words meaning "and it will come to be because … ." This underlines that Moses is dealing with the consequences of doing what God says.

[168] There is no real reason for inserting the word "gracious" in 7:9 but leaving it out here. The Hebrew phrase is the same. The two nouns "covenant" and "steadfast love" are in apposition. The different translation options arise from prioritizing one or the other. Given the weight of usage in Deuteronomy, it seems more likely that "love" qualifies covenant here.

is thoroughly appropriate for the setting on the plains of Moab.[169] The produce of the land, summed up as grain, new wine, and olive oil (see also 11:14; 12:17; 14:23; 18:4; 28:51), as well as the young of cattle ("herds") and sheep and goats ("flocks") will also be abundant, providing a tangible expression of Yahweh's favor (see also 28:4, 18, 51).[170]

The particularly Deuteronomic emphasis on Israel's blessing taking place before an audience of watching nations (see 4:5–8) is picked up in 7:14, where the blessing which flows from being in covenant with Yahweh is said to far outstrip any enjoyed by any other nation (see also 28:1–11). In Israel, this displays itself in the absence of anything that might interrupt the flow of the expansion of the nation or material blessing, in this case, the infertility of either people or breeding animals.[171] The prospect of uninterrupted blessing with Yahweh in their land is then contrasted with life in Egypt. This "blessed life" in the land is in marked contrast to their past experience in Egypt (which sets up the depiction of the "cursed life" as a return to Egypt (see also 11:26–32; 28:15–68). In particular, God will guarantee the health of his people in the land, "remov[ing] all sickness" from them. Instead of the "terrible diseases of Egypt," they will apparently enjoy perfect health; their enemies, however, can expect to be cursed with these very illnesses.[172]

One could be forgiven for thinking that these statements seem a little over the top. In fact Moses's extravagance at this moment does sound like a prototype of the prosperity gospel, proponents of which are quick to use Old Testament passages like this as a basis for guaranteeing health and wealth to their followers. However, in the context of Moses's preaching, it must be remembered that these promises are (a) *national* rather than individual; (b) *redemptive-historical* (or even *missional*) rather than simply personal; and (c) *symbolic* rather than strictly literal. This is not to say that God's blessing does not carry with it certain real-time benefits (such as protection from particularly Egyptian diseases, Exod 15:26), but it would

---

[169] The word for "land" (אֲדָמָה) used here is not the one used in 7:1 (אֶרֶץ), probably to emphasize the fertility idea.

[170] Hos 2:7–9 uses the same language to describe Israel's attribution of these to other gods. It may be that the words used for the produce, including the "lambs of your flocks," are echoing the names of Canaanite deities, with the clear implication that they are under the control of God himself,

[171] A similar idea is present in Exod 23:26.

[172] Pliny, the Roman Historian, called Egypt "the mother of skin diseases." See Tigay, *Deuteronomy*, 89.

be pushing the rhetoric of Moses's preaching too far to insist that no Israelite would ever get sick and die (unless they sin and fall under the curse of God). The contrast is between a life of loving God, in which the beneficence of God is enjoyed by the nation, and a life of "hatred" of God, in which the beautiful life in the land cannot be experienced.

This basic contrast, which undergirds the entirety of Moses's preaching in this book, necessitates the destruction of the Canaanites in 7:16. In this context, the Israelites' attitude to the occupants of the land is an index of their commitment to Yahweh. A commitment to love rather than hate Yahweh will lead inexorably to them following his instructions to the letter, and "destroying" (lit., "eating" or "devouring") the Canaanite tribes, and showing them no mercy.[173] The fact that this is backed up with a prohibition on worshiping their gods lest they be "ensnared" underlines that Moses's rhetoric continues to be underpinned by a deep realism. It is the Israelites' propensity to wander off the straight and narrow that, in this context, necessitates the removal of every last vestige of Canaanite idolatry. The focus is not on the wickedness of the nations, but on the weakness of God's people. Moses knows they will struggle to carry out God's commands. He also is convinced that should they waver, they will inevitably be susceptible to pagan idolatry.

7:17–26. It is this twofold suspicion (that Israel won't be able to take the land and as a result will be ensnared by idolatry) that gives rise to Moses's double warning in 7:17–26.

In verses 17 to 24, he piles up reasons against faltering in the impending conquest. If the Israelites are daunted by the thought (or sight) of the military strength of the seven Canaanite nations, questioning their ability to dispossess them, then in the first place, they are to remember the exodus. In 7:18, they are to recall "what the Lord your God did to Pharaoh and all Egypt" (as in 4:34 and 6:22). The call to "remember" is intensive (qal imperfect plus infinitive absolute). Moses summarizes the events of the escape from Egypt in familiar terms as "the great trials that you saw, the signs and wonders, the strong hand and outstretched arm."[174] But the point here is that God will repeat these actions in order to deal with "all the peoples you fear." He is not, of course, limited to these

[173] See Deut 13:8–9; 19:13, 21; 25:12, for cases where Israelites may be tempted to be too lenient.

[174] See Deut 4:34; 5:15; 6:21; 11:2; 26:8; 29:3; 34:11 for various combinations of these terms.

methods. Moses reminds them that he has also promised to deploy "hornets" against these nations (7:20, also Exod 23:28; Josh 24:12) to thwart both those who fight and those who flee.[175] There is no need to fear, for the defeat of those who oppose God and his people will be absolute. However, Moses's assumption is that they will fear the Canaanites, rather than fearing the God of the covenant.

As if the promise of *divine intervention* were not enough, Moses backs that up with a reassurance of guaranteed *divine presence.* Yahweh "their God," who is both "great" and "awesome" (derived from the verb "to fear," יָרֵא), is "among you." From the climactic events of Sinai onwards, this is a key idea in the life of the nation. The God who heard their cry in Egypt, brought them out with signs and wonders, made his presence visible to them in cloud and fire, spoke to them "out of the midst of the fire," and established his temporary dwelling with them in the tent, is perennially "among them." For Moses, this is the primary distinctive of Israel (4:5–8).[176] He is "for" them, so there is no need to panic (also 1:29–30).

The tone changes, however, in verse 22. Despite the assurance of the presence of the "great and awesome God" and the clear, repeated promise of a straightforward conquest (should Israel obey), the process of occupation will be slow and gradual. Recalling Exodus 23:30, Moses reminds the people that Yahweh has undertaken to deal with them "little by little," adding the explanation that a *blitzkrieg* would leave Israel vulnerable to being overwhelmed by the "wild animals." This is another example of the strange mixture of idealism and realism that Moses displays in his preaching. On the one hand, he is completely unequivocal on both God's commitment to the conquest and Israel's responsibility. But on the other, he regularly adds comments that reflect a keen grasp on the realities of the situation.[177] In this case, the warning about the wildlife should be taken as highlighting the challenge of a small nation (7:7) attacking, securing, and occupying a land currently held by a much larger population.

---

175 The word is translated "hornet" under the influence of the Septuagint. McConville argues that the parallelism in Exod 23:7–8 suggests simply translating it as "panic" (*Deuteronomy*, 149).

176 This also undergirds Moses's explanation of the "place God chooses," as we shall see when discussing ch. 12.

177 For example, the prohibition of intermarriage, coming right after the command to destroy. Similarly, the critique of the request for a king and the qualifications for a suitable candidate in 17:14–20 reflect this balance.

The exigencies of a campaign to take over an entire country, however, should not be allowed to detract from their absolute confidence in God. It is reiterated in 7:23 that God will overcome the Canaanites, throwing them into "great confusion" prior to their defeat. No king will be able to stand against Israel (7:24), and their names (and dynasties) will be consigned to the dustbin of history, as in Joshua 12:7–24 (see also the judgment on the Amalekites in Exod 17:14; Deut 25:19). No one will be able to withstand their divinely guaranteed advance, and Canaanite civilization will be destroyed.

For Moses at this point in his address, the primary concern is to ensure that Israel is clearly and exclusively committed to Yahweh, which will entail eradicating every vestige of pagan worship from the land they are entering. Carved idols must be burned (7:25). Where wooden idols have a veneer of gold or silver, these metals must be put beyond use (since the metals can't be "destroyed," this presumably means something like the process of Exod 32:20). The decadence of Canaanite religion posed a multivalent threat—worshiping other gods, bowing down before images and "coveting," with the result that they would "bear Yahweh's name unworthily." This would be "detestable" to God. This is the first occurrence of the word "detestable" in Deuteronomy (תועבה). In Genesis (43:32; 46:34) and Exodus (8:26), it refers to Israelite practices that are unconscionable for Egyptians, but in Leviticus (see ch. 18, especially 18:26–27), it is used to denote the abominable behavior of Canaanites in the land. To be "detestable" is both to be tainted with idolatry and morally repugnant. This is why nothing with Canaanite associations is to be brought into an Israelite home, but is to be "set apart for destruction" (חֵרֶם). If an Israelite contravenes this, then he or she is to be treated like a Canaanite and be "set apart for destruction."[178] In this context, this is a helpful translation of the term חֵרֶם because the focus is *not* on the destruction itself, but on the spiritual necessity which stands behind it. This is confirmed by the final statement of the chapter: emphatically, Israel is to "abhor" and "detest" (the verbal form of "detestable") everything connected with Canaanite idolatry with a passion, because it has been condemned by God.

Bridge

This chapter takes us to the very heart of the nature of our relationship with God. It is God who initiates, who chooses, who rescues and who

---

[178] This is played out in real time in the story of Achan in Josh 7.

reveals himself to his people. Consequently, it is only God who can guarantee our future with him. For God's people, it is all of grace. As Paul so memorably says in Romans 8:29–30:

> [29] For those he foreknew he also predestined to be conformed to the image of his Son, so that he would be the firstborn among many brothers and sisters. [30] And those he predestined, he also called; and those he called, he also justified; and those he justified, he also glorified.

The unconditionality of our covenantal relationship with God is staggeringly plain. And yet Moses in this chapter is not slow to spell out the far-reaching covenantal obligations that grace brings to those who have been freely chosen by God. The way of blessing is continued obedience in wholehearted worship of Yahweh. But how can this be maintained? How can the unconditionality and conditionality be reconciled? The answer remains unclear until the Lord Jesus, God in the flesh, perfectly meets the requirements of torah, living a beautiful life, fulfilling every condition which God has laid down, so that we might bask in the unconditional love of the Father. And he does all this by living a flawless life and dying a substitutionary death for us to achieve our redemption.

The jarring note in the chapter is, for many people today, the fact that the Canaanites must be destroyed completely. It is helpful to remember that (1) this was a common feature of ancient warfare; (2) Moses's preaching tends to use extravagant, sweeping language, but this is accompanied by a deep realism about how hard it will be for God's people to obey; and (3) the focus is ultimately not on the details of warfare, but Israel's exclusive allegiance to Yahweh himself. This unique and challenging historical situation ensures that the judgment of God cannot be taken lightly and prepares the way for the New Testament insistence that only in Christ can we find life and safety and that to reject him is to be exposed to the full fury of the wrath of God forever.

5. Learning from the Wilderness: Covenantal Dependence (8:1–20)

> [1] "Carefully follow every command I am giving you today, so that you may live and increase, and may enter and take possession of the land the Lord swore to your ancestors. [2] Remember that the Lord your God led you on the entire journey these forty years in the wilderness, so that he might humble you and test you to know what was in your heart, whether or not you would keep his commands. [3] He humbled

> you by letting you go hungry; then he gave you manna to eat, which you and your ancestors had not known, so that you might learn that man does not live on bread alone but on every word that comes from the mouth of the Lord. 4 Your clothing did not wear out, and your feet did not swell these forty years. 5 Keep in mind that the Lord your God has been disciplining you just as a man disciplines his son. 6 So keep the commands of the Lord your God by walking in his ways and fearing him. 7 For the Lord your God is bringing you into a good land, a land with streams, springs, and deep water sources, flowing in both valleys and hills; 8 a land of wheat, barley, vines, figs, and pomegranates; a land of olive oil and honey; 9 a land where you will eat food without shortage, where you will lack nothing; a land whose rocks are iron and from whose hills you will mine copper. 10 When you eat and are full, you will bless the Lord your God for the good land he has given you.
>
> 11 "Be careful that you don't forget the Lord your God by failing to keep his commands, ordinances, and statutes that I am giving you today. 12 When you eat and are full, and build beautiful houses to live in, 13 and your herds and flocks grow large, and your silver and gold multiply, and everything else you have increases, 14 be careful that your heart doesn't become proud and you forget the Lord your God who brought you out of the land of Egypt, out of the place of slavery. 15 He led you through the great and terrible wilderness with its poisonous snakes and scorpions, a thirsty land where there was no water. He brought water out of the flint rock for you. 16 He fed you in the wilderness with manna, which your ancestors had not known, in order to humble and test you, so that in the end he might cause you to prosper. 17 You may say to yourself, 'My power and my own ability have gained this wealth for me,' 18 but remember that the Lord your God gives you the power to gain wealth, in order to confirm his covenant he swore to your ancestors, as it is today. 19 If you ever forget the Lord your God and follow other gods to serve them and bow in worship to them, I testify against you today that you will certainly perish. 20 Like the nations the Lord is about to destroy before you, you will perish if you do not obey the Lord your God."

8:1–6. At this point, attention switches back to the exodus and wilderness experiences of God's people. Rather than focusing on the surrounding nations to stir them up (as in chs. 1–3), Moses now turns to the details of their experience as a source for motivation. Once more, Israel's response to God is crystalized to a single act: "The entire commandment that I am commanding you today you are to guard by doing" (my translation).[179]

---

[179] Block (*Deuteronomy*, 226) argues that 6:5 is in view, which may be the case. On balance, I prefer to take it as referring to the Deuteronomic torah as a whole.

The focus is on "guarding" God's command throughout the chapter (8:1, 6, 11), for this "single" act will determine the future of the nation.[180] This is the way to thrive and multiply (in fulfillment of the Adamic and Abrahamic promises). This is the way to enter and take the land (1:8) that was promised to them as the people of God. This is the way to life, a theme that comes to dominate the message of the book (e.g., 30:15–20). God's prior actions (promises) call forth a response of covenant loyalty (or faith), articulated and embodied as obedience, that holds the key both to occupation and flourishing. The gospel-shape of the obedient life (the grace of promises preceding a response of faith) is evident.

Moses is quick to highlight the fact that God's prior interactions with his people have been targeted to produce the humility that would in turn move them to trust him and not themselves. If they "remember" what happened, it will shape their lives.[181] In this case, their memories should recall the events which unfolded over the forty years post-Horeb. As in 5:1–5, not every individual actually experienced these events, but the recollection of the tradition needs to shape their national consciousness.

The entire journey from Horeb to Moab was designed to expose the designs and intentions of the hearts of God's people (rather than revealing to Yahweh anything that he did not already know). In Hebrew anthropology, the heart is the control center of the personality, where key decisions are made and the basic character of a person is revealed.[182] During the wilderness period, God subjected his people to a searching examination. The key question was: Would they listen to God and do what he commanded?[183] In the context, it seems clear that the results of this exercise were not flattering, and should have had the effect of humbling them, so that they threw themselves on God's kindness and provision in faith.

According to verse 3, the regular experience of hunger and the subsequent unprecedented (and ongoing) provision of manna throughout this wilderness period (see Exod 16; Num 21; Josh 5:12), were intended to

---

[180] See also 5:31, 6:1 and 27:1.

[181] For the classic discussion of the importance of remembering in Deuteronomy, see Edward P. Blair, "An Appeal to Remembrance: The Memory Motif in Deuteronomy," *Int* 15 (1961): 41–47.

[182] See my *Changed into His Likeness*, 44–45.

[183] It is interesting that the other place in Deuteronomy where this idea occurs is 13:3, which is also dealing with the issue of the people's willingness or unwillingness to discern and listen to the truth.

teach them to rely on Yahweh. Some have suggested that manna is sweet edible honeydew found in droplets up to the size of a pea on Sinai tamarisk bushes. These droplets are thought to be produced by insects which then deposit the sticky crystalline material on the tamarisk.[184] However, the fact that these only appear seasonally, alongside the absence of the provision on the Sabbath, underlines the fact that whatever the means used, this was another example of God's supernatural provision for his people.[185] In Exodus 16, the manna was to be a test of obedience to Yahweh's torah, specifically tied to Sabbath observance. Now it becomes an index of their entire response to God. The irony in these verses, of course, is that Moses's audience already knows that the result of this particular test was a spectacular fail, which led to their parents' generation dying in the wilderness.

The reassurance that Yahweh could be relied on to nourish them as they negotiated some fairly inhospitable terrain should have taught them that he can be relied on to provide for our deepest needs, and in particular, the resources needed to obey "the entire commandment." The famous statement, quoted by Jesus in the Judean desert during his confrontation with the Evil One in Matthew 4:4 ("Man does not live on bread alone but on every word which comes from the mouth of the Lord") should then be read as a clear statement of our inability to do what God asks of us apart from his gracious provision. McConville helpfully comments that "the thought in this place is not directly a contrast between the material and the spiritual, but an assertion that people do not secure their wellbeing in their own strength."[186] The message of the wilderness years was that listening to the God who speaks (as flagged in chs. 4–6) and doing what he says is the way to ensure present and future blessing both for God's people as they enter and settle in the land of Canaan, and also for all humanity.

At this point, Moses also adds two more concrete expressions of God's overarching care for and equipping of his people. In verse 4, he reminds them that their outer clothing miraculously lasted right through this period (also 29:4–5), and they were also preserved from podiatric issues (a fact picked up by Nehemiah in his prayer in Neh 9:21). The point is that with swollen feet, one could not wear sandals, and therefore couldn't easily make any progress through the rough terrain. This evidence of

---

184 For more detail, see Tigay, *Deuteronomy*, 93. See also the discussion in Alexander, *Exodus*, 324–326.

185 See the helpful discussion in Lundbom, *Deuteronomy*, 349.

186 McConville, *Deuteronomy*, 169.

God's fatherly, covenantal love in relatively insignificant details further emphasizes that he can be relied on in every dimension of life moving forward. They are to "know with their hearts" (lit.) that this is part of God's parental training (or discipline), which is designed to humble them, equipping them for a life of faith.

The idea that Yahweh trains and disciplines his people, passing on instruction to them as a father to a son, is a crucial building block of the wisdom literature (e.g., Prov 3:11–12; 4:1; 19:18; Job 5:17), but it is here in Deuteronomy that the idea is first articulated.[187]

The thinking is also close to that of Hebrews 12:11–13, which given the references to both discipline and foot issues, may well be a reflection on these verses:

> 11 No discipline seems enjoyable at the time, but painful. Later on, however, it yields the peaceful fruit of righteousness to those who have been trained by it. 12 Therefore, strengthen your tired hands and weakened knees, 13 and make straight paths for your feet, so that what is lame may not be dislocated but healed instead.

This is a further illustration of the continuity between the shape of the faithful life in Deuteronomy and after the coming of the Lord Jesus.

Verse 6 returns to obedience as the central response of faith. Throughout this section of the book, Moses freely mixes and matches his injunctions. The combination of "walking in his ways" (see also 5:33; 11:22; 19:9; 26:17; 28:9; 30:16) and "fearing him" (e.g., 4:10; 6:13; 10:20; 13:4; 17:19) occurs only here and 10:12, but is part of the fabric of covenantal life that Moses commends and commands to his people. God is a father who disciplines and who must also be respected and obeyed.

8:7–10. The scene now shifts from the painful memories of the barren past to the prospect of a verdant future. The extravagant description of the land occupies three verses, as Moses piles up rich images of Canaan that seem to deliberately echo the description of the pristine garden created in Eden in the opening chapters of Genesis.[188] The simple designation of the land as "good" (8:7, 10) may well be a throwback to the persistent rhythm of Genesis 1.[189] The emphasis on the abundant supply of water

---

[187] See also 1:31; 4:36. The connection between Deuteronomy and the Wisdom tradition is often highlighted, but seldom discussed in any great detail.

[188] Tigay describes the language as "elevated and quasi-poetic." *Deuteronomy*, 93.

[189] See also Deut 1:25, 35; 3:25; 4:21, 22; 6:18; 9:6; 11:17. It is slightly unexpected that this designation does not occur after ch. 11.

(coming from "streams, springs, and deep water sources") throughout the land as a whole may also be an echo of the depiction of the newly created land in Genesis 2:10–14, where two of four rivers (Pishon and Gihon) are explicitly said to flow through entire lands, and the others are the Tigris and the Euphrates, which are known as two of the major water sources in the region. Here, the sources of irrigation are simply called "waters," which includes both wadis (seasonal "springs") and "deep water sources" (וּתְהֹמֹת; cf. Gen 1:2, and, using different language, Deut 4:18). This, as well as the stark contrast with the desert, highlights how easy it will be to settle down.

The abundance of the water not surprisingly leads to an abundance of produce: the list of "wheat, barley, vines, figs, and pomegranates" has no parallel in the Old Testament (although all are common enough, e.g., Num 13:23), nor is the designation "a land of olive oil and honey" a common one.[190] The fairly obvious point is made explicit in 8:9—this is a land where God's people will be able to eat as much food as they want when they want, for they will not experience poverty, but rather will "lack nothing" (see Neh 9:21; cf. Ps 34:9). The richness of their diet is matched only by the extent of their mineral resources. The rocks of the land are rich in iron ore (presumably what is intended by "whose rocks are iron"), and there are copper deposits in the highlands.[191] Presumably the emphasis is on these elements because of their utility at the dawning of the Iron Age, although it may also recall the list of Genesis 2:14. There has been discussion over the extent to which Moses has exaggerated the extent of mineral deposits; however the contrast of life in the land with their experience in the wilderness may be more than enough to explain the extravagant language.[192]

All this beneficence should lead the people to "bless" (essentially the same as thanking him in this context) Yahweh, the one who has given them this "good land" (the seventh and climactic use of the word). The

[190] The two terms "oil" and "honey" occur together in Deut 32:13 (in the Song of Moses), but the way in which they are used seems a little different. In 2 Chr 31:5 (and also Jer 41:8; Ezek 16:13, 19 and 27:17) the combination occurs in what looks like a sacrificial context, which again, is not identical. Many suggest that because "honey" can denote other sweet substances derived from dates or figs, this fits more naturally into a list of produce proper. However, this may be pedantic: given passages such as Judg 14:8 and the evidence provided by the *DCH*, it seems most straightforward to take it at face value.

[191] Only here and in Job 28:2 are these two resources paired like this.

[192] Lundbom, *Deuteronomy*, 352–353, has a detailed discussion of these issues.

rabbis argued that this is the only blessing explicitly commanded in torah, and used it as a justification for the practice of saying grace after meals.[193] However, even as Moses makes this explicit, there is a sense that this will simply function as an indictment of Israel's guilt. There is no doubt that in this place, God's promised blessing can (and should) be tasted by faith. Israel has every reason to be grateful. However, the course of their national history to date does not give substantial grounds for optimism—a fact confirmed in the verses that follow.

8:11–20. The years spent in the wilderness were designed by God, Moses explains, to promote a single-minded, focused obedience to God (and his entire command). However, their leader is very aware that there is a strong possibility that rather than remembering and learning from this journey, they will "forget Yahweh their God"(4:9, 23; 6:12). And what does this forgetfulness look like? It will be defined by a failure to keep God's commands, ordinances, and statutes (מִצְוֹתָיו וּמִשְׁפָּטָיו וְחֻקֹּתָיו), which cover every conceivable aspect of life and which God is in the process of giving them. As we have already discussed, it seems most natural to take this reference to the stipulations as referring to the material to come in chapters 12–26, rather than forcing the language into a straitjacket by arguing that the Mosaic preaching is described as rules and regulations.

If God's faithfulness in hunger and hardship on the way and the richness of the land when they arrived were (or should have been) strong incentives to obey, according to 8:12–13, there were significant snares waiting for them as they settled down. Coping with a vastly improved diet in the land would present a challenge: satiety can give rise to thankfulness (8:10) or forgetfulness (8:12; also 6:11–12; 32:15–18). Similarly, settling down in a "good" land (3:7) may produce humble gratitude, but moving into beautiful designer (lit., "good") houses can just as easily lead to complacency (8:12). The problem is, of course, that this land is so good that over time, the successful animal husbandry programs and an increased wealth base (which are almost bound to come Israel's way) can in themselves turn out to be a real issue.[194] Amassing silver and gold is always problematic for God's people (as in 17:17 where the king is warned against such accumulation), and the fact that everything else they have increases too just exacerbates the issues.

---

[193] See Jakob J. Petuchowski, "Not by Bread Alone," *Judaism* 7:229–43.

[194] Three forms of the same verb (to increase or multiply) are used in 8:13.

The trouble is that all this comfort and ease can so easily make them proud: God's wilderness discipline was designed to humble them, but these things threaten to "lift up their hearts" (8:14, lit.; cf. 17:20). It is interesting that this pride leads swiftly to forgetting their roots. Arrogance expresses itself in forgetting "Yahweh your God, who brought you out of Egypt, out of the *house* of slavery" (my translation). It seems slightly ironic that bringing them out of one awful "house" in Egypt to the beautiful houses of Canaan would cause the Israelites no end of trouble. But it all begins with an exalted "heart." There is a growing sense in these chapters that Israel's problems run deep, and that Moses's impassioned calls for obedience may founder on the rock of the nation's heart.

Moses then appeals to God's care for the nation which was on display all the way from Egypt to the verge of the land, high on the Moabite plains. God led them through the "great and terrible wilderness" (also 1:19; 32:10; Jer 2:6). He protected them from poisonous snakes and scorpions, recalling Numbers 21:6–9 (see also Isa 30:6). The fact that it was a "thirsty land" proved no object to Yahweh, who effortlessly provided water even from the hardest of rock (see both Exod 17:6; Num 20:7–11) and, once more, supplied their wilderness staple of manna. As he did in 8:3 and again in verse 5, in verse 16 Moses reminds them that the purpose of all this was to "humble and test [or: refine] you, so that in the end he might cause you to prosper." God is in the business of doing us good. The phrase "in the end" is literally "at your end": God reassures them that this is their destiny. And yet, they refuse to obey. More than that, they choose hubris over humility.

Despite God's avowed intent to prosper them, the people are envisaged as saying, "My power and my own ability have gained this wealth for me." God has brought them out by his "power and outstretched arm" (4:37; 9:29) but the people have no problem in appropriating that designation for themselves. The correction in verse 18 is a blunt warning that to defy reality like this is to undermine God's covenant commitment both to their fathers (whether the patriarchs or the Horeb generation) and to them. The use of "today" here is another example of the way in which Deuteronomy treats the covenant as both historic and continually current in the life of the nation, as it faces the future in Canaan.

The transition to the possibility of idolatry in verse 19 seems a little jarring and abrupt. But the logic is clear: to embrace hubris and reject Yahweh's covenant is, in effect, to open the door wide to idolatry, and it is only a matter of time before they start to "follow other gods to serve them and bow in worship to them." The consequences of such actions, as always, are dire: "today" God says, "you will certainly perish." The verbal form is intensive, and the mood is intense, as a covenantal curse is spelled out.[195] The repetition of "today" sets this up as a perpetual and pressing obligation, for as verse 20 makes clear, to ignore Yahweh and worship other gods will lead inexorably to suffering the same fate as the former occupants of the land, falling under the judgment of God (as also in Lev 18:24–28). In the case of Israel, however, the sole cause of their demise would be clear: refusing to "obey [the voice of] Yahweh" their God (8:20).

Bridge

It is not particularly surprising that at this stage in Moses's preaching, there is significant overlap of language and ideas, as he continues to expound the importance of listening to the words of Yahweh and doing them, or "keeping the entire commandment," as he says. For the Christian reader two things jump out. The first is the pervasiveness of the gospel shape of biblical faith. Here, just as clearly as in the New Testament, we can see that it is God's gracious action (in the promises to the patriarchs, the exodus, and his care for Israel in the wilderness) that lays the foundation for the response of faith, which, as is so often the case, is to be expressed in wholehearted obedience. The second is that the relentless grace of Yahweh, expressed, perhaps, most powerfully in the fact that he speaks to us through his word (8:4), should lead us to deep humility, as we realize that he is God and we are not and that the only hope we have of living as he asks of us is to throw ourselves on the limitless resources that he holds out to us in Christ.

It is interesting that these twin themes are actually drawn out at some length in the book of James, so often decried for its lack of overt gospel shape. But the reality is that the Lord Jesus's brother has grasped both the sweeping gospel imperative that flows from the death and resurrection of the Lord Jesus, that we keep the "perfect law of freedom" (see Jas 1:25; 2:12), displaying faith and "works" in perfect synergy, and also that, in the words of James 4:10, we are to "Humble yourselves before the Lord,

[195] The form of words here is similar to 4:26, with Moses himself this time acting as a witness against the nation.

and he will exalt you." By the end of chapter 8, it's clear that Moses would have said a loud "Amen" to both of these.

This chapter also speaks powerfully to the numbing effect of wealth and comfort and the profound dangers of self-satisfaction (incidentally, both themes that occupy James, as he addresses the problem of favoritism and the particular challenges facing the "rich"). The importance of listening continues to be the controlling theme in Moses's address, as it is in the book of James: "But be doers of the word, not hearers only, deceiving yourselves ... the one who looks intently into the perfect law of freedom and perseveres in it, and is not a forgetful hearer but a doer who works—this person will be blessed in what he does" (Jas 1:22, 25).

6. Learning from the Golden Calf: Covenantal Humility (9:1–10:11)

> 1 "Listen, Israel: Today you are about to cross the Jordan to enter and
> drive out nations greater and stronger than you, with large cities for-
> tified to the heavens. 2 The people are strong and tall, the descendants
> of the Anakim. You know about them and you have heard it said about
> them, 'Who can stand up to the sons of Anak?' 3 But understand that
> today the Lord your God will cross over ahead of you as a consuming
> fire; he will devastate and subdue them before you. You will drive them
> out and destroy them swiftly, as the Lord has told you. 4 When the Lord
> your God drives them out before you, do not say to yourself, 'The Lord
> brought me in to take possession of this land because of my righteous-
> ness.' Instead, the Lord will drive out these nations before you because
> of their wickedness. 5 You are not going to take possession of their land
> because of your righteousness or your integrity. Instead, the Lord your
> God will drive out these nations before you because of their wickedness,
> in order to fulfill the promise he swore to your ancestors Abraham,
> Isaac, and Jacob. 6 Understand that the Lord your God is not giving you
> this good land to possess because of your righteousness, for you are a
> stiff-necked people.
>
> 7 "Remember and do not forget how you provoked the Lord your God
> in the wilderness. You have been rebelling against the Lord from the
> day you left the land of Egypt until you reached this place. 8 You pro-
> voked the Lord at Horeb, and he was angry enough with you to destroy
> you. 9 When I went up the mountain to receive the stone tablets, the tab-
> lets of the covenant the Lord made with you, I stayed on the mountain
> forty days and forty nights. I did not eat food or drink water. 10 On the
> day of the assembly the Lord gave me the two stone tablets, inscribed
> by God's finger. The exact words were on them, which the Lord spoke

to you from the fire on the mountain. 11 The LORD gave me the two stone
tablets, the tablets of the covenant, at the end of the forty days and
forty nights.

12 "The LORD said to me, 'Get up and go down immediately from here.
For your people whom you brought out of Egypt have acted corruptly. They have quickly turned from the way that I commanded them;
they have made a cast image for themselves.' 13 The LORD also said to
me, 'I have seen this people, and indeed, they are a stiff-necked people. 14 Leave me alone, and I will destroy them and blot out their name
under heaven. Then I will make you into a nation stronger and more
numerous than they.'

15 "So I went back down the mountain, while it was blazing with fire, and
the two tablets of the covenant were in my hands. 16 I saw how you had
sinned against the LORD your God; you had made a calf image for yourselves. You had quickly turned from the way the LORD had commanded
for you. 17 So I took hold of the two tablets and threw them from my
hands, shattering them before your eyes. 18 I fell down like the first time
in the presence of the LORD for forty days and forty nights; I did not eat
food or drink water because of all the sin you committed, doing what
was evil in the LORD's sight and angering him. 19 I was afraid of the fierce
anger the LORD had directed against you, because he was about to destroy you. But again the LORD listened to me on that occasion. 20 The LORD
was angry enough with Aaron to destroy him. But I prayed for Aaron
at that time also. 21 I took the sinful calf you had made and burned it. I
crushed it, thoroughly grinding it to powder as fine as dust, and threw
its dust into the stream that came down from the mountain.

22 "You continued to provoke the LORD at Taberah, Massah, and Kibroth-hattaavah. 23 When the LORD sent you from Kadesh-barnea, he said,
'Go up and possess the land I have given you'; you rebelled against the
command of the LORD your God. You did not believe or obey him. 24 You
have been rebelling against the LORD ever since I have known you.

25 "I fell down in the presence of the LORD forty days and forty nights
because the LORD had threatened to destroy you. 26 I prayed to the LORD:

Lord GOD, do not annihilate your people, your inheritance, whom you redeemed through your greatness and brought out of Egypt with a strong
hand. 27 Remember your servants Abraham, Isaac, and Jacob. Disregard
this people's stubbornness, and their wickedness and sin. 28 Otherwise,
those in the land you brought us from will say, 'Because the LORD wasn't
able to bring them into the land he had promised them, and because he
hated them, he brought them out to kill them in the wilderness.' 29 But
they are your people, your inheritance, whom you brought out by your
great power and outstretched arm.

> [10:1] "The LORD said to me at that time, 'Cut two stone tablets like the first ones and come to me on the mountain and make a wooden ark. [2] I will write on the tablets the words that were on the first tablets you broke, and you are to place them in the ark.' [3] So I made an ark of acacia wood, cut two stone tablets like the first ones, and climbed the mountain with the two tablets in my hand. [4] Then on the day of the assembly, the LORD wrote on the tablets what had been written previously, the Ten Commandments that he had spoken to you on the mountain from the fire. The LORD gave them to me, [5] and I went back down the mountain and placed the tablets in the ark I had made. And they have remained there, as the LORD commanded me."
>
> [6] The Israelites traveled from Beeroth Bene-jaakan to Moserah. Aaron died and was buried there, and Eleazar his son became priest in his place. [7] They traveled from there to Gudgodah, and from Gudgodah to Jotbathah, a land with flowing streams.
>
> [8] "At that time the LORD set apart the tribe of Levi to carry the ark of the LORD's covenant, to stand before the LORD to serve him, and to pronounce blessings in his name, as it is today. [9] For this reason, Levi does not have a portion or inheritance like his brothers; the LORD is his inheritance, as the LORD your God told him.
>
> [10] "I stayed on the mountain forty days and forty nights like the first time. The LORD also listened to me on this occasion; he agreed not to annihilate you. [11] Then the LORD said to me, 'Get up. Continue your journey ahead of the people, so that they may enter and possess the land I swore to give their ancestors.' "

9:1–3. The key command in the first eleven chapters of Deuteronomy is clearly the call to hear or "listen" (see 4:1; 5:1; 5:27; 6:3, 4; 7:12; and now 9:1). The reality that God speaks to his people from heaven, making his presence known to them on earth, as expounded at length in chapter 4, then drives the overwhelming and persistent need to listen to him come what may. The God of Horeb still speaks and continues to say essentially the same thing (e.g., 6:3; 8:1). This goes some way to explaining why this section of the book exhibits a certain sameness, as the eddies and flows of Moses's preaching continue to circle around the same basic point. This pattern continues in chapter 9, as their leader homes in on the innate self-righteousness of Israel and, in particular, mines the events that took place while Moses was with God on the mountain to call the people once more to face their own stubborn sinfulness and then hear and obey in response to God's grace.

The language of 9:1–2 echoes that of 1:28, picking up the slightly exaggerated and fearful report of the ill-fated spying mission of Numbers 13, as well as that of 7:1 (where the emphasis is on God's grace, rather than the people's sin). In the opening three chapters of the book, Moses mocked the faithlessness of the people by presenting a highly ironic take on their journey post-Horeb. Now, much more directly, he takes on the root attitude that hampered their advance into Canaan forty years earlier. The spies' report had explicitly linked the tall Anakim with the mysterious Nephilim of Genesis 6:1–4 (Num 13:33). Irrespective of how one views the Nephilim, it is clear that there was something unhealthy in the attitude of those responsible for reconnaissance in the land.[196] In fact, it seems to border on superstition. The nations may be larger and militarily superior, their settlements well-protected (see the comment on 1:28) and their warriors physically—and spiritually—intimidating, but their experience to date should have made it clear that any fears that may have lingered from the days of Numbers 13 and 14 were essentially groundless.

The fundamental need of the people is to acknowledge and grasp ("understand") a fundamental theological truth according to 9:3. They are to know this *today*. Given the fact that Moses's use of "today" is a key rhetorical strategy to ensure that the obligation to listen to God is impressed on both the Moab generation and all who would follow after, it is more likely that the emphasis is on understanding *today* rather than God acting today, as the occupation itself begins.[197] This is confirmed by the similar calls to acknowledge theological truth "today" in 4:39.

In this instance, the truth to be grasped is that the God who will cross the Jordan before them (thus enabling their crossing) is a "consuming fire."[198] This phrase was used in 4:24, paired with the epithet "a jealous God," in the context of the terrible impact of Israel's idolatry.[199] Here, however, the focus is on the consequences for the Canaanites who stand under this God's judgment. The distinctive feature of this campaign is that it is prosecuted by this awesome, irresistible God: Moses says first that *he* will "devastate and subdue" them. The means he uses, however,

---

[196] None of the possible ways of interpreting Gen 6 are entirely without problems, but I take it that the incidents described involve human beings (with the "sons of God" taken to be the line of Seth), which is then a material factor in the judgment that follows in the Flood.

[197] See Millar, *Time and Place in Deuteronomy.*

[198] For similar language and imagery see Deut 32:22; Isa 29:6; 30:27, 30; Jer 5:14, 17. Block calls this a "quasi-titular designation." *Deuteronomy*, 244.

[199] This language has previously been associated with God acting in judgment against his disobedient people in Lev 9:24; 10:2; Num 11:1; 16:35.

will be the Israelites themselves, who, as God's agents, will "drive them out and destroy them swiftly." This destruction is a persistent note in the chapter (an intensive of שָׁמַד occurs six times in the chapter: verses 3, 8, 14, 19, 20, 25).[200] The word "swiftly" here requires some comment, not least because it is qualified by the fact that Yahweh himself stands behind this.

At first glance, this does seem to contradict the declaration of 7:22, where Moses explains that God will drive out the nations "little by little." It may be that this is simply a claim that individual battles will, like Jericho in Joshua 6, be rapid affairs when conducted in line with God's instructions.[201] However, there may well be a more nuanced theological approach to conquest behind these words.

It is important to notice two distinct perspectives on the conquest in Moses's preaching: (1) When speaking of the challenge presented by the resistance of the warlike Canaanites, the emphasis falls on God's overwhelming superiority and his effortless ability to overcome them in an instant (hence "swiftly"). (2) In contrast, when Moses addresses the fine-grain detail of what it will take for the Israelites to secure the entire region and start to live as God's people under his rule in his land, then the text is quick to point out that this messy process will take a long time (usually because of the sinfulness of the people).

9:4–6. Maintaining perspective on their responsibilities and capabilities in relation to God's will will be crucial as Israel moves forward to "possess the land."[202] In an added twist to 8:14 and 17, Moses now warns the people not simply of the dangers of forgetfulness but also of self-righteousness. Picking up on the ideas introduced in 7:7–9, Moses insists that any success that the nation tastes in the land (whether in taking it in the first place or living in it) cannot be interpreted as a reward for their goodness. Having already made clear that Israel has been chosen purely by grace, he now flips his argument to clarify that they were definitely *not* chosen because of their "righteousness." Neither Israel's election nor military success can be traced back to their innate qualities. Similarly, the Canaanites are not dispossessed and driven out because Yahweh prefers Israelites: God is acting in just judgment against them because of "their

---

[200] The multiple uses of the verb "drive out" (יָרַשׁ) in this section (9:1, 3, 4, 5, 6) creates a sense of momentum.

[201] See Lundbom, *Deuteronomy*, 362; Tigay, *Deuteronomy*, 97, for this position.

[202] It is important to remember that the final focus of Deuteronomy is not the destruction of the Canaanites, but the possession of the land (see also 9:23; 10:11).

wickedness," which has now presumably becoming "full" (Gen 15:16). His use of Israel as his means of judgment does not imply anything about their purity.

In order to drive home his point, Moses then explicitly stresses that no individual Israelite will ever be able to claim that they have been brought into the land because of their "righteousness" (see on 6:25), or their "integrity" (lit., "uprightness of heart"). Both their actions and motivation come up short. The explanation for their good fortune in what is about to happen is found in the overlap of two realities: the kindness and faithfulness of God in keeping his freely made promises ("the word he swore") to Abraham, Isaac, and Jacob (see also 7:8); and the wickedness of the current occupants of the land, which has been percolating for hundreds of years. Moses the preacher has not quite finished, but rams home his point with one more thing that the Israelites really do need to know.

Alongside the realities that God is a consuming fire and that he has not acted on their behalf because of their righteousness, Israel needs to come to terms with the fact that, in his mercy, he has overlooked the one contribution they have actually made to the situation: their stubbornness, for they are literally a "stiff-necked people" (9:6). From Horeb onwards, Israel can justly be characterized like this. The first use of the phrase comes in the Exodus narratives that Moses is about to revisit (see Exod 32:9; 33:3, 5; 34:9). In the context of Deuteronomy, this stiff-neckedness prevents attentive listening (as in the English word "headstrong"). Jeremiah also uses the phrase in 7:26; 17:23 and 19:15 (see also 2 Kgs 17:14; Neh 9:16, 17, 29; Prov 29:1).[203] As such it may be the opposite of the phrase "incline your ear" used elsewhere, e.g., 2 Kgs 19:16; Ps 10:17).[204] This spiritual stubbornness exhibited in ignoring God's words necessitates not only Moses's approach in this chapter, but this entire sermon, and ultimately the transforming work of God through the gospel (see, e.g., Deut 10:16; 30:6). Moses's preaching in this section is clearly born of a lifetime of leading and cajoling this reluctant and recalcitrant nation.

9:7–21. 9:7 serves as a transition to the evidence that the nation has been consistently "stiff-necked"—evidence that is not hard to find! From

---

[203] 2 Chr 30:8 and 36:13 however, do use the phrase in a more general sense of rebellion.

[204] Lundbom (*Deuteronomy*, 364) suggests that "the image is one of an obstinate, intractable animal, sufficiently strong to resist the yoke on the back of the neck (cf. Isa 48:4)" (see also Block (*Deuteronomy*, 244). There may even be the implication that Israel is acting like the calf that they make at Horeb!

the moment they left Egypt all the way to Moab, they have furnished multiple examples of their spiritual hardness. The journey from Horeb was basically a procession of insurrections. As Moses has insisted from the beginning of his address, their great need is to "remember and not forget" this. Moses then unpacks this double imperative at some length, as he returns to the events in the wake of their rescue from Egypt. The cadences of Moses's actual preaching are clearly evident here.

Israel may have made it to "this place," the valley opposite Beth-Peor (3:29; 4:46), but this is not a moment for unalloyed joy. Rather they need to reflect on the journey. Moses's point is highly confronting: their stubbornness revealed itself not simply in failing to listen, but in "provoking" Yahweh their God (9:8). The word is a strong one: the actions of God's people stirred up his righteous anger (also 9:19, 22; 1:34), as they refused to heed or obey the God who had both made and rescued them. In the next phrase, Moses insists that they have made a lifelong, national habit of rebelling against God.[205] The fact that at the very moment the nation proper was "born" at Mount Horeb (9:8), they managed to push Yahweh to the point of destroying them is indicative of what the future would hold.[206] Moses points out that the anger they had stirred up in Yahweh almost led to the instant destruction of the nation—a fact that had cast a long shadow over subsequent events.

From verse 9, Moses walks the people painstakingly through the disastrous events on Mount Horeb which have proven characteristic of their behavior. This entire section draws heavily on both Exodus 24 and 32–34, but is not slavishly dependent on those texts. It reads and sounds like a slightly loose homiletical first person reflection of these events (the exodus account is in the third person), which includes changes of emphasis and previously unknown details that are particularly relevant for the Moab generation.

Moses begins by summarizing his own experience during the "forty days and forty nights" on the mountain (Exod 24:18), an expression that seems to be intentionally repeated to set up a contrast with the forty years of aimless wandering in the desert that followed (see Deut 9:9, 11,

---

[205] The form of the verb "rebel" is intensive (a hiphil participle), used with the verb "to be" to indicate continuing action (see GKC §116r).

[206] The word order (the sentence begins with "At Horeb") emphasizes that the events on the mountain are typical of Israel.

18, 25; 10:10).[207] Interestingly, while on the mountain, Moses insists that he "did not eat food or drink water." The most natural way of reading this is that in the presence of Yahweh, Moses was miraculously sustained physically (as was also the case on his return visit to the mountain in Exod 34:28).[208] The dramatic provision of manna and quail (and water) in the wilderness for the whole people was a parallel experience. In Luke 4:2, the Gospel writer carefully describes Jesus's experience in the wilderness as identical with Moses (fasting for forty days).[209]

The key element of Moses's encounter with God was clear and definitive communication inscribed by the very finger of God on two stone tablets (see Exod 31:18; 32:16). In Exodus 31, these tablets are described as the "tablets of the testimony," emphasizing that they are the very words of God. Here Moses describes these stones as the "tablets of the covenant" (also verses 11 and 15; see also Heb 9:4), because the focus is firmly on their relationship with Yahweh and the role of the "Ten Words" in outlining the shape of covenant loyalty.[210]

This handover took place, according to 9:10, on "the day of the assembly." This expression doesn't occur in Exodus and may refer to the final day of the revelation at Horeb or may more generally set up a parallel between the "day" at Moab and the "day" at Horeb, as part of Moses's careful rhetorical strategy to call the people to obedience.[211] The careful and repetitive language of verses 10–11 underlines that God has spoken *these very words* defining covenant loyalty to *them*. As in chapter 4 (4:10, 12, 33, as well as 5:22–27; 10:4; 18:16), Yahweh spoke out of the middle of the fire on Horeb. There can be no doubt what he asked of them, as he not only spelled out his requirements, but wrote them down with his very own finger and then set in stone for his people. Surely they can do nothing but obey? The summary statement of

---

[207] Five of the nine occurrences of this phrase in the Old Testament are in this section.

[208] With Tigay (*Deuteronomy*, 99), who says that "during this intimate encounter with God, inside the cloud, Moses was beyond human needs and concerns." More prosaically, he also points out that this would remove the need for bathroom breaks!

[209] In the verses which follow in Luke 4, it becomes clear that Jesus is both a "better" Moses and a "better Israel" as he resists the temptations dangled before him by the Evil One.

[210] In Exod 34:28, it is said explicitly that the "words of the covenant" are inscribed on the stone tablets. See also Block, *Deuteronomy*, 247 n. 9, for this view.

[211] The phrase is also used in 10:4 and 18:16 but nowhere else in the Hebrew Bible. The gathering at Moab is described as "the entire assembly of Israel" in 31:30, which may underline the connection between Moab and Horeb made explicit in 29:1.

verse 11, which underlines that the giving of the covenant tablets (as a written confirmation of the covenantal agreement) came at the end of this dramatic period, may well be intended to increase the tension, as both listeners and readers already know what is happening back at the foot of the mountain.[212]

The abruptness of the transition in verse 12 is designed to capture the shocking nature of Israel's behavior. God interrupted Moses's sojourn on the mountain to tell him to get up and go as quickly as possible. The issue is described in striking terms: "*your* people whom *you* brought out of Egypt have acted corruptly." In speaking like this, God highlights that the leader and the people share the same basic issue. The sinful choices of the people on Horeb will later be repeated by the leader on the journey to the land (Num 20:1–13). The terms for their rebellion quickly pile up: they "acted corruptly," turned from the way of Yahweh, and made a metal idol (literally, a "thing").[213] The earlier verdict of 9:6 was now dramatically confirmed, even as they waited for Moses to descend from the mountain of God. They were indisputably "stiff-necked" (9:13).

The narrative here moves more quickly than that of Exodus, where Moses pauses to intercede for the nation. Here, Moses omits this exchange, emphasizing that he was told to go "immediately" because the people had "quickly turned" from the ways of God. The details of his intercession do not particularly serve his purpose in pressing the Moab generation to obedience, and so they are omitted from his (necessarily) selective account. Moses's role as covenant mediator is not central here.

At this point, the substantial weight of God's condemnation conveyed through Moses's relentless preaching threatens to become too much to bear. Verse 14 is chilling. This is the only place in the Hebrew Bible where God commands that he be "left alone" (the earlier account of events in Exodus 32:10 has a weaker expression: "let me rest").[214] The fact that God expressed his intention to act in judgment (and "blot out their name under heaven") is extremely disturbing. The verb used here provides a graphic reminder of God's judgment in the flood narrative (Gen 6:7; 7:4,

---

[212] On this, see Weinfeld, *Deuteronomy 1–11*, 408–9.

[213] The idol may well have had a wooden core, which was then overlaid with gold. William H. C. Propp, *Exodus 19–40*, AB 2A (New York: Doubleday, 2006), 550, 559.

[214] The idea in Jer 7:16; 11:14; and 14:11 is similar, although the language is different. This text reflects an astonishing degree of intimacy between Moses and Yahweh.

24) and the verdict on the Amalekites in Exodus (17:14).[215] Once again, God's people were in danger of experiencing the same deserved fate as those who neither know nor serve Yahweh.

As recorded in Exodus 32:10 and Numbers 14:1–24, God expressed the intention to create a nation post-judgment from Moses, both as a kind of "new Noah" and a "new Abraham."[216] However, the language here is a little different, with the emphasis on the creation of a *superior* nation. While the relatively small Israelite population is used at points by Moses to highlight the grace of Yahweh (7:7), there is another strand of thought that presents the size and strength of the people as evidence of his favor. In Exodus (e.g., 1:7, 9, 20; 5:5), picking up on the motifs of the promises to Abraham, Isaac, and Jacob, the fact that Israel is strong and numerous is a clear indicator that they will overcome their Egyptian "hosts." The description of other nations using the same language in Deuteronomy 2:10, 21 and 7:1 suggests that although Yahweh will have to intervene in the short-term to overcome their relative weakness in order to bring them safely into the land, the fulfillment of his promises will involve Israel becoming "stronger and more numerous" than the other nations. For Moses here, it seems, God is still committed to delivering on his (Abrahamic) promises, even if the preacher himself may now play an unexpectedly prominent role.

In this passage (in contrast to Exod 32:11–14), there is no discussion of Moses's intercession for the people (advocating on the basis of God's reputation and his promises, and then later, in 32:32, putting his own future on the line for their sake). Rather Moses seems to intentionally downplay his own actions. The focus here is firmly on the persistent failure of the people, rather than either the grace of God or the key role of Moses.[217]

As he recreates the scene from Horeb in 9:15, Moses paints a vivid and dramatic picture: the mountain itself is described as "blazing with fire,"

---

[215] See also Deut 29:19. The same reality is described in different language in 7:24. There are thirty-three occurrences of the verb "wipe away" or "blot out" in the Old Testament: the vast majority carry theological weight. See *TWOT*, entry 1178.

[216] As my colleague Doug Green first pointed out to me, the Exodus passage sounds like an explicit rejection of the covenant with Abraham, with Moses replacing the patriarch and his line. However, in Deuteronomy, it reads more like a recalibration of God's covenant purposes that embraces both a new post-judgment existence (the expression "forty days and forty nights" [Gen 7:4, 17] is a clear link to Noah) and a fresh fulfillment of the promises to Abram in Gen 12 and elsewhere.

[217] This fits with the Deuteronomic emphasis on Moses being caught up in the sin of the nation, rather than him being the one whom God uses in exercising his mercy.

symbolizing Yahweh's revelatory presence as in chapter 4, and as the prophet descended, he did so clutching the very words of God, carved by the Almighty One himself (again described as "the tablets of the covenant"). He then describes what he saw as he descended in verse 16: "I saw how you had sinned against the LORD your God." The Hebrew is more striking: "I saw—and *behold* …" The salient issue is sin. Whatever the original intent of their actions, it quickly spilled over into rebellion. Making a "calf image" was the specific sin, which clearly broke the second commandment on the tablets. Israel quickly departed from the way of Yahweh.

Moses's response to this idolatry was as dramatic as it is appropriate. According to 9:17, smashing the tablets explicitly took place "before your eyes." Shattering the tablets was the ancient equivalent of tearing up a contract and provided a vivid illustration of the covenant breaking of the people. [218] However, Moses's action did not stop there, as he continued to pile up evidence of the seriousness of their behavior.

Israel's behavior imperiled their covenant relationship, which led Moses to throw himself prostrate before God "for forty days and forty nights" once more.[219] This evokes the wilderness years (as in 9:9), and given the wider context of judgment, there are almost certainly overtones of the flood (Gen 7:17; 8:6). Once more, the future of the nation is clearly in the balance. In explaining the reason for throwing himself on his face (a detail added to his recollection of the events of Exodus), Moses makes it clear that the "fierce anger" of Yahweh had brought him to the very point of destroying his people.[220] The physical action underlined both the seriousness and urgency of the situation (see verse 25 and also Ezra 10:1). Moses's own summary of his role is understated once more ("the LORD listened to me on that occasion"): as we have seen, he pushes the people to face their sin ("doing evil in the eyes of the LORD"; also 4:25–26), not to recognize his role as mediator.

In the same way that Moses's own later failure is pressed into homiletical service (e.g., 3:36–29) to confront the people, Aaron is now held up as

---

[218] Block comments "Moses declared the covenant null and void even before the people had a chance to see the divinely produced written documentation" (*Deuteronomy*, 250).

[219] Some commentators raise questions over the sequencing of the events in Exodus and Moses's rehearsal of the story here. If the text is taken at face value as a fairly loose retrospect, in which Moses is preaching on those events, arranging his account to highlight the key lessons for the people, then these issues basically disappear.

[220] The phrase is "wrath and blazing heat/fury."

a warning. This is in sharp contrast to the narrative of Exodus 32, where no reprieve for Aaron is noted. There, the primary interaction is between the brothers, as Moses asks Aaron to explain his actions, with Moses's own (righteous) anger and desire to avert the death of their nation filling the frame. Here, the issue is much more stark: Yahweh "was angry enough with Aaron to destroy him." Moses expresses his fraternal shock in strong and unusual language (the verb only occurs here, in 28:60; Job 3:25; 9:28; and Ps 119:39), but then highlights bluntly that his brother's survival was purely a matter of Yahweh's grace (in responding to his intercession). The original high priest of Israel came within a whisker of losing his life for sin! This is further evidence that the nation in its entirety was born in sin and shaped in iniquity (Ps 51:5).

Moses then reminds the people that rapid and decisive action is always what is called for in the face of disobedience and idolatry (9:21). The metal idol (bluntly described as "your sin" in Hebrew) was burned (burning the wooden core, if there was one, and also melting the gold), crushed, ground down or filed into powder and thrown into a Horeb stream (9:21; see also Josiah's actions in 2 Kgs 23:6, 12, 15).[221] He makes no mention of the people having to drink the golden water (Exod 32:20), but focuses on the way in which he dealt with the "sinful thing," thus encouraging this generation of Israelites and those who follow to take a similar zero tolerance approach to sin and temptation. Moses retells the story in the hope that these people, who have already been given multiple chances by God, will sit up and listen. But he isn't finished yet.

9:22–29. Lest the people are tempted to defend themselves by arguing that this was a momentary aberration, Moses quickly reminds them in 9:22–24 of three more moments of rebellion that followed hot on the heels of the events of Horeb: Taberah (lit., "burning," where Yahweh's anger "burned" against them; Num 11:1–3); Massah/Meribah (where Israel "tested" Yahweh by complaining about a lack of water; Exod 17:1–7; see also Deut 6:16) and Kibroth-hattaavah ("Graves of Craving," where Israel complained about having no meat; Num 11:4–34). What should have been a straightforward walk to Canaan (see Deut 1:2) was punctuated by regular, costly acts

---

[221] See Christopher T. Begg, "The Destruction of the Calf (Exodus 32,20/Deut 9,21)," in *Das Deuteronium: Enstehung, Gestalt und Botschaft*, ed. Norbert Lohfink, BETL 68 (Leuven: Leuven University Press 1985), 208–51, for an extended discussion of the ancient Near Eastern parallels to destroying images in this way. This tradition would also have had a particular resonance in the days of Jeroboam I (see 1 Kgs 12:28–29).

of rebellion, as the people continue to "provoke" Yahweh's wrath. This selective summary of their propensity to complain and/or disobey reached its climax at Kadesh-barnea (Num 13,14; see also 1:26–43), where they disregarded the "command" (lit., "mouth") of God. Their refusal to enter the land, already exposed as utterly foolish in chapters 1–3, is described as rebellion, faithlessness, and disobedience. Moses's summary is damning: "You have been rebelling against the Lord ever since I have known you," echoing 9:7 (see also 31:27), a note that is also repeated throughout the book of Jeremiah (3:24–25; 11:7–8; 22:21; 25:4–7; 26:4–5; 29:19; 32:30; 35:14–15).

Through this entire section from 9:1, Moses emphasizes the utterly predictable sinfulness of the people. While Yahweh has been gracious in the past, the relentless refusal of the people to respond to his grace is surely wearing away any sense of optimism concerning the impending conquest and occupation of the land. Is there really any hope for Israel? As in so much of the Old Testament, the answer is "no" in the short term, but ultimately a resounding "yes."

For a third time in this chapter (see 9:9, 18) it is recorded in verse 25 that Moses spent forty days and nights prostrate before God (the phrase "fell prostrate" is repeated in Hebrew for emphasis) in view of the threat to bring his people to an end.[222] It is probably easiest to take it as a reference to verse 18. However, in the flow of Moses's argument, the timing of these words is irrelevant. Moses's conversations with God are finally presented in verses 26–29 not as a slavish recapitulation of the events of Horeb in Exodus 32 (or Kadesh-barnea or anywhere else, although there are similarities with the earlier accounts).[223] His point is theological rather than chronological. The summary of this interaction with Yahweh at this juncture in his sermon (whenever it occurred in the timetable of events) captures the *theological* problem that the nation faces and that Deuteronomy eventually seeks to answer.[224]

Moses presented two interlocking reasons to God as he asked him to spare his people. The logic of God's own covenant faithfulness is the

---

[222] Similar repetition is found in 1:46 and 29:15, in both cases to underline the position of those involved.

[223] For the points of contact, see the table in Block, *Deuteronomy*, 257–258.

[224] Contrary to some, this section is not tacked on at the end out of a scribal desire to preserve the tradition. Nor is Deuteronomy overly concerned with chronology (contra McConville, *Deuteronomy*, 184). It is rather a vital *rhetorical and theological* moment in the sermon.

first. The fact that Yahweh had chosen Israel as his "people" and "inheritance," which has been demonstrated in their dramatic emancipation from Egypt, led Moses to appeal to divine faithfulness in the face of their disobedience (9:26, in contrast to God's words in v. 12). God's "greatness" is regularly affirmed in Deuteronomy (3:24; 5:24; 9:26; 10:17; 11:2; 32:3), encompassing his rescue of Israel from Egypt and his self-revelation at Horeb, as well as the full-orbed extent of his character and nature. This appeal was then backed up and expanded in 9:27 on the specific grounds of the covenantal commitments that Yahweh had made to Abraham, Isaac, and Jacob. The people's thoroughgoing sinfulness was not in doubt, but Moses asked God to "disregard" it on the basis of his prior gracious promises, which he called on God to "remember" for the clear benefit of Israel (as he does in Exod 32:13).[225]

In verse 28, Moses moved from appealing to God's intrinsic motivation, to that of his reputation in the world, and the possible perception that the end of Israel was a result of either the weakness or the caprice of God. The idea of a god's reputation hanging on the fate of his worshipers seems to have been a common one in the ancient Near East and recurs in many places in the Old Testament.[226] The death of God's chosen people in the wilderness could imply that rather than loving them with an everlasting love, God hated his people. Verse 29 insists that, as the exodus has made clear, that cannot be true: Israel is God's people and his inheritance. Yahweh's own character provides the basis for any hope for the future.

10:1–5 The temporal notes in 10:1, 8 and 10 ("at that time ... at that time ... like the first time/on this occasion") tie these apparently parenthetical details into the flow of the book.

First, Yahweh's commitment to covenant faithfulness and his repeated willingness to forgive is illustrated from the aftermath of the golden calf incident in Exodus 34, although once again, Moses's account of events is a fresh retelling, which includes several previously undisclosed details. As in Exodus 34:1–4, Moses was instructed to come back up the mountain, this time with new, pre-prepared stone tablets, as the covenant appears to be "renewed." Moses also adds another extra

---

[225] According to both *HALOT* and *DCH*, the idea behind "disregarding" is turning away (and possibly walking away) from Israel's sin.

[226] See for example the Hittite Prayer of Mursilis (14th Century BC) in *ANET*[3], 396. In the Old Testament, we find the idea, for example, not only in Deut 32:26–27 but also in Exod 32:12; Num 14:13–16; Josh 7:9; Jer 14:7; Ezek 36:22–23; Joel 2:17; Pss 25:11; 79:9–10; 115:1–2.

detail not appearing in the Exodus narratives: that God asked that he make a wooden box ("ark") for the stone "documents."

Moses duly made both the stone tablets and a box from acacia wood (10:3). This box is clearly a temporary receptacle for the new edition of the Ten Commandments (or Words), rather than the much grander, permanent version made from the same material (*the* ark, constructed by Bezalel and Oholiab in Exod 35:30–36:1).[227] Although there is no mention of this first box in any other narratives, given the way in which Moses has included a range of previously unknown details in his recollections, this is hardly surprising and should not simply be dismissed. This Mosaic temporary ark, like its more elaborate successor, performs an important function in Deuteronomy—ensuring that the words inscribed by God are lodged firmly at the heart of the nation.[228]

As in 9:10 (and also 18:16), Yahweh (the Hebrew has simply "he," as in Exod 34:6, perhaps to preserve a sense of awe at this moment) writes on the stones "on the day of the assembly" (10:4). This is not mentioned in Exodus or the Septuagint. In Deuteronomy, however, the picture of God's people assembled as one on this definitive day before him to listen to his word is an important one, and here serves to underline their shared responsibility to do exactly what God tells them. This is underlined as words spoken by God "to you" are first committed to stone and then carefully placed by Moses in his purpose-built box at the center of the camp. The fact that "they have remained there" as intended by God makes it clear that Israel has (and had) no excuse for failing to pay attention to these words, which lay out the basic terms and conditions of the covenant relationship.[229] The question before them now at Moab is: Will life in the land be any different?

10:6–11. At this point, the flow of Moses's preaching is disturbed by a couple of explanatory notes, which, like the historical notes in chapters

---

[227] For fourteenth century examples of Hittites storing treaty documents in a box, see Block, *Deuteronomy*, 262 n. 9. The fact that *the* (permanent) ark of the covenant is referred to in Deut 31:9, 25 suggests that the temporary box has essentially the same significance in Moses's sermon. Both arks are evidence that the speaking covenant God has told his people how they are to live with him. Block, *Deuteronomy*, 261, also points out that the lack of a definite article here strongly suggests that this is a temporary container.

[228] See also Exod 24:4, 12. There is some discussion of how this fits with Exod 34:28. Who wrote the Ten Words on the tablets? It is best to read these texts as providing a record of how God inscribed the Ten Words while Moses transcribed the book of the covenant. See the excellent discussion in Alexander, *Exodus*, 649.

[229] The texts in the ark will later be augmented with the Song of Moses, according to 31:26.

1–3, may be intended to underline the importance of some details in the previous section that might otherwise have been missed. They are, however, deftly woven into the flow of the argument.

The itinerary in 10:6–7 clears up some details from Numbers 33:31–39, but it is hard both to identify the places named and to work out how the two accounts relate, particularly in the light of the clear statement in Numbers 33:38–39 that Aaron was buried at Mount Hor. Despite this uncertainty, the brevity of the note abruptly highlights the importance of the death of Aaron outside the land (despite Yahweh extending grace to him at Horeb), even as it prefigures Moses's own exclusion from Canaan. It also underlines the consequences of the events at Horeb, even though they took forty years to unfold. As Eleazar takes Aaron's place, there is little to suggest that his son will fare any better. The note of 10:7, however, does at least hint at progress toward a better place, where wadis are plentiful.[230]

Similarly, the explanatory comment in verses 8–9 concerning the Levites is also important. This first mention of the tribe in the book ("backdated" to Horeb: "at that time") quickly establishes their importance, as well as affirming the centrality of the word in the life of God's people. In Exodus 32:25–29, the Levites are the guardians of orthodoxy, as they respond to Moses's urgings. In the light of that, they are dedicated to Yahweh. Now Moses expands on this: the key roles of the tribe are described by purpose clauses: to carry the ark, which in this context means guarding Yahweh's words; to stand before Yahweh and to serve him, an expression that points to their role in ensuring the sacrificial system functions; and to pronounce blessings on the people (which fits with the key role played by Aaron and his sons in Num 6:24–26, which is the centrepiece of the ideal picture of the nation camped around the Tent of Meeting at Horeb in Num 1:1-10:10. before they begin the journey to Canaan).[231]

These basic functions are reflected not just in Deuteronomy, but throughout the Old Testament. As the book progresses, the tribe of Levi plays an increasingly significant role. Their "landless" relationship with Yahweh (because, as Yahweh himself has said, *he* is their inheritance) is both the ideal and a constant reminder (Num 18:21–24) that the ultimate goal of the gift of the land is to enable Israelites to enjoy this same

---

[230] As in the previous verse, the identity of these places is uncertain. See, e.g., Lundbom, *Deuteronomy*, 385, for a list of possibilities.

[231] 10:8 implies a date for this section shortly after the occupation of Canaan. A similar perspective can be seen in, e.g., 3:11, 14.

"unbounded" relationship with their covenant God.[232] This is reflected in Deuteronomy 12:12; 14:27, 29; 18:1–5; as well as Joshua 13:14, 33; 18:7.

The statements of 10:10–11 are clearly resumptive, although it is not entirely clear whether verse 10 is simply picking up events in verse 4 or verses 18–19 or is suggesting that Moses spent a third such period on the mountain. Whichever is preferable, this section concludes with the people having been spared once more and the journey of Israel having, against all odds, continued to the point where they are at Moab, staring down the prospect of seeing the next phase of God's promise fulfilled as they step into the land.

Despite the people's continuing stubbornness and the multiplicity of fresh starts and repeat offences, incredibly God was willing to continue to extend his grace to his people (even if he needed some persuasion) and instructed Moses to lead his people forward toward the land he had promised them: "Get up. Continue ..." (10:11; cf. 2:24, in contrast to 9:12 where he is told to "get up and go down"). God's people are again on the move. Surely this time *they* will make the most of this opportunity, even if Moses himself has already been excluded?

Bridge

Israel's history post-Egypt, and particularly the events at Horeb itself, add weight to Moses's insistence that they are innately sinful and desperately need the grace of God. This is spelled out bluntly and directly in 9:1–7 and then echoed through Moses's highly nuanced rehearsal of the narratives in Exodus 32–34. Even as the nation proper comes into existence, they rebel against the God who has just rescued them so dramatically. Recalling their covenantal history should lead to a renewed humility and a desire to throw themselves on the mercy and grace of God. The ongoing pattern of repeated failures through the wilderness period, however, contributes to a growing sense that Israel is more likely to repeat this pattern in the land than to manage to live well with Yahweh. A radical intervention will be needed if Israel is ever to live the beautiful life to which God calls them.

God's dramatic intervention in Christ is such very good news for us. Our God has made it possible for those of us who have tasted grace in him to embody the vision that was first revealed to Israel. So Peter can write in 1 Peter 2:9–10 that

---

[232] On the complex relationship between the priests and the Levites in Deuteronomy, see McConville, *Law and Theology in Deuteronomy*, 124–153.

> [9] You are a chosen race, a royal priesthood, a holy nation, a people for his possession, so that you may proclaim the praises of the one who called you out of darkness into his marvelous light. [10] Once you were not a people, but now you are God's people; you had not received mercy, but now you have received mercy.

Through his "exodus," Christ has made us his people, even though we were strangers, living in darkness and rebellion against him. We deserved to be excluded but have been included in Christ and equipped to live lives of praise and gratitude and delight. To do anything less is incredibly foolish and a complete contradiction of who we are, not just as those who have been chosen, but as those who have been, and are being, and will be transformed into the likeness of Christ.

7. What God Requires (10:12–11:7)

> [12] "And now, Israel, what does the LORD your God ask of you except to fear the LORD your God by walking in all his ways, to love him, and to worship the LORD your God with all your heart and all your soul? [13] Keep the LORD's commands and statutes I am giving you today, for your own good. [14] The heavens, indeed the highest heavens, belong to the LORD your God, as does the earth and everything in it. [15] Yet the LORD had his heart set on your ancestors and loved them. He chose their descendants after them—he chose you out of all the peoples, as it is today. [16] Therefore, circumcise your hearts and don't be stiff-necked any longer. [17] For the LORD your God is the God of gods and Lord of lords, the great, mighty, and awe-inspiring God, showing no partiality and taking no bribe. [18] He executes justice for the fatherless and the widow, and loves the resident alien, giving him food and clothing. [19] You are also to love the resident alien, since you were resident aliens in the land of Egypt. [20] You are to fear the LORD your God and worship him. Remain faithful to him and take oaths in his name. [21] He is your praise and he is your God, who has done for you these great and awe-inspiring works your eyes have seen. [22] Your ancestors went down to Egypt, seventy people in all, and now the LORD your God has made you numerous, like the stars of the sky.
>
> [11:1] "Therefore, love the LORD your God and always keep his mandate and his statutes, ordinances, and commands. [2] Understand today that it is not your children who experienced or saw the discipline of the LORD your God:
>
> His greatness, strong hand, and outstretched arm; [3] his signs and the works he did in Egypt to Pharaoh king of Egypt and all his land; [4] what he did to Egypt's army, its horses and chariots, when he made the water of the Red Sea flow over them as they pursued you, and he destroyed them completely; [5] what he did to you in the wilderness until you reached this place; [6] and what he did to Dathan and Abiram, the

> sons of Eliab the Reubenite, when in the middle of the whole Israelite camp the earth opened its mouth and swallowed them, their households, their tents, and every living thing with them.
>
> 7 "Your own eyes have seen every great work the LORD has done."

10:12–22. From 10:12 to the end of chapter 11, Moses presses home his exhortations with a sustained and intense passage of persuasive preaching, before moving on to fill out the shape of the life to which God is calling his people in the land. A rhythm of command and supporting motivation drives this section, which focuses on the underlying attitudes of the people.[233]

As in 4:1, 26:10, and 31:19, the marker "and now" focuses all that Moses has been saying on the present moment.[234] It is right now at Moab that Israel must respond fulsomely and appropriately to Yahweh. But what should this response to God's grace look like? The description in verse 12 consists of a chain of four infinitive constructs: they are to (1) fear God, (2) walk in all his ways, (3) love him, and (4) serve him wholeheartedly. Verse 13 then presents a fifth link in this chain of infinitives, with the final instruction (keep his good commandments) presumably functioning as a summary. These five should not be thought of as separate responses, but as different ways of describing the beautiful life that God calls his covenant people to embrace and embody in the land they are about to enter.[235]

Moses characteristically piles up overlapping instructions like this, as he presents probably the fullest picture of life with God in the canon. To "fear God" is not a new idea in the Pentateuch (see, e.g., Gen 20:11; 22:12; 31:42, 53; 42:18; Exod 9:30, 20:20; Lev 19:14, 32; 25:17, 36, 43; Num 21:34) but in Deuteronomy, this becomes a key description of life with Yahweh.[236] "Fear" for us has an implicitly negative connotation, with overtones of oppression and even abuse. This is not the case in the biblical text. On the contrary, "fear" captures the scope and even thrill of a relationship with a transcendent God who is, despite all odds, committed to showing grace and favor to Israel as his sons. The call to "fear" God encapsulates relational warmth, unquestioning allegiance, and even existential *frisson*,

---

233 See the helpful comments of Tigay, *Deuteronomy*, 107.

234 The same word concludes this section in 10:22.

235 Lundbom calls this "a tidy summary of Deuteronomic theology, which calls for total commitment to Yahweh." (*Deuteronomy*, 389).

236 So Deut 4:10; 5:29; 6:2, 13, 24; 10:12, 20; 11:25; 13:4; 14:23; 17:19; 25:18; 31:12, 13; 32:17.

and should be read in the context of the full-orbed picture of relationship that Moses presents here.

"Walking in all his ways" (see 8:6; 11:22; 13:5; 19:9; 26:17; 28:9; 30:16) appears to be a phrase coined by Moses that then is picked up regularly in the rest of the Bible (most notably in the assessment of the kings of Judah and Israel in the books of Kings). As with "fearing God," it is an all-encompassing, all-of-life depiction of the faithful obedience to which God's people are called.

The treaty associations of "loving God" have already been discussed (see on 6:5), but the fact that the simple command can be used in parallel with these other descriptions of the shape of covenant life is another reason not to exclude an affective component. After the headline statement of 6:5, backed up in both 7:9 and 13, the prominence of this term rises sharply as Moses continues to call his people to a fulsome response to Yahweh (see also 10:20; 11:1, 13, 22).[237]

The call to "worship" is interesting. The verb used basically means to "work" (as in Gen 2:15), but from the beginning of the Bible, this kind of service has had all-of-life connotations. To "serve" God wholeheartedly, all day every day, in every day of life is exactly the kind of "worship" that God asks of those whom he loves and rescues (see Rom 12:1–2). The phrase "with all your heart and all your soul" has already occurred in 4:29, and is repeated in 11:13; 13:3 (both in the plural); 26:16; 30:2, 6, 10.[238] The fact that Israel is called to serve, love, obey, and return to Yahweh wholeheartedly emphasizes the overarching nature of the response that Moses is aiming for.

Verse 13 backs this up this multifaceted call with another simple but far-reaching command: "Keep the Lord's commands and statutes I am giving you today." What's striking about this summary is the motive clause: God's people are to live according to God's words each day in the future (the force of "today" extends far beyond Moab) "for your own good." To live in this "good" world (Gen 1) involves listening to the words of the good God, who has the good of his creatures at heart in all his work.[239] This is, of course, not the only motive for obedience (as we have

---

[237] It is also no accident that the term then recurs in 30:6, 16, 20 as Moses turns to talk about the results of God's intervention to transform his people. There is only one other occurrence in the book (13:3).

[238] See also Josh 22:5; 23:14; 1 Kgs 2:4; 8:48.

[239] Similar ideas are expressed in the longer phrases of 4:40; 5:33 and 6:24–25.

already seen repeatedly), but it is crucial, highlighting in particular the foolishness of rebellion and the damage caused to those who disobey. However, 10:12–13 also has the effect of setting the bar so high for God's people that one begins to wonder if any generation of God's people will be able to maintain this level of commitment, even for a moment.

It is not simply that these requirements are good for his people. The very fact that God has handed them down is compelling evidence for his dramatic, condescending generosity. This is stated in no uncertain terms in 10:14. The emphatic phrase "[*Look,*] the heavens, indeed the highest heavens, belong to the Lord your God" has no real parallel anywhere in Scripture.[240] In the flow of Moses's preaching however, it clearly serves to make the point that the Lord of *all* ("the earth and everything in it" are included almost as an afterthought!) has graciously condescended to choose and then speak to his people, spelling out to them how they should live with him *for their good.*

This kindness arises from the equally astonishing fact (10:15) that Yahweh "had his heart set on your ancestors and loved them" (see also 7:7).[241] The verb used here (חָשַׁק) is not common but is used either literally or metaphorically to mean to attach something firmly. When used of human desire (e.g., Gen 34:8; 1 Kgs 9:19), it involves the strongest of emotions (confirming incidentally that "love" here cannot be limited to the sphere of treaty obligation). Yahweh's covenantal commitment, which began with Abraham and continued with Isaac and Jacob and now encompasses the whole family of Israel, is not vacillating or fickle. His loving "choice" of his people, expressed in the covenant made with Abraham, has not wavered: "He chose you out of all the peoples, as it is today." In the same way that the Israelites are described as being part of the covenantal exchanges at Horeb (Deut 5:1–4), so too with the earliest promises made to Abraham.

Given all that God has done for his people, it is entirely reasonable that God should make some far-reaching demands of them. Deuteronomy 10:16 now sums up this required response in what is probably the most important (and certainly the most graphic) metaphor in the book: Israel

---

[240] The phrase is literally "the heavens of heavens," which is puzzling as there is no suggestion of a multilayered cosmology in ancient Israel, in contrast to both Babylon and the Greek-influenced world of the New Testament (see, e.g., 2 Cor 12:2; Eph 4:10).

[241] The particle רַק is a strong word that creates a sharp contrast between the choice of one nation and the ruling of the whole cosmos.

is to deal with their ongoing stubbornness by circumcising their hearts and not being "stiff-necked any longer" (see also 9:6, 13, 27; also Lev 26:41).

The call to (lit.) "circumcise the foreskin of your hearts" is as striking as it is unique in the Old Testament. While the image is picked up directly in Jeremiah 4:4 (see also the condemnation of 9:26) and implicitly in the description of the new covenant in Jeremiah 31:31–34 (as well as by Paul in Rom 2:25–29; Col 2:11; 3:11), it is only in Deuteronomy (here and in 30:6) that the details of the metaphorical procedure are described so graphically.[242] The power of the image conveys several things: (1) Israel must make a radical, far-reaching *inner* commitment (in contrast to the *external* acts of 6:4–9). (2) This commitment will require significant (perhaps painful) change at the level of motivation, if these words are to penetrate their thinking and decisions. (3) The (unspoken) implication is that performing such surgery on oneself (even metaphorical surgery) is impossible, a point that is later confirmed by Yahweh's own intervention in 30:6. As Moses's preaching reaches a crescendo, there is a growing sense that he is simply asking too much. The issue is not simply mental or cognitive, but spiritual.

The parallel command supports reading the text like this: "don't be stiff-necked any longer." If this is Israel's natural condition, which they have demonstrated in multiple ways over generations, a simple call to stop will hardly be enough to effect change, as it does not address their underlying, perennial problem: they aren't just sinners; they are inherently sinful. If the people are to respond to God as they should, then something dramatic will have to happen. Moses does not dwell on this unnerving insight but will return to this theme in due course.

In the meantime, Moses shifts the focus from the innate recalcitrance of Israel to the power and beauty of God in 10:17–18. The ascription to Yahweh of the double title "God of gods and Lord of lords" is unique.[243] The epithets "great," "mighty" (like a warrior, as in, e.g., Ps 24:8; Isa 9:6 [Heb. 9:5]), and "awe-inspiring" (derived from the common verb "to fear") add to a compelling picture of the transcendent God before whom Israel

---

242 The language is also found in the Dead Sea Scrolls, e.g., in *The Manual of Discipline*, 1QS 5:5.

243 Although see Ps 136:3 and the New Testament designation of "King of kings and Lord of lords" in 1 Tim 6:15; Rev 17:14; 19:16. According to GKC §133i, these expressions are superlatives. The pattern is a common one in the ancient Near East, especially among kings (see Lundbom, *Deuteronomy*, 392, for more details).

should gasp, bow, and tremble.[244] Surprisingly, Moses's focus shifts to the *integrity* of Yahweh, the God who does not "lift up faces" or take bribes. The imagery captures a situation where a ruler or judge pays attention to one applicant while refusing to look at the next (which is prohibited in 1:17 and 16:19). There is no such inconsistency with Yahweh. Instead, he shows grace and tenderness to those who have nothing to offer him, clearly including his wayward people.

God's concern for the fatherless, the widow, and the resident alien, first expressed here, is typical of Deuteronomy (e.g., 14:29; 16:11, 14; 24:17, 19, 20, 21; 26:12, 13; 27:19; see also Ps 94:6; Jer 7:6; 22:3; Ezek 22:7; Zech 7:10; Mal 3:5). Yahweh is both a God of justice (here, in the sense of fairness) in ensuring that those who are bereaved in Israel are cared for as they should be, as well as extending love to outsiders who are part of the extended community of Israel and therefore separated from the usual family support networks that provided the social fabric of ancient middle eastern society.[245] Providing food and an outer garment (presumably to enable them to keep warm at night) is a concrete expression of care and compassion.

This repeated call to "love" is striking, especially given the covenantal dimension of "love" in Deuteronomy. In 10:19, Israel must show the same "love" to the resident alien as Yahweh has shown them. The exodus itself provides a powerful theological rationale from the nation's own experience (see also Exod 22:21; 23:9; Lev 19:34).[246] Loving one's "neighbor" like this seems to be indicative of having embraced and responded to the grace of God, as Moses moves seamlessly to another multifaceted call to wholehearted covenantal obedience in verse 20: "You are to fear the Lord your God and worship him. Remain faithful to him and take oaths in his name."

As we have seen before, to "fear Yahweh and worship him" is to respond to him with a mixture of both trembling and delight, as befits

---

[244] Two of the attributes ("great" and "awe-inspiring") occur together in 7:21. Block (*Deuteronomy*, 272) argues that this is a direct polemic against the Canaanite god El.

[245] It may be that "widow" here, for example, is actually a woman who has no male relatives to support her, rather than simply one who has lost her husband. See, e.g., H. Hoffner's article on *'almānâ* in *TDOT* 1:287–91. This explains why some women whose husbands have died are never referred to by the obvious term "widow" (e.g., Tamar, Ruth).

[246] Depending on the context, Moses refers to the people as having been resident aliens or "slaves" in Egypt (Lev 25:42; Deut 6:21; 16:12 and by implication, 28:68) as a rationale for caring for widows, orphans, and resident aliens in their community. It is slightly puzzling that v. 19 jumps straight to the resident alien, omitting any mention of the fatherless or the widow. This may simply be because the resident alien is the hardest case.

flawed humans like us encountering the "God of gods and Lord of lords." This affective response must however also produce real action. The verb "remain faithful" is literally "stick" (the archaic word was "cleave," used famously in the KJV's rendering of Gen 2:24) with such dedication to Yahweh that it results in a determination to make only promises of which he would approve and that would bring honor to him.

Yahweh himself and Yahweh alone is to be the object of their affection, admiration, and allegiance: he is their "praise" (a word used in the Psalms to describe songs of praise) and their "God." This "great, mighty, and awe-inspiring God" (10:17) has done "great and awe-inspiring works" (10:21) in front of their very eyes. Yet again Moses insists that the experience of the exodus should have transformed this people forever. Yahweh has honored his promises to Abraham (Gen 22:17) and Isaac (Gen 26:4) and Jacob (Exod 32:13). The family of seventy (Gen 46:27; Exod 1:5) has become a nation.[247]

The call to obedience is relentless through this section. It is hard to imagine an image or an exhortation that Moses does not press into service. However, despite the rhetorical power of this passage, the content poses deeply disturbing questions: Can Israel keep this up? Can God's people change? Can they do what he asks? But Moses isn't quite finished his extended exhortation yet.

11:1–7. Chapter 11 begins with another composite call to obedience, made up of several broadbrush statements of what Yahweh requires. Once more, God's people are called to "love" Yahweh (characteristic of this whole section from 6:4 onwards but see especially 10:12).[248] This is backed up by a call to "keep his mandate." This phrase is used only here in Deuteronomy (but see also Gen 26:5, used of Abraham; Josh 22:3; 1 Kgs 2:3). Literally, the text says "guard the thing that is guarded" (presumably by God).[249] The nature of this mandate is then spelled out in more familiar Deuteronomic terms, as once more the people are called to guard or keep the "statutes, ordinances, and commands," despite the fact that the content of these commands remains slightly hazy.

---

[247] See also 1:10; 26:5; 28:62.

[248] Loving Yahweh by keeping his commands is also the key idea in 6:5–9; 7:9, 12; 10:12–13; 11:13, 22; 13:4; 19:9; 30:6, 20.

[249] Num 18:3 actually has a triple use of this verb when describing the Levites' role in caring for the tent of meeting.

Returning to the approach of chapter 5 (and 8:2–6), in 11:2–6 Moses again directly identifies the Moab generation in front of him with those who experienced the exodus and subsequent events in the wilderness. This time, however, he insists that it isn't their "children" who have "seen" and must respond to the events of the exodus (in ch. 5, he says it is not their parents), but *them*.[250] "Children" may be excused from grasping the full significance of the events he has been talking about—but they are not children. As adults, they have "experienced" (known) and "seen" the "discipline of the Lord your God." This is the only occurrence of the noun "discipline" in Deuteronomy, although it is common elsewhere, especially in the wisdom literature (Proverbs and Job in particular), adding some support to the idea that Deuteronomy may have shaped the wisdom tradition. [251]

Discipline often takes the form of punitive action in the Old Testament (e.g., notably Isa 53:5; see also Jer 2:30; 5:3; 30:14) but in this context, the emphasis is on God *teaching* his people through the events of the past forty years. An extremely succinct summary of their recent history follows, summed up in the phrase in 10:2: "his greatness, strong hand, and outstretched arm." God's greatness has been highlighted previously (3:24; 5:24 in association with his "strong hand" in the exodus), but this particular collocation of terms is a fresh one.[252]

The specific demonstrations of God's power cited by Moses in verses 4–6 include the "signs and the works he did in Egypt,"[253] his complete rout of Pharaoh's forces in the Sea of Reeds (Exod 14:23–28), the slightly vague (but nonetheless disturbing) "what he did *to you* in the wilderness," and then finally a reference to the rebellion led by Dathan and Abiram among others in Numbers 16.[254] In the Numbers account, Korah the Levite is named as leading the rebellion. However, as the story unfolds, not only are Dathan and Abiram (Reubenites) implicated alongside Korah, but their refusal to submit to Moses even when challenged directly brings them to the forefront. Their persistent stubbornness (given what Moses has been

---

[250] The syntax of the Hebrew is tricky, but this may simply be because of the looseness of the spoken style, with 11:2–7 comprising one sentence. See Craigie, *Deuteronomy*, 208. On the "solidarity" of the generations of Israel, see McConville, *Deuteronomy*, 202.

[251] The verbal form does occur in 4:36; 8:5; 21:18; 22:18. Tigay argues that the term encapsulates "both punishment and the lesson it teaches." *Deuteronomy*, 110.

[252] The combination "strong hand and outstretched arm" appears in 4:34; 5:15 and 7:19.

[253] The normal word for "wonders" (see, e.g., 4:34) is replaced here by the word "works."

[254] This is the only explicit mention of the crossing of the Re(e)d Sea in Deuteronomy.

saying about the Moab generation) is probably the reason why they are front and center here.[255] The dramatic, shocking, and instant judgment on these men, their families, and those who "followed them" (lit., "every standing thing," presumably referring to the 250 men of Num 16:2) is a powerful reminder that the obligation to respond to the whole gamut of Yahweh's words and actions is a serious matter. The earth "open[ing] its mouth and swallow[ing] them" presumably consigns them to Sheol, the abode of the dead. 11:7 reiterates this: the fact that "your own eyes" have "seen" "every great work" (perhaps better "this whole great work," emphasizing the unified saving work of Yahweh), whether in real time or as the accounts have been passed down by their parents and grandparents, makes it all the more obvious that they now need to respond.

Bridge

Moses's powerful preaching in this section highlights the core issue all human beings face: Yahweh, the God of Israel, is actually the God of the universe. He is sovereign, and he asks unquestioning, unlimited obedience from all of us. Moses captures that in a powerful range of images and commands, culminating in the demand that we "circumcise our hearts," an acknowledgement that in the last analysis, the most significant obstacles to obedience are internal rather than external. However, the fact that God's people are inveterately stubborn and "stiff-necked" takes us to the basic tension that is resolved only in the life and work of the Lord Jesus and the outpouring of the Spirit. As Paul points out, "there is no one righteous, not even one" (Rom 3:10), for we are all dead in sin. The inner surgery we require is not simply cutting out evil; we actually need to be brought to life, and there is only one who can perform that operation (John 10:10).

8. Blessing or Curse? (11:8–32)

> [8] "Keep every command I am giving you today, so that you may have
> the strength to cross into and possess the land you are to inherit, [9] and
> so that you may live long in the land the Lord swore to your ances-
> tors to give them and their descendants, a land flowing with milk and
> honey. [10] For the land you are entering to possess is not like the land
> of Egypt, from which you have come, where you sowed your seed and

[255] It may also be that the positive role of the Levites in the book, modeling a healthy relationship with God, has led Moses to leave out any discussion of Korah.

irrigated by hand as in a vegetable garden. 11 But the land you are entering to possess is a land of mountains and valleys, watered by rain from the sky. 12 It is a land the LORD your God cares for. He is always watching over it from the beginning to the end of the year.

13 "If you carefully obey my commands I am giving you today, to love the LORD your God and worship him with all your heart and all your soul, 14 I will provide rain for your land in the proper time, the autumn and spring rains, and you will harvest your grain, new wine, and fresh oil. 15 I will provide grass in your fields for your livestock. You will eat and be satisfied. 16 Be careful that you are not enticed to turn aside, serve, and bow in worship to other gods. 17 Then the LORD's anger will burn against you. He will shut the sky, and there will be no rain; the land will not yield its produce, and you will perish quickly from the good land the LORD is giving you.

18 "Imprint these words of mine on your hearts and minds, bind them as a sign on your hands, and let them be a symbol on your foreheads. 19 Teach them to your children, talking about them when you sit in your house and when you walk along the road, when you lie down and when you get up. 20 Write them on the doorposts of your house and on your city gates, 21 so that as long as the heavens are above the earth, your days and those of your children may be many in the land the LORD swore to give your ancestors. 22 For if you carefully observe every one of these commands I am giving you to follow—to love the LORD your God, walk in all his ways, and remain faithful to him—23 the LORD will drive out all these nations before you, and you will drive out nations greater and stronger than you are. 24 Every place the sole of your foot treads will be yours. Your territory will extend from the wilderness to Lebanon and from the Euphrates River to the Mediterranean Sea. 25 No one will be able to stand against you; the LORD your God will put fear and dread of you in all the land where you set foot, as he has promised you.

26 "Look, today I set before you a blessing and a curse: 27 there will be a blessing, if you obey the commands of the LORD your God I am giving you today, 28 and a curse, if you do not obey the commands of the LORD your God and you turn aside from the path I command you today by following other gods you have not known. 29 When the LORD your God brings you into the land you are entering to possess, you are to proclaim the blessing at Mount Gerizim and the curse at Mount Ebal. 30 Aren't these mountains across the Jordan, beyond the western road in the land of the Canaanites, who live in the Arabah, opposite Gilgal, near the oaks of Moreh? 31 For you are about to cross the Jordan to enter and take possession of the land the LORD your God is giving you. When you possess it and settle in it, 32 be careful to follow all the statutes and ordinances I set before you today."

11:8–17. As the sustained burst of exhortation that began in earnest at the start of chapter 5 (but was anticipated in chs. 1–4) reaches a crescendo, Moses reiterates just how much is dependent on Israel's response to the word of Yahweh.

In the first place, keeping "every command" (lit., "the whole commandment," as in 5:31, 6:1–2; 8:1) is a prerequisite for receiving the strength from God to make it to the other side of the Jordan and to permanently overcome the current occupants of the land (11:8). This is the first time the necessity of such flawless obedience has been mentioned. On top of that, wholehearted obedience will be necessary if Israel is to live well in the beautiful land (the land "flowing with milk and honey," as it was described to Moses in Exod 3:8, 17 and was rejected by the people in Num 14:8, 16:13–14; see also Deut 6:10–11; 8:7–10) for generations to come.[256] Moses's interest here is not simply in short-term gain, but in urging the people to live in covenant faithfulness into the distant future.

God has, it seems, done everything in his power to ensure that the environment in Canaan is set up in a way that is most conducive to covenant-keeping. This even extends to the way the land is supplied with water. The Egyptians had used the waters of the River Nile to develop a complex system of irrigation-based agriculture, although the Israelite slaves did not have access to the fertile flood plains. In any case, irrigation was exacting work.[257] Instead, their (presumably small) vegetable gardens were sowed and maintained "by hand" (11:10). The phrase is actually "by foot," which presumably is simply the idiom for manual labor. The land God is giving them, however, comes with a permanent maintenance contract guaranteed by Yahweh himself. He will supply the moisture, so that the land can (lit.) "drink water by the rain." But divine provision far exceeds that: this beautiful land "of mountains and valleys" (in contrast to both the flood plains of Egypt and the arid flatlands of Moab, which they have just trekked through) is one that God himself "cares for." This care takes the form of unbroken,

---

[256] To "live long in the land" (11:9) is symbolic of living as God intended and so enjoying him (see also Exod 20:12; Deut 5:33; 6:2; 32:47).

[257] See the description of one primitive device (a *shadûf*) that raised buckets of water when the Nile was not in flood, see George Adam Smith, *Historical Geography of the Holy Land* (London: Hodder & Stoughton, 1918), 147.Tigay suggests that the phrase may refer to using the foot to break down or redirect irrigation channels (*Deuteronomy*, 112).

all-year-round attention.[258] The point of all this is simple: given that life in the land is so generously underwritten by God, there will be no excuse for his people not enjoying life with him and living wholeheartedly for him in the land.

At this point, Moses introduces a new point to drive home to them how much is riding on Israel's obedience, as he moves to the end of this phase of his address. He has made it very clear (from 6:4–5 onward in particular) that all-encompassing obedience is vital: he instructs them both "to love the LORD your God" and "worship him with all your heart and all your soul," expanding on the Shema in a typical fashion (see also 10:12–13).[259] It is what comes next that is a little unexpected. It turns out in verse 14 that the very fertility of the land will be affected by their response to God, who assures them that: "I will provide rain for your land in the proper time, the autumn and spring rains, and you will harvest your grain, new wine, and fresh oil."[260] This reflects the shape of covenant life with Yahweh, where he makes promises and spells out Israel's response, which will become even clearer as this chapter continues.

The specific details reflect the reality of life in Canaan: the "early rain" in the late Autumn, was needed to soften the hard-baked ground for sowing, and the "late rain" in the growing season of Spring was essential to ensure steady growth and a good harvest of the necessities of life in the region. [261] God's personal involvement extends to ensuring that there is sufficient fodder for Israel's livestock (11:15), increasing both the effectiveness of the working animals as well as the quality of their meat, with the overall result that "You will eat and be satisfied." Despite the desirability of this satisfaction, it will bring real temptation to the people of Israel. The fertility of the land itself, then, will be a reliable index of the obedience of God's people.

This is an important connection for us to understand, particularly in a context where such promises are readily appropriated by proponents of

---

[258] The verb is "to seek" which has the sense of active interest in something (hence "care"). This 24/7 care may also contain an implied criticism of other gods (e.g., Baal, the Canaanite storm god, responsible for rainfall, who was viewed as being absent for large parts of the year because he was held captive by the god Mo't. See Block, *Deuteronomy*, 285).

[259] Lundbom rightly calls this combination "bedrock Deuteronomic theology"(*Deuteronomy*, 405).

[260] As occasionally happens, Moses speaks in God's voice here (see also 7:4).There may be an allusion to this verse in Jas 5:7.

[261] See Jer 5:24, and Block, *Deuteronomy*, 287, for a detailed explanation of rainfall patterns in Canaan.

prosperity theology. There is a very specific link between this particular land given by God at a particular moment, particular kinds of behavior in this land, and the meteorological experiences of the people who occupy the land. As we shall see in a moment, this is a real-time expression of the "state of the covenant" between God and his people *in the land of Canaan.* This dramatic, visual arrangement comes to an end and is recalibrated under the new covenant (to which Deuteronomy itself so clearly alludes in ch. 30). Verses 16–17 make this plain.

Should Israel in their newfound life of luxury be deceived and so "turn aside, serve, and bow in worship to other gods," there will be dire (and rapid) consequences (an idea that is picked up later in 32:13–18). Such idolatry will prove fatal. God's wrath will be expressed in "shutting the sky [lit., heavens] against you." This triggers a very obvious chain of events: the crops will fail, life in the land will become impossible, and the people will, like the pagan nations who preceded them (6:15; 9:3), "perish quickly from the good land." This explains why in the books that follow (see, e.g., the beginning of the Elijah narrative in 1 Kgs 17:1–7; also Jer 3:3; 14:1–11, 17–22), drought is always viewed primarily as a theological, rather than an agricultural, problem. When God's covenant people have been disobedient, God withholds the rain. Drought, then, is always an indicator that God's people are estranged from him or, as the verses that follow make clear (11:26–32), that they are living under the curse, rather than the blessing, of the covenant.[262]

11:18–25. The connection with chapter 6, and the accompanying sense that Moses is coming to the end of the sustained burst of exhortation that began in earnest in 6:1, is confirmed in verses 18–20, which forms a loose inclusio with that material. As we have seen repeatedly in the previous two chapters, earlier expressions are picked up and selectively restated or augmented in a way that is entirely consistent with the natural rhetorical variation of an actual, real-time address.

In 6:6, Moses insisted that his words were simply to be "on the hearts" of his people. Now he sharpens that demand by saying that they should be "imprinted" there.

The verb here simply means "place" or "put." Given that in 10:2, 5, it is used of putting the tablets in the ark (rather than God inscribing them), it seems likely that the image is not that of *writing* on the heart,

---

[262] Interestingly, a similar idea is found in Egypt around the same time. See *ANET*[3], 257.

but of either keeping them next to the heart or "installing" them as a kind of operating system for the whole person.[263] The command to display God's words on their hands and heads is repeated from 6:8 (with the tiny alteration that "hands" is plural). In fact, all of 6:8–9 is repeated, although the order is slightly different (and a different word for "teach" is used in 11:19). However, the reason for pursuing this lifestyle is set up differently.

In 6:2–3, the goal of obedience is introduced before the long list of injunctions: "Do this so that you may fear the LORD your God all the days of your life ... so that you may have a long life. Listen ... so that you may prosper and multiply greatly ... [in] a land flowing with milk and honey." Now in chapter 11, the focus falls explicitly on the *occupation* of the land, with both the initial conquest and long-term enjoyment of the land being tied to an obedient response to the words they are to write and display.

The terms of the promise in 11:21 are unusual, not only in that the duration of the prosperity is described in terms of "your days and those of your children," but also in that there is a second layer of longevity ("as long as the heavens are above the earth"). There seems to be no exact parallel to this expression, although the idea of the permanence of the heavens is commonplace.

Moses then presses home the fact that carefully obeying "*all* this commandment" (rather than "every one of these commands" [CSB]) is the key to occupying the land (11:22–23). There really only is one command, but again, the all-embracing nature of the response required is captured by piling up three instructions: God's people are to "love" him (as in 11:13); "walk in all his ways" (as in 8:6; 10:12) and "remain faithful" (lit., "cleave") to him (as in 4:3–4;10:20). God commits to "drive out all these nations." The second half of verse 23, which calls the Israelites to do what God himself has undertaken to bring about, shows that Moses is operating with a nuanced understanding of the relationship between human and divine action. To put it bluntly, this conquest requires both.

If Israel will carry out their mission as instructed, the results will be spectacular: the full extent of the promised land will be theirs without exception ("every place the sole of your foot treads"; see Josh 1:3; cf. Deut 2:5). By focusing on the key thing God asks of them, they will take the full extent of the land that has been promised to them, sketched here in general terms (as in 1:7, which is again picked up in Josh 1:4; cf. Deut 34:1–2).

---

263 For a similar thought, albeit one expressed in different language, see Ps 119:11.

However, the way in which this conditional promise is set up at this juncture does raise significant questions. God can clearly be relied on, but can the people?[264] The relentless insistence that God's people must carry out God's instructions to the letter—even "circumcising their hearts" (10:16)—and, in particular, that the successful occupation of the land depends on it, has, by this point in the book, started to create a nagging fear that all may *not* go well in the land, and even that God's people may not succeed in taking and holding it. There is little doubt that Yahweh can inspire "fear and dread," but the deeper question is: Can his people obey?

11:26–32. The passage that brings Moses's exhortation to a powerful climax is highlighted in two key ways: (1) the imperative form "look!" (רְאֵה) is used here as elsewhere (see, e.g., 1:8; 1:21; 2:24; 4:5; 30:15) at a key moment when God's people have a decision to make involving following God's instructions (and usually moving forward to a new place), and (2) the language of "today," which has already played an important role in the book, is used again to highlight the importance of the choice now facing the people in the light of Moses's address.[265]

The unique element at this point is the fact that the choice facing them is now presented in the most concise—and stark—terms: it is a choice between blessing and curse. This pairing occurs in key texts in Genesis (Gen 12:3; 27:29), but in both places it is an expression of divine benevolence and protection. Those who interact with the family of Abraham will experience divine curse or blessing as a result. Leviticus 26, in sketching out the consequences of covenantal obedience and disobedience, lays the foundation for what is said here but does not use the terms "blessing/curse" to sum up its message. For that, we must wait until Deuteronomy 11:26 and the climax of the Mosaic preaching.[266]

Moses clearly uses "a blessing and a curse" as the diametrically opposite experiences arising from covenant faithfulness and unfaithfulness (11:27–28). The "blessing" is intended to embrace the full scope of the fulfillment of

---

[264] Some of these issues are raised right at the beginning of Joshua. In Josh 2, for example, Rahab says the people are terrified of Israel, despite the slightly embarrassing (and clearly fearful) antics of the spies!

[265] For an extended discussion of the significance and use of the phrase "today" in Deuteronomy, see Millar in McConville and Millar, *Time and Place in Deuteronomy.*

[266] This, of course, does imply that the books belong in the canonical order. If Leviticus was a later work, it is hard to see why it would have avoided making use of such a powerful pair of antonyms.

God's covenantal promises that Moses has been expounding. This "blessing" in Deuteronomy encompasses enjoyment of God's presence and pleasure, population growth, length of life, prosperity, and national security in the land. Experiencing the "curse" means not only missing out on these "blessings," but also experiencing God's displeasure in the form of losing the land, being sent back to Egypt (at least metaphorically), and being treated like the nations whom they are to dispossess. Three times in consecutive verses (11:26, 27, 28) they are called to make the right choice "today," which, in keeping with the binary nature of the choice, means obeying Yahweh their God and not turning aside from the path (lit., "way," דֶּרֶךְ) of his commands to go after "other gods you have not known." This phrase, which clearly includes not simply recognition but experience, is used here for the first time, but becomes an important one in the rest of the book (13:2, 6, 13; 28:26, 64; 29:26; 32:17).[267] It provides a neat link with the laws concerning surviving in Canaan that follow and a shift to the primary challenge facing Israel being that of full-blown idolatry, rather than simply disobedience.

In order to ensure that this "day of decision" is enshrined at the heart of the new life of the nation, Moses foreshadows the introduction of a ritual that will be described in more detail in chapter 28 (and then enacted in Josh 8). It is to take place near Shechem (modern Nablus), roughly in the middle of the territory of the Canaanites. Mount Gerizim and Mount Ebal are twin peaks, about 3,000 feet above sea level, which, aside from this ritual, play no other part in the events of the Old Testament narrative.[268] The inclusion of the directions of 11:30 from Moab appear ancient (a singular oak at Moreh is mentioned in Gen 12:6; probably 35:4 and perhaps Josh 24:26; Judg 9:6), and would make sense if these mountains were actually of little religious significance before this time.[269]

11:31–32 bring us back once more to the immediacy of the decision facing Israel, echoing the words of 5:1 (among others). They are on the move,

---

[267] The only other place in the Old Testament where this phrase occurs is in the book of Jeremiah (e.g., Jer 7:9; 16:13; 19:4; 44:3).

[268] By Jesus's day, however, Mount Gerizim had become the focus of Samaritan religious practice. They believed that Gerizim was the place where Abraham had prepared to sacrifice Isaac and that it was chosen by God as the site of the temple. Jesus alludes to Gerizim in his conversation with the Samaritan woman in John 4:21–24 ("this mountain" referring to Gerizim, which provided a backdrop for the conversation taking place at Jacob's Well in Shechem).

[269] Some confusion is caused by the inclusion of Gilgal here, which is some distance away. It may be that it refers to an unknown "Gilgal" (perhaps a local landmark) in the Shechem region, or alternatively, Gilgal may denote the location of the Canaanite settlements, rather than the hills. The vagueness may reflect a preconquest perspective.

and now is the moment for them to take heed to Moses. The summary is simple. Go in. Trust God to overpower the inhabitants. Listen to God's words "today" and every day, as you live as his covenant people in his land.

Bridge

The key to living with and for God is simple. Remember who he is and what he's done. Listen to him, and do what he says. This is covenant faithfulness, which will lead to tasting the extravagant, grace-filled blessings of the covenant. Such is the generosity of God's provision, past, present, and future, that loving him, fearing him, walking in his ways, obeying him, worshiping him seem like the least his people could do. The problem is that they are completely incapable of producing this kind of response, as the past forty years of Israel's history in the wilderness have shown. Moses's rhetoric is both reasonable and highly persuasive. Yet there is a growing sense that the only thing that his plaintive appeals can produce is despair. Only the intervention of God himself, bringing us to new life by the Spirit and "circumcising our hearts," can put people like us in the position to live the life to which we are called.

The best way to read these chapters is through the lens of Paul's words in Romans 7:21–25: "So I discover this law: When I want to do what is good, evil is present with me. For in my inner self I delight in God's law, but I see a different law in the parts of my body, waging war against the law of my mind and taking me prisoner to the law of sin in the parts of my body. What a wretched man I am! Who will rescue me from this body of death? Thanks be to God through Jesus Christ our Lord!"

IV. Moses Preaches Torah (12:1–26:19)

A. Outline

12:1–32	Worshiping God's Way
13:1–18	Worshiping God Alone
14:1–21	Living as God's Treasured Possession
14:22–16:17	The Rhythm of Covenant Life
16:18–18:22	Living under God's Appointed Leaders
19:1–22:12	Death as the Ultimate Covenant Sanction
22:13–25:19	Covenant Righteousness in All of Life
26:1–19	Living All of Life for God

B. Relation to Surrounding Context

Throughout chapters 4–11, Moses has been urging the people of Israel to respond wholeheartedly to God's covenantal, rescuing grace. The rhythm of God speaking and the people responding in obedience was established at Horeb. Chapter 4 is an extended meditation on the God who makes his presence obvious to his people by speaking. The theology of Chapter 4 is then backed up and illustrated by the inclusion of the "sketch" of the obedient covenant life handed down by God himself in the Ten Words, and the extended appeal to heed these words of God.

From the outset, it is clear that the requirements of this covenant are extremely far-reaching. The Ten Words are only the beginning. We have seen that 6:4 has established that Israel's entire national life is to be built on listening. The growing intensity of the rhetoric of chapters 7–11 (where the shape of this response is repeatedly emphasized in broad terms like "keeping the whole commandment"; "fearing God"; "loving Yahweh with heart, soul, and might") has led the reader to the point where a more fulsome definition (or perhaps better, exposition) of the nature of the obedient life is expected. The "statutes and ordinances" that have been promised and anticipated from chapter 4 onward (see, e.g., 4:1; 5:1; 6:1; 8:11; 11:1), are now are enumerated at some length in the largest collection of legal and instructional material in the Bible.

C. Structure and Style

What exactly are we dealing with in these chapters? There are three important questions to consider: (1) What is the relationship between the Decalogue and these chapters? (2) What is the relationship between these chapters and other similar collections of laws in the Bible and the ancient Near East? (3) What is the role of these chapters (or "this torah") in the unfolding theology of the Bible?

(1) Deuteronomy 12–26 and the Ten Commandments

Over the past forty years, there has been much discussion of the relationship between the Ten Commandments and the laws of Deuteronomy 12–26.[270] It seems fair to say that a *broad correspondence* between the

---

[270] See Millar, *Now Choose Life*, 99–108, and John H. Walton, "The Decalogue Structure of the Deuteronomic Law," in *Interpreting Deuteronomy: Issues and Approaches*, ed. David

order of the Ten Words and the massive collection of stipulations in Deuteronomy has been established.

The literary structure of chapters 1–11, as we have seen, demands that the initial, indicative revelation at Horeb be augmented by a new, all-encompassing exposition of God's covenantal requirements. In other words, the internal structure of Deuteronomy itself drives us to read chapters 12–26 in the light of the Decalogue.

Then there is the fact that the flow of laws from chapter 12 on bears a remarkable similarity to the flow of the Ten Commandments. The insistence that God alone should be worshiped and idolatry resisted; that God's reputation must be upheld, familial relationships honored, the rhythm of life maintained in a way that reflects God's ordering of national life; and that human life is sacred can be mapped onto the Sinai revelation (relatively) easily and neatly.[271]

However, there are several problems with establishing a neat (or even definite) *correspondence*. (1) The first is the shape of Deuteronomy itself. If a hard and fast correspondence with the Decalogue had been Moses's intention, one might expect that the markers of this structure would have been highlighted more clearly. It is, for example, not entirely clear whether the "exposition" of Exodus 20 begins at chapter 6 or chapter 12. (2) The uncertainties over the structure of the Decalogue itself (as reflected in the differences between the Reformed, Lutheran, and Roman Catholic traditions are illustrative of this) muddy the waters considerably. (3) Perhaps the most significant factor is the difficulty in identifying any neat (or convincing) pattern, let alone a Decalogue pattern in the latter chapters of the Deuteronomic collection.[272]

It seems best then to understand the relationship between the revelation at Moab in Deuteronomy 12–26 as a dynamic expansion and

---

G. Firth and Philip S. Johnson (Downers Grove: InterVarsity, 2012), 93–117, for an overview and a discussion of the seminal work of Georg Braulik (e.g. *Studien zur Theologie des Deuteronomiums*, [Stuttgart: Kath. Bibelwerk, 1988] and Stephen Kaufman ("The Structure of the Deuteronomic Law." *Maarav* 1, no. 2 [1978–1979]: 105–58). The suggestion that Deut 12-26 is patterned on the Decalogue goes back at least as far as Luther. See Martin Luther, *Lectures on Deuteronomy*, Luther's Works 9 (Fort Wayne: Concordia, 1960) 67.

[271] Jack Lundbom (*Deuteronomy*, 417–18) provides a clear and simple table of proposed correspondences (and where they break down), enabling readers to make at least an initial assessment of the proposal easily.

[272] The attempts of editors in many English versions of the Bible to gather laws under heading such as "Miscellaneous Law" and "Various Laws" is a reflection of this difficulty!

exposition of the initial sketch of life with Yahweh in his land given first at Horeb. Moses essentially preaches on the Decalogue in a way which is broadly recognizable to his hearers but isn't constrained by any attempt to stick rigidly to the categories of the original.

(2) Deuteronomy 12–26 and Ancient Near Eastern Laws

This section of the book is often referred to as the "law code" (in line with other ancient collections like that of Hammurabi, King of the city-state of Babylon from c. 1800 BC).[273] However, this description is slightly misleading, for at least two reasons.

First, unlike Hammurabi's "law code," the rules of Deuteronomy 12–26 (like all the legal material in the Bible) are deeply embedded in a *narrative context*. Rather than the briefest of introductions, detailing the authority of the king and lawgiver, eleven chapters of preaching precede the laws of Deuteronomy. This has given rise to all kinds of arguments over whether the rules or the story came first: some see the laws as the earliest material, which was then set in a narrative context; others argue that the values of the ancient narratives are codified in laws; and still others take a redactional approach.[274] I would suggest that it is ultimately more fruitful to read Deuteronomy on its own terms as weaving together both "law" and narrative as part of its overall goal to urge God's people to obey.

James Watts, in his excellent short book *Reading Law*, comes at this whole question from a different angle, thinking through the rhetorical purpose and use of law codes in the ancient Near East. Watts points out that "the combination of story and list [and divine sanction] ... should be regarded as a strategy of persuasion employed by many cultures in a variety of literary genres for the purpose of convincing readers

---

[273] The stele bearing the Law Code of Hammurabi can be viewed in the Louvre in Paris, and translations readily accessed online (see, e.g., http://avalon.law.yale.edu/subject_menus/hammenu.asp).

[274] In *Story as Torah*, Wenham argues that the narratives back up the values in the law (73–107). Barton ("Law and Narrative," 137), takes the reverse position, arguing that the laws provide the rationale for the judgments made in the narratives. Sailhamer takes a different approach again, proposing a complex redactional history in which a legalistic Mosaic mindset was eventually overcome and overwhelmed by an earlier, more grace-driven Abramic dogma (*Meaning of the Pentateuch*, 315, also ch. 10, "The Purpose of the Mosaic Law in the Pentateuch," 537–62).

and hearers of the document's, and its author's, authority."[275] In other words, both law and narrative work together, employing complementary strategies of persuasion.

Watts also goes on to point out that when compared to other collections of law both in the Bible and in the ancient Near East generally, the Pentateuch with its variety of legal material is "truly *sui generis*, without parallel in size, scale, contents in Israel's or any other culture's earlier or contemporary literature. Yet the rhetoric of story, list and sanction still shapes its maze of genres and traditions."[276]

The second key difference between the Deuteronomic material and comparable ancient Near Eastern material is the nature (and couching) of the individual requirements themselves. The laws of Hammurabi are typically straightforward, taking the form "If you do this, then this will happen to you" (usually called "case" or "casuistic" law). There is little or no attempt at persuasion or motivation. Hammurabi, claiming extravagant, divine authority as the king, simply makes demands in order to preserve the peace and order of *his* kingdom for his own primary benefit. This is quite typical of similar ancient material (generally known as "cuneiform" law, because of the style of text used on the clay tablets on which it is written), but quite different from the biblical material, which displays a rich variety of material.[277]

These biblical rules are, unlike the contemporary material, very clearly preached. These chapters are full of motive clauses. They are also very clearly rooted in grace. Both the context of chapters 1–11 and the constant explicit reminders of Yahweh's grace in the text (e.g., 12:28–29; 13:5; 14:1–2) make it clear that God acts first in kindness and then invites them to respond. The key concerns of right worship, right relationships, and right behavior (which can be summed up as a concern for "righteousness," as we shall see) are quite different from those of cuneiform law. There is no effort to be comprehensive, but rather a picture is painted of life in the land (or perhaps better, a model is provided of how to work out

---

[275] Watts, *Reading Law*, 45.

[276] Watts, *Reading Law*, 60.

[277] In contrast to Hammurabi's laws, Deut 12–26 contains, e.g., "apodictic" address ("thou shalt not"); motive clauses, repetition for effect, variation, selectivity, hypothetical case law, and purpose statements at a specific and general level. For a brief discussion of these features with bibliography see Millar, *Now Choose Life*, 104–6.

what to do in the land).[278] This goes some way to explaining why, while some of the laws are really quirky (e.g., 25:11–12), overall the thrust is a clear, positive and heartwarming call to live a grace-shaped life, as chapter 26, which is deliberately held back as a suitable conclusion to these laws, makes plain.

Taking all these features into account, it becomes clear that these chapters of Deuteronomy are deeply theological, and reflect the same concerns as the rest of Moses's preaching. This is in marked contrast to the bare stipulations of cuneiform law. For example, chapters 12–26 repeatedly insist that:

- God is absolutely and utterly sovereign (*he* will choose the place in which Israel must worship)
- Worshiping God his way is the only way to joy (which is also why idolatry is such a terrible idea)
- Celebrating in his presence is right at the heart of life in the land (which is why poor and landless people get to join in celebrations at the sanctuary)
- The gift of land is an expression of relationship with Yahweh, and so must be deeply respected

Given all of this, it would be a mistake to underestimate the distinctiveness of these remarkable chapters even in their ancient context.

(3) A Biblical Theology of Torah

Unlike the English word "law," which conjures up restrictions, accusations, and an overarching sense of guilt, the Hebrew idea of torah (lit., "instruction") has a generally positive and constructive emphasis. Psalm 19 makes this very clear:

> [7] The instruction of the Lord is perfect,
> renewing one's life;
>
> the testimony of the Lord is trustworthy,
> making the inexperienced wise.
>
> [8] The precepts of the Lord are right,
> making the heart glad;

---

[278] This is partly why Block's reading of these laws as a "national constitution" for Israel, while attractive, is not ultimately compelling. There are too many gaps and too much that is apparently random for this to be persuasive.

> the command of the LORD is radiant,
>   making the eyes light up.
>
> [9] The fear of the LORD is pure,
>   enduring forever;
>
> the ordinances of the LORD are reliable
>   and altogether righteous.
>
> [10] They are more desirable than gold—
>   than an abundance of pure gold;
>
> and sweeter than honey
>   dripping from a honeycomb.
>
> [11] In addition, your servant is warned by them,
>   And in keeping them there is an abundant reward.

The question is, how can the psalmist, along with the rest of the Old Testament writers be so positive about "law" (the word is torah)?[279] In one way, Deuteronomy is an extended answer to that question. From the headline statement of 4:8 ("And what great nation has righteous statutes and ordinances like this entire law I set before you today?") all the way through the laws themselves in chapters 12–26, there is an enduring note of celebration and joy. The torah defines a response to God which can be summed up as "choosing life" (see 30:15–20).

Deuteronomy in particular sets the parameters for the biblical theology of law in at least three ways: (1) Torah (and the accompanying expressions that describe God's instruction and commands) is viewed as an entirely positive term. To follow God's instruction is to live richly within the right boundaries that God has laid down. (2) Torah is an expansive and expanding idea.[280] Rather than a strictly delimited list of rules (as, for example, the Pharisees understood it in Jesus's day), torah is an all-embracing concept. [281] (3) Torah is an early depiction of the "beautiful life" fulfilled, embodied, and made possible by Jesus. This view of torah prepares for us to read these chapters prophetically, both at the level of recognizing details that

---

[279] I am indebted to my friend Daniel Block for capturing this emphasis. See, e.g., *How I Love Your Torah*.

[280] The diagram in Block, *Deuteronomy*, 369, highlights how Israel's "constitutional tradition" expands from the Decalogue through the Holiness Code to Deuteronomy. However, Jesus's ministry is then depicted as focusing that tradition. I would argue that Jesus's ministry continues the expansion, opening up the possibility of enjoying life to the full (John 10:10) with him.

[281] This is reflected in Jesus's constant insistence that the righteousness of the Pharisees was minimalistic ("you have heard it said ... but I say to you ... ").

appear to be an anticipation of Christ himself (e.g., 17:14–20) and of reading the whole collection as a foreshadowing of the all-encompassing, gospel-shaped life delivered to us by Christ. Deuteronomy anticipates the fact that life in Christ will be more vivid, more joyful, more whole-hearted, more far-reaching than anything else we have seen. This "expansionist" reading of the Old Testament opens up all kinds of possibilities in applying the Old Testament responsibly to the life of God's new covenant people.[282]

In Deuteronomy 12–26 then, Moses continues to preach as he both presents an expansive, all–of–life vision of the life of freedom lived in the presence of the Lord in the land that he has given them by grace in fulfillment of his promises to Abraham, Isaac, and Jacob and seeks to persuade Israel to embrace this vision.

1. Worshiping God's Way (12:1–32)

> 1 "Be careful to follow these statutes and ordinances in the land that
> the Lord, the God of your ancestors, has given you to possess all the
> days you live on the earth. 2 Destroy completely all the places where
> the nations that you are driving out worship their gods—on the high
> mountains, on the hills, and under every green tree. 3 Tear down their
> altars, smash their sacred pillars, burn their Asherah poles, cut down
> the carved images of their gods, and wipe out their names from ev-
> ery place. 4 Don't worship the Lord your God this way. 5 Instead, turn
> to the place the Lord your God chooses from all your tribes to put his
> name for his dwelling and go there. 6 You are to bring there your burnt
> offerings and sacrifices, your tenths and personal contributions, your
> vow offerings and freewill offerings, and the firstborn of your herds
> and flocks. 7 You will eat there in the presence of the Lord your God and
> rejoice with your household in everything you do, because the Lord
> your God has blessed you.
>
> 8 "You are not to do as we are doing here today; everyone is doing
> whatever seems right in his own sight. 9 Indeed, you have not yet
> come into the resting place and the inheritance the Lord your God is
> giving you. 10 When you cross the Jordan and live in the land the Lord
> your God is giving you to inherit, and he gives you rest from all the
> enemies around you and you live in security, 11 then the Lord your

[282] For example, the Old Testament food laws can be dispensed with as markers of distinctiveness but are an anticipation of a deeper distinctiveness that now rests on our union with Christ and possession of (and by) the Holy Spirit, which issues in love (and the other parts of the "fruit of the Spirit").

God will choose the place to have his name dwell. Bring there everything I command you: your burnt offerings, sacrifices, offerings of
the tenth, personal contributions, and all your choice offerings you
vow to the Lord. 12 You will rejoice before the Lord your God—you,
your sons and daughters, your male and female slaves, and the Levite
who is within your city gates, since he has no portion or inheritance
among you. 13 Be careful not to offer your burnt offerings in all the
sacred places you see. 14 You must offer your burnt offerings only in
the place the Lord chooses in one of your tribes, and there you must
do everything I command you.

15 "But whenever you want, you may slaughter and eat meat within
any of your city gates, according to the blessing the Lord your God
has given you. Those who are clean or unclean may eat it, as they
would a gazelle or deer, 16 but you must not eat the blood; pour it on
the ground like water. 17 Within your city gates you may not eat the
tenth of your grain, new wine, or fresh oil; the firstborn of your herd
or flock; any of your vow offerings that you pledge; your freewill
offerings; or your personal contributions. 18 You are to eat them in
the presence of the Lord your God at the place the Lord your God
chooses—you, your son and daughter, your male and female slave,
and the Levite who is within your city gates. Rejoice before the Lord
your God in everything you do, 19 and be careful not to neglect the
Levite, as long as you live in your land.

20 "When the Lord your God enlarges your territory as he has promised
you, and you say, 'I want to eat meat' because you have a strong desire
to eat meat, you may eat it whenever you want. 21 If the place where
the Lord your God chooses to put his name is too far from you, you may
slaughter any of your herd or flock he has given you, as I have commanded you, and you may eat it within your city gates whenever you
want. 22 Indeed, you may eat it as the gazelle and deer are eaten; both
the clean and the unclean may eat it. 23 But don't eat the blood, since
the blood is the life, and you must not eat the life with the meat. 24 Do
not eat blood; pour it on the ground like water. 25 Do not eat it, so that
you and your children after you will prosper, because you will be doing
what is right in the Lord's sight.

26 "But you are to take the holy offerings you have and your vow offerings and go to the place the Lord chooses. 27 Present the meat and
blood of your burnt offerings on the altar of the Lord your God. The
blood of your other sacrifices is to be poured out beside the altar of
the Lord your God, but you may eat the meat. 28 Be careful to obey all
these things I command you, so that you and your children after you
may prosper forever, because you will be doing what is good and right
in the sight of the Lord your God.

[29] "When the Lord your God annihilates the nations before you, which
you are entering to take possession of, and you drive them out and
live in their land, [30] be careful not to be ensnared by their ways after they have been destroyed before you. Do not inquire about their
gods, asking, 'How did these nations worship their gods? I'll also do
the same.' [31] You must not do the same to the Lord your God, because
they practice every detestable act, which the Lord hates, for their gods.
They even burn their sons and daughters in the fire to their gods. [32] Be
careful to do everything I command you; do not add anything to it or
take anything away from it."

12:1–7. From the very beginning of chapter 12, it is evident that the collection of legal material is quite different from any other ancient law code.[283] This is "law preached."[284] As we have seen, Moses has urged the people repeatedly to commit wholeheartedly to obey Yahweh in chapters 6–11; now he fills out the shape of this obedience. The "statutes and ordinances" have been anticipated in the preceding material (notably 4:1; 5:1; 6:1, etc.), and now they are revealed.[285]

According to 12:1, these rules are inextricably embedded in a context of covenant promise. There is no stark contrast between law and grace here. These commands are to be lived out in the land that is a free gift from Yahweh. The free gift itself is the result of a longstanding, ill-deserved promise made to your "ancestors" ("fathers"), a term that generally refers particularly to Abraham, Isaac, and Jacob. But this verse reaches not only back to Genesis 12, but all the way back to the beginning of Genesis, as the "land" is situated "on the earth," which the man Adam was commissioned to fill and subdue (Gen 1:28).[286] Whatever we make of the material that follows, it is no "bolt-on" collection of disconnected material: it is a key part of the "Deuteronomic project," which involves lifelong obedience to the word of Yahweh (see also, e.g., 4:9).

---

[283] It is not even clear that "law code" is the right term for Deut 12–26.

[284] A term memorably coined by Gerhard von Rad, *Studies in Deuteronomy*, Studies in Biblical Theology 9 (London: SCM Press, 1956), 16. Tigay rightly comments that Moses devotes "more attention to exhorting the people to obey the laws as the laws themselves." *Deuteronomy*, 117.

[285] It is also important to note that this new section is closely tied to 11:31–32, with some seeing a chiastic relationship to the preceding verses (see McConville, *Deuteronomy*, 212–13).

[286] The words "land" and "earth" are used interchangeably in Deuteronomy, but in this instance, they seem to refer to the local and global.

Moses has already made it clear (in, e.g., 7:1–6) that dealing with the Canaanites will be the primary challenge of the occupation. This is not simply to be a matter of overcoming their military might, but rather of destroying every vestige of their influence, worship, and theology. This is why the laws begin with a command to "Destroy completely all the places where the nations that you are driving out worship their gods" (12:2). The verbal form is intensive (piel), for this intervention needs to be decisive. Israel must obliterate every place where pagan worship and fertility rituals took place in Canaan. This is not a new idea—it occurs several times earlier in the Pentateuch (Exod 23:24; 34:10–16; Num 33:50–52)—but the urgency of carrying out these commands is now clear.

Obedience here is designed to have a dual effect: on the one hand, it is a clear reminder that the land belongs to Yahweh, not the gods of Canaan; and on the other, it instantly removes the temptation for Israel to follow the ways of the Canaanites, which have already been repeatedly denounced as anathema. The fact that these places are apparently ubiquitous ("on the high mountains, on the hills, and under every green tree"), sounds an ominous warning to the people of God: no half-hearted attempt to keep this command will be sufficient.[287] It is all or nothing.

The subsequent commentary on Israel's life in Canaan repeatedly highlights the failure to keep this most basic of commands. In the books of Kings, for example, the repeated refrain is that throughout the preexilic period, these places remained in (often heavy) use (see, e.g., 1 Kgs 3:1–3; 11:7; 14:23; 15:14). The "high places" (as they are called elsewhere, but not in Deuteronomy) sadly remained a feature throughout the nation's time in the land.[288]

According to 12:3, every single piece of cultic apparatus is to be obliterated. The language is slightly different to 7:4 (here the Asherah poles are to be burned and the carved images cut down, once more surely the result of natural variation in oral communication), but

---

[287] The phrase "On every high hill and under every green tree" becomes a virtual shorthand for the prevalence of idolatry in Israel (see, e.g., 1 Kgs 14:23; 2 Kgs 17:10; Jer 2:20; 3:6; 17:2–3; Ezek 6:13; 20:28). Block comments that the threefold description "highlights the pervasiveness, intensity and futility of pagan worship." Block, *Deuteronomy*, 304.

[288] There is plentiful archaeological evidence for Israel continuing to worship at "high places." See the helpful list in Lundbom, *Deuteronomy*, 424.

rather than appealing to God's holiness for motivation (7:5), here the purpose is more dramatic: to "wipe out their names from every place." These gods cannot be allowed to co-exist with Israel's God in the land.[289] Yahweh is supreme and will brook no rivals. Life in the land is a life to be lived with him alone.

The blunt truth of monotheism immediately gives rise to a key principle that is fundamental for much of what follows. 12:4 states plainly that "Don't worship the Lord your God this way." Yahweh and Yahweh alone determines how Yahweh shall be worshiped. Practically, this means that Israel has no freedom to be creative, nor to adapt Canaanite worship for their purposes, but must worship in the way God himself commands. This has been anticipated throughout the previous chapters (and also in Exod 23:24), notably in the insistence that they need to listen carefully to all Yahweh's words, but now it is made explicit.

This insistence finds its first unique and fundamental expression in Yahweh's selection of the location of their worship center in verse 5: "Instead, turn to the place the Lord your God chooses from all your tribes to put his name for his dwelling and go there." The translation is slightly misleading here. The people are to "seek" this place (rather than "turn" to it), which underlines a deliberate choice to submit their desires and practices to the will of Yahweh by making a pilgrimage to this "chosen" place. Only one place will bear his name (in contrast to the many "places" in v. 2), and as they have journeyed with God to the land, now they will journey to this one place in the land, where the whole gamut of national religious (sacrificial) activity will take place. But this is not simply a religious venue. This is where God will make his "name dwell." The verb here (שָׁכַן) and its associated noun (מִשְׁכָּן) are generally associated with the tabernacle (so older translations generally, and rightly, used the verb "tabernacle" in this context). The point is not simply that Yahweh will take up residence, but that he will establish a way to meet with him and enjoy his presence through the sanctuary described in such detail earlier in the Pentateuch. As we saw in 4:32–40, this is not simply an expression of ownership, but a pointer to the fact that he is actually present with his people. The question then is: Will

[289] A reality which, sadly, persisted throughout the history of Israel and Judah. For references to the Asherim alone see 1 Kgs 14:15, 23; 16:33; 2 Kgs 17:10; 18:4, 22; 21:3, 7; 23:6, 14–15; Mic 5:13; Isa 27:9; Jer 2:27; 3:9; 17:2. On erasing the name, see Zech 13:2.

his people submit to his revealed will and sovereign rule, and so enjoy life with him in this land? The key will be setting up this "place within a place," a worship center at the heart of the land, to which they continue to journey as those who trust Yahweh.[290]

This emphasis on *going* to the place chosen by Yahweh, rather than on the precise details of what is to be done there, is underlined by the non-specific but all-encompassing list of sacrifices in 12:6.[291] Despite the fact that Deuteronomy will go on to ease some requirements around killing animals away from the sanctuary (in order to make life workable in the land), this is clearly the headline principle: the entire religious life of the nation is to be lived according to Yahweh's commands. "Burnt offerings and sacrifices" are the main sacrifices prescribed in the earlier laws in Exodus and Leviticus. Tigay calls the burnt offering (see Lev 1) the "gift *par excellence*."[292] "Tenths" are those voluntary gifts offered in response to particular events in the life of the nation or the individual, especially harvest offerings of grain, wine and olive oil, as well as requisite offerings from herds and flocks (Lev 27:32). "Personal offerings" (traditionally "wave" or "heave offerings") is used in Exodus to describe a variety of voluntary offerings (see, e.g., Exod 25:2–3; 29:27–28), but here may refer to the firstfruits (Deut 26:4). "Vow offerings" and "freewill contributions" generally refer to spontaneous expressions of gratitude and commitment to Yahweh. The offering of the "firstborn" punctuated the natural rhythm of the life of the nation, reminding them of who they were and their underlying obligation to Yahweh who had rescued them (see Exod 13:1–2), and that too should be brought to Yahweh's designated place. Every cultic expression of Israel's faith in Yahweh is now to be

---

[290] Much earlier, Exod 20:24–25 appears to allow for a plurality of *altars*, of which Yahweh says "I will come to you and bless you." At this earliest stage of the nation, before the journey to the land has even begun, this is completely understandable. This is an early expression of the kindness of Yahweh meeting with his people. However, Deut 12 takes things to a new level, where Yahweh will make his *name* dwell with the people, which implies a new level of intimacy.

[291] Tigay understands this representative list as covering "animal sacrifices, taxes on agricultural products, voluntary offerings and firstlings of cattle." *Deuteronomy*, 120.

[292] Tigay, *Deuteronomy*, 128. The term "sacrifices" presumably covers the "peace offerings" of Lev 3, and perhaps also various guilt offerings. Strictly speaking, the burnt offering was not eaten (12:7), but Moses is laying out broadbrush principles for how the sacrificial system will operate, rather than dealing carefully with every exception.

enacted at the very heart of the nation, in the place chosen by Yahweh at his generous invitation.[293]

It is important that we understand that, whatever else Moses says on the theme of sacrifice and whatever the particular distinctives of these laws when they speak about the worship of the nation, the starting point is simply that Israel must embrace the full scope of the revealed practices of the sacrificial system in the land and enact them at the place which Yahweh chooses, *because this is the key to enjoying life with Yahweh in the land.*

One of the particular emphases of Deuteronomy makes explicit what is implied in all the earlier sacrificial legislation (and briefly mentioned in Lev 23:40): the goal of sacrifice is to enjoy Yahweh's presence as his people in his land. This is explicit in 12:7: "You will eat there in the presence of the Lord your God and rejoice with your household in everything you do, because the Lord your God has blessed you." McConville comments: "The plain meaning is that he is actually present, just as he has been present with Israel during their journeyings to the land (1:31)."[294] This is the first of nine occasions where people are commanded to enjoy in Deuteronomy (see 12:7, 12, 18; 14:26; 16:11, 14, 15; 26:11; 27:7; and see also the consequences of not rejoicing in 28:47–48). The source of this joy is the blessing of Yahweh, given as part of his gracious covenant. The entire people of God get to rejoice in his presence. And they get to do it in all of life (lit., "in every undertaking of your hand"), because of the relentless blessing of Yahweh.

From the outset of the laws, it is important to notice that Moses's concerns are sweeping and theological, rather than detailed and prescriptive. The absence of any role for the priest in these verses, for example, is significant, but only in revealing that Moses's emphasis lies on the sovereignty of God and the joy of the people. This is preached law, which aims to move people to enjoy life in the land with the God who loves them and has rescued them and to deal wisely and decisively with the nations who threaten their life and future.

12:8–14. According to Moses, Israel stands on the threshold of an entirely new way of living. Despite all that has already been said to his people by Yahweh (in Genesis to Numbers), now is the moment when

---

293 Block helpfully points out that the verbs in vv. 5–7 are "come" and "bring" (rather than "go" and "take"), which conveys this sense (*Deuteronomy*, 305–7).

294 McConville, *Deuteronomy*, 223.

everything is about to change: "You are not to do as we are doing here today." The transitional nature of life in the wilderness is then characterized as "everyone ... doing whatever seems right in his own sight." In view of the climactic verdict of Judges 21:25, describing the declension of life in Israel to preconquest chaos, it is hard to view this as a positive. The current *laissez-faire* approach to worship *en route* to the land clearly needs to change and to be brought into line with God's fulsome and life-giving provision for their new life.

There is an apparent tension here between Moses's description of pre-entry religious practice and Leviticus 17:1–7, which insists that all slaughter take place at the sanctuary. However, in all likelihood, Moses is simply drawing attention to the fact that Israel has already fallen far from the ideal of obedience before they actually get into the land.

Life in the land is to be characterized by rest, security and richness. The word for "rest" here is from the same root (נוח) used to describe the pleasing aroma produced by Noah's sacrifice in Genesis 8:21.[295] This may well imply that this moment is as significant as Noah's new beginning into a refreshed creation after the judgment of the flood, and the "resting place" is where God's people will be able to enjoy the life which God has created them for.[296] That the land is their inheritance conveys the fact that God himself is their generous guarantor, who stands behind their occupation and who gives them all the good things which are awaiting them. This rest is later tasted under Joshua's leadership (Josh 21:44; 22:4; 23:1); in the reigns of David (2 Sam 7:1, 11), Solomon (1 Kgs 5:4 [Heb. 5:18]; 8:56), Asa (2 Chr 15:15) and Jehoshaphat (2 Chr 20:30), but ultimately brought within our grasp by the Lord Jesus (see Heb 4:9). The pattern of sinfulness followed by displays of Yahweh's grace followed by declension is, it seems, already entrenched deeply in the life of God's people.

Yahweh's ownership of the land, and their status as favored sons receiving an inheritance, is to be (literally) enshrined by his choice in verse 11 of "the place to have his name dwell." As we have already seen, this is one of the most important phrases in Deuteronomy and is front and center in the laws. There are two important elements in this theologically

---

[295] The fact that Noah's name is made up of the first and third letters of the root makes an allusion even more probable.

[296] It is also likely that this is an allusion to the "Sabbath rest" of God himself in Gen 2:1–3. The word used however, does not have any demonstrable links to the Sabbath, making this hard to prove. However, Yahweh's words in Exod 33:14 display a similar concern.

weighty phrase: (1) the sovereignty of God, which stands behind his right to choose the place where Israel meets him, and (2) the reality of his presence with his people in the land. It is here, at the chosen place, which Israel's journey to the land culminates, and to which Israel's "journey" within the land continues.[297] The determining factor in the longevity and quality of their life in the land will be the way they relate to Yahweh and respond to the privilege and challenge of his actual presence with them.

For Moses in Deuteronomy, the operational details of the sacrificial system are taken as read. The language of verse 11, which simply reels off a list of generic sacrifices ("burnt offerings, sacrifices, offerings of the tenth, personal contributions, and all your choice offerings you vow to the Lord") is more concerned to emphasize the theological principle of wholehearted obedience than to ensure the worshiper follows proper procedure. That's confirmed by the addition of "choice" offerings to the list of verse 8.[298]

Verse 12 then placards two of the most obvious distinctives of the Deuteronomic material concerning the worship of Israel. The first of these is *joy*. The journeys to the place chosen by Yahweh that punctuate the life of the people are to be characterized above all by this note of glad celebration, as they "rejoice before the Lord your God." This joy flows from Yahweh's gracious care and provision for them, both past and present, rather than arising directly from the sacrifices. However, the goal of both their journey within the land and the offerings is to enable them to enjoy God's presence. The phrase "before the Lord your God" should be taken at face value: God is actually present at the sanctuary (see, e.g., 4:32–40), and his people are to rejoice both in and because of his presence with them.

The second key distinctive of Israelite worship in 12:12 is *inclusivity*. The entire covenant community is to share in the privilege and delight of celebrating with Yahweh. This includes both natural families ("you, your sons and daughters"), wider households (interestingly, including "your male and female slaves," despite the non-ideal nature of the existence of slavery in Israel), as well as the local Levite, "since he has no portion or inheritance among you." The Levite is now not simply a pointer to the primacy of knowing Yahweh; he gets to participate in the enjoyment of

---

[297] See L. Michael Morales, *Who Shall Ascend the Mountain of the Lord? A Biblical Theology of the Book of Leviticus*, NSBT 37 (Downers Grove: InterVarsity Press, 2015).

[298] Interestingly, one could argue that Leviticus also displays a similar lack of interest, but this feature is clearly even more pronounced in Deuteronomy.

the relationship with Yahweh to which the entire life of his tribe points. This is reiterated in 14:27, 29; 16:11, 14; 18:6–8; and 26:11–13. These prescriptions are clearly highly theological: they are based on the ideal of all of God's people enjoying his presence in the land which he has given them.[299]

It is this positive theological concern that undergirds the prohibition of making use of the proliferation of high places at the land which they are entering (12:13). The warning to "Be careful not to ..." is a crucial part of the rhetoric of these chapters. These high places were to prove an index of Israel's faithfulness in the generations to come. But for Moses, the matter is simple: Yahweh makes his presence known only at the place he chooses. The vague expression "in one of your tribes" here, as in 12:5, underlines that Yahweh alone will choose this place. This means that opting to make sacrifices anywhere else is both direct disobedience (the command to "do everything I command you" undergirds everything here) and a rejection of the offer of relationship that is built in to almost every passage in this book. Israel must listen to Yahweh, rather than allowing their eyes to be drawn to the vestiges of Canaanite idolatry.

12:15–19. The provision made in these verses for killing animals and eating their meat has given rise to a huge amount of discussion over the years. It is often said that Deuteronomy is desacralizing the slaughter of animals. However, this is one of those places in the Old Testament where the simplest explanation is surely the best. This material simply presents itself as a common-sense adjustment of practice for life in the land. Up to this point, Israel had lived, moved, and camped together. A central spot designated for slaughter made perfect sense. As they moved into the land, this was clearly no longer going to be practicable. Given the preponderance of "high places" (v. 13), a very real danger would be that the people would naively make their way to the nearest pagan religious site. In the light of that, God through Moses establishes a new practice for life in Canaan in 12:15: "whenever you want, you may slaughter and eat meat within any of your city gates."

There is no limitation to this provision. It is to be driven simply by the "desires" of appetite or need (the preposition is general and can cover both the time of eating and the amount of food). Eating fresh meat in the

---

[299] This goes some way to explaining why Deuteronomy is relatively uninterested in the workings of the tribe of Levi. It is clear that all those who function as priests are Levites, but not all Levites are priests, but beyond that, nothing is said.

ancient world was a luxury, generally requiring a large number of people to make it worthwhile, given that it had to be consumed at one sitting in pre-refrigeration days. Life in the land will clearly enrich Isarel's diet and their common life. However, it is vital that the Israelites continue to remember that all their eating and drinking in the land, and especially eating meat, is "according to the blessing the Lord your God has given you." As this torah will make plain over and over again, all of life is to be lived with and for Yahweh, including killing and eating animals.

The theological symbolism of eating meat at home is clarified in the last clause of verse 15. Moses explains that this is a simplification, not a complication, and so no further ritual restrictions are to be added. While the general dietary distinctives of Israel are obviously to be preserved, the vivid system of cleanness/uncleanness does not impinge on eating meat at home, in the same way as it made no claims on those hunting game (animals such as gazelle and deer were never to be sacrificed).

It would, however, be misleading to call this "profane slaughter." For Yahweh's people in Yahweh's land there is to be no such thing. The word "only" (CSB: "but") introduces a strong exception. First and foremost, they must not "eat the blood."

This was prohibited by God as early as Genesis 9:4 (see also Lev 3:17; 7:26–27; 19:26), but here Moses draws on a seminal passage in Leviticus 17, which is worth quoting in full:

> [10] Anyone from the house of Israel or from the aliens who reside among them who eats any blood, I will turn against that person who eats blood and cut him off from his people. [11] For the life of a creature is in the blood, and I have appointed it to you to make atonement on the altar for your lives, since it is the lifeblood that makes atonement. [12] Therefore I say to the Israelites: None of you and no alien who resides among you may eat blood. (Lev 17:10–12)

There is much discussion on the precise meaning of verse 11 in particular, but it is clear that the prohibition on eating blood in any circumstance is a symbolic action arising from the fact that blood plays a key (substitutionary) role in the system of atonement. This is reiterated in the following verses in Leviticus 17, which deal with what to do when hunting:

> [13] Any Israelite or alien residing among them, who hunts down a wild animal or bird that may be eaten must drain its blood and cover it with dirt. [14] Since the life of every creature is its blood, I have told the

> Israelites: You are not to eat the blood of any creature, because the life of every creature is its blood; whoever eats it must be cut off.

This is a simple but solemn reminder that all life, like Israel itself belongs to God. Deuteronomy now takes these basic insights and applies them to the "new normal" in Canaan. When eating meat in the towns and villages of their new land, God's people are to continue to remember their need for atonement (and the associated importance of blood) by refraining from eating it and "pour[ing] it on the ground like water."

It is important to remember that this statement reads somewhat differently for semi-nomadic people in an arid climate than for those who are privileged enough to have clean water perpetually (and literally) "on tap." Water is a most precious resource, not a commodity enjoyed in such superabundance that it can be wasted without a thought. The blood is not simply to be disposed of in any old way, but "poured out" with a reverent awareness that enjoying life with God itself depends on it.

Always realistic, Moses is highly aware of the danger that such "liberalization" will lead to a *laissez-faire* attitude to the importance of worshiping God together at the place which Yahweh will choose. This leads Moses to back up the instructions of 12:7–9, casting much of the same language in the negative ("Within your gates you *may not* eat"). After that, verses 18–19 reiterate that the primary note of this celebration should be shared joy in the presence of Yahweh.

The main addition in verse 19 highlights his overwhelming concern: "Be careful not to neglect the Levite, as long as you live in your land." The Levites in Deuteronomy, as we have already seen, function both as a reminder that relationship with Yahweh is everything (surpassing even the gift of the land, because the land is given to facilitate *relationship*), and also as an index of Israel's response to Yahweh's grace. The landless Levites depend on the theological memory of the rest of the nation, if they are to be included in the tangible celebrations of God's goodness in his presence at the place he chooses. If the people do not maintain the rhythm of traveling to worship, the landless Levites (who lived in urban centers) may well be excluded from enjoying the blessings of the land.

12:20–28. The highly unusual nature of this collection of rules and instructions quickly becomes apparent, as Moses circles back to reiterate both the necessity and the generosity encapsulated in this change of practice. This self-evidently is preached law.

The provision in verse 20 is remarkable: God's extension of their territory (actually from zero to having an entire land of their own!) is not the end of his generosity.[300] Yahweh actually anticipates and accommodates their strong desire to "eat meat" (presumably any kind of meat other than quail).[301] In the ANE it was relatively unusual to eat meat, so this clearly points to a completely new level of prosperity and provision in the land. It is so striking that this kind of "legislation" is right at the beginning of the Deuteronomic collection, and speaks volumes of the generosity of Yahweh.

The statement at the end of 12:20 is completely unambiguous. Any reluctance to embrace this new provision is countered head-on: "you may eat it whenever you want." God's provision for his people is inherently expansive rather than restrictive. He wants them to live the beautiful life in his good land. In the verses which follow, Moses now makes this permission completely explicit. The realities of life in Canaan will mean that distance from the chosen place is an issue for many people (12:21), and as a result, "any of your herd or flock" (i.e., any domesticated, clean animal) may be killed and eaten by anyone with minimum fuss. [302]

In 12:23–25, the concern of verse 15 is reiterated in three successive verses. It could hardly be more strongly expressed. Lundbom suggests that this is because of the new prospect of unsupervised slaughter.[303] The blunt instruction is backed up in various ways. In verse 23, we find the added rationale that "you must not eat the life with the meat." While graphically expressed, there is nothing to suggest that we have moved beyond a symbolic understanding of the significance of blood. The fact that blood speaks of and represents the life of the animal (and of people) undergirds the substitutionary logic of the entire sacrificial system. This precludes a magical (or even physiological) view of the power of the blood.

The repetition of the command to dispose of the blood "like water" is backed up in verse 25 by a typically Deuteronomic incentive to obey in this sphere: "Do not eat it, so that you and your children after you will prosper, because you will be doing what is right in the LORD's sight." God, it seems, is the only master of life and death, and recognizing this even in

---

[300] A similar pattern is found in 19:8–10, which also deals with expansion.

[301] Given the fact that God appears to have provided quail only twice during the exodus (Exod 16:12–13; Num 11:30–35), this seems completely understandable!

[302] The Qumran Temple Scroll (11QT 52:11) defines being "near" the temple as within a three day journey.

[303] Lundbom, *Deuteronomy*, 437.

the mundane details of butchering animals to eat, is a key to prospering with Yahweh in the land (on "prospering," see also 19:13; 28:11, 63; 30:5, 9; on "doing what is right in Yahweh's sight, see 6:18; 13:18; 21:9).

The following verses (12:26–28) complete the circle by reminding Israel of what still should only be done at the tabernacle. The "holy offerings," that is their sacrificial obligations, as well as their voluntary expressions of gratitude and commitment, need to be discharged at God's place in God's way. The blood poured out on the altar (rather than simply on the ground) expresses the fact that the offerer owes God everything (even deserving death). In God's kindness, the meat can be eaten, but the message of the blood cannot be overlooked. The note of verse 25 is then sounded again, as Moses emphasizes once more listening to Yahweh; obeying him in every detail is the way to enjoying the beautiful balance of rich provision of food *and forgiveness* promised through sacrifice. This is the key to living the beautiful life ("what is good and right") with God in the land, and strikingly doing so "forever."

12:29–32. At the end of chapter 12, Moses returns to the threats posed to the life of the covenant people in the land by the current occupants. It is possible to take these verses with the chapter that follows, but they also make sense as the conclusion of chapter 12 (which is hardly surprising, given the flowing nature of Moses's address). The translation "annihilate" is actually "to cut off" (כָּרַת), which has overtones of drastic judgment (see Gen 9:11). However, given the fact that verse 30 contains a double warning against being "ensnared by their ways after they have been destroyed before you" or "inquiring about their gods," it seems unlikely that the intention of verse 29 is to anticipate the elimination of every single Canaanite. It does, however, underline the importance of taking the *whole* land if the system laid out in chapter 12 is to function smoothly and safely for Israel.

The scenario painted in 12:30 is typically conversational ("How did these nations worship their gods? I'll also do the same"). The laws of Deuteronomy are uniquely loose in their approach and framing and are clearly primarily homiletically rather than "constitutionally" shaped. But either way, Moses's main point is made abundantly clear: God is not eliminating the Canaanite nations before them for Israel to model their life on the very behavior and worship that led to this just judgment.[304] Already

---

[304] "Canaanite worship must not be reborn as Yahweh worship, which is the sort of thing that happened in ANE religion and classical religion generally." Lundbom, *Deuteronomy*, 439.

it has been hammered home in a multiplicity of ways: God must be worshiped his way. There is no room for creativity or innovation. Rather God's people need to listen to him and do what he says. The alternative is to embrace "detestable act[s], which the Lord hates." The word used to sum up Canaanite practice is "detestable," which stretches even to child sacrifice: "They even burn their sons and daughters in the fire to their gods."[305]

The slogan of 12:32 provides a fitting conclusion to the chapter: "Do everything [lit., every word] I tell you; do not add anything to it or take away anything from it" (also 4:2). God's provision for life in the land spoken through his servant is flexible and generous, but he is the one who must set the agenda for his covenant people if they are to flourish with him in the land.

Bridge

The gulf between the life that Yahweh holds out to his people with him in the land and the Canaanite way is stark. The blessing and curse motif introduced at the end of chapter 11 is now sketched out in vivid colors. There are only two ways to live. The way of self-determination leads to judgment and death; the way of humble submission, dependence, and gratitude leads to joy and life in the land with Yahweh.

The emphasis on joy in Yahweh's presence at the place he chooses is enhanced by the strikingly relaxed provisions for life in the land. But the contrast between that life and the abominable idolatry of the current occupants could hardly be greater. Moses's preaching is deeply moving at both ends of the emotional register and raises the question "how could anyone refuse to do what God asks?" God is present with his people—a theme picked up and amplified by Solomon in 1 Kings 8, and ultimately embodied in the Lord Jesus himself (John 1:14; 4:21–24). It always falls to his people to live an open-ended life of submission to him, as long as it remains "today."

2. Worshiping God Alone (13:1–18)

> [1] "If a prophet or someone who has dreams arises among you and
> proclaims a sign or wonder to you, [2] and that sign or wonder he has

[305] There is evidence of these practices in Phoenicia at the time, which suggests that we can reasonably assume that this assessment of the Canaanites" behavior is accurate. See George C. Heider, *The Cult of Molech Reassessed, JSOTSup* 43 (Sheffield: JSOT, 1985), 196–203. See also Deut 18:9–12; Lev 18:21; 20:2–5; Jer 7:31; 19:5; 32:35; Ezek 16:20–22; 20:25–26, 31; 23:37–39; Ps 106:37–39 and the tragic events recounted in 2 Kgs 3:27; 16:3; 17:17; 21:6.

promised you comes about, but he says, 'Let's follow other gods,' which
you have not known, 'and let's worship them,' 3 do not listen to that
prophet's words or to that dreamer. For the Lord your God is testing
you to know whether you love the Lord your God with all your heart
and all your soul. 4 You must follow the Lord your God and fear him.
You must keep his commands and listen to him; you must worship him
and remain faithful to him. 5 That prophet or dreamer must be put to
death, because he has urged rebellion against the Lord your God who
brought you out of the land of Egypt and redeemed you from the place
of slavery, to turn you from the way the Lord your God has commanded
you to walk. You must purge the evil from you.

6 "If your brother, the son of your mother, or your son or daughter, or
the wife you embrace, or your closest friend secretly entices you, saying,
'Let's go and worship other gods'—which neither you nor your ancestors
have known, 7 any of the gods of the peoples around you, near you or
far from you, from one end of the earth to the other—8 do not yield to
him or listen to him. Show him no pity, and do not spare him or shield
him. 9 Instead, you must kill him. Your hand is to be the first against
him to put him to death, and then the hands of all the people. 10 Stone
him to death for trying to turn you away from the Lord your God who
brought you out of the land of Egypt, out of the place of slavery. 11 All
Israel will hear and be afraid, and they will no longer do anything evil
like this among you.

12 "If you hear it said about one of your cities the Lord your God is giving
you to live in, 13 that wicked men have sprung up among you, led the
inhabitants of their city astray, and said, 'Let's go and worship other
gods,' which you have not known, 14 you are to inquire, investigate,
and interrogate thoroughly. If the report turns out to be true that this
detestable act has been done among you, 15 you must strike down the
inhabitants of that city with the sword. Completely destroy everyone
in it as well as its livestock with the sword. 16 You are to gather all its
spoil in the middle of the city square and completely burn the city and
all its spoil for the Lord your God. The city is to remain a mound of ruins
forever; it is not to be rebuilt. 17 Nothing set apart for destruction is to
remain in your hand, so that the Lord will turn from his burning anger
and grant you mercy, show you compassion, and multiply you as he
swore to your ancestors. 18 This will occur if you obey the Lord your God,
keeping all his commands I am giving you today, doing what is right in
the sight of the Lord your God."

13:1–5. Given the emphasis on the word of Yahweh in chapters 4–11, it is not entirely surprising that attention turns to the issue of discerning whether or not a message comes from Yahweh. The focus shifts abruptly at the beginning of chapter 13 from the sinful propensities of the Israelites themselves to the activities of a "prophet" or "dreamer" whose actions imperil the nation.[306]

There has been little discussion of the role or significance of prophets (נָבִיא) in the Pentateuch (and 18:15–22 is the only other passage in the legal material addressing prophecy). Biblical prophecy as a "movement" is essentially unknown before Samuel. The term does occur in Genesis 20:7 (of Abraham); Exodus 7:1 (of Aaron); and in the comments of Numbers 11:29 and 12:6, but there is no real discussion or explanation of what being a prophet involves (or how to spot a real one).[307] However, there is no question that charismatic figures claiming some kind of divine inspiration were well known (whether they are described as "prophets" or not; see, e.g., the Balaam narratives of Num 22–24). The prospect of someone "arising" to lead the nation astray is hardly difficult to imagine.

Neither the term "prophet" nor "someone who has dreams" is pejorative in itself (as the Joseph narratives demonstrate), but the danger posed to Israel is clear.[308] They may perform a "sign or wonder" in order to commend apostasy to Israel, thus making it obvious that signs and wonders are, in themselves, inherently unreliable (as exhibited by the magicians of Egypt in Exod 7). The key question to ask is not regarding the veracity of the sign, but the message which is proclaimed. The verdict of 13:2 is blunt: if the message is "let's follow other gods" (that is, other than Yahweh), then it must be rejected.[309] Worshiping gods whom "you have not known" is a radical rejection of the covenant God who has made himself known to the patriarchs and to Israel at the exodus, bringing them out of Egypt and redeeming them (13:5).

Up to this point, Yahweh himself has led and directed Israel.[310] Once the nation enters Canaan, it is anticipated that the threat will come from

---

[306] This could possibly be based on the thought of Exod 20:3–4.

[307] The feminine form is used in Exod 15:20 of Miriam, who joins Deborah (Judg 4:4), Huldah (2 Kgs 22:14; 2 Chr 34:22), and Noadiah (Neh 6:14) on the list of named prophetesses in the Old Testament. It is not clear if Isa 8:3 is designating Isaiah's wife as a prophetess in her own right.

[308] Although see Jer 23:25–28.

[309] Samuel A. Meier, *The Messenger in the Ancient Semitic World* (Atlanta: Scholars Press, 1988), 171, highlights a Hittite text where if a messenger says one thing and the message he bears another, then the written source is to be believed. For other possible ancient treaty parallels, see McConville, *Deuteronomy*, 236–37.

[310] Generally, Yahweh does this without sending a prophet. Although the term is applied to Moses (so 18:18, and by implication, 34:11–12), the emphasis in Deuteronomy is on Yahweh himself speaking to his people.

so-called prophets promoting idolatry. Because the occupation may take time (7:22) and may be messy (see, e.g., Josh 19:47–48), the nation will need to guard carefully against resurgences of false worship and must act swiftly when it happens. Once more, the persistence of Canaanite theology (and therefore, presumably, some stubborn Canaanites) is assumed. But the key thing is that they must not listen to anyone other than Yahweh (see 4:28, 35, 39).

Back in chapter 8 (8:2, 16), Moses had insisted that part of the purpose of the period spent in the wilderness was to test Israel. At the end of 13:3, this idea recurs: "For the Lord your God is testing you to know whether you love the Lord your God with all your heart and all your soul." Both the language and the thought here are very similar to the way Moses argues in earlier chapters.[311] Given what we have seen so far, we are left with the nagging feeling that the reason that Yahweh needs to test his people, is that he knows that sooner or later they will surely fail.

Verse 4 makes it plain that Moses is expounding the same all-encompassing response to Yahweh's grace that he has been demanding throughout the book. The people must "follow," "fear," "listen," "worship," and "remain faithful" ("cleave") to Yahweh, whose name emphatically comes first in every clause. All this they do by "keeping his commands." The vocabulary and tone have not changed (see, e.g., 10:20), but the application has sharpened: in this case, the one who speaks falsely "must be put to death."

This insistence that worshiping any other god is a capital offence seems to be unique in the ancient world.[312] The seriousness of this verbal crime is highlighted in multiple ways: first and foremost, the death penalty is mandated for the false prophet; second, the crime is described as "urging rebellion (סָרָה)" against Yahweh, which is always a deeply serious matter (as it is in Jer 28:16; 29:32); third, this is a rejection of the God who "brought you out of Egypt and redeemed you from the place of slavery" (perhaps echoing the first commandment in 5:6–7); fourth, this

---

311 This demonstrates how important it is not to differentiate too strongly between the various sections of the book. Moses continues to "preach" (including persuading), even when strictly speaking he has moved into his exposition of torah. Block says "this is not the style of legislation, but the language of a pastor, passionate about the spiritual wellbeing of his flock after he is gone." *Deuteronomy*, 325.

312 See Edwin M. Good, "Capital Punishment and its Alternatives in Ancient Near Eastern Law," *Stanford Law Review* 19 (1967): 947–77.

false speaking seeks to "turn (or: drive) Israel from the way" of Yahweh. All of this leads to the conclusion that Israel must "purge the evil from you." The verb "purge" may also mean "sweep" (1 Kgs 14:10), but the point is clear: this poison must be completely eradicated from the nation.

The command to "purge the evil from among you" recurs in Deuteronomy 17:7, 12; 19:19; 21:21; 22:21, 22, 24 and 24:7. It captures both the idea that Yahweh demands wholehearted (and morally pure) obedience from his united people and that they will always remain vulnerable to people who either through their words or their actions imperil the life of the covenant nation. The people must deal quickly and decisively with such spiritual and moral toxicity.[313]

13:6–11 Given the recent history of the nation recounted in chapters 1–11 (and in particular, the events involving the Baal of Peor as well as the golden calf incident), it makes perfect sense that Moses moves from the external threat posed by any failure to eliminate the Canaanite nation and their theology to the very real possibility of such rebellion arising from within Israel itself.

Rather than simply saying "if *anyone*," Moses the Preacher names four of the closest possible relationships: "If your brother, the son of your mother, or your son or daughter, or the wife you embrace, or your closest friend secretly entices you ..." It is unusual that a brother is called "the son of your mother" (Gen 43:29; Judg 8:19; Pss 50:20; 69:8). This could refer to a stepbrother, but is more likely simply to be an emphatic designation to highlight the appalling prospect of idolatry arising in Israel (reflecting the special bond between full brothers in a world where childbirth was often fatal and blended families common). In any case, within the family, the danger is being subtly enticed (סות) by close relatives. This danger extends even to children, spouse (the phrase "the wife you embrace" delicately refers to marital intimacy), and best friend.

The invitation to idolatry is also expanded from simply "other gods which neither you nor your ancestors have known" to the gods of other nations in 13:7. These are called "the gods of the peoples around you" (Baal and the Canaanite pantheon), but are extended to include the non-gods worshiped by every other nation, irrespective of their

---

[313] There are similarities between the loyalty demanded here and that expected in ancient documents, including both vassal treaties and loyalty oaths. See especially Moshe Weinfeld, "The Loyalty Oath in the Ancient Near East," *Ugarit-Forschungen* 8 (1976): 379–414. See also Block, *Deuteronomy*, 327 n. 14, for bibliography on this issue.

geographical distance from Israel. Monotheism is to be the perpetual distinctive of the people in the land.

The arresting words of 13:8 underline the seriousness of the issue. To embrace idolatry is to threaten the very existence of the nation. Therefore, it must be resisted. There can be no concessions to idolaters or idolatry, nor can their poison be entertained even for a second. Yahweh's people must listen to Yahweh and Yahweh alone. But resistance is not enough. Decisive action must be taken against this toxic teaching. The person seeking to woo people away from Yahweh must be shown no pity nor lenience, nor be protected from the community (13:8b). Rather the community must be protected from him: "Instead you must kill him." Idolatry requires death. That short sentence may raise all kinds of questions—and hackles—for us, but it is clearly a non-negotiable in the mind of Moses. This is an act of high treason against Yahweh the King of kings. And what comes next demands not simply theoretical assent, but personal involvement.

Every Israelite without exception must take responsibility for ensuring faithfulness to Yahweh, which includes acting against even their closest friends and most precious family members. The insistence that "Your hand is to be the first against him to put him to death, and then the hands of all the people" is a powerful statement that allegiance to Yahweh trumps every human relationship, and also that the decision to embrace and promote idolatry not only imperils the nation, but inevitably drives a wedge through the closest of family ties. It also parallels the principle in 17:7 that eyewitnesses should take the lead in enacting the sentence.[314]

Death by stoning is rarely enacted in the Old Testament. It is prescribed here; in 17:1–7 for idolatry; in 21:21 (where a rebellious son threatens the fabric of community life in a broadly parallel way) and in 22:24 for a man sleeping with another's fiancée. The only records of such a judicial sentence being carried out come in Numbers 15:35–36 and in 1 Kings 21:10, where the innocent Naboth's death is engineered by Queen Jezebel. It is impossible to overstate the gravity of these matters for Moses.

In typically Mosaic fashion, even this severest of punishments is tied directly to Israel's salvation history. The God they are in danger of

---

[314] Like many in the book, this passage switches back and forth between the singular and plural. This stylistic feature (shared with some ancient treaties) should not be mapped onto how the actions specified should be carried out.

rejecting is "your God who brought you out of the land of Egypt, out of the place of slavery." Idolatry cannot exist in the context of a covenant relationship with the God who has rescued them. It imperils the very existence of Israel, which is why these drastic steps must be embraced by the whole people. Only then will there be a sufficient deterrent to safeguard the life of the nation.

The purpose of these steps is that "All Israel will hear and be afraid" (also 17:13; 19:20; 21:21), and so will together resolve to pursue covenant faithfulness in the future.

Again, it is important to notice the nature of this material. This is not simply legislation in any straightforward sense but is deeply theologically rooted and persuasively expressed. Moses preaches not simply to exclude unacceptable behavior in the life of the community, but also to secure the present and future covenant loyalty of the people as a whole.

13:12–18. Having begun with the immediate external threat of the nations facing them in the land, and then having tackled the possibility of idolatry arising within the people, Moses now anticipates future issues that may arise in the land itself. Looking beyond the conquest, at some point one of the now Israelite-occupied walled towns of Canaan may become a hotbed of heterodox theology. The source of the toxicity this time is vague: "wicked men who have sprung up among you." The phrase is "sons of b/Belial" (lit., "sons of worthlessness"),[315] but these indeterminate interlopers are pushing the same message that caused the issues in 13:1–5 and 6–11, encouraging Israel to worship "gods you have not known." The situation envisaged is clearly serious. The false teaching has taken root: all the inhabitants have been "led astray" by the invitation to apostasy. As soon as the rumors of such a breach of covenant faithfulness start to circulate, the people as a whole must act.

It is noticeable that the approach prescribed by Moses here is vague and general. It displays no particular knowledge of Canaan, nor gives any specific guidance on who is responsible for prosecuting the steps recommended or what weight of evidence is sufficient to warrant action. Like the discussions of the conquest itself, it is an *in principle* approach to a significant threat facing Israel.

---

[315] It is uncertain if this refers to a quality or a personal name, which later came to be used of the Evil One in, e.g., 2 Cor 6:15. James Hamilton helpfully suggested in a personal communication that it may denote the seed of the Serpent, rather than the seed of Adam (see Gen 3:15).

The seriousness of the matter is reflected by the care in which investigations are to be undertaken: the people as a whole are to "inquire, investigate, and interrogate thoroughly" (17:4 and 19:18 have only one verb). If the rumors prove to be true, and the entire walled town has been gripped by idolatry, then swift and drastic action must be taken. In essence, the city is to be treated as "Canaanite": "you must strike down the inhabitants of that city with the sword. Completely destroy (חָרַם) everyone in it as well as its livestock with the sword." The repetition of "the sword" is a reminder that this is effectively a call to launch a civil war against Israel's own people and that this action will, in all likelihood, be resisted. But as with the conquest, this "war" is divinely sanctioned, and the underlying assumption is that the idolaters, standing under the judgment as they are, will lose.

Israelites basically becoming Canaanites demands specific remedial action to ensure that this spiritual cancer does not spread. All the spoil is to be collected and dumped "in the middle of the city square" (13:16). The public spectacle of burning the spoil will be superseded as the entire settlement is to be (lit.) "burned with fire." This is to be done "for" or "to" Yahweh, presumably as a kind of burnt offering (see Lev 6:8–9) to atone for the idolatry, as well as an enduring sign for the people: "The city is to remain a mound of ruins forever; it is not to be rebuilt." The charred "heap" is to stand as a perpetual warning to anyone who sees it. Again, the emphasis is on instant deterrence, rather than an ongoing program of law enforcement.

Did this ever happen? There is no record of this practice ever being enacted in Israel (and the rabbis went to some lengths to mitigate its demands).[316] However, the joint witness of Joshua 6:28; 8:28; 1 Kings 16:34 and Jeremiah 49:2, and the events of Judges 19:22; 20:27–30, 48, makes clear that the concept was clearly embedded in Israel's consciousness.

In 13:17–18, Moses expands on the principle of חָרַם, explaining that it is a crucial part of living in the land enjoying Yahweh's favor. Here for the first time, it is said to play a propitiatory role, turning aside the anger provoked by the idolatrous city and allowing the people to continue to experience the blessings of the covenant, and in particular his compassionate mercy.[317] It will also ensure that the fulfillment of the promises to the patriarchs is not derailed, as God continues to multiply them.

---

[316] Tigay, *Deuteronomy*, 134.

[317] The words for "compassion" and "mercy" here are from the same root. The first is the nominal form (give mercy) and the second an intensive (piel) verb.

The key to all this is once more articulated in terms that are very familiar from chapters 6–11. Enjoying the extravagant blessing of God is dependent on a wholehearted response to his grace. Israel must "obey the LORD your God, keeping all his commands I am giving you today, doing what is right in the sight of the LORD your God." Once more, we see that the main thing is listening to the voice of God, not those who would lead his people astray, and doing what is "right."

Bridge

Listening to—and following—Yahweh alone is the central issue not simply in Deuteronomy 13 but in the whole book. This key issue will, according to Moses, determine the course of their life in the land. Before they have even entered Canaan however, the danger of idolatry looms large. Whether Israelite or not, as Paul argues so powerfully in Romans 1, we are born with a propensity to exchange the truth of God for a lie and to worship gods made in our own image, rather than Yahweh, the God of the covenant and the cosmos.

Both the clarity and the urgency of wholehearted allegiance to Yahweh is communicated passionately, but also continually raises the specter of our inability to reach or maintain this level of commitment. Moses's "torah-preaching" makes it clear from the outset that living the blessed, gospel-shaped life of the covenant is a glorious prospect but one that would have remained beyond our reach, had it not been for Jesus Christ, the true Israelite and the second Adam, doing what we simply could not do for ourselves. In dealing with God's pure and holy wrath on the cross, and in living a faithful life on our behalf, he has opened up unimaginable riches for us, as we live with and for him. We cannot for a second think of preaching—or believing—another gospel. As Paul highlights in Galatians 1:6–12, which may well draw on this chapter, that would be anathema.

3. Living as God's Treasured Possession (14:1–21)

> [1] "You are sons of the LORD your God; do not cut yourselves or make a bald spot on your head on behalf of the dead, [2] for you are a holy people belonging to the LORD your God. The LORD has chosen you to be his own possession out of all the peoples on the face of the earth.
>
> [3] "You must not eat any detestable thing. [4] These are the animals you may eat:
>
> oxen, sheep, goats,
> [5] deer, gazelles, roe deer,

wild goats, ibexes, antelopes,
and mountain sheep.

[6] "You may eat any animal that has hooves divided in two and chews
the cud. [7] But among the ones that chew the cud or have divided hooves,
you are not to eat these:

camels, hares, and hyraxes,
though they chew the cud, they do not have hooves—
they are unclean for you;
[8] and pigs, though they have hooves, they do not chew
the cud—
they are unclean for you.
Do not eat their meat or touch their carcasses.

[9] "You may eat everything from the water that has fins and scales, [10] but
you may not eat anything that does not have fins and scales—it is unclean for you.

[11] "You may eat every clean bird, [12] but these are the ones you may
not eat:

eagles, bearded vultures,
black vultures, [13] the kites,
any kind of falcon,
[14] every kind of raven, [15] ostriches,
short-eared owls, gulls,
any kind of hawk,
[16] little owls, long-eared owls,
barn owls, [17] eagle owls,
ospreys, cormorants, [18] storks,
any kind of heron,
hoopoes, and bats.

[19] "All winged insects are unclean for you; they may not be eaten. [20] But
you may eat every clean flying creature.

[21] "You are not to eat any carcass; you may give it to a resident alien
within your city gates, and he may eat it, or you may sell it to a foreigner.
For you are a holy people belonging to the Lord your God. Do not boil
a young goat in its mother's milk."

14:1–2. In chapters 12 and 13, we have clearly been moving in the world of Deuteronomy 5:7–8 (usually construed as commandments 1 and 2). In chapter 14, we move to a discussion of Israel's distinctiveness. On a traditional understanding of the third commandment ("Do not take the name of the Lord your God in vain"), it is hard to see how the rules around Israel's diet could possibly be part of any Decalogue structure. If, however, Block's convincing argument that "to *take* the name" actually means "to *bear* the name" is correct, then chapter 14 fits beautifully into the unfolding exposition of the Ten Words.[318] Israel is to live in a way which befits who she is.

Twice so far in the book (1:31; 8:5), it has been implied that Israel is Yahweh's son (see also Exod 4:22–23; Hos 11:1; Isa 1:2, 4; Jer 31:20).[319] Now in 14:1, for the first time, it is made explicit that "You are sons of the Lord your God." It is striking that this is not simply a national privilege: each member of the people of Israel can rightly be described as sons of Yahweh. This deep, covenantal belonging has immediate, real-time consequences.

Israel's distinctiveness is to be expressed first by refraining from (a) cutting themselves or (b) making a bald spot on their heads (lit., "make baldness between your eyes") "on behalf of the dead." The underlying reason for this is clear: as already stated in 7:6, God's people are a "holy people" by virtue of belonging to Yahweh, who himself is "holy" (also Lev 20:26; 21:5–6, which applies specifically to priests). God's holiness embraces both moral purity and separateness (or uniqueness), both of which have moral implications for Israel, as does the fact that Yahweh has chosen them as his treasured "possession out of all the peoples on the face of the earth" (see also 7:6; 26:18; Exod 19:5; Ps 135:4).[320] In Deuteronomy 7, this phrase is embedded in a discussion of the extravagant nature of God's grace. Now in this chapter, the focus falls firmly on the need for God's people to live differently.

The particular expressions of differentness in these verses are slightly unexpected, although similar (but not identical) prohibitions are found in Leviticus 19:27–28. It is not immediately apparent why Israel would want to cut themselves or to shave part of their hair "on behalf of the dead." Later in the Old Testament, this is exactly the kind of thing that the people did (Jer 41:5; 47:5; 48:37; Hos 7:14; also Isa 15:2; 1 Kgs 18:28). It is also reasonable to read these prohibitions in the context of the emphasis throughout the chapter on the need for Israel to demonstrate clear distinctiveness from the nations around by way of their diet. One can then only assume that these acts would have been clearly recognized as part of the fabric of the religion of the Canaanites, and for Israel to succumb

---

[318] See Block, "Bearing the Name," 61–72. See also Imes, "Bearing YHWH's Name at Sinai."

[319] This is also implied but not stated in the ritual of the firstborn, introduced in the wake of the Passover in Exod 13.

[320] For a literal use of the term see Eccl 2:8, 1 Chr 29:3.

to copycat behavior would have completely undermined the purpose for which God had called them.[321]

14:3–21. The basic concern to ensure that Israel does not drag the name of Yahweh through the mud is amplified through the rest of this section, as Moses turns his attention to their national diet. The overarching principle is spelled out in verse 3: "You must not eat any detestable thing." The idea of avoiding anything which is "detestable" has already occurred in 7:25–26, 12:31; and 13:14, each time in connection with behavior that is intrinsically Canaanite. This seems to be at the heart of the concept.[322] Israel's menu must set the nation apart. This principle was established as early as Genesis 2, in the garden of Eden, when God spelled out to Adam and Eve what they could and could not eat.

The list of animals that follows falls broadly into four categories: (1) medium to large land animals (14:4–8); (2) aquatic creatures (14:9–10); (3) birds (14:11–18); and (4) insects (14:19–20). A similar list occurs in Leviticus 11, but the tone seems very different. Leviticus 11 uses the term "detest" eight times, which does not occur here. In the earlier book, there is more explanation, with significant emphasis placed on avoiding contact with carcasses and the vileness of creeping creatures (see in particular Lev 11:42, alluding to Gen 3).[323] In Deuteronomy, there seems to be little concern to provide a theological rationale for this system. The fact that hooves and cud-chewing are used to demarcate what is acceptable is simply stated here, for the primary idea is that, as in chapter 12, God exercises his absolute right to tell his people how they should live and specifically what they should eat. The inclusion of the list of what they *may eat* (no such list is included in Leviticus) also maintains the positive emphasis of the discussion of eating that has characterized chapters 12 and 13. Covenant life with Yahweh embraces and enhances every part of life.

In the case of larger animals, the rule is simply stated in verse 6: "any animal that has hooves divided in two and chews the cud" can

---

[321] See Hallo and Younger, *The Context of Scripture*, 1:267–68, where in *CTA* 5 it is said of Ba'lu that "He pours dirt of mourning on his head, dust of humiliation on his cranium. ... With a stone he scratches incisions on (his) skin, with a razor he cuts cheeks and skin."

[322] The fact that in Gen 43:32; 46:34 and Exod 8:26, the word is used to describe what is unacceptable to Egyptians, plus the sense in Lev 18:22–30 that the actions prohibited there are associated with the current occupants of the land, confirms this.

[323] See G. Geoffrey Harper, *Teaching Leviticus: From Text to Message* (Fearn: Christian Focus, 2022), 169.

be eaten. No reason at all is given for this. One could say that they are divinely arbitrary.[324] This finds support in the fact that the animals in verses 7 and 8 that meet only one of the two criteria are simply said to be "unclean for you." This may well betray that fact that there is no spiritual nor ethical reason for abstaining from eating these animals. It is simply a concrete expression of obedience. Unlike Leviticus, the animals that may be eaten are listed. There are no particular surprises in the list broadly comprising cattle, sheep, goats, deer, and antelope. The emphasis on the positives is typical of Deuteronomy, which stresses the enjoyment of Yahweh's provision.[325]

The list of prohibited animals (on the basis of not being both cloven-hoofed and cud-chewing)[326] is the same as Leviticus 11, although camels, hares, and hyraxes are grouped together here, perhaps to highlight the particular emphasis on not eating pork. The fact that pigs are the only routinely farmed animal to be designated "detestable" probably necessitated this reinforcement. There is some anatomical looseness in the classification: looking like a cud-chewer and having feet that look like hooves.

Both the language of "unclean for you" and not eating their meat or touching their carcasses (14:8) are drawn from Leviticus 11. The idea that contamination flowed from both ingesting and touching is a key part of the elaborate ritual system that aimed to demonstrate to onlookers (as well as to remind the Israelites themselves) that they were a holy people belonging to a holy God.

The discussion of aquatic creatures in 14:9–10 is much more cursory than that of mammals of the preceding verses (as well as the parallel passage in Lev 11:9–12). This is presumably because this was not a pressing problem on the plains of Moab, nor was it likely to be in the near future. This fits with the absence of any nuance when discussing fish in the Old Testament as a whole (where "fish" are just "fish"!). The

---

[324] Attempts to root these designations in factors such as the toxicity or digestibility of the flesh are not ultimately persuasive. See Tigay, *Deuteronomy*, 137, who points out that this approach began with medieval Jewish commentators with a medical background!

[325] For a detailed discussion of the identification of animals that may be eaten, see Lundbom, *Deuteronomy*, 465–66. The main uncertainty is around the "mountain sheep."

[326] Jacob Milgrom, *Leviticus 1–16*, AB (New York: Doubleday, 1991), 646, argues that it is simply animals with hooves (rather than cloven hooves) that are permitted. While his argument has some linguistic merit, it is clear from Deut 14 that "divided in two" is what is intended.

use of "fins and scales" as the determining factor for cleanness here is not developed further.[327]

In contrast, more birds are mentioned than any other kind of animal. This may well be because of Israel's experience in the wilderness, where they had acquired a taste for airborne game! On the positive side, Moses simply says they may eat all "clean birds" (without naming them), before listing the same birds to be avoided as Leviticus 11:12–19.[328] The precise identification of most of these birds is uncertain, but most appear to be either birds of prey or scavengers.[329]

As with aquatic creatures, the note on insects is extremely brief in 14:19–20. The prohibition is simple: "All winged insects [lit., swarming things] are unclean for you; they may not be eaten." The exceptions are equally straightforward in 14:20, allowing for the consumption of "every clean flying creature," without detailing which kinds of flying creature are meant here (in contrast with Lev 11:20–22, which goes into some detail, clarifying that locusts and grasshoppers are consumable), but Moses does not pause to discuss this.

This highlights a couple of important features of these laws: (1) It seems clear that Moses is assuming a relatively detailed knowledge of an earlier body of laws (including Leviticus). (2) The laws, as with the rest of the book, are clearly *preached*. Moses is making no attempt to be comprehensive but is rather selecting from a body of ideas and legislation in order to make a rhetorical point, which is clearly focused on the necessity of Israel demonstrating a profound distinctiveness. The final instructions in this section confirm that these two Mosaic principles govern the chapter.

In 14:21, God insists that hiss people must not eat "any carcass," that is, the body of an animal that has died in an accident or by natural causes and therefore has not been slaughtered in the prescribed way (including the careful draining of its blood). Once more, however, the symbolic nature of this material comes to the fore. Eating this meat would not be wrong *in itself*; it is simply not to be done in Israel. The fact that the meat may be shared with the

---

[327] In contrast to Lev 11, where other aquatic life forms are compared to the "swarming" things, and therefore to be avoided.

[328] The only minor variation is that the "Egyptian vulture" of Lev 11 is replaced by the "black vulture" here. Presumably these refer to the same bird.

[329] Again, see the extensive discussion of Lundbom (*Deuteronomy*, 470–75) for the possible classification of these birds.

"resident alien within your city gates" or even sold to a non-Israelite demonstrates that the issue here is not one of *morality* but of the distinctiveness of God's people. This is confirmed by the unambiguous statement "for you are a holy people belonging to the Lord your God." Along with 14:2, this makes clear that this chapter is designed to encourage and ensure that Israel lives in a way that befits the treasured possession of the holy God.[330] Which takes us to the final enigmatic statement of the section in 14:21b.

At face value, the command in this verse is simple: "Do not boil a young goat in its mother's milk." In Leviticus 22:8, this practice was forbidden for priests, but in Exodus 23:19b; 34:26b and also here, it is extended to the whole nation (perhaps because Moses has emphasized that they are a nation of priests). The challenge is uncovering what precisely this rule is prohibiting, why it was necessary to include it, and why, given its apparently elusive nature, it occupies such a prominent position, appearing to summarize and sharpen the (already clear!) point of 14:1–21.

It has been suggested that the explanation may lie in the chemical composition of a mother goat's milk, with the colostrum making the mixture turn red when heated, giving it the appearance of blood.[331] This may be possible, but still doesn't explain why such an apparently strange practice (to which there is no direct ancient parallel) needs to be addressed in the first place. The situation is eased slightly if, following Augustine and Luther, the phrase is translated as "*at* its mother's milk" (i.e., still a suckling), but even this does not completely solve the puzzle.[332] It is still not clear why this rule appears four times in the Pentateuch.[333]

Given the argument in the rest of the chapter, it may well be best to treat this prohibition (along with the cutting of hair and body in 14:1) as alluding to an otherwise unknown Canaanite practice, which thus brings the material on standing out from the nations to a vivid conclusion.

---

[330] Block describes this section on eating as a sandwich, with these verses providing the "theological bread." *Deuteronomy*, 341.

[331] C.J. Labuschagne, "'You Shall Not Boil a Kid in Its Mother's Milk': A New Proposal for the Origin of the Prohibition," in *The Scriptures and the Scrolls,* ed. F.G. Martinez et al. *VTSup* 49 (Leiden: Brill, 1992), 6–17.

[332] See the helpful discussion of Stefan Schorch, "A Young Goat in its Mother's Milk? Understanding an Ancient Prohibition," *VT* 60 (2010): 116–30.

[333] It has also been suggested that the verse prohibits conjoining life and death. This is possible and would account for the ban on cooking a kid in the milk that should have been its source of life (from its mother), but this still doesn't really explain its connection with the context.

Bridge

The idea that God's people should stand out is a key biblical theological theme. From Exodus 19:6 the trajectory is set. It is then developed substantially in Deuteronomy 4:5–8; 7:1–11; and then this chapter. It is picked up memorably by Isaiah in 42:6 and 49:6, before exploding in the kingdom ministry of Jesus, who makes it possible for us to live in a way that far exceeds the righteousness of the Pharisees and the Scribes and that is radically different from the Gentiles. This is gathered up beautifully by the apostle Peter, who writes in 1 Peter 2:9–12:

> [9] But you are a chosen race, a royal priesthood, a holy nation, a people for his possession, so that you may proclaim the praises of the one who called you out of darkness into his marvelous light. [10] Once you were not a people, but now you are God's people; you had not received mercy, but now you have received mercy. [11] Dear friends, I urge you as strangers and exiles to abstain from sinful desires that wage war against the soul. [12] Conduct yourselves honorably among the Gentiles, so that when they slander you as evildoers, they will observe your good works and will glorify God on the day he visits.

This is the life to which we are called and for which we are equipped in Christ.

Jesus's direct teaching in Mark 7:14–23, as well as the vision of Peter in Acts 11 and the ensuing discussions at the Council of Jerusalem in Acts 15, all make it clear that the concrete dietary restrictions designed to make the nation of Israel stand out in the Old Testament have now been superseded on this side of Jesus's death and resurrection. In the supranational people of God that is the church, our differentness is not built on what we eat (or wear, or even how we organize), but on the same love that God has lavished on us in Christ (John 13:34–35).

4. The Rhythm of Covenant Life (14:22–16:17)

> [22] "Each year you are to set aside a tenth of all the produce grown in your fields. [23] You are to eat a tenth of your grain, new wine, and fresh oil, and the firstborn of your herd and flock, in the presence of the Lord your God at the place where he chooses to have his name dwell, so that you will always learn to fear the Lord your God. [24] But if the distance is too great for you to carry it, since the place where the Lord your God chooses to put his name is too far away from you and since the Lord your God has blessed you, [25] then exchange it for silver, take the silver in your hand, and go to the place the Lord your God chooses. [26] You may spend the

silver on anything you want: cattle, sheep, goats, wine, beer, or anything you desire. You are to feast there in the presence of the Lord your God and rejoice with your family. 27 Do not neglect the Levite within your city gates, since he has no portion or inheritance among you.

28 "At the end of every three years, bring a tenth of all your produce for that year and store it within your city gates. 29 Then the Levite, who has no portion or inheritance among you, the resident alien, the fatherless, and the widow within your city gates may come, eat, and be satisfied. And the Lord your God will bless you in all the work of your hands that you do.

15:1 "At the end of every seven years you must cancel debts. 2 This is how to cancel debt: Every creditor is to cancel what he has lent his neighbor. He is not to collect anything from his neighbor or brother, because the Lord's release of debts has been proclaimed. 3 You may collect something from a foreigner, but you must forgive whatever your brother owes you.

4 "There will be no poor among you, however, because the Lord is certain to bless you in the land the Lord your God is giving you to possess as an inheritance—5 if only you obey the Lord your God and are careful to follow every one of these commands I am giving you today. 6 When the Lord your God blesses you as he has promised you, you will lend to many nations but not borrow; you will rule many nations, but they will not rule you.

7 "If there is a poor person among you, one of your brothers within any of your city gates in the land the Lord your God is giving you, do not be hardhearted or tightfisted toward your poor brother. 8 Instead, you are to open your hand to him and freely loan him enough for whatever need he has. 9 Be careful that there isn't this wicked thought in your heart, 'The seventh year, the year of canceling debts, is near,' and you are stingy toward your poor brother and give him nothing. He will cry out to the Lord against you, and you will be guilty. 10 Give to him, and don't have a stingy heart when you give, and because of this the Lord your God will bless you in all your work and in everything you do. 11 For there will never cease to be poor people in the land; that is why I am commanding you, 'Open your hand willingly to your poor and needy brother in your land.'

12 "If your fellow Hebrew, a man or woman, is sold to you and serves you six years, you must set him free in the seventh year. 13 When you set him free, do not send him away empty-handed. 14 Give generously to him from your flock, your threshing floor, and your winepress. You are to give him whatever the Lord your God has blessed you with. 15 Remember that you were a slave in the land of Egypt and the Lord your God redeemed you; that is why I am giving you this command today. 16 But

if your slave says to you, 'I don't want to leave you,' because he loves you and your family, and is well off with you, [17] take an awl and pierce through his ear into the door, and he will become your slave for life. Also treat your female slave the same way. [18] Do not regard it as a hardship when you set him free, because he worked for you six years—worth twice the wages of a hired worker. Then the LORD your God will bless you in everything you do.

[19] "Consecrate to the LORD your God every firstborn male produced by your herd and flock. You are not to put the firstborn of your oxen to work or shear the firstborn of your flock. [20] Each year you and your family are to eat it before the LORD your God in the place the LORD chooses. [21] But if there is a defect in the animal, if it is lame or blind or has any serious defect, you may not sacrifice it to the LORD your God. [22] Eat it within your city gates; both the unclean person and the clean may eat it, as though it were a gazelle or deer. [23] But you must not eat its blood; pour it on the ground like water.

[16:1] "Set aside the month of Abib and observe the Passover to the LORD your God, because the LORD your God brought you out of Egypt by night in the month of Abib. [2] Sacrifice to the LORD your God a Passover animal from the herd or flock in the place where the LORD chooses to have his name dwell. [3] Do not eat leavened bread with it. For seven days you are to eat unleavened bread with it, the bread of hardship—because you left the land of Egypt in a hurry—so that you may remember for the rest of your life the day you left the land of Egypt. [4] No yeast is to be found anywhere in your territory for seven days, and none of the meat you sacrifice in the evening of the first day is to remain until morning. [5] You are not to sacrifice the Passover animal in any of the towns the LORD your God is giving you. [6] Sacrifice the Passover animal only at the place where the LORD your God chooses to have his name dwell. Do this in the evening as the sun sets at the same time of day you departed from Egypt. [7] You are to cook and eat it in the place the LORD your God chooses, and you are to return to your tents in the morning. [8] Eat unleavened bread for six days. On the seventh day there is to be a solemn assembly to the LORD your God; do not do any work.

[9] "You are to count seven weeks, counting the weeks from the time the sickle is first put to the standing grain. [10] You are to celebrate the Festival of Weeks to the LORD your God with a freewill offering that you give in proportion to how the LORD your God has blessed you. [11] Rejoice before the LORD your God in the place where he chooses to have his name dwell—you, your son and daughter, your male and female slave, the Levite within your city gates, as well as the resident alien, the fatherless, and the widow among you. [12] Remember that you were slaves in Egypt; carefully follow these statutes.

> [13] "You are to celebrate the Festival of Shelters for seven days when you have gathered in everything from your threshing floor and winepress. [14] Rejoice during your festival—you, your son and daughter, your male and female slave, as well as the Levite, the resident alien, the fatherless, and the widow within your city gates. [15] You are to hold a seven-day festival for the LORD your God in the place he chooses, because the LORD your God will bless you in all your produce and in all the work of your hands, and you will have abundant joy.
>
> [16] "All your males are to appear three times a year before the LORD your God in the place he chooses: at the Festival of Unleavened Bread, the Festival of Weeks, and the Festival of Shelters. No one is to appear before the LORD empty-handed. [17] Everyone must appear with a gift suited to his means, according to the blessing the LORD your God has given you."

If the connection between the preceding section and the Decalogue (via reading the third commandment as "You shall not *bear* the name of Yahweh your God in vain") may seem a little tenuous, the proposed link between the section that runs from 14:22 to 16:17 and the Sabbath command is both more persuasive and much easier to see. The punctuation of the life of the covenant people with a steady pattern of offerings and practices (over months and years), built around enjoying the gifts and freedoms that Yahweh has given them, flows from the same theological source as the command to enjoy regular rest in the land with the God of rest.[334]

14:22–27. At first glance, the inclusion of the arrangement for tithes ("tenths") at this point may seem a little strange. The annual "setting aside" of a portion of all agricultural "produce," including livestock, seems almost prosaic beside the drama and excitement of the three festivals of chapter 16 but heads this section partly because it anticipates the shared joy of these occasions.[335] It is in the mundane, hands-on rhythm of harvesting, gathering, storing, and setting aside that the trajectory of national life is to be set. It is the perpetual invitation to rejoice in the presence of the divine host, Yahweh himself, that the goal of life in the land is to be found.

---

[334] One puzzle, of course, is the absence of any reference to the Sabbath itself. The likely solution, however, is not complex: as the Decalogue itself has already been quoted verbatim in ch. 5 and Moses is offering a loose exposition of its teaching, he sees no need to repeat what already seems to have been enshrined in the life of the nation.

[335] According to Lev 27:32 (also 2 Chr 31:6), the animals are to be counted as part of the "tenth."

This practice has its roots very early in Israel's history.[336] Abraham offers a tenth of the spoils of war to Melchizedek in Genesis 14:20, and Jacob offers to do the same to Yahweh, albeit in certain (typical!) conditions (Gen 28:20–22). The basic principle is extremely simple: "Each year you are to set aside a tenth of all the produce grown in your fields" (14:22). Tithes are to be taken to the chosen place on years 1, 2, 4 and 5, with years 3 and 6 being dealt with by verses 28–29. No tithe is to be offered in the sabbatical year, because the land is to be given rest.[337]

The subsequent reference to the firstborn livestock in verse 23 shows that this is to be an all-inclusive statement.[338] The entirety of agricultural output is to be tithed. This is to be a fulsome, all-embracing practice.[339]

The basic agricultural staples of the fertile crescent are listed: "grain, new wine, and fresh (olive) oil," the predominant crops, alongside the "herd and flock," which covers various kinds of livestock. Rather than being a tax leading to resentment, the tithe is an expression of God's kindness, with the people feasting together "in the presence of the Lord your God at the place where he chooses to have his name dwell."

No comment is made on when this is actually supposed to happen: timing is not the central concern here, *theology is*.[340] One may have been able to bring tithes at any time, or it may have been part of one of the other major festivals (perhaps Weeks or Booths).[341]

This combination of key Deuteronomic expressions confirms beyond all doubt that Moses understands the life of the people to be lived out in the real-time presence of God in the heart of the land. God has voluntarily chosen to make his presence obvious with them as they celebrate

---

336 Tithing was a common practice in the ancient Near East (see Lundbom, *Deuteronomy*, 483, for more details.)

337 Block suggests that these years may have even been staggered to ensure a continuous supply of food. *Deuteronomy*, 359.

338 The lack of interest in detail is fairly typical of Deuteronomy. It is simply stated that the offering of the firstborn animals is part of this practice, without any further comment. There is no need to attribute this to divergent traditions. The two rituals are also linked in 26:1–15.

339 It is important to appreciate that the Pharisees' error in, e.g., Matt 23:23 and Luke 11:42 (where they tithe even the smallest herb), is not that they are too scrupulous, but that they have misunderstood God's gracious provision. They are missing out on the expansiveness and joy of giving gratefully and wholeheartedly to God.

340 See McConville's seminal work *Law and Theology in Deuteronomy*.

341 See the helpful comments of Lundbom, *Deuteronomy*, 484. He also speculates on how any excess might have been stored for use in later years, especially the sabbatical year.

his goodness with him. The reason for this gracious intervention is then made clear: "so *that you will always learn to fear the* LORD *your God.*"

"Fearing God" in Deuteronomy is a key component of covenant life (4:10). It captures the nature of wholehearted response to the God who makes the nation his son through rescuing them and committing to them. It is an all-encompassing response, which embraces joy, deep respect, obedience, gratitude, enjoyment, and awe. And it is the core of Moses's concern here, which is deeply practical.

This is underlined by the provision for the tithe to be cashed in at the source, to relieve the difficulty of everyone transporting large amounts of produce and animals to the chosen place. However, this concession for convenience must lead to "taking the silver [proceeds] in your hand," as one would have taken the produce to the chosen place, and converting it into provisions for an inclusive family celebration. The silver currency is literally to be "bound in your hand," presumably in some kind of makeshift pouch, until it is spent, which is where the generosity at the heart of this practice becomes evident.

The insistence in verse 27 that "You may spend the silver on anything you want: cattle, sheep, goats, wine, beer, or anything you desire" is striking. Nowhere else in Scripture is such explicit warrant given to personal taste, or such encouragement to lay on a family feast. This is also the first reference to beer in the Bible and, as with the allusion to wine, it is clearly positive.[342]

"Rejoicing with your family" in the presence of Yahweh lies at the heart of Moses's understanding of the rhythm of covenant life, as is, once more, the inclusion of the Levite, who probably also represents other vulnerable groups here. Ensuring the Levite is able to enjoy the goodness of God expressed through the abundance of the land is particularly important, "since he has no portion or inheritance among you." The Levite's presence is also a visible reminder that the ultimate goal of this feasting is the enjoyment of Yahweh himself (rather than simply the relief of poverty), which is perhaps the central distinctive emphasis of the Mosaic exposition of the beautiful life to be built by Israel in the land.[343]

---

[342] See KBL 972 for the meaning "beer." Also Michael M. Homan, "Beer and Its Drinkers: An Ancient Near Eastern Love Story," *Near Eastern Archaeology* 64 (2007): 84–95.

[343] Tigay (*Deuteronomy*, 143) points out that it would likely have been impossible to consume all the tithe during the festival. As is the case throughout these chapters, Moses is

14:28–29. Such is the generosity of Yahweh that the joy of the annual tithe celebration is augmented (uniquely in Deuteronomy) by the provision for a triennial tithe to be gathered locally. This time, the focus is not so much on eating and drinking (as in 14:23), but on *providing for* those who are potentially excluded from enjoying the bounty of the land. The tithe is to be stored "within your city gates," and then made available to the Levite, resident alien, orphan, and widow. These marginalized groups are then able to "come, eat, and be satisfied." It is not clear whether or not the producer and the family are to share in this meal, presumably because, in this context, that isn't the point. The focus falls on "the Levite, who has no portion or inheritance" (because Yahweh is his inheritance), and the others. The position of the Levite as a visual aid of God's self-giving is reinforced by God ensuring that the landless ones still get to join in and celebrate his blessing (see also 10:18–19).

When the Levites (and others) are supported like this, they experience the satisfaction which comes from being part of Yahweh's people (14:29, cf. 4:5–8).

It is worth noting at this juncture that Moses's point here is profoundly theological. There is little interest in the details of gathering, presenting, storing, or even eating the tithe. Some more information is given in 26:12–15, but even there, the triennial tithe functions primarily as a kind of theological capstone to the collection of laws. The emphasis in both passages is firmly on the rhythm of thankfulness and celebration that is to dominate the life of God's people.

15:1–6. At the start of chapter 15, Moses's focus switches from the inclusive celebration of the blessings of Yahweh in the triennial tithe to the provision for the remission of debts every seven years. There is no precedent for this legislation. This in itself is hardly surprising, as the prospect of transitioning to a settled existence in the land would clearly occasion the need for some new provisions. Given the fact that Leviticus 25:1–7 provides for "rest" for the land every seventh year, the cancellation of debts seems to be a further example of a "Sabbath principle" at work in shaping the national life of God's people.[344]

---

not concerned by such mundane details! The perspective of his speech is looking forward to a life in the land that cannot yet be fully envisaged.

[344] The connection to Sabbath supports the view that Moses is expounding the Decalogue at this point. The provisions of Lev 25 (also Exod 23:10–11) and Deut 15 are clearly different but are not incompatible.

As is often the case in the Deuteronomic torah, the emphasis falls squarely on theological principle rather than on the detail of how such a scheme might actually be enacted.[345] Far more time is spent giving reasons to live like this than spelling out what it might actually involve. The basic requirement is simple: at the end of each seven year period, every Israelite must "cancel debts."[346] The circumstances are specified in verses 2–3. A neighbor borrows something (the statement is deliberately vague; presumably this could be agricultural equipment, animals, land, or even capital). The loan is secured against property (perhaps in the form of grazing rights). Moses stipulates that this arrangement will lapse at the end of seven years, releasing the neighbor (necessarily a brother Israelite) from all obligation. This probably means that the debt was completely erased, although it could be that the terms are renewed for another seven years.[347]

That this arrangement applies only to neighbors or "brother Israelites" unlocks the theological principle standing behind this legislation. Verse 3 states that even though wealth can be accrued from foreigners in this way, "you must forgive whatever your brother owes you." The presence of such long-term, crippling economic hardship among God's people cannot be allowed, because it would bring into question the very goodness of God himself.[348] The way in which God has set up his covenant people (with blessing and curse as the real-time indicators of their covenant faithfulness) means that the default of national life must be prosperity. Economic stress and failure should be the direct result of disobedience only. The public proclamation (lit., "to Yahweh," most likely meaning "in his honor") of this remission of debts (15:2) is to serve as an open statement of the reality of being part of the people of Yahweh.

The statement of 15:4 is striking: "There will be no poor among you, however, because the LORD is certain to bless you in the land the LORD

---

[345] Deut 31:10 suggests that this was to take place as part of the Feast of Booths.

[346] There is some discussion over whether the remission is to occur at the start or the end of the seventh year. Jewish tradition has the release taking place on the last day of year 7, but it may be that Driver (*Deuteronomy*, 174) is right to suggest on the basis of v. 12 that freedom came at the beginning of the calendar year. Yet again, however, Moses is typically disinterested in clarifying such operational details!

[347] For a discussion of what this might mean in practice, see Wright, *God's People in God's Land*, 170–72.

[348] As demonstrated by the terms of repentance and recommitment in Neh 10:31.

your God is giving you to possess as an inheritance."[349] This is the ideal situation in Israel, where God's people (as envisaged in 4:5–8) embrace the full range of prescriptions that he has given them, and as a result their beautiful life commends God himself to the watching nations. This is explicit in verse 6: the prosperity and independence of God's people speaks powerfully to the world. Because God is with them, and has blessed them, they will be lenders, not borrowers, and rulers, not subjects (see also Prov 22:7). The blessing of Yahweh (see vv. 4, 6, 10, 14, 18) is everywhere around them. The caveat added in verse 5—that this is contingent on wholehearted, all-embracing obedience—suggests, however, that this may not always be the case in Israel. Given the nature of God's people, there is a very real possibility that this blessing will rebound in curse (cf. 28:12, 43–44).

15:7–11. The note of realism implied in 15:1–6 becomes explicit in verses 7–11. Despite the provision to allow landowners to escape a downward spiral of debt, individual Israelites may still find themselves trapped in poverty. The fact that this happens "within ... your city gates in the land that the Lord your God is giving you" may suggest that this "urban" poverty will arise among those who are no longer able to live on an inherited plot of land. However, Moses's main concern here is that God's people do not mistreat those who find themselves in this situation. The call here is "for an open heart and an open hand."[350]

The idealism of 15:4 is, as always for Moses, tempered with a realism forged by an unrelenting awareness of human sin. The temptation for God's people to "be hardhearted or tightfisted" in their treatment of their brother who is poor is very real.[351] To act like this is to deny who they are as the people of Yahweh and to refuse to treat one another as they have been treated by their generous God. Rather they are to be "openhanded" (see Pss 104:28; 145:16), and "freely loan him enough for whatever need he has." Interestingly, the injunction is to lend rather than give. This is built on the understanding that God's blessing will ensure a return to prosperity, and that when God's people are living as they should in his land, such poverty should only ever be a temporary issue.

---

[349] *Targum Onqelos* captures the sense well: "There *should* be no poor among you."

[350] Lundbom, *Deuteronomy*, 490. Block argues that this is the central panel of this entire section (*Deuteronomy*, 355).

[351] See also 1 John 3:17.

The main obstacle to the consistent enjoyment of this kind of beautiful life by all, however, is not external threats, but the sinful hearts of the people. 15:9–10 is striking.

One key difference between this collection of preached laws and similar ancient material is the way Moses presses beyond mere legislation to diagnosis of the sinfulness of the human heart. In these verses, he anticipates self-interest and greed trumping God's command to be generous (as the Pharisees did with the "Corban" rules in Mark 7). God has given to them, so they must give to others. This is a basic responsibility of God's people.

Refusing to help the poor on the basis that the term of the loan (whether it be land or money) is unattractive to the lender is simply unacceptable.[352] The motivation to lend to a brother Israelite who is struggling was never supposed to be financial gain, but the relentless generosity of God himself to all his people. To be "stingy" in this context is not simply reprehensible in the eyes of society, but in the eyes of God himself. Within God's people, God himself is always the final arbiter in any dispute, and in this case, if or when the poor brother cries out "to the Lord against you," you will have no excuse. "Non-lenders" have no defense, and their sinful actions will be exposed (see also Exod 22:23–24).

After the blunt, all-encompassing command to "give to him" (15:10), reasons to behave generously are piled up in a typically Mosaic fashion. Besides fearing exposure before God, his people are to be generous to the poor without having a "stingy heart" because of the marvelous prospect of God "bless[ing] you in all your work and in everything you do." This expansive expression underlines that acting like God by being generous replicates the core experience of the nation and enables them to live a life of grace together. As Block helpfully sums up: "The antidote to such twisted thinking is a generous heart concerned about the wellbeing of the poor rather than one's own advantage."[353]

In the light of 15:4, verse 11 comes as a shock. It should not be so, but Moses insists that "there will never cease to be poor people in the land." There is a significant gulf between the way things should be and the way they are. This is because of the enduring effects of sin. In the short term,

---

[352] Interestingly, later Judaism encountered just such a problem, which led Rabbi Hillel to propose a mechanism that allowed lenders to offer a loan that wasn't subject to this regulation (see *m.* Šeb. 10.3).

[353] Block, *Deuteronomy*, 368.

the way to address this is clear: "Open your hand willingly to your poor and needy brother in your land." Generosity like this is a clear reflection of the goodness and kindness of God. However, there is no real evidence that the quality of kindness described in 15:7–11 was ever consistently lived out. It remained an aspiration throughout the history of God's people. But this is exactly what Moses's words in 15:12–18 lead us to expect.

15:12–18. These verses take the non-ideal situation of 15:7–11 a significant step farther. The slightly terse language cannot hide the seriousness of the situation: one of your brother or sister Israelites "is sold to you." This is not now short-term financial pressure, but long-term poverty leading to a desperate attempt to remedy the situation by selling oneself into indentured service. The idea that a "fellow Hebrew, a man or woman, is sold to you" cuts across the very identity of the covenant people. They may have once been slaves (the term "Hebrew" probably alludes to their time in Egypt), but God has set them free. How can they possibly countenance enslaving one another? Whether what is envisaged is voluntary or not, this is clearly an extreme situation, but nevertheless one that is anticipated and has no short-term solution. Hence the injunction of verse 12: when he "serves you six years, you must set him free in the seventh year."

Both Exodus 21:1–11 and Leviticus 25:39–46 deal with the messy reality of slavery/indentured service, which was a normal part of life in the ancient Near East, but Moses here adopts a unique tone and focuses on the responsibility of the master, irrespective of the actions or conditions that have led to this situation. It also appears to extend the scope of the provision to cover women and to shorten the possible term of service from forty-nine years to six![354] What is clear is that the ongoing legacy of the exodus and God's continuing loving kindness have created a dynamic of increasing generosity as his people enter the land, ensuring that debt-servitude can last for only a substantial but limited time.[355]

---

[354] Lev 25:40 seems to imply that release only happens in the Year of Jubilee (once every fifty years). However, the accompanying language around children seems to imply a much shorter period, perhaps as envisaged here. It may also be that Exod 21 is referring to a different situation: (a) there the slave is "bought" and (b) the woman may well be "sold" to be married, rather than being caught up in debt slavery (see McConville, *Deuteronomy*, 262; Tigay, *Deuteronomy*, 149).

[355] Both Jer 34:14 and Neh 5:1–13 make clear that this is not an implausible situation.

This provision seems to be an extension of the "law of release" in 15:1, although the timings are slightly different. The "law of release" appears to operate on a fixed calendar (giving rise to the problems addressed in vv. 7–11), whereas in this six-year period, the clock starts to run down the moment the indentured service begins.

It is also striking that the main concern of this passage is to ensure that the formerly enslaved individual should be set up to flourish in future. It is incumbent on the "owner" to be radically generous. Although there are parallels to the release from debt slavery, there is nothing like the provision of verses 13–14 anywhere else in the ancient world.[356]

The obligation on the former master is not to "send him away empty-handed." This is based on a deep-rooted conviction that all Israel are brothers, and so their relationships can never be viewed in purely economic terms. Rather, the generosity of God in which they all share together is to be re-expressed to this newly freed servant, as it was nationally when they fled from Egypt (Exod 3:21–22; 11:2–3; 12:35–36). The "owner" is now to hold nothing back: "Give generously to him from your flock, your threshing floor, and your winepress." The brother is to be set up with livestock and produce, presumably to enable him to resume life with Yahweh in the land that he has given to his people. All of this is a gift of grace, as verse 14 makes explicit: "You are to give him whatever the Lord your God has blessed you with." The word for "give" here is a rare one, with lavish overtones. Everything that God's people have has been gifted to them, and so they must be poised to pass it on wherever there is need.

The theological rationale behind this severance pay is not unexpected, but that hardly diminishes its force: "Remember that you were a slave in the land of Egypt and the Lord your God redeemed you."[357] Given this soaring reality, the people of Israel can never sit easily with enslaving one another. It can only ever be a temporary measure, with the whole community taking responsibility to ensure that even in the direst economic straits, there is always a pathway to recovery. Moses self-consciously adds, "That is why I am giving you this command today." This torah is so much more than a list of rules. It is a rich theological vision of

---

[356] Surprisingly, the Code of Hammurabi insists that the wife or children of a citizen sold into slavery because of bad debt should be released in the fourth year (*ANET*³, 170–71), but there is no equivalent of the generous provision that follows.

[357] So Tigay, *Deuteronomy*, 149.

the life of freedom, a beautiful life to be lived in covenant with Yahweh in the land he provides for his people, a life of freedom to be lived with God in his strength for his glory.

This richly theological vision of the way things should be is coupled with a deep sensitivity to the vagaries of real life. In 15:16–18, Moses considers the possibility that the indentured servant asks to stay as part of the household.[358] If Israel captures and lives out the vision of these chapters, this would surely be a very real possibility. The special ritual, involving taking "an awl and pierc[ing] through his ear into the door," regularizes this situation and makes it permanent, attaching the person to his master's "house," but it also underlines that this is a voluntary arrangement. The final phrase of verse 17 highlights that this measure applies to women as well as men.

The awl-piercing ritual then on the one hand preserves the principle that all Israel has been set "free," whilst allowing for an individual (in very unusual circumstances) to opt in to lifelong service of the household. To be a "slave for life" is a unique situation—it provides permanent security and dependence to a vulnerable member of the community in the context of a loving household .

The injunction in 15:18 ("Do not regard it as a hardship when you set him free") probably refers back to the actions of verses 12–14. To act grudgingly in this context this would be to forget the kindness of God to all his people in setting them free from Egypt, and to fail to show similar compassion to the one who had ended up in dire economic straits. This is why the attitude of the master matters. Even in non-ideal situations, Yahweh is committed to safeguarding his blessing in every aspect of the nation's life.

15:19–23. It is slightly surprising that at this point Moses turns to the discussion of how to handle the firstborn of the flock. However, it does seem that these laws tend to flow from one paragraph to another via a chain of associations, where one aspect of a law is then picked up in the next. In this case, there is an apparently seamless transition from a discussion of the dignity of every Israelite to that of the consecration of firstborn animals. The idea of the "firstborn" was enshrined at the

---

[358] See also Exod 21:5–6, where the servant actually expresses familial love for his master. No comment is made on the significance of this ritual or whether the slave wears a ring from this point on as a badge or marker.

heart of the nation's consciousness in the exodus (see Exod 13:1–16; also 22:29–30, and even Gen 4:4). The fact that this seminal ritual embraced both human beings and animals being "consecrated" to Yahweh almost certainly provides the rationale for this transition.[359]

In 15:19–23, Moses picks up the central concern of the ritual (without any attempt to cover every detail), which is that the life of God's people is to be built around shared joy. He again reminds Israel of the exodus, but now spells out how this principle should be worked out in the land, where some will be too far away to make repeated trips to the tent of meeting on the eighth day as prescribed in Exodus 22:29–30. Not only should all these animals be consecrated to Yahweh, but they are also precluded from both working the land (oxen) and being sheared (sheep). Instead, as already highlighted in 14:23, these animals are to be eaten annually at Yahweh's chosen place in his presence as part of the tithe festival.[360]

It becomes increasingly clear that the Deuteronomic legislation is concerned to begin the process of shaping earlier provisions to fit the realities of life in the land. The earlier principles are now worked out in sensible, manageable ways as the prospect of daily life in Canaan looms large. This includes a word on dealing with firstborn animals that have any defect or imperfection (as in Mal 1:6–8). Rather than being taken to the place chosen by Yahweh, they are to be eaten "at the city gates," i.e., in the heart of the community (also 12:15–16, 22–25). Perhaps surprisingly, "both the unclean person and the clean may eat it, as though it were a gazelle or deer," although the usual care must be taken with the blood (15:23). Despite the symbolic importance of the purity laws, these appear to be trumped by the goodness and generosity of God, who allows all of his people to celebrate together regularly at the heart of his land. With that, attention turns to the most fundamental rhythm of the life of the nation—the three major annual festivals.

16:1–8. In a position broadly analogous to that of the Sabbath command in the Decalogue, 16:1–17 now deals with the trio of national festivals that

---

[359] See also Exod 13:2, 11–16; 22:29–30; Lev 27:26–27; Num 18:15–18 for other discussions of this key practice. There is no discussion here of how the provision for the priests fits in. According to Block, the move from the statement that all firstborn animals belong to Yahweh in Exodus to the need to sacrifice only male, perfect clean animals means that only about 15% have to be sacrificed (*Deuteronomy*, 379).

[360] The general principle of Exod 13:11–13 is now worked out: rather than an Israelite making repeated trips to the chosen place every time an animal reaches eight days old, these firstborn animals are included in the tithe festival. This assumed in 12:6–7, 17–18; 14:23.

are to punctuate the life of the people of God in the land. Chapter 16 opens the discussion with an expanded Passover Festival in verses 1–8.

In the Exodus narratives, both the Passover itself and eating unleavened bread feature centrally.[361] In Exodus 12:17; 23:15; and 34:18, Israel is told to mark the events of the exodus by celebrating the Festival of Unleavened Bread. No explicit instructions are given on how this relates to future Passover meals or how the two are to be integrated. Once they arrive in Canaan, however, it seems that these two linked commemorations are to be combined into one super-festival, to be celebrated in the first month of the year, Abib (later known by its Babylonian name, Nisan). Presumably the fact that God had brought them out on Abib 14 was already so deeply engrained in the national consciousness that there was no need to specify the date.[362]

As we have seen throughout these chapters, Moses's primary concern seems to be with theological principle rather than the mechanics of the celebration itself.[363] He begins by emphasizing the historical roots of the festival: Passover is to be celebrated "because the Lord your God brought you out of Egypt by night in the month of Abib." [364] In Deuteronomy, the departure takes place at night (a detail omitted in Exod 34:18, and apparently at odds with Num 33:3; however, Moses here views the events beginning with the death of the Egyptian firstborn during the hours of darkness), providing the rationale for this meal being the only one to be enjoyed in the evening.

The first major shift in practice, however, is revealed in verse 2: rather than simply being celebrated at home (or up to this point, presumably in each family's tent), the primary action takes place when sacrifice is made "in the place where the Lord chooses to have his name dwell." Having traveled to this place, the nation celebrates together.[365] Rather than the emphasis being on the application of blood, Passover is swept

---

[361] On the importance of unleavened bread see Exod 12:8, 15–20, 34, 39; see also Num 9:1–14; 28:16–25; Lev 23:5–8.

[362] In a similar way many people today will speak simply of "Christmas" without spelling out the date.

[363] Lundbom comments that there is "a minimum of detail and a maximum of theological overlay" (*Deuteronomy*, 504).

[364] The festival is to *dominate* the whole month rather than necessarily lasting for thirty days. Although see the options discussed in Tigay, *Deuteronomy*, 153.

[365] While only the men of Israel are required to attend the festival, it seems that everyone is included.

up in Deuteronomy's concern to ensure that God's people worship his way (at the place he designates).

In addition, unlike Exodus (12:24–25), according to Deuteronomy 16:2, it is now permissible to eat from the "herd" (i.e., beef) as well as the "flock" (lamb). Tigay helpfully suggests that this relaxation may simply have been a matter of logistics, as a transition is made from household meals to a community celebration.[366]

The third innovation involves the careful combination of the celebration of the nation's rescue from Egypt with the enjoyment of God's presence and rest in fulfillment of his promises at the heart of the land, symbolized by eating unleavened bread, now characterized as the "bread of hardship." The rushed, panicked departure from Egypt ("you left the land of Egypt in a hurry") is translated into a week of rejoicing, accompanied with a side of unleavened bread!

There is a looseness in the description of the ritual itself in verses 4–7 (particularly around the culinary details: there is no mention of bitter herbs or of no bones being broken in the cooking process, Exod 12:8, 46), but the key steps and the basic timetable to be followed are clear. Initially, all yeast is to be removed from within their borders (CSB: "in your territory") for the duration of the festival.[367] It should not even be "seen" (16:4, lit.; CSB: "found"). This is presumably designed to be a definitive, public statement of allegiance to Yahweh (rather than flowing from the evils of yeast!). This was already flagged in Exodus 12:19–20, but the ban is extended from "households" to the entire nation. In addition, 16:4b insists that "none of the meat you sacrifice in the evening of the first day is to remain until morning." This Passover requirement recalls the manna and quail in the wilderness, which was also to be consumed on the same day. The implication is that even in the land, the people are to be continually dependent on God.

The repetition in 16:5–7 that the sacrifice for the Passover must be killed *and eaten* in the place chosen by God is emphatic: "You are to cook and eat it in the place the LORD your God chooses." The entire nation is to gather, to eat and then "you are to return to your tents in the morning."[368]

---

[366] Tigay, *Deuteronomy*, 153. See also 2 Chr 35:7.

[367] McConville helpfully points out that the whole land is the context in which this feast is to be celebrated. *Deuteronomy*, 273.

[368] These tents are not their present portable dwellings, but temporary shelters erected for the duration of the festival.

The word for "cook" here is normally translated "boil," which would be in direct contravention of Exodus 12:8–9 (which insists on roasting and prohibits boiling). The most likely explanation here is that the word can also be used generically of cooking (as in 2 Chr 35:13) and does not reflect another innovation.[369] The fact that the people are told to "eat unleavened bread for six days" may simply mean six *more* days, or that in the new arrangements, rather than being baked along with the Passover lamb, unleavened bread was reserved for the days after the feast. The joint festival then concludes with a "solemn assembly" (the translation does not exclude rejoicing, which has been the keynote of the festival) on which God's people rest, before they disperse again to live with God in the land.[370]

The insistence that the nation journey to the place chosen by God both enshrines perpetual movement/pilgrimage at the heart of life in the land and ensures that their identity as one covenant people is regularly reinforced. This same emphasis lies at the heart of the other festivals which make up this chapter.[371]

16:9–12. The timing of the second of the three national festivals in this chapter is dependent on when the grain harvest ripens and "the sickle is first put to the standing grain" (16:9). However, according to Leviticus 23:15–16, this was not strictly speaking a moveable feast, as the countdown began the day after the beginning of the Feast of Unleavened Bread (so Passover was held on 14 Nisan, the special sabbath which began the Feast of Unleavened Bread on 15 Nisan, and then on 16 Nisan, Firstfruits, the seven weeks begins). This meant that the Festival of Weeks began on the fiftieth day after that of Unleavened Bread (which later gave rise to the Greek name for the festival, "Pentecost" or "fifty days").[372]

In his instructions for this second trip to the place chosen by Yahweh, Moses gives no detail on the appropriate offerings to be made (in contrast to Lev 23 and Num 28:26–31), but rather issues a simple call in verse 10 to

---

[369] It may also simply be a relaxation of the earlier prescription. It is good to note that Exod 12 is a narrative of what happened rather than specifying specific ritual actions.

[370] It is possible that returning to their tents could mean going home on day two to eat unleavened bread at home, but this is less likely. It seems best to take "tents" literally here, as the nation camps around the chosen place.

[371] It is worth underlining that although only the males must attend (16:16), each of the festivals assumes that other family members will be there.

[372] Later Jewish tradition associates Pentecost with the giving of the torah (by working out dates from Exod 19), but there is no direct connection drawn either here or in Exodus.

make a "a freewill offering that you give in proportion to how the Lord your God has blessed you."

If Passover and Unleavened Bread are designed to celebrate God's *past* goodness, the Festival of Weeks extends the celebration to include God's continued generosity to his people in the present. The foundation of their joy (v. 11) is still to be their identity as the nation whom God has rescued from Egypt and made his own (stated explicitly once more in v. 12), but this second inclusive and exuberant national holiday enshrines their ongoing experience in the land in their calendar. Once more the people of God (including the marginalized and the landless) rejoice together in his presence at his chosen place (although this time, only for a single day).

As Moses continues to preach this torah, it is clear that, in the context of Deuteronomy, the origins and details of this festival are relatively unimportant. What matters is that it now plays its part in maintaining a rhythm of joyful thankfulness in the life of God's people in the land. Hence the section concludes with a command: "carefully follow these statutes."

16:13–15. Moses's description of the third of these annual national pilgrimage-celebrations, the Festival of Shelters, shares the same theological emphasis as Passover/Unleavened Bread and Weeks—rejoicing together in the presence of Yahweh.

Shelters is to be celebrated when the harvest (primarily grain, olives, and grapes) has not only been gathered, but has been processed, ready for consumption, storage, or sale.

Once again, much more detail is supplied elsewhere: both Leviticus 23:33–44 and Numbers 29:12–39. Leviticus again ties down the date—to the "fifteenth day of the seventh month," five days after the Day of Atonement (Lev 23:26, 39)—and ties the celebration directly to the experience of the nation on the move in the exodus (Lev 23:42–43). In Numbers 29, there is no mention of previous camping experiences, but the focus is placed firmly on the diet of specific sacrifices to be offered on each day of the eight-day festival. In Deuteronomy, Moses places the theological emphasis on yet another facet of the feast.

As with Passover/Unleavened Bread and Weeks, enjoying God together with the entire community at the place he chooses in the land is front and center. There is also a distinct future emphasis in Moses's description of Shelters: verse 15 speaks of the fact that Yahweh will bless his people. Sleeping in tents is a reminder of what God has done and is yet to do.[373] In addition, the culmination of this annual cycle is "you will have abundant joy" (16:15). God has rescued his people and brought them into the land so that they might rejoice in his presence, a glorious reality that is to be built into the celebration of this festival, as the Torah is read aloud (31:9–13).

16:16–17. The final verses in this section reiterate the concerns that lie at the heart of Moses's theological vision. The obligation on all adult males (presumably as the heads of households) to come to the place chosen by Yahweh three times a year is to set the rhythm of life in the land of God's people. The invitation extended to whole families is a mark of God's generosity. When they come to the chosen place, they are to rejoice in the presence of Yahweh, as they celebrate with their households and the full spectrum of the community. This is to be the grateful rhythm of national life.

These three festivals in the first, third, and seventh months of the year establish a pattern of gathering and celebrating at the heart of life in the land. In Deuteronomy, the central element of each festival is a celebration rooted in gratitude—past gratitude (Passover/Unleavened Bread), present gratitude (Weeks), and future gratitude (Shelters).

This emphasis is made explicit in 16:16, as gratitude is enshrined at the heart of the national consciousness. God has blessed them, and so each one must acknowledge that by "a gift suited to his means," with God's goodness precluding anyone showing up "empty-handed." God makes this annual rhythm of gratitude possible. Their obedience must bring it to reality. The fact that both 2 Kings 23:22 and Nehemiah 8:17 provide evidence that this pattern was never really established in the life of the people is a tragic indictment of the heart problem of the chosen people.

Bridge

According to this long section (14:22–16:17), the rhythm of the life of God's covenant people is to be one of gratitude leading to joy.

The events of their history have clearly established that they owe God everything. Moses now makes it clear that the way they are to flourish in the land is by living out of that gratitude, as they ensure that their life

---

[373] Similar shelters are mentioned in, e.g., Gen 33:17 (shepherds); 1 Kgs 20:12, 16 (camouflage for soldiers); Job 27:18 and Isa 1:8 (watchmen).

together is shaped by powerful and dramatic reminders of God's goodness, which leads to enjoying him.

This immensely positive vision of life with God is one which is embodied, proclaimed, and made possible by Jesus himself, the one who says "I have come that you might have life, and have it in abundance" (John 10:10) and "I have told you these things so that my joy may be in you and your joy may be complete" (John 15:11).

The New Testament establishes a similar rhythm of gratitude and joy as it calls God's people to meet together weekly, before scattering again throughout the community. When we gather, we are to hear the gospel proclaimed and illustrated in the Lord's Supper, and we are to speak the gospel into one another's lives, as we "encourage one another ... all the more as we see the day approaching" (Heb 10:25). United to Christ and empowered by his Spirit, we are to live the reality of a gospel-shaped life of gratitude-fueled joy in a way that Israel simply never managed to pull off.

5. Living under God's Appointed Leaders (16:18–18:22)

> [18] "Appoint judges and officials for your tribes in all your towns the Lord
> your God is giving you. They are to judge the people with righteous
> judgment. [19] Do not deny justice or show partiality to anyone. Do not
> accept a bribe, for it blinds the eyes of the wise and twists the words of
> the righteous. [20] Pursue justice and justice alone, so that you will live
> and possess the land the Lord your God is giving you.
>
> [21] "Do not set up an Asherah of any kind of wood next to the altar you
> will build for the Lord your God, [22] and do not set up a sacred pillar;
> the Lord your God hates them.
>
> [17:1] "Do not sacrifice to the Lord your God an ox or sheep with a defect
> or any serious flaw, for that is detestable to the Lord your God.
>
> [2] "If a man or woman among you in one of your towns that the Lord your
> God will give you is discovered doing evil in the sight of the Lord your
> God and violating his covenant [3] and has gone to serve other gods by
> bowing in worship to the sun, moon, or all the stars in the sky—which
> I have forbidden—[4] and if you are told or hear about it, then investigate
> it thoroughly. If the report turns out to be true that this detestable
> act has been done in Israel, [5] you are to bring out to your city gates
> that man or woman who has done this evil thing and stone them to
> death. [6] The one condemned to die is to be executed on the testimony
> of two or three witnesses. No one is to be executed on the testimony
> of a single witness. [7] The witnesses' hands are to be the first in putting

him to death, and after that, the hands of all the people. You must purge the evil from you.

8 “If a case is too difficult for you—concerning bloodshed, lawsuits, or assaults—cases disputed at your city gates, then go up to the place the Lord your God chooses. 9 You are to go to the Levitical priests and to the judge who presides at that time. Ask, and they will give you a verdict in the case. 10 You must abide by the verdict they give you at the place the Lord chooses. Be careful to do exactly as they instruct you. 11 You must abide by the instruction they give you and the verdict they announce to you. Do not turn to the right or the left from the decision they declare to you. 12 The person who acts arrogantly, refusing to listen either to the priest who stands there serving the Lord your God or to the judge, must die. You must purge the evil from Israel. 13 Then all the people will hear about it, be afraid, and no longer behave arrogantly.

14 “When you enter the land the Lord your God is giving you, take possession of it, live in it, and say, ‘I will set a king over me like all the nations around me,’ 15 you are to appoint over you the king the Lord your God chooses. Appoint a king from your brothers. You are not to set a foreigner over you, or one who is not of your people. 16 However, he must not acquire many horses for himself or send the people back to Egypt to acquire many horses, for the Lord has told you, ‘You are never to go back that way again.’ 17 He must not acquire many wives for himself so that his heart won’t go astray. He must not acquire very large amounts of silver and gold for himself. 18 When he is seated on his royal throne, he is to write a copy of this instruction for himself on a scroll in the presence of the Levitical priests. 19 It is to remain with him, and he is to read from it all the days of his life, so that he may learn to fear the Lord his God, to observe all the words of this instruction, and to do these statutes. 20 Then his heart will not be exalted above his countrymen, he will not turn from this command to the right or the left, and he and his sons will continue reigning many years in Israel.

18:1 “The Levitical priests, the whole tribe of Levi, will have no portion or inheritance with Israel. They will eat the Lord’s food offerings; that is their inheritance. 2 Although Levi has no inheritance among his brothers, the Lord is his inheritance, as he promised him. 3 This is the priests’ share from the people who offer a sacrifice, whether it is an ox, a sheep, or a goat; the priests are to be given the shoulder, jaws, and stomach. 4 You are to give him the firstfruits of your grain, new wine, and fresh oil, and the first sheared wool of your flock. 5 For the Lord your God has chosen him and his sons from all your tribes to stand and minister in his name from now on. 6 When a Levite leaves one of your towns in Israel where he was staying and wants to go to the place the Lord chooses, 7 he may serve in the name of the Lord his

God like all his fellow Levites who minister there in the presence of the LORD. [8] They will eat equal portions besides what he has received from the sale of the family estate.

[9] "When you enter the land the LORD your God is giving you, do not imitate the detestable customs of those nations. [10] No one among you is to sacrifice his son or daughter in the fire, practice divination, tell fortunes, interpret omens, practice sorcery, [11] cast spells, consult a medium or a spiritist, or inquire of the dead. [12] Everyone who does these acts is detestable to the LORD, and the LORD your God is driving out the nations before you because of these detestable acts. [13] You must be blameless before the LORD your God. [14] Though these nations you are about to drive out listen to fortune-tellers and diviners, the LORD your God has not permitted you to do this.

[15] "The LORD your God will raise up for you a prophet like me from among your own brothers. You must listen to him. [16] This is what you requested from the LORD your God at Horeb on the day of the assembly when you said, 'Let us not continue to hear the voice of the LORD our God or see this great fire any longer, so that we will not die!' [17] Then the LORD said to me, 'They have spoken well. [18] I will raise up for them a prophet like you from among their brothers. I will put my words in his mouth, and he will tell them everything I command him. [19] I will hold accountable whoever does not listen to my words that he speaks in my name. [20] But the prophet who presumes to speak a message in my name that I have not commanded him to speak, or who speaks in the name of other gods—that prophet must die.' [21] You may say to yourself, 'How can we recognize a message the LORD has not spoken?' [22] When a prophet speaks in the LORD's name, and the message does not come true or is not fulfilled, that is a message the LORD has not spoken. The prophet has spoken it presumptuously. Do not be afraid of him."

16:18–20. The importance of the "judicial system" in Israel features at several key moments in the history of God's people (see, e.g., Exod 18:13–27; Deut 1:9–18). Alongside appointing Moses, God insists that there should be a plurality at the heart of the life of Israel. This basic principle is now developed and applied to the life of the nation in the land.[374]

The system of "judges and officials" (the terminology is quite distinct from 1:9–18) seems to replace the more informal arrangements suggested

---

[374] Once again, "no attempt is made to regulate the details of the institution, such as the method by which the judges are to be selected, their numbers, the organization of the courts, etc." (Driver, *Deuteronomy*, 200). Presumably these people are chosen from among the elders of each place.

by Jethro in Exodus and reflected by Moses in chapter 1.[375] The new system of community-led appointments is based less on helping Moses to cope (and so by implication, delegating his "personal" authority) and more on emphasizing that Yahweh's own authority is now to be carefully devolved to cover every person and place throughout the land ("in all your towns").[376]

No comment is made on the specific responsibilities of the "judge" and the "official" (who is presumably some kind of clerk) who are to be appointed by the community, but it is clear that they are to work together to "judge the people with righteous judgment." This is a unique phrase (מִשְׁפַּט־צֶדֶק), which deliberately roots fair human legal decisions to the righteousness of God (although both ideas occur in, e.g., Gen 18:19; Lev 19:15; 1 Kgs 10:9; 1 Chr 18:14; Job 8:3; 37:23; Amos 5:7; Isa 1:21; 9:7; Jer 22:3; Pss. 33:5; 72:1–2; 99:4). The implications of this approach are significant: fairness and just decisions are not to be denied to anyone, and the entire system is to be built upon the assumption that all are equal in God's eyes (which clearly excludes "partiality"; see also Exod 23:2–3, 6–8; Deut 1:17). This lays the foundation for the prophetic critique of power that is so prominent in the rest of the Old Testament.[377] In particular, it is vital that those with financial resources cannot subvert the system, and so bribes (or any kind of gifts) are completely prohibited (10:17). According to Moses, a bribe "blinds the eyes of the wise and twists the words of the righteous." This is an extremely unusual means of persuasion in Deuteronomy (having all the hallmarks of a wisdom saying, an emphasis which is absent in, e.g., Exod 23, although see Deut 1:13, 15), but it is both graphic and persuasive.

The striking (and again unparalleled) expression in verse 20 ("Pursue justice and justice alone" or more literally "Righteousness! Righteousness! you shall seek") emphasizes that a godly legal system is a prerequisite for taking and holding the land and enjoying life with Yahweh in it.

---

[375] McConville helpfully suggests that the model in 1:9–18, while suitable for a people "on the march," would not have been fit for purpose in the land (*Deuteronomy*, 262). Contra Block (*Deuteronomy*, 402), these seem to be two related but separate roles, rather than "scribal judges."

[376] No effort is made to spell out how different authority figures are to relate (or work together). Generally it seems that elders deal with most domestic matters. In 21:1–9, the elders and the judges work together. In 17:8–12 and 19:15–19, it is the judges and the priests who must cooperate. For more details, see Lundbom, *Deuteronomy*, 521.

[377] A point helpfully made by Tigay, *Deuteronomy*, 159.

16:21–17:7. The statements of 16:21–17:1 (and in fact, this entire section) seem at first glance out of place, given that they deal with matters not normally conceived of as judicial. It seems that the intention of these prohibitions is to underline that there can be no separation of powers among God's people. "Righteous judgment" is dependent on right worship. This presumably explains why Moses turns immediately to ensuring that the heart of the worship of God ("the altar you will build for the Lord your God") is safeguarded from potential idolatry by prohibiting setting up a wooden pole of any kind or erecting a stone pillar which might function as an "Asherah" or a "sacred pillar" (probably a representation of Baal) near the sanctuary (16:21–22).[378] The visual symbolism is clear: the place chosen for Yahweh must clearly be for the worship of Yahweh alone in the same way that the justice system established by Yahweh must be shaped and empowered by his righteousness alone. The connectedness of the entire life of the people of God, lived under his authority, is obvious. The Lord hates both injustice and idolatry.

This "all of life" perspective is also reflected in 17:1, which excludes the offering of any "ox or sheep with a defect or any serious flaw." The logic is simple: God has given us everything and can never be repaid, but nonetheless demands the very best (see also Lev 22:17–25). Anything else is tantamount to idolatry in that it is giving a higher priority to someone or something else, thus dethroning God. Such behavior is "detestable" to God. As we have seen, this term is generally used in Deuteronomy of actions which are inconsistent with being God's people, but rather typify the idolatrous present inhabitants of the land (see, e.g., Deut 7:26; 12:31; 13:14; 14:3; 17:1, 4; 18:9, 12; 20:18; 22:5; 23:18; 24:4; 25:16).

These verses then reflect a view of life in the land in which the whole nation has a responsibility to uphold the covenant with Yahweh. The specific legal functions of 16:18–20 are part of the fabric of the beautiful life God has invited them to enjoy in the land. This is made explicit in 17:2–7.

Although it is not obvious at first glance, these verses *seem* to be addressing the judges and officials of 16:18–20 in an indirect way that is unique to Deuteronomy (see 21:1; 22:22; 24:7). This is apparently confirmed in 17:8–9, where provision is made for difficult cases to

---

[378] The verb used here can mean "plant," but there is no reason to insist that the Asherah must then be a living tree. Tigay simply says the intent is to ban "any treelike object" (*Deuteronomy*, 161), as well as stone pillars (7:5).

be referred to the Levitical priests and "the judge who presides" on appeal. So why does Moses not make it clearer that these are instructions for law officers? His concern, as demonstrated consistently through this collection of legislation, is not primarily with administrative process, but with casting a theological vision of the life of the people of God. The entire community must be committed to the righteous life.[379] As part of this vision (which develops the material in chapter 13), he wants to underline that the responsibility for covenantal faithfulness is shared by every member in the people of God. Idolatry within their "towns" (lit., "gates") is not simply the problem of law enforcement officers, but a shared problem for the whole people of God. "Doing [the] evil in the sight of the Lord your God" (which is further defined explicitly as idolatry in vv. 3–4) is a breach of the covenant with Yahweh: it affects everyone, and therefore is everyone's problem. The phrase "the stars in the sky" is literally "the host of heaven (which occurs elsewhere in 2 Kgs 17:16; 21:3, 5; 23:4–5; Jer 19:13 and Zeph 1:5 in the context of idolatry, and perhaps specifically Astarte worship[380]). Matters of idolatry are so threatening to the life of God's people that every rumor of such behavior must be investigated carefully (again, presumably by the judges and officials). Even in a case like this, "righteous judgment" must be on display.

Verses 5–7 outline what such due process looks like. There are three interlocking parts to the process: (1) the penalty for idolatry, if proven, remains public stoning, as befits an act that imperils the existence of the entire community; (2) the accused must be treated fairly; in particular, eyewitness testimony must be corroborated by either one or (preferably) two others, providing a safeguard against personal vendettas being carried out (for a statement of the general principle, see 19:15); (3) as in 13:9, those who have uncovered the idolatrous acts must take the lead in carrying out the punishment, and then they must be joined by the entire community in stoning the guilty party at the city gates.[381] In God's eyes, covenant-breaking has

---

[379] So Peter T. Vogt, *Religious Concepts in the Theology of Deuteronomy* (Gloucester: University of Gloucestershire Press, 2003), 224–26.

[380] See Jack R. Lundbom, *Jeremiah 1-20*, AB 21A (New York: Doubleday, 1999), 476–77 for this suggestion.

[381] In both Lev 24:14 and Num 15:35, this is to take place outside the camp (i.e., in an unholy place). Once Israel is in the land, no such places exist, for the entire land is holy.

consequences for the entire community, and so it is necessary for the entire community to act in "purging the evil from you."[382]

17:8–13. The fact that Moses has the judges and officials primarily in mind becomes clear, as he now makes provision for cases that are "too difficult for you," where "you" can really refer only to local judges and officials.[383] Whether dealing with murder (lit., "blood on blood"), complex civil cases (lit., "claim on claim") or assault (lit., "blow on blow"), sometimes the judicial process in the community will reach an impasse (17:8). In these "disputed" cases (a term that is vague enough to encompass those in which the judges themselves cannot agree, as well as those in which the verdict is hotly opposed by either the plaintiff or the accused), the matter can be escalated to "the Levitical priests and to the judge who presides at that time" (17:9). They are to hear the case, which may have involved seeking God's guidance.

This is the first mention of this presiding judge (perhaps also mentioned in 25:2), who appears to one chosen from among the Levites to chair such appeals.[384] The fact that the decisions of this body *must* be accepted is underlined in the strongest possible terms in verses 10–11. Their ruling is spoken "at the place the LORD chooses," which invests it with the very authority of Yahweh himself. Like his other commands through Moses, his verdict through this court of appeal must be carried out to the letter (v. 10b, reiterated in 11a). Israel has previously been told not to "turn to the right or to the left" in the context of the revelation at Horeb (5:22), and now the ruling of this tribunal is given the same weight. The word "instruction" is actually "torah," which links their verdict to Moses's exposition of the righteousness of Yahweh in action.

This explains why refusing to accept this judicial pronouncement is tantamount to rebelling against the word of Yahweh. So verse 12: "The person who acts arrogantly, refusing to listen either to the priest who stands there serving the LORD your God or to the judge, must die." Because

---

[382] Israel is commanded to "purge the evil" from among them in 13:5; 17:7, 12; 19:19; 21:21; 22:21, 22, 24; and 24:7. In each case, the "crime" to be punished strikes at the heart of the life of the community: covenant-breaking idolatry; refusal to submit to the leaders of the family or the nation; perjuring a brother Israelite; promiscuity or adultery; and kidnapping. Although this sounds repressive to modern ears, it is completely consistent with Deuteronomy's rich and nuanced understanding of what it means to be the people of Yahweh.

[383] See the parallel provision of 1:17 for a time after Moses himself has departed.

[384] Block, *Deuteronomy*, 408, concurs.

this judge speaks from God's place with his delegated authority, his ruling *must* be accepted as coming from God himself (in contrast to e.g. 18:22; see also Jer 5:30–31. There is to be no negotiation, for this would undermine the fabric of the life of the covenant nation. The word of the priest(s) or the judge in this context must be obeyed, for Israel must be a holy nation. Any attempt to resist this rule must itself be "purged," both as a punishment and a future deterrent, promoting the fear of Yahweh and safeguarding the nation against arrogance (17:13; also 13:11).

It is fascinating that in Moses's conception of the one people of God, there is no divide between secular and religious authority: the judges guard against idolatry in 17:2–7, and the Levitical priests rule on judicial matters in 17:8–13. To be the covenant people shapes every element of the life of the nation. Theology saturates every sphere of thinking and action. This is also displayed in the massively influential discussion of the future kings of Israel.

17:14–20. If confirmation were needed that this is not a conventional law code, it can be found in 17:14–20, as Moses turns to discuss an institution which does not yet exist in Israel, but is common in the ancient Near East. The anticipated request is couched in terms of having "a king ... like all the nations." In the context of Deuteronomy, wanting to do anything "like the nations" cannot be a good thing. However, it is important to differentiate having a king, which seems, in itself, to be a neutral proposition, and having a king "like all the nations," which is self-evidently *not* a good thing. Ancient Near Eastern kingship usually claimed both divine origin and unconstrained divine authority (the king's word *was* law), which quite clearly could not be allowed to happen within the covenant people of Israel.[385] The focus then is not on the unacceptability of having any king, but on the foolishness of mimicking the nations.[386]

Foundationally, the impulse to "set a king over me" must be subjected to Yahweh's lordship over his people. Like the place to which they must go to worship, the king must be God's appointment. This king is set apart from the beginning because he is "the king the Lord your God chooses."

---

[385] See the helpful discussion of kingship in the ancient world in John H. Walton, *Ancient Near Eastern Thought and the Old Testament* (Grand Rapids: Baker, 2006), 278–86.

[386] It is worth noting that despite the claims that Deuteronomy is closely modeled on an international treaty, Yahweh is not named as Israel's King until the Blessing of Moses in 33:5. This weakens the likelihood that the anticipated request for a king here is a rejection of Yahweh as king. This becomes explicit in 1 Samuel but is not so here.

This basic differentiation from other kings is then filled out in detail in the verses which follow.

The parameters within which this divinely appointed king will operate begin with the assertion that the king is to be chosen "from your brothers." The rest of Moses's description will make clear that the king is to be (and must remain) a "brother," that is, a faithful member of Yahweh's people. This already precludes two things: (1) the king setting himself up above his people (and regarding himself as above "the law," and by extension Yahweh himself), and (2) being a foreigner, which here is less a matter of ethnicity and more an emphatic assertion that the king must be part of *Yahweh's people.*

Part of the underlying concern of these prescriptions is exactly that which shaped chapters 1–3: God's people must press forward in obedience, rather than going back to Egypt, either literally or metaphorically. This is reflected in verse 16: "However, he must not acquire many horses for himself or send the people back to Egypt to acquire many horses, for the LORD has told you, 'You are never to go back that way again.' "[387] Deliberately building military strength and making dubious alliances with neighboring powers, whether with Egypt or anyone else, is ruled out as incompatible with trust in Yahweh, the God who rescued them from Egypt. In the rest of the Old Testament, any dalliance with Egypt in particular is a sign that all is not well with either the king or the kingdom. God's king and people are to live in dependence on Yahweh alone, not on either their own strength or the comforting strength of other nations around them. This leads naturally to the prohibition of verse 17.

Yahweh's king must not "acquire many wives for himself." Three overlapping concerns lie behind this. The first is the simplest: the king is not to become self-indulgent in any area (see also v. 17b), particularly that of sexuality (the same rules apply to the king as to the rest of the brotherhood of Israel). Second, he is not to follow the contemporary pattern of using marriage as a mechanism to forge political alliances with surrounding nations (as, for example, Solomon was to do with the daughter of Pharaoh in 1 Kgs 3:1, and subsequently with many others, 1 Kgs 11:1–7).[388] The final reason for rejecting this royal version of polygamy is simply "so that his heart won't go astray." The implication is that

[387] This may be an allusion to Exod 14:13; see also Deut 28:68.

[388] It is also possible that providing an heir is in view, but I think this is less likely.

these "many women" will include those who worship other gods and, in an extension of the principle applied so rigorously in chapters 12–14, there is no place for close relationships with those who worship false gods among any of God's people, let along the king.

The focus on the king's "heart" is an important one. In Hebrew anthropology, the "heart" is the seat of our decisions, affections, and commitments. For one's "heart" to go astray is not simply to be swayed emotionally; it is to undergo a complete change in allegiance or transfer of loyalty.[389] The heart of the king is particularly important, as is reflected in the narrative of David's anointing and rise (see 1 Sam 10:9; 13:14; 16:7).

In the same way that power and sex are alluring dangers, so too is money, as is stated in verse 17b: "He must not acquire very large amounts of silver and gold for himself" (see also 8:13–14). The king must trust Yahweh, not his fortune. In Moses's discussion, it quickly becomes apparent that the king chosen by Yahweh is to be unlike any other king ever seen anywhere!

The radically different nature of the kingship anticipated by Moses is underlined in 17:18–20. On ascending to the throne, the new king's first act is no less surprising than what we have already seen: he is to "write a copy of this instruction [torah] for himself on a scroll."[390] The act of writing out Deuteronomy by hand is not simply to be a ceremonial statement. This priestly certified (and therefore accurate) copy is to provide the perpetual template and reference point both for the nation and for the reign of the king.[391] So important is this copy of the torah, that "it is to remain with him, and he is to read from it all the days of his life" (17:19). Keeping it on his person (or at least in a readily accessible place) at all times and devoting himself to reading it (probably reciting it aloud) regularly for the rest of his life will have the effect of enabling the king to be *the* model Israelite, "that he may learn to fear the Lord his God, to observe all the words of this instruction, and to do these statutes."[392] The

---

[389] See the discussion in my *Changed into His Likeness*, 32–50.

[390] There is much discussion of what "this torah" refers to. The simplest solution, in my view, is that it refers to the speeches of Moses in their entirety (i.e., essentially the book of Deuteronomy).

[391] As is often noted, "Deuteronomy" is derived from a (mis)translation of this verse as a "second law." It is not certain just what was to be copied out. Given the normal reference of *tôrâ* in Deuteronomy, the most natural reading is the entirety of Moses's sermon.

[392] A similar instruction is given to Joshua (Josh 1:8).

king's response to the words of Yahweh is precisely what is expected of the people. Once more, we see that this king is to be the model Israelite.[393]

It is impossible to overemphasize the importance of this king modeling humble obedience. That is underlined in verse 20: "Then his heart will not be exalted above his countrymen" (8:14). The king's heart is not to be "turned aside" or now "lifted up." Idolatry and arrogance are the twin temptations that the king must resist at all times.[394] However, if the king listens to the word of Yahweh to him through his personal scroll, "he will not turn from this command to the right or the left" (also 5:31–32). Should the king live like this, then there is every reason to expect that God's people might flourish under him (and his descendants) for many years.[395]

18:1–8. At the beginning of chapter 18, Moses returns to discuss the "Levitical priests" (or "the priests who are Levites"). There is much discussion about Deuteronomy's predilection for this description (already seen in 10:8–9). In 18:1, Moses underlines his theological concerns. Given that the location of the sanctuary has not yet been chosen, with the emphasis falling firmly on Yahweh's *right* to choose, it should not come as a surprise that the focus is not on priestly functions. Rather, the Mosaic emphasis is on the role of the tribe of Levi as a whole within his vision of God's people living happily under his rule in his land. This passage (unlike Numbers) pays no attention to the distinctions within the tribe, but rather to the function the tribe plays in this theological world.[396] Hence the headline statement of 18:1–2: "The Levitical priests, the whole tribe of Levi, will

---

[393] Desi Alexander suggests that Jesus quotes extensively from Deuteronomy in his interactions with the devil in Matt 4 as evidence that he is the ultimate messiah (personal communication).

[394] I would argue that these twin concerns explain the evaluation of all the kings of Israel from Saul onwards. David is the ideal king and the measure against which all later kings are assessed, not because he is perfect, but because in these two areas (devotion to Yahweh, not idols, and a humble commitment to his brothers, rather than self-promotion), he is consistently faithful to Yahweh and his covenant and can even at points claim (and be acclaimed) to be "blameless."

[395] This is a foundational text that provides the theological foundation of the critique of the kings of Israel and Judah, beginning in 1 Samuel and stretching through to the end of 2 Kings (see, e.g., the appraisal of Solomon in 1 Kgs 10:23–11:8). However, it is important to notice that there are elements of this prescription that are strangely not emphasized in the later narratives (lifting up one's heart only appears in 2 Kgs 14:10 in a message sent from Jehoash of Israel to Amaziah of Judah, and no king is ever said to have copied out the torah). It makes most sense to read these words as the prescient warning of Moses, rather than a neatly crafted piece of "Deuteronomistic" reverse engineering.

[396] Although according to 10:6 and 31:25, Moses is clearly aware of the distinctions.

have no portion or inheritance with Israel. ... The Lord is his inheritance, as he promised him."

Although not dealing with leadership directly like the preceding verses, the tribe of Levi clearly occupies a visibly significant place in the life of the nation. Their dependence on God through the generosity of the other tribes, and their share in what is set aside for Yahweh himself (so v. 1b: "They will eat the Lord's food offerings; that is their inheritance"), is a clear and present statement that the nation belongs to God, is accountable to God, and was called and created for the enjoyment of God. In inviting Levi to "sit at his table," Yahweh reminds Israel of the very purpose of their calling.[397]

In the present context, this grand vision of what it means to be a nation in covenant with Yahweh relativizes all other leaders (even the king), making all leaders both accountable to and representative of the rule of God.

The significance of this living, breathing symbolism is emphasized by the detailed description of the parts of any sacrifice to be made by fire (probably the fellowship offering) that are available to the Levites: the priests are to be given the shoulder, jaws (better, "cheeks"), and stomach (18:3).[398] Prized cuts of meat are to be accompanied by the "firstfruits" of both the staple produce of the nation (grain, new wine, and olive oil as in Num 18:12–13) and any wool produced. The "firstfruits" are not simply the earliest batches of produce, but part of the best of the harvest, to be offered when production is at its optimum. Typically, Moses makes no comment on any such practicalities (e.g., how this system actually operates): his focus is firmly on the theological message enshrined at the heart of the nation by the existence and life of Levi.

Moses is particularly concerned to ensure that the role and life of the Levites is preserved permanently. This is not an optional extra for God's people. The language of verse 5 is strong: "For the Lord your God has chosen him and his sons from all your tribes to stand and minister in his name from now on." The final phrase is literally "for all the days." Levi is to be a perpetual, permanent reminder that God's goal in giving them the land is actually to give them himself. This, in turn, means that no one can be allowed to play power games with the priesthood or the priestly tribe.

---

[397] So Block, *Deuteronomy*, 427.

[398] This is slightly different from Lev 7:32–34, which assigns the breast and one thigh to the priests serving at the tent. The concerns of Deuteronomy are much broader, dealing with the entire tribe of Levi.

Moses insists on the right of *any* Levite to participate in the life of the cult at the place chosen by God. While the majority of Levites at any moment will be living at home (in a Levitical "city," v. 6), they must not be excluded from their right. Despite any existing rostering arrangements, any Levite has the right to serve alongside "all his fellow Levites who minister there in the presence of the Lord." There is no such thing as a second-class Levite! Nor is there to be any attempt to restrict access to the provision generated from the sacrificial system: "They will eat equal portions besides what he has received from the sale of the family estate" (17:8).

The allusion to the proceeds of a "sale of the family estate" may seem slightly strange given the fact that the Levites are landless. However, it is important to remember that Levites still had homes and personal property in urban settlements, which presumably, over time, would have meant houses being sold and resources shared out in order to allow successive generations to provide homes for their families.[399]

While this material is slightly unexpected at this point in the collection of laws, it displays many of the key convictions that have undergirded the discussion of leadership among God's people so far. The overriding concern of the discussion is to make a theological point: Yahweh himself stands at the center of the people, and he is both the ultimate leader and the ultimate goal of their life together. The role of the Levites then is a perpetual reminder that ultimately, Israel has only one leader and only one God.

18:9–14. The discussion of the symbolical role of the Levitical priests among God's people prompts a series of fresh warnings against mimicking the "detestable customs" of the nations (building on 12:29–31). Yet again, the concerns of this torah are focused not simply on legal (or even constitutional matters), but on the theological engine room of the life of God's people. God's self-giving kindness (as most recently expressed and embodied in the tribe of Levi) should lead to wholehearted obedience. They should learn from Yahweh and his commands (4:1; 5:1), not the practices of the nations.

Of course, it should be self-evident that copying the nations whose behavior is about to lead to God's judgment, expressed through the Israelite conquest, is a really bad idea. But Moses's view of human nature

---

[399] Jer 32:6–15 and 37:12 where Jeremiah (a priest) buys a field from a cousin is probably an example of this.

is dim enough to require regular repetition of even the most obvious theological principles. In verses 10–11, he then steps through a list of defining Canaanite customs: "No one among you is to sacrifice his son or daughter in the fire, practice divination, tell fortunes, interpret omens, practice sorcery, cast spells, consult a medium or a spiritist, or inquire of the dead." It is not easy to identify all of the prohibited activities with confidence (and there may well be significant overlap between them), but they clearly include child sacrifice (see 12:31, as well as Lev 18:21; 20:2–5; 2 Kgs 16:3; 17:17; 21:6; Jer 7:31–32; 19:1–13; 32:35; Ezek 16:20–21; 20:25–26, 31; 23:37, 39) and various attempts to extract special knowledge of the future. These included augury and divination, harnessing dark powers through sorcery and magic, and contacting the realm of the dead through necromancy.[400] Moses's verdict in 18:12 on those who act like this (as well as the acts themselves) is blunt: "Everyone who does these acts is detestable to the Lord." Repeating the "detestable" acts of the Canaanites is foolish in the extreme.[401]

In stark contrast, God's people must live God's way: "You must be blameless before the Lord your God" (18:13). The word "blameless" is often used of a flawless animal, fit for sacrifice to a holy God. The image is graphic and arresting. God's people must be "pure," with no gross blemishes marking their national life. The same epithet is applied to Noah (Gen 6:9) and Job (1:1), and both Abraham (Gen 17:1) and the nation of Israel as a whole (Josh 24:14) are called to live like this.

Despite the fact that these activities led to the judgment of the Canaanites, Moses anticipates that the Israelites, though called to be "blameless," may well be sucked into similar behavior, and so adds a final warning in verse 14. The Lord who has given them the land had not (lit.) "given them to do this." Rather, they should devote themselves to listening to and living for the God who speaks and invites them to live in relationship with him in this land. Once more, Moses the preacher shapes the way in which Moses the lawgiver speaks!

---

400 See excellent discussion and bibliography on these verses in Block, *Deuteronomy*, 437.

401 G. Ernest Wright comments "Pagan magic is an abomination to God. His will cannot be learned, forced or coerced by it. He cannot be tricked into revelation. He will make himself known when and by the means that he himself chooses., i.e., by his herald the prophet, whose word shall be clearly spoken and clearly understood in contrast to the devious and mysterious world of the occult." G. Ernest Wright, "Deuteronomy" in *The Interpreter's Bible*, ed. George Arthur Buttrick et al., vol. 2 (New York: Abingdon, 1953), 311–37, 447.

18:15–22. In 18:15, the flow of legislation takes another unexpected turn when Moses announces that "The Lord your God will raise up for you a prophet like me from among your own brothers." The word "prophet" is placed first in the sentence in Hebrew, making the transition even more emphatic. It is important to understand that while on the one hand, this section is completely unprecedented—there is no similar prediction anywhere else in the Pentateuch—yet on the other hand, Moses himself states that this is a natural development of his ministry (and the request of the people) at Horeb.[402]

The goal of such a prophetic ministry is to enable people to "listen" to the words of God. As Moses looks to the future and life in the land, the key challenge before the people of Yahweh is to continue to listen (as made so clear in, e.g., 6:4–5). Now Moses states that future listening will need a future "Moses" to speak God's word to the people. This rich vein of thought is laid out in 18:16–18.

The same principle that was operative at Horeb is applied to the future provision of a Mosaic Prophet. Back on the mountain, the people said (v. 16): "Let us not continue to hear the voice of the Lord our God or see this great fire any longer, so that we will not die!"(cf. 5:22). They realized that they needed an intermediary to enable them to receive and embrace the word of Yahweh. Looking back to these events, God himself affirms the wisdom in their words (18:17) and affirms his intention to provide a similar figure in the future. In typically Deuteronomic fashion, the words spoken at Horeb are taken as a timeless statement applying to "today" at Moab, and also future "todays" in the land. Yahweh's response is to promise a repeat of the events of Horeb, with a new Moses speaking his words—so verse 18: "I will raise up for them a prophet like you from among their brothers. I will put my words in his mouth, and he will tell them everything I command him."

This is a truly astonishing promise. Nowhere else in Deuteronomy is it envisaged that there will be a repeat of the formative and foundational events of Horeb. This comparison suggests that this figure (and it is best taken as an individual) will come at a decisive moment in the life of God's people and presumably have a similar impact to the events of the

[402] In Gen 20:7, Abraham is called a prophet by God in his appearance to Abimelech. Num 12:6 and Deut 13:1, 5 allow the existence of prophets. In Exod 7:1, Aaron is called a prophet, acting in support of the God-like ministry of Moses, and in Exod 15:20 Miriam is referred to as a prophetess, but nowhere is there anything quite like this statement.

exodus and Horeb.[403] The words of this prophet must be treated in the same way as those of Moses: as the very words of Yahweh (so v. 19: "I will hold accountable whoever does not listen to my words that he speaks in my name"). It is worth noting that no one in the Old Testament comes close to matching this description, which eventually finds its fulfillment in the Lord Jesus Christ.[404]

The promise of such a significant one to come clearly opens up the question of how he is to be identified. How will the people recognize this prophet (or conversely, when someone claiming to be this figure or another messenger from God is a charlatan)? The consequences of anyone simply *claiming* to have this kind of authority are severe: this kind of presumption, whether arising from an attempt to co-opt Yahweh's approval or from idolatry, means that "that prophet must die" (as in 17:12–13). But how is this to be discerned or determined (18:21)? The test is straightforward: according to 18:22, if the message is or comes true, then the prophet is the real deal. If he speaks falsely (or in the name of another god) however, he is to be killed. Such is the weight of responsibility of claiming to speak with God's authority.

Moses's words here lay the foundation for the Old Testament understanding of prophecy (see, e.g., Jer 28:1–17 and the demise of the false prophet Hananiah). Somewhat surprisingly, however, the idea of a prophet like Moses to come does not figure large in the rest of the Old Testament (which once more suggests that this is an ancient text, rather than reverse-engineered to suit the purposes of Josiah or the exiles).[405] Nor is there any clear evidence that this text was understood to provide a procession of such people through Israelite history. However, in later texts from Qumran and elsewhere, there is a clear expectation that God

---

[403] Some have argued that the sense of "raise up" here is distributive and suggests that a succession of prophets are in mind. This is not persuasive, and it is best to take these verses as referring to an individual.

[404] See in particular Acts 3:18–24; 7:37–38, as well as the references to "the Prophet" in John 1:45; 6:14; 7:40 and Matthew's depiction of Jesus as the new Moses throughout his Gospel. See Grant R. Osborne, *Matthew*, Zondervan Exegetical Commentary on the New Testament (Grand Rapids: Zondervan, 2010) 1089–90; also Dale W. Allison, *The New Moses: A Matthean Typology* (Repr., Eugene: Wipf & Stock, 2013), especially 73–84.

[405] Although see Christopher R. Seitz, "Prophet Moses and the Canonical Shape of Jeremiah," *ZAW* 1 (1989): 3–27. Seitz argues that Jer 1 identifies Jeremiah as a prophet like Moses and that this shapes his ministry. His argument has merit but isn't completely persuasive.

will send an individual who meets these criteria.[406] In Acts 3:33 and 7:37, Jesus is identified explicitly as being this figure, and the fulfillment of this promise given through Moses.

Bridge

The vision of the beautiful life of God embodied in his people living in righteousness (including “righteous justice”) in the land is a compelling one. As he puts flesh on the longed-for situation of 4:5–8, where the surrounding nations gasp at their quality of life, and especially their justice system, it is not hard to see the way Moses is seeking to motivate God’s people to obey. Like Jesus in the Sermon on the Mount, he lays out a compellingly attractive picture of the godly life. But just like Matthew 5–7, the realization of the vision ultimately depends on a radically different leader to bring it to fulfillment.

In the middle of the slightly mundane description of judges, officials, and priests, two figures stand out: the king and the “prophet like Moses.” In both cases, the envisaged figure is dramatically different from anyone who follows in the pages of the Old Testament. It is clear that if Israel were to have a king like this, everything would be very different. The king is to be humble, single-minded, and above all, godly. The future prophet is likewise to be peerless: his revelation of God’s plans and intentions will far exceed anything that has been seen before. When this prophet shows up, nothing can ever be quite the same again.

There is little to suggest that Moses realized that these two sketches are actually of the same person: the Lord Jesus Christ, the one whose single-minded devotion and staggering humility are like no other, the one of whom God said, “This is my Son: listen to him.” He is the one in whom this life is not only embodied, but in whom we too can share in the reality Moses could only describe.

6. Death as the Ultimate Sanction (19:1–22:12)

> 1 “When the Lord your God annihilates the nations whose land he is
> giving you, so that you drive them out and live in their cities and hous-
> es, 2 you are to set apart three cities for yourselves within the land
> the Lord your God is giving you to possess. 3 You are to determine the
> distances and divide the land the Lord your God is granting you as an

---

406 See, e.g., the “Teacher of Righteousness” in 1QpHab 8:2–3 and *i*.

inheritance into three regions, so that anyone who commits manslaughter can flee to these cities.

4 “Here is the law concerning a case of someone who kills a person and flees there to save his life, having killed his neighbor accidentally without previously hating him: 5 If, for example, he goes into the forest with his neighbor to cut timber, and his hand swings the ax to chop down a tree, but the blade flies off the handle and strikes his neighbor so that he dies, that person may flee to one of these cities and live. 6 Otherwise, the avenger of blood in the heat of his anger might pursue the one who committed manslaughter, overtake him because the distance is great, and strike him dead. Yet he did not deserve to die, since he did not previously hate his neighbor. 7 This is why I am commanding you to set apart three cities for yourselves. 8 If the LORD your God enlarges your territory as he swore to your ancestors, and gives you all the land he promised to give them—9 provided you keep every one of these commands I am giving you today and follow them, loving the LORD your God and walking in his ways at all times—you are to add three more cities to these three. 10 In this way, innocent blood will not be shed, and you will not become guilty of bloodshed in the land the LORD your God is giving you as an inheritance. 11 But if someone hates his neighbor, lies in ambush for him, attacks him, and strikes him fatally, and flees to one of these cities, 12 the elders of his city are to send for him, take him from there, and hand him over to the avenger of blood and he will die. 13 Do not look on him with pity but purge from Israel the guilt of shedding innocent blood, and you will prosper.

14 “Do not move your neighbor’s boundary marker, established at the start in the inheritance you will receive in the land the LORD your God is giving you to possess.

15 “One witness cannot establish any iniquity or sin against a person, whatever that person has done. A fact must be established by the testimony of two or three witnesses.

16 “If a malicious witness testifies against someone accusing him of a crime, 17 the two people in the dispute are to stand in the presence of the LORD before the priests and judges in authority at that time. 18 The judges are to make a careful investigation, and if the witness turns out to be a liar who has falsely accused his brother, 19 you must do to him as he intended to do to his brother. You must purge the evil from you. 20 Then everyone else will hear and be afraid, and they will never again do anything evil like this among you. 21 Do not show pity: life for life, eye for eye, tooth for tooth, hand for hand, and foot for foot.

20:1 “When you go out to war against your enemies and see horses, chariots, and an army larger than yours, do not be afraid of them, for the LORD your God, who brought you out of the land of Egypt, is with you. 2 When

you are about to engage in battle, the priest is to come forward and
address the army. [3] He is to say to them, 'Listen, Israel: Today you are
about to engage in battle with your enemies. Do not be cowardly. Do
not be afraid, alarmed, or terrified because of them. [4] For the LORD your
God is the one who goes with you to fight for you against your enemies
to give you victory.'

[5] "The officers are to address the army, 'Has any man built a new house
and not dedicated it? Let him leave and return home. Otherwise, he may
die in battle and another man dedicate it. [6] Has any man planted a vineyard and not begun to enjoy its fruit? Let him leave and return home.
Otherwise he may die in battle and another man enjoy its fruit. [7] Has
any man become engaged to a woman and not married her? Let him
leave and return home. Otherwise he may die in battle and another
man marry her.' [8] The officers will continue to address the army and
say, 'Is there any man who is afraid or cowardly? Let him leave and
return home, so that his brothers won't lose heart as he did.' [9] When the
officers have finished addressing the army, they will appoint military
commanders to lead it.

[10] "When you approach a city to fight against it, make an offer of
peace. [11] If it accepts your offer of peace and opens its gates to you, all
the people found in it will become forced laborers for you and serve
you. [12] However, if it does not make peace with you but wages war
against you, lay siege to it. [13] When the LORD your God hands it over
to you, strike down all its males with the sword. [14] But you may take
the women, dependents, animals, and whatever else is in the city—all
its spoil—as plunder. You may enjoy the spoil of your enemies that
the LORD your God has given you. [15] This is how you are to treat all the
cities that are far away from you and are not among the cities of these
nations. [16] However, you must not let any living thing survive among
the cities of these people the LORD your God is giving you as an inheritance. [17] You must completely destroy them—the Hethite, Amorite,
Canaanite, Perizzite, Hivite, and Jebusite—as the LORD your God has
commanded you, [18] so that they won't teach you to do all the detestable acts they do for their gods, and you sin against the LORD your God.

[19] "When you lay siege to a city for a long time, fighting against it in
order to capture it, do not destroy its trees by putting an ax to them,
because you can get food from them. Do not cut them down. Are
trees of the field human, to come under siege by you? [20] But you may
destroy the trees that you know do not produce food. You may cut
them down to build siege works against the city that is waging war
against you, until it falls.

[21:1] "If a murder victim is found lying in a field in the land the LORD your
God is giving you to possess, and it is not known who killed him, [2] your

elders and judges are to come out and measure the distance from the
victim to the nearby cities. [3] The elders of the city nearest to the victim
are to get a young cow that has not been yoked or used for work. [4] The
elders of that city will bring the cow down to a continually flowing
stream, to a place not tilled or sown, and they will break its neck there
by the stream. [5] Then the priests, the sons of Levi, will come forward,
for the LORD your God has chosen them to serve him and pronounce
blessings in his name, and they are to give a ruling in every dispute
and case of assault. [6] All the elders of the city nearest to the victim will
wash their hands by the stream over the young cow whose neck has
been broken. [7] They will declare, 'Our hands did not shed this blood;
our eyes did not see it. [8] LORD, wipe away the guilt of your people Israel
whom you redeemed, and do not hold the shedding of innocent blood
against them.' Then the responsibility for bloodshed will be wiped away
from them. [9] You must purge from yourselves the guilt of shedding
innocent blood, for you will be doing what is right in the LORD's sight.

[10] "When you go to war against your enemies and the LORD your God
hands them over to you and you take some of them prisoner, and [11] if
you see a beautiful woman among the captives, desire her, and want to
take her as your wife, [12] you are to bring her into your house. She is to
shave her head, trim her nails, [13] remove the clothes she was wearing
when she was taken prisoner, live in your house, and mourn for her
father and mother a full month. After that, you may have sexual relations with her and be her husband, and she will be your wife. [14] Then
if you are not satisfied with her, you are to let her go where she wants,
but you must not sell her or treat her as merchandise, because you
have humiliated her.

[15] "If a man has two wives, one loved and the other neglected, and both
the loved and the neglected bear him sons, and if the neglected wife
has the firstborn son, [16] when that man gives what he has to his sons
as an inheritance, he is not to show favoritism to the son of the loved
wife as his firstborn over the firstborn of the neglected wife. [17] He must
acknowledge the firstborn, the son of the neglected wife, by giving him
two shares of his estate, for he is the firstfruits of his virility; he has
the rights of the firstborn.

[18] "If a man has a stubborn and rebellious son who does not obey his
father or mother and doesn't listen to them even after they discipline
him, [19] his father and mother are to take hold of him and bring him to
the elders of his city, to the gate of his hometown. [20] They will say to
the elders of his city, 'This son of ours is stubborn and rebellious; he
doesn't obey us. He's a glutton and a drunkard.' [21] Then all the men of
his city will stone him to death. You must purge the evil from you, and
all Israel will hear and be afraid.

[22] "If anyone is found guilty of an offense deserving the death penalty and is executed, and you hang his body on a tree, [23] you are not to leave his corpse on the tree overnight but are to bury him that day, for anyone hung on a tree is under God's curse. You must not defile the land the Lord your God is giving you as an inheritance.

[22:1] "If you see your brother Israelite's ox or sheep straying, do not ignore it; make sure you return it to your brother. [2] If your brother does not live near you or you don't know him, you are to bring the animal to your home to remain with you until your brother comes looking for it; then you can return it to him. [3] Do the same for his donkey, his garment, or anything your brother has lost and you have found. You must not ignore it. [4] If you see your brother's donkey or ox fallen down on the road, do not ignore it; help him lift it up.

[5] "A woman is not to wear male clothing, and a man is not to put on a woman's garment, for everyone who does these things is detestable to the Lord your God.

[6] "If you come across a bird's nest with chicks or eggs, either in a tree or on the ground along the road, and the mother is sitting on the chicks or eggs, do not take the mother along with the young. [7] You may take the young for yourself, but be sure to let the mother go free, so that you may prosper and live long. [8] If you build a new house, make a railing around your roof, so that you don't bring bloodguilt on your house if someone falls from it. [9] Do not plant your vineyard with two types of seed; otherwise, the entire harvest, both the crop you plant and the produce of the vineyard, will be defiled. [10] Do not plow with an ox and a donkey together. [11] Do not wear clothes made of both wool and linen. [12] Make tassels on the four corners of the outer garment you wear."

19:1–14. At the beginning of chapter 19, there seems to be an abrupt shift of focus from leadership to dealing with death in the community. It may be that Moses is picking up on matters of "righteous judgment," introduced back in chapter 17. However, this is one of the places where a Decalogue structure is most compelling, as it would account for the transition from a discussion of authority figures (fifth commandment) to that of killing (sixth commandment).

While it is true to say that this collection of laws becomes less ordered as we make our way through chapters 12–26, there is a still a clear thread linking the material in this section, as Moses deals with safeguards and stipulations around justified (and unjustified) killing, whether carried out by armies or individuals, in a time of war or peace.

The translation "When the Lord your God *annihilates* the nations" in 19:1 (see also 12:29) is a little unfortunate. The verb is simply "to cut," which can have a wide range of meanings but does not necessitate using such a strong word in English. The author's intention does not seem to be to make any particular statement about the nature of the conquest at this point, but simply to point forward to the days when Israel has taken over the land.[407]

In Deuteronomy, cities of refuge take on a significant theological role. In the same way that the tribe of Levi functions as a reminder that God himself is their inheritance, these cities are a concrete reminder that God is the guarantor of their peace.

As in 4:41–43, Moses names three such cities—not this time in the Transjordan, but carefully located in the northern, central, and southern parts of the land (19:1–3; Josh 20:7). The provision of such places has, from the beginning, tempered the legislation around killing with mercy (see Exod 21:12–14, which enunciates the principle without naming any places, and the much fuller discussion in Num 35:9–34, which focuses on the evidence). The mathematical precision with which they are to be operated according to verse 3 is a further expression of the mercy of Yahweh: "You are to determine the distances and divide the land the Lord your God is granting you as an inheritance into three regions, so that anyone who commits manslaughter can flee to these cities." This ensures every citizen has roughly equal access to these safe places. The phrase translated "determine the distances" is literally "prepare for yourself the road," which may refer to creating the routes, rather than simply mapping them out.[408]

This does, of course, raise the question of when an individual can make use of this provision, which Moses answers with an extended worked example in verses 4–7. The key principle in verse 4 is contained in the final phrase: "without previously hating him." Moses is addressing causing someone's death "without malice aforethought." The way in which this provision is introduced (וְזֶה דְּבַר) is highly unusual, probably highlighting the extremely limited scope of these provisions. Moses's almost conversational approach continues in verse 5, as he specifies the kind of incident he has in mind: "If, for example, he goes into the forest with his neighbor to cut timber, and his hand swings the ax to chop down a tree,

---

[407] See the extended discussion in *DCH* 288.6.53 of the possible meanings of כָּרַת.

[408] P. E. Dion, "Deuteronomy 9:13: Prepare the Way or Estimate the Distance?" *Eglise et théologie* 25 (1994): 333–41.

but the blade flies off the handle and strikes his neighbor so that he dies, that person may flee to one of these cities and live." No detail is given regarding how long he can stay.[409] The point is simply that he is safe.

One may be forgiven for thinking that this kind of industrial accident can hardly have been common (and certainly not common enough to warrant the development of case law!). But this is a misunderstanding of the nature of the Mosaic torah. Moses here, as everywhere, is painting a picture of a rich and righteous life in God's land, which extends to the protection of those involved in tragic accidents.

Such protections, however, are not theoretical. There is a very real danger, according to verse 6 that "the avenger of blood" (lit., "redeemer" of blood) might visit revenge on the unfortunate axman "in the heat of his anger." There is no discussion of this "avenger/redeemer" might be or of how a person might be designated as such.[410] The focus is instead on the fact that the cities of refuge create the opportunity for a cooling off period for those in hot pursuit. For this proposal to work, however, it is imperative that every Israelite live close enough to safety to enable him to find refuge before he is overtaken "because the distance is great." Taking revenge on the fugitive would clearly be unjust for, as verse 7 restates, "he did not previously hate his neighbor." The rationale behind the establishment of these cities is clear.

Looking ahead, Moses anticipates that this provision of places of refuge will need to be expanded to ensure that the "accessibility principle" continues to be met. Verses 8–9 bring together the promises made to the patriarchs, the conquest of the land as a whole, and complete obedience in a fresh way and capture the Deuteronomic tension between idealism and realism (and unconditionality and conditionality) beautifully. If (and it is a real "if") God's people manage to deliver on wholehearted obedience, these three east bank cities of refuge will need to be augmented by three more. The reason for this is spelled out in verse 10: "In this way, innocent

---

[409] But according to Num 35:25, 28, 32; Josh 20:6, such a person would live in the city of refuge for the rest of his life or until the death of the high priest.

[410] Lundbom, *Deuteronomy*, 568, suggests that this is probably the next of kin. Tigay argues that to "redeem" here essentially carries the sense of "to rectify" by atoning for the death (*Deuteronomy*, 181). McConville highlights the possibility that the "redeemer's" role might actually be to the blood itself, rather than the deceased (*Deuteronomy*, 311). See also the article by Robert L. Hubbard, "גָּאַל"in *NIDOTTE* 1:789–94. It is hard to resolve this with any certainty.

blood will not be shed, and you will not become guilty of bloodshed" in Yahweh's land. The motivation behind this is more than simple justice: it is to prevent innocent bloodshed in the land, because this bloodguilt will impair Israel's relationship with God. For Moses, there is more at stake than fairness or even due process. Israel's relationship with Yahweh is intrinsically linked to the land, and unrighteousness in the land cannot but impair that relationship. However, there is no sign that these three extra cities were ever created, largely due to Israel's struggle to take the land, coupled with their tendency to defile the territory they had taken (see Judg 2:20–3:4).

The painful reality that such events will take place in Israel is highlighted further in the scenario described in verses 11–13, which is the antithesis of that in verses 5–7. In this case, there is no mistaking the motive: for this person "hates his neighbor." Nor is there any doubt that this is premeditated, according to verse 11, for he "lies in ambush for him" before inflicting a mortal wound and attempting to find sanctuary in one of these cities. In this case, any claim for protection is rendered null and void. Interestingly, the "elders of his city" (19:12) are to take the lead in recalling him and ensuring that justice is done.

As we have seen, there is no definitive demarcation of the various roles of those involved in the Israelite judicial system: judges, officials, priests, and elders all play their part at various times. The elders in particular are involved here, as well as in 21:1–9 (an unsolved murder); 21:18–21 (a rebellious son); 22:13–21 (a virgin who is exploited); and 25:5–10 (a male refusing to honor his family obligations).

In this case, the role of the elders involves "hand[ing] him over to the avenger of blood." The passive construction ("he will die") de-emphasizes the action of the avenger: this is to be understood as a necessary act of "righteous judgment" rather than as a simple act of revenge. This is reiterated in verse 13, which mirrors the thought of verse 11: this is not just a matter of ensuring justice for an individual, but rather of safeguarding the entire nation's relationship with Yahweh. Following this course of action is the only way to thrive with Yahweh in the land. Although there is (typically) no detail given on how this process is to be carried out, there can be no commuting of the sentence ("Do not look on him with pity") because Israel's very relationship with Yahweh is at stake: they must "purge from Israel the guilt of shedding innocent blood" if they are to flourish in the land.

This explains why stealing your neighbor's land by moving boundary markers is included here in verse 14 (see also 27:17; Job 24:2–4; Prov 22:28; 23:10; Hos 5:10). To interfere with the land of a fellow Israelite is so serious because the land is the context in which each individual enjoys his relationship with Yahweh. The foundational nature of this divine gift is captured in verse 14 by the statement that these boundaries were "established at the start in the inheritance you will receive in the land the LORD your God is giving you." While not a capital offence, this is, nonetheless, a profoundly serious matter among the people of Yahweh, who are called, above all, to righteousness.[411]

19:15–21. There is one further loose end to be dealt with before Moses moves on to the rules surrounding killing in the context of armed conflict: ensuring that evidence is weighed properly and is admissible, especially when dealing with the serious issues ("any iniquity or any sin") addressed in this section.[412] The primary goal here is not simply ensuring good process: it is the righteousness of the people of God in his land.

The threshold for relying on testimony is that it must be presented by "two or three witnesses" (19:15, which is cited in Matt 18:16; 2 Cor 13:1 and 1 Tim 5:19). The underlying principle is stated forcefully: "One witness cannot establish any iniquity or sin against a person, whatever that person has done." This bespeaks a very strong view of human sinfulness, which is clearly the main issue here. This needs to be factored into any reading of these chapters. Again, Moses's main concern is neither legal process nor retributive justice, but rather dealing with the problem of the human heart, here described in terms of the "iniquity or sin" that flows from it.

This awareness of our innate deceitfulness leads immediately to Moses's provision of a procedure for dealing with false accusations. In 19:16–17, a specific scenario is again presented as an example, in which "a malicious witness" (lit., a "witness of injustice") makes an accusation against an individual. The process to be followed is spelled out in verse 17: "The two people in the dispute are to stand in the presence of the LORD before the priests and judges in authority at that time." Two things jump out about this procedure: (1) the hearing is to take place explicitly

---

[411] Similar prohibitions are found in other ancient sources, including Hittite laws from around 1300 BC: see HL 168 *ANET*[3], 195.

[412] 17:6 deals with this requirement in capital cases. It now appears that all serious matters (of which capital crimes are just a subset) are to be dealt with like this.

in the presence of Yahweh. He "stands" in all these cases, as the ultimate judge of his people. (2) There is a familiar vagueness about the precise details of the legalities. This time, the case is to be heard by "the priests and judges in authority." There is a consistent looseness in this legislation (if it can even be called that), and Moses seems more concerned to assert Yahweh's authority (as the one who appoints priests and judges, including those mentioned in 17:8–13) than to clarify who should stand in which case, whether those appearing need to swear oaths or any other procedural detail.

If Moses seems slightly uninterested in the identity of the court officials, there is no lack of clarity around the way in which this case is to be conducted. This must be done with appropriate care and due diligence ("the judges are to make a careful investigation" of the allegations against the "brother," 19:18) and ensure proportionality in the sentence.

That the baseless allegations rebound on the perjurer is fascinating. On the one hand, it is explicitly said to "purge the evil" from the land of Israel, the phrase that is routinely used of actions that prevent the interruption of Yahweh's relationship with his people, preserving "righteous judgment" in the land. But it clearly also acts as a deterrent to such behavior. The punishment is not simply to be that for lying, but for committing whatever crime is alleged. The aim of this provision is clearly stated in verse 20: "Then everyone else will hear and be afraid, and they will never again do anything evil like this among you" (see 13:11; 17:13; 21:21) Things are to be different among the family of God.

The Deuteronomic version of the *lex talionis* in 19:21 *must*, then, be read in this context. Its inclusion at this point in the collection of laws adapts and deploys this common ancient Near Eastern adage (also Exod 21:23–25; Lev 24:18–20) to limit the damage done to the community by false accusations: "Do not show pity: life for life, eye for eye, tooth for tooth, hand for hand, and foot for foot." While this principle is a succinct expression of just proportionality, limiting and prescribing judicial sentences at the same time, here the focus is firmly on ensuring that Yahweh's people do not drift away from the high standards that their God has laid before them, particularly in the realms of truth and justice.

20:1–4. While it is clearly true that the war about to be waged by Israel is the most morally and theologically problematic feature of the book of Deuteronomy, Moses's discussion of the details of the prosecution of both this campaign and all subsequent wars in Israel really is surprisingly gentle and nuanced. The discussion of warfare, as we may have come to expect by now, starts not with logistics, but with theology, and in particular with the security and confidence which flows from fearing Yahweh alone.[413] It is the only extended discussion of warfare in the Old Testament.

In 20:1–4, the contours of faith are traced out in terms of not approaching battle on the basis of what can be seen. Numerical superiority (whether reckoned by "horses, chariots" or the sheer size of the opposing army) should not be allowed to outweigh the glorious fact that "the Lord your God, who brought you out of the land of Egypt, is with you." One of the key lessons of the exodus was that the God who was clearly present with his people would fight their battles for them (so Exod 14:14). Now this principle is extended to the conquest of the land (as in 1:21, 29–31; 7:17–21; 9:1–3; 31:3).

To underline this spiritual reality, just before hostilities the priest is to speak to the army. During the flight from Egypt, it was Moses himself who took the lead in directing, reassuring, and encouraging the people (the army here is clearly a "citizen army"). Now he envisages a different scenario, as the "priest" takes over theological leadership of the people. Once more, Moses's instructions are light on detail (there is no explanation of which priest, or how he is to be selected) because his concerns are inherently theological. Moses does, however, lay out exactly what the priest(s) should say at that moment, reminding them that there is no need to flinch or panic, for God will fight for his people.

According to verse 3, this "day" is another of those significant "todays" in the unfolding history of God's people according to Moses. At this moment, on the verge of conflict, as at all others, they are to "listen" and to trust God. The piling up of alternative reactions ("Do not be cowardly. Do not be afraid, alarmed, or terrified because of them") clearly suggests that there is a real danger of them wilting in the face of the powers arrayed against them. But there really is no need to panic. As in Exodus 14, according to verse 4 "the Lord your God is the one who goes with you to fight for you against your enemies to give you victory [lit., deliverance]." How could Israel be afraid? It is important to note that none of this gives Israel a license for expansionist aggression: God's undertaking is to stand with them and fight for them *against Canaan*. For more general instructions, we need to read on.

---

413 Although the word "fear" does not appear here, the thought is clearly similar to that of Deut 5:29; 6:2, 13, 24; 10:12, 20; 13:4; 14:23; 17:19.

20:5–9. That Moses turns to the subject of exemptions from military service at this point is surprising to say that least, as is the fact that it is the "officials" (see 1:15; 16:18; also 1 Chr 27:1; 2 Chr 26:11) who are to organize the army.[414] The conditions that allow for a man to step back from fighting (subsequent to the conquest itself) are as follows: (1) "Has any man built a new house and not dedicated it? Let him leave and return home" (20:5). A key part of the issue seems to be the man not having the opportunity to carry out the dedication step, which presumably strips him from the opportunity to be thankful to Yahweh.[415] This would seem like a minor thing compared to his possible death, but for Moses, it seems to be bound up in enjoying the good inheritance of Yahweh. (2) "Has any man planted a vineyard and not begun to enjoy its fruit? Let him leave and return home" (20:6). This seems to confirm the interpretation of verse 5: what is in view is the opportunity to enjoy the tangible blessing of God in the land. In this case, it also clarifies that we have shifted from the immediate context of the conquest to a wider discussion of the conduct of war (and the terms of conscription in Israel) more generally. Leviticus 19:23–25 lays down a five year process for vines reaching maturity, so this exemption could extend for quite some time. (3) "Has any man become engaged to a woman [lit., paid the bride-price] and not married her? Let him leave and return home" (20:7). This is the best known (and most easily understandable and transferrable) exemption. Each of the first three exemptions allows the individual to enjoy the good provisions of God in the land. This is more generous than any contemporary provision and is an expression of God's kindness. The fourth, however, is quite different. (4) Rather than investigating if anyone is being overzealous in his commitment to Yahweh, at the expense of enjoying his generosity, in 20:8 the officers are to test the motivation of the soldiers, asking "Is there any man who is afraid or cowardly?" Given what has already been said in 20:1–4, this isn't simply an inquiry into the emotional state of the troops but is essentially a matter of faith—or to be more accurate, a matter of the absence of the "fear of Yahweh." There is no discussion of how

---

[414] *HALOT* helpfully sets out the variety of meanings attached to this term, which seems to be a non-priestly, non-royal official (e.g., the Israelite foremen in Egypt as in Exod 5:6, 10, 14, 19).

[415] This is a very unusual idea, and the verb is scarcely used in the Old Testament. 1 Kgs 8:63 suggests it can mean "dedicate," but it also may simply denote "moving in." See also 28:30.

this matter is to be determined (presumably it is left to the conscience of the individual?), but if such a deficit is identified, "Let him leave and return home, so that his brothers won't lose heart as he did." Rather than protecting the ability of the individual to enjoy the goodness of God, this exception protects the morale of God's people, protecting the army from infectious and ungodly panic, and maintains their corporate ability to trust Yahweh when they are drawn into battle. It is only at this point that the prosecution of the campaign is handed over to the "military men" (v. 9).

20:10–20. The transition from the prosecution of the war of conquest to the situation once the nation is settled in the land, implicit in verses 5–9, is now made explicit in verses 10–20, which lay out the normal way in which the nation shall fight against other cities *after the conquest* (i.e., non-Canaanite cities). This is confirmed by the clarification in verses 18–20.

When the people of God become embroiled in a conflict at some point in the future, they are to follow a five step process: (1) they to offer the city terms of peace (שָׁלוֹם, probably in the sense of a "peace treaty" (20:10). (2) If accepted, they are to make the people their subjects, allowing them to "become forced laborers" and to serve them (as Joshua made a "peace treaty" with the Gibeonites in Josh 9). (3) if the city chooses to resist and fight, then Israel is to lay siege to it (as in, e.g., Ezek 4:2). (4) Given the fact that victory is a matter of course in a divinely sanctioned war (which would seem to imply that this is inherently a defensive act), they are to "strike down all its males with the sword." The males here are almost certainly the members of the army. There are to be no civilian casualties. However, the males are to be struck "to the mouth of the sword" (lit.). (5) God's people are to "take plunder" or "spoil." According to 20:14, they are to be allowed to take "the women, dependents, animals, and whatever else is in the city." They are to "enjoy" this spoil as a gift from Yahweh. This is fairly disturbing for most people today: the idea of one group of people owning others is a difficult one. However, it is important to remember that the way Israel is to treat captives is carefully circumscribed and is decidedly more benign than both usual ancient Near Eastern practice and the way that Israel has been treated by the nations in the land.[416]

---

[416] Block suggests that this whole discussion is moderated by its proximity to the *lex talionis* at the conclusion of the previous chapter. *Deuteronomy*, 467.

The distinction between these nations that may or may not be encountered and the Canaanites that they are about to encounter in the land is striking. 20:16–18 states baldly once again that the six nations listed (basically all the Canaanites) should be put to death as God has commanded on the basis of his judgment (Gen 15:16–20). Israel is to put an end to their evil (and dangerous) practices. The goal of these actions is to ensure that "they won't teach you to do all the detestable acts they do for their gods" (also 7:4; 12:29–31; 13; 18:12). These nations must not be allowed to assume the teaching role that belongs to Yahweh alone. However, if these stringent measures are not followed, then it is inevitable that Israel will "sin against the Lord." These instructions are deeply challenging, but it is important, however, to remember several things: (1) This is a one–off judgment of God, traced back to the sin of the Canaanites. (2) In the ancient world, an entire community sharing in the consequences of actions was completely comprehensible. (3) The text itself prohibits this being made a policy. These are extreme measures designed to safeguard the future of the people of God are striking for their carefully circumscribed scope. And (4) the same fate would befall an Israelite city that fell into idolatry (13:13–19).

The fact that God's people are never simply let loose to wage war as they see fit (and certainly not with divine sanction for whatever measures they deem necessary to win) is underlined by the unexpectedly humanitarian measures of 20:19–20. When cities are being besieged (presumably even in Canaan), there is to be no scorched-earth policy. In particular, Moses says, "Do not destroy its trees by putting an ax to them." The reason for this is not primarily ecological. However, the fact that they are a valuable source of food (which often require both time and care to bring them to the point of bearing fruit), coupled with the theological rationale that they are not accountable to God for their actions (so v. 19: "Are trees of the field human, to come under siege by you?"), means that they should not be cut down. No such ban applies to non-fruit-bearing trees, whose wood may be used in mounting a successful siege against the enemy.

Once more, the rhetorical nature of these chapters comes to the fore. Speaking of the trees in this way highlights both the wickedness of the Canaanites, who stand under the judgment of Yahweh, and the radically different way in which God's people must conduct themselves in every other circumstance—even when they themselves come under threat—for it is their role to demonstrate the calm attractiveness of the beautiful life with Yahweh. [417]

21:1–9. At the beginning of chapter 21, Moses turns from warfare to the rules surrounding an unsolved murder within the land.[418] At first glance, this seems like a rather clunky transition. However, once it is recognized that his main concern is not *primarily* with judicial or investigative processes (like identifying the culprit, for example), but rather with ensuring that the people's relationship with God is not interrupted by the "shedding of innocent blood," which is made clear at the end of the unit in 21:8–9. Moses's main focus is theological, not legal: God's people must understand that their relationship with God is built on the need for atonement and forgiveness.

When a corpse is discovered (presumably stabbed), and there is no obvious explanation of what has happened, a series of precise steps is to be followed.[419] Initially, "your elders and judges are to come out and measure the distance from the victim to the nearby cities" (21:2). This is typically vague, but as events unfold, it becomes clear that the "elders" here include representatives from any settlement in the vicinity, along with appointed "judges," whose role is to settle any arguments over which city is closest (and therefore responsible), and to ensure that internal conflict does not develop within the nation. It is then the responsibility of the elders of the settlement closest to the spot where the body is discovered to oversee the judicial process, and also to perform a ritual, which is described in verses 3–8.[420]

There are several surprising features of this ritual: it does not seem to be a sacrifice "proper" (particularly since no blood is shed) and it is to be performed instantly (by implication) and locally (at the nearest stream).[421] This underlines that such rituals (including all sacrifices)

---

[417] Block argues that v. 20 should not be read as a question, but as a statement, which simply insists that humanity *depends on* the trees for food. It is then simply a reminder not to "bite the hand that feeds you." This is plausible, but not completely conclusive. *Deuteronomy*, 479.

[418] This law is unique in the Old Testament.

[419] Lundbom points out that the verb clearly means "stabbed" in Gen 34:25–27 and Num 19:16 (*Deuteronomy*, 592). Also Tigay, *Deuteronomy*, 191.

[420] McConville (*Deuteronomy*, 328) helpfully suggests that once the measuring is done and responsibility allocated, the judges step back.

[421] For a comprehensive discussion of the problems raised, see Tigay, "Excursus 19: The Ceremony of the Broken-necked Heifer" in *Deuteronomy*, 472–76.

speak to the willingness of God to find a way to forgive. They operate on a principle of *grace*, where God accepts an action in the place of the actual payment. In that sense, all such rituals are simply an anticipation of the one true sacrifice to come, the Lord Jesus Christ and illustrate the many facets of his work for us.

This ritual centers on "a young cow that has not been yoked or used for work" (21:3; also Num 19:1–10). That the young heifer has not yet been put to work may imply that it is unblemished and may also mean that it is easier to kill by a blow to the neck or head (implied by v. 5). The location is unusual: the elders are to go to "a continually flowing stream, to a place not tilled or sown." The choice of virgin country with a river (rather than a seasonal wadi) running through it in 21:4 may well be intended to allude to Eden, the archetypal place where God enjoyed fellowship with his "people," Adam and Eve.[422] The land is the context of Yahweh's relationship with Israel, and nothing must be allowed to sully that relationship.

In this ritual, no blood is to be shed, which is why the neck of the animal is to be broken. This is not a sacrifice per se (as in Exod 13:13), which explains why there is no need to go to the place chosen by Yahweh. However covenantal ideas are still prominent.

The Levites are front and center, as verse 5 makes clear: "Then the priests, the sons of Levi, will come forward, for the Lord your God has chosen them to serve him and pronounce blessings in his name, and they are to give a ruling in every dispute and case of assault." Their combined role here seems slightly awkward. On the one hand, they are the tribe charged with blessing the nation (as in Num 6:24–26), which places them in the position of ensuring that matters are resolved, so that the relationship between God and people is not disrupted. To our eyes, on the other hand, the responsibility granted to the priests to rule on "every dispute and case of assault" seems odd. It may be that Moses is keen to ensure that Israel does not become merely a civil society. Israel's highest allegiance must always be to Yahweh himself. The result is the primacy of the Levites in those areas of life that directly impact the nation's relationship with Yahweh lived out in his land.

---

[422] See Gershon Brin, "The Firstling of Unclean Animals" *JQR* 68 (1977–1978): 12–14. The absence of sowing or cultivation may well imply that this is a reset of the process of filling and subduing the earth. Also Block, *Deuteronomy*, 489. Alternatively, it may suggest that this ritual renders the site unusable in future, although this seems less likely.

This makes some sense of the requirement of verse 6, where the elders of the nearest community must assert their innocence, as they "wash their hands by the stream over the young cow whose neck has been broken" (cf. Ps 26:6; Matt 27:24). As they perform this symbolic act, they are to say, "Our hands did not shed this blood; our eyes did not see it" (v. 7). Because they did not shed blood, the blood of the heifer is not to be shed. However, the striking atonement language in 21:8–9 rests on the fact that God alone can (and must) atone for this crime and forgive his people.

The unsolved crime does still bring guilt on the people of Israel, and according to verse 8, that guilt must still be wiped away. Moses insists that the threat of "guilt" is the major challenge faced by the people in the land. They need God to act in a way that allows the "shedding of innocent blood" to be dealt with. Almost without explanation, verse 8 asserts that performing this ritual will protect the elders of the city concerned and the entire nation: "the responsibility for bloodshed will be wiped away from them." No comment is made on how this might work. It is simply by grace. This is always the case with sacrifice ("it is impossible for the blood of bulls and goats to take away sins," Heb 10:4), and to say otherwise is to slide toward paganism.

Israel's focus (and the focus of every community within Israel) must be on ensuring that nothing interrupts their relationship with their God, which requires following Moses's impassioned plea in 21:9: "You must purge from yourselves the guilt of shedding innocent blood, for you will be doing what is right in the Lord's sight." This is the way of righteousness in the land.

21:10–14. Although the transition to a discussion of how to treat captives taken in future wars, rather than the conquest, is a little abrupt, the flow of thought is not hard to follow. Whether in wartime or peace, Israel is to act with righteousness, and any maltreatment of the innocent threatens the very life of the nation. However that does not take away the startingly kind (and countercultural) provisions in these verses.

The situation is sketched out in verse 10: at some indeterminate point in the future, when Israel fights a legitimate war (i.e., with divine sanction) and "the Lord your God hands them over to you and you take some of them prisoner," how are the captives to be treated? What follows needs to be read against an ancient background in which captives were essentially to be regarded as the property of the captor, with neither rights nor limitations on how they could be treated. In Israel, things are to be a little different.

This is an emotionally intense scenario. If an Israelite warrior is drawn to a captive woman by her beauty and "desires her and wants to take her as his wife" (the language is the same as 7:7 and 10:15 where Yahweh "sets his love" on his people), this is permissible ("you are to bring her into your house," 21:12). However, safeguards must be set in place for both the woman's own safety and protection for the community from any possible introduction of pagan practices.

The makeover in 21:12–13 both insists that she divests herself of the markers of her own (idolatrous) culture ("She is to shave her head, trim her nails, remove the clothes she was wearing when she was taken prisoner") and allows for her to come to terms with the traumatic events of the recent past, including the loss of her family (the woman is to "live in your house, and mourn for her father and mother a full month").[423] At this point, the marriage can take place: "After that, you may have sexual relations with her and be her husband, and she will be your wife."

Perhaps surprisingly, Moses is very sensitive to the danger of such women being abused, and so legislates to ensure that the woman is protected if the marriage does not work out (if the husband "is not satisfied with her," 21:14). There is clearly a power dynamic at work here—the wife being both a woman and a member of a defeated enemy. This probably explains why, rather than speaking to the shameful actions of the husband in changing his mind instead of honoring his commitment, Moses simply specifies protections for the divorced woman: "You are to let her go where she wants, but you must not sell her or treat her as merchandise [a verb used in the Old Testament only here and in 24:7], because you have humiliated her." The phrase "humiliated her" implies had sexual relations with her and then cast her off (see also 22:24, 29; Gen 34:2; 2 Sam 13:12).

These prescriptions are unprecedented in the ancient world and show remarkable tenderness and flexibility in dealing with an immensely problematic situation. A key part of "righteousness" is ensuring that the weak and the vulnerable are protected, even in situations where there is no perfect outcome.

21:15–17. After having dealt with the protection of recently captured foreigners whose marriages go badly wrong, one can see why Moses pauses to address the messy realities surrounding bigamy in 21:15–17.

---

[423] Lundbom disputes the idea that these actions are connected with a rejection of a pagan past, but sees them simply as representing mourning and (on the basis of 2 Sam 19:24) improving her appearance, presumably after the traumatic events that led to her capture (*Deuteronomy*, 598–99).

Verse 15 sets out a scenario—a man has two wives, "one loved and the other neglected"[424]—that is all too familiar from the patriarchal narratives, notably the situation in Jacob's household, which is echoed in the opening chapter of Samuel. As in the previous verses, the text makes no comment on any underlying issues (ignoring the bigamy itself), but the clear concern is to ensure that the rights of the unloved wife and her son are protected. The prohibition in 21:16 is unambiguous: "He is not to show favoritism to the son of the loved wife as his firstborn over the firstborn of the neglected wife." It may well be that this is an allusion to the case of Leah and Rachel, where Joseph supplanted Reuben as the official "firstborn," receiving a double share of the inheritance.[425] The practice of the father's estate being divided into "the number of sons plus one" portions, with the firstborn getting the extra portion as well as his own is well attested throughout the ancient world.[426]

Moses's concern for the weak on the one hand and his deep realism about life in Israel, where both quick divorces of powerless women and bigamy are part of the social fabric, is very obvious.

21:18–23. Returning to the subject of death, Moses deals with the seriousness of rebellion within the family, which is tantamount to a breach of the covenant. If a son is "stubborn and rebellious" (probably best taken together to mean something like "completely incorrigible"), repeatedly resisting and rejecting all attempts to discipline him (21:18), then both his parents, highlighting the high view of mothers in Israel, must take drastic action, for behavior like this threatens the covenant itself.[427]

Behavior like this needs to be addressed not simply at a parental level (thus neutralizing any attempts to play one parent against the other, or the son manipulating his parents: both must act together). They are to "take hold of him and bring him to the elders of his city, to the gate of his hometown." Interestingly, the parents" indictment of their son is to go beyond what has already been revealed: they are to say "This son of

---

[424] The Hebrew reads "loving one and hating the other." But as Mal 1:2 shows, the word has a much broader semantic range than the English "hate," and the translation "neglected" is to be preferred.

[425] The fact that Reuben slept with one of his father's wives, however, also played into this change.

[426] See the excellent discussion in Lundbom, *Deuteronomy*, 602–3.

[427] See also McConville, *Deuteronomy*, 331. The importance of disciplining children lies at the heart of the book of Proverbs (e.g., 13:24; 19:18; 22:15; 23:13–14; 29:17). In Deuteronomy, it is Israel (8:5) and then, uniquely, this rebellious son who receive this discipline.

ours is stubborn and rebellious; he doesn't obey us. He's a glutton and a drunkard." The combination of not "listening" to his parents, as well as overindulging in food and wine, is tantamount to rejection of Yahweh himself, for parents speak with God's delegated authority. Gluttony and drunkenness are an implicit rejection of the beautiful life that Yahweh holds out to his people. Ironically, this is the very accusation levelled at Jesus in Matthew 11:18–19!

This is why the response to the son is so harsh in 21:21: "Then all the men of his city will stone him to death." Only here and in 13:10 (which is a response to a close family member attempting to lure others into idolatry) is the community to take matters into their own hands like this. Nothing is said about judicial procedure here, because that's not the point. Moses wants to make plain that behavior that imperils the covenant must be dealt with in the most drastic terms for the sake of the whole nation: "You must purge the evil from you, and all Israel will hear and be afraid." Unlike the preceding provisions, this law is *harsher* than other ancient Near Eastern sanctions on such sons. This is because such behavior places the entire covenantal relationship between God and his people in jeopardy. One of the best known (if least understood) statements in Deuteronomy picks up and develops this idea in 21:22–23.

If someone is executed in Israel (e.g., for the kind of lifestyle described in the previous verses or a similar capital crime), then they are understood to have experienced the curse, rather than the blessing, of the covenant. The point is probably not that the means of execution brings a curse (which fits with the fact that in most cases, hanging was probably not the means of execution). Rather the common practice was to suspend or impale the corpses of those who have been executed on a tree (or a pole), *as a mark of disgrace* (and in the light of 21:21, presumably as a warning to others). Such people have clearly been abandoned by their god(s) (see Gen 40:19, 22; Josh 8:23, 29; 10:26; 2 Sam 4:12; 21:12). This is spelled out in verse 23: "you are not to leave his corpse on the tree overnight but are to bury him that day, for anyone hung on a tree is under God's curse."[428] The temporary exposure of the corpse seems to announce that the individual has paid the price for their apostasy, coming under God's curse. However, Moses says that the corpse should then quickly be buried, presumably

428 Unusually, the word for "God" here is *Elohim*. For a helpful discussion of the alternative ways of understanding this verse, see Block, *Deuteronomy*, 500–502.

as a symbol that the curse has been dealt with by Yahweh. Once more, the mechanism for this remains a mystery, but following these steps will ensure that the land is not further defiled, and the nation's relationship with Yahweh can continue.

The apostles Luke, John, and Paul all pick this verse (Acts 5:30; 10:39; John 19:31; Gal 3:13) to explain that, on the cross, Christ bore both our sin and the covenantal curse flowing from that. By bearing God's wrath in our place, Jesus dealt with the curse of the covenant in order that we might know the covenantal blessing of God. The shame of Roman crucifixion is an echo of the shame of covenant breakers being exposed on a tree or pole and a vivid announcement of Christ bearing our sin and shame.

22:1–12. Up to this point, this legal material has been carefully ordered, and it is not difficult to pick up threads that link the larger blocks of material. However here, at the beginning of chapter 22, everything starts to unravel! The "Decalogue template" from which Moses seems to have been working appears to be thrown away (or at least to become much more speculative), as grouping laws by catchword or broad theme appears to overwhelm any larger structural considerations and attempts to fit the bewildering array of laws into a neat pattern becomes more and more speculative. Rather than invest significant energy in trying to fashion some kind of neat scheme from the variety that follows, I suspect it is truer to Moses's intention simply to embrace the growing chaos. It may be that applying the Decalogue is still his overwhelming aim, but this exposition now takes on the shape of a broad-brush, all-encompassing, scattergun representation of the beautiful life with Yahweh that touches every conceivable situation (and a few inconceivable ones as well!).

This eclectic approach starts to become apparent in 22:1–12, where a series of instructions concerning two familiar intertwined themes are included: the "brotherhood of Israel" and remaining distinct from the Canaanites.

The focus in the first four verses falls (somewhat surprisingly) on stray livestock (see also Exod 23:4–5). If anyone sees a stray animal belonging to a brother then it is their responsibility to see it returned to their brother. One cannot "hide" from (CSB: "ignore it") this responsibility. To live as God's people in God's land is to be part of a family, a brotherhood, that carries substantial obligations. Not only is it important to take responsibility for the stray animal (rather than just ignoring it), according to verse 2 the person who finds it must care for it indefinitely. Going much further than Exodus 23, Moses says: "If your brother does not live near you or you don't know him, you are to bring the animal to your home to remain with you until your brother comes looking for it; then you can return it to him." Every member of God's people is "family."[429]

Lest anyone tries to wriggle out of their obligations by limiting this practice to particular animals, 22:3 extends the provision to donkeys and then to "his garment, or anything your brother has lost and you have found. You must not ignore it." In God's land, the care that God's people are to show one another is all-embracing and relentless! There is no room for casuistry: Moses presses on to make sure that they have grasped the intention behind his words in verse 4: "If you see your brother's donkey or ox fallen down on the road, do not ignore it; help him lift it up." A (over?) laden or yoked animal would not be easy to rescue if it had fallen—but the primary focus is attitudinal: every Israelite must care for the property (including animals) of his brothers as if it were his own. [430]

It is hard to see any possible connection with what comes next in 22:5, which prohibits cross-dressing. The ban is simple and straightforward: "A woman is not to wear male clothing, and a man is not to put on a woman's garment," but no direct explanation is given for the rule. That the word for "man" here is "strong man/warrior" (גֶּבֶר) underlines the fact that we are talking about behaviors that blur the differences between men and women (the word for clothing actually means men's "stuff") and do not fit with the righteousness required of the nation. However, the fact that Moses says that "everyone who does these things is detestable to the Lord your God" (cf. Lev 18:22) makes it likely that this is viewed as "Canaanite behavior." Given the preoccupations and practices of worshipers of Baal and Asherah, this may prohibit the practice of "sympathetic magic," sexual acts associated with fertility rites.[431]

---

[429] Houses in the ancient Near East often had a stable on the lower floor; hence, bringing an animal to your home was a completely normal step (see 1 Sam 28:24).

[430] The emphasis on the "brotherhood" of Israel is based on the assumption (common throughout the ancient Near East) that property was generally in the hands of men. It would be grossly unfair to accuse Moses of sexism, particularly given the plethora of laws sitting alongside these provisions that defend and extend the rights of women.

[431] See Willliam, W. Hallo, "Biblical Abominations and Sumerian Tattoos," *JQR* 76 (1985–1986): 21–40; also Calum M. Carmichael, *The Laws of Deuteronomy* (Ithaca: Cornell University Press, 1974), 147; Tigay, *Deuteronomy*, 201. For an extended discussion of transvestitism in Israel, see Nili Sacher Fox, "Gender Transformation and Transgression: Contextualizing the Prohibition of Cross-Dressing in Deuteronomy 22:5" in *Mishneh Todeh: Studies in Deuteronomy and its Cultural Environment in Honor of Jeffrey H. Tigay*, eds. Nili Sacher Fox, David A. Glatt-Gilad, and Michael J. Williams (Winona Lake: Eisenbrauns, 2009), 47–71.

The following verses (22:6–7) seem to have no such association with pagan practice, but the commandment here is much closer to natural law. The beautiful life that Israel is called to in the land is to be a sustainable one, in which they are to make sure that they don't treat even wildlife in a reckless way (see also Lev 22:28). In particular, God's people are to treat mother birds who are either incubating eggs or feeding their young with gentleness. They are allowed to take the young (and presumably the eggs) from the nest, but are to "be sure to let the mother go free." Presumably to take the healthy adult bird is to threaten the survival of the species (thus denuding the land).[432] This is confirmed by the motive clause: "so that you may prosper and live long." The ultimate goal of Israel in the land is to live in the way which God dictates, displaying the peerless goodness of this life to the watching world (see 4:5–8).

The building regulations of 22:8 return to the idea of death—in this case, avoiding unnecessary deaths through irresponsible building practices (cf. Exod 21:33–34 with its legislation on pits!) Flat roofs—used for storage, socializing, and even sleeping—are to be built with a guard rail "so that you don't bring bloodguilt on your house if someone falls from it." The underlying theological principle seems to be that to be part of the people of Yahweh is both to be different from those around and to be deeply committed to and responsible for the welfare of those within.

The theme of distinctiveness is then picked up in the four instructions in verses 9–12 (cf. Lev 19:19). The ban on mixing seeds in a vineyard is slightly confusing—it is not entirely clear why anyone would be sowing anything other than grapes in a vineyard, nor is it apparent how this intersects with the rules for newly-planted trees in Leviticus 19:23–35—but the overall intent is clear enough: having two crops intermingled would "defile" (perhaps better, "forfeit") the entire crop.[433] It may well be that the primary concern here is for the visual impact of the landscape in Israel: every aspect of their life is to speak of their single-minded commitment to Yahweh and his covenant.

[432] This is a little like the prohibition of 14:21, but here it seems that, in the wild, the precariousness of life means that it is more serious to kill the mother.

[433] The expression here is unusual. The verb normally means "to regard as holy," but here appears to denote the opposite (being defiled and so forfeit—presumably to Yahweh). According to *DCH* 7:190, there is one parallel use from Qumran (4QInstrd 103.29). Block (*Deuteronomy*, 514–15) may be right to see this as a prohibition on "intercropping"—sowing other crops between rows of vines—but gives no real explanation of why this might be problematic.

If the appearance of the landscape is in view, it would explain both the reluctance to team up an ox and a donkey when plowing (22:10) and to wear garments made from mixed yarns (specifically a wool-linen mix, 22:11).[434] Neither of these prohibitions appears to be a matter of utility: neither harnessing an ox and a donkey nor combining wool with linen promise much of an improvement in performance. The intention is most likely to display everywhere one looks that the people of God are focused on one thing: following Yahweh wholeheartedly.[435]

This emphasis on the visual is continued by the instruction to "make tassels on the four corners of the outer garment you wear" in 22:12.[436] This picks up an earlier instruction in Numbers 15:37–41, which is worth including in full:

> [37] The Lord said to Moses, [38] "Speak to the Israelites and tell them that throughout their generations they are to make tassels for the corners of their garments, and put a blue cord on the tassel at each corner.
> [39] These will serve as tassels for you to look at, so that you may remember all the Lord's commands and obey them and not prostitute yourselves by following your own heart and your own eyes. [40] This way you will remember and obey all my commands and be holy to your God.
> [41] I am the Lord your God who brought you out of the land of Egypt to be your God; I am the Lord your God.

It seems then that the insistence that Israel is distinct from the nations lies behind all four initially opaque requirements in verses 9–12: mixing seed, teaming different kinds of animals, and combining fabrics may all compromise the symbolism of Israel's uniqueness.

Bridge

Embracing the torah of Moses is, at heart, a matter of life and death. The life that Israel is called to live really is "life to the full," which touches every part of their existence. In particular, it demands that their national life be structured in a way that embodies "righteous judgment," values

---

434 As Block points out (*Deuteronomy*, 515 n. 22) the priestly garments in Exod 28:5–6, 8, 15; 39:1–3, 5, 8 appear to violate this, although that may be because the symbolic purpose of their garb is different. On the Day of Atonement, however, where the high priest is clearly representing the nation, he wears only linen (Lev 16:4, 23, 32).

435 The fact that the ox is a clean animal and the donkey unclean may support this reading. See also Paul's comments in 2 Cor 6:14. Tigay comments "The rabbis could think of no reason for this prohibition." *Deuteronomy*, 203.

436 McConville (*Deuteronomy*, 338–39) argues that there is a sexual connotation in 22:9–12, but this is not entirely persuasive.

human life immensely, and orders every detail of their existence to demonstrate and embody the goodness of Yahweh.

Both of these interlocking perspectives—that there are only two ways to live, and that life in Christ is to be eminently attractive—are deeply embedded both in the ministry of Jesus and the New Testament as a whole. So Peter writes in 1 Peter 2:9–10:

> [9] But you are a chosen race, a royal priesthood, a holy nation, a people for his possession, so that you may proclaim the praises of the one who called you out of darkness into his marvelous light. [10] Once you were not a people, but now you are God's people; you had not received mercy, but now you have received mercy.

As those who have received God's mercy, being credited with Christ's righteousness even as he took God's righteous judgment for us, we are called and equipped to live in him and with him—to live a beautiful life now that will reach its full consummation in the world to come.

7. Righteousness in All of Life (22:13–25:19)

> [13] "If a man marries a woman, has sexual relations with her, and comes to hate her, [14] and accuses her of shameful conduct, and gives her a bad name, saying, 'I married this woman and was intimate with her, but I didn't find any evidence of her virginity,' [15] the young woman's father and mother will take the evidence of her virginity and bring it to the city elders at the city gate. [16] The young woman's father will say to the elders, 'I gave my daughter to this man as a wife, but he hates her. [17] He has accused her of shameful conduct, saying, "I didn't find any evidence of your daughter's virginity," but here is the evidence of my daughter's virginity.' They will spread out the cloth before the city elders. [18] Then the elders of that city will take the man and punish him. [19] They will also fine him a hundred silver shekels and give them to the young woman's father, because that man gave an Israelite virgin a bad name. She will remain his wife; he cannot divorce her as long as he lives. [20] But if this accusation is true and no evidence of the young woman's virginity is found, [21] they will bring the woman to the door of her father's house, and the men of her city will stone her to death. For she has committed an outrage in Israel by being promiscuous while living in her father's house. You must purge the evil from you.
>
> [22] "If a man is discovered having sexual relations with another man's wife, both the man who had sex with the woman and the woman must die. You must purge the evil from Israel. [23] If there is a young woman who is a virgin engaged to a man, and another man encounters her in the city and sleeps with her, [24] take the two of them out to the gate

of that city and stone them to death—the young woman because she
did not cry out in the city and the man because he has violated his
neighbor's fiancée. You must purge the evil from you. 25 But if the man
encounters an engaged woman in the open country, and he seizes and
rapes her, only the man who raped her must die. 26 Do nothing to the
young woman, because she is not guilty of an offense deserving death.
This case is just like one in which a man attacks his neighbor and mur-
ders him. 27 When he found her in the field, the engaged woman cried
out, but there was no one to rescue her. 28 If a man encounters a young
woman, a virgin who is not engaged, takes hold of her and rapes her,
and they are discovered, 29 the man who raped her is to give the young
woman's father fifty silver shekels, and she will become his wife because
he violated her. He cannot divorce her as long as he lives.

30 "A man is not to marry his father's wife; he must not violate his
father's marriage bed.

23:1 "No man whose testicles have been crushed or whose penis has been
cut off may enter the Lord's assembly. 2 No one of illegitimate birth may
enter the Lord's assembly; none of his descendants, even to the tenth generation, may enter the Lord's assembly. 3 No Ammonite or Moabite may
enter the Lord's assembly; none of their descendants, even to the tenth
generation, may ever enter the Lord's assembly. 4 This is because they did
not meet you with food and water on the journey after you came out of
Egypt, and because Balaam son of Beor from Pethor in Aram-naharaim
was hired to curse you. 5 Yet the Lord your God would not listen to Balaam,
but he turned the curse into a blessing for you because the Lord your
God loves you. 6 Never pursue their welfare or prosperity as long as you
live. 7 Do not despise an Edomite, because he is your brother. Do not despise an Egyptian, because you were a resident alien in his land. 8 The children born to them in the third generation may enter the Lord's assembly.

9 "When you are encamped against your enemies, be careful to avoid
anything offensive. 10 If there is a man among you who is unclean because
of a bodily emission during the night, he must go outside the camp; he
may not come anywhere inside the camp. 11 When evening approaches,
he is to wash with water, and when the sun sets he may come inside the
camp. 12 You are to have a place outside the camp and go there to relieve
yourself. 13 You are to have a digging tool in your equipment; when you
relieve yourself, dig a hole with it and cover up your excrement. 14 For
the Lord your God walks throughout your camp to protect you and deliver
your enemies to you; so your encampments must be holy. He must not
see anything indecent among you or he will turn away from you.

15 "Do not return a slave to his master when he has escaped from his
master to you. 16 Let him live among you wherever he wants within
your city gates. Do not mistreat him.

17 “No Israelite woman is to be a cult prostitute, and no Israelite man is to be a cult prostitute. 18 Do not bring a female prostitute’s wages or a male prostitute’s earnings into the house of the Lord your God to fulfill any vow, because both are detestable to the Lord your God.

19 “Do not charge your brother interest on silver, food, or anything that can earn interest. 20 You may charge a foreigner interest, but you must not charge your brother Israelite interest, so that the Lord your God may bless you in everything you do in the land you are entering to possess.

21 “If you make a vow to the Lord your God, do not be slow to keep it, because he will require it of you, and it will be counted against you as sin. 22 But if you refrain from making a vow, it will not be counted against you as sin. 23 Be careful to do whatever comes from your lips, because you have freely vowed what you promised to the Lord your God.

24 “When you enter your neighbor’s vineyard, you may eat as many grapes as you want until you are full, but do not put any in your container. 25 When you enter your neighbor’s standing grain, you may pluck heads of grain with your hand, but do not put a sickle to your neighbor’s grain.

24:1 “If a man marries a woman, but she becomes displeasing to him because he finds something indecent about her, he may write her a divorce certificate, hand it to her, and send her away from his house. 2 If after leaving his house she goes and becomes another man’s wife, 3 and the second man hates her, writes her a divorce certificate, hands it to her, and sends her away from his house or if he dies, 4 the first husband who sent her away may not marry her again after she has been defiled, because that would be detestable to the Lord. You must not bring guilt on the land the Lord your God is giving you as an inheritance.

5 “When a man takes a bride, he must not go out with the army or be liable for any duty. He is free to stay at home for one year, so that he can bring joy to the wife he has married.

6 “Do not take a pair of grindstones or even the upper millstone as security for a debt, because that is like taking a life as security.

7 “If a man is discovered kidnapping one of his Israelite brothers, whether he treats him as a slave or sells him, the kidnapper must die. You must purge the evil from you.

8 “Be careful with a person who has a case of serious skin disease, following carefully everything the Levitical priests instruct you to do. Be careful to do as I have commanded them. 9 Remember what the Lord your God did to Miriam on the journey after you left Egypt.

10 “When you make a loan of any kind to your neighbor, do not enter his house to collect what he offers as security. 11 Stand outside while

the man you are making the loan to brings the security out to you. [12] If he is a poor man, do not sleep with the garment he has given as security. [13] Be sure to return it to him at sunset. Then he will sleep in it and bless you, and this will be counted as righteousness to you before the Lord your God.

[14] "Do not oppress a hired worker who is poor and needy, whether one of your Israelite brothers or one of the resident aliens in a town in your land. [15] You are to pay him his wages each day before the sun sets, because he is poor and depends on them. Otherwise he will cry out to the Lord against you, and you will be held guilty.

[16] "Fathers are not to be put to death for their children, and children are not to be put to death for their fathers; each person will be put to death for his own sin. [17] Do not deny justice to a resident alien or fatherless child, and do not take a widow's garment as security. [18] Remember that you were a slave in Egypt, and the Lord your God redeemed you from there. Therefore I am commanding you to do this.

[19] "When you reap the harvest in your field, and you forget a sheaf in the field, do not go back to get it. It is to be left for the resident alien, the fatherless, and the widow, so that the Lord your God may bless you in all the work of your hands. [20] When you knock down the fruit from your olive tree, do not go over the branches again. What remains will be for the resident alien, the fatherless, and the widow. [21] When you gather the grapes of your vineyard, do not glean what is left. What remains will be for the resident alien, the fatherless, and the widow. [22] Remember that you were a slave in the land of Egypt. Therefore I am commanding you to do this.

[25:1] "If there is a dispute between men, they are to go to court, and the judges will hear their case. They will clear the innocent and condemn the guilty. [2] If the guilty party deserves to be flogged, the judge will make him lie down and be flogged in his presence with the number of lashes appropriate for his crime. [3] He may be flogged with forty lashes, but no more. Otherwise, if he is flogged with more lashes than these, your brother will be degraded in your sight.

[4] "Do not muzzle an ox while it treads out grain.

[5] "When brothers live on the same property and one of them dies without a son, the wife of the dead man may not marry a stranger outside the family. Her brother-in-law is to take her as his wife, have sexual relations with her, and perform the duty of a brother-in-law for her. [6] The first son she bears will carry on the name of the dead brother, so his name will not be blotted out from Israel. [7] But if the man doesn't want to marry his sister-in-law, she is to go to the elders at the city gate and say, 'My brother-in-law refuses to preserve his brother's name in Israel.

He isn't willing to perform the duty of a brother-in-law for me.' [8] The elders of his city will summon him and speak with him. If he persists and says, 'I don't want to marry her,' [9] then his sister-in-law will go up to him in the sight of the elders, remove his sandal from his foot, and spit in his face. Then she will declare, 'This is what is done to a man who will not build up his brother's house.' [10] And his family name in Israel will be 'The house of the man whose sandal was removed.'

[11] "If two men are fighting with each other, and the wife of one steps in to rescue her husband from the one striking him, and she puts out her hand and grabs his genitals, [12] you are to cut off her hand. Do not show pity.

[13] "Do not have differing weights in your bag, one heavy and one light. [14] Do not have differing dry measures in your house, a larger and a smaller. [15] You must have a full and honest weight, a full and honest dry measure, so that you may live long in the land the Lord your God is giving you. [16] For everyone who does such things and acts unfairly is detestable to the Lord your God.

[17] "Remember what the Amalekites did to you on the journey after you left Egypt. [18] They met you along the way and attacked all your stragglers from behind when you were tired and weary. They did not fear God. [19] When the Lord your God gives you rest from all the enemies around you in the land the Lord your God is giving you to possess as an inheritance, blot out the memory of Amalek under heaven. Do not forget."

The final section of the collection of laws will be discussed under the umbrella heading "righteousness in all of life." That is not to say that there is no order or sense of progression through these laws (from 22:13 onwards, for example, there is significant space devoted to matters of sexual purity, corresponding broadly to the seventh commandment), but the sense that Moses has carefully arranged prescriptions thematically to fit neatly with a strict Decalogue pattern diminishes. Rather than a topical arrangement, these chapters display a "scattergun" approach, which relies more on catchwords and allusion to create an overall effect of comprehensiveness.

22:13–21. Sexual misconduct dominates the next series of laws, beginning a local equivalent of the situation with captured foreign women in 21:10–11.[437] The wording of verse 13 strongly suggests that the man's decision to spurn his wife is culpable. He has chosen to abandon his commitment to her ("If a man marries a woman, has sexual relations with

[437] With the exception of 22:8–9, which concerns a situation addressed also in Exod 22:16–17, the laws in the rest of this chapter are unique to Deuteronomy.

her, and comes to hate her"). Everything that follows is predicated on protecting the vulnerable woman from the covenant-breaking man. This is a key part of what makes this legislation unique in the ancient world.

Everything in this section is profoundly theological and is further illustration of the worldview of Deuteronomy. Covenant-breaking has massive ramifications for the entire community. The life of God's people is to be built on righteousness. The sexual misconduct sketched out in this section is completely inconsistent with a righteous life. The accusation of 2:14 impugns the woman, her parents, and the entire community she is from. Should it be upheld, it strikes at the heart of the life of the covenant people. However, should the accusation be found to be false and to flow from a desire to break faith with the wife, it is utterly antithetical to the life to which God's people are called.

Once the allegation of "shameful conduct" prior to marriage is made and the husband "brings out against her a wicked name" (lit.,), a definite process must be followed. In this case, according to verse 15, the women's parents (as in 21:19, both parents are involved) are to produce the evidence of his daughter's virginity (the word means "cloak," but as Exod 22:26–27 shows, this garment could also be used for sleeping—in this case, on one's wedding night).

The father (v.17) then has the opportunity to repudiate the accusation, echoing the words that threaten to destroy the reputation of his daughter and family, and presenting the evidence to the elders. The description of what is to happen is simple: "They will spread out the cloth before the city elders."[438] Once this is produced, no further discussion is needed. The truth of the matter is obvious.

On seeing the evidence, if it is apparent that the husband's accusation is false, "the elders of that city will take the man and punish him." The verb can mean "flog" (1 Kgs 12:11; 2 Chr 10:11) and probably carries the sense of physical punishment here. But that is not the only consequence of his false accusation. In verse 19, Moses adds: "They will also fine him a hundred silver shekels and give them to the young woman's father." This seems to be double the normal bride price which he would have received.[439] This is restoration for the damage done to his wife's

[438] Presumably, the garment was entrusted to the bride's family after the marriage was consummated as protection for the bride.

[439] In Deut 22:29, the amount of money to be repaid if a man sleeps with a woman who is not betrothed is 50 silver shekels. However, when this scenario is described in Exod

reputation ("because that man gave an Israelite virgin a bad name"), as well as for the damage he has done to the entire community. Although contemporary readers may struggle with the implication that the woman is "owned," it is important to realize that, in an ancient context, this payment spoke primarily to the value of the woman.

Moses's determination to protect the woman is remarkable. These instructions flow from the deep-rooted commitment to righteousness that suffuses the life of Israel. Covenant faithfulness is so important to the community that the women is protected for the rest of her life: "she will remain his wife; he cannot divorce her as long as he lives." False accusations threaten the very fabric of the covenant people, and these rules guard against them.

If, however, the evidence points in the other direction and the woman is guilty, the consequences are even more severe: "the woman shall be executed for adultery." The designation "adultery" is important here. Sex before marriage is a serious matter in Israel, but "adultery" is on a different plane because it is breaking a covenant made before Yahweh. As the rest of the chapter makes clear, irrespective of whether the guilty party is the man or the woman, the penalty for this kind of covenant breaking is death. But here, the focus is on the impact that this kind of behavior has on the entire community. This is why the woman is to be taken "to the door of her father's house." This is a very public reminder that her sin took place right in the middle of the community, which is why "the men of her city" are commanded to stone her to death (as in 21:21). Having allowed this to happen and sharing the in the shame of the exposure of these events, the community itself is to be involved in the punishment.

The final statement in this section underlines that this is an issue for the entire community. Because she has committed an "outrage" (נְבָלָה, a word used only here in Deuteronomy) among them, they must "purge the evil" from among them. Once more, such behavior strikes right at the heart of the covenant.

22:22–30. The basic principle (laid out initially in the seventh commandment) assumed in verses 13–21, is now made explicit in 22:22: "If a man is discovered having sexual relations with another man's wife, both the man who had sex with the woman and the woman must die. You must

22:16–17, it is stated that the normal bride price should be paid—hence 50 shekels seems to have been the normal bride price, although it is nowhere stated explicitly.

purge the evil from Israel." Adultery is covenant breaking. It is at odds with the righteous life to which God calls his people. It is deeply wrong and is punishable by death for both parties (the text is emphatic about this). The language here is so strong because dealing with this issue is vital for the survival of Israel as a covenant people. Having stated this plainly, Moses then gives three case studies to enable Israel to negotiate the complexities of real life in the land.

The three scenarios that follow (23:23–24, 25–27, 28–29) involve (a) a single man with a betrothed woman (also described as a "wife," because she was that in all but name (and consummation) in the town (23:23–24); (b) a single man with a betrothed woman in a rural area (23:25–27); and (c) a single man with an unattached virgin (23:28–29).

It is important for readers to remember that in the cultural setting of the ancient Near East, women and men would never have spent time alone. The assumption is that such liaisons in an urban setting would have been the result of careful planning (and therefore mutual agreement). This is the situation envisaged in verse 23. The "young woman who is engaged to a man" is *found* by another man in the city and they have sex. The verb underlines what is already implied. The woman is a willing party in this tryst, and "because she did not cry out" (v. 24), both parties are to be "taken out to the gate of that city and stoned to death." The reason for this is that, once more, "You must purge the evil from you." This is a clear example of covenant breaking and cannot be tolerated in Israel.

If the incident occurs in the countryside, a very different approach is taken: "If the man encounters an engaged woman in the open country, and he seizes and rapes her, only the man who raped her must die." Unlike the previous situation, the man uses force here. This provision is fascinating in that it is framed entirely in favor of the woman. It is assumed in verse 27 that "when he found her in the field, the engaged woman cried out, but there was no one to rescue her." One can only assume that this is done out of a deep desire to protect vulnerable women should they find themselves isolated and unprotected. The statement of verse 26 is striking: "Do nothing to the young woman, because she is not guilty of an offense deserving death" (see 21:22). The woman is to be treated as a victim. Only the man is deemed to be a covenant breaker in this scenario.

In verse 28, the focus shifts to a young woman who is not engaged. There is some discussion over the best way to translate the verb "lie with" (CSB: "rapes"), and whether or not "taking hold" of the woman implies that this sexual encounter is nonconsensual. Given the stance of the preceding laws (which are so concerned to protect the woman), it seems likely that this is not dealing with an instance of rape, but rather with premarital consensual sex.[440] This would explain the insistence of verse 29 that the couple get married, with the man giving "the young woman's father fifty silver shekels, and she will become his wife because he violated her." This is half the amount in verse 19, and either represents the bride price or a fine.[441] The added clause ("He cannot divorce her as long as he lives") underlines that this is a real, lifelong marriage and not something that can be conveniently avoided.

It is surprising at this point to read a prohibition of marrying a woman who had previously been married to your father ("A man is not to marry his father's wife"). This possibility presumably emerged after the father's death (especially as men often married much younger women) and may imply a polygamous situation (rather than dealing with incest). The reason given is not immediately clear: "he must not violate his father's marriage bed." The phrase literally reads "he must not uncover or lift up his father's corner [or: wing or edge]." It may imply climbing into his father's marriage bed. Given the consistent emphasis on breaking covenant, it may imply that such an arrangement would be an implicit breach of the covenant made between one's father and his wife. To do that would be to bring shame on the family, and thus the covenant people as a whole.

23:1–8. From this point on, attempts to tie the order of stipulations into a Decalogue pattern become completely strained and speculative, as Moses turns to the subject of admission to the assembly of God's covenant people in 23:1–8.

The criteria applied in the verses that follow are hard to discern and do not, on first glance at least, appear to be entirely consistent. Some of the principles laid down are entirely unexpected, and bald pronouncements sit alongside detailed historical justifications.

23:1 begins the list with the assertion that "No man whose testicles have been crushed or whose penis has been cut off may enter the LORD's assembly." No clue is given as to how or why the man concerned has been so afflicted.[442] But given that eunuchs (those who had been emas-

[440] See the discussion in Lundbom, *Deuteronomy*, 638.

[441] Tigay argues that the bride price was normally much lower (*Deuteronomy*, 208).

[442] "Crushed" here is not a common word, but occurs several times in the Old Testament, including famously in Isa 53:10.

culated either by illness, accident, or deliberate action, which may be what v. 1 is covering) often had a role in the life and worship of pagan courts, excluding such pagan influence may be in view. The verses that follow may support this.[443] On the other hand, it could also be based on the inability of those mentioned in verse 1 to play a full part in filling the earth and subduing it, and as a result they are excluded from the "assembly."[444] On balance, I think the former view is to be preferred. It is striking that by the end of the Old Testament, this exclusion has been replaced by a promise of inclusion (so Isa 56:4–5, famously fulfilled in Acts 8:26–39).

The next prohibition (v. 2) seems extremely harsh in a contemporary context: "No one of illegitimate birth may enter the LORD's assembly; none of his descendants, even to the tenth generation, may enter the LORD's assembly." The repeated exclusion order signals that this is not a small matter, as does the extent of the exclusion: "to the tenth generation," while stopping short of being a permanent moratorium, is a very long time! So what it being referred to? The word translated "illegitimate birth" (מַמְזֵר) occurs only here and possibly in Zechariah 9:6. Given the strength of the penalty, the context of Zechariah, and the treatment of illegitimacy in the Old Testament, it seems likely that something more than a child being conceived out of wedlock is in view. [445] Moses seems to be backing up his earlier strictures against marrying Canaanite women, perhaps extending it to cover liaisons with cult prostitutes (an issue which is addressed specifically in vv. 17–18) in future. The assembly of Israel—the nation gathered before Yahweh, whether to listen or make decisions (see 4:10; 5:22; 9:10; 10:4; 18:16; 31:30)—must be made up only of those whose allegiance to Yahweh is unquestionable.

---

[443] There may also be a connection with 14:1. Josephus (*Ant* 4.290) takes this view.

[444] The "assembly" is the general term used to describe gatherings of all the people of Israel. At times, it refers to all free males (often related to judgment or war), and at others, the entire worshiping community. See Eugene Carpenter, "קהל", *NIDOTTE*, 3:888–91.

[445] Writing in *TWOT* 1:498, entry 1174a, 1184, Walter Kaiser says, "Only found in Deut 23:2, it is used of an illegitimate child who is refused entrance to the congregation of the Lord until the tenth generation. Zech 9:6 may refer to an individual, but more likely it figuratively depicts the mixed population of Ashdod. It is possible that the Deut reference also refers to a child of mixed parentage-Hebrew and pagan." Also McConville, *Deuteronomy*, 349 and Block, *Deuteronomy*, 535. Lundbom (*Deuteronomy*, 647) argues that it refers to those with birth defects arising from incestuous marriages, but this seems unduly speculative, and had this been the case, one would have expected it also to be reflected in the following verses concerning Ammon and Moab.

Moses then turns to deal with relationships with individuals from neighboring nations who find themselves in Israel, beginning with those who share kinship with them through the patriarchs. In the first place, those from Ammon and Moab (related to Israel through Lot) are to be barred permanently from playing a full role in the covenant community. So in verses 3–4, we read "No Ammonite or Moabite may enter the Lord's assembly; none of their descendants, even to the tenth generation, may ever enter the Lord's assembly." The thought may be that both Ammon and Moab were the result of incest (Gen 19:30–38). Whether or not that is the case, this has every appearance of being an ancient prescription. Given the family history of King David, for example, it seems highly unlikely that this would have made it into Deuteronomy without significant qualification had it been the product of a later age![446]

According to Moses here, the particular prohibitions on Ammonites and Moabites are based on the events of Numbers 21–24. The Ammonites do not receive much attention either in Numbers (21:20) or in Moses's retrospect on the journey to Kadesh in Deuteronomy 2 and 3. Here, however, they are treated as sharing in the culpability of the Moabites, who, rather than helping their "cousins" in their hour of need, conspired against them (perhaps with the notable exception of those living in Ar, Deut 2:29).

Two reasons are given for this permanent exclusion from the family of God: (1) they did not proactively offer Israel food and water on their wilderness journey; (2) "Balaam son of Beor from Pethor in Aram-naharaim was hired to curse" God's people (Num 22–24). The text of Numbers does not deal explicitly with their failure to offer support to Israel (in contrast to the discussion of the Edomites). However, an argument from silence is hardly implausible given the terrain and the details that are supplied. There is no such shortage of evidence when it comes to the Moabite attempt to use Balaam against Israel. The whole narrative of Numbers 22–24 is a grand demonstration of God's generosity to and in particular his love for his people, as he "turned the curse into a blessing."

This settled and determined opposition to Yahweh leads to the unambiguous command of 23:6: "Never pursue their welfare [good] or prosperity [wellbeing] as long as you live." No treaties or covenants are to be

---

[446] Presumably Ruth's faith and "conversion" was viewed as overcoming this obstacle to David's inclusion in the assembly of Israel! Interestingly, this verse is quoted in full in Neh 13:1–2.

made with these nations (see the allusion to this verse in Ezra 9:12). In the case of the Moabites and Ammonites, proximity to the people chosen by Yahweh (and perhaps the grace experienced by Lot through his relationship with Abram) seems to have had a negative effect.[447] It may be that a similar principle to Hebrews 6 is in operation (so Heb 6:4–5: "For it is impossible to renew to repentance those who were once enlightened, who tasted the heavenly gift, who shared in the Holy Spirit, who tasted God's good word and the powers of the coming age").

In contrast, the Edomites, descendants of Esau, are to be treated as "brothers." This implies that any Edomite who wishes to can become a member of the covenant people (presumably because of the direct relationship with Abraham). This is puzzling for at least two reasons. First, the narrative of Numbers 20 describes in some detail how the Edomites not only failed to offer Israel support as they passed by but actively threatened them.[448] On top of that, there is the contrast with the strongly anti-Edomite sentiment of Obadiah (directly linked to the Edomites' part in and gloating over the destruction of Jerusalem) and Malachi (see 1:1–4).

The best explanation of this is that in the early days of Israel, despite the "blip" of Numbers 20, the relationship between Israel and Edom was relatively warm, largely as a result of their joint descent from Abraham and Isaac. Unlike the Ammonites and Moabites, the descendants of Esau did not prosecute a sustained, aggressive plan against God's people. Later in their history, relationships soured in the wake of the Babylonian attacks on Judah.

---

447 This is reflected in the ongoing enmity between these nations: see, e.g., 2 Kgs 3:36–27; 24:2; Jer 40:13–41:15; Ezek 25:1–6; Zeph 2:8.

448 "Moses sent messengers from Kadesh to the king of Edom, 'This is what your brother Israel says, "You know all the hardships that have overtaken us. Our fathers went down to Egypt, and we lived in Egypt many years, but the Egyptians treated us and our ancestors badly. When we cried out to the Lord, he heard our plea, and sent an angel, and brought us out of Egypt. Now look, we are in Kadesh, a city on the border of your territory. Please let us travel through your land. We won't travel through any field or vineyard, or drink any well water. We will travel the King's Highway; we won't turn to the right or the left until we have traveled through your territory." ' But Edom answered him, 'You will not travel through our land, or we will come out and confront you with the sword.' 'We will go on the main road,' the Israelites replied to them, 'and if we or our herds drink your water, we will pay its price. There will be no problem; only let us travel through on foot.' Yet Edom insisted, 'You may not travel through.' And they came out to confront them with a large force of heavily-armed people. Edom refused to allow Israel to travel through their territory, and Israel turned away from them." (Num 20:14–21)

Surprising though the discussion of the Edomites may be, the real surprise comes in the provision made for Egyptians in 23:7 (see also 10:18–19). The description of Israel's experience in Egypt as being "a resident alien in the land" owes more to the days of Joseph than the lead-up to the exodus. Given Moses's own upbringing and the increasing influence of the tribe of Joseph, it is perhaps not surprising that forty years after the exodus a more positive attitude to Egypt emerges. The fact that in 22:8 allowance is made for third-generation Egyptian immigrants to become full-fledged Israelites ("the children born to them in the third generation may enter the Lord's assembly"), while not exactly welcoming them with open arms, is still more positive than one might expect. In Isaiah 56:3–8, this is relaxed further, envisioning a day when all those who express real faith in Yahweh are included in his people.

23:9–14. The focus now shifts abruptly to the extremely mundane details of maintaining ritual purity during a military campaign (like the one which is about to start). The people must ensure in verse 9 that there is not "anything offensive" (lit., "an evil thing") anywhere in the camp. Suddenly, we find ourselves in the thought-world of Leviticus (see, e.g., Lev 15:1–33, also Num 5:1–4), although it seems that the standards of purity in the military camp are to exceed even those of the people "on the way."

Verses 10–11 give very specific instructions on dealing with nocturnal emissions among the troops when they are on a campaign. It is assumed that the reader understands that this renders a man ritually unclean (as in Lev 15:16–18), and so Moses moves straight to the procedure for dealing with the issue: after spending the day outside the camp (isolated from others to avoid contaminating them), "when evening approaches, he is to wash with water, and when the sun sets he may come inside the camp."[449]

If this seems extremely scrupulous, it pales beside the rules surrounding defecation when the army is on the move. When the soldiers strike camp, according to verse 12, a suitable site for a latrine "outside the camp" must be identified (according to the Qumran War Scroll, it was to be "two thousand cubits" away). To facilitate the process, "You are to have a digging tool in your equipment; when you relieve yourself, dig a hole with it and cover up your excrement" (v. 13). This is all remarkably specific, from the requirement to carry a "spike" or tent-peg down to the instruction to "squat." But the reason for all this care is striking.

---

[449] Lev 15:18 makes a similar demand of those who have had sexual intercourse.

In what may be an echo of Genesis 3:8 (where Yahweh first walks among his people like this), it is the fact that God himself walks around the camp that necessitates this care.[450] Nothing unholy (literally "nakedness of a thing") must be allowed to drive him away—not least because victory depends on it!

23:15–16. The surprises just keep coming in verses 15–16, as it turns out that the land God gives his people is to be a place of refuge for those seeking asylum from neighboring countries—and in particular, those who are escaped slaves. This particular blessing to the nations is in stark contrast to all comparable contemporary legislation, which demanded the return of slaves both locally and internationally.[451] This radically different approach (which was presumably unpopular among Israel's neighbors) is based on the fact that ideally, there is to be no slavery in Israel (so, e.g., Deut 15:12). Moses even goes so far as extending to such people the right to choose where to live: "Let him live among you wherever he wants within your city gates." The language of choice has surprising echoes of God's actions on behalf of Israel. The additional injunction not to "mistreat" the escapee does not have a motivation attached, but by this stage the fact that the Israelites had been slaves in Egypt may be taken as read.

23:17–18. Up to this point, allusions to pagan practices have tended to be slightly veiled. But no longer. The prohibition of illicit sexual religious activity among God's people (presumably associated with the place chosen by God) is extremely blunt in verse 17: "No Israelite woman is to be a cult prostitute, and no Israelite man is to be a cult prostitute."[452] The underlying assumption is the regularly expressed concern that the people will, sooner or later, fall into idolatry with all its associated practices. The language in verse 18 is particularly striking: the terms used are not actually "female and male prostitute," but "harlot" and "dog." It is hard to envisage a circumstance where the proceeds of illicit sexual activity are brought "into the house of the Lord your God to fulfill any vow," but

[450] Block pictures Yahweh "inspecting his troops" (*Deuteronomy*, 539). Tigay contends that this only refers to the presence of Yahweh to fight for his people (*Deuteronomy*, 214) but this seems unduly restrictive. See also Lev 26:11–12.

[451] See Lundbom, *Deuteronomy*, 655 for a discussion of the ancient Near Eastern material.

[452] There is much discussion of the actual practices being condemned here, and the extent to which cultic prostitution was institutionalized in the religious world of the ancient Near East. Block's suggestion (based on Akkadian precedent) that these male and female shrine functionaries often became caught up in orgiastic activity is a sensible solution (*Deuteronomy*, 545–46). Moses's point, however, remains clear.

given Israel's propensity to fall into syncretism, perhaps one should not be so skeptical. Although the precise details of the practices prohibited here remain slightly obscure, it is clear that all sexually promiscuous behavior fits into the category of "detestable" to Yahweh and has no place in the land which he is giving to his people.

23:19–25. The goodness of God in giving Israel the land and blessing them in it is to shape the entire economic system, and in particular, to remove any need to charge interest. The family dynamic of the brotherhood of Israel leads to the rule of 23:19: "Do not charge your brother interest on silver, food, or anything that can earn interest" (see also Exod 22:25–27; Lev 25:35–38). The blanket ban underlines the fact that charging interest is essentially an act of unfaith that undermines the very nature of life in the family of God. Unlike the laws in Exodus and Leviticus, no reference is made to the economic status of the borrower (the usual reason for borrowing).[453] The point here is a far-reaching, theological one. To eschew interest is part and parcel of living as a people of promise, enjoying the blessing of God.[454]

Interestingly, this ban does not extend to dealing with foreigners (presumably foreign merchants working for profit). There is nothing wrong with charging interest per se; it just not to be a feature of the brotherly relations in Israel (a point that is reiterated in verse 20).[455] This act of faith, according to Moses, is a necessary precursor to ensuring that "the Lord your God may bless you in everything you do in the land you are entering to possess."

The requirement that Israel embody the righteousness of God also extends to following through on any kind of solemn commitment made to Yahweh. An ancient part of Israel's piety was to underscore requests

---

[453] Klaus Issler argues that the distinction is purely an economic one, prohibiting lending at interest to poor "brothers" but allowing commercial loans to "(foreign) traders" (with the emphasis falling on their job rather than their ethnicity). Issler surveys the debate very helpfully, but ultimately, the wider context seems to suggest that the contrast between Israel and the nations is most important here. Klaus Issler, "Lending and Interest in the OT: Examining Three Interpretations to Explain the Deuteronomy 23:19–20 Distinction in Light of the Historical Usury Debate," *JETS* 59 (2016): 761–89.

[454] Some argue that these rules are based on the eighth commandment, fitting in to the overall Decalogue pattern. However, the variety of the surrounding material makes this hard to sustain.

[455] Attitudes to interest vary in the ancient world. Again, see Lundbom's thorough discussion (*Deuteronomy*, 663–65).

made to God with a practical expression of "good faith." In this new world of "righteousness," such piety is allowed but must be authentic. God takes such commitments seriously because he is righteous and expects his people to be the same.

This explains why Moses insists that for Israel to give your word is essentially to make a vow to God that must be honored if you are to avoid sinning: "Be careful to do whatever comes from your lips, because you have freely vowed what you promised to the Lord your God" (cf. Num 30:3). Israel must be relentlessly truthful. This matters more than any particular form of words. There is no compulsion to make promises or vows (v. 23), but once you have made it, Moses says "do not be slow to keep it, because he will require it of you, and it will be counted against you as sin [lit., it will be a sin in you]." Israel's words are to mirror those of God himself.[456] Israel is to speak as God has spoken to them.

This is the foundation for the kind of trust that lies behind 23:24–25, which allows for everyone to enjoy the produce of the land (which is, after all, God's ultimate possession) without attempting to exploit one another for material gain. Eating as many grapes or as much grain as one can, without attempting to defraud your neighbor by using a container to gather grapes or a sickle to harvest his grain, is a snapshot of the righteous life. God's people really can depend on the overflowing generosity and provision of God.

24:1–7. Chapter 24 opens with a cluster of laws dealing with human relationships, starting with the only Old Testament laws dealing with divorce. It seems that any semblance of thematic arrangement or order has vanished.

The statement in 24:1 is puzzling for several reasons. The first is that the reality of divorce is simply assumed, and unlike other discussions of sexual ethics in chapters 12–26, there is neither provision for the protection of the woman nor any real attention paid to the reason given for ending the marriage. The instruction that "he may write her a divorce certificate, hand it to her, and send her away from his house" seems almost cursory. Part of the explanation is undoubtedly the phrase "finds something indecent about her" (עֶרְוַת דָּבָר), which could be translated "a thing/matter of nakedness." Surprisingly, this does not refer to sexual immorality. The same phrase occurred in 23:14 when stipulating toilet

[456] These verses shed some light on the issues raised by the behavior of Ananias and Sapphira in Acts 5.

arrangements in the camp to ensure that such unholy behavior is kept from the sight of Yahweh. It seems safe to assume that Moses has in mind some gross (and indisputable) act of indecency.[457] This is confirmed by the fact that his focus is *not* on the reason for the marital breakdown, but on preserving ongoing "righteousness" in the conduct of community life.

In addition, it should be noted that 24:1 does not stand alone: it is the opening phrase of a series of provisions. The "if clause" (protasis) finds its conclusion in the "then clause" (apodosis) of verse 4. This makes it likely that 24:1 is *descriptive rather than permissive* (let alone prescriptive). Moses is not addressing the morality of writing a divorce certificate but dealing with the fallout after the event. The overall intention is to prohibit remarrying after divorce. This verse then does not grant *permission* for men to divorce their wives on specific grounds, nor does it even discuss those grounds.

In verses 2–3, the potential scenario is fleshed out. The disgraced wife "goes and becomes another man's wife," at which point events repeat themselves, and her second husband also "writes her a divorce certificate, hands it to her, and sends her away from his house." Of course, it is hard to envisage this being a regular occurrence, but that isn't the point. Moses is dealing with broad principles that can be applied to a variety of unforeseen circumstances, which is why he adds "or if he dies" at the end of verse 3. Moses makes a strong point in verse 4: once broken, a covenant cannot be remade. The first man "may not marry her again after she has been defiled, because that would be detestable to the Lord."[458] The language of defilement (an unusual hothpael form, הֻטַּמָּאָה) is typical of Leviticus rather than Deuteronomy, but presumably speaks either of the "indecent" actions that led to each divorce or (in the case of the second husband's death) simply from the woman having had sexual relations with another man.[459] However, that the putative situation is denounced as "detestable". Israel must deal with these events so that they do not "bring guilt on the

[457] Block's suggestion that it refers to menstrual bleeding that renders the wife perpetually ritually unclean, thus preventing normal marital relations, is plausible but probably too specific (*Deuteronomy*, 558–59).

[458] This is precisely how these verses are understood in Jer 3:1. It has been suggested that the underlying motive for the action of the men here is profit (see McConville's discussion of this and other possibilities, *Deuteronomy*, 358–59), but the lack of detail points rather in the direction suggested above.

[459] The verb only occurs here and in 21:23.

land the Lord your God is giving you as an inheritance." This moves the whole discussion into the sphere of Israel's distinctive, divinely inspired righteousness, set against the dark background of the surrounding cultures.[460] Righteousness and trust must characterize Israel's ethical life in every sphere, including marriage and even the sadness of divorce. To act any other way would be tantamount to a breach of covenant.

From considering the implications of multiple divorces, Moses returns to the celebration and protection of marriage. In 20:7–8, newlywed males were excused from military service (preeminently during the conquest). Now the provision is extended to all kinds of public service ("any duty" or even "matter"). However, this legislation in 24:5 goes even further than chapter 20, with an emphatic statement of the positive delights of marriage: "He is free to stay at home for one year, so that he can bring joy to the wife he has married." The underlying premise is that to deny a husband or wife sexual and relational intimacy would be inherently wrong and a denial of "righteousness" in its fullest sense. Life in the land should be a celebration of God's kindness, and any action which interrupts the enjoyment of that kindness, experienced as the "good life" in the land, is deeply problematic.

This is why depriving a brother of "a pair of grindstones or even the upper millstone as security for a debt" (24:6) is unacceptable. Repayment cannot be forced like this in Israel. The first term ("a pair of grindstones") refers to the small milling device found in most homes, and the second to the top or rider stone of a larger communal mill. Neither should be taken as a pledge for a debt. There are two reasons for this: taking these stones would, of course, undermine the ability of the person to grind and therefore feed himself and presumably his family, risking plunging a brother into a downward spiral of poverty (see also Job 24:3, 9 and 2 Kgs 4:1 for other examples of unacceptable pledges). More than that, taking such a pledge effectively denies the ability of one of Yahweh's people to enjoy his beautiful (righteous) life. The life that is taken as security is more than mere existence: it is the life to the full, which is given by God himself.

The restriction on kidnapping (whether in order to recover a debt or for any other reason) in verse 7 then takes this principle a step further.

---

[460] The situation is like that of Lev 18:22—the focus is on the action itself being detestable, rather than apportioning blame.

Removing the freedom of (stealing) a brother is punishable by death (also Exod 21:16). The motive for such an action ("whether he treats him as a slave or sells him") is irrelevant. Lording it over someone like this (which may be the literal meaning of the phrase)[461] is a violation of God's covenant with his people, and the response must be unequivocal: "the kidnapper must die. You must purge the evil from you." This simply cannot be allowed to happen in the family of God.

24:8–9. An abrupt change of focus introduces the community response to the kind of skin condition dealt with at length in Leviticus 13–14. Here, however, the issue is not actually treating skin disorders, but rather submission to the appropriate authority—in this case, "following carefully everything the Levitical priests instruct you to do." The core concern of these verses is underlined by the statement at the end of verse 8: "Be careful to do as I have commanded them." The Levites speak as those who have been commissioned by Moses to deliver the very words of God (presumably another allusion to the provisions of Lev 13–14). And all of this is backed up in the briefest of references to the events of Numbers 12:1–10 in verse 9: "Remember what the Lord your God did to Miriam on the journey after you left Egypt." The issue in Numbers 12 was rebellion against Moses's leadership, and specifically against the authority of his words.[462] This opposition led to Miriam becoming leprous, which explains the connection between skin complaints and submission to authority. These verses then provide reinforcement to the basic concern, displayed throughout the book, that God's people live by listening in the land which God is giving them.

24:10–25:4. From 24:10, Moses presents a wide range of material, mostly unique to Deuteronomy, designed to protect those who are vulnerable and disadvantaged. Irrespective of the cause of such people's plight, the community of God's people must offer care and support.

Although the idea of the brotherhood of Israel is not invoked specifically, treating one's neighbor well expresses the fundamental mutual responsibilities of the covenant people. This is illustrated in verses 10–11,

---

461 Driver, *Deuteronomy*, 274.

462 Numbers highlights that the roots of the conflict seem to have been personal and relational: "Miriam and Aaron criticized Moses because of the Cushite woman he married (for he had married a Cushite woman)" (Num 12:1), but then were expressed in a clear rejection of Moses's authority: "They said, 'Does the Lord speak only through Moses? Does he not also speak through us?' " (12:2).

where a strict limit is placed on what may be done when a loan repayment becomes due: "Do not enter his house to collect what he offers as security." This would be both invasive and humiliating. Instead of forcing entry, Moses's instruction is clear: "Stand outside while the man you are making the loan to brings the security out to you" (24:11). Every Israelite should be allowed the chance to deal with the difficulty of falling into debt with dignity.[463] Interestingly, there is no discussion of how one is to recover the debt if the person is unable to pay. In the world of Deuteronomy, that is a matter of lesser concern!

In the verses that follow, Moses adds further restrictions—specifically with regard to dealing with the poor. Those who are struggling economically should not be deprived of the cloak that doubles up as a sleeping bag. Even if a poor person offers you his cloak as a down payment, Moses insists, "Be sure to return it to him at sunset." The consequences of such kindness are significant: it will result in a right relationship between you ("he will bless you") and also guarantees the approval of God himself. The fact that "this will be counted as righteousness to you before the Lord your God" provides yet more evidence that the overarching purpose of these laws is to ensure that God's righteousness is embodied in every aspect of the life of his people.

This relational righteousness, according to 24:14–15, is even to be extended to struggling hired workers, whatever their ethnicity. The attitude to slavery among God's people is remarkable in itself, but the insistence on compassion for "hired workers" (even those who are migrants) is dramatically different from anything else seen in the ancient Near East. The general prohibition of treating such workers unfairly is backed up by a positive requirement to ensure that they are paid each day, in the same way as Israelites (Lev 19:13): "You are to pay him his wages each day before the sun sets, because he is poor and depends on them." This will enable the worker to provide for himself and his family. To refuse to do this is a denial of the righteousness to which they are called and puts the oppressor at odds with Yahweh himself. This explains why in 24:15, if the oppressed worker cries out to God (cf. Exod 22:22–23), his prayer will be heard and "you will be held guilty." This is "the antithesis of the spirit of the covenant."[464]

---

[463] See David A. Daube, "The Culture of Deuteronomy," *Orita* 3 (1969): 27–52.

[464] McConville, *Deuteronomy*, 362. See also Jas 5:4.

Many of these requirements are basically a matter of natural justice, albeit a natural justice shaped by Israel's own experience of God's kindness. It is not really a surprise that Moses insists that individuals should be answerable for their own sin (24:16) and that the vulnerable should not be denied justice or protection, whether non-Israelites passing through, the fatherless, or widows.

The principle of 24:16 ("each person will be put to death for his own sin," rather than anyone being punished for the crimes of relatives) is a classic expression of the righteousness of God.[465]

Such fair treatment is also to be extended consistently to those who are most vulnerable in Israelite society (24:17), with "resident aliens," "fatherless children," and "widows" all being singled out for special attention (as in 10:18). And the motivation for all this? Once more, Israel's experience in captivity themselves is to shape the way they treat others: "Remember that you were a slave in Egypt, and the Lord your God redeemed you from there" (24:18). Simply "remembering" should, of course, be more than enough to mold their behavior, but Yahweh leaves his people without excuse: "Therefore I am commanding you to do this."

The statements that follow in 24:19–22 give particular shape to the way the needy are to be protected and cared for. Profit and productivity should not be pursued at their expense, but rather there should be a studied inefficiency in harvesting grain, grapes, and olives (see Lev 19:9–10; 23:22). When harvesting grain, if a sheaf is forgotten, Moses says "do not go back to get it." The reason for this is simple but far-reaching: "so that the Lord your God may bless you in all the work of your hands" (as in 23:20). God's beneficence can be relied on. His people have no need to pursue higher yields at the expense of the poor. The same principle applies when harvesting olives ("do not go over the branches again," 24:20) and grapes ("do not glean what is left," 24:21): "what remains will be for the resident alien, the fatherless, and the widow." The experience of the exodus should shape the life of God's people in the land in permanent

---

[465] This is not contradicted by texts such as Exod 20:5 (Deut 5:9) and 34:7 which deal with the enduring consequences of sinful behavior, rather than the (judicial) punishment itself. Lundbom (*Deuteronomy*, 693–94) cites some examples in contemporary legislation that demand such punishment. He argues that God retains the right to punish the many for the sins of the few, but this is not persuasive.

and profound ways, not least in their generous provision for the poor.[466] This is the road to experiencing the blessings of the covenant as a nation.

In this "righteous" environment, even the guilty are protected. The statement of 25:1 should be unnecessary ("the judges ... will clear the innocent and condemn the guilty"), but given the nature of people, nothing is left to chance. 25:2–3 ensures that sentences handed down by the judges are proportional, limiting corporal punishment to what is "appropriate for his crime," prescribing the setting ("before the judges") and establishing an upper limit of "forty lashes" for crimes demanding corporal punishment (e.g., 22:18; see also 2 Cor 11:24–25). There is a specific reason for this: even the criminal is a "brother Israelite" and as such must not be needlessly "degraded."

It is not easy to see the link between verses 1–3 and verse 4. The statement "Do not muzzle an ox while it treads out grain" sounds proverbial—the hard-working ox shouldn't be forced to smell the food it is providing without being allowed to eat it—and acts as a summary of the LORD's commitment to justice for the weak.[467] To be righteous means to treat people (and animals) fairly. Interestingly, Paul picks up on this principle (and the specific example of 25:4) when talking about support for teachers in 1 Corinthians 9:9 and 1 Timothy 5:18.

Throughout this section, the overwhelming burden of Moses is to see God's righteousness embodied in the life of the nation, and particularly in the protection of the vulnerable on the basis of the exodus.

25:5–10. At this point, as we move to the conclusion of Moses's grand presentation of the shape of the beautiful life, we encounter a series of typically Deuteronomic worked examples. These scenarios are hardly typical. If anything, they seem to have been chosen to demonstrate that being the covenant people of Yahweh, called to righteousness, should shape Israel's behavior in even the most arcane and outlandish circumstances. This both highlights that these chapters (12–26) cannot be adequately characterized as either case law or as a constitution for the nation. This torah really is *sui generis.*

It is clear from verses 5–10 that righteousness in Israel means both caring for the vulnerable and taking family responsibilities deeply

---

466 As displayed by Boaz in Ruth 2.

467 Ancient artwork (notably from Egypt) has been found depicting oxen nibbling grain even as they thresh it (Lundbom, *Deuteronomy*, 701).

seriously. This time, the situation, while probably uncommon, is not hard to envisage. The crucial detail is that two brothers are "living on the same property": this means that both are dependent on the land (a shared inheritance). If "one of them dies without a son" (25:5), this would have the effect of exposing the widow to great financial risk. Without an heir to secure a share of the property, she is extremely vulnerable. However, of more pressing significance is the threat of the inheritance (and name) of the dead brother being eradicated: his place and that of his family in Israel would effectively be lost. This explains why the woman is prohibited from marrying a "stranger" (that is, someone outside the family). The way in which this law is cast may suggest that it is designed not to prevent the woman following her heart but rather to stop the remaining brother from getting rid of his obligation by fobbing her off on another man and presumably retaining the full share of the land himself, thus disrupting the pattern of inheritance and erasing the memory of his brother.

Rather than pursuing such a selfish action, he "is to take her as his wife, have sexual relations with her, and perform the duty of a brother-in-law for her" (v. 5). The details are sparse. It would seem likely that this situation applies only if the remaining brother is single (rather than prescribing bigamy as the answer to the inheritance issue). What is clear, however, is that the focus is on ensuring the continuance of the dead brother's name (thereby preserving his inheritance). The mechanism involves the firstborn son of the new union receiving the inheritance of the dead brother ("so his name will not be blotted out from Israel") and then normal service being resumed for any other offspring. There is an apparent tension here with the prohibitions of Leviticus 18:16 (having sex with one's brother's wife) and 20:21 (marrying one's brother's wife), but this is best understood as the difference between normal life and the exceptional circumstances described here, in which levirate marriage was appropriate.[468]

Although the situation seems slightly arcane, the principles underlying this provision could hardly be more serious. Provision is made for a widow to go the elders at the city gate and say "My brother-in-law refuses to preserve his brother's name in Israel" (v. 7). This is clearly his

[468] The story of Numbers 27:1–11, where Zelophehad's daughters inherit land, also shows that there could be real flexibility in exceptional circumstances on how inheritance laws were applied. At the end of the day, we do not have enough information to construct a full picture of how these various practices fitted together.

solemn duty (as in Gen 38 and the story of Tamar and Onan). Refusal to meet this obligation will lead to public humiliation, in front of the elders, at the hands of the woman, who in verse 9 is to "remove his sandal from his foot, and spit in his face."

Removing his sandal like this is basically to "unman" the brother: one can neither work properly nor fight barefoot. Spitting in the face is the highest expression of disgust (see Num 12:14; Job 30:10). The brother is opting out of all responsibility to his family, his nation, and his God and is therefore only worthy of contempt. So serious is this matter, that the stigma on the individual is to remain: "And his family name in Israel will be 'the house of the man whose sandal was removed' " (25:10).

It is not completely clear why this particular sequence of events should be singled out for attention. Other scenarios (like a couple simply having no [surviving] children) would surely have been more common! However, in this collection, Moses seems to delight in choosing slightly more arcane situations in order to illustrate underlying principles and the overarching righteousness that must characterize the life of Yahweh's people in the land. This approach is illustrated even more vividly in the material that follows.

25:11–12. The intervention envisaged in 25:11–12 has to be the most unexpected in the Old Testament! We are not told what causes the fight between these two men, nor what motivates the wife of the underdog to intervene. However, what is clear is that the wife's action is shameful: when she "puts out her hand and seizes him by the private parts." Literally she grabs the man's "parts of shame." Presumably this action imperils the man's ability to procreate, which goes some way to explaining the uniquely severe penalty.[469]

We should not ignore the fact that this is the only example of a command to sever a body part anywhere in the Old Testament. It is literally her "palm" (כַּף) that is to be cut off. It is not entirely clear what is envisaged.[470] Given the fact that physiological differences preclude the usual "eye for an eye" equivalence in sentencing, this shocking punishment nonetheless fits the crime. It is still a "like for like" provision, rather

[469] The Middle Assyrian Laws (see *ANET*³, 181) contain legislation for punishing women who damage a man's testicles by mutilation, but the text is damaged and one cannot be sure of the nature of the penalty. The scenario here however is much more detailed and specific.

[470] See Block, *Deuteronomy*, 585, and Lundbom, *Deuteronomy*, 712–13, for a range of possibilities.

than an excessively punitive mutilation. But what lies behind this strange provision? At the heart of Moses's concern here is the disruption of the life of the covenant people. Ensuring that "your eye shall show no pity" (lit.) is the demand made earlier in the book in response to idolatry (13:8), cold-blooded murder (19:13), and perjury (19:21). This suggests that the woman concerned here is making a deliberate attempt to prevent her husband's opponent ever having children. In any event, one suspects that Moses's inclusion of this incident in his presentation after thirteen chapters would have had the effect of making even the most drowsy listener sit up and start to take notice!

25:13–16. The demand for "righteousness" is not limited to more outlandish occurrences but must saturate every interaction and transaction between the people of Yahweh. This includes using "full and honest" (lit., "whole and righteous") measures (25:15; see also Lev 19:35–36, where "righteous" [צֶדֶק] is also used). The point of keeping "differing measures, a larger and a smaller" at home was to use the lighter weight to calculate your debts and the heavier one to work out what other people owe you. Seeking to exploit the people of God like this just will not do (as in, e.g., Hos 12:7; Amos 8:5; Mic 6:11). On the contrary, as 25:16 states: "You must have a full and honest weight, a full and honest dry measure." This is the way to live out God's righteousness, and therefore this is the way of blessing, as befits a covenant people.

To defraud each other is the way of the nations. To act like this is to expose oneself to the displeasure of God himself (so 25:16: "For everyone who does such things and acts unfairly is detestable to the Lord your God"). To act like this is to reject the ways of Yahweh and go the way of the nations.

25:17–19. The final section of the main body of the collection of laws draws directly on either the events of Exodus 17:8–16 or Numbers 14:43–45. In both accounts, the Amalekites launched unprovoked attacks on God's people.[471] Here Moses adds the extra detail in verse 18 that "they met you along the way and attacked all your stragglers from behind when you were tired and weary." The reason behind this cowardly attack is actually quite simple: "they did not fear God" (25:18b).

---

[471] Given the contrasting outcomes of the encounters in Exodus and Numbers, it may be more likely that Moses has the post-Horeb clash in mind. However, Exod 17:14 suggests that it is the initial clash that settled things.

In this case, "righteousness" requires that the people of Yahweh execute his judgment against Amalek with the same level of care and obedience as they must against the Canaanite nations. The instruction of verse 19 is crystal clear: when they have secured the land (and have "rest from all the enemies around you") then they must "blot out the memory of Amalek under heaven." The abortive attempts of Saul to do just that are recorded in 1 Samuel 15.[472] The command of Exodus 17:14 is reiterated, with Moses adding a further imperative: "Do not forget!" God's people must be relentless in the pursuit of the righteous life to which God has called them.

Bridge

While at one level, these chapters of Moses's torah seem slightly random and unpredictable, at another they relentlessly depict the righteousness of Yahweh that must control and be displayed in every single aspect of the life of his people. From family life to commerce, from the treatment of animals to neighbors, every facet of life must be shaped by and conform to the full-orbed justice and kindness (the righteousness of) Yahweh himself. This is the righteousness that exceeds that of the Pharisees which Jesus came to put within our grasp by the power of the Spirit.

The coming of Christ makes a rich and radical difference to our life as the people of God. That's why Paul can write in Ephesians 4:17–18, "Therefore, I say this and testify in the Lord: You should no longer walk as the Gentiles do, in the futility of their thoughts. They are darkened in their understanding, excluded from the life of God, because of the ignorance that is in them and because of the hardness of their hearts."

As God's people we are called to live a dramatically different, righteous life. Paul continues in Ephesians 4:21–23: we were "taught by him, as the truth is in Jesus, to take off your former way of life, the old self that is corrupted by deceitful desires, to be renewed in the spirit of your minds, and to put on the new self, the one created according to God's likeness in righteousness and purity of the truth."

---

[472] A conflict that plays a central role in the book of Esther, as Haman and Mordecai clash.

8. Conclusion: Living All of Life for God (Firstfruits and Tithes) (26:1–19)

1 "When you enter the land the Lord your God is giving you as an inheritance, and you take possession of it and live in it, 2 take some of the
first of all the land's produce that you harvest from the land the Lord
your God is giving you and put it in a basket. Then go to the place
where the Lord your God chooses to have his name dwell. 3 When you
come before the priest who is serving at that time, say to him, 'Today I
declare to the Lord your God that I have entered the land the Lord swore
to our ancestors to give us.'

4 "Then the priest will take the basket from you and place it before
the altar of the Lord your God. 5 You are to respond by saying in the
presence of the Lord your God:

> My father was a wandering Aramean. He went down to
> Egypt with a few people and resided there as an alien. There
> he became a great, powerful, and populous nation. 6 But the
> Egyptians mistreated and oppressed us, and forced us to
> do hard labor. 7 So we called out to the Lord, the God of our
> ancestors, and the Lord heard our cry and saw our misery,
> hardship, and oppression. 8 Then the Lord brought us out
> of Egypt with a strong hand and an outstretched arm, with
> terrifying power, and with signs and wonders. 9 He led us
> to this place and gave us this land, a land flowing with
> milk and honey. 10 I have now brought the first of the land's
> produce that you, Lord, have given me.

You will then place the container before the Lord your God and bow down
to him. 11 You, the Levites, and the resident aliens among you will rejoice in
all the good things the Lord your God has given you and your household.

12 "When you have finished paying all the tenth of your produce in the
third year, the year of the tenth, you are to give it to the Levites, resident
aliens, fatherless children, and widows, so that they may eat in your towns
and be satisfied. 13 Then you will say in the presence of the Lord your God:

> I have taken the consecrated portion out of my house; I
> have also given it to the Levites, resident aliens, father-
> less children, and widows, according to all the commands
> you gave me. I have not violated or forgotten your com-
> mands. 14 I have not eaten any of it while in mourning, or
> removed any of it while unclean, or offered any of it for
> the dead. I have obeyed the Lord my God; I have done all
> you commanded me. 15 Look down from your holy dwell-
> ing, from heaven, and bless your people Israel and the

land you have given us as you swore to our ancestors, a
land flowing with milk and honey.

[16] "The LORD your God is commanding you this day to follow these statutes and ordinances. Follow them carefully with all your heart and all your soul. [17] Today you have affirmed that the LORD is your God and that you will walk in his ways, keep his statutes, commands, and ordinances, and obey him. [18] And today the LORD has affirmed that you are his own possession as he promised you, that you are to keep all his commands, [19] that he will elevate you to praise, fame, and glory above all the nations he has made, and that you will be a holy people to the LORD your God as he promised."

At the conclusion of his exposition of the torah, Moses turns to a pair of rituals that express the very heart of what God ask of his people: a wholehearted commitment to live for and with him, the God of the covenant, in the land which he is giving them.

26:1–11. Chapter 26 picks up many of the elements of chapter 12, as the people are called to go to the place chosen by God to rejoice in his presence, and so it provides a fitting conclusion to this long central panel of Moses's preaching.

Moses's careful ordering of material obviously resumes at the conclusion of the collection of laws. The fact that the ritual of firstfruits was associated with the Feast of Weeks, means that the details included here could very naturally have been included in chapter 16 (or even where it is mentioned in connection with the Levites in 18:4), but for rhetorical reasons, it is held back until now, so that the "confession of faith" of this ritual provides a fitting response and conclusion to this section of the book.[473]

The basic idea of the ritual is beautifully simple according to verse 2: "Take some of the first of all the land's produce that you harvest from the land the LORD your God is giving you and put it in a basket. Then go to the place where the LORD your God chooses to have his name dwell." As is often the case in Deuteronomy, the details are fairly vague ("some of the first of all" your produce) because Moses's agenda is primarily theological rather than liturgical.[474] Although it is not stated explicitly here, the implication is surely that the best of the produce should be selected. It also extends the provision of 18:4 to cover all possible produce.

[473] With McConville, *Deuteronomy*, 378.

[474] The offering of firstfruits is also prescribed or described in Exod 23:16, 19; 34:22, 26; Lev 23:17; Num 15:19–21.

In this section, twelve actions are described—five by the worshiper, two by the priest and then five more by the worshiper—but these actions are deeply embedded in a rich theological framework.[475] At the heart of the ceremony is the idea of gratitude: God has ordered history to give them this land (26:1, 2, 3), and now the people must express their thanks, both in terms of this offering and the confession that accompanies it.

In 26:3, the offering is taken to the "priest who is serving at that time" (another vague allusion to the inner workings of the sanctuary; see 17:9; 19:17), and an initial declaration made: "Today I declare to the Lord your God that I have entered the land the Lord swore to our ancestors to give us." The foundational statement in this ritual emphasizes both the past ("I have entered the land") and the present ("today"). This is a key feature of the whole book: the key to living well for Yahweh is to make godly choices today that are informed by the key todays of the past and to acknowledge that the journey of Israel in future will hinge on making repeated choices to pursue Yahweh on the procession of todays that are yet to come. Yahweh has "brought" them into the land; now they must "bring" the firstfruits to the priest.[476]

After the priest receives the basket and places it "before the altar" (26:4), the individual is to "respond" or "answer" with the prescribed statement. To describe this as an answer is both deliberate and important: this entire ritual is predicated on the prior goodness and grace of Yahweh. No actual words have been spoken to the worshiper, but this is clearly an answer to the grace that Yahweh has "announced" to his people in a myriad of ways in the recent past. The response is also "spoken" not to the priest, but "in the presence of Yahweh your God." This answer is given to the God who graciously speaks to his people.[477]

The confession itself runs from verse 5 to verse 10. It sums up, or at least alludes to, the key elements of the history of God's people from the patriarchal narratives to the conquest extremely succinctly. In 26:5, the public statement begins (perhaps slightly surprisingly) with Jacob: "My father was a wandering Aramean ..." The designation "Aramean" is unusual but easily understood, tying Jacob to his forebears, Isaac and

---

[475] See the helpful diagram in Block, *Deuteronomy*, 599.

[476] The verb "to come" (בּוֹא) is woven into the structure of this text (see McConville, *Deuteronomy*, 378).

[477] The theological underpinnings of this chapter are clearly the same as those of chapter 4.

Abraham, who came from and moved around ancient civilizations that could be generically described as Aramean. One may have expected a reference to Abraham at this point as the "father of the nation," but throughout the Old Testament, this accolade is awarded to both him and his grandson, Jacob, the physical progenitor of the heads of the twelve tribes, with the emphasis depending on context. It is particularly appropriate to describe Jacob as an Aramean, given the origins of his mother (Gen 24:10), and the time he spent there with Laban, his uncle (e.g., 25:20), even marrying his Aramean cousins, Leah and Rachel.[478]

As the focus here is on the actual (impending) occupation of the land, it is not surprising that Jacob is mentioned. Jacob's enforced move to Egypt ("wandering" here may even imply *de facto* refugee status, as in Ps 105:13) and experience of exclusion and oppression ("as a resident alien") led to the fulfillment of promises that had their origin with Yahweh's commitment to his grandfather, initially in Genesis 12:1–3: "There he became a great, powerful, and populous nation" (also Exod 1:7–20). Part of the genius of this recap of Israel's history is that it manages to encapsulate the importance of the promises to Abraham and the birth of the nation through Jacob and his sons in a very few words.

The account of the exodus in verses 6–8 is similarly economical, drawing on a range of familiar (and stereotypical) terms familiar from both Deuteronomy itself and earlier pentateuchal material (e.g., Exod 1:11–12; 2:24–25; 3:14–15; 6:9) . The persecution of God's people (v. 6), their appeal to "Yahweh, the God of our ancestors" (presumably Abraham, Isaac, and Jacob once more), his loving response (he "heard our cry and saw our misery, hardship, and oppression," v. 7), and his direct action in rescuing Israel "with a strong hand and an outstretched arm, with terrifying power, and with signs and wonders" (v. 8) are well-worn phrases (4:34; 6:21; 8:14). Interestingly, given the prominence of the events of Horeb in the book, there is no reference to those formative events here. While in the past some have made much of this omission, in this context, with its focus on the fulfillment of patriarchal promises, it is surely a matter of enough already having been said on the subject!

The forty-year catalogue of events that takes up most of Exodus and Numbers is condensed into a single line in 26:9: "He led us to this place

---

[478] Block suggests the term is deliberately vague, applying to all three patriarchs, in line with Moses's convention (*Deuteronomy*, 601–2).

and gave us this land, a land flowing with milk and honey." At the heart of the land ("this place"), Yahweh chooses a place where this confession should be made. Again, this has been amply covered earlier in Moses's sermon, so we move straight to the climactic statement of verse 10: "I have now brought the first of the land's produce that you, Lord, have given me."[479] This simple act, and the straightforward commentary encapsulate a wholehearted response to the grace of God and a moment-to-moment commitment to live out the torah that Moses has been preaching. These simple words are to be underlined by a simple act, as the basket is placed before Yahweh and the worshiper "bows down to him" (26:10).

Such faith-driven actions then unlock the joy that is at the heart of the attractive and inclusive righteousness of God (see 4:5–8). All Israel is once more to rejoice together in God's presence "in all the good things" that God has given them all, including the Levites and those foreigners who have made their home in Israel.

In many ways, this is a simple rerun of the shape of national life that is set out in chapter 16. However, the added element of the confession of faith on behalf of the worshiper and the all-encompassing nature of the ritual, drawing together the promises to the patriarchs, the exodus, and the conquest, makes it a suitable, full-orbed conclusion to Moses's preaching.

26:12–15. The presentation of the triennial tithes (i.e., those to be periodically made available to the Levites and other disadvantaged members of the community) was dealt with in 14:28–29. Now Moses revisits this ritual, presumably to hammer home the model of obedient response to grace embodied in the preceding verses. The common elements of community rejoicing and verbal affirmation clearly bind the two ceremonies together, and Moses returns to the tithe to underscore the message of the first half of the chapter.

Yet again, the primary focus is not on the mechanics of the obligation. Moses jumps straight to the conclusion of events ("when you have finished paying all the tenth"), where the entire community (this time specifying all "disadvantaged" groups: "the Levites, resident aliens, fatherless children, and widows") has been enabled to feast together across the nation ("in all your towns").

---

[479] The Hebrew is more emphatic, requiring something like "Look!" or "Here it is!'

Even though the tithe is distributed locally (away from the place chosen by Yahweh), the confession itself still takes place "in the presence of Yahweh." This shows that Yahweh's presence is both real and localized and not limited to the sanctuary in operation at that time, but, as chapter 4 makes clear, primarily tied to the divine word.[480]

Unlike the public affirmation of verses 5–10, the emphasis is not on salvation history, but on the individual response of the worshiper. The list of actions in verses 13–14 reads like a disclaimer: (1) I have shared the tithe, providing for the community feast (26:13), rather than eaten it myself; (2) I have not "violated or forgotten your commands" (26:13), presumably referring to blatant or egregious sins; (3) I have not engaged in any questionable (probably Canaanite) religious practices: "I have not eaten any of it while in mourning, or removed any of it while unclean, or offered any of it for the dead" (26:14); and (4) "I have obeyed Yahweh my God," and have lived according to the torah.[481]

This final statement reminds Moses's listeners of the tension that runs throughout this book and will come into sharper focus in the closing chapters: God's people are called to the wholehearted obedience of a torah-shaped life, and yet can never manage to reach that standard in the fullest sense (as visible in, e.g., 6:4–5). However, Israel can avoid idolatry and other blatant forms of disobedience and ensure their corporate life conforms to the patterns laid down in the torah.[482] If they manage to do this, it does create the conditions for God to continue to bless his people in his land from his "holy dwelling," that is, "heaven."

This blessing of Yahweh results in the people living a beautiful, righteous life in close relationship with him in fulfillment of all that was

---

[480] With, e.g., Tigay, *Deuteronomy*, 243. However, Ian Wilson, "Central Sanctuary or Local Settlement? The Location of the Triennial Declaration (Dtn 26,13–15)," *ZAW* 120 (2008): 323–40, among others, argues that the confession still takes place at the chosen place.

[481] Lundbom sees these statements as a simple affirmation that the tithe has not been misused as part of otherwise allowable Jewish burial rites (*Deuteronomy*, 732), but allows that it may be linked to necromancy and other pagan rites. It is hard to see why normal burial practices would occupy such a prominent position in the laws.

[482] This finds a parallel in the responsibilities of the king in Deut 17, and the assessment of the Davidic line in the light of that in both Kings and Chronicles (despite their differing agendas and emphases) and reflected in the Psalms. There is no suggestion anywhere that even David is sinless, but he is held up as one whose "heart was not turned aside" nor "lifted up above his brothers," or as the Psalms prefer, "blameless" (rather than sinless).

promised to Abraham, in the new Eden of the land "flowing with milk and honey." This is the pinnacle of Moses's idealism.

26:16–19. In 26:16–19, Moses deliberately provides a conclusion to his expansive exposition of torah, summarizing not just the requirement for righteousness, laid out so powerfully in chapters 12–26 (the "statutes and ordinances"), but also the message of his address as a whole up to this point.

The persistent emphasis on responding to Yahweh "this day" (or simply "today") continues in verses 16, 17, and 18. "Today" at Moab will set the tone for the "days" to come in the land (as in, e.g., 26:3). This moment of decision implicitly demands that every moment in the land be treated similarly. And what does Yahweh ask of his people? The long version has been expounded in chapters 12–26: the short version is to "follow the statutes and ordinances" and, picking up on 6:4, to "follow them carefully with all your heart and with all your soul."

Verse 17 could possibly refer to the declaration to be made on presentation of the triennial tithe, but it seems much more likely that Moses is referring to "the covenant at Moab" (29:1) and their in-the-moment response to his preaching on the plains of Moab. These verses strike a rich and delicate balance between the primacy of Yahweh's covenantal grace and both the necessity and consequences of obedient response. This covenant involves both grace and responsibility. Moses is well aware of the asymmetry of God's statement "I will be your God; you will be my people" and captures the delicate nuance of that statement beautifully.

Unusually, Israel's response (v. 17) comes before the gracious commitment of Yahweh (vv. 18–19) in these verses. Here, the emphasis is on the further blessings that Israel's response to grace will unlock. There is a lot riding on this. Should Israel manage to maintain wholehearted obedience, listening to Yahweh and doing exactly what he says (which is completely reasonable, given that they are Yahweh's "treasured possession," as in 7:6, a people of "promise"), the ramifications will be huge. According to verse 19, "he will elevate you to praise, fame, and glory above all the nations he has made, and that you will be a holy people to the Lord your God as he promised" (see also 28:1). The vision anticipated in 4:5–8 will become reality.[483] They really will be a "people holy to God."[484]

It is important to notice that the relationship between God's grace and Israel's response here is complex. It is not simply "Do this and you will get this." Yahweh's action is important at the beginning, middle, and end of this process. What God asks of his people, and promises to his people is clear. But it is also clear that if they are to meet their side of the deal, they will need God's help every step of the way.

Bridge

Chapter 26 brilliantly captures both the urgency and the extent of the response that Yahweh requires from his people. Moses's vision of the beautiful life is expansive, even all-encompassing. In every part of life, Yahweh's people are to love him and others, obeying him wholeheartedly. That obedience is dramatically represented and summed up in the liturgy of the firstfruits festival, and then backed up by a reminder of the symbolism of the triennial tithe. Israel must listen and obey today and every day. And yet even in these rituals, the comprehensive affirmations that must be made are deeply worrying: Israel may be able to fulfil her obligations on the surface (albeit with a gargantuan effort), but at the level of motivation? The signs are ominous.

This chapter is a brilliant exposition of the dynamics of grace in the life of the people of God. We do not simply need God to tell us what to do, or even to set us up in a context that is conducive to obedience; we need Yahweh to work in us at the deepest level and to enable us day after day to make godly choices in the power he supplies. Only in the resources he supplies can we hope to live the beautiful life.

The apostle Peter at the start of his second letter tells us the glorious news that we need to hear; the news of what God has done for us in the Lord Jesus: "His divine power has given us everything required for life and godliness through the knowledge of him who called us by his own glory and goodness" (2 Pet 1:3).

---

[483] This vision is later picked up and developed in Isa 42:6 and 49:6, where the Servant of Yahweh embodies the nation as they should be and is a light to the nations.

[484] The form of the double declaration here resembles an ancient treaty between "equals" (e.g., that between Rameses II of Egypt and the Hittite Hattusili III); see *ANET*[3], 199–203. However, the correspondence is not exact, and it is not clear that this is reflecting a specific covenant ceremony.

This is the truth we need to hear over and over as we take hold of the gospel again and again. This is what we need to say to one another over and over again, as we speak the gospel into one another's lives. As the writer to the Hebrews says, "Encourage each other daily, while it is still called today, so that none of you is hardened by sin's deception" (Heb 3:13).

In Deuteronomy 12–26, then, Moses gives the fullest, most wide-ranging picture of righteousness (construed in terms of right worship, right relationships, and right behavior) in Scripture. It is a stunning picture of the beautiful life in God's presence in his land. Expanding on the Decalogue, Moses applies and illustrates what a righteous life with God looks like, mixing commands with persuasion, examples with exhortation. This is a collection of legal material unlike any other in the ancient world in its scope, intent, and vision. What God asks of his people is clear. However, it is equally clear that if they are to have any hope of doing what Yahweh requires of them, they desperately need his enabling, equipping, and forgiving grace.

V. Moses Preaches Blessing and Curse (27:1–28:68)

> [1] Moses and the elders of Israel commanded the people, "Keep every
> command I am giving you today. [2] When you cross the Jordan into the
> land the LORD your God is giving you, set up large stones and cover them
> with plaster. [3] Write all the words of this law on the stones after you
> cross to enter the land the LORD your God is giving you, a land flowing
> with milk and honey, as the LORD, the God of your ancestors, has prom-
> ised you. [4] When you have crossed the Jordan, you are to set up these
> stones on Mount Ebal, as I am commanding you today, and you are to
> cover them with plaster. [5] Build an altar of stones there to the LORD your
> God—do not use any iron tool on them. [6] Use uncut stones to build the
> altar of the LORD your God and offer burnt offerings to the LORD your God
> on it. [7] There you are to sacrifice fellowship offerings, eat, and rejoice
> in the presence of the LORD your God. [8] Write clearly all the words of
> this law on the plastered stones."
>
> [9] Moses and the Levitical priests spoke to all Israel, "Be silent, Isra-
> el, and listen! This day you have become the people of the LORD your
> God. [10] Obey the LORD your God and follow his commands and statutes
> I am giving you today."
>
> [11] On that day Moses commanded the people, [12] "When you have crossed
> the Jordan, these tribes will stand on Mount Gerizim to bless the peo-

ple: Simeon, Levi, Judah, Issachar, Joseph, and Benjamin. [13] And these tribes will stand on Mount Ebal to deliver the curse: Reuben, Gad, Asher, Zebulun, Dan, and Naphtali. [14] The Levites will proclaim in a loud voice to every Israelite:

[15] 'The person who makes a carved idol or cast image, which is detestable to the Lord, the work of a craftsman, and sets it up in secret is cursed.'

And all the people will reply, 'Amen!'

[16] 'The one who dishonors his father or mother is cursed.'

And all the people will say, 'Amen!'

[17] 'The one who moves his neighbor's boundary marker is cursed.'

And all the people will say, 'Amen!'

[18] 'The one who leads a blind person astray on the road is cursed.'

And all the people will say, 'Amen!'

[19] 'The one who denies justice to a resident alien, a fatherless child, or a widow is cursed.'

And all the people will say, 'Amen!'

[20] 'The one who sleeps with his father's wife is cursed, for he has violated his father's marriage bed.'

And all the people will say, 'Amen!'

[21] 'The one who has sexual intercourse with any animal is cursed.'

And all the people will say, 'Amen!'

[22] 'The one who sleeps with his sister, whether his father's daughter or his mother's daughter is cursed.'

And all the people will say, 'Amen!'

[23] 'The one who sleeps with his mother-in-law is cursed.'

And all the people will say, 'Amen!'

[24] 'The one who secretly kills his neighbor is cursed.'

And all the people will say, 'Amen!'

[25] 'The one who accepts a bribe to kill an innocent person is cursed.'

And all the people will say, 'Amen!'

[26] 'Anyone who does not put the words of this law into practice is cursed.'

And all the people will say, 'Amen!'

[28:1] "Now if you faithfully obey the LORD your God and are careful to follow all his commands I am giving you today, the LORD your God will put
you far above all the nations of the earth. [2] All these blessings will come
and overtake you, because you obey the LORD your God:

> [3] You will be blessed in the city
> and blessed in the country.
> [4] Your offspring will be blessed,
> and your land's produce,
> and the offspring of your livestock,
> including the young of your herds
> and the newborn of your flocks.
> [5] Your basket and kneading bowl will be blessed.
> [6] You will be blessed when you come in
> and blessed when you go out.

[7] "The LORD will cause the enemies who rise up against you to be defeated before you. They will march out against you from one direction but flee from you in seven directions. [8] The LORD will grant you
a blessing on your barns and on everything you do; he will bless you
in the land the LORD your God is giving you. [9] The LORD will establish
you as his holy people, as he swore to you, if you obey the commands
of the LORD your God and walk in his ways. [10] Then all the peoples of
the earth will see that you bear the LORD's name, and they will stand
in awe of you. [11] The LORD will make you prosper abundantly with offspring, the offspring of your livestock, and your land's produce in the
land the LORD swore to your ancestors to give you. [12] The LORD will open
for you his abundant storehouse, the sky, to give your land rain in its
season and to bless all the work of your hands. You will lend to many
nations, but you will not borrow. [13] The LORD will make you the head
and not the tail; you will only move upward and never downward if
you listen to the LORD your God's commands I am giving you today and
are careful to follow them. [14] Do not turn aside to the right or the left
from all the things I am commanding you today, and do not follow
other gods to worship them.

[15] "But if you do not obey the LORD your God by carefully following all
his commands and statutes I am giving you today, all these curses will
come and overtake you:

> [16] You will be cursed in the city
> and cursed in the country.
> [17] Your basket and kneading bowl will be cursed.
> [18] Your offspring will be cursed,
> and your land's produce,
> the young of your herds,
> and the newborn of your flocks.

[19] You will be cursed when you come in
and cursed when you go out.

[20] "The LORD will send against you curses, confusion, and rebuke in
everything you do until you are destroyed and quickly perish, because
of the wickedness of your actions in abandoning me. [21] The LORD will
make pestilence cling to you until he has exterminated you from
the land you are entering to possess. [22] The LORD will afflict you with
wasting disease, fever, inflammation, burning heat, drought, blight,
and mildew; these will pursue you until you perish. [23] The sky above
you will be bronze, and the earth beneath you iron. [24] The LORD will
turn the rain of your land into falling dust; it will descend on you
from the sky until you are destroyed. [25] The LORD will cause you to be
defeated before your enemies. You will march out against them from
one direction but flee from them in seven directions. You will be an
object of horror to all the kingdoms of the earth. [26] Your corpses will
be food for all the birds of the sky and the wild animals of the earth,
with no one to scare them away.

[27] "The LORD will afflict you with the boils of Egypt, tumors, a festering
rash, and scabies, from which you cannot be cured. [28] The LORD will
afflict you with madness, blindness, and mental confusion, [29] so that
at noon you will grope as a blind person gropes in the dark. You will
not be successful in anything you do. You will only be oppressed
and robbed continually, and no one will help you. [30] You will become
engaged to a woman, but another man will rape her. You will build
a house but not live in it. You will plant a vineyard but not enjoy its
fruit. [31] Your ox will be slaughtered before your eyes, but you will
not eat any of it. Your donkey will be taken away from you and not
returned to you. Your flock will be given to your enemies, and no
one will help you. [32] Your sons and daughters will be given to another
people, while your eyes grow weary looking for them every day. But
you will be powerless to do anything. [33] A people you don't know will
eat your land's produce and everything you have labored for. You
will only be oppressed and crushed continually. [34] You will be driv-
en mad by what you see. [35] The LORD will afflict you with painful and
incurable boils on your knees and thighs—from the sole of your foot
to the top of your head.

[36] "The LORD will bring you and your king that you have appointed
to a nation neither you nor your ancestors have known, and there
you will worship other gods, of wood and stone. [37] You will become
an object of horror, scorn, and ridicule among all the peoples where
the LORD will drive you.

[38] "You will sow much seed in the field but harvest little, because
locusts will devour it. [39] You will plant and cultivate vineyards but

not drink the wine or gather the grapes, because worms will eat
them. [40] You will have olive trees throughout your territory but not
moisten your skin with oil, because your olives will drop off. [41] You
will father sons and daughters, but they will not remain yours, because
they will be taken prisoner. [42] Buzzing insects will take possession of
all your trees and your land's produce. [43] The resident alien among
you will rise higher and higher above you, while you sink lower and
lower. [44] He will lend to you, but you won't lend to him. He will be the
head, and you will be the tail.

[45] "All these curses will come, pursue, and overtake you until you are
destroyed, since you did not obey the LORD your God and keep the commands and statutes he gave you. [46] These curses will be a sign and a
wonder against you and your descendants forever. [47] Because you didn't
serve the LORD your God with joy and a cheerful heart, even though you
had an abundance of everything, [48] you will serve your enemies that
the LORD will send against you, in famine, thirst, nakedness, and a lack
of everything. He will place an iron yoke on your neck until he has
destroyed you. [49] The LORD will bring a nation from far away, from the
ends of the earth, to swoop down on you like an eagle, a nation whose
language you won't understand, [50] a ruthless nation, showing no respect
for the old and not sparing the young. [51] They will eat the offspring of
your livestock and your land's produce until you are destroyed. They will
leave you no grain, new wine, fresh oil, young of your herds, or newborn
of your flocks until they cause you to perish. [52] They will besiege you
within all your city gates until your high and fortified walls, that you
trust in, come down throughout your land. They will besiege you within
all your city gates throughout the land the LORD your God has given you.

[53] "You will eat your offspring, the flesh of your sons and daughters
the LORD your God has given you during the siege and hardship your
enemy imposes on you. [54] The most sensitive and refined man among
you will look grudgingly at his brother, the wife he embraces, and the
rest of his children, [55] refusing to share with any of them his children's
flesh that he will eat because he has nothing left during the siege and
hardship your enemy imposes on you in all your towns. [56] The most
sensitive and refined woman among you, who would not venture to
set the sole of her foot on the ground because of her refinement and
sensitivity, will begrudge the husband she embraces, her son, and her
daughter, [57] the afterbirth that comes out from between her legs and
the children she bears, because she will secretly eat them for lack of
anything else during the siege and hardship your enemy imposes on
you within your city gates.

[58] "If you are not careful to obey all the words of this law, which
are written in this scroll, by fearing this glorious and awe-inspiring
name—the LORD, your God—[59] he will bring wondrous plagues on you

> and your descendants, severe and lasting plagues, and terrible and chronic sicknesses. [60] He will afflict you again with all the diseases of Egypt, which you dreaded, and they will cling to you. [61] The Lord will also afflict you with every sickness and plague not recorded in the book of this law, until you are destroyed. [62] Though you were as numerous as the stars of the sky, you will be left with only a few people, because you did not obey the Lord your God. [63] Just as the Lord was glad to cause you to prosper and to multiply you, so he will also be glad to cause you to perish and to destroy you. You will be ripped out of the land you are entering to possess. [64] Then the Lord will scatter you among all peoples from one end of the earth to the other, and there you will worship other gods, of wood and stone, which neither you nor your ancestors have known. [65] You will find no peace among those nations, and there will be no resting place for the sole of your foot. There the Lord will give you a trembling heart, failing eyes, and a despondent spirit. [66] Your life will hang in doubt before you. You will be in dread night and day, never certain of survival. [67] In the morning you will say, 'If only it were evening!' and in the evening you will say, 'If only it were morning!'—because of the dread you will have in your heart and because of what you will see. [68] The Lord will take you back in ships to Egypt by a route that I said you would never see again. There you will sell yourselves to your enemies as male and female slaves, but no one will buy you."

After the conclusion of the collection of legal material in 26:16–19, Moses's attention shifts to specific rituals to be performed immediately on entering the land. As we might expect, these rituals are laden with theological significance and pave the way for the conclusion of the book in both the rhetorical climax of chapters 29–30 and the embodiment of its message in the "postscript" of chapters 31–34. In these chapters, Moses, now joined by the other leaders of God's people, spells out what has been merely a gnawing sense of unease thus far. The cavernous gulf between what God requires and what Israel is capable of is starting to come into full view.[485]

27:1–8. Now joined for the first time by the "elders of Israel" in 27:1, Moses reiterates his clarion call to obey, and to do it *today*. The language could hardly be more emphatic: Moses and the elders "*command*" the people to keep "the whole *commandment*" that they are *commanded* (here by Moses) today (see also 4:1–2, 5–6; 7:11; 8:1; 11:22, etc.). The addition of

---

[485] There is much discussion about the structure of these chapters and how they fit into the flow of the book (see, e.g., Block, *Deuteronomy*, 623–24). This part of the book consciously picks up the thought of 11:26–32 and develops it.

the elders here (and presumably the Levitical priests in 27:9) anticipates the fact that Moses's days are drawing to a close. Soon it will fall to others to ensure that all-encompassing obedience is the defining characteristic of the life of God's people.

As soon as the people set foot on dry land on the other side of the Jordan, they are to "set up large stones and cover them with plaster" (27:2). This ceremony has strong echoes of the covenant confirmation at Horeb (Exod 24:1–11), but here the focus falls on writing the torah *on the stones themselves*, so that the very words of Yahweh are on display at the heart of the new nation. Plastering stones like this enables the torah to be inscribed in black ink (probably made from soot) and, crucially, to be easily read.[486] Erecting these stones, however, is a one-off ritual, rather than the commissioning of a permanent, readable monument. Both the plaster and ink would quickly weather when exposed to the elements. These actions enshrine *obedience* at the heart of the nation from day one.[487]

The instructions specify inscribing "all the words of this law" on the stones (27:3). These words could be chapters 12–26 or, perhaps even more likely, Moses's words at Moab in their entirety.[488] Torah here once again captures the throughgoing response demanded by Yahweh's action in enabling them to cross the Jordan (which is depicted as a recapitulation of the crossing of the Red Sea), take possession of his land-gift, and enjoy the good life with him in that land, all in fulfillment of the promises to the patriarchs. The fact that Shechem was the place where Abram first received the promise of a gift of land (Gen 12:6–7) and where Jacob first bought land (Gen 33:18–19) makes the location of these actions deeply appropriate.

---

[486] Craigie, *Deuteronomy*, 328 (following Driver, *Deuteronomy*, 296) suggests that this technique is typically Egyptian, rather than Palestinian or Mesopotamian. For other ancient examples of writing on plaster, see Lundbom, *Deuteronomy*, 740.

[487] There is a slight delay until this ritual is carried out in Josh 8:30–35. Given the varied use of "day" in Deuteronomy, there is no need to insist on the actions taking place within 24 hours of fording the river (with Tigay, *Deuteronomy*, 248, *pace* Lundbom, *Deuteronomy*, 739, et al.) This ritual is not to be confused with the way (smaller?) stones from the Jordan are piled up at Gilgal as the river is crossed.

[488] This phrase is normally used as a general, non-specific summary term to refer to the total of the preaching of Moses at Moab. Tigay, *Deuteronomy*, 248, rightly points out that two stone pillars the size of the Law Code of Hammurabi could easily have contained all of Moses's words (Block, *Deuteronomy*, 627–28).

Moses reminds them that they have arrived in a land "flowing with milk and honey" (6:3; 11:9; 26:9, 15; 31:20), just as Yahweh promised in the exodus (Exod 3:8, 17; 13:5).

Verse 4 clarifies that the stones are to be set up on the limestone-rich Mount Ebal, one of the twin 3,000 foot peaks above Shechem on the east of the land above the Jordan Valley. These mountains are around 7.5 miles from the Jordan, which suggests that they are to source the stones when they get there, rather than carrying them from the Jordan. This ceremony designates Ebal (and Gerizim) as a permanent visual aid to the goodness of God at the heart of the land.

As well as setting up these temporary whiteboards on Ebal, the Israelites are to build a simple altar (27:5). As in Exodus 20:25, the altar is made from natural, undressed stones (presumably to distinguish Israelite altars from the long-established, chiseled Canaanite shrines). The purpose of the altar is to enable God's people to mark their entry into the land by presenting "burnt offerings." As is typical of the Old Testament, sacrifice marks this key moment in the life of the nation (see, e.g., Gen 9; 12; 1 Kgs 8; also 1 Chr 28; Ezra 6:16). There is no comment on the reason these particular sacrifices are offered, although in this case it is probable that the burnt offering encapsulates Israel's complete obligation to Yahweh, and the "fellowship" (or "peace") offering celebrates the covenantal relationship that is cemented by the gift of the land (the same offerings are made in Exod 24:6). It is completely appropriate then that here on Mount Ebal, the people are to "rejoice in the presence of Lord your God" for the first time. This initial sacrifice presumably precedes the practice required by in 12:6–7, 11–12, and 18 coming into effect at the place chosen by Yahweh: (or alternatively, Ebal is the first sanctioned place).[489]

The restatement of the requirement to write the torah on the stones in verse 8 is not simply redundant. The repetition underlines the inherent connection between obedience and life in the land. The immediate function of these stones (and the enduring function of the mountain on which they stand) is to make God's instructions not just clear but binding, so that Israel has no excuse should they depart from them. It

---

[489] So McConville, *Deuteronomy*, 390.

also ensures that the teaching, rather than the sacrifices, is the central element in this event.[490]

To "write clearly" conveys a Hebrew construction that is hard to capture in English (lit., "making it clear well"). The nuance of the adverbial form of the verb "to do good" is often missed: the goal of this torah is to convey "good" to God's people, and to write "well" is not simply to ensure that the handwriting on the rock is legible, but also that God's people have access to the "good" and life-giving words of God.[491]

This ritual unexpectedly takes place on Mount Ebal, which, according to the verses that follow (e.g., 27:11), is the mountain of curse, rather than Mount Gerizim, the mountain of blessing. This anticipates the rising note of pessimism in this final part of the book. It turns out that this highly significant event (and its stones) will come to function as an indictment of the people in years to come.

27:9–10. In 27:9, rather than the elders, it is the priests who are Levites who share the stage with Moses. Now the people are called not to enact a ritual on entering the land, but to embrace a significant theological reality before they cross the border. In an echo of the repeated calls of 6:4 and elsewhere, now uniquely with the added element of a call for silence, Moses insists that the people shut up and listen. This is to be the basic stance of those who have "become the people of God" (v. 9; see also 26:18; 29:13).

It usually Horeb that is spoken of as the definitive "day" for Israel (and the moment when they became the people of God; see Exod 19:3–6; Deut 4:20, 34; but also Exod 6:6–7). Here, however, Moab is described as a "new Horeb." The expanded revelation of torah, coupled with the long overdue completion of the journey to the land, together constitute a significant reboot for the people of Yahweh, as they come of age as the people of Yahweh.

The emphatic "this day" in verse 9 is further intensified by the reminder that "today" (that is, the day they hear these words on the plains of Moab) is crucial for setting a trajectory of obedience for the

---

[490] As Tigay, *Deuteronomy*, 250, helpfully points out.

[491] Similar verbal forms are used in 4:40; 5:16, 28; 6:3, 18; 8:16; 9:21; 12:25, 28; 13:15; 17:4; 18:17; 19:18; 22:7; 28:63; 30:5. In every case except 9:21 (which is picked up from Exod 32), there is a strong moral component in the use of the verb, dealing with the prospering of the nation. This is almost certainly the implication here.

nation.[492] God has spoken (as he did on the "day" at Horeb). He has made them his own. Every "today" from now on must be a day of listening and obedience. As the focus shifts from the near future to the immediacy of the present, there is a heightening in Moses's rhetoric. The moment for decision is now here.

27:11–26. The importance of this moment in the life of the nation is underlined from verse 11 on, as Moses returns to the actions to be carried out on the hills above Shechem (this time apparently speaking alone). As well as erecting the altar on Mount Ebal (27:1–8), they are to enact a dramatic covenant ritual on the twin peaks.

As is typical of rituals in Deuteronomy, there is little specific detail. Moses's primary concern is overtly theological. According to verses 12–13, the nation must divide into two groups: six tribes are to climb Mount Gerizim (viewed from Shechem, the peak to the south/left); the other six are to ascend to the summit of Mount Ebal, where the altar is to be built.

The grouping of the tribes is not explained but reflects the period before Joseph is divided into Ephraim and Manasseh. The group on Mount Gerizim deliver the blessing of God. This group consists of the children of Leah and Rachel, Jacob's wives. Reuben, the eldest may well be excluded because of his sexual sin (see Gen 35:22; 49:4). Zebulun is also relegated to the second group, but that simply may be to even up the numbers. The second group contains the sons borne by the servants of Leah and Rachel (Zilpah and Bilhah), as well as Reuben and Zebulun.[493] Both of these groups stand on their respective mountains in order to "bless" and "deliver the curse." The translation here reflects the Hebrew: to "stand to bless" is a straightforward intensive verb, whereas the second group of tribes are, literally, to "stand on/for the curse."[494] No explicit reason is given for this, but it may imply that whereas the

---

[492] For an extended discussion of the significance of the success of key "days" in Deuteronomy, see Millar in *Time and Place in Deuteronomy*, 42–49 and *Now Choose Life*, 67–98.

[493] Alternatively, the tribes could be divided along geographical lines, with the southern tribes occupying the mountain of blessing.

[494] Driver argues that the translation "for," although rare, is appropriate here (*Deuteronomy*, 298 n.9). McConville agrees, arguing that if the tribes simply stand for the blessing and curse, rather than pronouncing them, it makes the whole account of the ritual cohere (*Deuteronomy*, 387).

blessing is conditional on their (unlikely) obedience, experiencing the curse of the covenant is almost a given.

This possibility finds support in what happens next.

Although in verses 12 and 13, the tribes themselves appear to make the pronouncements, in verse 14, it becomes clear that the actual speaking is left to the Levites. No specific instructions are given concerning the position from which the Levites are to proclaim the words which follow. Joshua 8:30–35, however, makes it plain that from the earliest times, these instructions were understood to require the Levites to leave their tribal position and split into two groups that placed themselves facing the two mountains.[495]

At this point, one might expect both blessing and curse to be pronounced (as happens in ch. 28). Instead, the Levites pronounce *only* a list of twelve curses, clearly matching the number of tribes (there is no corresponding *pronouncement* of blessing, but see below on ch. 28).

The phrase "in a loud voice" is an unusual one (lit., an "exalted" voice, which may be a play on the fact that the words are to be intoned from the top of a mountain!), but it is the content of the curses that is most interesting.

There is some overlap with the Decalogue of chapter 5 (the prohibition of idolatry at the head of this list in v. 15, and the obligation to honor one's parents in v. 16), although the tone of these execrations is decidedly Deuteronomic. As is the case in the rest of the book, these curses reflect an understanding of covenant faithfulness that begins with the Ten Commandments but is not exhausted by them (see also Jer 11:1–3). In fact, it is the fine-grained vision of righteousness expounded at some length in chapters 12–26 that seems to undergird most of these warnings.

This is why, for example, idolatry, which is prohibited in secret, as well as in public, is cursed (27:15). It is why dishonoring parents is so strongly denounced (v. 16, also 5:16). It is why there is to be no place

---

[495] According to C. W. Wilson ("Ebal and Gerizim, 1866," *Palestine Exploration Fund Quarterly Statement* [1873], 66–71), the saddle between the mountains forms a natural amphitheater, where voices could easily be heard on either side: "There is no other place in Palestine so suitable for the assembly of an immense body of men within the limits to which a human voice could reach, and where at the same time each individual would be able to see what was being done. The recesses in the two mountains which form the amphitheatre, are exactly opposite to each other, and the limestone strata running up to the very summits in a succession of ledges present the appearance of a series of regular benches" (70).

in Israel for moving fences (v. 17; 19:14), exploiting the vulnerable (v. 19; 24:17) or committing bribery (v. 25; 16:19), all of which have already been explicitly prohibited by Moses. The focus of the people should be on ensuring sexual propriety in every relationship and justice in every situation. As verse 26 makes explicit, it is nothing less than failure to obey all the words of God conveyed through Moses that will bring down the curses of the covenant ("Anyone who does not put the words of this law into practice is cursed.")

The fact that some of the curses to be uttered address issues not previously addressed by Moses in Deuteronomy (27:18, 21–22 deal with misleading the blind, bestiality, and incest) further strengthens the view, expressed above, that the torah of Moses is indicative rather than definitive, as even within Deuteronomy itself there is clear evidence of a dynamic understanding of the responsibilities of God's people as they enter the land. God has not spelled out exhaustively everything he asks of them. But by listening to his words, they will know very well what a righteous life looks like.

Here, however, the focus seems to fall on egregious sinful actions. Deliberately misleading the blind is cruel and spiteful. Exploiting the weak and vulnerable through the judicial system is reprehensible. The particular forms of sexual immorality condemned here—whether sleeping with one's step-mother, mother-in-law, bestiality or incest (27:20–23)—simply cannot be allowed in Israel.[496] Killing another member of the brotherhood of Israel, whether for some indeterminate personal reason (v. 22) or as a contract killing (v. 23), is so far from the ideal laid out in Deuteronomy as to beggar belief. This list of curses is designed to shock and to stop Israel in their tracks, even as they first set foot in the land. And Moses is at pains to point out that obedience is an all or nothing thing: "Anyone who does not put the words of this law into practice is cursed." And all the people will say, "Amen!" (27:26).[497]

The importance of the people's twelvefold "Amen" in 27:11–26 should not be overlooked. At the outset of their time in the land, the people are required to acknowledge that God has spoken, and

---

[496] The only curse in this section with a motive clause is 27:20: "for he has violated his father's marriage bed" (lit. "uncovered the skirt of his father").

[497] This verse is quoted by Paul in Gal 3:10, where he extends Moses's logic to cover the law as a whole.

that he has spoken clearly. After Moses's final words on the plains of Moab, underlined and affirmed on Gerizim and Ebal, there can be no doubt that he requires his people to be a righteous nation. This is the responsibility that flows from his covenantal commitment to be their God. Should they choose to reject this, experiencing the curse of the covenant is inevitable. The twelve tribes must acknowledge that their future can only be one of blessing or curse. There is no third way.

Unexpectedly (and confusingly), there is no corresponding list of blessings, as seems to be promised by verse 12. Various explanations have been offered but the simplest and most persuasive is that the blessings are deliberately omitted at this point for rhetorical reasons to highlight the growing likelihood of Israel's disobedience. The bluntness of the final curse in 27:26 supports this. The words of Joshua 8:34 (where "Joshua read aloud all the words of the law—the blessings as well as the curses—according to all that is written in the book of the law") offers implicit confirmation that the omission of the blessings in the ritual itself was both deliberate and ancient.

Whatever unfolds in the subsequent history of Israel, if God's people do not manage to obey Yahweh wholeheartedly, reproducing his righteousness in the land, first at Shechem and then on into the future, they will stand condemned by their very own words.

28:1–14. Chapter 28 is best understood as Moses's reflection on the ritual he has just sketched out.[498] In 11:26–32, Moses establishes that Israel's response to the torah that he is expounding can be viewed through the twin lenses of "blessing" and "curse." The abbreviated account of the ritual to be enacted once in the land in chapter 27 reiterates the importance of the basic choice Israel faces: a choice Moses expands on in chapter 28.

In the final form of the book of Deuteronomy, the collection of rituals, extracts of preaching, and narrative accounts, as well as the Song and Blessing of Moses are carefully arranged to support the central message: the faithful God has spoken to his people, bringing them into this land and calling them to live in his righteousness; but the problem is that without the direct intervention of God himself, his people simply

---

[498] Some (e.g., Block) have suggested that as the book was assembled, ch. 27 was inserted into Moses's speech which ran smoothly from ch. 26 to 28. This is unnecessary. Despite the slight roughness, the logic of the text flows very well as it stands.

cannot deliver on what is required, and will inevitably experience curse rather than blessing.

From 28:1–14, Moses provides a brief guide to the blessings that have been promised should the people chose to obey "this day," that is, at Moab and each day they live in the land.

28:1 picks up the overall promise of 26:19, promising preeminence for Israel in God's economy (stated here as God putting them "far above all the nations of the earth"). This will be expressed in their being "overtaken" by blessings, if and when they obey the voice of Yahweh (28:2; see also 7:12–16; 11:13–15; 15:4–6).

The extent of these blessings is sketched out in a series of pictures of comprehensiveness: (a) *everyone* will be blessed by Yahweh (both urban and rural dwellers (28:3); (b) *every sphere of life* will be blessed, including children, agricultural produce, livestock (both "herds" and "flocks"), and even domestic food preparation (28:4–5). The blessing of God will be experienced and evidenced in all the activity of life, captured by the words of verse 6: "You will be blessed when you come in and blessed when you go out."

Moses continues to expand on the nature of this blessing in verses 7–14. This section is both wide-ranging and slightly repetitive. Covenant blessing guarantees protection from enemies, whose aggression will result in them being scattered in "seven directions" (28:7), probably an allusion to the normal depiction of the Canaanites as seven nations, although it may simply denote a large number (as in Isa 4:1; 11:15; Prov 24:16). It also ensures that their "barns" will be full (v. 8, and elsewhere only in Prov 3:10), and that Yahweh's provision will stretch to "everything they do," repeating the thought of verse 6 (see also 12:7).

As in 26:18–19 (and 7:6–9), the blessing of Yahweh that flows from covenantal obedience also underwrites Israel's internal holiness and international reputation. 28:9 underlines that "walking in Yahweh's ways" (also, e.g., 5:33) is the way to be established as Yahweh's holy people before a watching world. All nations will see that they "bear the Lord's name" (lit., "that the name of Yahweh is called on you"), and so will fear them, and presumably refrain from attacking them (27:10).[499]

---

[499] The idea (although not the vocabulary) are similar to that of the third commandment in Deut 5:11 (see the discussion above).

Verse 11 picks up the language and thought of verse 4. The phrase "prosper abundantly" carries the idea of more than enough, before making explicit that blessing will result in large families, burgeoning herds and flocks, and rich harvests in the land (or perhaps here, "soil") given by God himself. All covenantal promises will be fulfilled (11:11–14), and the nation will stand tall on the international stage. In a remarkable image, this is ascribed to the direct action of Yahweh himself, who is not only behind all this prosperity, but according to verse 12, is pulling the necessary levers to bring this about: "The LORD will open for you his abundant storehouse, the sky, to give your land rain in its season and to bless all the work of your hands."[500]

Moses points to a divinely engineered fertility, which will mean that they will not be put in a position of dependence on other nations (as in 15:6). Rather, their national fortunes will soar, if they maintain their loyalty to Yahweh. The "head not tail" language occurs only in this chapter (also 28:44) and Isaiah 9:14–15; 19:15. Moses then uses clever directional language, stating that they will only move up (not down) if they do not veer to the right or the left in idolatry (28:14, in marked contrast to 26:19).

This section (28:1–14) has the overall character of a summary of Moses's earlier appeals to stay true to Yahweh in order to experience the blessings of the covenant. However, these blessing are dwarfed by the exposition of the curses that will fall on Israel should they disobey all that God commands.[501]

28:15–68. The language and form of the curses in 28:15–19 mirrors that of 28:1–6.[502] Moses now envisages the nation being "overtaken" by the consequences of disobedience (almost personified here), with a clear statement of results of *not* listening followed by a list of six curses. The style is loose (presumably arising from the oral nature of the original material) with the reversal of blessing following a slightly

---

500 See also Job 37:9; 38:22; Ps 135:7; Jer 10:13; 51:16 for the idea of Yahweh's storehouse. The rain is also provided in Deut 11:11,14,17.

501 There is some ancient precedent for this: the curses in Lev 26 far outnumber the blessings; Ps 109:8–19 has no blessings at all. The Code of Hammurabi has a much longer curse at the end than a promise of blessing, as do some ancient treaties (see, e.g., the Vassal Treaties of Esarhaddon, *ANET*[3], 538–41). However, unlike Hammurabi, Yahweh does not threaten his people, but simply warns them of the consequences of choosing disobedience.

502 For a detailed proposal concerning the structure of the curse list, see Lundbom, *Deuteronomy*, 757–61. It is not clear that there is such careful ordering.

different order from verses 3–6, but the same point is being made. Like the blessings, the curses will be experienced in all Israel ("in the city and the country," v. 16), will affect every sphere of life (including childbirth, crop yield, and animal husbandry, vv. 17–18) and every activity ("coming in" and "going out," v. 19).[503]

As with the blessings in verses 7–14, Moses adds to the initial description of the consequences of disobedience in verses 20–26. He underlines that Yahweh instigates everything in this chapter. God's actions in bringing the curse are essentially the mirror image of those associated with blessing.

Rather than the protection and flourishing associated with the fulfillment of covenant promises, 28:20–24 details the destruction of the nation. Initially in verse 20, Israel is faced with "curses, confusion, and rebuke," but then it becomes clear that, like the Canaanite nations in the land, they will "quickly perish." The wickedness of their actions, summed up as "abandoning" Yahweh (v. 20) leads to the nation being treated as those who are opposed to God. The "confusion" envisaged is the panic brought about by war (as in 7:23). The "rebuke" relentlessly exposes every part of Israel's behavior.[504]

The language of verse 21 is particularly graphic: "The Lord will make pestilence cling to you until he has exterminated you from the land you are entering to possess." The covenant that Yahweh has made with them depends on their obedience and compliance. They were to "stick" to him; now plagues will "stick" to them. They cannot ignore this and experience his blessing. There is no middle ground: disobedience leads to experiencing the curse of the covenant.

The language of blessing and curse is extremely important at a biblical-theological level. It provides a way to encapsulate both the conditionality and unconditionality of the covenant. Disobedience both breaks the covenant and cannot ultimately break it. Yahweh will both divorce his unfaithful wife and refuse ultimately to let her go. He will expel his people from the land, and yet promise to bring them home. This tension will ultimately be resolved in the new covenant, which noticeably has no place for blessing and curse as key categories.

---

[503] Jeremiah makes significant use of these verses: see, e.g., Jer 5:17; 14:18; 20:14, 18; 29:32.

[504] Again, this language of "abandoning Yahweh" is picked up by the prophets, particularly Jeremiah: see 1:16; 2:13, 17, 19; 5:7, 19; 9:13; 16:11; 17:13.

The highly emotive descriptions of the consequences of disobedience continue in verse 22, with the weight of God's displeasure being expressed in human disease, climatic extremes, and fungal infestation of crops and property.[505] These threats are personified: "these will pursue you until you perish." In the same way that Israel pursued the original occupants of the land, they will be driven out by the curses of the covenant. In a similar vein, according to 28:23, both the sky (which will be "bronze") and the earth ("iron") will conspire against the people (also Lev 26:19). A lack of rain as evidence of the curses of the covenant being poured out is a strong motif in Jeremiah's preaching (so 3:3–3; 5:24–25; 12:4; 14:1–6 and 23:10; see also 1 Kgs 8:35–35; 17:1; 18:8; Amos 4:4–8). Rather than opening his "abundant storehouse" to provide rain (v. 12), in verse 24, Yahweh will "turn the rain of your land into falling dust" (lit., "powder and dust"). This anti-precipitation will have a catastrophic effect not only on the land, but also on the people themselves.

The focus switches in 28:25–26 to actual military adversaries. The allusions to the original conquest of the land continue, as any attempts by the nation to repel aggressors will lead to the mirror image of the experience of the conquest. Rather than expelling seven nations, they will "flee from them in seven directions." The net result of their experience of the curse of the covenant is that rather than being a light to the nations (as in 4:5–8), they "will be an object of horror to all the kingdoms of the earth."[506] The abject defeat of Israel is described graphically in verse 26, as Moses depicts the bodies of the fallen troops as carrion strewn on the battlefield.[507]

In the next stanza of curses (28:27–35), if anything, things get worse. God's people are hit with a plague of diseases and other afflictions, beginning with "the boils of Egypt." This is clearly a reference to Exodus 9:8–12 (the sixth plague). The very exodus unravels, and Israel is taken back to Egypt (in contrast to, e.g., Deut 17:14–20). This note emerges repeatedly throughout the rest of the chapter. However, this "new slavery" as the curses of the covenant are poured out, is significantly worse than that previously experienced by the nation.

---

[505] The diseases (both human and plant) are not easy to identity. See the extended discussion in Lundbom, *Deuteronomy*, 772.

[506] This idea is picked up by Jeremiah in 15:4; 24:9; 29:18 and 34:17. See also 2 Chr 29:8.

[507] This is a common biblical image: Gen 40:19; 1 Kgs 14:11; 16:4; Isa 18:6; Ezek 39:17–20; Ps 79:2, and in multiple places in Jeremiah (e.g 7:33, 15:3, etc.).

These boils, like the "tumors, festering rash, and scabies" that come with them, are "incurable."[508] This is compounded in verse 28 by "madness, blindness, and mental confusion"(also Zech 12:4), which leads to the desperately sad situation in the following verse, where the nation "gropes as a blind person gropes in the dark."[509] God's people are confused, ineffective, vulnerable, and isolated. The words of verse 29 are arresting: "You will not be successful in anything you do. You will only be oppressed and robbed continually, and no one will help you." (words later spoken by Jeremiah to King Zedekiah in Jer 32:5). This is a far cry from the flourishing envisaged and commended in the earlier part of Moses's sermon.

Having left the metaphor of blindness behind, Moses now raises the emotional temperature even further, as he describes the pain of having glimpsed the fulfillment of the promises of God, but having everything stripped away.[510] The multi-layered trauma of the rape of a fiancée (28:30) sits alongside the frustration of building a home but not being able to move in and patiently waiting for the vineyard you planted to reach maturity but never tasting the wine (20:6). This savage reversal of 6:10 also involves cattle being slaughtered, pack animals being removed, and grazing flocks being acquired by someone else. At every stage, "no one will help you." The classic covenantal statement "I will be your God; you will be my people" is apparently suspended as these curses are rolled out.

However, it is not simply possessions that are lost. As in the case of Job, even family is catastrophically affected: "Your sons and daughters will be given to another people, while your eyes grow weary looking for them every day. But you will be powerless to do anything" (28:32). The idiom is like that of "crying your eyes out." Even the commands to be fruitful and multiply, filling the earth and subduing it, prove to be beyond Israel as the curse takes hold.

---

[508] There is much discussion over the precise nature of the medical complaints. "Tumors" for example, probably refers to hemorrhoids, but precise identification is ultimately impossible.

[509] Possibly a reference to the ninth plague in Exod 10:22; similar imagery is found in Isa 59:9–10.

[510] See also, e.g., Jer 6:11–12; 8:10; Amos 5:11; Micah 6:15; Zeph 1:13 for similar language and ideas.

Throughout Deuteronomy, the specter of being expelled from the land has lurked in the shadows (see, e.g., 4:25–31; 11:17): now it emerges into the spotlight. Another nation is apparently responsible for the carnage of the previous verses. "A people you don't know" despoil the land, and Israel "will only be oppressed and crushed continually" (28:33). For the covenant people of Yahweh to experience all this can only be maddening (v. 34), but they must not overlook the fact that behind all this stands God himself (20:35). It is he who afflicts them with these incurable "boils" (as in v. 27, except now affecting the legs). This idea of dual agency, where foreign nations are both held responsible for their actions and clearly acting in line with God's actions is a constant and consistent feature of the Old Testament.

The description of the future expulsion from the land in 28:36–37 is fascinating for at least three reasons: (1) for the first time, the king anticipated in Deuteronomy 17 is included (and presumably implicated) in the departure of the nation from the land;[511] (2) as in 4:28, the "destination" of the people is worshiping "other gods, of wood and stone." This is a western semitic perspective on "exile," which doesn't fit with a Babylonian context (in Palestine, wooden gods were normal, whereas in Babylon gods routinely seem to have been made of stone);[512] (3) the form of the verb (a hiphil imperfect jussive form) of "to walk" highlights how, rather than Israel "walking in the ways of Yahweh," they are compelled *by* Yahweh to walk into exile. All of this happens in full view of the watching nations, with the result that God's people become "an object of horror, scorn, and ridicule among all the peoples," the very antithesis of the situation envisaged in the promises to Abraham in Genesis 12.[513] It is important to remember that throughout the ancient Near East (and for much of Israel's history), dispossession and expulsion (exile) were part

---

[511] The entire structure of the book of Kings is built around the culpability of the kings (beginning with David and Solomon, and including every subsequent king) in the fate of the nation. See my "1–2 Kings," in *1 Samuel–2 Chronicles*, ESV Expositional Commentary 3 (Wheaton: Crossway, 2019), 491–898.

[512] See, e.g., Isa 44. and Motyer's comments in J. Alec Motyer, *The Prophecy of Isaiah* (Leicester: InterVarsity Press, 1993), 27. In addition, there is little suggestion in the exilic and post-exilic literature that idolatry was an issue for Judah in the wake of the Babylonian intervention. If that is the case, then these words make sense only in an early setting.

[513] Although it could be argued that even this warning is a form of "blessing" to any nation that sees and takes heed.

and parcel of normal life. There is no need to see the shadow of Babylon in every mention of the idea.[514]

The relentless exposition of the consequences of disobeying Yahweh continues in 28:38–44. In fact the sheer volume of this "curse" material is the standout feature of this chapter. Moses now turns to warn (again) that all their activity will literally be fruitless (28:38–40), because of locusts devouring crops (Exod 10:4–19), worms attacking vines and grapes, and an unspecified issue that causes olives to fall from their trees prematurely. This declension from the beautiful life that God has invited them to enjoy is also reflected in sons and daughters being seized (28:41, as in vv. 4, 11, 18, 30–33), presumably by foreign marauders, as well as the serious issues caused by "buzzing insects."[515] According to verses 43 and 44, the blessing of 28:13 will be flipped on its head, and the nation will become subject to sojourners (28:44; contrast with 5:13–14; 10:18; see also Lev 25:47–55; Prov 22:7). The picture is a graphic one, not found anywhere else in the Old Testament, with the resident alien flourishing at the expense of the actual people of Yahweh.

From verse 45, the curses are once again personified as a relentless pursuer, who will bring the nation to an end. Such is the importance of covenant faithfulness, expressed in listening and obedience.

Moses, as he has done throughout this section, makes the connection between Israel's future experience of these curses and Egypt's past experience of the plagues (Exod 6–12). Israel's fate will become "a sign and a wonder against you and your descendants forever" (27:46; cf. 4:34; 6:22; 34:11). Unlike the plagues however, this experience of covenant curse is to be a *perpetual* reminder to every generation of what it means to be the people of Yahweh. Envisaging a day that he seems to view as almost inevitable, he anticipates the reason for their catastrophic failure: "Because you didn't serve the Lord your God with joy and a cheerful heart, even though you had an abundance of everything, you will serve your enemies that the Lord will send against you, in famine,

---

[514] Lundbom, *Deuteronomy*, 783, helpfully points out that Israel and Judah had experienced at least five "exiles" before 586. Also Tigay, *Deuteronomy*, 266, adds that the Bible speaks of exiles in Phoenicia, Ammon, Moab, Syria, Assyria, Babylonia, Media, Persia, Elam, Asia minor, Egypt, Nubia, and elsewhere!

[515] According to *HALOT* 1031, the two occurrences of this word in the Old Testament (here and Isa 18:1) seem to come from different roots, but the idea of a whirring noise caused by insects seems to be in view. It may refer to crickets.

thirst, nakedness, and a lack of everything." Israel's future does not rest on legalistic observance, but on the kind of wholehearted response to the word of Yahweh called for in 6:3–4. As has been the case throughout the book, Moses is not slow to insert commentary on what might happen. In 28:47–8 he makes clear that if this fate befalls them, it will be because they refused to "obey the Lord your God and keep the commands and statutes he gave you." A lack of joy and delight in keeping the torah will lead inexorably to disaster (as in 6:10–12), described at the end of verse 48 as experiencing hunger, thirst, nakedness, and want (in contrast to the abundance of having every good thing), as they are slowly crushed to death by an iron yoke.[516]

In 28:49–57, the focus falls once more on the human agent who is responsible for all this. Moses describes "him" as "swooping down like an eagle." Both Isaiah 5:25–27 and Jeremiah 5:15–17 pick up on this language and imagery, applying it to the Assyrians and Babylonians respectively (see also Jer 48:40; 49:22; Hos 8:1; Hab 1:8). According to verse 49, this destroyer is a nation which comes from far away and does not speak Hebrew. The other distinguishing marks of this nation include looking scary, attacking people of all ages and consuming all the produce of the land (vv. 50–51), reducing it to a state of barrenness (as in 27:18, 30–31). As the Israelites had done to Jericho, so this nation will do to them: "They will besiege you within all your city gates until your high and fortified walls, that you trust in, come down throughout your land (28:52)." This enemy will quickly set up stall within the very heart of the cities of Israel (the city gates in ancient towns were not simply an entrance portal but the center of community and commercial life). Misplaced trust (dealt with only here in Deuteronomy among God's people, but see 1:28; 3:5; 9:1 for such an attitude among the Canaanites) is a recipe for disaster.

The curse of the covenant is also felt as the fabric of the life of God's people falls apart under siege, according to verses 53–57, which are as viscerally disturbing as any in the Old Testament. It is hard to overstate the horror of the extremities to which these people are driven, choosing to "eat your offspring, the flesh of your sons and daughters the Lord your God has given you" in order to survive (28:53; see also Lev 26:29; Jer 19:9; Ezek 5:10 for similar warnings, and 2 Kgs 6:26–29; Lam 2:20; 4:10 for incidences in Israel's history). Whether this is eating the flesh of children

---

[516] This is probably the inspiration behind Jeremiah's actions in Jer 28:13–14.

who have just died of starvation (which seems most likely) or killing one's own children in desperation, the situation is clearly dire.[517] Even the "most sensitive and refined" men (vv. 54–55) and women (vv. 56–57) of the community are reduced to barbarism, in the "dog eat dog" world of the curse. The picture of men clamoring to share in the flesh of a child is a truly terrible one. The most delicate of women ("who would not venture to put the sole of her foot on the ground because of her refinement and sensitivity"—in other words, who is used to being carried around) is transformed by this extremity into a state of ravenous, desperate selfishness. The image of a new mother secretly eating both her own placenta and her infant children as they emerge from her body, lest her much-loved husband or older children get a taste of it, is both gruesome and disturbingly sad. However, such are the consequences of breaking the covenant with Yahweh.

This dark material comes to a climax in 28:58–68, which sums up this covenant-breaking behavior and its attendant consequences as a "return to Egypt." Verses 58–60 recapitulate what Moses has now said countless times: only through a careful and thoroughgoing attention to the commands of Yahweh ("all the words of this torah," as in 17:19; 27:3, 8; and also 29:29; 31:12; 32:46) and by "fearing this glorious and awe-inspiring name" (see Ps 72:19; Neh 9:5; see also Pss. 99:3; 111:9; Mal 1:14) can they avoid going back from whence they came. "Wondrous plagues," "severe and lasting plagues," and "terrible and chronic sicknesses" will be their lot if they choose the way of unfaithfulness: "He will afflict you again with all the diseases of Egypt, which you dreaded, and they will cling to you" (28:60).[518] As if that weren't enough, in verse 61, Moses adds that Yahweh will also afflict them with "every sickness and plague *not* recorded in the book of this law"! Nothing is spared in the attempt to urge people to faithful obedience. This also explains the importance of a written record of these words (see also 29:21; 30:10; 31:26).

One by one, from verse 62, the promises made by God from the beginning are systematically reversed. The undertaking given to Abraham that his descendants would be "as numerous as the stars in the sky" (Gen 15:5) is rolled back. They will be reduced to "a few people" again (10:22;

[517] Extreme actions like this are alluded to in a range of ancient Near Eastern documents (see Lundbom, *Deuteronomy*, 791–92). However, it is one thing to note similarities; it is quite another to prove dependence (see McConville, *Deuteronomy*, 402–3).

[518] This language is picked up by Jeremiah in 6:7; 10:19; 14:17; 15:18; 19:8; 30:12,14.

26:5). In 28:63, the commission to "be fruitful and multiply" given to Adam is turned on its head as Yahweh now "will be glad to cause you to perish and to destroy you." The gift of land is snatched away, as God's people are "ripped" out of it. To reject Yahweh and his covenant is to invite a "new Babel," as God's people are "scattered among all peoples from one end of the earth to the other" (as in 4:27; Lev 26:33), where they will no longer worship the one true God, but other man-made godlets "which neither you nor your fathers have known" (28:64, also, e.g., 4:28; 11:28; 13:2,6,13; 29:26).

The full extent of the covenant curses is underlined in 28:65–67, where the loss of the material blessings of covenant with Yahweh is accompanied by the personal impact of turning their backs on him. There will be no "peace," nor a "resting place for the sole of your foot" (Gen 8:9): instead, Yahweh will give them a "trembling heart, failing eyes, and a despondent spirit." Rest is replaced by anxiety, fear, confusion and misery. Assurance of God's goodness will be replaced by an existential angst that cannot be shaken off: "Your life will hang in doubt before you. You will be in dread night and day, never certain of survival" (28:66). Their reality will consist of a deep discontent that is dominated by fear, with a constant longing for both day and night in turn to be over, because of both "the dread you will have in your heart" and the events unfolding before their eyes (28:67).

The very covenant itself seems to have unraveled by verse 68: "The Lord will take you back in ships to Egypt by a route that I said you would never see again. There you will sell yourselves to your enemies as male and female slaves, but no one will buy you." The expressed hope of 17:16 has been overturned by Israel's own rebellion. It is puzzling that ships are mentioned here. While it is possible to sail from Israel to Egypt, it was not the usual route, and neither nation was known for its love of the ocean. The most likely explanation is simply that Moses is flagging that this is a metaphor rather than an explicit prediction of a return to the land in which the nation of Israel was born. The point is rather that they will be scattered and abandoned. Rather than being rescued as Yahweh's treasured possession (as in Exod 19:6), they will languish in slavery—a slavery they themselves have chosen—without even being able to attract the attention of a possible master.

Bridge

After beginning with a powerful reminder of the choice that Israel will perpetually face in the land as the refreshment of the covenant at Moab gives way to the covenant renewal at Shechem—one of obedience or disobedience, blessing or curse—this chapter takes on an increasingly dark tone, as the curses of the covenant trace the unraveling of God's promise as his people choose to "go back to Egypt." The shape of the chapter and the sheer weight of the curse material creates a growing sense of inevitability: it is hard to see how God's people could avoid this fate. One could even say that there is a strong sense that Moses's mind is already turning to the question of what happens beyond this experience of covenant curse.

At a biblical-theological level, the idea of blessing and curse is extremely powerful, but also potentially misleading. It is deeply embedded in the historical particularities of God's choice of one nation at a particular moment in history. *Their* progress as the covenant people of God can be mapped using these external metrics of produce, weather, wealth, and national security. Even here there is more to be said, but this is a reliable starting point. In the New Testament, however, the kingdom of God is not limited to one nation-state, but is scattered across every nation, across time and space. This explains why the language of blessing and curse is so rare in the New Testament.[519]

Positively speaking, however, the language of blessing and curse encapsulates the tension at the heart of Yahweh's covenant with his people: there is no question whether he can be relied on, but can they? Experiencing the curse really is inevitable, but hope can be found in the fact that these curses are *covenant* curses. Even though the relationship has been badly damaged, it somehow remains intact (even if it is hanging by a thread). This then anticipates the work of one who would not only deal with the curse, bringing us unimagined blessing, but would take the curse of the covenant for us. This is why Paul could write in Galatians 3:10, 13–14:

> [10] For all who rely on the works of the law are under a curse, because it is written, Everyone who does not do everything written in the book of the law is cursed. … [13] Christ redeemed us from the curse of the law

---

[519] An exception to this is Jesus's teaching in Matt 5 and 23, as well as the blessings and woes in Luke 6. However, it is important to realize that he is, in effect, re-preaching the message of Moses to his own generation: God calls them as his people to enjoy a beautiful life of blessing, but they have chosen a life of "woe."

by becoming a curse for us, because it is written, Cursed is everyone
who is hung on a tree. 14 The purpose was that the blessing of Abraham
would come to the Gentiles by Christ Jesus, so that we could receive the
promised Spirit through faith.

VI. Moses Preaches the New Covenant (29:1–30:20)

1 These are the words of the covenant that the Lord commanded Moses
to make with the Israelites in the land of Moab, in addition to the covenant he had made with them at Horeb. 2 Moses summoned all Israel and
said to them, "You have seen with your own eyes everything the Lord
did in Egypt to Pharaoh, to all his officials, and to his entire land. 3 You
saw with your own eyes the great trials and those great signs and wonders. 4 Yet to this day the Lord has not given you a mind to understand,
eyes to see, or ears to hear. 5 I led you forty years in the wilderness;
your clothes and the sandals on your feet did not wear out; 6 you did
not eat food or drink wine or beer—so that you might know that I
am the Lord your God. 7 When you reached this place, King Sihon of
Heshbon and King Og of Bashan came out against us in battle, but we
defeated them. 8 We took their land and gave it as an inheritance to
the Reubenites, the Gadites, and half the tribe of Manasseh. 9 Therefore,
observe the words of this covenant and follow them, so that you will
succeed in everything you do.

10 "All of you are standing today before the Lord your God—your leaders,
tribes, elders, officials, all the men of Israel, 11 your dependents, your
wives, and the resident aliens in your camps who cut your wood and
draw your water—12 so that you may enter into the covenant of the Lord
your God, which he is making with you today, so that you may enter
into his oath 13 and so that he may establish you today as his people
and he may be your God as he promised you and as he swore to your
ancestors Abraham, Isaac, and Jacob. 14 I am making this covenant and
this oath not only with you, 15 but also with those who are standing
here with us today in the presence of the Lord our God and with those
who are not here today.

16 "Indeed, you know how we lived in the land of Egypt and passed
through the nations where you traveled. 17 You saw their abhorrent
images and idols made of wood, stone, silver, and gold, which were
among them. 18 Be sure there is no man, woman, clan, or tribe among
you today whose heart turns away from the Lord our God to go and
worship the gods of those nations. Be sure there is no root among
you bearing poisonous and bitter fruit. 19 When someone hears the
words of this oath, he may consider himself exempt, thinking, 'I
will have peace even though I follow my own stubborn heart.' This
will lead to the destruction of the well-watered land as well as the

dry land. [20] The LORD will not be willing to forgive him. Instead, his
anger and jealousy will burn against that person, and every curse
written in this scroll will descend on him. The LORD will blot out
his name under heaven, [21] and single him out for harm from all the
tribes of Israel, according to all the curses of the covenant written
in this book of the law.

[22] "Future generations of your children who follow you and the
foreigner who comes from a distant country will see the plagues
of that land and the sicknesses the LORD has inflicted on it. [23] All its
soil will be a burning waste of sulfur and salt, unsown, producing
nothing, with no plant growing on it, just like the fall of Sodom and
Gomorrah, Admah and Zeboiim, which the LORD demolished in his
fierce anger. [24] All the nations will ask, 'Why has the LORD done this
to this land? Why this intense outburst of anger?' [25] Then people
will answer, 'It is because they abandoned the covenant of the LORD,
the God of their ancestors, which he had made with them when he
brought them out of the land of Egypt. [26] They began to serve other
gods, bowing in worship to gods they had not known—gods that
the LORD had not permitted them to worship. [27] Therefore the LORD's
anger burned against this land, and he brought every curse written
in this book on it. [28] The LORD uprooted them from their land in his
anger, rage, and intense wrath, and threw them into another land
where they are today.' [29] The hidden things belong to the LORD our
God, but the revealed things belong to us and our children forever,
so that we may follow all the words of this law.

[30:1] "When all these things happen to you—the blessings and curses I
have set before you—and you come to your senses while you are in
all the nations where the LORD your God has driven you, [2] and you and
your children return to the LORD your God and obey him with all your
heart and all your soul by doing everything I am commanding you
today, [3] then he will restore your fortunes, have compassion on you,
and gather you again from all the peoples where the LORD your God
has scattered you. [4] Even if your exiles are at the farthest horizon, he
will gather you and bring you back from there. [5] The LORD your God will
bring you into the land your ancestors possessed, and you will take
possession of it. He will cause you to prosper and multiply you more
than he did your ancestors. [6] The LORD your God will circumcise your
heart and the hearts of your descendants, and you will love him with
all your heart and all your soul so that you will live. [7] The LORD your
God will put all these curses on your enemies who hate and persecute
you. [8] Then you will again obey him and follow all his commands I am
commanding you today. [9] The LORD your God will make you prosper
abundantly in all the work of your hands, your offspring, the offspring
of your livestock, and the produce of your land. Indeed, the LORD will

> again delight in your prosperity, as he delighted in that of your ancestors, [10] when you obey the LORD your God by keeping his commands and statutes that are written in this book of the law and return to him with all your heart and all your soul.
>
> [11] "This command that I give you today is certainly not too difficult or beyond your reach. [12] It is not in heaven so that you have to ask, 'Who will go up to heaven, get it for us, and proclaim it to us so that we may follow it?' [13] And it is not across the sea so that you have to ask, 'Who will cross the sea, get it for us, and proclaim it to us so that we may follow it?' [14] But the message is very near you, in your mouth and in your heart, so that you may follow it. [15] See, today I have set before you life and prosperity, death and adversity. [16] For I am commanding you today to love the LORD your God, to walk in his ways, and to keep his commands, statutes, and ordinances, so that you may live and multiply, and the LORD your God may bless you in the land you are entering to possess. [17] But if your heart turns away and you do not listen and you are led astray to bow in worship to other gods and serve them, [18] I tell you today that you will certainly perish and will not prolong your days in the land you are entering to possess across the Jordan. [19] I call heaven and earth as witnesses against you today that I have set before you life and death, blessing and curse. Choose life so that you and your descendants may live, [20] love the LORD your God, obey him, and remain faithful to him. For he is your life, and he will prolong your days as you live in the land the LORD swore to give to your ancestors Abraham, Isaac, and Jacob."

Throughout Moses's addresses, there has been a growing sense that he is convinced that eventually, God's people will break the covenant and so forfeit the right to enjoy the beautiful life in the land that he is holding out to them. That impression takes shape and becomes clearer in his exposition of the ritual to be enacted at Gerizim and Ebal and his ensuing preaching on the inevitability of the experience of the curse in chapter 28. This then leads into the climax of the book in chapters 29 and 30, as Moses introduces the prospect of a future new covenant, in which God does for his people what they cannot do for themselves by changing their hearts.

29:1–9. Chapter 29 begins by introducing the "Moab covenant," mentioned explicitly only here in the Bible.[520] This covenant is described as "in

---

[520] There is significant discussion over whether this verse refers back to the events in chs. 27 and 28 or forward to 29. There are good arguments both ways, but ultimately, that 29:1–9 refer to events at Moab and the previous chapters are set on Ebal and Gerizim suggests that this is the introduction to the covenant summary that follows. For a detailed discussion of the possibility that this entire unit (29–30) is structured as a covenant renewal ceremony, see McConville, *Deuteronomy*, 413–4.

addition to" that made at Horeb (29:1).[521] This simple statement encapsulates the perspective reflected in the exposition of torah in chapters 12–26, as well as the book as a whole. There is no suggestion at this point that the covenant made at Horeb (which effectively constitutes the nation) needs to be replaced, but rather, as the Decalogue needs to be applied to the richness of life in the land, so this covenant sharpens the demands of faithfulness to Yahweh in the new context. Not only does this refreshed covenant underline the importance of continuing to obey Yahweh in the days ahead; it also provides a vital window into God's covenantal dealings with his people.

As we have already noted, disagreement over the nature and relationship of the biblical covenants runs deep.[522] I am persuaded that the covenants of the Pentateuch are a series of overlapping divine commitments, each of which picks up and expounds some aspect (or aspects) of the relationship that Yahweh has with his people.[523] The text makes no systematic attempt to rationalize these covenants; they seem to happily overlap or develop one another. This is why Moses can speak freely and easily of the Moab Covenant. It is not that the people can move on from what was revealed at Horeb—Moses has already told them repeatedly to remember what God said there—but that as they move into a new context, they will need to rise to face different challenges to those endured in the wilderness, hence the Moab Covenant.

The language also highlights the importance of Moses's role in establishing this covenant. Yahweh "commands" Moses to make the covenant with the Israelites, as he (presumably also Moses) had made with them at Horeb. No other leader is ever spoken of in this way. It is Moses and Moses alone in the Old Testament who can legitimately be called the "covenant maker," a fact that paves the way for Jesus to be portrayed as

---

[521] The expression occurs only here and in 4:35 in Deuteronomy but is relatively common elsewhere in the Old Testament (e.g., Gen 26:1; 46:26; Lev 9:17; 23:38; Num 5:8; 6:21).

[522] See the discussion of "Covenant" in Biblical and Theological Themes in Deuteronomy above.

[523] As Block has pointed out (see his huge work *Covenant*), some of the biblical covenants are with the nation, others with a representative figure (like David), and some with the earth or the cosmos. I would argue that all of these covenants are a single reality: Yahweh's commitment to create a people for himself to enjoy life with him in the new creation. A very similar idea has been expressed classically in Reformed theology by speaking of the "covenant of grace," which has different expressions or administrations.

the new Moses (see, e.g., Matt 1–4), instituting the very new covenant that Moses foreshadows later in this chapter.

In 29:2–9 however, Moses summons all Israel again (presumably after some days, during which they are camped on the plains of Moab) as he did at Horeb (5:1) and presses home what really is the key message of his combined addresses. Verses 2–4 encapsulate his point:

> [2] You have seen with your own eyes everything the LORD did in Egypt to Pharaoh, to all his officials, and to his entire land. [3] You saw with your own eyes the great trials and those great signs and wonders. [4] Yet to this day the LORD has not given you a mind to understand, eyes to see, or ears to hear.

The seeing that really matters—which here is clearly hearing God's word and living the beautiful life described there (loving Yahweh and other people)—is currently beyond them. Some of them (those over forty) may remember the events of the exodus. The rest have seen the recent events in the Transjordan. But they cannot see what really matters. The results of the test in 8:2 are now clearly in!

For the first time it is spelled out that listening, seeing, and trusting are gifts of God that Israel does not yet possess. While Moses has made it very clear that they themselves are both culpable and responsible for this failure, at another level they are trapped in their disobedience because Yahweh has not yet given them the ability to discern and act on the truth.[524]

Moses maintains a delicate theological balance here. Their spiritual perception may be extremely limited, but that doesn't change the fact that God has given his people every reason to obey. Without missing a beat, Moses continues to rehearse God's kindness in the wilderness (29:4–5; as in 8:4), even assuming the voice of Yahweh (as he also did in 28:20) as he alludes to the spiritual benefits of a wilderness diet of manna rather than bread, wine or beer (29:6), and then reminds them of the ease of conquering the Amorite kings Sihon and Og in the Transjordan, as a dry run for taking the land (29:7–8; also 2:26–3:8). This is why the command of verse 9 ("Therefore, observe the words of this covenant and follow them, so that you will succeed in everything

---

[524] The thought here is very similar to that of Isa 6, which is then picked up by Jesus himself in the context of Mark 4 and his explanation of his parables. Some writers (e.g., Block, *Deuteronomy*, 676 and Tigay, *Deuteronomy*, 275–76) see 29:6–7 as a statement that Israel *can* now discern the truth. This simply does not fit with the flow of these chapters.

you do") is perfectly reasonable. God has every right to expect (and insist on) covenant faithfulness, whether the people are capable of delivering or not.

Initially, this seems hard to grasp: Isn't it unreasonable for Moses (and more importantly, Yahweh) to expect God's people to do what they cannot do? But to argue like that is to misunderstand the nature of the covenant relationship. Israel owes Yahweh the allegiance which he is seeking. The obligation stands irrespective of the ability to discharge it. It is also worth noting that this is one of the basic premises of biblical religion. Paul's entire argument in Romans, for example, rests on the fact that all humanity is answerable to God. Those who are "dead in sin" are incapable of living righteously and are justly subject to God's wrath.[525]

29:10–15. Building on the pattern of 5:2–5, where Moses deliberately forges a link between the past at Horeb and the present ("today") at Moab, emphasizing that the Horeb covenant is dynamic and enduring, in 29:10–15, he establishes that the Moab covenant will be the key to Israel's future. Life in the land is to be an unbroken series of "todays" that are marked by a decisive commitment to obey Yahweh.

Just as they all stood before Yahweh at Horeb, Moses insists that "all of you are standing today before the Lord your God" at Moab. Yahweh's presence for Moses is conveyed primarily through his word: where he chooses to speak, there he is present. Moses is quick to underline that he is with *all* of his people. The list in 29:10–11 is deliberately (and unusually) all-inclusive, listing "your leaders, tribes, elders, officials, all the men of Israel, your dependents, your wives, and the resident aliens in your camps who cut your wood and draw your water." In other words, Yahweh is speaking to the entirety of his people, from the various leaders (see 1:15; 19:12) right down to those, presumably part of the mixed crowd who came out of Egypt, who have attached themselves to the nation but act as servants.[526]

Moses issues this commanding invitation on Yahweh's behalf. The word order in 29:12–13 (Heb. 29:11–12) is slightly unusual but seems

---

[525] For a contrary view, which regards these verses as a general statement of the nation's propensities, see Michael A. Grisanti, "Was Israel Unable to Respond to God? A Study of Deuteronomy 29:2–4," *Bibliotheca Sacra* 163 (2006): 176–96.

[526] The numbers of this group would soon be swelled by the addition of the Gibeonites, according to Josh 9:16–27.

to have the sense that God has brought them to him, so that (a) they might "enter [cross] into the covenant" of Yahweh their God;[527] (b) they might "enter into his oath"; and (c) "he may establish you today as his people and he may be your God." As they cross the border, they start a new phase of their covenantal existence, so they need to "enter" this covenant. However, they must not allow this newness to obscure the fact that this is essentially the same covenant that Yahweh made with Abraham, Isaac, and Jacob, (the "oath"), reiterated and expanded at Horeb, summed up as usual in the phrase "I will be your God, you will be my people" (so Exod 6:7; Lev 26:12; Jer 7:23; 11:4; 24:7; 30:22; 31:1; Ezek 36:28; Hos 2:23).[528]

The emphasis on "today" (vv. 10, 12, 13) is quite deliberate. In the same way that every generation shares in the covenant made at Horeb, so every generation is to live at Moab, even when they have crossed into the land. This is made explicit in 29:14–15: "I am making this covenant and this oath not only with you, but also with those who are standing here with us today in the presence of the Lord our God and with those who are not here today." This ever-current Moab covenant is the key to life in the land for future generations.[529]

In Hebrews 3 (especially vv. 7–19, which quote Ps 95), we find that this same basic principle is picked up and applied directly to the people of God living under the new covenant.[530] A gospel-shaped life is still one that is lived out as a series of "todays" in which we continue to respond wholeheartedly to all that God has done for us and given to us in the Lord Jesus Christ.

29:16–29. The basic choice which God's people face is now sketched out against the background of Israel's own past experience. Once more, the aged Moses appeals not simply to the lived experience of those who were under twenty years old before the exodus (and so have at least some recollection of life in Egypt), but to the collective memory of the

---

[527] Lundbom (*Deuteronomy*, 807), Tigay (*Deuteronomy*, 277), and McConville (*Deuteronomy*, 415) all suggest that the verb may imply passing through the halves of a calf which had been cut in two, as in Gen 15:19–21 and Jer 34:18–20. I think this is possible but not persuasive. The verb is generally used in Deuteronomy of crossing into the land.

[528] Block's suggestion that this is a hendiadys (his "sworn covenant") is surely theologically accurate (*Deuteronomy*, 678).

[529] On this idea see Timothy A. Lenchak, "*Choose Life*": *A Rhetorical-Critical Investigation of Deut 28,69–30,20*, AnBib 129 (Rome: Pontifical Biblical Institute, 1993), 103–4.

[530] Paul takes a similar approach in 1 Cor 10:1–11.

nation as a whole. Both Egypt and the nations through which God's people traveled (including Edom, Ammon, and Moab, and perhaps their brief foray into Canaan itself) provided ample opportunity to see idolatry in action and even to practice it (Deut 4:3; Num 25:1–3). No kind of idol—whether an "abhorrent image" (שִׁקּוּץ) or an "idol" (גִּלּוּל, literally a "dung pellet")—can offer the kind of beautiful life that Yahweh had rescued them for, and holds out to them in the land (29:17–18).[531] The two terms capture both the vile nature of idols (reflected in, e.g., 1 Kgs 11:5; 2 Kgs 23:13; Jer 7:30; Hos 9:10) and their inability to respond (e.g., Lev 26:30; Jer 50:2; and over forty times in Ezekiel).

After all that Moses has said on the edge of the land (including, e.g., 13:1–18), the instruction of verse 18 almost seems superfluous: "Be sure there is no man, woman, clan, or tribe among you today whose heart turns away from the Lord our God to go and worship the gods of those nations." To do so would be to allow a "root ... bearing poisonous and bitter fruit" (often identified as hemlock; see Hos 10:4) to grow up at the heart of the people of Yahweh.[532] There can be no compromise when it comes to idolatry among the people of Yahweh.

What might give rise to such a toxic root in the life of God's people? The answer is hardly surprising: *arrogant complacency*. When someone "hears the words of this oath" (29:19) (presumably referring to the prohibition of v. 18), there is a possibility that he "considers himself blessed in his heart" (lit., CSB: "exempt"; the same idea is found in Jer 7:8–10). The thought seems to be that someone trusts his or her own feelings, and in particular the sense that even should they follow their own "stubborn heart," everything will be fine. They say to themselves "I will have peace." The problem is that they are deluded, for the consequences of this behavior will be both drastic and all-encompassing. It will lead to "the destruction of the well-watered land as well as the dry land."

---

[531] For the meaning of "sheep droppings" for the second term, see D. Bodi, "Les *gillûlim* chez Ézéchiel et dans l'Ancien Testament et les different pratiques cultuelles associées à ce terme," *Revue biblique* 100 (1995): 481–510.

[532] This statement is quoted in Heb 12:15: "Make sure that no one falls short of the grace of God, and that no root of bitterness springs up causing trouble and defiling many." It is clear that the writer of Hebrews is equating "falling short of the grace of God" with the idolatry condemned in Deuteronomy. To miss out on God's grace because one has valued someone or something else more highly is a form of idolatry

The original is slightly ambiguous here: it simply says that the "saturated" and the "thirsty" will both be destroyed. There are two possible interpretations: (1) as the CSB suggests, the words may simply apply to the land itself, in which case 29:19 simply refer to the land itself being obliterated as a result of idolatry; (2) two groups of people are being described (those who are well-hydrated and those who are parched; or even those who are fruitful and those who are barren and unproductive) as a way of representing all of God's people (see Isa 58:11 and Jer 31:12, the other two Old Testament occurrences of the adjective, where the language is clearly figurative). It is hard to choose between the alternatives, although 29:22 may imply that it is the land itself that is in view.[533]

If the precise consequences of his actions on the land and/or its inhabitants are hard to pin down, the same cannot be said of the fate of the perpetrator of the idolatry.

One of the most terrifying statements in all of Scripture follows in 29:20: "The Lord will not be willing to forgive him." For Moses, deliberate idolatry among the covenant people of God, who have seen his actions on their behalf and benefited repeatedly from his goodness, is an unforgivable sin (Exod 34:6–7; Deut 6:15).[534] This goes some way to explain why as well as withholding his forgiveness, God's "anger and jealousy will burn against that person," expressed in "every curse written in this scroll" coming down on him. The twin images are smoke and fire coming from Yahweh's nostrils, and the curses lying like a predator in wait (as in 33:13). The final clause of verse 20 states bluntly that "The Lord will blot out his name under heaven." This phrase is used in Genesis 7:23 of the generation brought to an end

---

[533] McConville suggests this translation: "so that plenty of water may put an end to the drought," taking it as part of the words of the wicked. This is an intriguing possibility (*Deuteronomy*, 417).

[534] Interestingly, the book of Hebrews again deals with such ideas: "For it is impossible to renew to repentance those who were once enlightened, who tasted the heavenly gift, who shared in the Holy Spirit, who tasted God's good word and the powers of the coming age, and who have fallen away. This is because, to their own harm, they are recrucifying the Son of God and holding him up to contempt. For the ground that drinks the rain that often falls on it and that produces vegetation useful to those for whom it is cultivated receives a blessing from God. But if it produces thorns and thistles, it is worthless and about to be cursed, and at the end will be burned" (Heb 6:4–8). It is intriguing that, as in Deut 29, reference is made to fruitful land that is sustained by rain and arid, barren soil.

by judgment in the flood. Yahweh has also threatened to do this to Israel at Horeb (9:14) and committed to do it to the Amalekites (25:19).[535] This is the very antithesis of the way life should be in covenant, as Yahweh "singles him out for harm" of the kind described in the curses of chapters 27 and 28.

For most of Deuteronomy, the emphasis has fallen on the responsibility of the people of God to honor their covenant promises. Here, as Moses's life and words draw to a close, the focus sharpens on the individuals who make up the people of God. Shockingly, the God of covenant love is also the God of covenant judgment. For those who reject his relentless commitment and spurn his direct and personal command for obedience, there will be a heavy price to pray. It is no small thing to reject the living God. The fact that God has provided this "book of torah" makes that undeniably clear.

Even here, however, things can still get worse. The consequences of idolatry are not limited to the original perpetrator. According to 29:22, the reverberations of unfaithfulness will be felt across both time and space. "Future generations" of Israelite children will be appalled when they see the enduring devastation of the land. "The foreigner who comes from a distant country" will be similarly shocked when he passes through and glimpse the after-effects of the "plagues of the land and the sicknesses the Lord has inflicted on it" (as "promised" in 28:21–22, 27–28, 35, 59–61). The post-apocalyptic landscape will be like that of Sodom and Gomorrah in Genesis 19: "All its soil will be a burning waste of sulfur and salt, unsown, producing nothing, with no plant growing on it, just like the fall of Sodom and Gomorrah, Admah and Zeboiim, which the Lord demolished in his fierce anger."[536] Covenant faithfulness leads to flourishing, but unfaithfulness leads only to barren devastation.

In 4:5–8, the surrounding nations were pictured as asking longingly about Israel's quality of life, as Moses celebrated their intimate relationship with Yahweh. Now the watching world will ask, "Why has the Lord done this to this land? Why this intense burst of anger? [lit. the heat of this great

---

[535] A similar phrase is used of the Canaanites in 7:24–25 and 12:3; see also Pss 9:5; 69:28; 109:13–14

[536] Admah and Zeboiim are both mentioned in connection with Sodom and Gomorrah in both Gen 9 and 14. Although they are not specifically named in Gen 19, it seems that these associated communities were also destroyed in judgment.

anger]" (29:24). The answer is repetitive, but powerful. Moses explains ahead of time: should Israel fall victim to the anger of Yahweh, covenant-breaking will be the reason (29:25; see also 1 Kgs 19:10, 14; Jer 22:9).

As we saw at the beginning of the chapter, covenant unfaithfulness grows more serious as time goes on. God has given precious promises to the patriarchs (Abraham, Isaac, and Jacob). He has rescued the nation from slavery in Egypt and brought them into the land (see the double explanation given in v. 25). And yet they "began to serve other gods, bowing in worship to gods they had not known" (29:26). To state the obvious, Yahweh, the covenant God who constantly demands exclusive allegiance, had not given them license to do this. Yahweh's action in 29:27 is both predictable and has been coming since the beginning of chapter 27: "Therefore the Lord's anger burned against this land, and he brought every curse written in this book on it."

The culmination of this envisaged unfaithfulness is expulsion from the land in verse 28: "The Lord uprooted them from their land in his anger, rage, and intense wrath, and threw them into another land where they are today."[537] This is not a clumsy, accidental "reveal" of the provenance of the book. There is very little reason to believe that this is a *post facto* explanation of how Israel ended up in Babylon (like 1 and 2 Kings, for example). Rather this is precisely what it appears to be—a blunt warning ahead of time, that if the people of Israel choose to worship other gods, they will forfeit Yahweh's favor. At the heart of a covenantal relationship lies an insistence on exclusivity: if they will not have "Yahweh alone" then they cannot have Yahweh, and by extension will lose the land that he is giving them. "Today" at Moab (and on every "today" in the land), they must choose Yahweh or they will wake up one morning to find that "today" we are in exile. Moses has carefully constructed a rhetorical world where living for God "today" is the key to everything, and this warning is a key part of it.

The apparently cryptic statement of 29:29 is the hinge that links chapters 29 and 30. It speaks of the "hidden things" that "belong" to God, and the "revealed things" that "belong" to the Moab generation and those who follow. There has been much discussion of this verse, but it seems clear that the "revealed things" are best taken as the content of the covenant at Moab, as the culmination of all that Moses has said in these addresses. All these words "belong" to the people, and so are to

[537] The same threefold phrase is found in Jer 21:5 and 32:37.

be listened to and acted upon. They are to take them to heart (so also, e.g., 6:4–9). And the "secret things"? They seem most naturally to refer to the precise course of Israel's future. Moses has hinted at the shape that their life will take, but as for the fine-grained detail of how life in the land will actually unfold for Israel and when the future events that Moses has hinted at, including what he is about to describe in chapter 30, might happen? That remains hidden in the will of God.[538]

30:1–10. Deuteronomy 30 is one of the most significant chapters in the entire Old Testament. It is here that, for the first time, God reveals his commitment to refresh the covenant to deal with his people's inability to keep it. It is here that the prophetic preaching of Jeremiah and Ezekiel finds its wellspring. It is here that the gospel-shape of the Old Testament becomes apparent, as the pervasive reality of sin, Israel's decisive need for intervention, and the grace-fueled willingness of God to do what it takes to transform people like us is brought into the light. It is here in Deuteronomy 30 that we are given the key to ensure that we read the torah properly and the lens through which to view the subsequent history of God's people. And it is here that the delicate balance of Moses's rhetoric, both calling people to wholehearted obedience and exposing their inability to maintain such faithfulness, finds its potential resolution.

From the beginning of chapter 27, there has been an air of inevitability surrounding the future failure of Israel. However, in chapter 30 the growing sense that Moses is convinced that, sooner or later, God's people will experience the curses of the covenant rather than simply basking in its blessings gives way to a clear statement of the fate that awaits them. The *if* gives way to a very definite *when.*

Chapter 30 opens with a succinct preview how the history of Israel will play out: "When all these things [better: words] happen to you—the blessings and curses I have set before you ..." (as in 11:26–31). The expectation is clear: an initial experience of blessing will give way to the loss and devastation that comes with the curses of the covenant, as God's own people abandon him. This section, however, is not simply another swathe of dire warnings about the consequences

---

[538] It is possible that Jesus has this statement in mind when he says, "I praise you, Father, Lord of heaven and earth, because you have hidden these things from the wise and intelligent and revealed them to infants" (Matt 11:25).

of disobedience but describes a future day when the shape of life for those who belong to him will change forever.

Importantly, this section (30:1–10) is arranged chiastically, rather than chronologically. Events do not unfold sequentially but revolve around the game-changing event of 30:6 that explains how Israel's return to Yahweh in repentance and faith has been made possible.[539] 30:1–10 describes what God will do at some indeterminate moment in the future.[540]

First, the people of Israel will "come to their senses," taking the words of verse 1 to heart (see also 4:39). This will happen while they are "in all the nations" where they have been scattered (30:1). Once more, the plural "nations" underlines that Moses's understanding of this scattering is a general, theological vision of the consequences of disobedience.[541] The key to this awakening is literally "returning to your heart/mind." This will be developed throughout the section, but clearly involves much more than clearer cognition. This is *repentance*.[542]

This is confirmed by the statement in verse 2: "you and your children *return* to the Lord your God and obey him with all your heart and all your soul by doing everything I am commanding you today." This is nothing short of the realization of the vision to which Moses has been calling the people from the very beginning of the book (e.g., 4:9, 29). Several elements are worth highlighting: (1) the envisaged response is intergenerational; (2) repentance ("return") is the foundation of the response; (3) this repentance is displayed by the kind of fulsome obedience which has been the heartbeat of the book; and (4) on that day, Israel will start to do what Moses has told them to do "today" at Moab.

At this time, Yahweh will "restore the fortunes" of his people (lit., "return your return"—a phrase that probably refers to bringing their time of captivity to an end), show them "compassion" (4:31; 13:17; also Exod 34:6; Jer 12:15; 31:20; 33:26), which entails pouring out blessing on the people rather than curse, and bring them back to the land (the primary blessing of the covenant).

---

539 See, e.g., the excellent discussion in Paul Barker, *The Triumph of Grace: Faithless Israel, Faithful Yahweh in Deuteronomy* (Carlisle: Paternoster, 2004). Also Block, *Deuteronomy*, 695. Others (including Tigay, McConville, and Lenchak, have v. 8 at the center).

540 With, e.g., Craigie, *Deuteronomy*, 361.

541 This is clear evidence that the perspective of Deuteronomy is clearly early, and is not influenced by the Babylonian exile.

542 See William L. Holladay's classic study, *The Root* שׁוּב *in the Old Testament (With Particular Reference to its Usage in Covenantal Contexts)* (Leiden: Brill, 1958).

The logic of this passage is built on Moses's description of a series of essentially contemporaneous future events. As they unfold, there is nothing to suggest that he has a particular sequence of causality in mind. It is not as simple as: Israel repents, and God brings them home. God's action and the response of his people are interwoven. A great reversal will take place, but the central point is that it will *all* be the Lord's doing, and it will be marked by a thoroughgoing repentance among all God's people and return to the land.

The return to the land from this great scattering is front and center, as emphasized by 30:4–5. The "return" to Yahweh and the "return" to the land are inseparable, as Yahweh puts his covenant back on a solid footing. Distance will be no object to God's determination to restore his people (the phrase in v. 4 is literally "at the end of the heavens"; see also 4:32). Wherever they are, they will be brought back home. Yahweh's ancient promises will be fulfilled, with this scattering proving to be no more than a temporary interruption. Verse 5 makes it plain that the promises to Abraham, Isaac, and Jacob will not only be honored ("The Lord your God will bring you into the land your ancestors possessed, and you will take possession of it"), but be far exceeded. God's grand plans to build and bless a people, initiated with Adam and amplified through Abraham and his family, will now be extravagantly realized: "He will cause you to prosper and multiply you more than he did your ancestors."

The central statement of this section, and probably the most important sentence in all of Deuteronomy comes in 30:6: "The Lord your God will circumcise your heart and the hearts of your descendants, and you will love him with all your heart and all your soul so that you will live." In 10:16, Moses had called on all Israel to "circumcise their hearts"; now he announces that a day is coming when Yahweh himself will do what they cannot ultimately do for themselves.

As in chapter 10, to "circumcise the heart" (also Jer 4:4; 9:26) is to perform radical surgery on the whole person, with the Hebrew word (לֵבָב) conveying the idea of "your whole self" (encompassing decisions, emotions, and even personality). A day is coming when individuals will be transformed, but Moses is quick to add that this is not simply a decisive *moment*, but a transition to a whole new era, when successive generations of God's people will be enabled to meet their covenantal obligations. In future, the prayer of 5:29 will be answered, and the command of 6:4 (to "love Yahweh with heart, soul and strength") will be firmly within Israel's reach. And the result? 30:6 makes it clear that then, "you will live."

Moses's understanding of life is full and rich. It is a precursor to the life Jesus offers to all who come to him, particularly in John's Gospel (see, e.g., John 10:10). On multiple occasions throughout the book, he has spoken of this beautiful life which God invites his people to share with him (see 4:1, 40; 5:16, 33; 8:1; 11:9; 16:20; 22:7; 25:15), but it is now, in chapter 30, that it becomes clear how this life is to be lived and enjoyed: it will take the direct intervention of God himself. At the climax of this sermon, Moses invites God's covenant people to embrace and enjoy this life (30:16, 19, 20; 32:47). This offer finds even fuller expression in the new covenant passages of Jeremiah (31:31–34; 32:39–40) and Ezekiel (36:24–27).[543]

If this great reversal leads to the curse being removed from Israel, to be replaced by divine blessing, the opposite is the case for those who have opposed and oppressed the people of Yahweh. The curses that Israel experienced as a result of breaching covenant will now be experienced as divine judgment by those who "hate and persecute" them (30:7).

In 30:8–9, Moses returns to describing the dramatic transformation in the life of the nation: they will again "return and obey." It is best to retain the verb "return" here, rather than simply say "again obey" (CSB). The idea of returning is thematic in this section, capturing both spiritual and spatial movement. A day is coming when Israel will obey like never before, because God will give them the ability to carry out his commands. The blessings promised in 28:3–6, 11 will also be restored (covering children, livestock, and crops), with the result that "the Lord will again delight in your prosperity, as he delighted in that of your ancestors." In Moses's vision, covenantal harmony will not only be restored, but enhanced and intensified.

Verse 10 is a separate sentence in Hebrew, and the "when" clause (כִּי) is best taken as a description of how things will be on that day: God's people will gladly and wholeheartedly obey everything recorded in "this book of torah," which suggests (again) a clear and firm expectation that Moses's words would quickly and fully be reproduced for succeeding generations

[543] For a rich discussion of the circumcision motif, see John D. Meade, "Circumcision of the Heart in Leviticus and Deuteronomy: Divine Means for Resolving Curse and Bringing Blessing," *Southern Baptist Journal of Theology* 18, no. 3 (2014): 59–85.

(as in 28:58, 61, and also, by implication, 17:18). In addition, the people will "return to him with all your heart and all your soul." Given the parallels between verses 6 and 10, this is best understood as a description of a life of repentance and faith, brought about by the transformation of God, rather than a single transformative experience. Although the phrase is not used here, Moses has clearly outlined what Jeremiah later describes as a "new covenant" (Jer 31:31–34)—that is, a refreshed covenant that actually works, ensuring that "I will be your God, you will be my people" describes an enduring reality.

30:11–14. Interpreting 30:11–14 is not straightforward. The key issue surrounds the time reference of the verse. "The command that I give you *today*" could refer to the present, and therefore to Moses's urging the people at Moab once again to pay attention to his word. It is possible that Moses has switched from envisaging the future to the present.[544] However, there are significant problems in reading the text in this way, not least the fact that in the light of 29:16–28 (building on the rhetoric of chs. 27 and 28), Moses has already insisted that it very definitely *is* "too difficult and beyond their reach" to listen to and obey his words. There is, however, an alternative.

In Hebrew, verse 11 is introduced by an emphatic word (כִּי) which can simply mean "indeed," and so ties the command to the situation in verses 1–10.[545] It is only on *that day* (the "day" when the new covenant is inaugurated and the hearts of God's people have been circumcised) that it can be said that obedience is achievable. Only after God's dramatic intervention can they live out this command, which here encompasses all that Moses has said and is being written down.[546]

This perspective is confirmed in 30:12–14. Something has had to happen in order to make obedience possible. God has had to bring the command to the people. So verses 12–13: "It is not in heaven so that you have to ask, 'Who will go up to heaven, get it for us, and proclaim it

---

[544] This is probably the view of the majority of interpreters.

[545] Lundbom, *Deuteronomy*, 821, supports the linguistic argument, although he seems to think the verses refer to the present (823). Similarly, Block accepts that 30:11–14 can refer only to a time after understanding has been given. However, because he sees 29:4 as having already happened (and disconnects it from 30:6), he can locate 30:11–14 in the present, rather than the future, which would seem more consistent.

[546] Obedience for Israel is theoretically possible (there is nothing physically stopping them from doing the right thing), but Moses knows that they will not choose to do what God asks.

to us so that we may follow it?' And it is not across the sea so that you have to ask, 'Who will cross the sea, get it for us, and proclaim it to us so that we may follow it?' " God has had to bring the word near to his people (as in Prov 30:4).

Now up to this point, it seems plausible that Moses is simply talking about what he has been doing since the start of Deuteronomy, that his own proclamation of God's words has done the trick. However, 30:14 makes it clear that he is thinking of something else: "But the message is very near you, in your mouth and in your heart, so that you may follow it."

Nowhere in his speeches has Moses spoken quite like this. The events of Horeb (as related in, e.g., 4:32–40) were remarkable, but the people only heard the words of Yahweh. Now these words penetrate to the very center of their lives. The statement in 30:14 is surely referring back to what God is committed to doing in 30:6. The ability to follow this message is predicated on the transforming work of Yahweh himself.

This way of reading the text finds support in Romans 10, where the apostle Paul sees 30:11–14 as anticipating the work of Christ announced in the gospel:

> [4] For Christ is the end of the law for righteousness to everyone who believes, [5] since Moses writes about the righteousness that is from the law: **The one who does these things will live by them**. [6] But the righteousness that comes from faith speaks like this: **Do not say in your heart, "Who will go up to heaven?"** that is, to bring Christ down [7] or, **"Who will go down into the abyss?"** that is, to bring Christ up from the dead. [8] On the contrary, what does it say? **The message is near you, in your mouth and in your heart.** This is the message of faith that we proclaim: [9] If you confess with your mouth, "Jesus is Lord," and believe in your heart that God raised him from the dead, you will be saved. [10] One believes with the heart, resulting in righteousness, and one confesses with the mouth, resulting in salvation." (Rom 10:4–10)

The apostle's logic is clear: there is no need for anyone to do anything more (including going to heaven or into "the abyss") because Jesus Christ has made the decisive difference (including "circumcising our hearts").[547] This means that all that needs to be done is to "confess Jesus is Lord,"

[547] Colin J. Smothers, *In Your Mouth and In Your Heart: A Study of Deuteronomy 30:10–12 in Paul's Letter to the Romans in Canonical Context,* (Eugene: Pickwick, 2022) has provided an excellent and provocative study of this passage that is well worth consulting, even though he comes to some slightly different conclusions.

which opens up the glorious possibility of living the kind of beautiful, righteous life that Moses has been describing in such painstaking detail. It is with some justification that Daniel Block calls Deuteronomy "the Gospel according to Moses!"

30:15–20. What then are we do with 30:15–20? Do these words also refer to that future day after God's decisive intervention, which we now know to have taken place in Christ? Several markers in the text suggest that in verse 15, Moses returns to the present, to round off his appeal to his own generation in his own day at Moab.

The word "See" (רְאֵה, imperative of רָאָה) is an important clue to what is going on here. Elsewhere in the book (see the key points at 1:8; 4:5; and 11:26, and also the reports of 1:21; 2:24, 31), a call to "see" or "look" is used to bring Moses's audience back to real time. Here, it is the sign that their leader is speaking once more of the *immediate* response the people need to what Moses has said on the very cusp of the land. Once more, "today" means *today*, as Moses underlines that "life and prosperity, death and adversity" are hanging in the balance. We are now back in the realm of blessing and curse, which is a further sign that we have returned to the present from 30:1–14.

In what proves to be the final passage of Moses's addresses proper, he reiterates what he has said one more time, calling Israel to wholehearted obedience in what have become familiar terms. It is a straight choice: life or death, "good" or "evil." In 30:16, Moses describes the choice in familiar terms: "For I am commanding you today to love the Lord your God, to walk in his ways, and to keep his commands, statutes, and ordinances." This is the only way they will be able to "live and multiply," enjoying the blessings of the covenant in the land that God will give them. The unconditionality of 30:1–14 has reverted to conditionality: only full obedience can lead to blessing and the fulfillment of promise. Moses reiterates that the converse is also true in 30:17. Anything less than consistent covenant faithfulness is tantamount to idolatry (as in 29:25–29) and will lead to disaster and the briefest of stays in the land (30:18).

As Moses's appeal reaches its final climax, he enlists the entire cosmos to witness the choice that has been clearly set before them (as it was in 4:26 and will be again in 31:28). The choice is presented at its most stark in verse 19: Moses has set before them "life and death, blessing and curse." There are only two ways to live, and Moses urges them to "Choose life so that you and your descendants may live." This choice is both demanding and far-reaching. As he has done so often, Moses calls them to "love the Lord your God, obey him, and remain faithful to him" (30:20). God himself is their only hope. In fact, Moses goes as far as to say "he is your life." Only in and through Yahweh can they hope to survive in the land, to enjoy the fulfillment of the promise, and to keep the covenant that he had made with their ancestors and was renewing with them at Moab.

How can Moses, on the one hand, insist that obedience to Yahweh is the only way to "live," while, on the other, remain adamant that Israel simply does not have the wherewithal to do what God is asking of them? This is the enduring puzzle of this chapter, which takes us to the very heart of the message of the book. So how can we resolve this?

Moses exposes the basic dilemma of human existence, which can ever be resolved only by the gospel of the Lord Jesus. As human beings, we are under an obligation to God that we can never hope to meet. Flawed human beings cannot simply reform themselves. Nor can they ultimately respond properly to even the best preaching. We need the intervention of God himself. For people today, the challenge lies in accepting that reality and submitting to the Lord Jesus Christ. For Moses's hearers, the challenge was different: to embrace reality and then to wait, choosing life by seeking to obey as best they could in the interim, while looking to Yahweh, the God of the covenant, to do what he committed to doing in Deuteronomy 30:6.

Bridge

These chapters crystallize the message of the book of Deuteronomy. The obedience that God rightly requires and Moses passionately preaches is now clearly declared to be beyond the reach of Israel. But there is no need for despair. God has already committed to doing what is necessary to enable people like us to live for him. He has committed to "circumcising our hearts," refreshing his covenant of grace in Christ to enable us to have life to the full with him, now and forever. What Moses's hearers could only long for, we have experienced in Christ.

The apostle Paul picks up on this image in a striking way in Colossians 2, tying together this new covenant circumcision and the work of Christ in his death and resurrection like this:

> 11 You were also circumcised in him with a circumcision not done
> with hands, by putting off the body of flesh, in the circumcision of
> Christ, 12 when you were buried with him in baptism, in which you
> were also raised with him through faith in the working of God, who
> raised him from the dead. 13 And when you were dead in trespasses
> and in the uncircumcision of your flesh, he made you alive with him
> and forgave us all our trespasses. 14 He erased the certificate of debt,
> with its obligations, that was against us and opposed to us, and has
> taken it away by nailing it to the cross. 15 He disarmed the rulers and
> authorities and disgraced them publicly; he triumphed over them
> in him. (Col 2:11–15)

Because of all that God has done for us and given us in union with Christ, surely we must choose life.

VII. Postscript 1: The Inevitability of Failure (31:1–32:47)

> 1 Then Moses continued to speak these words to all Israel, 2 saying, "I
> am now 120 years old; I can no longer act as your leader. The LORD has
> told me, 'You will not cross the Jordan.' 3 The LORD your God is the one
> who will cross ahead of you. He will destroy these nations before you,
> and you will drive them out. Joshua is the one who will cross ahead of
> you, as the LORD has said. 4 The LORD will deal with them as he did Sihon
> and Og, the kings of the Amorites, and their land when he destroyed
> them. 5 The LORD will deliver them over to you, and you must do to them
> exactly as I have commanded you. 6 Be strong and courageous; don't be
> terrified or afraid of them. For the LORD your God is the one who will go
> with you; he will not leave you or abandon you."
>
> 7 Moses then summoned Joshua and said to him in the sight of all Israel,
> "Be strong and courageous, for you will go with this people into the land
> the LORD swore to give to their ancestors. You will enable them to take pos-
> session of it. 8 The LORD is the one who will go before you. He will be with
> you; he will not leave you or abandon you. Do not be afraid or discouraged."
>
> 9 Moses wrote down this law and gave it to the priests, the sons of Levi,
> who carried the ark of the LORD's covenant, and to all the elders of Isra-
> el. 10 Moses commanded them, "At the end of every seven years, at the
> appointed time in the year of debt cancellation, during the Festival of Shel-
> ters, 11 when all Israel assembles in the presence of the LORD your God at the
> place he chooses, you are to read this law aloud before all Israel. 12 Gather
> the people—men, women, dependents, and the resident aliens within your
> city gates—so that they may listen and learn to fear the LORD your God and
> be careful to follow all the words of this law. 13 Then their children who do
> not know the law will listen and learn to fear the LORD your God as long as
> you live in the land you are crossing the Jordan to possess."

[14] The Lord said to Moses, "The time of your death is now approaching. Call Joshua and present yourselves at the tent of meeting so that I may commission him." When Moses and Joshua went and presented themselves at the tent of meeting, [15] the Lord appeared at the tent in a pillar of cloud, and the cloud stood at the entrance to the tent.

[16] The Lord said to Moses, "You are about to rest with your ancestors, and these people will soon prostitute themselves with the foreign gods of the land they are entering. They will abandon me and break the covenant I have made with them. [17] My anger will burn against them on that day; I will abandon them and hide my face from them so that they will become easy prey. Many troubles and afflictions will come to them. On that day they will say, 'Haven't these troubles come to us because our God is no longer with us?' [18] I will certainly hide my face on that day because of all the evil they have done by turning to other gods. [19] Therefore write down this song for yourselves and teach it to the Israelites; have them sing it, so that this song may be a witness for me against the Israelites. [20] When I bring them into the land I swore to give their ancestors, a land flowing with milk and honey, they will eat their fill and prosper. They will turn to other gods and worship them, despising me and breaking my covenant. [21] And when many troubles and afflictions come to them, this song will testify against them, because their descendants will not have forgotten it. For I know what they are prone to do, even before I bring them into the land I swore to give them." [22] So Moses wrote down this song on that day and taught it to the Israelites.

[23] The Lord commissioned Joshua son of Nun, "Be strong and courageous, for you will bring the Israelites into the land I swore to them, and I will be with you."

[24] When Moses had finished writing down on a scroll every single word of this law, [25] he commanded the Levites who carried the ark of the Lord's covenant, [26] "Take this book of the law and place it beside the ark of the covenant of the Lord your God so that it may remain there as a witness against you. [27] For I know how rebellious and stiff-necked you are. If you are rebelling against the Lord now, while I am still alive, how much more will you rebel after I am dead! [28] Assemble all your tribal elders and officers before me so that I may speak these words directly to them and call heaven and earth as witnesses against them. [29] For I know that after my death you will become completely corrupt and turn from the path I have commanded you. Disaster will come to you in the future, because you will do what is evil in the Lord's sight, angering him with what your hands have made." [30] Then Moses recited aloud every single word of this song to the entire assembly of Israel:

> [32:1] "Pay attention, heavens, and I will speak;
> listen, earth, to the words from my mouth.

[2] Let my teaching fall like rain
and my word settle like dew,
like gentle rain on new grass
and showers on tender plants.
[3] For I will proclaim the LORD's name.
Declare the greatness of our God!
[4] The Rock—his work is perfect;
all his ways are just.
A faithful God, without bias,
he is righteous and true.
[5] "His people have acted corruptly toward him;
this is their defect—they are not his children
but a devious and crooked generation.
[6] Is this how you repay the LORD,
you foolish and senseless people?
Isn't he your Father and Creator?
Didn't he make you and sustain you?
[7] Remember the days of old;
consider the years of past generations.
Ask your father, and he will tell you,
your elders, and they will teach you.
[8] When the Most High gave the nations their inheritance
and divided the human race,
he set the boundaries of the peoples
according to the number of the people of Israel.
[9] But the LORD's portion is his people,
Jacob, his own inheritance.
[10] "He found him in a desolate land,
in a barren, howling wilderness;
he surrounded him, cared for him,
and protected him as the pupil of his eye.
[11] He watches over his nest like an eagle
and hovers over his young;
he spreads his wings, catches him,
and carries him on his feathers.
[12] The LORD alone led him,
with no help from a foreign god.
[13] He made him ride on the heights of the land
and eat the produce of the field.
He nourished him with honey from the rock
and oil from flinty rock,
[14] curds from the herd and milk from the flock,
with the fat of lambs,
rams from Bashan, and goats,
with the choicest grains of wheat;

you drank wine from the finest grapes.
15 "Then Jeshurun became fat and rebelled—
you became fat, bloated, and gorged.
He abandoned the God who made him
and scorned the Rock of his salvation.
16 They provoked his jealousy with different gods;
they enraged him with detestable practices.
17 They sacrificed to demons, not God,
to gods they had not known,
new gods that had just arrived,
which your ancestors did not fear.
18 You ignored the Rock who gave you birth;
you forgot the God who gave birth to you.
19 "When the Lord saw this, he despised them,
angered by his sons and daughters.
20 He said, 'I will hide my face from them;
I will see what will become of them,
for they are a perverse generation—
unfaithful children.
21 They have provoked my jealousy
with what is not a god;
they have enraged me with their worthless idols.
So I will provoke their jealousy
with what is not a people;
I will enrage them with a foolish nation.
22 For fire has been kindled because of my anger
and burns to the depths of Sheol;
it devours the land and its produce,
and scorches the foundations of the mountains.
23 I will pile disasters on them;
I will use up my arrows against them.
24 They will be weak from hunger,
ravaged by pestilence and bitter plague;
I will unleash on them wild beasts with fangs,
as well as venomous snakes that slither in the dust.
25 Outside, the sword will take their children,
and inside, there will be terror;
the young man and the young woman will be killed,
the infant and the gray-haired man.
26 I would have said: I will cut them to pieces
and blot out the memory of them from mankind,
27 if I had not feared provocation from the enemy,
or feared that these foes might misunderstand
and say, "Our own hand has prevailed;
it wasn't the Lord who did all this."

28 Israel is a nation lacking sense
with no understanding at all.
29 If only they were wise, they would comprehend this;
they would understand their fate.
30 How could one pursue a thousand,
or two put ten thousand to flight,
unless their Rock had sold them,
unless the LORD had given them up?
31 But their "rock" is not like our Rock,
as even our enemies concede.
32 For their vine is from the vine of Sodom
and from the fields of Gomorrah.
Their grapes are poisonous;
their clusters are bitter.
33 Their wine is serpents' venom,
the deadly poison of cobras.
34 "'Is it not stored up with me,
sealed up in my vaults?
35 Vengeance and retribution belong to me.
In time their foot will slip,
for their day of disaster is near,
and their doom is coming quickly.'
36 The LORD will indeed vindicate his people
and have compassion on his servants
when he sees that their strength is gone
and no one is left—slave or free.
37 He will say, 'Where are their gods,
the "rock" they found refuge in?
38 Who ate the fat of their sacrifices
and drank the wine of their drink offerings?
Let them rise up and help you;
let it be a shelter for you.
39 See now that I alone am he;
there is no God but me.
I bring death and I give life;
I wound and I heal.
No one can rescue anyone from my power.
40 I raise my hand to heaven and declare:
As surely as I live forever,
41 when I sharpen my flashing sword,
and my hand takes hold of judgment,
I will take vengeance on my adversaries
and repay those who hate me.
42 I will make my arrows drunk with blood
while my sword devours flesh—

> the blood of the slain and the captives,
> the heads of the enemy leaders.'
> 43 "Rejoice, you nations, concerning his people,
> for he will avenge the blood of his servants.
> He will take vengeance on his adversaries;
> he will purify his land and his people."

> 44 Moses came with Joshua son of Nun and recited all the words of this
> song in the presence of the people. 45 After Moses finished reciting all
> these words to all Israel, 46 he said to them, "Take to heart all these
> words I am giving as a warning to you today, so that you may command
> your children to follow all the words of this law carefully. 47 For they
> are not meaningless words to you but they are your life, and by them
> you will live long in the land you are crossing the Jordan to possess."

After the climax of Moses's preaching at the end of chapter 30, the rest of the book details the transition of leadership to Joshua and the final words and death of Moses, including the song of chapter 32 and the blessing of chapter 33. Although it is made up of a collection of loosely connected material, this addendum to the book emphasizes and reinforces the key theological concerns of the book in a surprisingly powerful way.

31:1–8. The opening phrase of 31:1 emphasizes the connection between these chapters and Moses's earlier preaching ("And Moses continued to speak all these words ..."), as he reminds the gathered assembly that his time is rapidly coming to an end. He will not enter the land: his time must come to an end in Moab. There are three reasons why this is so: (1) he is now 120 years old (although see 34:7);[548] (2) he is no longer capable of "going out and coming in," which seems to refer to leading, especially in battle (Num 27:17; although Deut 28:6 seems to have a more general reference); and (3) Yahweh himself had told Moses "You will not cross the Jordan" (also 1:37; 3:23–27). It is this last reason that is the most significant in the context of Deuteronomy.

Moses's death outside the land as a result of his arrogant response to the sinful behavior of the people casts a long shadow over the entire book and comes into sharp focus in the closing chapters.[549] The fact that

---

[548] After Moses, no one in the Old Testament is recorded as reaching this age (although Joshua comes close, reaching 110 years old, according to Josh 24:29). From this point on, to quote Moses himself, "Our lives last seventy years, or if we are strong, eighty years" (Ps 90:10).

[549] A point made powerfully by Dennis T. Olson in *Deuteronomy and the Death of Moses: A Theological Reading* (Minneapolis: Fortress, 1994).

Moses himself announces his fate (see also 3:21–26) adds to the rhetorical impact of the exclusion of such a great leader from the fulfillment of promise in the land. If Moses falls outside the land, then what hope do the people of Israel have of avoiding falling inside it? The brute fact of the death of Moses joins the ritual above Shechem and the content of Moses's preaching in chapters 29 and 30 in painting a dark picture of the future of the nation.

In one sense, failure is not inevitable—as Moses himself makes plain in 31:3: "The Lord your God is the one who will cross ahead of you." Not only does Yahweh guarantee that he will be with them, but also (as in 9:3), he will deal with the nations currently occupying the land. Strikingly, Moses will not be at the head of the army. That honor and responsibility will fall to Joshua.[550] But there is no doubt that their God, the God of Israel, will bring about their certain victory. Once more the Transjordan provides irrefutable evidence that the God who is with them can be trusted. He will deal with the Canaanites as he dealt with the Amorite kings, Sihon and Og (31:4). In the light of that, they should do exactly as they are told in order to ensure victory (as in 7:1–5; 20:16–18). Moses then leaves them with the ringing call to "Be strong and courageous."

For Israel, being brave is simply to refuse to cower before the enemy. Such terror or panic is the antithesis of trust in Yahweh. Their hope is not to be in Moses, or Joshua for that matter, but in the simple fact that "the Lord your God is the one who will go with you; he will not leave you or abandon you." Once more, this exposes the crack in the covenant relationship between Yahweh and Israel. Yahweh's presence and power are utterly dependable. Israel's trust is not.

The fact that Moses repeats his charge to "be strong and courageous" to Joshua in front of the entire nation at least hints that it will not be straightforward leading a people who are prone to balking at the slightest challenge—something that Joshua himself already knew well (see Num 13–14).[551] As the new leader, he must "go with the people" and "enable them to take possession" of the land (31:7), but Moses insists that Yahweh himself will "go before" him, "be with him," and never "leave or abandon"

[550] Interestingly, the same phrase is used to describe Yahweh and Joshua leading out the army. Again, human and divine agency are working in tandem.

[551] The longer account of this incident in Josh 1 confirms this, where the Reubenites, Gadites, and half the Manassites attempt to reassure Joshua by saying "We will obey you, just as we obeyed Moses in everything!" (Josh 1:17).

him (31:8; see also 4:31; 3:22). The God of the covenant can be trusted. But can the same be said of the people?[552]

31:9–13. The enduring question remains: Will the people listen to the voice of Yahweh, as he has spoken through Moses at Horeb and now at Moab? What happens next ensures that should they forget the words of Yahweh, they are without excuse, for Moses has "written down this law" (31:9).

At key points throughout Deuteronomy, God, Moses, and others *write things down* (4:13; 5:22; 10:4; 17:18; 27:3, 8; 29:21; 30:10). As the nation is about to enter the land, recording the words of this sermon is a vital part of God's provision for his people. So now in 31:9, Moses himself transcribes the words of his address (presumably on leather or parchment scrolls, rather than a physical book as we know it) and deposits it with the Levites and elders. The fact that the Levites "carry the ark of the covenant," which contains the twin tablets of Exodus 34, underlines the fact that Moses's words at Moab are considered to be on a par with those at Horeb: they are the very words of Yahweh himself.[553]

Part of the reason for keeping written records of covenant obligations like this was to facilitate periodic renewal of the covenant commitments set out in the document.[554] According to Moses in 31:10–11, such a covenant renewal is to punctuate the life of the nation of Israel: "At the end of every seven years, at the appointed time in the year of debt cancellation, during the Festival of Shelters, when all Israel assembles in the presence of the Lord your God at the place he chooses, you are to read this law aloud before all Israel." Embedded in the calendar of events in the year of debt cancellation (described in ch. 15) is to be a public reading by the leaders of this entire torah (which is at least the book of Deuteronomy) in the presence of Yahweh in his place and in the hearing of all the people. The joy-filled festival of shelters is the context of this public reading and a refreshment of joy-fueled covenant commitment the goal.

Moses emphasizes that for *this* event (unlike the annual festivals), *all* the people (rather than just the males, 16:16) are to gather at the chosen place for a fresh encounter with God himself through his words. "Men,

---

552 In 31:17, Yahweh says that if they break the covenant, he will forsake them, but as the book as a whole points out, this will only be a temporary measure, despite the provocation of Israel's faithlessness.

553 This is also part of the (often implicit) tradition that the Levites in particular are to be the teachers of Israel (e.g., 2 Chr 15:3; 17:8–9; 35:3; Jer 18:18; Ezek 7:26; Hag 2:10–14; Mal 2:7).

554 So Moshe Weinfeld, *Deuteronomy and the Deuteronomic School*, 63–64.

women, dependents, and the resident aliens within your city gates" are all to be included, because this event is to be an important part of keeping the nation on track, that they may "listen and learn to fear the Lord your God and be careful to follow all the words of this law" (also 4:10). This is remarkably progressive for the ancient world.

Even if parents neglect the responsibilities laid out so clearly in 6:4–9, for example, this festival will ensure that even "their children who do not know the law will listen and learn to fear the Lord your God as long as you live in the land you are crossing the Jordan to possess" (31:13).

With the exception of the glorious scenes of Nehemiah 8, where, led by Ezra, who reads the torah, the Levites "explained the law to the people as they stood in their places. They read out of the book of the law of God, translating and giving the meaning so that the people could understand what was read" (Neh 8:7–8), there is no sign that this event ever became a regular part of the life of the people of Yahweh. To paraphrase G. K. Chesterton, "The Old Testament ideal was not tried and found wanting. It was found difficult; and left untried."[555]

31:14–30. If 30:1–20 is the most theologically far-reaching passage in Deuteronomy, then 31:14–30 is probably the most surprising. We have heard a growing note of pessimism throughout Moses's speech. Now, finally, he expresses the settled, decisive conviction that God's people cannot sustain obedience in the land and will disobey, eventually forfeiting God's gift of the very land itself. There is no longer any room for ambiguity. Astonishingly, this theologically rooted pessimism is confirmed by the direct affirmation of Yahweh himself. No detail is given on how God appeared to Moses: as is typical in Deuteronomy, the focus remains squarely on the words spoken. But as Yahweh speaks, he leaves no room for doubt or misunderstanding.

Initially, Yahweh confirms that Joshua is to be Moses's successor. God tells Moses that his death is imminent (see the similar phrases in Gen 47:29 and 1 Kgs 2:1) and instructs him to bring Joshua to the tent of meeting "so that I may commission him." This is unusual, in that no other biblical commissioning takes place at the tent like this.[556] In this case, however, it is emphasizing that Joshua is now taking over Moses's role as the one

---

[555] See G. K. Chesterton, *What's Wrong with the World* (London: Cassell, 1910), 39.

[556] The closest parallel seems to be the commissioning of the temple in 1 Kgs 8. Block (*Deuteronomy*, 727) argues plausibly that this is a portable "appointment" tent outside the camp, to which God came for special meetings with his people (e.g., Exod 33:7–11; Num

who interacts with Yahweh on behalf of the people. This is made clear by the surprising appearance of Yahweh in 31:15: "The Lord appeared at the tent in a pillar of cloud, and the cloud stood at the entrance to the tent" (as in Num 12:5, also 14:14). This is the first time since the journey to the land was aborted, that Yahweh has appeared before his people in this way, and the last time in the canon that such a phenomenon occurs. Joshua is established as the new Moses, and God commits to continue to meet with his servant. However, once Joshua has led the people into the land, and they have found "rest from all their enemies" (Josh 23:1), this line of succession comes to an end.

In 31:16, rather than proceeding straight to the commissioning itself, God speaks to Moses in unprecedented terms about the inevitability of the apostasy to come: "You are about to rest with your ancestors, and these people will soon prostitute themselves [lit., go whoring] with the foreign gods of the land they are entering. They will abandon me and break the covenant I have made with them."[557] Any interpretation of the message of Deuteronomy must take this direct divine statement seriously: God himself confirms that sooner or later, his people will choose death rather than life. It is not a question of *if* but *when.* The tension between Moses's preaching and his pessimistic view of Israel's future is ultimately a tension between what God rightly asks of his creatures and what we deliver. This tension is as old as Adam and Eve and is now played out in God's gracious election of Israel as his covenant people and the painful reality that the people he has chosen (referred to pejoratively as "this people," as in Exod 32:9, 21; Num 14:11; Isa 6:9–10, 11–12; see also Luke 15:30, "this son of yours") are ultimately incapable of loving their God as they should.

When that "day" comes (31:17), their covenant breaking (this strong verbal form also occurs in Lev 26:15; Jer 11:10; Ezek 16:59; 44:7) will lead to a burning outpouring of divine wrath, as God withdraws from his people, abandoning (or forsaking) them and hiding "his face from them, so that they will become easy prey." Without the protection of God's presence, "many troubles and afflictions will come to them," as we have already seen in the long exposition of the curses of the covenant in chapters 27

12:4–5). However, Alexander (*Exodus*, 635) disputes this, seeing that tent as merely a temporary precursor to the tabernacle.

557 The language of whoring after other gods occurs in Exod 34:15–16; Judg 2:17; 8:33.

and 28. Covenant breaking always has this result: "I will certainly hide my face on that day because of all the evil they have done by turning to other gods" (31:18).[558]

In order to impress the seriousness of the choice facing Israel yet again and to force them to confront the basic, brutal reality that, if they will not listen to him, they will have to live *without* his presence and *with* the fearful reality of his wrath, Yahweh instructs Moses and Joshua (the command is plural) to "write (down) this song for yourselves and teach it to the Israelites" (31:19).

Although routinely called the Song of Moses, this song is really the Song of Yahweh. Moses and Joshua simply teach it to the people, explain it to the people, and ensure that they sing it. Yahweh himself insists that the song is a "witness for me against the Israelites." This is a strong statement. The idea seems to be that the song will be a warning ahead of time that the people are wired for disobedience, and sooner or later, even as they enjoy the God-given prosperity of a land "flowing with milk and honey" (as in 6:3, etc.), will become complacent and selfish, "despising" Yahweh and turning to other gods (31:20). If they keep singing this "national anthem," as Block helpfully calls the song, it will remind them, even when they have rebelled (31:21), that they have no excuse because God had warned them repeatedly ahead of time.[559]

The idea of a "witness against the people" recurs in 31:26, where it is the torah scroll itself that is the witness, and in Joshua 24:27 (a large stone erected at Shechem, at the foot of Ebal and Gerizim). In the New Testament, Jesus's command to shake the dust off one's feet when leaving a village where the gospel receives a hostile reception, and James's insistence that trusting corrosive wealth destroys, function in similar ways.

If they are taught this song well and it becomes part of the national consciousness, it will provide a theological anchor for the people of God, even in their disobedience. According to 31:21, "When many troubles and afflictions come to them, this song will testify against them, because their descendants will not have forgotten it." God's grace even extends

---

[558] See 32:20; also Job 13:24; 34:29; Ps 10:11; 13:1; 22:24; 27:9; 30:7; 69:17; 88:14; 102:2; 104:29; 143:7; Isa 8:17; 54:8; 59:2; 64:7; Jer 33:5; Ezek 39:23–24; 39:29; Mic 3:4). This is the antithesis of what was held out to Israel in Num 6:25–26.

[559] See Daniel I. Block, "The Power of Song: Reflections on Ancient Israel's National Anthem (Deuteronomy 32)," in *How I Love Your Torah O LORD! Studies in Deuteronomy* (Eugene: Cascade, 2011), 162–184.

to providing a mechanism ahead of time to bring them to their senses. In the final part of the verse, Yahweh adds "For I know what they are prone to do, even before I bring them into the land I swore to give them." Literally, Yahweh says he knows יֵצֶר (their "imagination," "intent," or even "nature"), an idea that first occurred in Genesis 6:5 and 8:21. His people are not essentially different from Noah's contemporaries, despite all that Yahweh has done for them.

It is a great tragedy that even though Moses "wrote down this song on that day and taught it" to them (31:21), as with the reading of the torah every seven years, there is scant evidence that this song ever became part of the theological foundation of God's people in the land. The Song of Yahweh/Moses is one of the most neglected parts of the Old Testament, even in the life of the church today. The words of Yahweh to the people in Deuteronomy 31, backed up and amplified by this song, are the necessary accompaniment to the extravagant promises to bless which litter Moses's preaching. Yes, Yahweh is a good, generous, and powerful God, but the world is populated by flawed, broken, and recalcitrant people who desperately need to be transformed if they are to enjoy life with him. Thus, when the commissioning of Joshua actually happens in 31:23, the call to "Be strong and courageous" takes on a more ominous hue, given the dark warnings of the previous verses.

Before we come to the song itself, Moses reiterates the expressed concerns of Yahweh from 31:24. Initially, we are told that Moses "finished writing down on a scroll every single word of this law." As in 31:9, the core of the book—that is, the words of Moses as he preaches this torah on the plains of Moab—is committed to parchment or vellum before the people enter the land.[560] The documents supporting the covenant at Moab take their place alongside those (stone) documents undergirding the covenant at Horeb by the ark of the covenant. Moses commissions the Levites in 31:25 to ensure that this happens and that his words remain at the center of national life. [561]

---

[560] Lundbom argues that this actually refers to the Song and is an attempt to attach the status of "law" to it. It seems much simpler to retain the usual reference of the phrase to the main body of Deuteronomy, which now includes the song (see *Deuteronomy*, 844–45).

[561] This mirrored the ancient Near Eastern practice of placing treaty documents in temples. Presumably the scroll was placed in a jar or similar vessel for safekeeping, although 1 Kgs 8:9 suggests that they may have been misplaced by the time of Solomon!

It is striking that even Moses's exposition of the beautiful life in the torah will ultimately join the song in functioning as a witness against the people (21:26).[562] Here we find the seeds of the later apostolic discussion of the role of the law in, for instance, Romans 7:7–13. There is no question that the law is a good and positive thing. The problem is that when God's people try to live it out, without God's intervention, bringing us to life and equipping us for obedience through union with Christ in the power of the Spirit, the end result can only be condemnation. It is important to see that the basic tension between a positive view of the goodness of torah and its function in exposing evil are not a new phenomenon but can be traced back to these chapters (and even earlier).

Like Yahweh himself, Moses knows that Israel's attempts to live out covenant faithfulness in the land can only ultimately end one way: "For I know how rebellious and stiff-necked you are. If you are rebelling against the Lord now, while I am still alive, how much more will you rebel after I am dead!" (31:27).[563] Any remaining ambiguity is removed. Moses says plainly that God's people will choose death rather than life, with all that entails.

Moses then commands the Levites to call the leaders of the nation (the "tribal elders and officers") together one final time, so that he may spell out this painful reality directly to them, "calling heaven and earth as witnesses against them" (31:28; see on 4:26 and 30:19). He does this in 31:29: "For I know that after my death you will become completely corrupt and turn from the path I have commanded you. Disaster will come to you in the future, because you will do what is evil in the Lord's sight, angering him with what your hands have made" (see 4:25–26). This clearly leaves no room for uncertainty.

This chapter is often overlooked in the unfolding of redemptive history. The stark verdict on Israel's future not only completes the paradoxical nature of Moses's preaching in Deuteronomy, but also sets the trajectory for Joshua and the historical books that follow, as well as laying a theological foundation for the ministry of the prophets. The conquest of the land is going to be a failure. The cracks start appearing as soon as Israel sets foot in the land (see, e.g., Josh 2, 7, 9), and the "rest" which they experience is always fragile and incomplete. The downward spiral of Judges does

---

[562] With Tigay, *Deuteronomy*, 297.

[563] The phrase "stiff-necked" is also found in 9:6, 13; 10:16.

not come as a surprise. Hope for Israel from this point on is ultimately to be found in a new covenant on the other side of judgment. The gradual evaporation of hope of a stable and God-centered national existence in God's land has already begun. This reality is reflected in almost every line of the song, to which we finally come, as "Moses recited aloud every single word of this song to the entire assembly of Israel" (31:30).

32:1–43. The Song of Moses (or the Song of the Lord transcribed by Moses), sung (or recited) and taught by Moses, is a roller-coaster ride of soaring descriptions of the power, beauty, kindness, and justice of God (e.g., 32:1–4, 10–14, 34–42) interspersed with searing criticism of the nature and behavior of Israel (e.g., 32:5–6, 15–22, 28–33). It is a careful blend of familiar language and ideas from Moses's preaching, with distinctive expressions and imagery that speak to the antiquity of the song.[564]

The structure of the song is reflected in the layout of the English text (with successive stanzas separated by blank lines), which will guide our discussion. A helpful outline is as follows:

Introduction (1–3)
The Greatness of Yahweh (4)
Israel's Betrayal of Yahweh their God (5–9)
Yahweh's Past Kindnesses (10–14)
Indictment of Israel (15–18)
Judgment on Israel (19–22)
The Extent of Israel's Punishment (23–25)
Yahweh's Motivation for Sparing Them (26–27)
Reflection on Israel (28–33)
Israel's Future Hope (34–38)
The Greatness of Yahweh (39–42)
Conclusion (43)[565]

32:1–4. Given Moses's expressed intention in 30:19 and 31:27 to call heaven and earth as witnesses, it is no surprise to hear that the song opens with broadly the same idea, calling the heavens to "pay attention" and the earth to "listen carefully." Right at the start of this song, the cosmos itself is enlisted as the audience for Israel's performance in the land. The singer is then to intone what is basically a prayer for the

[564] The reference in v. 14 to the conquest of Bashan (in the Transjordan) fits the context at Moab on the way to the land perfectly.

[565] This is a modified version of Lundbom's outline. For this, and a detailed and extremely helpful analysis of the poetics of the Song, see *Deuteronomy*, 859–71.

reception of the "teaching" of the song (see Prov 1:5), presumably in both his own consciousness and that of any hearers of the song. The metaphor is powerful: "Let my teaching fall like rain and my word settle like dew, like gentle rain on new grass and showers on tender plants." (32:2)[566] Interestingly, despite the function of the song as a witness *against* Israel, conviction of their sin is seen as an inherently good thing. This is surely because even as it prosecutes its case, the song opens up the possibility of forgiveness for the repentant people of God.

The reason why embracing this teaching will prove refreshing, should the singers and hearers choose to do so, is ultimately because this is a song about Yahweh. According to 31:3, the song "proclaims Yahweh's name" (see also Exod 33:19; 34:5; Ps 105:1–2) and "declares his greatness." In particular, it celebrates God's dependability, consistency, integrity, and justice.

31:4 opens with a single word in Hebrew: God is "The Rock" (also vv. 18, 30, 31). While the idea that God is Israel's "rock" is common, it is unusual for it to appear without qualification.[567] The contrast between the utter solidity and dependability of Yahweh and the unreliability of his covenant people is deliberately extreme. Six epithets are attached to God and his works: (1) "perfect" (see Deut 18:13), which carries the sense of morally flawless; (2) "just," in other words, his decisions are completely fair and beyond question; (3) "faithful," as in dependable and consistent, particularly in the realm of covenant-keeping; (4) "without bias" (the word here is normally translated as "iniquity," carrying the idea of veering off track, hence "bias"); (5) "righteous," a word used in 4:8 of the torah, and 16:19 and 25:1 of those who are innocent or beyond reproach; and (6) "true," or upright (used with "righteousness" in Ps 119:137).

The effect of all this is twofold: first, it is clear that God himself models precisely what he requires of Israel as his covenant partner, and second, it anticipates any attempt to attach blame to him for their failure. Yahweh's

---

[566] Similar language is used of the effect God's words in Isa 55:10–11 and of the king's rule in Psalm 72:6.

[567] So, e.g., in Gen 49:24, he is described as "the Rock of Israel" (also 2 Sam 23:3; Isa 30:29). In Psalm 89:26, God is the "rock of my salvation," and in 94:22, "the rock of my protection." Isa 17:10 refers to the "rock of your strength"; Isa 51:1 the "rock from which you were cut." It may also be that Jesus has this image (if not this specific text?) in mind when he speaks of the house built on the rock in Matt 7:24–25.

commitment to them is unshakeable and his actions unimpeachable. The same, however, cannot be said for the people.

32:5–9. In the light of all this, the response of Israel to Yahweh's constancy is shocking. The Hebrew of 32:5 is abrupt: just two words in the original announce that "He [the people] has acted corruptly toward him [Yahweh]" (see 9:12). And the problem? Their "defect" (a term that usually describes an issue making something or someone unholy or unacceptable to Yahweh, but see Prov 9:7, Job 11:15 for metaphorical uses) is that they are not (lit.) "his sons."[568] They are not behaving as those who are fit to share in the Father's inheritance. Rather they are a "devious and crooked generation."[569] Given the way Moses has routinely conflated the past, present, and future in his preaching, it is clear that this, sadly, is a song that every generation of God's covenant people can sing with conviction!

The words of this song, however, do not simply detail the painful reality, but they also address it head on. Yahweh himself preaches to his people through the proxy of this song. In 32:6, a triple question is asked: "Is this how you repay the Lord, you foolish and senseless people? Isn't he your Father and Creator [cf. 1:31; 8:5]? Didn't he make you and sustain [or: establish] you?" Ingratitude is not the only sin of which God's people are guilty, but it is the most basic. God made them, chose them, rescued them, and provided for them. In their stupidity, they have turned their backs on him.

32:7–9 starts to trace God's kindness to his people from ancient times. The time reference of verse 7 is uncertain, but seems most naturally to refer to early human history, presumably as recounted in Genesis 1–11 and alluded to in the next verse. One's "father" and the "elders" will be able to explain what happened not because they are ancient, but because the tradition has been passed on to them. The salient fact here is that when God, referred to here by the ancient title "the Most High" (e.g., Gen 14:19–20) "gave the nations their inheritance" in verse 8 and divided the sons of Adam (probably an allusion to the events at Babel in Gen 10:32; 11:1–9), he set things up ("set the boundaries of the peoples") "according to the number of the people of Israel."[570] The point is that

---

568 The Hebrew is tricky here, but this is clearly the point. See also 1:31; 8:5.

569 These ideas recur in both Job (5:13; 9:20, where the word is rendered "guilty" in the CSB) and Proverbs (8:8; 11:20; 17:20; 19:1; 28:6, 18).

570 According to one of the Dead Sea Scrolls (4QDeut[j]) and the LXX the text should read "sons of God/gods." Neither form is without difficulty.

from the beginning, God ensured that the course of world history was ordered for the benefit of the nation that he would choose. Rather than starting verse 9 with "But," then, it seems more natural to render the conjunction (כִּי) as "Because," supplying the reason for this preferential treatment: it is because Israel is Yahweh's own "portion" or "allocation" (cf. the dividing line in Amos 7:17; Mic 2:5), and the people of Jacob "his inheritance." Yahweh set up the world to facilitate intimacy with his people Israel. That alone should have given enough reason to listen to him. But it really is only the beginning.

32:10–14. The nation is then to sing of Yahweh's history with his people in vivid and emotive terms, starting with verse 10. Yahweh "found" Israel in a desert, in a featureless wilderness, and then "surrounded," "cared for," and "protected him as the pupil of his eye" (see Jer 2:2; 31:2–3; Ezek 16:1–7; Hos 9:10). The image is of the reflection of the person one is looking at in the center of the eye—hence the "pupil" (also Prov 7:2).[571] Israel is right at the center of the attention—and the affection—of God himself. So, verse 11, "he watches over his nest" (or perhaps better, "stirs up," in the sense of fluffing it up to make it comfortable and secure), "hovering" protectively over his young. He even taught the young Israel to "fly": "he spreads his wings, catches him, and carries him on his feathers." In 32:12, using language reminiscent of 6:4 (and Hos 13:4), it is affirmed that Yahweh alone did this, "with no help from a foreign God," and so Israel should express their gratitude in covenant faithfulness.[572]

As the song turns to Yahweh bringing his people to the verge of the land in verses 13–14, the lyrics are dramatic: "He made him ride on the heights of the land [see also Isa 58:14] and eat the produce of the field. He nourished him with honey from the rock [wild honey was common in Canaan, where it can be found even in rock fissures; see Gen 43:11, Deut 8:8; 1 Kgs 14:3; Ps 81:16] and oil from flinty rock." The oil here is olive oil. Olive trees can, at times, grow in the most inhospitable places. It's as if the land itself is feeding Israel. Yahweh's care for his people in the wilderness, and presumably his ongoing

---

[571] Traditionally, this figure was translated as "the apple of his eye," but unfortunately, this is almost certainly wrong.

[572] It is interesting that there is no explicit reference to the exodus here, but this actually fits with where the narrative in Deuteronomy begins (i.e., in the wilderness, rather than in Egypt). See Tigay, *Deuteronomy*, 304.

care for them in the land they are about to enter, is stunning, as they enjoy a diet of "curds ... milk ... the fat of lambs, rams [lit., sons] from Bashan, and goats," as well as the "choicest grains of wheat" and freshly fermented wine."[573] This is a Transjordan diet fit for kings, but in this case is provided by a loving God.

32:15–18.[574] Israel's response to this extravagant generosity is summed up in 32:15–18. Jeshurun, used only in Isaiah 44:2 outside this chapter and the next, is an ancient name for Israel and ironically means "the straight (or upright) one." But they have become like a cow fattened and ready for slaughter, which, oblivious to the fact that it is simply hastening its impending fate, rebels against its master. In 32:15, adjectives are piled up ("fat, bloated, and gorged") to convey that this situation is utterly disgraceful. They are then to sing of their actions ("He abandoned the God who made him") and the attitudes driving them ("scorned" or "treated as a fool the Rock of his salvation" [cf. Mic 7:6; Nah 3:6]).

The litany of sin continues in verses 16–18, as a string of verbs adds further definition to their rejection of Yahweh: they "provoked ... enraged ... sacrificed [to demons, not God] ... ignored ... forgot." The full gamut of sin is covered here. The song depicts Yahweh as a rightly jealous lover, the upholder of what is right and good, the God who has made himself known over generations (unlike the "demons ... gods they had not known, new gods that had just arrived"), and the Rock (32:5) who was also their parent ("who gave birth to you").[575] It is as if the past history of the nation, and what will unfold in the years to follow, is summed up in a few brief lines.

32:19–22. Inevitably, the envisaged response in verses 19–35 is exactly as chapters 27–31 have envisaged. In verse 19, the singers are to imagine Yahweh seeing all this, reacting to it as a holy God must (he was "angered by his sons and daughters"), and then responding. The words "he despised them" are chilling (see also Lam 2:6). There is surely no question that had this song become a part of the life of the nation, it would have had an arresting effect.

---

[573] Judging from Ps 22:12 and Ezek 39:18, these "sons of Bashan" may be cattle rather than sheep. The phrase "the blood of the grape" is used here, as in Gen 49:11.

[574] Some manuscripts (4QPhil 141, Sam and LXX) have an extra phrase at the start of v. 15: "Jacob ate his fill." This may be original, but in any case, the point is made by the next clause.

[575] For demons, see Ps 106:37, and "no-gods" Hos 8:6; Jer 2:11; 5:7; 16:20.

Deuteronomy 32:20 presents Yahweh as "hiding his face from them" (as in 31:17–18). In this context, Yahweh is clearly stepping back to allow the consequences of their actions to unfold. "I will see what will become of them" is not a statement of helplessness or complete disengagement, but rather a deliberate withholding of help in order to bring on what is inevitable.

The verdict "for they are a perverse generation" and, literally, "sons in whom there is not faithfulness" goes far beyond behavior to expose the core issue which Moses has been tackling in the previous chapters: they have uncircumcised hearts.[576] The fact that every "generation" is expected to sing these words is a subtle but ultimately damning indictment of the covenant people of Yahweh.

In verse 21, the language of verse 16 is picked up once more, but this time to bring a simple symmetry to the actions of the people and their God: the idolatry of the people in going after a no-god has "provoked jealousy" and "enraged" Yahweh; now Yahweh's action (and deliberate inaction) will seek to reignite their spiritual sensibilities by using a "no people" (as in a nation or nations which are not in covenant with him) and a "foolish nation" to provoke them.[577]

There can be no mistaking the seriousness of the predicament in which God's people will find themselves, if and when they rebel against Yahweh. His white-hot, settled wrath finds expression in judgment that is all-consuming: once kindled, Yahweh's anger produces a fire which "burns to the depths of Sheol," consuming the land and everything in it, and even "scorches the foundations of the mountains."

32:23–25. Having been instructed to proclaim the curses of the covenant from the mountains above Shechem in chapters 27 and 28, now Israel is to sing them in 32:23–25. "Disasters" (lit., "evil things") will be heaped on them; Yahweh himself will empty his quiver, launching his "arrows" at them (also Ezek 5:16). Verse 24 lists a plethora of sufferings that will strike them: "hunger ... pestilence ... plague ... wild beasts with fangs ... venomous snakes." This part of the picture is completed by the description of almost unspeakable destruction wreaked on Yahweh's

---

[576] Again, the language of perversity is picked up mainly in Proverbs: 2:12, 14; 6:14; 8:13; 10:31–32; 16:28, 30; 23:33.

[577] See Ps 74:18 and Rom 10:19, where Paul quotes this verse in the context of God using the gentiles' acceptance of the gospel to provoke Jewish people. On worshiping "nothings" see Jer 8:19; 10:8; 14:22; 1 Kgs 16:13,26; Ps 31:6, and also Jer 2:5, where he refers to Baal as "the Nothing."

disobedient people. There really is no hiding place. The children (presumably playing) outside will be the first to suffer, before the "sword" enters the homes of the people, wreaking terror and sparing no one: "the young man and the young woman will be killed, the infant and the grey-haired man."[578]

It is true that there are several texts in Deuteronomy concerning other nations that can seem morally problematic in our day. But those texts need to be read in the light of the song that was supposed to be the national anthem of Israel. There is no license for jingoistic imperialism or racist violence. There will always be punishment and justice. The God of Deuteronomy is pure, holy, and active. All peoples on earth—including Israel, his chosen, covenant people—are accountable to him, and a failure to honor, treasure, and love him will always have terrible consequences in the long-term. On this, the Bible speaks with one voice.

32:26–27. In verses 26 and 27, the words of Yahweh himself continue as he speaks in the most dramatic and fearsome terms. It now becomes clear that the only thing that stays his hand, avoiding the complete destruction of the nation and the permanent annulment of the covenant, is the possibility of mixed messages going to the watching nations, encouraging them in their arrogance to say: "Our own hand has prevailed; it wasn't the Lord who did all this." The strong messages of 7:7–11 and 9:1–6 concerning the grace of Yahweh and the unworthiness of the people are reinforced in the most dramatic way, as the nation is forced to sing of their survival by the skin of their teeth. The only reason why Yahweh himself did not pick up a weapon and "cut them to pieces," eradicating them from history, is the progress of his overarching plan of redemption: to allow his covenant people to vanish would inevitably bolster the hubris of other nations. In a bold anthropomorphism, this is what Yahweh "feared." It is not hard to see why this most searching of songs appears to have been quickly shelved.

32:28–33. Even though the voice of the singer is now Moses, there is no let-up in 32:28, which is a damning indictment of the people to whom God has spoken (e.g., 4:5–8): "Israel is a nation lacking sense with no understanding at all."[579] As they stand on the verge of entering

---

[578] See a similar picture in Jer 9:21.

[579] The Hebrew does not name which nation this is, so the verse could refer to vv. 26–27. It seems more natural (with the CSB) to read these verses as dealing with Israel.

the land, there is no sense that they have learned from the previous forty years. The song makes it clear that Yahweh does not expect this trajectory to change. "If only they were wise, they would comprehend this" (32:29), but the unavoidable truth is that they are not. They have no interest in thinking about their "fate" (lit., their "ultimate end"). Already it seems clear that their only real hope is that God himself will provide them with his wisdom.[580]

This epic song pauses to ask a question in 32:30, which, had God's people possessed any of the wisdom alluded to in the previous verse, would be easily answered: how could they slump to such an ignominious defeat, routed with so little effort by so few people (with one defeating one thousand, two beating ten thousand)? The answer is obvious: Yahweh "their Rock" has "sold them" and "given them up" (v. 31). There can be no question whether the non-gods of the nations who oppress them are superior: "their "rock" is not like our Rock"—even the other nations concede that (again, 4:5–8 is apposite). Nor does the downfall of Israel vindicate these nations: the vivid imagery makes it plain that they will ultimately face judgment for their attitudes and actions, for "their vine is from the vine of Sodom and from the fields of Gomorrah."[581] Their idolatrous DNA is what leads to their toxic behavior, as their "poisonous and bitter grapes" produce wine that is "serpents' venom, the deadly poison of cobras."

This denunciation then gives way to an extended explanation in 32:34–42 of how the one and only God, the righteous God of the covenant can use such people as his tools, if his chosen people have reneged on their commitment to him, without compromising his own righteousness.[582]

32:34–38. When Yahweh starts to speak again in verse 34, his statement, while slightly cryptic, is clearly an assertion of his absolute sovereignty: "Is it not stored up with me, sealed up in my vaults?" It is not entirely obvious *what* is locked away. It is probably the "wine" of verse 33, although it may be the "vengeance and retribution" alluded to at the start of verse 35, or more generally, the *explanation* of how divine justice

---

[580] A theme which Paul expounds at some length in 1 Cor 1–2, and notably in 1:26–31, where he explicitly calls the Lord Jesus Christ "the wisdom of God."

[581] These cities have already been mentioned by Moses in 29:23.

[582] This is a question which is taken up repeatedly in the Old Testament, most notably in the book of Habakkuk.

operates when using other nations to discipline the covenant people.[583] Whichever it is, the song reminds Israel that divine justice does not necessarily keep in step with our desired timing: "In time their foot will slip," for both their "day of disaster" and their "doom" are fast approaching. [584] While one always has to factor in that according to the words attributed to Moses in Psalm 90:4, "in your sight a thousand years are like yesterday that passes by, like a few hours of the night," there is no doubt that Yahweh has both the right and the ability to carry out vengeance and retribution in due time.[585]

The song takes an unexpected turn in verse 36, with the expectation not simply that God will act with justice, dealing with those nations that wreak havoc on Israel, but that "Yahweh will indeed vindicate his people." This "vindication" is in parallel to having "compassion" (or relenting), and this happens when he sees that they (probably his people rather than their enemies) have hit rock bottom and "their strength is gone." This idea is picked up repeatedly in Isaiah (47:3–4; 59:17–20; 61:2; 63:4). The "vindication" then is not an affirmation of their behavior, or an acknowledgement that they have been dealt with harshly or unfairly, but rather that their status as the freely chosen, much loved people of Yahweh has been affirmed by his (eventual) announcement that they have suffered enough and that those who have attacked them now must pay. The final phrase of 32:36 ("and no one is left—slave or free") is hard to interpret, but probably implies that everyone has been brought "to their knees" in dependence upon God, and there is no one left to help Israel apart from Yahweh.[586]

The future words of Yahweh to the idolatrous nations who brought such pain to God's people are recorded in verse 37. Initially, Yahweh will mock these people for having trusted in non-gods. In the same way as Elijah would on Mount Carmel (1 Kgs 18:27–29), he mocks these false gods ("Where are they?"), questioning their ability to be a rock for anyone and

---

[583] Yahweh keeps various things (including wind, rain, hail and snow) in storehouses, ready to be released as needed for the good or ill of human beings (e.g., Deut 28:12; Job 38:22–24; Ps 33:7; Jer 10:13).

[584] This is the text on which Jonathan Edwards preached his famous sermon, "Sinners in the Hands of an Angry God."

[585] This idea is expressed repeatedly throughout the Bible (e.g., Lev 26:25; Num 31:3; Ps 94:1–3; Isa 1:24; Jer 46:10; Ezek 25:14,17; Rom 12:19; Heb 10:30).

[586] See the helpful discussion of Tigay, *Deuteronomy*, 312.

asking "Who ate the fat of their sacrifices and drank the wine of their drink offerings?" (32:38), thus exposing the sham of their supposed existence. The challenge to "let them rise up and help you ... and be a shelter to you" leaves no room for protest.[587]

32:39–42. The declaration that begins in verse 39 is a powerful statement of the sovereignty of the God of the covenant, which is akin to 6:4 and 32:12 (see also Isa 43:11–13). The call to "see" again signals a shift in perspective as in 30:15, but here from speaking to the enemies of God's people when Israel's time of punishment is finished to the time of the singers. God says that all people must acknowledge that "I, I am he." There is only one God, and his name is Yahweh (Exod 15:11; Deut 3:24; 4:7, 32–39; 6:4). There is no other God but him. The implications flowing from this are massive: (1) it is Yahweh who "bring[s] death and give[s] life"; (2) it is Yahweh who "wounds and heals" (Job 5:18; Isa 19:22; 30:26; Hos 6:1); (3) it is Yahweh alone who rescues, and no one can rescue anyone from his grasp (Job 10:7; Ps 50:22; Isa 43:13; Hos 2:10; 5:14).

This means that when Yahweh says "[indeed] I raise my hand to heaven" (32:40) in order to "sharpen my flashing sword" and take "hold of judgment," nothing can stand in his way. It is possible that Yahweh is taking an oath here (swearing by himself), but what is certain is that his enemies will experience his "vengeance" (39:41, as in v. 35) and will be "repaid" for their contempt of him. None can stand against him: "I will make my arrows drunk with blood while my sword devours flesh—the blood of the slain and the captives, the heads of the enemy leaders." The Hebrew reads "the long-haired head of the enemy" (as in Ps 68:21), and is to be preferred.

Now the weapons unleashed on Israel (32:23) are aimed at the enemy, who has shown contempt to God himself. This is based on the premise that to oppose Yahweh's people is to oppose Yahweh.

32:43. In 32:43 the song ends in a similar place to where it began, although this time, it is the nations who are enlisted as the audience

[587] The pronoun at the end of 32:38 is singular ("it"), which jars with the "them" of the line before. The manuscript evidence strongly suggests that this is original. The switch to the singular may simply be a device to imply that whether one worships one idol or many, it makes no difference—non-gods are, by definition, completely ineffectual.

to Yahweh's victory.[588] More than that, they are urged to "rejoice" at the just treatment of the enemies of his people, in particular those who have shed the blood of his "servants." The fact that he will not only "take vengeance on his adversaries" but will also "purify his land and his people" underlines that ultimately, this song is a celebration of God's eschatological determination to establish a people for himself who can live with him and enjoy him forever.

32:44–47. In 32:44, it is reiterated that these words were "recited" (sung?) publicly by Moses, this time with Joshua's name added to the credits (31:22, 30). Having heard them, the people are now without excuse. These words should be sung and lived by the covenant people of God.

It is clear that Moses regards this song as capturing the heart of the message of his final preaching, which is why he urges them in verse 46: "Take to heart all these words I am giving as a warning to you today, so that you may command your children to follow all the words of this law carefully." The future of the nation depends on the way in which they respond to—and live out—these words. For these are not "empty" or "meaningless" words (32:47): "they are your life, and by them you will live long in the land you are crossing the Jordan to possess" (see also 4:1; 30:20). Singing this song of sin and grace (and doing this word) is the key to the future—both in the land, and beyond it.

Bridge

The message of Moses's sermon, which makes up the vast bulk of Deuteronomy, is hammered home both by the direct words of Yahweh himself and the mediated words of Israel's national anthem. Israel is deeply sinful, and ultimately their only hope is to be found in the future grace of God.

One cannot downplay the gospel shape of Moses's words. The painful truth is that even though the torah describes the beautiful life that Yahweh holds out to his people, the people themselves are utterly unable

---

[588] There is a textual issue here, with the LXX and 4QDeut[q] including extra lines not present in the MT. They begin by invoking the heavens (and the angels/sons of God) to praise the God of Israel. In the LXX, this happens alongside the nations. In Rom 15:10, Paul quotes the third line of the LXX in the context of the Gentiles acknowledging the work of God (i.e., what is common to the LXX and MT). Heb 1:6 however seems to quote from material in the LXX rather than the MT (although the line may actually come from elsewhere, e.g., Ps 97:7).

to live this life. Sooner or later, they will rebel. Human beings are inveterate idolaters, and left to ourselves, we will choose the death that comes from worshiping non-gods. But the glorious reality is that even though judgment must come, for Yahweh is a pure and righteous God, he is absolutely committed to bringing salvation to his people—and his world—on the other side of judgment.

VIII. Postscript 2: The Death of Moses (32:48–34:12)

> [48] On that same day the LORD spoke to Moses, [49] "Go up Mount Nebo in
> the Abarim range in the land of Moab, across from Jericho, and view
> the land of Canaan I am giving the Israelites as a possession. [50] Then
> you will die on the mountain that you go up, and you will be gathered
> to your people, just as your brother Aaron died on Mount Hor and was
> gathered to his people. [51] For both of you broke faith with me among
> the Israelites at the Waters of Meribath-kadesh in the Wilderness of
> Zin by failing to treat me as holy in their presence. [52] Although from
> a distance you will view the land that I am giving the Israelites, you
> will not go there."
>
> [33:1] This is the blessing that Moses, the man of God, gave the Israelites
> before his death. [2] He said:
>
> "The LORD came from Sinai
> and appeared to them from Seir;
> he shone on them from Mount Paran
> and came with ten thousand holy ones,
> with lightning from his right hand for them.
> [3] Indeed he loves the people.
> All your holy ones are in your hand,
> and they assemble at your feet.
> Each receives your words.
> [4] Moses gave us instruction,
> a possession for the assembly of Jacob.
> [5] So he became King in Jeshurun
> when the leaders of the people gathered
> with the tribes of Israel.
>
> [6] Let Reuben live and not die
> though his people become few."
>
> [7] He said this about Judah:
>
> "LORD, hear Judah's cry and bring him to his people.
> He fights for his cause with his own hands,
> but may you be a help against his foes."

8 He said about Levi:

> "Your Thummim and Urim belong to your faithful one;
> you tested him at Massah
> and contended with him at the Waters of Meribah.
> 9 He said about his father and mother,
> 'I do not regard them.'
> He disregarded his brothers
> and didn't acknowledge his sons,
> for they kept your word
> and maintained your covenant.
> 10 They will teach your ordinances to Jacob
> and your instruction to Israel;
> they will set incense before you
> and whole burnt offerings on your altar.
> 11 LORD, bless his possessions,
> and accept the work of his hands.
> Break the back of his adversaries and enemies,
> so that they cannot rise again."

12 He said about Benjamin:

> "The LORD's beloved rests securely on him.
> He shields him all day long,
> and he rests on his shoulders."

13 He said about Joseph:

> "May his land be blessed by the LORD
> with the dew of heaven's bounty
> and the watery depths that lie beneath;
> 14 with the bountiful harvest from the sun
> and the abundant yield of the seasons;
> 15 with the best products of the ancient mountains
> and the bounty of the eternal hills;
> 16 with the choice gifts of the land
> and everything in it;
> and with the favor of him
> who appeared in the burning bush.
> May these rest on the head of Joseph,
> on the brow of the prince of his brothers.
> 17 His firstborn bull has splendor,
> and horns like those of a wild ox;
> he gores all the peoples with them
> to the ends of the earth.
> Such are the ten thousands of Ephraim,
> and such are the thousands of Manasseh."

18 He said about Zebulun:

> “Rejoice, Zebulun, in your journeys,
> and Issachar, in your tents.
> 19 They summon the peoples to a mountain;
> there they offer acceptable sacrifices.
> For they draw from the wealth of the seas
> and the hidden treasures of the sand.”

20 He said about Gad:

> “The one who enlarges Gad’s territory
> will be blessed.
> He lies down like a lion
> and tears off an arm or even a head.
> 21 He chose the best part for himself,
> because a ruler’s portion was assigned there for him.
> He came with the leaders of the people;
> he carried out the LORD’s justice
> and his ordinances for Israel.”

22 He said about Dan:

> “Dan is a young lion,
> leaping out of Bashan.”

23 He said about Naphtali:

> “Naphtali, enjoying approval,
> full of the LORD’s blessing,
> take possession to the west and the south.”

24 He said about Asher:

> “May Asher be the most blessed of the sons;
> may he be the most favored among his brothers
> and dip his foot in olive oil.
> 25 May the bolts of your gate be iron and bronze,
> and your strength last as long as you live.
> 26 There is none like the God of Jeshurun,
> who rides the heavens to your aid,
> the clouds in his majesty.
> 27 The God of old is your dwelling place,
> and underneath are the everlasting arms.
> He drives out the enemy before you
> and commands, ‘Destroy!’
> 28 So Israel dwells securely;
> Jacob lives untroubled
> in a land of grain and new wine;
> even his skies drip with dew.

[29] How happy you are, Israel!
Who is like you,
a people saved by the Lord ?
He is the shield that protects you,
the sword you boast in.
Your enemies will cringe before you,
and you will tread on their backs."

[34:1] Then Moses went up from the plains of Moab to Mount Nebo,
to the top of Pisgah, which faces Jericho, and the Lord showed
him all the land: Gilead as far as Dan, [2] all of Naphtali, the land of
Ephraim and Manasseh, all the land of Judah as far as the Mediterranean Sea, [3] the Negev, and the plain in the Valley of Jericho, the
City of Palms, as far as Zoar. [4] The Lord then said to him, "This is
the land I promised Abraham, Isaac, and Jacob, 'I will give it to your
descendants.' I have let you see it with your own eyes, but you will
not cross into it."

[5] So Moses the servant of the Lord died there in the land of Moab, according to the Lord's word. [6] He buried him in the valley in the land of
Moab facing Beth-peor, and no one to this day knows where his grave
is. [7] Moses was one hundred twenty years old when he died; his eyes
were not weak, and his vitality had not left him. [8] The Israelites wept
for Moses in the plains of Moab thirty days. Then the days of weeping
and mourning for Moses came to an end.

[9] Joshua son of Nun was filled with the spirit of wisdom because Moses had laid his hands on him. So the Israelites obeyed him and did as
the Lord had commanded Moses. [10] No prophet has arisen again in Israel
like Moses, whom the Lord knew face to face. [11] He was unparalleled for
all the signs and wonders the Lord sent him to do against the land of
Egypt—to Pharaoh, to all his officials, and to all his land—[12] and for all
the mighty acts of power and terrifying deeds that Moses performed
in the sight of all Israel.

The final movement of the book of Deuteronomy also functions as a conclusion to the "five books of Moses." The preaching of Moses reached its climax in chapter 30 and was then backed up by the words of Yahweh and the song of chapter 32. The final section of the book now focuses almost exclusively on Moses's death. As we have seen, Moses's death outside the land has been an important focus in Deuteronomy itself, so the conclusion is not alien to the thought or purpose of the book. However, the death of the towering figure who has led Israel through its formative years in Egypt and the wilderness, and the man through whom God revealed his torah at Sinai and Moab takes on an even greater significance in the flow of redemptive history as an era comes to an end.

32:48–52. On the very same day that Moses and Joshua teach and sing "the song," Yahweh speaks to Moses a final time. He tells him to "Go up Mount Nebo in the Abarim range in the land of Moab, across from Jericho, and view the land of Canaan I am giving the Israelites as a possession" (32:49; also 3:27; Num 27:12–14). On a clear day, one can see Jerusalem and the Dead Sea in the south, and all the way to the mountains in the north (as well as Jericho, less than nine miles away across the Jordan Valley). This is one last kind concession to Moses, the servant of Yahweh, before he dies, which according to verse 50, is about to happen on that very mountain.

Yahweh underlines that, like his brother Aaron, who died and was buried on Mount Hor in Edom (Num 33:37–39), Moses will die outside the land.[589] The journey that began with the reunion of these brothers in Exodus 4:27 is about to end, as God's covenant people enter his land. But neither of them will complete the journey. And the reason? The sinful frailty of even the best of humanity. Even these two foundational leaders, Moses, who spoke God's words, and Aaron, with whom the hereditary high priesthood began, "broke faith" with Yahweh according to 32:51.[590] The events surrounding the catastrophic and costly failure are described in Numbers 20 (see also Deut 1:19–46). While Israel was at "the Waters of Meribath-kadesh in the Wilderness of Zin," Moses (and Aaron) "failed to treat Yahweh as holy" before all the people. In that incident, Yahweh had told Moses to speak to the rock to bring water from it, thereby demonstrating that God himself was performing the miracle. Rather than speaking, Moses ostentatiously struck the rock twice with his staff, even as he said "Listen, you rebels! Must *we* bring water out of this rock for you?" (Num 20:10, italics mine). This act of hubris could not go unpunished, and even now, at the very end of Moses's life, is a tangible demonstration that what Yahweh rightly demands from his people (wholehearted, lifelong

---

[589] The precise location of Mount Hor is disputed, with at least two preferred options: Jebel Harun and Jebel Madurah, both near Petra in southern Jordan. Jebel Madurah has the advantage of being on the Edomite border (Num 33:37).

[590] The choice of word here is interesting. "Breaking faith" is first used in Lev 5:15–21 of defrauding Yahweh, but is then picked up and much used by the Chronicler (e.g., 1 Chr 2:7; 5:25; 10:13) in explaining the heart of Israel's spiritual problems down through the generations.

obedience) will ultimately prove beyond even the best of them. So Moses shares the same fate as his entire generation (completing the picture of Deut 3:26). In his case, he does have the privilege of gazing over the land, but in 32:52, God underlines that he cannot enter: "Although from a distance you will view the land that I am giving the Israelites, you will not go there."

As has been pointed out multiple times, Moses's death casts a long shadow. Both those who hear his words at Moab and the future generations who will occupy the land need to pay close attention to the brute fact of his death on the border. The fact that both Deuteronomy and the Pentateuch as a whole (coupled with all that we have seen in chs. 27–32 in particular) end with his passing is an arresting warning of the inevitable consequences of breaking faith with Yahweh.

33:1–5. Chapter 33 consists entirely of the final words of Moses, in which he blesses the people of Israel before his death (33:1).

There is only one biblical parallel to such a blessing—that uttered by Jacob, the father of the nation, prior to his death in Genesis 49. The significance of this should not be overlooked. It recognizes Moses's foundational role in the life of the covenant people, alongside the progenitor of the twelve tribes.

However, Moses's blessing, unlike that of the patriarch, does not simply follow the birth order of the sons of Israel. As we shall see, Levi (in keeping with the role of the Levites in the book) and Joseph are much more prominent, with Judah slipping out of the spotlight and Simeon, whose territory was within Judah's, slipping out of the list altogether. Possible reasons for this will be explored below. In addition, Jacob's words have a more prophetic cast, sketching out the future of his sons in varying detail. Deuteronomy 33 consists of expressed wishes, descriptions, and occasionally commands, launched with a succinct summary of redemptive history to date (33:1–5) and concluded (in vv. 26–29) with a soaring, theologically rich benediction.[591]

Moses, described as "the man of God" in 33:1 (despite 32:51–52; see also Josh 14:6; Ps 90:title [Heb. 90:1]). He speaks first in verse 2 of Yahweh

---

[591] Tigay comments: "This poem is one of the most difficult texts in all ancient literature. It is full of rare words, syntactic difficulties, grammatical inconsistencies and opaque allusions. Some of these difficulties are probably due to its rare vocabulary and poetic forms; others to the poem's aphoristic style, which expresses things in a terse, symbolic way and is filled with allusions no longer understandable to us." *Deuteronomy*, 318.

coming in all his (military) might and glory from the Sinai region which here includes Seir (1:44) and Mount Paran (Hab 3:3–4). This is the only reference to Sinai in Deuteronomy (Moses usually preferring Horeb), which may well strengthen the view that this blessing functions as the conclusion not just of Deuteronomy, but the entire Pentateuch.

Yahweh is then depicted as coming with "ten thousand holy ones with lightning in his right hand." As the text stands, this is a vivid picture of God arriving with his "hosts" to take on all comers (and in context, presumably Egypt in particular).[592]

This intervention flows from Yahweh's "love" for his people (lit., "peoples") (33:3). However, the rest of verse 3 is almost as tricky as verse 2. The Hebrew reads "All his holy ones are in your hand," which is not easy to interpret. The word translated "assemble" is literally to "be followed" or "follow," but this does not fit easily with "to your feet." The final phrase ("Each receives your words") does, however, suggest that the overall picture is of Yahweh acting in power to gather his people at his feet to speak to them at Sinai. [593]

This is then confirmed in 33:4, albeit by a surprising third person reference to Moses himself. It may be that this is part of a confession of faith that had become current within Moses's own lifetime. The torah of Moses was a genuinely precious gift for the "assembly of Jacob" (cf. 9:10; 10:4; 18:16), now listening not to the patriarch as in Genesis 49:1, but to Moses, the man of God.

Such a confessional understanding would also go some way to explaining the strangeness of 33:5: "So he became King in Jeshurun when the leaders of the people gathered with the tribes of Israel." The first puzzle concerns who is being referred to here. *Presumably* this is Yahweh, but it seems very odd that this would be omitted, unless this is following some traditional formulation. Then there is the fact that this is the only explicit

---

[592] There are some textual issues in v. 2: the word for "lightning" here can easily be divided into two words meaning "fiery law" without altering the text. Alternatively, the whole phrase "with lightning in his right hand" can be read to say "from his southland to the mountain slopes," as the CSB footnote makes clear. In addition, it may be that Yahweh comes "from" his hosts (coming to Israel) rather than "with" them. It is also possible that "holy ones" is actually a reference to Kadesh. The Hebrew is not straightforward, but on balance, it seems best to retain the translation adopted above.

[593] Some take this to refer to the ten thousand holy ones in the previous verse, but it seems much more natural to take this to apply to Yahweh's people, Israel (with McConville, *Deuteronomy*, 468–69).

reference to God as King in the entire book.[594] The obscure language ("Jeshurun," used only in 32:15; 33:5, 26; Isa 44:2) gives the whole unit an archaic feel. The last question concerns when this coronation happened. The most likely scenario is when God spoke at Sinai, declaring them to be his own covenant people. However, given the way the book collapses covenant moments at Moab, Horeb, and the future, some flexibility here is not surprising.

But why does Moses begin his blessing like this? Unlike Jacob, Moses's contribution to the life of the nation is not biological. He is not the progenitor of those who would in turn father the twelve tribes of Israel. His role has been very different. He simply passed on the instructions that God their Rescuer and King gave to him, both to enable their escape and shape their future life. Now he knows that their future flourishing depends on their response to the words he has spoken. This gives his blessing a very different shape and tone.

33:6–25: The Blessing of the Tribes. The blessing itself begins with a slightly muted wish for the tribe of Reuben: "Let Reuben live and not die, though his people become few" (33:6). As in Gen 49:3–4, this isn't exactly brimming with positivity, although there is no explicit mention here of his sexual indiscretion. It seems that through the wilderness period, the tribe has not flourished, but despite their determination to settle in the Transjordan, Moses's great concern is to see them survive.

Perhaps the most unexpected feature of this blessing is that Simeon, Leah's second son, is completely omitted from the list. Simeon was absorbed by Judah very early in Israel's history (see, e.g., Josh 19:9, which points out that Simeon's land was encircled by Judah). Some take this as evidence that this ancient blessing must be post-Mosaic. A simpler solution (and one that doesn't demand such a glaring anachronism to have found its way into the text) is simply to take this as a pointer to the fact that for some reason, even preconquest, the tribes had begun to coalesce.

Surprisingly (especially given Gen 49:8–12), Judah also receives little attention (33:7). On the one hand, the preeminence of the royal tribe means that it is elevated to second place in the blessing, but Moses makes

---

[594] I think this ultimately proves to be an insurmountable problem for works like Meredith G. Kline's *The Treaty of the Great King: The Covenant Structure of Deuteronomy* (Grand Rapids: Eerdmans, 1963), which views the entire book as an ancient covenant document that is closely modeled on Hittite treaties.

no *explicit* mention of any role in ruling.[595] However, while Moses's prayer that Yahweh will "hear Judah's cry and bring him to his people" is a little cryptic, it is probably best understood as an allusion to Judah's emerging leadership (asking that God would establish his preeminence). A comment is added concerning Judah's independent spirit ("He fights for his cause with his own hands"), to which Moses adds the wish that God would come to his aid ("but may you be a help against his foes").

The scope of the blessing on Levi is probably the most strikingly different to the blessing pronounced by Jacob. While the patriarch simply alludes negatively to the bloody events surrounding Shechem, Hamor, and Dinah (Gen 34), Moses's blessing reflects all that he has subsequently said about his own tribe, and the particular roles they are to take in the life of the nation.

In 33:8–10, Moses makes a series of statements about the tribe of Levi, largely based on events or instructions in Exodus–Deuteronomy. The first (33:8) is a little tricky to interpret. The Masoretic Text reads, "Your Thummim and Urim to your faithful man whom you tested at Massah and contended with at the Waters of Meribah."[596] A main verb must be supplied, and opinion is divided on whether this should be an imperative (so JPS, ESV) or an indicative (CSB, NIV). On balance, the CSB rendering seems more likely in light of Exodus 28:30 (see also Lev 8:8; Num 27:21; 1 Sam 14:41; 28:6; Ezra 2:63; Neh 7:65, which are the other references to the mysterious Thummim and Urim in Scripture). It is also unusual that the tribe is personified as a single, faithful individual. What is clear is that the tribe of Levi has already been invested with the means of divine guidance for the nation. However, it is not so obvious how Levi was tested and approved at Massah and Meribah (Exod 17:1–7).[597] Perhaps the most satisfactory solution is to ascribe this comment to Moses's personal knowledge of events, there being no other obvious reason for its inclusion.

The second statement about the Levites in 33:9 is much easier to fathom. Exodus 32:25–29 records how the Levites sided with Moses in the

---

[595] Given Moses's teaching concerning a future king (17:14–20), it seems that at this point, Moses has more interest in the character of any future ruler of God's people than in his tribal origins.

[596] Both the LXX and the Dead Sea Scrolls seek to smooth this out by saying "Give to Levi your Thummim, and your Urim to the faithful one."

[597] Psalm 95, which also alludes to these events, sheds no light on the issue, making no mention of the Levites.

chaos instigated by the forging and worship of the golden calf at Mount Sinai. In Exodus, this expressed itself in a willingness to "go against son and brother." Here, Moses extends that to being ready to say of parents "I do not regard them." Their faithfulness is captured in the phrase "they kept your word and maintained your covenant."[598] Any hope of the nation remaining faithful to Yahweh depends to a large degree on the Levites continuing to model and defend covenant fidelity.

This is reflected by the statement in 33:10a that they will "teach your ordinances to Jacob and your instruction (torah) to Israel." Moses has hinted at this role in 27:14 and 31:25. Now it becomes more explicit.[599] This teaching role, however, is augmented with the more conventional function of, literally, "setting incense before your nose and whole things on your altar," presumably referring to burnt offerings. Moses then understandably asks God to "bless his strength" (so perhaps "efforts" rather than "possessions") and "accept the work of his hands," and also, in a graphic description, to smash the "loins" of his enemies, thus disabling them by striking at the source of their strength and preventing further attacks.

Moses's statement about Benjamin is brief but glowing: "The Lord's beloved rests securely on him." There is some uncertainty (as throughout the chapter) over whether the form of the verb is jussive ("Let him rest securely") or indicative ("he does rest securely"), but not much is affected by this, particularly since it is followed by a statement of Yahweh's care of Benjamin: "He [Yahweh] shields him [Benjamin] all day long, and he [Benjamin] rests on his [Yahweh's] shoulders."[600] The metaphor in view is almost certainly that of Yahweh as shepherd. Why Benjamin is promoted to fourth place in the list of sons is less clear, particularly given the extensive and fulsome treatment given to his older brother, Joseph in 33:13–17.

The blessing sought for Joseph is longer even than that of Levi. It is here that the connections between Genesis 49 and the blessing of Moses

---

[598] This attitude is also displayed by Phinehas in Num 25:11–12.

[599] It should be noticed however that there is not much evidence of the Levites performing this role throughout Israel's history (see only 2 Chr 35:3; Neh 8:7, although also 2 Chr 15:3; Jer 18:18; Hos 4:6; Mic 3:11 and Mal 2:7 on the failure of priests more generally to teach the truth).

[600] If it is Yahweh who rests on Benjamin's shoulders, it has been suggested that this is a reference to the sanctuary being in Benjamin. However, it is much simpler to see a switch of subject here.

are most apparent. In Jacob's case, the narrative of Genesis has made clear both a father's (not always helpful) special affection for his son and also the unique role played by Joseph in preserving the family in the face of famine. For Moses, it is the way in which God worked through Joseph in Egypt that explains his positivity. It may even be that his own experience of favor, being raised by the daughter of Pharaoh as a direct result of Joseph's legacy, may be reflected in these words.

In 33:13, Moses asks Yahweh to bless "his" (presumably Joseph's) land "with the dew of heaven's bounty and the watery depths that lie beneath."[601] This moisture will enable the sun (33:14) to produce a "bountiful harvest" and the "abundant yield of the seasons [lit., moons]"—an all-year-round yield of "the best products of the ancient mountains and the bounty of the eternal hills"(33:15).[602] Moses envisages Joseph's line enjoying the "choice gifts of the land and everything in it," and more than that, the very favor of God himself at the heart of the land which he has given. Yahweh is described as the one "who dwells in the bush," tying all of this back to Moses's own experience in Exodus 3:2–4.

The final clause of verse 16 ("May these rest on the head of Joseph, on the brow of the prince of his brothers") is a direct quotation of Genesis 49:26, but the remainder of the Joseph material, though reflecting similar sentiments to Jacob's blessing, is quite different. The descendants of Joseph, the prince of Egypt, are likened to a splendid "firstborn bull," with "horns like those of a wild ox" (presumably his sons, Ephraim and Manasseh).[603] Unexpectedly, the "ten thousands of Ephraim" and the "thousands of Manasseh" are depicted as "goring" the nations, even "to the ends of the earth." Such claims only make sense in the immediate context of the blessing—that is, the conquest of Canaan. Ephraim is Joshua's tribe, and Moses envisages them taking the lead as the people of God engage the inhabitants of the land, as the plans orchestrated by God and instigated through Joseph finally come to fruition.

---

[601] See the very similar conception in Prov 3:20. The "watery depths" are alluded to in Gen 1:2; 6:11; 8:2; Exod 15:8; Job 38:30; Prov 8:24. For the blessing of "dew," also in connection with Jacob (when he "stole" his brother Esau's blessing) see Gen 27:28, 39.

[602] The phrase "eternal hills" is identical to the "ancient hills" of Gen 49:26. See also Hab 3:6.

[603] In 1 Chr 5:1, it is said that Reuben's birthright is given to Joseph as a result of the eldest brother's sexual sin.

In 33:18–25, Moses deals with the remaining six northern tribes much more briefly. He calls Zebulun and his older sibling Issachar to rejoice (33:18). The goal for Zebulun is that they find joy as they travel; for Issachar, the challenge is to find delight at home ("in your tents"). According to verse 19, both tribes are united in calling people to offer "acceptable sacrifices" (lit., "righteous sacrifices") on a "mountain" (perhaps Mount Tabor, which lay at the edge of their territory).[604] As in Genesis 49, Zebulun's connection with the sea and Issachar's with getting down and dirty is highlighted. There is much here that remains mysterious, but the key elements are once more right worship and enjoying divinely provided wealth.

Blessing is then invoked for anyone who supports Gad in his determination to take and hold his (Transjordanian) land (33:20). As in 1 Chronicles 12:8, Gad's reputation as a tribe of fierce fighters is mentioned: "He lies down like a lion and tears off an arm or even a head." The reference to the "head" is linked to his choosing "the best part for himself, because a ruler's portion was assigned there for him." This may well refer to Gad laying claim to the lands of Gilead during the Transjordan campaign (Num 32:1–40; for Gad's eventual allocation of land, see Josh 13:24–28). Moses also commends Gad for playing their part in carrying out "the Lord's justice [better: righteousness] and his ordinances for Israel" (32:21; see also 6:25).

The single sentence spoken of Dan (33:22) is reminiscent of the description of Gad (33:20) and Judah in Genesis 49:9, rather than the unflattering description of Dan itself in Genesis 49:17. The comparison of Dan to a young lion from Bashan is much more positive than Jacob's "snake by the road." This is typical of the greater positivity of the Mosaic blessing compared to that of Jacob. That is backed up by the encouragement given to Naphtali in 33:23: "Naphtali, enjoying approval, full of the Lord's blessing, take possession to the west and the south."[605] Even those tribes of which little is said in Genesis 49 and who would turn out to play little part in the key moments of Israel's unfolding history, are depicted as enjoying a blessed life with Yahweh in the land.

---

604 This may be an example of the thinking that sees Israel's sanctuary (and then the temple) as a representation of the "Mountain of Yahweh," which in turn is a representation of his heavenly dwelling. See the excellent discussion of these ideas in Morales, *Who Shall Ascend*, 257–306.

605 Lundbom (*Deuteronomy*, 936) takes the phrase "west and south" to be "sea and south," a hendiadys referring to the Sea of Galilee.

This general positivity may be why the blessing on Asher is withheld to take the final position in the list. The tribe whose name is "blessed" receives the most fulsome commendation: "May Asher be the most blessed of the sons; may he be the most favored among his brothers and dip his foot in olive oil," presumably flowing down from the fertile hills. The point seems to be less about the preeminence of Asher per se and more about the peace and security that Yahweh is poised to lavish on his people—so verse 25: "May the bolts of your gate be iron and bronze, and your strength last as long as you live."[606]

Moses's recent theological exposé in chapters 27–32 notwithstanding, this final blessing of the tribes picks up the relentless determination of Yahweh to bless his people which begins in Eden, continues with Abraham, and unfolds through the exodus and even the wilderness wandering, bringing them to the very edge of the land. Israel's record to date has hardly been stellar, but Yahweh remains the good and generous God who has invited them to share a beautiful, torah-shaped life with him in the land.

33:26–29. At the end of his blessing, Moses returns to proclaiming the uniqueness of Yahweh. In 33:26, he affirms simply that "there is none like the God of Jeshurun," picking up the rare term used in 32:15 and 33:5, and describing him as the one "who rides the heavens to your aid, the clouds in his majesty." This idea of Yahweh riding in the clouds recurs in Psalm 68:4 and Isaiah 19:1, in the context of his acting against Egypt, as well as in Psalm 104:3. This seems to be part of an ancient exodus tradition and is also the basis of Israel's deep-rooted trust in him.

According to verse 27, the security of God's people comes from the fact that they live "in" him ("The God of old is your dwelling place"), and, in one of the most comforting pictures in the entire Bible, that "underneath are the everlasting arms." This God is eternally committed to the welfare of his people. They can never slip out of his grasp or wander or fall beyond his reach. This metaphorical care is expressed concretely in the reality that "he drives out the enemy before them"—a promise that most immediately refers to the present occupants of Canaan (and perhaps the recently dispossessed occupants of the Transjordan), who already stand under his judgment.

"Israel dwells securely" simply because of Yahweh (see 12:10; 33:12 also Lev 25:18–19; 26:5; Jer 23:6; 33:16; Ezek 28:26). The phrase "Jacob lives untroubled" in 33:28 is an attempt to make sense of the Hebrew

[606] This language is picked up in describing the ministry of Jeremiah; see Jer 1:18; 15:12.

which literally reads "Jacob is a spring alone." The following phrases ("in a land of grain and new wine ... his skies drip with dew") make it plain that whatever the precise nuance of the tricky phrase, it is a description of their blissful existence of his people in an idyllic land.

Moses's last words proclaim the kindness of the rescuing God to his people leading to their unparalleled contentment (as in 4:5–8): "How happy you are, Israel! Who is like you, a people saved by the LORD?" He sums up all that he has said about Yahweh by describing him as their protective "shield" (Gen 15:1; Pss 3:3; 5:12; 18:2, 30, etc.) and, uniquely, as "the sword you boast in." With this God on their side, there is no reason to fear. On the contrary, "your enemies will cringe before you, and you will tread on their backs."[607]

34:1–8. After Moses pronounces his peerless blessing, which draws together Yahweh's character as a rescuer and a tender father, we finally reach the account of his death. The transition to Moses walking up Nebo, to the top of Pisgah (probably the ridge of which Nebo forms part; also Num 23:13–14), and overlooking the Jordan Valley toward Jericho, is highly emotive.

At this point, Moses sees the full extent of the land, now described in terms of tribal territories: "Gilead as far as Dan, all of Naphtali, the land of Ephraim and Manasseh, all the land of Judah as far as the Mediterranean Sea, the Negev, and the plain in the Valley of Jericho, the City of Palms, as far as Zoar." This echoes the experience of Abram in Genesis 13:10. Moses looks north to Gilead and then does a counterclockwise circle. Given that the land has not been allocated yet, the use of the tribal names for the areas he looks at shows that this was written up after the events of the conquest. It has also been pointed out that this exceeds what can be seen with the naked eye (up to 60 miles, but also hindered by topography). This either means that the writer of these verses intends us to use our imagination (as in "Gilead is way over there in that direction") or that Yahweh, in his kindness, gave Moses a vision that far exceeded what even his "undimmed eyes" (34:7) could see. The fact that Yahweh says in verse 4 that "This is the land I promised Abraham, Isaac, and Jacob, 'I will give it to your descendants.' *I have let you see it with your own eyes*, but you will not cross into it" suggests that the latter may be the case.

---

[607] The word "backs" could more easily be translated as "high places" as in 32:13, which given the impending occupation of Canaan, seems to make perfect sense.

God will keep his promises, but the unavoidable truth is that not even Moses could keep covenant.

The simple yet moving note of 34:5 underlines this: "So Moses the servant of the Lord died there in the land of Moab, according to the Lord's word." Ultimately, only Yahweh can be trusted. The form of the verb at the start of verse 6 may, astonishingly, have the implication that Yahweh himself buried Moses somewhere "in the valley in the land of Moab facing Beth-peor." This accords with the fact that "no one to this day knows where his grave is," referring to the later time when this note on Moses's death was added to the book.[608] It is enough to say that Moses is buried near Beth–Peor, adding further to the sense of sadness.

Once more, 34:7 notes that Moses reached the age of 120 (also 31:2). We are told that both his eyesight and "vitality" (perhaps his mental capacities; the precise meaning of the word לֵחַ is unclear, which leads Tigay to suggest it may refer to an absence of wrinkles!) were undiminished right to the end. The preceding speeches are ample evidence of that. Unsurprisingly, the people mourned his passing. As in the days of Aaron (Num 20:29), the people mourned for their leader for thirty days. However, as befits a book which aims to equip Israel for its future spiritual journey, it was then time to move on (34:8).

34:9–12. As we have seen already, Joshua is a worthy successor for Moses and is appointed by God himself. It now becomes apparent that God himself has equipped and endorsed him through Moses's himself: he is "filled with the spirit of wisdom because Moses had laid his hands on him." Initially, at least, the transition is smooth, and the Israelites follow his lead, as together they do "as the Lord had commanded Moses" (34:9), an issue that is picked up again in Joshua 1:16–18, where the people insist that their record under Moses was blemish-free! All of this takes place, however, against a backdrop of a sermon that has exposed the inveterate sinfulness of the people (e.g., chs. 1–3), and the death *outside the land* of perhaps the greatest individual ever to lead God's people.

This note is sounded one last time in the closing sentences of Deuteronomy, and of the Pentateuch as a whole: "No prophet has arisen again in Israel like Moses, whom the Lord knew face to face" (34:10; also 5:4; Exod 33:11; Num 12:8). Both in the privileges Yahweh granted him

---

[608] This may well have been when the book as we know it took on its final form. Everything we have seen suggests that this was relatively soon after the conquest of Canaan.

and the ways in which Yahweh used him ("He was unparalleled for all the signs and wonders the Lord sent him to do against the land of Egypt," 34:11), there would never be another quite like Moses. And yet, as this book, and the preceding verses have made completely clear, even Moses ultimately fell short. The end of this book underlines the same message Moses has preached from the very beginning of this book: Israel's only hope and security can be found only in God himself.

Bridge

The blessing of Moses in chapter 33 is a remarkable piece of literature, which celebrates the power and goodness of our rescuing God, even while highlighting the messy brokenness of the people he chooses. God has intervened in the exodus. He has spoken at Horeb. He will bring his people into his land. He will work with the family of Jacob to enable them to hear his words and taste his forgiveness and experience his goodness in the land. He will teach them that security and joy can be found only in belonging to him. No ordinary human being—not even Moses—can secure that for himself, let alone lead others to it.

Deuteronomy ends, then, on a disquieting and ominous note. The curses, the song, the death of Moses, and the words of Yahweh himself have pushed the inevitability of Israel's sin and failure in the land into full view. But even in doing that, they have promised and heralded the fact that God's relentless grace will ultimately prevail. God has already committed to providing a way back for his sinful people through a new, transformative covenant that will bring to reality everything he has promised from the very beginning, putting a beautiful life with him within the grasp of people like us—an everlasting covenant that we know has been established in the Lord Jesus Christ himself.

BIBLIOGRAPHY

Alexander, T. Desmond. *Exodus*. AOTC. Downers Grove: InterVarsity, 2017.
———. *Face to Face with God: A Biblical Theology of Christ as Priest and Mediator*. Downers Grove: IVP Academic, 2022.
Allison, Dale W. *The New Moses: A Matthean Typology*. Repr., Eugene: Wipf & Stock, 2013.
Aquinas, Thomas. *Summa Theologica*. Translated by the Fathers of the English Dominican Province. 3 Volumes. New York: Benziger Brothers, 1947.
Arnold, Bill T. "Deuteronomy as the 'Ipsissima Vox' of Moses." *Journal for Theological Interpretation* 4 (2010): 53–74.
Ballard, Bruce. "The Death Penalty: God's Timeless Standard for the Nations?" *JETS* 43 (2000): 471–87.
Barker, Paul A. "Contemporary Theological Interpretation of Deuteronomy." Pages 60–90 in *Interpreting Deuteronomy: Issues and Approaches*. Edited by David G. Firth and Philip S. Johnson. Downers Grove: InterVarsity Press, 2012.
———. *The Triumph of Grace: Faithless Israel, Faithful Yahweh in Deuteronomy*. Carlisle: Paternoster, 2004.
Barton, John. "Law and Narrative in the Pentateuch." *Communio Viatorum* 51 (2009): 126–40.
Begg, Christopher T. "The Destruction of the Calf (Exodus 32,20/Deut 9,21)." Pages 208–51 in *Das Deuteronium: Enstehung, Gestalt und Botschaft*. Edited by Norbert Lohfink. BETL 68. Leuven: Leuven University Press 1985.
Blair, Edward P. "An Appeal to Remembrance: The Memory Motif in Deuteronomy." *Int* 15 (1961): 41–47.
Block, Daniel I. *Covenant: The Framework of God's Grand Plan of Redemption*. Grand Rapids: Baker, 2021.
———. *Deuteronomy*. NIV Application Commentary. Grand Rapids: Zondervan, 2012.
———. *How I Love Your Torah, O LORD! Studies in the Book of Deuteronomy*. Eugene: Wipf and Stock, 2011.

———. *The Gospel According to Moses: Theological and Ethical Reflections on the Book of Deuteronomy*. Eugene: Cascade, 2012.

Boda, Mark J. *Return to Me: A Biblical Theology of Repentance*. NSBT 35. Downers Grove: IVP, 2015.

Bodi, D. "Les *gillûlim* chez Ézéchiel et dans l'Ancien Testament et les different pratiques cultuelles associées à ce terme." *Revue biblique* 100 (1995): 481–510.

Braulik, Georg. *Studien zur Theologie des Deuteronomiums.* SBAB 2. Stuttgart: Kath. Bibelwerk, 1988.

———. *The Theology of Deuteronomy: Collected Essays of Georg Braulik.* Richland Hills: Bibal, 1994.

Brin, Gershon. "The Firstling of Unclean Animals." *JQR* 68 (1977–1978): 12–14.

Burge, Gary M. *Jesus and the Land: The New Testament Challenge to "Holy Land" Theology*. Grand Rapids: Baker, 2010.

Carmichael, Calum M. *The Laws of Deuteronomy*. Ithaca: Cornell University Press, 1974.

Carpenter, Eugene. "קהל", *NIDOTTE*, 3:888–91.

Chesterton, G. K. *What's Wrong with the World.* London: Cassell, 1910.

Christensen, Duane L. *Deuteronomy 1:1–21:9.* 2nd ed. Word Biblical Commentary 6a. Nashville: Thomas Nelson, 2001.

———. *Deuteronomy 21:10–34:12.* 2nd ed. Word Biblical Commentary 6b. Nashville: Thomas Nelson, 2002.

Cook, Stanley A. *The Laws Of Moses and the Code of Hammurabi.* London: A&C Black, 1903.

Copan, Paul. *Is God a Moral Monster? Making Sense of the Old Testament God.* Grand Rapids: Baker, 2011.

Craigie, Peter C. *The Book of Deuteronomy*. New International Commentary on the Old Testament. Grand Rapids: Eerdmans, 1976.

Cross, Frank Moore. *Canaanite Myth and Hebrew Epic.* Cambridge, MA: Harvard University Press, 1973.

Daube, David A. "The Culture of Deuteronomy." *Orita* 3 (1969): 27–52.

DeRouchie, Jason. *A Call to Covenant Love: Text Grammar and Literary Structure in Deuteronomy 5–11.* Piscataway: Gorgias, 2007.

de Tillesse, Minette. "Sections 'tu' et sections 'vous' dans le Deutéronome." *VT* 12 (1962): 29–87.

Dion, P. E. "Deuteronomy 9:13: Prepare the Way or Estimate the Distance?" *Eglise et théologie* 25 (1994): 333–41.

Driver, S. R. *Deuteronomy*. International Critical Commentary. Edinburgh: T&T Clark, 1902.

Ford, William. "The Challenge of the Canaanites." *TynBul* 68, no. 2 (2017): 161–84.

Fox, Nili Sacher. "Gender Transformation and Transgression: Contextualizing the Prohibition of Cross-Dressing in Deuteronomy 22:5." Pages 47–71 in *Mishneh Todeh: Studies in Deuteronomy and its Cultural Environment in Honor of Jeffrey H. Tigay*. Edited by Nili Sacher Fox, David A. Glatt-Gilad, and Michael J. Williams. Winona Lake: Eisenbrauns, 2009.

Frankena, R. "The Vassal-Treaties of Esarhaddon and the Dating of Deuteronomy." *Old Testament Studies* 14 (1965): 122–54.

Good, Edwin M. "Capital Punishment and its Alternatives in Ancient Near Eastern Law." *Stanford Law Review* 19 (1967): 947–77.

Grisanti, Michael A., "Was Israel Unable to Respond to God? A Study of Deuteronomy 29:2–4." *Bibliotheca Sacra* 163 (2006): 176–96.

Hallo, William W. "Biblical Abominations and Sumerian Tattoos." *JQR* 76 (1985–1986): 21–40.

Hallo, William W. and K. Lawson Younger, eds. *The Context of Scripture*. 3 vols. Leiden: Brill, 1997.

Harper, G. Geoffrey. *Teaching Leviticus: From Text to Message*. Fearn: Christian Focus, 2022.

Heider, George C. *The Cult of Molech Reassessed*. *JSOTSup* 43. Sheffield: JSOT, 1985.

Holladay, William L. *The Root* שׁוּב *in the Old Testament (With Particular Reference to its Usage in Covenantal Contexts)*. Leiden: Brill, 1958.

Homan, Michael M. "Beer and Its Drinkers: An Ancient Near Eastern Love Story." *Near Eastern Archaeology* 64 (2007): 84–95.

Hubbard, Robert L. "גָּאַל"in *NIDOTTE* 1:789–94.

Hundley, Michael. "To Be or Not To Be: A Reexamination of Name Language in Deuteronomy and the Deuteronomistic History." *VT* 59 (2009): 541–43.

Issler, Klaus. "Lending and Interest in the OT: Examining Three Interpretations to Explain the Deuteronomy 23:19–20 Distinction in Light of the Historical Usury Debate." *JETS* 59 (2016): 761–89.

Imes, Carmen Joy. *Bearing YHWH's Name at Sinai: A Reexamination of the Name Command of the Decalogue*. Bulletin for Biblical Research Supplement 19. University Park: Eisenbrauns, 2018.

Kalluveettil, Paul. *Declaration and Covenant: A Comprehensive Review of Covenant Formulae from the Old Testament and the Ancient Near East*. AnBib 88. Rome: Pontifical Biblical Institute, 1982.

Kaufman, Stephen A. "The Structure of the Deuteronomic Law." *Maarav* 1, no. 2 (1978–1979): 105–58.

Kitchen, Kenneth A. *On the Reliability of the Old Testament*. Grand Rapids: Eerdmans, 2003.

Kline, Meredith G. *The Treaty of the Great King: The Covenant Structure of Deuteronomy*. Grand Rapids: Eerdmans, 1963.

———. "The Two Tables of the Covenant." *Westminster Theological Journal* 22 (1960): 133–46.

Labuschagne, C. J. "'You Shall Not Boil a Kid in Its Mother's Milk': A New Proposal for the Origin of the Prohibition." Pages 6–17 in *The Scriptures and the Scrolls*. Edited by F. G. Martinez et al. *VTSup* 49. Leiden: Brill, 1992.

Lemaire, André, Baruch Halpern, and Matthew J. Adams. *The Books of Kings: Sources, Composition, Historiography and Reception*. *VTSup* 129. Leiden: Brill, 2010.

Lenchak, Timothy A. *"Choose Life": A Rhetorical-Critical Investigation of Deut 28,69–30,20*. AnBib 129. Rome: Pontifical Biblical Institute, 1993.
Lohfink, Norbert. *Das Hauptgebot: Eine Untersuchung literarischer Einleitungsfragen zu Deuteronomium 5–11*. AnBib 20. Rome: Pontifical Biblical Institute, 1963.
Lundbom, Jack R. *Deuteronomy: A Commentary*. Grand Rapids: Eerdmans, 2013.
——. *Jeremiah 1–20*. AB 21A. New York: Doubleday, 1999.
Luther, Martin. *Lectures on Deuteronomy*. Luther's Works 9. Fort Wayne: Concordia, 1960.
MacDonald, Nathan. "The Literary Criticism and Rhetorical Logic of Deuteronomy I–IV." *VT* 56 (2006): 203–24.
McConville, J. Gordon. "1 Kings VIII and the Deuteronomic Hope." *VT* 42 (1992): 67–69.
——. *Deuteronomy*. AOTC. Leicester: IVP, 2002.
——. *God and Earthly Power: An Old Testament Political Theology*. London: T&T Clark, 2006.
——. *Grace in the End: A Study in Deuteronomic Theology*. Grand Rapids: Zondervan, 1993.
——. *Law and Theology in Deuteronomy*. *JSOTSup* 33. Sheffield: JSOT Press, 1984.
——. "The Theology of Deuteronomy." *NIDOTTE* 5:537–44.
McConville, James Gordon, and J. G. Millar. *Time and Place in Deuteronomy*. JSOTSup 179. Sheffield: Sheffield Academic, 1994.
McKay, J. W. "Man's Love for God in Deuteronomy and the Father/Teacher—Son/Pupil Relationship." *VT* (1972): 426–35.
Meade, John D. "Circumcision of the Heart in Leviticus and Deuteronomy: Divine Means for Resolving Curse and Bringing Blessing." *Southern Baptist Journal of Theology* 18, no. 3 (2014): 59–85.
Meier, Samuel A. *The Messenger in the Ancient Semitic World*. Atlanta: Scholars Press, 1988.
Milgrom, Jacob. *Leviticus 1–16*. AB. New York: Doubleday, 1991.
Millar, J. Gary. *1–2 Kings*. Pages 491–898 in *1 Samuel–2 Chronicles*, ESV Expositional Commentary 3 (Wheaton: Crossway, 2019).
——. *Calling on the Name of the Lord: A Biblical Theology of Prayer*. NSBT 38. London: Apollos, 2016.
——. *Changed into His Likeness: A Biblical Theology of Personal Transformation*. NSBT 55. London: Apollos, 2021.
——. "Deuteronomy." Pages 159–65 in *NDBT*. Edited by Brian S. Rosner, T. Desmond Alexander, Graeme Goldsworthy, and D. A. Carson. Downers Grove: IVP Academic, 2000.
——. "Land." Pages 623–26 in *NDBT*. Edited by Brian S. Rosner, T. Desmond Alexander, Graeme Goldsworthy, and D. A. Carson. Downers Grove: IVP Academic, 2000.
——. *Now Choose Life: Theology and Ethics in Deuteronomy*. NSBT 6. Leicester: Apollos, 1998.

Millard, Alan R. "King Og's Bed and Other Ancient Ironmongery." Pages 481–92 in *Ascribe to the Lord: Biblical and Other Essays in Memory of Peter C. Craigie*. Edited by Lyle Eslinger and Glen Taylor. *JSOTSup* 67. Sheffield: JSOT Press, 1988.

Moberly, R. W. L. "Yahweh is One: The Translation of the Shema." Pages 209–15 in *Studies in the Pentateuch*. Edited by J. A Emerton. *VTSup* 41. Leiden: Brill, 1990.

Morales, L. Michael. *Exodus Old and New: A Biblical Theology of Redemption*. Downers Grove: IVP Academic, 2020.

——. *Who Shall Ascend the Mountain of the Lord? A Biblical Theology of the Book of Leviticus*. NSBT 37. Downers Grove: InterVarsity Press, 2015.

Moran, William L. "The Ancient Near Eastern Background of the Love of God in Deuteronomy." *Catholic Bible Quarterly* 25 (1963): 77–87.

Nelson, Richard D. *Deuteronomy*. OTL. Louisville: Westminster John Knox, 2002.

Nolland, John A. *The Gospel of Matthew: A Commentary on the Greek Text*. New International Greek Testament Commentary. Grand Rapids: Eerdmans, 2005.

Noth, Martin. *The Deuteronomistic History*. *JSOTSup* 15. Sheffield: JSOT Press, 1981.

Olson, Dennis T. *Deuteronomy and the Death of Moses: A Theological Reading*. Minneapolis: Fortress, 1994.

Osborne, Grant R. *Matthew*. Zondervan Exegetical Commentary on the New Testament. Grand Rapids: Zondervan, 2010.

Paul, Shalom M. *Studies in the Book of the Covenant in the light of Cuneiform and Biblical Law*. *VTSup* 18. Leiden: Brill, 1970.

Petuchowski, Jakob J. "Not by Bread Alone." *Judaism* 7 (1958):229–43.

Powlinson, David. "Revisiting Idols of the Heart and Vanity Fair." *JBC* 27, no. 3 (2013): 37–42.

Propp, William H. C. *Exodus 19–40*. AB 2A. New York: Doubleday, 2006.

Rad, Gerhard von. *Deuteronomy*. OTL. London: SCM, 1966.

——. *Studies in Deuteronomy*. Studies in Biblical Theology 9. London: SCM, 1956.

Robertson, O. Palmer. *The Christ of the Covenants*. Phillipsburg: Presbyterian and Reformed, 1980.

Robson, James. "The Literary Composition of Deuteronomy." Pages 19–57 in *Interpreting Deuteronomy: Issues and Approaches*. Edited by David G. Firth and Philip S. Johnson. Downers Grove: InterVarsity Press, 2012.

Sailhamer, John H. *The Meaning of the Pentateuch: Revelation, Composition and Interpretation*. Downers Grove: IVP Academic, 2009.

Schnittjer, Gary. *Old Testament Use of the Old Testament: A Book by Book Guide*. Grand Rapids: Zondervan, 2021.

Schorch, Stefan. "A Young Goat in its Mother's Milk? Understanding an Ancient Prohibition." *VT* 60 (2010): 116–30.

Seitz, Christopher R. "Prophet Moses and the Canonical Shape of Jeremiah." *ZAW* 1 (1989): 3–27.

Smith, George Adam. *Historical Geography of the Holy Land*. London: Hodder & Stoughton, 1918.

Smith, James K. A. *Desiring the Kingdom: Worship, Worldview, and Cultural Formation*. Grand Rapids: Baker Academic, 2009.

Smothers, Colin J. *In Your Mouth and In Your Heart: A Study of Deuteronomy 30:10–12 in Paul's Letter to the Romans in Canonical Context*. Eugene: Pickwick, 2022.

Tigay, Jeffrey H. *Deuteronomy*. JPS Torah. Philadelphia: Jewish Publication Society, 1996.

Trimm, Charles. "Recent Research on Warfare in the Old Testament." *Currents in Biblical Research* 10 (2012): 1–46.

van Goudoever, Jan. "The Liturgical Significance of the Date in Dt 1, 3." Pages 145–48 in *Das Deuteronomium: Einstehung, Gestalt und Botschaft*. Edited by Norbert Lohfink. BETL 68. Leuven: Leuven University Press, 1985.

Vogt, Peter T. "Centralization and Decentralization in Deuteronomy." Pages 118–38 in *Interpreting Deuteronomy: Issues and Approaches*. Edited by David G. Firth and Philip S. Johnson. Downers Grove: InterVarsity Press, 2012.

———. *Deuteronomic Theology and the Significance of Torah: A Reappraisal*. Winona Lake: Eisenbrauns, 2006.

———. *Religious Concepts in the Theology of Deuteronomy*. Gloucester: University of Gloucestershire Press, 2003.

Walton, John H. *Ancient Near Eastern Thought and the Old Testament*. Grand Rapids: Baker, 2006.

———. "The Decalogue Structure of the Deuteronomic Law." Pages 93–117 in *Interpreting Deuteronomy: Issues and Approaches*. Edited by David G. Firth and Philip S. Johnson. Downers Grove: InterVarsity Press, 2012.

———. "Deuteronomy: An Exposition of the Spirit of the Law." *Grace Theological Journal* 8 (1987): 213–25.

Waterhouse, S. Douglas. "A Land Flowing with Milk and Honey." *Andrews University Seminary Studies* 1 (1963): 152–66.

Watts, James W. *Reading Law: The Rhetorical Shaping of the Pentateuch*. Edinburgh: T&T Clark, 1999.

Weinfeld, Moshe. "The Covenant of Grant in the Old Testament and the Ancient Near East." *Journal of the American Oriental Society* 90 (1970): 184–203.

———. "The Decalogue: Its Significance, Uniqueness and Place in Israel's Tradition." Pages 3–47 in *Religion and Law: Biblical-Judaic and Islamic Perspectives*. Edited by E. B. Firmage et al. Winona Lake: Eisenbrauns, 1990.

———. *Deuteronomy 1-11*. AB. New York: Doubleday, 1991.

———. *Deuteronomy and the Deuteronomic School*. Oxford: Clarendon, 1972.

———. "The Loyalty Oath in the Ancient Near East." *Ugarit-Forschungen* 8 (1976): 379–414.

Wenham, Gordon J. *Story as Torah: Reading the Old Testament Ethically*. Grand Rapids: Baker, 2004.

Williamson, Paul R. *Sealed with an Oath: Covenant in God's Unfolding Purpose*. NSBT 23. Downers Grove: InterVarsity Press, 2007.

Wilson, C. W. "Ebal and Gerizim, 1866." *Palestine Exploration Fund Quarterly Statement* (1873): 66–71.

Wilson, Ian. "Central Sanctuary or Local Settlement? The Location of the Triennial Declaration (Dtn 26,13–15)." *ZAW* 120 (2008): 323–40.

——. *Out of the Midst of the Fire: Divine Presence in Deuteronomy*. Society of Biblical Literature Dissertation Series 151. Atlanta: Scholars Press, 1995.

Work, Telford. *Deuteronomy*. Brazos Theological Commentary on the Bible. Grand Rapids: Brazos, 2009.

Wright, Christopher J. H. *Deuteronomy*. New International Biblical Commentary. Peabody: Hendrickson, 1996.

——. *God's People in God's Land: Family, Land, and Property in the Old Testament*. Exeter: Paternoster, 1990.

Wright, G. Ernest. "Deuteronomy." Pages 309–537 in *The Interpreter's Bible*, ed. George Arthur Buttrick et al. Vol. 2. New York: Abingdon, 1953.

Younger, K. Lawson. *Ancient Conquest Accounts: A Study in Ancient Near Eastern and Biblical History Writing*. *JSOTSup* 98. Sheffield: JSOT Press, 1990.

SCRIPTURE INDEX

OLD TESTAMENT

Exodus

Numbers

Deuteronomy

Joshua

Judges

Ruth

1 Samuel

2 Samuel

1 Kings

2 Kings

1 Chronicles

2 Chronicles

Ezra

Nehemiah

Job

Psalms

Proverbs

Ecclesiastes

Song of Solomon

Isaiah

Lamentations

Ezekiel

NEW TESTAMENT

ANCIENT SOURCES INDEX

ANCIENT NEAR EASTERN TEXTS

DEAD SEA SCROLLS

RABBINIC WORKS